CONSTITUTIONAL LAW

UNDERGRADUATE EDITION

Second Edition, Volume 1

GREGORY E. MAGGS
JUDGE
U.S. COURT OF APPEALS FOR THE ARMED FORCES

PETER J. SMITH
ARTHUR SELWYN MILLER RESEARCH PROFESSOR OF LAW
GEORGE WASHINGTON UNIVERSITY LAW SCHOOL

WEST ACADEMIC PUBLISHING

444 Cedar Street, Suite 700
St. Paul, MN 55101
1-877-888-1330

Printed in the United States of America

ISBN: 978-1-63659-328-9

Preface

The meaning of the Constitution is far too important a subject to leave solely to lawyers and those who want to become lawyers. All adults should know about the powers that the Constitution grants the federal government and rights that it gives to individuals. Many widely debated issues, such as health insurance, same-sex marriage, free speech on campus, and so forth, require some understanding of the Constitution. College and graduate school are ideal places to study these subjects in depth, whether a student is focusing on history, political science, or some other subject. Accordingly, this book is specifically designed for use by non-law students in undergraduate or graduate constitutional law courses.

Non-law students, however, face a disadvantage in tackling a course on constitutional law because studying the subject requires them to understand Supreme Court cases, which are often technically complicated. Law students do not have the same difficulty; they generally excel at reading cases because they receive thorough instruction on how to do it and practice the skill in all their courses. Some textbooks for non-law students attempt to deal with this issue by summarizing Supreme Court decisions, and thus eliminating the need to read them. This book takes a different approach because the authors believe that non-law students can read Supreme Court cases if they are given some initial instruction on the subject and the cases are appropriately edited. The book contains over one hundred explanatory text boxes that clarify legal terms in cases.

We have selected the principal cases very carefully, and we have tried to avoid the problem created by the aggressive editing in many books, which present excerpts so brief that the students in effect read only *about* what the Supreme Court has decided. Supreme Court opinions should be presented as more than a series of conclusory assertions that have been stitched together by a space-sensitive editor. We have tried to edit the principal cases to ensure that they are short enough to read, but rich enough to give the students a clear sense of the Court's reasoning. We have also chosen not to create the illusion of breadth that characterizes many books in the field. Rather than provide summaries of dozens of decisions in each area that we take up, we focus on fuller excerpts of the principal cases, which are designed to be illustrative. Our book is self-consciously a casebook, and does not aspire to be a treatise.

Rather than follow the principal cases with pages and pages of notes and questions—an ineffective approach that students universally resent—we include multiple sidebars in the excerpts of each principal case to focus the students' attention on important questions at the very moment when they are reading the relevant portions of the opinion. Among other things, the sidebars focus attention on particularly salient passages of the opinions; draw connections between the discussion in the case and other topics that the students have explored (or will explore) in the book; supply food for thought; and direct the students to secondary materials to enrich their studies. After each case, we provide brief points for discussion, to focus the students' attention on the central themes in the case. Each chapter also contains hypothetical problems—often drawn from real cases—to encourage the students to apply the doctrine that they have learned, and ends with an "executive summary" of the material, to identify the main themes and doctrines covered in the chapter.

Throughout the book we include "Point-Counterpoints," in which we provide arguments for and against central questions raised by the materials in the book. To be sure, throughout the book—in the points for discussion and in short excerpts from scholarly articles by leading experts in the field—we present a diversity of views on every subject. But the Point-Counterpoint discussions are presented in our own voices and reflect our genuine points of disagreement on the many disputed questions raised in the book. We think that the students will find these discussions rich and stimulating.

Although we have attempted to provide fuller excerpts of the principal cases than is perhaps common in casebooks in the field, we of course nevertheless have had to do substantial editing. We have used three asterisks to indicate that text has been omitted within a paragraph, although we have often omitted entire paragraphs without providing a similar indication. We have omitted most footnotes from the cases; when we have included them, we have used the original numbering from the cases. Footnotes that we have inserted in the cases, on the other hand, are indicated by an asterisk and conclude with the notation "—Eds." We have also omitted many of the citations, but we have attempted to preserve the most important ones.

This book is based on the fifth edition of *Constitutional Law: A Contemporary Approach*, a textbook that we wrote for law students. Many people helped us with the law school edition. At the risk of inadvertently leaving some out, we wish to acknowledge Brad Clark, Tom Colby, Ronald Collins, Elizabeth Joh, William Kelley, Chip Lupu, Alan Morrison, Jeff Powell, Michael Rappaport, David Stras, and Robert Tuttle for their helpful comments.

Gregory Maggs dedicates his contributions to the book to his patient family and to the many generations of law students at the George Washington University who have contributed to his understanding of constitutional law. Peter Smith dedicates his contributions to the book to Eileen Smith, the memory of David Smith, and to Laurie, Jonah, and Sarah, whose highly refined sense of justice has consistently challenged his own.

We hope that reading this book is as enjoyable for you as writing it was for us.

Gregory E. Maggs
Peter J. Smith

June 2021
Washington, DC

Table of Contents

PART IV. SEPARATION OF POWERS

PART V. CONSTITUTIONAL LIMITATIONS ON NON-GOVERNMENTAL CONDUCT

Table of Cases

The principal cases are in bold type.

CONSTITUTIONAL LAW

UNDERGRADUATE EDITION

Second Edition, Volume 1

PART I

Introduction

CHAPTER 1

History and Overview

This book concerns the constitutional law of the United States. As you will see in reading it, the book focuses mostly on how the Supreme Court has interpreted various provisions of the U.S. Constitution. This introductory chapter provides some background for understanding the Court's cases. The chapter starts by describing the historical setting in which the Constitution came into being. It then briefly outlines the structure and content of the Constitution. Finally, it presents conflicting theories about how courts should interpret the Constitution.

A. HISTORICAL SETTING OF THE CONSTITUTION

In the mid-1700s, the United Kingdom of Great Britain[1] possessed a number of colonies in North America. Thirteen of these colonies later declared their independence and joined together to form the United States of America: Connecticut, Delaware, Georgia, Maryland, Massachusetts, New Hampshire, New Jersey, New York, North Carolina, Pennsylvania, Rhode Island, South Carolina and Virginia.[2]

Go Online

Many students feel that they would benefit from a quick refresher on American history. For a concise and easily accessible survey, visit the U.S. State Department's "Outline of U.S. History," available at https://time.com/wp-content/uploads/2015/01/history_outline.pdf. Chapters 3 and 4 of this outline, titled "The Road to Independence" and "The Formation of a National Government," are especially relevant.

[1] "Great Britain" is the name of the large island that England, Scotland, and Wales occupy. The Kingdom of England annexed Wales through Acts of Parliament passed in 1536 and 1543. In 1707, the Act of Union merged the Kingdom of England and the Kingdom of Scotland to form a new nation called the "United Kingdom of Great Britain." Historical discussions often shorten the lengthy name of this nation to the "United Kingdom" or "Great Britain" or just "Britain."

[2] In North America, the United Kingdom also possessed the colonies of Quebec, Nova Scotia, Prince Edward Island, East Florida, and West Florida, but these colonies did not seek independence at the time of the American Revolution. Prior to the Revolution, the territory that later became Vermont was not recognized as a separate colony; instead, it was claimed by the colonies of both New York and New Hampshire. Vermont

What led these colonies to seek independence? What did they hope to accomplish in forming a new nation? How did they organize their government? These are questions that anyone studying the Constitution must consider.

1. Colonial Governance and Events Preceding the Revolution

The thirteen colonies that later formed the United States exercised a fair degree of self-governance for many years. Each of the colonies had an elected assembly or legislature, which had authority to pass laws. In addition, these assemblies generally had the sole power to impose taxes and the sole authority to set the budget. The assemblies' enactments were subject to disapproval by a governor (who was appointed by the King of England in all of the colonies except Connecticut and Rhode Island) and by an appointed legislative council (except in Pennsylvania). But actual disapproval of legislation was very rare, and until the mid-1700s, few disputes arose between the colonies and the King or Parliament.

Serious challenges to the colonies' self-governance did not come about until the end of the French and Indian War. In this conflict, which lasted from 1754 until 1763, the United Kingdom fought against France and France's American Indian allies in North America. Although the United Kingdom ultimately prevailed, it incurred enormous expenses in the process. To help recover some of that money, Parliament passed several acts that sought to raise revenue from the colonies. These acts included the Stamp Act of 1765 and Townshend Act of 1767, both of which imposed taxes on various goods within the colonies.

Many colonists believed that these acts exceeded the power of Parliament. They asserted that any taxation imposed on the colonists must come from their own assemblies. Some of the colonists consequently protested the legislation with petitions and civil disobedience. In 1770, to alleviate tensions, Parliament repealed the taxes on almost all goods. But Parliament retained a tax on tea, largely to demonstrate that it did have power to tax the colonies if it so chose.

Colonists responded to the remaining tax by boycotting British tea and by smuggling tea into the country without paying taxes on it. (John Hancock, who later played a key role in the formation of the United States, was indicted on criminal charges for illegally purchasing and reselling tea from Holland.) Parliament in turn passed the Tea Act of 1773, which allowed the English East

---

declared its independence from Great Britain and from New York and New Hampshire in 1777, but did not participate in the government formed by the Articles of Confederation. It joined the United States, after ratification of the Constitution, in 1791. Massachusetts assumed control over Maine in the mid-1600s and retained that control until 1820. Maine accordingly did not sign the Declaration of Independence.

India Company to import and sell tea at lower prices than what the colonial merchants were charging, with the hope of inducing Americans to stop their boycott of British tea. To thwart this measure, on December 16, 1773, a group called the Sons of Liberty boarded ships in Boston Harbor that were carrying East India Company tea and threw the tea into the water.

In 1774, in response to this famous "Boston Tea Party," Parliament passed five laws that the colonists called the "Intolerable Acts" or the "Coercive Acts." These acts, among other things, severely limited the civil and political rights of colonists in Massachusetts. The goal was to force the colonists to make restitution for the tea and generally cease their defiance of Parliament. The founders of the United States remembered the loss of their liberty when they later drafted the Constitution and Bill of Rights.

> **FYI**
>
> The **Intolerable Acts** consisted of five individual acts. The Boston Port Act closed Boston to commercial shipping. The Quartering Act allowed a governor to order that British soldiers be quartered in private buildings if quarters were not provided for them within 24 hours following a request. The Massachusetts Government Act gave the royal government the exclusive power to appoint judges and prosecutors and prohibited town meetings without the permission of the royal governor. The Administration of Justice Act allowed the governor to order trials of persons arrested in Massachusetts to take place in other colonies, in order to prevent magistrates and juries from acquitting local residents who were hostile to the governor. The Quebec Act permitted the free exercise of the Roman Catholic Religion in Quebec, but it also provided no elected legislative assembly, creating—as the other colonists saw it—a tyranny that might spread to the other colonies.

2. The First and Second Continental Congresses

The Intolerable Acts and other factors led concerned colonists from all of the colonies except Georgia to send delegates to a meeting in Philadelphia. The meeting became known as the "First Continental Congress." The delegates met peacefully between September 5 and October 26, 1774. In total, fifty delegates attended. They included many famous figures of the era, such as John Adams, Samuel Adams, Patrick Henry, John Jay, Richard Henry Lee, Peyton Randolph, Roger Sherman, and George Washington.

The delegates to the First Continental Congress did not act as if they had the power to pass laws or take any other governmental actions. Instead, the delegates merely adopted resolutions and submitted letters and petitions of grievances to the King. Before adjourning, the First Continental Congress agreed to reconvene on May 10, 1775, in Philadelphia.

Before the appointed date for the Second Continental Congress arrived, war broke out in Massachusetts. The fighting started with the battle of Lexington and Concord on April 19, 1775. In that battle, local militiamen defeated British troops who had come to seize their stores of weapons. Following the battle, colonists drove the British troops back to Boston and surrounded the city.

FYI

The records of the First and Second Continental Congress are collected and published in the Journals of the Continental Congress, 1774–1789 (Worthington C. Ford *et al.* eds. 1904–37), the full text of which is available at the Library of Congress's website: http://memory.loc.gov/ammem/amlaw/lwjc.html.

It was in these circumstances that the Second Continental Congress began to meet in Philadelphia on May 10, 1775. The Congress included delegates from each of the thirteen colonies. These delegates included many famous men of the founding era, such as John Hancock, John Adams, Benjamin Franklin, George Washington, and Thomas Jefferson. Like the First Continental Congress, the Second Continental Congress had no clear legislative authority. It could adopt resolutions, but could not pass laws or impose taxes.

Nevertheless, on June 15, 1775, the Second Continental Congress decided to assume authority over the American forces surrounding Boston, resolving that "a General be appointed to command all the continental forces, raised, or to be raised, for the defence of American liberty." It then unanimously selected George Washington for this position. The Second Continental Congress also appointed additional subordinate officers, and it agreed to finance the military (although obtaining the funds for this purpose proved difficult). Over the course of the next eleven months, fighting between American and British forces continued.

By the summer of 1776, the war had convinced the colonists that the colonies could no longer remain a part of the United Kingdom. Accordingly, on July 4, 1776, the Second Continental Congress adopted the Declaration of Independence. With this declaration, the fighting with Great Britain became a war for independence. The war for independence—known now as the "Revolution" or "Revolutionary War"—lasted seven years. The American forces lost most of the battles, but held together and eventually prevailed. In 1783, the United Kingdom acknowledged the independence of the United States in the Treaty of Paris, and the war ended.

3. The Articles of Confederation and the Calling of a Constitutional Convention

The Declaration of Independence proclaimed that the colonies had become "free and independent states." But these independent states needed to work together to prevail against the United Kingdom. In 1777, while the Revolutionary War was still being fought, the Continental Congress drafted a document called the Articles of Confederation. This document was finally approved by all of the states in 1781.

The Articles of Confederation was more like a multilateral treaty among allies than a formal constitution for a new national government. The document announced that its purpose was to create a "firm league of friendship" among the former colonies, which had now become something more akin to separate states. It emphasized that each "state retains its sovereignty, freedom, and independence."

Under the Articles of Confederation, the states would continue to send delegates to a Congress just as they had done before. The Congress had limited power to pass laws, with each state having one vote. But the government was not effective. All measures required the unanimous assent of the states. The Congress had no way to enforce laws or collect taxes. There were no national courts. In addition, the unity of the states became strained over trade and other issues.

> **Food for Thought**
>
> The newly independent states did not create a strong national government in the Articles of Confederation. Why might they have felt reluctant to do that even though the Revolutionary War clearly showed that the states needed to work together?

In 1787, the weaknesses in the Articles of Confederation led the Congress to call for a convention "for the sole and express purpose of revising the Articles of Confederation and reporting to Congress and the several legislatures such alterations and provisions therein as shall when agreed to in Congress and confirmed by the states render the federal constitution adequate to the exigencies of Government & the preservation of the Union." Notwithstanding the Congress's mandate, the convention quickly adopted as its task the drafting of a new Constitution. Accordingly, the convention became known as the "Constitutional Convention of 1787" (or sometimes the "Philadelphia Convention" or the "Federal Convention").

The states each could send as many "deputies" as they wanted to the Constitutional Convention. At the Convention, however, the delegates decided that each state would have only one vote. In total, fifty-five men attended the Convention. These men represented all of the states except Rhode Island, which chose not to participate. The deputies, whom we now call the "Framers" of the Constitution, included grand eminences such as George Washington and Benjamin Franklin; visionary political thinkers such as James Madison, Alexander Hamilton, James Wilson, and Roger Sherman; and masters of written expression such as Gouverneur Morris, who did most of the final stylistic editing of the Constitution. The deputies also included dissenters, such as George Mason of Virginia, who refused to vote for the document because it did not contain a bill of rights, and Robert Yates and John Lansing, Jr., who left the Convention early because they believed that their instructions from the New York legislature did not permit them to participate in creating a new constitution.

> **FYI**
>
> Although the Constitutional Convention met in secret and the members agreed not to discuss what took place, we now know a great deal about what transpired at the proceedings. The Convention appointed a secretary, who kept an official journal. In addition, at least eight of the fifty-five members took notes at the Convention. By great fortune, James Madison, who was the intellectual leader of the delegates, took the most extensive notes. The records and notes are collected in *The Records of the Federal Convention of 1787* (Max Farrand, ed., 1911), a source cited by more than 100 Supreme Court cases. The Library of Congress's website contains the full text of this work at http://memory.loc.gov/ammem/amlaw/lwfr.html. For guidance in using these records, see Gregory E. Maggs, *A Concise Guide to the Records of the Federal Constitutional Convention of 1787 as Evidence of the Original Meaning of the U.S. Constitution*, 80 Geo. Wash. L. Rev. 1707 (2012).

4. Proceedings of the Constitutional Convention

As the cases in this book will show, in interpreting the Constitution, the Supreme Court often looks very carefully at what the deputies argued and decided at the Constitutional Convention.[3] To understand the Court's frequent references to the deputies' debates, readers of the Court's opinions should know what happened in Philadelphia. Basically, the Convention took place in nine chronological segments:

1. *Full Convention (May 14–May 29).* The Convention began by unanimously selecting George Washington to serve as the Convention's president. It then

[3] As discussed in Part C of this chapter, many writers disagree about whether it is possible to discern the original meaning of the Constitution from these debates and, in any event, whether the original meaning should govern modern interpretation of the Constitution.

adopted rules governing the proceedings. These rules specified, among other things, that each state present and fully represented would have one vote and that the proceedings would be kept secret.

On May 29, 1787, Edmund Randolph offered 15 resolutions, each just one sentence in length. These resolutions—which became known as the "Virginia Plan" for government—reflected the ideas of James Madison. Under the plan, there would be a national legislature that would have two chambers, one directly elected and the other appointed by the state legislatures. The plan generally favored the states with large populations (Massachusetts, Pennsylvania, New York, and Virginia) because it called for proportional representation in both houses. After Randolph made this proposal, the Convention decided to deliberate as a committee of the whole (i.e., a gathering where all of the deputies could discuss the issues under informal rules of debate).

2. *Committee of the Whole (May 30–June 13).* On the first day when the deputies met as a committee of the whole, Gouverneur Morris urged Randolph to modify his resolutions to include the following proposal: "Resolved, that a national government ought to be established consisting of a supreme Legislature, Executive, and Judiciary." The committee of the whole voted to adopt this resolution. With this action, the committee of the whole implicitly endorsed creating a new Constitution as the goal of the Convention, rather than merely amending the Articles of Confederation.

3. *Full Convention (June 13–June 15).* The Convention formally debated the Virginia Plan from June 13 to June 15. The small states opposed the Virginia Plan because they believed that their votes would be diluted in a national legislature with proportional representation. On June 15, William Paterson of New Jersey proposed a set of nine alternative resolutions, which became known as the "New Jersey Plan." The New Jersey Plan favored small states. Most significantly, the plan called for a unicameral legislature with equal representation for each state. The Convention again decided to meet as a committee of the whole, this time to discuss the New Jersey Plan.

4. *Committee of the Whole (June 16–June 19).* The committee of the whole debated and ultimately rejected the New Jersey Plan. It also considered an alternative plan proposed by Alexander Hamilton. Hamilton's plan called for an executive elected for life and senators chosen for life. The plan would have reduced state sovereignty by allowing the national executive to appoint executives for each state government.

5. *Full Convention (June 19–July 26).* Important debates about representation in the legislative branch followed the rejection of the New Jersey Plan. The large and small states could not agree on the composition of the legislative branch. Ultimately, a modified version of the Virginia Plan became acceptable to the Convention after the delegates agreed to what has become known as the "Great Compromise" (or alternatively as the "Connecticut Compromise"). In this compromise, the states would have equal representation in the Senate and proportional representation in the House. This compromise balanced the interests of large and small states. The Convention also adopted the closely related three-fifths rule, under which only three-fifths of a state's slave population would be counted for determining representation in the House. This feature split the difference between Southern states, which wanted all slaves counted for this purpose, and Northern states, which opposed counting any slaves in determining state entitlement to representation in the House.

In addition to the Great Compromise, the Convention also addressed a variety of other important topics. These included the term of the executive's service, the appointment of judges, and the process for ratifying the Constitution. On July 26th, with the general structure of the government settled, the Convention created a "Committee of Detail" to turn the plan into a draft. The Convention recessed while the Committee of Detail performed its work.

6. *Committee of Detail (July 27–August 5).* John Rutledge, Edmund Randolph, and James Wilson did most of the work of the Committee of Detail. In addition to describing the government and the selection of its members, the Committee of Detail added the list of congressional powers and the list of limitations on state powers now found in Article I. When the Committee of Detail finished, its draft was printed and distributed to all of the deputies.

7. *Full Convention (August 6–September 6).* The Full Convention then debated the Committee of Detail's draft and other important matters. They considered suffrage qualifications, immigration, slavery, and the veto power. During this time, the Convention referred some matters to separate committees, which met and reported back to the Convention. After reaching final conclusions on most items, the Convention appointed a "Committee of Style" (sometimes called the "Committee on Style and Arrangement"). The Committee of Style was charged with the task of putting the Constitution in a consistent form.

8. *Committee of Style (September 6–September 12).* The Committee of Style put all of the Convention's changes into the draft and polished the text. Gouverneur Morris did much of the work, although the Committee also included James Madison, William Johnson, Rufus King, and Alexander Hamilton. Their work is

seen as very important because they formulated the precise expression of many of the Constitution's great clauses. The Committee of Style finished its assignment on September 12, and a printer made copies of its draft for all of the deputies.

9. *Full Convention (September 12–September 17).* The Convention then debated the Committee of Style's draft for several days. During this time, George Mason and Elbridge Gerry proposed the inclusion of a bill of rights. The Convention debated but rejected this proposal. Two days later, on September 17, 1787, the state delegations present at the Convention unanimously approved the Constitution. All of the individual delegates present except for Gerry, Mason, and Randolph signed the Constitution. The Convention then adjourned.

The U.S. Constitution
National Archives

5. Ratification of the Constitution

The Constitution, by its own terms, could not go into effect until ratified. Article VII said: "The Ratification of the Conventions of nine States, shall be sufficient for the Establishment of this Constitution between the States so ratifying the Same." Under this provision, each state legislature was expected to form a ratifying convention to debate and vote on the Constitution. In the fall of 1787 and spring and early summer of 1788, the states held these ratifying conventions.

Whether the proposed Constitution would be ratified was an open question. The Constitution would make many substantial changes to the status quo. Although some people favored ratification, many others did not. Public debate spread throughout the states on the subject. Supporters of the Constitution became known as the "Federalists," while opponents became known as the "Anti-Federalists."

Three of the best known Federalists were Alexander Hamilton, James Madison, and John Jay. In the fall of 1787 and spring of 1788, they wrote a series of 85 essays explaining the Constitution and urging its ratification in the State of New York. Each of these essays was titled "The Federalist" followed by a number

> **FYI**
>
> The Federalist Papers are clearly the most influential source of the original meaning of the Constitution other than the text of the Constitution itself. The Supreme Court has cited the Federalist Papers in more than 400 cases. The Library of Congress's website contains the full text of the Federalist Papers: https://www.loc.gov/rr/program//bib/ourdocs/federalist.html. For more information on the Federalist Papers, see Gregory E. Maggs, *A Concise Guide to the Federalist Papers as a Source of the Original Meaning of the United States Constitution*, 87 B.U. L. Rev. 801 (2007).

designating its order in the series. Historians typically refer to the 85 essays as the "Federalist Papers." These essays, all of which are available online, address nearly every aspect of the Constitution. Although the essays are advocacy documents and not dispassionate legal analyses, they have been remarkably influential. As you will see in reading the cases in this book, the Supreme Court regularly relies on these essays in attempting to discern the original meaning of the Constitution.

The Anti-Federalists opposed the Constitution for a number of reasons. Two of the most important concerned the protection of state sovereignty and individual rights. Opponents felt that the Constitution gave too much power to the federal government at the expense of the states. They also worried that the Constitution did not contain a bill of rights that would limit the powers of the government. In thinking about these opponents of the Constitution, modern readers should remember that their concerns stemmed from having lived through Parliament's oppression of the colonies.

By the summer of 1788, conventions in nine states had approved the Constitution, putting it into effect among the ratifying states. As the following table indicates, ratification was uncontroversial in Delaware, New Jersey, and Georgia. Each of these small states unanimously ratified the document.

But the Constitution was much more controversial in other states. Indeed, switching just a few votes in big states like New York or Virginia might have scuttled the entire project.

> **FYI**
>
> Many records from the state ratifying conventions are collected in The Debates in the Several State Conventions on the Adoption of the Federal Constitution, As Recommended by the General Convention at Philadelphia, in 1787 (Jonathan Elliot, ed. 1836–59). This work, often called Elliot's Debates for short, has been very influential; the Supreme Court has cited it in over 100 cases. The full text is available online at the Library of Congress's website: http://memory.loc.gov/ammem/amlaw/lwed.html. For guidance on using these records, see Gregory E. Maggs, *A Concise Guide to the Records of the State Ratifying Conventions as a Source of the Original Meaning of the United States Constitution*, 2009 U. Ill. L. Rev. 457.

State	Date of Ratification	Vote
Delaware	Dec. 7, 1787	30–0
Pennsylvania	Dec. 12, 1787	46–23
New Jersey	Dec. 18, 1787	38–0
Georgia	Jan. 2, 1788	26–0
Connecticut	Jan. 9, 1788	128–40
Massachusetts	Feb. 6, 1788	187–168
Maryland	Apr. 28, 1788	63–11
South Carolina	May 23, 1788	149–73
New Hampshire	Jun. 21, 1788	57–47
Virginia	Jun. 25, 1788	89–79
New York	Jul. 26, 1788	30–27
North Carolina	Nov. 21, 1789	195–77
Rhode Island	May 29, 1790	34–32

6. The First Congress

Federal elections took place during the fall of 1788, and the new government under the Constitution began in 1789. George Washington, of course, became the first President. In the First Congress, which met from March 1789 to March 1791, a total of 29 persons served as senators and 66 served as representatives.

Many of these senators and representatives justifiably could consider themselves experts on the Constitution. Ten of the senators and eleven of the representatives had served as deputies at the Constitutional Convention. Some of them, including James Madison, Oliver Ellsworth, and Roger Sherman, had played prominent roles in the Constitution's drafting. Other members of the First Congress, such as Richard Henry Lee, had participated at state ratifying conventions even though they had not attended the Constitutional Convention.

FYI

Because the First Congress laid so much of the foundation for the new nation, the Supreme Court often looks to its acts for guidance in determining the original meaning of the Constitution. The acts of the First Congress are published in volume 1 of *The Public Statutes at Large of the United States of America* (1845), the citation of which is abbreviated as "1 Stat." The Library of Congress has the full text at its website: http://memory.loc.gov/ammem/amlaw/lwsl.html.

During its two-year term, the First Congress passed an astounding 96 acts. Among its many other accomplishments, the First Congress:

- imposed taxes on imported goods and on vessels entering United States ports, providing the first source of federal revenue;
- shaped the executive branch by establishing the Departments of Foreign Affairs, War, and Treasury;
- created the federal judicial system;
- passed laws on naturalization, patents, copyrights, and other subjects still governed by federal law;
- established a system of lighthouses, the post office, and the Bank of the United States;
- provided for the assumption of state revolutionary war debts and paying of the national debt; and
- located the seat of government in the District of Columbia and admitted Kentucky and Vermont into the Union.

The First Congress also proposed twelve amendments to the Constitution, ten of which (now known as the Bill of Rights) received quick ratification by the states.

B. ORGANIZATION OF THE CONSTITUTION

The Constitution contains a number of different parts. No one expects a new student of constitutional law to commit the document to memory or to master its provisions in one reading. But before going further, you should take some time to become familiar with its organization.

Preamble

The Constitution starts with an introduction, or "Preamble," which lists the six goals of the People in adopting the Constitution: "to form a more perfect Union, establish Justice, insure domestic Tranquility, provide for the common defence, promote the general Welfare, and secure the Blessings of Liberty to ourselves and our Posterity." Although lofty in tone, the courts mostly have concluded that the language of the Preamble is precatory. In other words, it does not create legal rights, duties, or powers. But the Preamble is still important. For example, it makes clear that the "People" rather than the states adopted the Constitution. We will consider this distinction in cases about the nature of the United States' sovereignty.

Article I

Following the Preamble, the Constitution contains seven articles. The first three articles reflect the Framers' vision that there are three branches of government: the legislative branch, the executive branch, and the judicial branch. Each has its own powers and has some ability to provide checks on the others. But as we will see in Chapter 6, sometimes questions arise about whether one branch is attempting to exercise powers belonging to another branch.

Article I contains ten sections that address the legislative branch. Section 1 establishes the fundamental point that "[a]ll legislative Powers herein granted shall be vested in a Congress of the United States, which shall consist of a Senate and House of Representatives." This means, among other things, that Congress has these powers, and that the President and the courts do not. You will read about this provision in famous cases like *Youngstown Sheet & Tube v. Sawyer*, 343 U.S. 579 (1952), in which the Court held that the President was unconstitutionally attempting to assert powers that were legislative in nature.

Sections 2 through 6 then tell how senators and representatives are selected, what their qualifications must be, how they are paid, and so forth. These provisions come up in the important case of *U.S. Term Limits v. Thornton*, 514 U.S. 779 (1995), a case invalidating an attempt to add what amounted to additional restrictions on who could run for the House or Senate.

Section 7 describes the procedure that Congress must follow in order to pass a law. As most high school civics classes teach, the House and Senate have to approve a bill, and the President must sign it. If the President vetoes a bill (i.e., rejects it), the House and Senate can override the veto with a two-thirds vote. But we will see in *INS v. Chadha*, 462 U.S. 919 (1983), that Congress has sometimes been tempted to look for ways to exercise power without involving the President.

Section 8 then lists the subjects upon which Congress may pass laws. It says that Congress may collect taxes, regulate commerce, establish a post office, and so forth. Chapter 3 of this book covers what Congress may and may not do under Article I, section 8. We will see in *Heart of Atlanta Motel v. United States*, 379 U.S. 241 (1964), and *Katzenbach v. McClung*, 379 U.S. 294 (1964), that Congress has the power to pass legislation protecting civil rights. On the other hand, we will see in *United States v. Lopez*, 514 U.S. 549 (1995), and *New York v. United States*, 505 U.S. 144 (1992), that the Supreme Court has struck down laws attempting to ban guns from schools or order the states to provide for the disposal of radioactive waste as being beyond the power of Congress to enact.

Sections 9 and 10 state various specific prohibitions. Section 9 says that Congress generally cannot suspend the writ of habeas corpus, pass ex post facto laws, tax exports from states, or give preference to one state's ports. Section 10 then tells us some of the things that the states may not do. They cannot enter treaties or coin money, impose duties on imports and exports, and so forth.

Article II

Article II concerns the executive branch. The Chief Executive, of course, is the President of the United States. Article II, section 1 says: "The executive Power shall be vested in a President of the United States of America." But the President does not act alone. The federal departments and agencies assist the President. The Constitution does not create these departments, but in various provisions it contemplates their existence. Congress has created many such departments, including the Department of Justice, the Department of Defense, the State Department, and so forth.

The President is the chief executive. In general, that makes everyone else in the executive branch subordinate to the President. The President generally exercises control by firing or threatening to fire those who will not carry out his lawful policies. But we will see in cases like *Humphrey's Executor v. United States*, 295 U.S. 602 (1935), and *Morrison v. Olson*, 487 U.S. 654 (1988), that Congress may place some limits on the ability of the President to control subordinates in this manner.

Section 2 puts the President in charge of the military, and allows him to grant pardons and appoint judges and other office holders. Section 3 requires the President to report to Congress, receive ambassadors, make sure that the laws are faithfully executed, and so forth.

Article III

Article III describes the power of the federal judiciary. The first sentence of Section 1 tells us that "[t]he judicial Power of the United States, shall be vested in one supreme Court, and in such inferior Courts as the Congress may from time to time ordain and establish." Section 2 specifies the "subject matter jurisdiction" of federal courts—in other words, the kinds of cases that the federal courts may decide. For example, it says that they can hear lawsuits between "Citizens of different States," which we know as diversity jurisdiction. We will see in the first case included in Chapter 2, *Marbury v. Madison*, 5 U.S. (1 Cranch) 137 (1803), that the Court struck down a federal statute that attempted to give the Court jurisdiction beyond the limits of Article III, section 2.

Articles IV–VII

Articles IV through VII contain a variety of different provisions. Article IV generally addresses relations among the states. As we will see in Chapter 4, the Privileges and Immunities Clause in Article IV limits discrimination by states against citizens of other states. Article V discusses the amendment process. The House and Senate can propose amendments by a two-thirds vote or two-thirds of the states can call a convention. (The latter route for amendment has never been used.) Proposals for amending the Constitution become effective when three-fourths of the states have ratified them in their legislatures or in conventions. Article VI tells us, among other things, that the "Constitution, and the Laws of the United States * * * shall be the supreme Law of the Land." Article VII describes the ratification process that had to occur before the Constitution could take effect.

Amendments

The Constitution now contains 27 amendments. The first 10 amendments, commonly called the Bill of Rights, protect a large number of individual rights. Amendments 13 through 15 are known as the "Civil War Era Amendments" or the "Reconstruction Amendments" because they were passed at the end of the Civil War during the process of Reconstruction. They abolish slavery, bar states from denying equal protection of the laws or due process of the law to any person, and protect voting rights. We will be looking extensively at the First Amendment's protection of Free Speech, Free Press, and Religion, and at the Fourteenth Amendment's guarantees of Equal Protection and Due Process, in the second half of this book.

C. METHODS OF INTERPRETING THE CONSTITUTION

One of the many things that distinguished the American Constitution at the time of its ratification was the simple fact that it was written down. (Although the United Kingdom—the nation from which the United States broke but from which it inherited its legal tradition—also had a "constitution," it was developed over time, in a common-law fashion, rather than codified.) At first blush, one might expect there to be little need for a thick casebook of judicial opinions for matters governed by a written document. But the study of American constitutional law has, from the very beginning, been as much a study of judicial interpretations of the Constitution as it has been of the document itself. We will see one of the reasons why this is so in Chapter 2 when we consider *Marbury v. Madison* and the topic of judicial review. But answering the question of who should get to interpret the Constitution—a question on which there is substantial continuing debate, as we will see in Chapter 2—does not tell us why a written Constitution should so frequently require interpretation in the first place. As it turns out, there has long been a need for interpretation of the Constitution because it is often not obvious, even after careful consultation of the text of the Constitution, what the Constitution tells us about important questions.

There are several reasons why this is so. First, the Framers of the Constitution (and those who ratified it) sought to preserve some degree of flexibility for subsequent generations to address pressing problems and, if necessary, to structure the government accordingly. Second, as described above, although the Framers were able to achieve consensus by compromising on some controversial questions, they masked their disagreement on other questions by writing general and vague provisions. Third, the Framers simply did not anticipate some of the questions that would arise in the future. Today's problems often look very different from the problems of 1789—or 1868, when the Fourteenth Amendment was ratified. Accordingly, the plain text of the Constitution often does not speak directly to questions that are likely to arise today.

One possible response to constitutional silence would be to conclude that if the Constitution does not expressly prohibit a particular action, it permits it. The Constitution, after all, is almost entirely about the limits on governmental, rather than private, action—the sole (and obviously incredibly important) exception being the Thirteenth Amendment, which prohibits slavery—and one could sensibly conclude that if the Constitution does not prohibit the government from taking a certain action, it implicitly permits it. There is great appeal to this approach; indeed, as we will see, among other things, it attempts to preserve democratic government by preventing judicial interference with the modern choices of democratically elected officials. But even if one is persuaded that it is the proper response to constitutional silence, it does not help us to determine when in fact the Constitution is silent on a particular question. This is because the Constitution's broad provisions arguably touch on a wide range of topics, even though they fail to provide specific guidance on most controversial questions that are likely to arise.

Indeed, the Constitution tends to speak at very high levels of generality. There is little doubt, for example, that the First Amendment protects the freedom of speech, but it does not define "freedom" or "speech." Is a contribution to a candidate for public office a form of "speech"? See *Buckley v. Valeo,* 424 U.S. 1 (1976), which we consider in Volume 2. What about publicly burning a draft card as a form of protest against an ongoing war? See *United States v. O'Brien,* 391 U.S.

367 (1968), which we also consider in Volume 2. And even if we can agree on what counts as speech, does a law imposing some limits on the ability to engage in a particular form of speech—but not prohibiting it entirely—"abridg[e]" the "freedom" protected by the Amendment? Similarly, the Fourteenth Amendment prohibits the States from denying to persons the "equal protection of the laws," but it does not give any more guidance about what those terms mean—whether, for example, the government is ever permitted to distinguish among citizens and, if so, whether some bases for classification are more problematic than others; and, if so, whether a State can justify a particular suspect classification—such as a requirement that drivers over 70 years old, but not younger drivers, get annual eye exams, or a ban on women serving in combat in the military—with sufficiently compelling reasons. Even determining whether the Constitution is "silent," therefore, requires interpretation of the document's broad terms.

Of course, the Constitution is not unusual among written texts in requiring interpretation to determine its meaning. Courts routinely are called upon, for example, to interpret statutes and contracts, written texts that only sometimes speak with great detail, and often speak in broad generalities—or, with respect to issues that are litigated, are entirely silent. Although interpretation of such documents is commonplace, there are a range of interpretive approaches that courts follow—and substantial debate over which are appropriate and defensible. In the context of statutory interpretation, for example, there are lively debates over whether judges should consider legislative history to determine statutory meaning, or whether courts should seek to discern congressional purposes in order to shed light on how Congress would have chosen to address particular circumstances about which the statute is silent. Similarly, there is a long-standing debate over whether, in interpreting a contract, courts should consider only the plain meaning of the contract's terms or instead may consider extrinsic evidence to determine a contract's meaning.

> **FYI**
>
> There is an extensive literature on the appropriate way for courts to interpret statutes. For a taste of the debate, compare John F. Manning, *Textualism as a Nondelegation Doctrine*, 97 Colum. L. Rev. 673 (1997), with Alexander Alienikoff, *Updating Statutory Interpretation*, 87 Mich. L. Rev. 20, 47–61 (1988).

But even assuming that there is a "correct" way to interpret statutes and contracts, matters are at least arguably more complex when the document at issue is the Constitution, because the Constitution is quite different from a statute or a contract in many important ways. First, as we will see when we consider *Marbury v. Madison* in Chapter 2, the Constitution is understood to be a form of "higher" law—that is, it cannot be superseded by an ordinary statute enacted by Congress, and (by its own express terms, in the Supremacy Clause of Article VI) it trumps state law that is inconsistent with its provisions. Second, by its own terms (in Article V), the Constitution can be amended only after obtaining a super-majority consensus—a two-thirds majority in both Houses of Congress and ratification by three-quarters of the States—that has rarely been achieved in over two hundred years. As noted above, there have been only 27 Amendments, and even that number tends to overstate the ease with which the Constitution may be amended: the ten Amendments in the Bill of Rights were adopted together two years after ratification of the original document, and one other (the Twenty-Seventh) was proposed along with the original Bill of Rights; three Amendments were adopted within only a few years after the Civil War; and two of the Amendments—the Eighteenth, enshrining Prohibition, and the Twenty-First, repealing it—effectively cancel each other out. Indeed, not only is it difficult to amend the Constitution, but Article V actually states that some of its provisions cannot be amended at all, even with the requisite support of two-thirds of both Houses of Congress and three-fourths of the states. Perhaps more strikingly, the provision that cannot be amended today is the one that gives each state an equal voice in the Senate, even though that provision arguably is the single most anti-democratic provision in the Constitution itself. Third, and particularly important in light of the first two distinctive features, the Constitution is over 200 years old.

Together, these features of the Constitution—its status as higher law, the difficulty of amending it, and its age—stand in uneasy tension with the notion of democracy. Indeed, the very notion of constitutionalism means that democratically elected majorities today cannot decide to govern themselves in the manner of their choosing if their choices would conflict with the Constitution. This tension is generally known as the "dead-hand problem": to embrace constitutionalism is to accept that the men who wrote and ratified the Constitution to govern them over 200 years ago should also be able to reach into the future, with their now-dead hands, and tell us how to live our lives.

> **Food for Thought**
>
> The provision in the Constitution providing the requirements for its ratification itself was inconsistent with the "constitution" that was in force at the time it was adopted. Although Article VII provided that the Constitution would become effective upon ratification by nine of the thirteen states, the Articles of Confederation expressly required *unanimous* consent of the states for any amendments to its terms. What does this suggest about the extent to which we should treat the *current* Constitution as binding?

One possible response to the dead-hand problem, of course, would be to deny the continuing binding force of the Constitution. It is, after all, merely a collection of words with no independent force beyond our willingness to follow it. But this response historically has held little appeal, because each successive generation has seen great value in binding itself to a charter for self-governance. First, it would be difficult for government to function without rules for the proper exercise of its power. Second, there is good reason to limit the power of democratic majorities. The Constitution is a form of self-imposed paternalism, to prevent us from letting the perceived exigencies of the moment lead us to decisions that, upon reflection and with the clarity of hindsight, we know are destructive of our most deeply held values.

And, as explained above, if we are to embrace the Constitution, then we must have some way to interpret it. The debate over how to interpret the Constitution is at least as old as the Constitution itself and tends to reflect the basic tension created by the very notion of constitutionalism. On the one hand, if we accept that the Constitution is a form of law (albeit higher law), then there is a strong argument that we should interpret it as we would any other law—to have a generally fixed content, determined by the will of those who enacted it, embodied either in their intentions, in the text itself, or in the understanding of that text at the time it was enacted. Indeed, one could forcefully argue that if the Constitution did not mean what its Framers thought it meant—or at least something closely approximating, at some level of generality, what they thought it meant—then the Constitution would not truly be a form of law in any conventional sense. This conception of the proper way to interpret the Constitution forms the theoretical basis of the approach to interpretation known as "originalism." Proponents of originalism argue that a provision of the Constitution must mean today what it meant, or perhaps was understood to mean, when it was ratified.

On the other hand, if we are concerned about the dead-hand problem and its seeming inconsistency with our democratic impulses today, then we might seek to interpret the Constitution in a way that reflects values that have enduring support, and not simply those that were important at the time of the Founding. According to this view, if the Constitution is binding principally because we agree to be bound by it, and we are eager to be bound by it only if we perceive it to be legitimate according to contemporary values, then we must update the Constitution in order to preserve it. This conception of the proper way to interpret the Constitution is often called "non-originalism," defined in contrast to what it is not. Most non-originalists rely to some degree on the original meaning of the Constitution, at least at a high level of generality, but also see room for constitutional meaning to evolve.

The debate over these competing views reflects the fundamental paradox of constitutionalism: if the Constitution is a form of law, then its meaning to the people who adopted it must be central to its meaning today. But do those people have a right to bind us to their choices? In the sections that follow, we consider the conventional arguments for and against originalism and non-originalism.

1. Originalism

Originalism is an approach to interpretation that accords dispositive weight to the original meaning of the Constitution. According to this approach, a provision of the Constitution must mean today what it meant when it was adopted. Under an originalist approach, for example, if the Constitution did not prohibit capital punishment in 1789—or in 1791, when the Bill of Rights was ratified, or in 1868, when the Fourteenth Amendment was ratified—then it does not prohibit it today. Conversely, under an originalist approach, if the Constitution in 1789—or, again, in 1791 or 1868—did not authorize Congress to rely on its authority under the Commerce Clause to regulate certain matters, then arguably Congress lacks that power today, as well. (We will consider in Chapter 3 whether changes in the nature of "commerce" inevitably should lead to the conclusion that Congress has greater power to regulate local matters today than it did at the time of the Framing.)

> **FYI**
>
> Some originalists seek the original "intent" of the Framers, some seek the original "understanding" of the Constitution by the Framers or the ratifiers, and still others seek the original "objective meaning" of the Constitution. What are the differences among those three concepts? Should judges apply different inquiries depending upon whether they seek original intent, understanding, or objective meaning?

Proponents of originalism generally offer five principal arguments in support of their approach to interpreting the Constitution. First, they argue that to interpret is, by definition, to seek the original meaning of the text. Second, they argue that originalism is the only approach to constitutional interpretation that properly recognizes the Constitution's status as law. Third, they argue that originalism is necessary to preserve democratic values. Fourth, they argue that originalism is uniquely promising for constraining the ability of judges to impose their own personal views under the guise of constitutional interpretation. Fifth, deciding constitutional issues in accordance with the original meaning of the Constitution is a methodology firmly established by precedent. We discuss these claims in turn.

First, originalists argue that to interpret a document is, by definition, to attempt to determine what its author or authors intended to convey. When we interpret a contract—or read a shopping list or any other written text, for that matter—we generally seek to determine what the author of the document meant, at the time that the author wrote it. It should be no different, originalists contend, when we seek to interpret the Constitution.

Second, originalists generally argue that because we have always treated written law as having a fixed meaning—this is true, for example, for statutes, whose meaning does not generally evolve over time—the Constitution, which is a form of law, must have a fixed meaning, as well. And, originalists argue, just as a statute's meaning is determined by reference to the understandings of the people who enacted it, the meaning of a provision of the Constitution must also be determined by reference to the people who were responsible for its enactment. Originalists do not necessarily deny the existence of the dead-hand problem, but they argue that if the Constitution is authoritative only to the extent that we agree with it today, then it is not really law at all but instead is simply a makeweight.

Third, proponents of originalism argue that only their approach is consistent with the proper judicial role in a democratic society. Any approach other than originalism, they argue, inevitably seeks constitutional meaning in evolving or current values. But a democratic system, they argue, does not need constitutional guarantees to ensure that its laws reflect current values. And it is fundamentally anti-democratic, they contend, to permit unelected judges to invalidate democratically enacted laws that are not inconsistent with the original meaning of the Constitution.

Fourth, originalists contend that because judicial review is by its very nature counter-majoritarian—a theme that we will explore in detail in Chapter 2—it is essential to ensure that judges employing it exercise, in Alexander Hamilton's words, "judgment" rather than "will," The Federalist No. 78—that is, that judges simply interpret the law rather than make the law. Because the original meaning of the Constitution is fixed, originalists argue, it can be objectively determined by a judge without reference to his own political preferences. In contrast, they argue, if the Constitution's meaning "evolves," but derives from something other than democratic enactments, then the judges seeking the Constitution's meaning will not be restrained in their ability to impose their own personal views under the guise of constitutional interpretation.

Fifth, deciding constitutional issues in accordance with the original meaning of the Constitution is a methodology firmly established by precedent from the 1790s to modern times. Indeed, all members of the Supreme Court today, whether they might be characterized as liberal or conservative, routinely justify their constitutional decisions, in whole or in part, by asserting that they are following the original meaning. Look for evidence of this practice as you read the cases in this book. In contrast, instances in which the Supreme Court expressly has rejected originalist methodology are extremely rare. To be sure, sometimes there are disagreements about what the original meaning of the Constitution was. But in these instances the Justices are usually disagreeing about conclusions and not about methods. Accordingly, even if other, non-originalist, interpretative methods might be legitimate or even preferable in some ways, originalists contend that respect for precedent should cause judges to hesitate to abandon a methodology so firmly rooted in the Supreme Court's decisions.

The basic approach of originalism, of course, is not a new approach to interpretation. But it has attracted renewed attention and support in the last few decades, in part as a response to the perceived non-originalism of the Supreme Court in the 1950s, 1960s, and 1970s, an era that saw a substantial judicial expansion of rights subject to constitutional protection.

Perspective and Analysis

Justice Antonin Scalia was arguably the most well-known and influential originalist. Consider his defense of the approach:

> [O]riginalism seems to me more compatible with the nature and purpose of a Constitution in a democratic system. A democratic society does not, by and large, need constitutional guarantees to insure that its laws will reflect "current values." Elections take care of that quite well. The purpose of constitutional guarantees * * * is precisely to prevent the law from reflecting certain changes in original values that the society adopting the Constitution thinks fundamentally undesirable.

He has also criticized the alternatives to originalism:

> [T]he central practical defect of nonoriginalism is fundamental and irreparable: the impossibility of achieving any consensus on what, precisely, is to replace original meaning, once that is abandoned. * * * [In contrast, originalism] establishes a historical criterion that is conceptually quite separate from the preferences of the judge himself.

Antonin Scalia, *Originalism: The Lesser Evil,* 57 U. Cin. L. Rev. 849, 862–64 (1989).

2. Non-Originalism

In contrast, non-originalists generally believe that the Constitution's meaning today is not always the meaning that it had when it was ratified. Non-originalists accordingly look to a range of sources in interpreting the Constitution. This is not to say that all non-originalists believe that the original meaning is irrelevant to constitutional interpretation; to the contrary, virtually all theories of constitutional interpretation accord significant—and in some cases dispositive—weight to the original meaning. Non-originalists often conclude that the original meaning of a constitutional provision, expressed at a very high level of generality, provides guidance for ascertaining the relevant constitutional rule. Non-originalists, for example, might read the Equal Protection Clause of the Fourteenth Amendment to announce a general rule about equal treatment, which they might be willing to apply in a manner that the Framers of the Fourteenth Amendment did not contemplate, such as to discrimination on the basis of gender. But, for the reasons discussed below, non-originalists sometimes are willing to depart from the original meaning.

Non-originalists also often look to judicial precedent in seeking constitutional meaning. In this way, many non-originalists view constitutional interpretation as something akin to common-law decision-making, with constitutional principles evolving gradually over time. Non-originalists also often look to state practices to determine whether broad consensus has developed that a particular action or practice is acceptable or unacceptable. For example, if public flogging is banned in all states but one—and has been illegal in all states but one for decades—then a non-originalist might conclude that public flogging today is a "cruel and unusual" punishment within the meaning of the Eighth Amendment, even though it likely was not thought to be cruel and unusual in 1791, when the Eighth Amendment was ratified, or in 1868, when the Fourteenth Amendment was ratified.

> **Make the Connection**
>
> As we will see in Chapter 7, the Supreme Court has held that the Due Process Clause of the Fourteenth Amendment "incorporated" most of the provisions in the Bill of Rights, applying their limits to state, as well as federal, action.

Non-originalists are willing to depart from the original meaning of the Constitution because of concerns about originalism itself. Non-originalists have generally disputed originalists' claims that originalism is likely to produce determinate constitutional meaning today. More fundamentally, non-originalists argue that departure from the original meaning often is necessary to ensure that the Constitution retains legitimacy, which is essential if the public is to continue to accept the Constitution's binding character. We discuss these claims in turn.

First, non-originalists contend that most difficult constitutional questions that arise today cannot be answered by simple reference to the original understanding. They observe that the historical record is silent on many important provisions of the Constitution; that when the Framers did discuss the meaning of a particular provision of the Constitution, they often disagreed about its meaning; and that, in any event, the Framers did not contemplate, let alone discuss, most of the difficult questions that arise today or how the Constitution would apply to those problems. Accordingly, non-originalists argue that resort to the original meaning is unlikely to produce determinate constitutional meaning today. Non-originalists also argue that this likely indeterminism undermines the claim that originalism is uniquely promising as a way to constrain judges from imposing their own views under the guise of constitutional interpretation; faced with an ambiguous or indeterminate historical record, non-originalists contend, judges have discretion to choose the evidence of original meaning that best reflects their own personal values.

Second, and more important, non-originalists argue that originalism fails to account for the dead-hand problem, and thus risks producing a Constitution that fails the test of legitimacy. Originalism, non-originalists note, by definition gives voice to the values of the framing generation, and thus risks producing results that the American public today might find problematic. An originalist approach to the Fourteenth Amendment, for example, arguably would have required the Court to conclude, contrary to the decision in *Brown v. Board of Education*, 347 U.S. 483 (1954), that racial segregation in public schools does not violate the Equal Protection Clause. Similarly, discrimination on the basis of gender was commonplace in 1868 when the Fourteenth Amendment was ratified; a faithfully originalist approach almost certainly would permit the states today to prohibit women from (among other things) serving as lawyers, as they did at the time that the Amendment was ratified. See *Bradwell v. Illinois*, 83 U.S. (16 Wall.) 130 (1873).

Food for Thought

There is a debate among scholars about whether *Brown* was correct as an originalist matter. Compare Robert H. Bork, *The Tempting of America* 76 (1990), and Michael W. McConnell, *Originalism and the Desegregation Decisions*, 81 Va. L. Rev. 947 (1995) (arguing that Brown was consistent with the original understanding of the Fourteenth Amendment), with Alexander Bickel, *The Original Understanding and the Segregation Decision*, 69 Harv. L. Rev. 1 (1955), and Michael Klarman, Brown, *Originalism, and Constitutional Theory*, 81 Va. L. Rev. 1881 (1995) (arguing that *Brown* was inconsistent with the original understanding of the Fourteenth Amendment). We will consider the decision in *Brown*, and discrimination on the basis of race and gender, in Volume 2.

Non-originalists recognize that the Constitution (in Article V) makes explicit provision for the adoption of amendments, but they argue that the potential of the amendment process to incorporate modern values into the Constitution is illusory. In 1954, for example, when the Court decided Brown, Southern resistance would have prevented the ratification of an amendment prohibiting racial segregation. Similarly, as recently as the 1970s, a proposed amendment to prohibit discrimination on the basis of gender failed to achieve ratification in the required three-quarters of the States. These results, non-originalists contend, would substantially undermine respect for the Constitution, and thus the public's willingness to be bound by the Constitution. Perhaps as a result, many of the Court's decisions cannot be explained simply by reference to the original meaning of the Constitution, and some of the Court's decisions are almost certainly inconsistent with the original meaning.

Perspective and Analysis

Justice William Brennan was an influential critic of originalism and a proponent of what some call "Living Constitutionalism." Consider his view:

> A position that upholds constitutional claims only if they were within the specific contemplation of the Framers in effect establishes a presumption of resolving textual ambiguities against the claim of constitutional right. * * * This is a choice no less political than any other; it expresses antipathy to claims of the minority to rights against the majority. * * *

Justice Brennan did not reject the notion that the Constitution has enduring principles, defined by the Framers' choices. But he disagreed with a formulaic application of those principles:

> Current Justices read the Constitution in the only way that we can: as twentieth-century Americans. We look to the history of the time of the framing and to the intervening history of interpretation. But the ultimate question must be: What do the words of the text mean in our time? For the genius of the Constitution rests not in any static meaning it might have had in a world that is dead and gone, but in the adaptability of its great principles to cope with current problems and current needs.

William J. Brennan, Jr., *The Constitution of the United States: Contemporary Ratification,* 27 S. Tex. L. Rev. 433, 436 (1986).

All of this discussion leads to an important question: Which interpretive method does the Supreme Court use? As you will see, this question has no simple answer. As you read the Court's cases, you will find three categories of decisions.

In some cases, especially older ones, the Supreme Court has insisted emphatically that only the original meaning of the Constitution matters. The decision in *South Carolina v. United States,* 199 U.S. 437 (1905), made this point with unmistakable clarity. The Court said: "The Constitution is a written instrument. As such its meaning does not alter. That which it meant when adopted, it means now." *Id.* at 448.

In other cases, however, the Court has squarely rejected the idea that it must follow the original meaning of the Constitution. For example, in *Home Building & Loan Assn. v. Blaisdell,* 290 U.S. 398 (1934), which we consider in Volume 2, the Court allowed a state law to alter the obligation of a mortgage contract even though it recognized that this result likely conflicted with the original understanding of Contracts Clause in Article I, Section 10. The Court unapologetically rejected the idea that "the great clauses of the Constitution must be confined to the interpretation which the framers, with the conditions and outlook of their time, would have placed upon them." *Id.* at 443.

Most modern cases fall somewhere in between these two extremes. Usually, the Court considers evidence of the original meaning without making broad pronouncements about whether the original meaning must control. Sometimes the Court follows the original meaning, and sometimes it does not. Interestingly, even though the current Justices have very different views on constitutional interpretation, they all cite the Federalist Papers, the records of the Constitutional Convention, and the state ratifying debates from time to time because they all consider these sources to be influential. In many cases, the Court tries to follow the original meaning, but simply cannot agree on what it was. For example, as we will see in Chapter 4 in *U.S. Term Limits, Inc. v. Thornton,* 514 U.S. 779 (1995), both the majority and dissenting opinions claim to follow the original meaning.

In reading the cases in this book, consider not only the results that the Supreme Court reaches, but also what interpretive methodology the Court is using.

This section has provided an overview of the competing approaches to constitutional interpretation. Although we directly address the arguments for originalism and non-originalism here, in many respects all of the material that follows in this book speaks, even if only indirectly, to the same question. Indeed, the judicial decisions in this book about what the Constitution means often are as much about the appropriate way to interpret the Constitution as they are about the meaning of the particular provisions at issue. As you read those materials, be sensitive to the relationship between arguments about the meaning of particular provisions of the Constitution and arguments about the appropriate way to interpret the Constitution more generally.

The United States Supreme Court
Architect of the Capitol

D. HOW CASES REACH THE SUPREME COURT AND ARE DECIDED

This book contains numerous edited Supreme Court opinions. In reading these opinions, it is important to understand a little bit about how cases reach the Supreme Court and how the Court decides them. Most lawsuits begin in a state or federal "trial" court. In a civil case, the plaintiff files a complaint against the defendant and asks for a remedy. For example, in *District of Columbia v. Heller*, 554 U.S. 570 (2008), which is included at the end of this chapter, a special police officer named Dick Heller sued the District of Columbia. Heller wanted to keep a functioning handgun at his home in the District of Columbia for self-defense, but the District of Columbia had a strict gun control statute that barred him from doing so. Heller, who was joined by several others in the same situation, sued the District of Columbia government in a federal trial court, the United States District Court for the District of Columbia, arguing that the gun control statute violated the Constitution's Second Amendment. In a criminal case, the government brings criminal charges against the defendant. For example, in *Loving v. Virginia*, 388 U.S. 1 (1967), which we consider in Volume 2, the state of Virginia charged Richard Loving and his wife, Mildred Loving, in a Virginia state trial court with violating a Virginia statute making interracial marriage a crime. The Lovings argued that the statute violated the Fourteenth Amendment, but the state trial court rejected this argument, found them guilty, sentenced them each to one year in prison, but suspended the sentence on the condition that they leave Virginia and not re-enter the state for 25 years.

After a federal or state trial court decides a case, an appeal may follow. In federal cases, appeals go to one of the U.S. Courts of Appeals. In *District of Columbia v. Heller*, Heller and the other plaintiffs appealed to the U.S. Court of Appeals for the District of Columbia Circuit. A panel of three judges reversed the decision of the U.S. District Court, and concluded that the District of Columbia

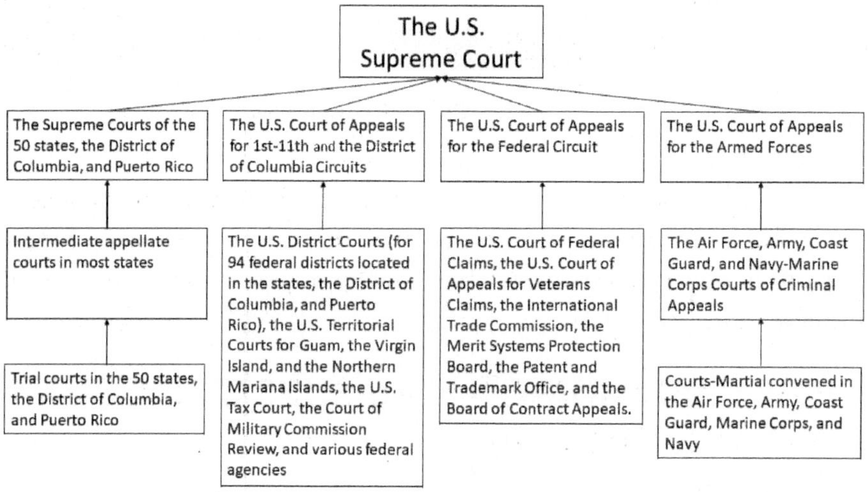

The Appellate Jurisdiction of the U.S. Supreme Court
Maggs & Smith

statute violated the Second Amendment. In *Loving v. Virginia*, the Lovings appealed their convictions to the Supreme Court of Appeals of Virginia, but that court upheld their conviction.

After losing in a U.S. Court of Appeals or the highest court in a state, a party may seek review of a decision involving a question of federal law—including federal constitutional law—in the U.S. Supreme Court. Prior to 1988, many litigants had a right to appeal to the Supreme Court in cases presenting certain constitutional questions. For example, Mr. and Mrs. Loving had a right to appeal, and exercised that right after the Virginia Supreme Court ruled against them. In the appeal, they were called the "appellants" and the state of Virginia was called the "appellee." But the rules regarding Supreme Court jurisdiction have changed over time. Since 1988, almost all litigants must ask the Supreme Court to review their case. They do this by a filing a "petition for writ of certiorari." The Supreme Court receives about 6000 such petitions each year and cannot review them all. The Supreme Court therefore has discretion to decide which cases to review. The Court typically selects about 80 cases to decide each year. In *District of Columbia v. Heller*, the District of Columbia asked the Supreme Court to review its case by filing a petition for writ of certiorari, and the Court granted the petition. In that case, the District of Columbia was called the "petitioner" because it filed the petition for writ of certiorari, and Heller and the other plaintiffs were called the "respondents." The Supreme Court is most likely to exercise its discretion to grant a petition when the decision in the court of appeals (or state supreme court) conflicts with the decision of another court, or when the case involves the constitutionality of a law, as in *Heller* and *Loving*.

When a case comes before the Supreme Court, the petitioner first files a written brief, typically about 50 pages long, setting forth the argument for why the Supreme Court should reverse the lower court. The respondent then files a response of the same length, arguing that the Supreme Court should affirm the lower-court decision. The plaintiff then has an opportunity to file a reply brief addressing the respondent's arguments. In addition, the Supreme Court may allow third-parties—called amici curiae (which means friends of the court)—to file briefs. In the *Heller* case, more than sixty private groups and governmental units filed amicus briefs. The Court also holds an "oral argument" at which each side's lawyers typically have 30 minutes to speak. During the oral argument, the Justices may ask the lawyers questions.

After the oral argument, the Justices hold a conference, and each of them votes on what the Court should do with the case. Sometimes the vote is unanimous. For example, in *Loving v. Virginia*, all nine Justices agreed that the Supreme Court should reverse the Virginia Supreme Court. Chief Justice Warren then wrote an opinion explaining the Court's decision. In other instances, the Court is divided. In *District of Columbia v. Heller*, five Justices thought that the Supreme Court should affirm the U.S. Court of Appeals for the District of Columbia Circuit, and four wanted the Supreme Court to reverse it. In this situation, Justice Scalia, representing the judges in the majority, wrote the Court's opinion. Justice Stevens and Justice Breyer both wrote dissenting opinions in which they explained their contrary views. Sometimes a Justice will write a concurring opinion, in which the Justice expresses agreement with the majority, but wishes to make additional points. In other instances, a Justice may file an opinion concurring in the judgment; in such cases, the Justice agrees with the majority about whether the case should be affirmed or reversed, but does not agree with the majority's reasoning.

Supreme Court opinions serve several purposes. The most immediate purpose is to let the parties and the lower court know whether the lower court's decision is affirmed or reversed. The opinions also explain the court's reasoning, showing the arguments that the Court accepted and rejected. Finally, an opinion serves as precedent upon which lower courts—and the Supreme Court itself—may rely in the future. But as you will see in the course, sometimes the Supreme Court overrules its prior decisions. For example, in *Plessy v. Ferguson*, 163 U.S. 537 (1896), included in Volume 2, the Supreme Court held that segregation did not necessarily violate the Fourteenth Amendment, but the Supreme Court later overruled that decision in *Brown v. Board of Education*, 347 U.S. 483 (1954), also included in Volume 2.

E. WHAT TO LOOK FOR WHEN READING SUPREME COURT OPINIONS

When you read Supreme Court opinions in this book, make sure that you first understand what lawyers call the **facts**. The facts are what happened in the case. In *Heller*, the facts are that Mr. Heller and others wanted to keep handguns in their homes but the District of Columbia had a law that prevented them from doing so. In *Loving*, Mr. and Mrs. Loving were married in the District of Columbia, and then moved to Virginia, where they were arrested for violating a Virginia statute.

Look next for the **issues** or questions presented in the case. All cases in this book involve constitutional issues. In some cases, the parties disagree about what rule or standard should govern a case. For example, in *Heller*, the issue was whether the Second Amendment's guarantee of a right to keep and bear arms creates an individual right to keep arms unrelated to militia service. In *Loving*, the issue was whether the Fourteenth Amendment makes a law that treats races equally (i.e., neither whites nor blacks can marry outside their race) but treats individuals of different races unequally (e.g., a white person can marry a white person, but a black person cannot marry a white person) violates the Fourteenth Amendment.

In still other cases, the parties will agree about the constitutional standard or rule, but will disagree about its application to the facts. For example, in *United States v. Lopez*, 514 U.S. 549 (1995), included in Chapter 3, the parties agreed that Article I, section 8, clause 3 gave Congress the power to regulate intrastate economic activities that in the aggregate might have a substantial effect on interstate commerce. But they disagreed about whether Congress could enact a law making it a crime to possess a gun within 1000 feet of a school because they had different views on whether such possession of a gun might have a substantial effect on interstate commerce. In reading any case, you should identify the **rules** that the Court determines should govern the case and be able to describe the Court's **application** of the rules to the facts.

After distilling the facts, the issues, the rules, and the application of the rules, your next step should be to think critically about what the Court decided. What was the majority's reasoning? Why did the dissent disagree? Which side do you think was correct and why? If the facts were different, would this case come out in a different way? How might the Court's decision affect other cases? Your instructors will surely ask you questions of these kinds, so it will help to think about them in advance.

F. AN ILLUSTRATIVE CASE

As we have discussed, constitutional interpretation often involves the need to ascribe concrete meaning to ambiguous text and the need to apply that text to concrete circumstances. What considerations are relevant in engaging in those inquiries?

In the case that follows, the Court considered the constitutionality under the Second Amendment of the District of Columbia's prohibition on the possession of handguns in the home. As you read the three opinions in the case—one for the Court and two in dissent—consider the roles that text, history, structure, and policy play in the interpretations that the Justices advanced.

DISTRICT OF COLUMBIA V. HELLER

554 U.S. 570 (2008)

JUSTICE SCALIA delivered the opinion of the Court.

The District of Columbia generally prohibits the possession of handguns. It is a crime to carry an unregistered firearm, and the registration of handguns is prohibited. See D.C.Code §§ 7–2501.01(12), 7–2502.01(a), 7–2502.02(a)(4) (2001). Wholly apart from that prohibition, no person may carry a handgun without a license, but the chief of police may issue licenses for 1-year periods. See §§ 22–4504(a), 22–4506. District of Columbia law also requires residents to keep their lawfully owned firearms, such as registered long guns, "unloaded and dissembled or bound by a trigger lock or similar device" unless they are located in a place of business or are being used for lawful recreational activities. See § 7–2507.02.

[Respondent Dick Heller, a D.C. special police officer authorized to carry a handgun while on duty at the Federal Judicial Center, wished to keep a handgun at home. He filed a lawsuit in District Court challenging these provisions under the Second Amendment. The trial court held for the District of Columbia, reasoning that the Second Amendment does not protect an individual right to own firearms. But the court of appeals reversed this decision. The District of Columbia then sought review in the Supreme Court.]

The Second Amendment provides: "A well regulated Militia, being necessary to the security of a free State, the right of the people to keep and bear Arms, shall not be infringed." * * * The two sides in this case have set out very different interpretations of the Amendment. Petitioners and today's dissenting Justices believe that it protects only the right to possess and carry a firearm in connection with militia service. Respondent argues that it protects an individual right to possess a firearm unconnected with service in a militia, and to use that arm for traditionally lawful purposes, such as self-defense within the home.

The Second Amendment is naturally divided into two parts: its prefatory clause and its operative clause. * * * Logic demands that there be a link between the stated purpose and the command. [That] requirement of logical connection may cause a prefatory clause to resolve an ambiguity in the operative clause * * *. But apart from that clarifying function, a prefatory clause does not limit or expand the scope of the operative clause. Therefore, while we will begin our textual analysis with the operative clause, we will return to the prefatory clause to ensure that our reading of the operative clause is consistent with the announced purpose.

Operative Clause

"Right of the People." The first salient feature of the operative clause is that it codifies a "right of the people." The unamended Constitution and the Bill of Rights use the phrase "right of the people" two other times, in the First Amendment's Assembly-and-Petition Clause and in the Fourth Amendment's Search-and-Seizure Clause. The Ninth Amendment uses very similar terminology * * *. All three of these instances unambiguously refer to individual rights, not "collective" rights, or rights that may be exercised only through participation in some corporate body. * * * What is more, in all [other] provisions of the Constitution that mention "the people," the term unambiguously refers to all members of the political community, not an unspecified subset. [This] contrasts markedly with the phrase "the militia" in the prefatory clause. As we will describe below, the "militia" in colonial America consisted of a subset of "the people"—those who were male, able bodied, and within a certain age range. Reading the Second Amendment as protecting only the right to "keep and bear Arms" in an organized militia therefore fits poorly with the operative clause's description of the holder of that right as "the people." We start therefore with a strong presumption that the Second Amendment right is exercised individually and belongs to all Americans.

"Keep and bear Arms." We move now from the holder of the right—"the people"—to the substance of the right: "to keep and bear Arms." Before addressing the verbs "keep" and "bear," we interpret their object: "Arms." The 18th-century meaning is no different from the meaning today. The 1773 edition of Samuel Johnson's dictionary defined "arms" as "weapons of offence, or armour of defence." 1 Dictionary of the English Language 107 (4th ed.) (hereinafter Johnson). * * * The term was applied, then as now, to weapons that were not specifically designed for military use and were not employed in a military capacity.

> **FYI**
>
> You will see throughout this book that opinions often cite 18th-century dictionaries as evidence of what words in the Constitution meant at the time of the Framing. For guidance on this practice, see Gregory E. Maggs, *A Concise Guide to Using Dictionaries from the Founding Era to Determine the Original Meaning of the Constitution*, 82 Geo. Wash. L. Rev. 358 (2014).

We turn to the phrases "keep arms" and "bear arms." Johnson defined "keep" as, most relevantly, "[t]o retain; not to lose," and "[t]o have in custody." Johnson 1095. * * * Thus, the most natural reading of "keep Arms" in the Second Amendment is to "have weapons."

At the time of the founding, as now, to "bear" meant to "carry." When used with "arms," however, the term has a meaning that refers to carrying for a particular purpose—confrontation. * * * Although the phrase implies that the carrying of the weapon is for the purpose of "offensive or defensive action," it in no way connotes participation in a structured military organization. From our review of founding-era sources, we conclude that this natural meaning was also the meaning that "bear arms" had in the 18th century. In numerous instances, "bear arms" was unambiguously used to refer to the carrying of weapons outside of an organized militia. The most prominent examples are those most relevant to the Second Amendment: Nine state

> **Food for Thought**
>
> As the Court's discussion makes clear, some state constitutions explicitly extended the right to bear arms to self-defense. Does this fact support or undermine the Court's interpretation?

constitutional provisions written in the 18th century or the first two decades of the 19th, which enshrined a right of citizens to "bear arms in defense of themselves and the state" or "bear arms in defense of himself and the state." It is clear from those formulations that "bear arms" did not refer only to carrying a weapon in an organized military unit.

Meaning of the Operative Clause. Putting all of these textual elements together, we find that they guarantee the individual right to possess and carry weapons in case of confrontation. This meaning is strongly confirmed by the historical background of the Second Amendment. * * * Between the Restoration and the Glorious Revolution, the Stuart Kings Charles II and James II succeeded in using select militias loyal to them to suppress political dissidents, in part by disarming their opponents. These experiences caused Englishmen to be extremely wary of concentrated military forces run by the state and to be jealous of their arms. They accordingly obtained an assurance from William and Mary, in the Declaration of Right (which was codified as the English Bill of Rights), that Protestants would never be disarmed * * *. This right has long been understood to be the predecessor to our Second Amendment.

By the time of the founding, the right to have arms had become fundamental for English subjects. Blackstone [cited] the arms provision of the Bill of Rights as one of the fundamental rights of Englishmen, [describing it as] "the natural right of resistance and self-preservation" * * *. Thus, the right secured in 1689 as a result of the Stuarts' abuses was by the time of the founding understood to be an individual right protecting against both public and private violence. And, of course, what the Stuarts had tried to do to their political enemies, George III had tried to do to the colonists.

There seems to us no doubt, on the basis of both text and history, that the Second Amendment conferred an individual right to keep and bear arms. [We now determine] whether the prefatory clause of the Second Amendment comports with our interpretation of the operative clause. * * *

Relationship between Prefatory Clause and Operative Clause

* * * The debate with respect to the right to keep and bear arms, as with other guarantees in the Bill of Rights, was not over whether it was desirable (all agreed that it was) but over whether it needed to be codified in the Constitution. During the 1788 ratification debates, the fear that the federal government would disarm the people in order to impose rule through a standing army or select militia was pervasive in Antifederalist rhetoric. Federalists responded that because Congress was given no power to abridge the ancient right of individuals to keep and bear

arms, such a force could never oppress the people. It was understood across the political spectrum that the right helped to secure the ideal of a citizen militia, which might be necessary to oppose an oppressive military force if the constitutional order broke down.

It is therefore entirely sensible that the Second Amendment's prefatory clause announces the purpose for which the right was codified: to prevent elimination of the militia. The prefatory clause does not suggest that preserving the militia was the only reason Americans valued the ancient right; most undoubtedly thought it even more important for self-defense and hunting. But the threat that the new Federal Government would destroy the citizens' militia by taking away their arms was the reason that right—unlike some other English rights—was codified in a written Constitution.

> **FYI**
>
> Article I, § 8, cl. 16 gives Congress the power "[t]o provide for organizing, arming, and disciplining, the Militia, and for governing such Part of them as may be employed in the Service of the United States, reserving to the States respectively, the Appointment of the Officers, and the Authority of training the Militia according to the discipline prescribed by Congress." Is it clear that this provision, especially when viewed in conjunction with cl. 15, authorizes Congress to determine the membership in the various state-controlled militias?

[P]etitioners' interpretation does not even achieve the narrower purpose that prompted codification of the right. If, as they believe, the Second Amendment right is no more than the right to keep and use weapons as a member of an organized militia, [then] it does not assure the existence of a "citizens' militia" as a safeguard against tyranny. For Congress retains plenary authority to organize the militia, which must include the authority to say who will belong to the organized force. * * * Thus, if petitioners are correct, the Second Amendment protects citizens' right to use a gun in an organization from which Congress has plenary authority to exclude them. It guarantees a select militia of the sort the Stuart kings found useful, but not the people's militia that was the concern of the founding generation.

> **FYI**
>
> The Supreme Court often looks to early state constitutions for evidence of the meaning of the U.S. Constitution. For guidance on this practice, see Gregory E. Maggs, *A Guide and Index for Finding Evidence of Original Meaning of the U.S. Constitution in Early State Constitutions and Declarations of Rights*, 98 N.C. L. Rev. 779 (2020).

Our interpretation is confirmed by analogous arms-bearing rights in state constitutions that preceded and immediately followed adoption of the Second Amendment. Four States adopted analogues to the Federal Second Amendment in the period between independence and the ratification of the Bill of

Rights. Two of them—Pennsylvania and Vermont—clearly adopted individual rights unconnected to militia service. Pennsylvania's Declaration of Rights of 1776 said: "That the people have a right to bear arms for the defence of themselves, and the state * * *." In 1777, Vermont adopted the identical provision, except for inconsequential differences in punctuation and capitalization. * * * North Carolina also codified a right to bear arms in 1776: "That the people have a right to bear arms, for the defence of the State * * *." Declaration of Rights § XVII. This could plausibly be read to support only a right to bear arms in a militia—but that is a peculiar way to make the point in a constitution that elsewhere repeatedly mentions the militia explicitly. We [believe] that the most likely reading of [these] pre-Second Amendment state constitutional provisions is that they secured an individual right to bear arms for defensive purposes. [That] is strong evidence that that is how the founding generation conceived of the right.

Justice STEVENS places overwhelming reliance upon this Court's decision in *United States v. Miller,* 307 U.S. 174 (1939). [According to Justice STEVENS, Miller held that] the Second Amendment "protects the right to keep and bear arms for certain military purposes, but that it does not curtail the legislature's power to regulate the nonmilitary use and ownership of weapons." [But] Miller did not hold that and cannot possibly be read to have held that. The judgment in the case upheld against a Second Amendment challenge two men's federal convictions for transporting an unregistered short-barreled shotgun in interstate commerce, in violation of the National Firearms Act, 48 Stat. 1236. It is entirely clear that the Court's basis for saying that the Second Amendment did not apply was [that] the type of weapon at issue was not eligible for Second Amendment protection: "In the absence of any evidence tending to show that the possession or use of a [short-barreled shotgun] at this time has some reasonable relationship to the preservation or efficiency of a well regulated militia, we cannot say that the Second Amendment guarantees the right to keep and bear such an instrument." 307 U.S. at 178 (emphasis added). "Certainly," the Court continued, "it is not within judicial notice that this weapon is any part of the ordinary military equipment or that its use could contribute to the common defense." *Ibid.* [H]ad the Court believed that the Second Amendment protects only those serving in the militia, it would have been odd to examine the character of the weapon rather than simply note that the two crooks were not militiamen. * * * We therefore read Miller to say only that the Second Amendment does not protect those weapons not typically possessed by law-abiding citizens for lawful purposes, such as short-barreled shotguns.

Like most rights, the right secured by the Second Amendment is not unlimited. * * * Although we do not undertake an exhaustive historical analysis today of the full scope of the Second Amendment, nothing in our opinion should be taken to cast doubt on longstanding prohibitions on the possession of firearms by felons and the mentally ill, or laws forbidding the carrying of firearms in sensitive places such as schools and government buildings, or laws imposing conditions and qualifications on the commercial sale of arms. * * * We also recognize another important limitation on the right to keep and carry arms. *Miller* said, as we have explained, that the sorts of weapons protected were those "in common use at the time." 307 U.S. at 179. We think that limitation is fairly supported by the historical tradition of prohibiting the carrying of "dangerous and unusual weapons."

We turn finally to the law at issue here. [As we have demonstrated,] the inherent right of self-defense has been central to the Second Amendment right. The handgun ban amounts to a prohibition of an entire class of "arms" that is overwhelmingly chosen by American society for that lawful purpose. The prohibition extends, moreover, to the home, where the need for defense of self, family, and property is most acute. Under any of the standards of scrutiny that we have applied to enumerated constitutional rights, banning from the home "the most preferred firearm in the nation to 'keep' and use for protection of one's home and family," 478 F.3d, at 400, would fail constitutional muster. * * * Whatever the reason, handguns are the most popular weapon chosen by Americans for self-defense in the home, and a complete prohibition of their use is invalid.

[T]he District's requirement (as applied to respondent's handgun) that firearms in the home be rendered and kept inoperable at all times [makes] it impossible for citizens to use them for the core lawful purpose of self-defense and is hence unconstitutional.

Before this Court petitioners have stated that "if the handgun ban is struck down and respondent registers a handgun, he could obtain a license, assuming he is not otherwise disqualified," by which they apparently mean if he is not a felon and is not insane. Respondent conceded at oral argument that he does not "have a problem [with] licensing" and that the District's law is permissible so long as it is "not enforced in an arbitrary and capricious manner." We therefore assume that petitioners' issuance of a license will satisfy respondent's prayer for relief and do not address the licensing requirement.

Justice BREYER [criticizes] us for declining to establish a level of scrutiny for evaluating Second Amendment restrictions. He proposes, explicitly at least, none of the traditionally expressed levels (strict scrutiny, intermediate scrutiny, rational basis), but rather a judge-empowering "interest-balancing inquiry" that "asks whether the statute burdens a protected interest in a way or to an extent that is out of proportion to the statute's salutary effects upon other important governmental interests." * * * We know of no other enumerated constitutional right whose core protection has been subjected to a freestanding "interest-balancing" approach. The very enumeration of the right takes out of the hands of government—even the Third Branch of Government—the power to decide on a case-by-case basis whether the right is really worth insisting upon. * * * Constitutional rights are enshrined with the scope they were understood to have when the people adopted them, whether or not future legislatures or (yes) even future judges think that scope too broad. [The Second Amendment] is the very product of an interest-balancing by the people—which Justice BREYER would now conduct for them anew. And whatever else it leaves to future evaluation, it surely elevates above all other interests the right of law-abiding, responsible citizens to use arms in defense of hearth and home.

In sum, we hold that the District's ban on handgun possession in the home violates the Second Amendment, as does its prohibition against rendering any lawful firearm in the home operable for the purpose of immediate self-defense. Assuming that *Heller* is not disqualified from the exercise of Second Amendment rights, the District must permit him to register his handgun and must issue him a license to carry it in the home.

We are aware of the problem of handgun violence in this country, and we take seriously the concerns raised by the many amici who believe that prohibition of handgun ownership is a solution. [But] the enshrinement of constitutional rights necessarily takes certain policy choices off the table. These include the absolute prohibition of handguns held and used for self-defense in the home. Undoubtedly some think that the Second Amendment is outmoded in a society where our standing army is the pride of our Nation, where well-trained police forces provide personal security, and where gun violence is a serious problem. That is perhaps debatable, but what is not debatable is that it is not the role of this Court to pronounce the Second Amendment extinct. [Affirmed.]

JUSTICE STEVENS, with whom JUSTICE SOUTER, JUSTICE GINSBURG, and JUSTICE BREYER join, dissenting.

The Second Amendment was adopted to protect the right of the people of each of the several States to maintain a well-regulated militia. It was a response to concerns raised during the ratification of the Constitution that the power of Congress to disarm the state militias and create a national standing army posed an intolerable threat to the sovereignty of the several States. Neither the text of the Amendment nor the arguments advanced by its proponents evidenced the slightest interest in limiting any legislature's authority to regulate private civilian uses of firearms. Specifically, there is no indication that the Framers of the Amendment intended to enshrine the common-law right of self-defense in the Constitution.

In 1934, Congress enacted the National Firearms Act, the first major federal firearms law. Upholding a conviction under that Act, this Court held that, "[i]n the absence of any evidence tending to show that possession or use of a 'shotgun having a barrel of less than eighteen inches in length' at this time has some reasonable relationship to the preservation or efficiency of a well regulated militia, we cannot say that the Second Amendment guarantees the right to keep and bear such an instrument." *Miller*, 307 U.S. at 178. The view of the Amendment we took in *Miller*—that it protects the right to keep and bear arms for certain military purposes, but that it does not curtail the Legislature's power to regulate the nonmilitary use and ownership of weapons—is both the most natural reading of the Amendment's text and the interpretation most faithful to the history of its adoption.

* * * The preamble to the Second Amendment [is] comparable to provisions in several State Declarations of Rights that were adopted roughly contemporaneously with the Declaration of Independence.[5] Those state provisions highlight the importance members of the founding generation attached to the maintenance of state militias; they also underscore the profound fear shared by many in that era of the dangers posed by standing armies. While the need for state militias has not been a matter of significant public interest for almost two centuries, that fact should not obscure the contemporary concerns that animated the Framers.

The parallels between the Second Amendment and these state declarations, and the Second Amendment's omission of any statement of purpose related to the right to use firearms for hunting or personal self-defense, is especially striking in light of the fact that the Declarations of Rights of Pennsylvania and Vermont did expressly protect such civilian uses at the time. Article XIII of Pennsylvania's 1776 Declaration of Rights announced that "the people have a right to bear arms for the defence of themselves and the state"; § 43 of the Declaration assured that "the inhabitants of this state shall have the liberty to fowl and hunt in seasonable times on the lands they hold, and on all other lands therein not inclosed." And

[5] The Virginia Declaration of Rights ¶ 13 (1776), provided: "That a well-regulated militia, composed of the body of the people, trained to arms, is the proper, natural, and safe defence of a free State; that Standing Armies, in time of peace, should be avoided, as dangerous to liberty; and that, in all cases, the military should be under strict subordination to, and governed by, the civil power." [Maryland, Delaware, and New Hampshire had similar provisions.]

Article XV of the 1777 Vermont Declaration of Rights guaranteed "[t]hat the people have a right to bear arms for the defence of themselves and the State." The contrast between those two declarations and the Second Amendment reinforces the clear statement of purpose announced in the Amendment's preamble. It confirms that the Framers' single-minded focus in crafting the constitutional guarantee "to keep and bear arms" was on military uses of firearms, which they viewed in the context of service in state militias.

The preamble thus both sets forth the object of the Amendment and informs the meaning of the remainder of its text. * * * The Court today tries to denigrate the importance of this clause of the Amendment by beginning its analysis with the Amendment's operative provision and returning to the preamble merely "to ensure that our reading of the operative clause is consistent with the announced purpose." That is not how this Court ordinarily reads such texts, and it is not how the preamble would have been viewed at the time the Amendment was adopted. * * * Without identifying any language in the text that even mentions civilian uses of firearms, the Court proceeds to "find" its preferred reading in what is at best an ambiguous text, and then concludes that its reading is not foreclosed by the preamble. Perhaps the Court's approach to the text is acceptable advocacy, but it is surely an unusual approach for judges to follow.

[T]he words "the people" in the Second Amendment refer back to the object announced in the Amendment's preamble. They remind us that it is the collective action of individuals having a duty to serve in the militia that the text directly protects and, perhaps more importantly, that the ultimate purpose of the Amendment was to protect the States' share of the divided sovereignty created by the Constitution.

Although the Court's discussion of [the words "to keep and bear Arms"] treats them as two "phrases"—as if they read "to keep" and "to bear"—they describe a unitary right: to possess arms if needed for military purposes and to use them in conjunction with military activities. * * * The term "bear arms" is a familiar idiom; when used unadorned by any additional words, its meaning is "to serve as a soldier, do military service, fight." 1 Oxford English Dictionary 634 (2d ed.1989). It is derived from the Latin arma ferre, which, translated literally, means "to bear [ferre] war equipment [arma]." * * * Had the Framers wished to expand the meaning of the phrase "bear arms" to encompass civilian possession and use, they could have done so by the addition of phrases such as "for the defense of themselves," as was done in the Pennsylvania and Vermont Declarations of Rights. The unmodified use of "bear arms," by contrast, refers most naturally to a military purpose, as evidenced by its use in literally dozens of contemporary texts. * * * When, as in this case, there is no [qualifier], the most natural meaning is the military one; and, in the absence of any qualifier, it is all the more appropriate to look to the preamble to confirm the natural meaning of the text.

The Amendment's use of the term "keep" in no way contradicts the military meaning conveyed by the phrase "bear arms" and the Amendment's preamble. To the contrary, a number of state militia laws in effect at the time of the Second Amendment's drafting used the term "keep" to describe the requirement that militia members store their arms at their homes, ready to be used for service when necessary. The Virginia military law, for example, ordered that "every one of the said officers, non-commissioned officers, and privates, shall constantly keep the aforesaid arms, accoutrements, and ammunition, ready to be produced whenever called for by his commanding officer." Act for Regulating and Disciplining the Militia, 1785 Va. Acts ch. 1, § 3, p. 2. "[K]eep and bear arms" thus perfectly describes the responsibilities of a framing-era militia member.

[T]he single right that [the clause describes] is both a duty and a right to have arms available and ready for military service, and to use them for military purposes when necessary. * * * When each word in the text is given full effect, the Amendment is most naturally read to secure to the people a right to use and possess arms in conjunction with service in a well-regulated militia.

Two themes relevant to our current interpretive task ran through the debates on the original Constitution. "On the one hand, there was a widespread fear that a national standing Army posed an intolerable threat to individual liberty and to the sovereignty of the separate States." *Perpich v. Department of Defense*, 496 U.S. 334, 340 (1990). On the other hand, the Framers recognized the dangers inherent in relying on inadequately trained militia members "as the primary means of providing for the common defense," *Perpich*, 496 U.S. at 340. * * * In order to respond to those twin concerns, a compromise was reached: Congress would be authorized to raise and support a national Army and Navy, and also to organize, arm, discipline, and provide for the calling forth of "the Militia." U.S. Const., Art. I, § 8, cls. 12–16. The President, at the same time, was empowered as the "Commander in Chief of the Army and Navy of the United States, and of the Militia of the several States, when called into the actual Service of the United States." Art. II, § 2. But, with respect to the militia, a significant reservation was made to the States: [the] States respectively would retain the right to appoint the officers and to train the militia in accordance with the discipline prescribed by Congress. Art. I, § 8, cl. 16.[20]

---

[20] The Court assumes—incorrectly, in my view—that even when a state militia was not called into service, Congress would have had the power to exclude individuals from enlistment in that state militia. That

But the original Constitution's retention of the militia and its creation of divided authority over that body did not prove sufficient to allay fears about the dangers posed by a standing army [because] it did not prevent Congress from providing for the militia's disarmament. * * * This sentiment was echoed at a number of state ratification conventions; indeed, it was one of the primary objections to the original Constitution voiced by its opponents.

[In response, upon ratifying the Constitution several states proposed amendments to the document.] The relevant proposals sent by the Virginia Ratifying Convention read as follows:

> "17th, That the people have a right to keep and bear arms; that a well regulated Militia composed of the body of the people trained to arms is the proper, natural and safe defence of a free State. That standing armies are dangerous to liberty, and therefore ought to be avoided, as far as the circumstances and protection of the Community will admit; and that in all cases the military should be under strict subordination to and be governed by the civil power."
>
> "19th. That any person religiously scrupulous of bearing arms ought to be exempted, upon payment of an equivalent to employ another to bear arms in his stead."

North Carolina adopted Virginia's proposals and sent them to Congress as its own * * *. New York produced a proposal with nearly identical language. Notably, each of these proposals used the phrase "keep and bear arms" [and] embedded the phrase within a group of principles that are distinctly military in meaning.

> **Take Note**
>
> Virginia's proposal—and Madison's original draft of the Second Amendment—included a provision to exempt conscientious objectors from service in the militias. What does this provision suggest about the contexts in which the Amendment protects the right to keep and bear arms?

By contrast, New Hampshire's proposal [described] the protection involved in more clearly personal terms[:] "Congress shall never disarm any Citizen unless such as are or have been in Actual Rebellion."

[James] Madison, charged with the task of assembling the proposals for amendments sent by the ratifying States, was the principal draftsman of the Second Amendment. [His] decision to model the Second Amendment on the distinctly military Virginia

assumption is not supported by the text of the Militia Clauses of the original Constitution, which confer upon Congress the power to "organiz[e], ar[m], and disciplin[e], the Militia," Art. I, § 8, cl. 16, but not the power to say who will be members of a state militia. It is also flatly inconsistent with the Second Amendment. * * *

proposal is therefore revealing, since it is clear that he considered and rejected formulations that would have unambiguously protected civilian uses of firearms. When [his draft proposal] was debated and modified, it is reasonable to assume that all participants in the drafting process were fully aware of the other formulations that would have protected civilian use and possession of weapons and that their choice to craft the Amendment as they did represented a rejection of those alternative formulations.

Until today, it has been understood that legislatures may regulate the civilian use and misuse of firearms so long as they do not interfere with the preservation of a well-regulated militia. The Court's announcement of a new constitutional right to own and use firearms for private purposes upsets that settled understanding * * *.

JUSTICE BREYER, with whom JUSTICE STEVENS, JUSTICE SOUTER, and JUSTICE GINSBURG join, dissenting.

[T]he protection the [Second] Amendment provides is not absolute. The Amendment permits government to regulate the interests that it serves. Thus, irrespective of what those interests are—whether they do or do not include an independent interest in self-defense—the majority's view cannot be correct unless it can show that the District's regulation is unreasonable or inappropriate in Second Amendment terms. This the majority cannot do.

The majority is wrong when it says that the District's law is unconstitutional "[u]nder any of the standards of scrutiny that we have applied to enumerated constitutional rights." [It] certainly would not be unconstitutional under, for example, a "rational basis" standard, which requires a court to uphold regulation so long as it bears a "rational relationship" to a "legitimate governmental purpose." *Heller v. Doe*, 509 U.S. 312, 320 (1993). The law at issue here, which in part seeks to prevent gun-related accidents, at least bears a "rational relationship" to that "legitimate" life-saving objective.

Respondent proposes that the Court adopt a "strict scrutiny" test, which would require reviewing with care each gun law to determine whether it is "narrowly tailored to achieve a compelling governmental interest." *Abrams v. Johnson,* 521 U.S. 74, 82 (1997). But the majority implicitly, and appropriately, rejects that suggestion by broadly approving a set of laws [whose] constitutionality under a strict scrutiny standard would be far from clear. Indeed, [almost] every gun-control regulation will seek to advance (as the one here does) a "primary concern of every government—a concern for the safety and indeed the lives of its citizens." *United States v. Salerno*, 481 U.S. 739, 755 (1987). * * * Thus, any attempt in theory to apply strict scrutiny to gun regulations will in practice turn into an interest-balancing inquiry, with the interests protected by the Second Amendment on one side and the governmental public-safety concerns on the other, the only question being whether the regulation at issue impermissibly burdens the former in the course of advancing the latter.

I would simply adopt such an interest-balancing inquiry explicitly. * * * "[W]here a law significantly implicates competing constitutionally protected interests in complex ways," the Court generally asks whether the statute burdens a protected interest in a way or to an extent that is out of proportion to the statute's salutary effects upon other important governmental interests. See *Nixon v. Shrink Missouri Government PAC*, 528 U.S. 377, 402 (2000) (BREYER, J., concurring). Any answer would take account both of the statute's effects upon the competing interests and the existence of any clearly superior less restrictive alternative.

The only dispute regarding [the trigger-lock] provision appears to be whether the Constitution requires an exception that would allow someone to render a firearm operational when necessary for self-defense * * *. The District concedes that such an exception exists. * * * And because I see nothing in the District law that would preclude the existence of a background common-law self-defense exception, I would avoid the constitutional question by interpreting the statute to include it. See *Ashwander v. TVA*, 297 U.S. 288, 348 (1936) (Brandeis, J., concurring).

No one doubts the constitutional importance of [the] basic objective [of the District's ban on handgun possession], saving lives. But there is considerable debate about whether the [provision] helps to achieve that objective. * * * Petitioners, and their amici, have presented us with [statistics about handgun violence.] * * * From 1993 to 1997, there were 180,533 firearm-related deaths in the United States, an average of over 36,000 per year. * * * In over one in every eight firearm-related deaths in 1997, the victim was someone under the age of 20. * * * From 1993 to 1997, 81% of firearm-homicide victims were killed by handgun. * * * Handguns also appear to be a very popular weapon among criminals. * * * Statistics further suggest that urban areas, such as the District, have different experiences with gun-related death, injury, and crime, than do less densely populated rural areas. A disproportionate amount of violent and property crimes occur in urban areas, and urban criminals are more likely than other offenders to use a firearm during the commission of a violent crime.

Respondent and his many amici [disagree] strongly with the District's predictive judgment that a ban on handguns will help solve the crime and accident problems that those figures disclose. * * * First, they point out that, since the ban took effect [in 1976], violent crime in the District has increased, not decreased. * * * Second, respondent's amici point to a statistical analysis that [concludes] that strict gun laws are correlated with more murders, not fewer. * * * Third, they point to evidence indicating that firearm ownership does have a beneficial self-defense effect. * * * Fourth, respondent's amici argue that laws criminalizing gun possession are self-defeating, as evidence suggests that they will have the effect only of restricting law-abiding citizens, but not criminals, from acquiring guns.

[T]he District and its amici [respond] with studies of their own. * * * The upshot is a set of studies and counterstudies that, at most, could leave a judge uncertain about the proper policy conclusion. [But] legislators, not judges, have primary responsibility for drawing policy conclusions from empirical fact. [D]eference to legislative judgment seems particularly appropriate here, where the judgment has been made by a local legislature, with particular knowledge of local problems and insight into appropriate local solutions. * * * For these reasons, I conclude that the District's statute properly seeks to further the sort of life-preserving and public-safety interests that the Court has called "compelling."

The District's statute burdens the Amendment's first and primary objective hardly at all. [T]here is general agreement among the Members of the Court that the principal (if not the only) purpose of the Second Amendment is found in the Amendment's text: the preservation of a "well regulated Militia." * * * To begin with, the present case has nothing to do with actual military service. [And] the District's law does not seriously affect military training interests. The law permits residents to engage in activities that will increase their familiarity with firearms. They may register (and thus possess in their homes) weapons other than handguns, such as rifles and shotguns. * * * And while the District law prevents citizens from training with handguns within the District, [the] adjacent States do permit the use of handguns for target practice, and those States are only a brief subway ride away. [G]iven the costs already associated with gun ownership and firearms training, I cannot say that a subway ticket and a short subway ride (and storage costs) create more than a minimal burden.

The District's law does prevent a resident from keeping a loaded handgun in his home. And it consequently makes it more difficult for the householder to use the handgun for self-defense in the home against intruders, such as burglars. [But] there is no clearly superior, less restrictive alternative to the District's handgun ban [because] the ban's very objective is to reduce significantly the number of handguns in the District * * *. [A]ny measure less restrictive in respect to the use of handguns for self-defense will, to that same extent, prove less effective in preventing the use of handguns for illicit purposes. If a resident has a handgun in the home that he can use for self-defense, then he has a handgun in the home that he can use to commit suicide or engage in acts of domestic violence. * * * [T]he District law is tailored to the life-threatening problems it attempts to address. The law concerns one class of weapons, handguns, leaving residents free to possess shotguns and rifles, along with ammunition. The area that falls within its scope is totally urban. * * *

The majority derides my approach as "judge-empowering." I take this criticism seriously, but I do not think it accurate. * * * Application of such an approach, of course, requires judgment, but the very nature of the approach—requiring careful identification of the relevant interests and evaluating the law's effect upon them—limits the judge's choices; and the method's necessary transparency lays bare the judge's reasoning for all to see and to criticize.

The majority's methodology is, in my view, substantially less transparent than mine. * * * "Putting all of [the Second Amendment's] textual elements together," the majority says, "we find that they guarantee the individual right to possess and carry weapons in case of confrontation." Then, three pages later, it says that "we do not read the Second Amendment to permit citizens to carry arms for any sort of confrontation." Yet, with one critical exception, it does not explain which confrontations count. It simply leaves that question unanswered.

Nor is it at all clear to me how the majority decides which loaded "arms" a homeowner may keep. The majority says that that Amendment protects those weapons "typically possessed by law-abiding citizens for lawful purposes." This definition conveniently excludes machineguns, but permits handguns, which the majority describes as "the most popular weapon chosen by Americans for self-defense in the home." But what sense does this approach make? According to the majority's reasoning, if Congress and the States lift restrictions on the possession and use of machineguns, and people buy machineguns to protect their homes, the Court will have to reverse course and find that the Second Amendment does, in fact, protect the individual self-defense-related right to possess a machinegun. On the majority's reasoning, if tomorrow someone invents a particularly useful, highly dangerous self-defense weapon, Congress and the States had better ban it immediately, for once it becomes popular Congress will no longer possess the constitutional authority to do so. * * * There is no basis for believing that the Framers intended such circular reasoning.

I am similarly puzzled by the majority's list [of] provisions that in its view would survive Second Amendment scrutiny. * * * Why these? Is it that similar restrictions existed in the late 18th century? The majority fails to cite any colonial analogues. * * *

The argument about method, however, is by far the less important argument surrounding today's decision. Far more important are the unfortunate consequences that today's decision is likely to spawn. Not least of these [is] the fact that the decision threatens to throw into doubt the constitutionality of gun laws throughout the United States. I can find no sound legal basis for launching the courts on so formidable and potentially dangerous a mission. In my view, there simply is no untouchable constitutional right guaranteed by the Second Amendment to keep loaded handguns in the house in crime-ridden urban areas.

POINTS FOR DISCUSSION

a. The Judicial Role and the Counter-Majoritarian Difficulty

In holding that the challenged regulations were unconstitutional, the Court noted that "the enshrinement of constitutional rights necessarily takes certain policy choices off the table." Notice that in making this statement, the Court is also asserting its authority both to determine the meaning of the Constitution and to invalidate democratically enacted laws. Is it problematic to permit the Court to act in such a counter-majoritarian, and arguably anti-democratic, fashion? Or is it essential that the Court do so? This question will be the subtext of all the material that follows, but it will be the particular focus of Chapter 2.

b. Structural and Institutional Arrangements or Individual Rights?

Justice Scalia concluded that the Second Amendment protects an individual right to keep and bear arms for purposes unrelated to participation in a state militia. Justice Stevens, by contrast, would have held that the Amendment is principally a structural protection to ensure that Congress cannot disarm the state militias. Which view do you find more convincing?

Notice that Justice Scalia did not deny the structural aims of the Second Amendment, and that Justice Stevens did not deny that its structural aims advance the interest in liberty. The first several Parts of this book will focus on the principal structural and institutional arrangements that the Constitution creates, federalism and separation of powers. As we will see in detail, the Framers clearly viewed these arrangements as essential to preserving individual liberty. The remainder of the book will focus on the Constitution's explicit and direct protections for individual rights. Does it make sense to treat structural provisions and rights provisions as separate and discrete features of the constitutional scheme?

c. Interpretive Methodology: Originalism v. Non-Originalism

In interpreting the Second Amendment, Justice Scalia sought to determine its meaning at the time of the Framing. He relied on contemporaneous sources, such as eighteenth-century dictionaries and state constitutional provisions. Justice Breyer focused on the competing state and individual interests implicated by the challenged regulation. Was his approach non-originalist? Or did he simply seek to apply the original meaning of the Second Amendment to modern circumstances? Which approach did you find more sensible or convincing?

d. Interpretive Methodology: Originalism v. Originalism

Like Justice Scalia, Justice Stevens took an originalist approach to the Second Amendment, but he reached a very different conclusion about the Amendment's meaning. To the extent that the two Justices relied on similar materials, whose arguments did you find more convincing? What does the fact that they relied in part on competing sources say about the viability of originalism as an approach to interpreting the Constitution?

Did their inquiries have the same objective? Notice that Justice Scalia focused principally on what the language of the Second Amendment likely would have meant at the time of its ratification. Justice Stevens spent considerable time addressing the Amendment's drafting history. Does that mean that Justice Stevens was attempting to discern Madison's—and the other Framers'—intent in ratifying the Amendment? Is there a difference between the original "objective meaning" and the original "intent"? Is there a difference in the evidence that one might use to establish meaning and intent?

Notice also that Justice Scalia read the individual phrases in the Second Amendment atomistically, asking what each phrase means before assembling those individual meanings into one, broader meaning. Justice Stevens, by contrast, read the Amendment more holistically, with a particular emphasis on what the preamble suggests about the meaning of what Justice Scalia referred to as the "operative" clause. Given that many of the Constitution's most important provisions are written at a high level of generality and often are ambiguous in their application, what is the role of text in constitutional interpretation? Whose approach in *Heller* to the text did you find most convincing?

e. Level of Scrutiny

As the competing opinions suggested, the Court often assesses the constitutionality of government action by evaluating the governmental interests advanced by the action and the burden that the action imposes on the constitutional right at issue. For example, the Court has never interpreted the Equal Protection Clause of the Fourteenth Amendment absolutely to prohibit the government from treating different classes of citizens differently. Some classifications—such as a law providing that only persons over sixteen years of age are eligible to obtain driver's licenses—do not seem problematic, and accordingly are subjected only to "rational basis review," under which they are upheld as long as the classification is reasonably related to some legitimate governmental interest. Other classifications—such as laws that deny government benefits on the basis of race—are deeply suspect, and accordingly are subjected to "strict scrutiny," under which they can be upheld only if they are narrowly tailored to achieve a compelling governmental interest. Still other classifications—such as those that distinguish on the basis of gender—are subjected to "intermediate scrutiny," which falls somewhere between rational basis review and strict scrutiny. The various levels of scrutiny generally reflect a judgment that few constitutional prohibitions are absolute, and that some government actions that burden protected rights nevertheless are defensible.

> **Make the Connection**
>
> We discuss levels of scrutiny in Volume 2, when we consider the Due Process Clause, the Equal Protection Clause, and the First Amendment.

What level of scrutiny did the majority apply to the challenged regulations? Did the majority consider the government's interest in the challenged regulations? Or did the majority simply suggest that regulations that would have been prohibited in 1791 are prohibited today? Does the majority's suggestion that many regulations of the right to bear arms would be constitutional shed any light on this question? What level of scrutiny did Justice Stevens apply?

Justice Breyer explicitly proposed a test under which the challenged regulation's constitutionality turns on whether the statute "burdens a protected interest in a way or to an extent that is out of proportion to the statute's salutary effects upon other important governmental interests." Is this approach preferable to the majority's apparent approach of recognizing categories of absolutely forbidden regulations and of clearly permissible regulations?

f. Role of Precedent

Before *Heller*, the Court had decided very few cases that even circumspectly interpreted the Second Amendment. Perhaps the most important was *United States v. Miller*, 307 U.S. 174 (1939), a brief opinion whose reasoning, as the competing approaches in *Heller* show, was far from clear. What is the role of precedent in interpreting the Constitution? Suppose that the Court in *Miller* had clearly held that the Second Amendment protects the right to keep and bear arms only in conjunction with participation in a state militia. Would the Court in *Heller* have been bound by that holding if it concluded that the Court in *Miller* had failed properly to discern the original meaning of the Amendment? When is it appropriate for the Court to overrule prior decisions that interpreted the Constitution? In answering this question, consider what remedies exist when the Court "errs" in interpreting the Constitution.

g. The Constitution and Ambiguity

The issue in *Heller* was both of great importance and seemingly fundamental. Why do you think it took the Court over 200 years squarely to resolve that issue? In fact, as we will see throughout this book, a surprising number of important constitutional questions have never been addressed by the Court. As you read the materials that follow, consider why, and whether constitutional ambiguity is a good or bad thing.

h. Role of the Dissenting Opinions

Why did Justices Breyer and Stevens write such extensive dissenting opinions? Dissenting opinions do not carry any precedential value, as they represent the views of a minority of Justices. Are dissenting opinions simply an expression of disagreement for disagreement's sake? Are they templates for criticism of the Court's decision? If so, to what end? Are they in effect intended as the groundwork for a future change of course on the Court? In this book, we will regularly see dissenting opinions. If nothing else, does the Court's frequent inability to achieve unanimity suggest anything about the nature of constitutional interpretation?

Problem

Police officers investigating a suspected shoplifting incident asked a customer if they could search her purse. The customer consented. The officers found no evidence of shoplifting but saw a stun gun in the purse. The police then arrested the woman for violating a Massachusetts law prohibiting private citizens from possessing a "portable device or weapon from which an electrical current, impulse, wave or beam may be directed." The woman asserted that she needed the weapon to protect herself from an abusive former boyfriend and claimed a Second Amendment right to possess it. In response, the government made the following three arguments, all of which it believed were consistent with the originalist methodology of *Heller*.

A. A "stun gun was not the type of weapon contemplated by Congress in 1789 as being protected by the Second Amendment" because stun guns "were not in common use at the time of the Second Amendment's enactment."

B. Even if stun guns are "arms," Massachusetts still can prohibit them because they "fall within the 'traditional prohibition against carrying dangerous and unusual weapons.'" Stun guns would have been considered "unusual" in 1789 because they are a "thoroughly modern invention."

C. There is no evidence that stun guns "are readily adaptable to use in the military."

Are these proper originalist arguments? The Massachusetts Supreme Judicial Court accepted all of these arguments, but the U.S. Supreme Court unanimously concluded that all of them were invalid. *Caetano v. Massachusetts*, 577 U.S. 411 (2016). The Court, however, rejected them as inconsistent with *Heller*, rather than concluding specifically that they were improper on originalist grounds.

POINT-COUNTERPOINT

Does *Heller* represent originalism's triumph or its failure?

POINT: GREGORY E. MAGGS

"Originalism" is a doctrine saying that judges should interpret the Constitution according to its original meaning. Proponents of originalism disagree on some points, such as whether judges should focus on the original intent of the Framers, the original understanding of the ratifiers, or the original objective meaning of the Constitution's text. But they all agree that none of these meanings change over time and that judges should not allow current policy considerations to affect their interpretation of the Constitution.

One common objection to originalism is that it does not produce certain results. The argument supporting this objection is that the text of the Constitution and the relevant historical materials are often too sparse or inconclusive to produce definitive answers to current constitutional issues. This deficiency may prevent judges from determining answers to important constitutional questions. Worse, it may allow judges to decide cases according to their own political preferences and then cover up what they are doing with make-weight arguments resting on vague historical documents.

At first glance, the Supreme Court's decision in *District of Columbia v. Heller*, 554 U.S. 570 (2008), might appear to support this objection to originalism. Justice Scalia's opinion for the Court and Justice Stevens's dissenting opinion both claim to use originalist methodology, but they reach different conclusions. This result may suggest to some that originalism cannot answer the question of what the Second Amendment means. In addition, the Court's conservatives concluded that the gun control law at issue was unconstitutional, while the Court's liberals concluded that it was not. Because conservative politicians tend to oppose gun control, and liberal politicians tend to favor it, this division of the Justices might suggest that politics determined the Justices' positions.

But further reflection should reveal that *Heller* does not represent a failure of originalism. Any method of constitutional interpretation may produce differing conclusions. But originalism appears to be generally more determinate than other interpretative methods. Most of the cases in this book contain both majority and dissenting opinions, yet in very few of these cases did both sides attempt to use originalist methodology. *Heller* is an example, as is *U.S. Term Limits v. Thornton*, 514 U.S. 779 (1995), but not many others come to mind. Has any other method of constitutional interpretation produced comparable certainty?

As for policy preferences, a closer look casts doubt on suspicions that either the majority or the dissent in *Heller* was just voting for the outcome that it favored as a matter of policy. The District of Columbia statute was among the most extreme gun control laws in the nation. Even without knowing what the individual Justices actually think about gun control, it is difficult to believe that all of the members of the dissent, who generally favor personal rights, would want laws that effectively ban all handgun ownership. The majority meanwhile went out of its way to make clear, in dicta, that many kinds of gun regulations are still constitutional. Again, it is hard to imagine that all of the Justices in the majority would favor every possible regulation. Instead, *Heller* appears to represent a good faith effort to determine what the Second Amendment originally meant, and is thus a triumph of originalism.

COUNTERPOINT: PETER J. SMITH

Originalism's proponents contend that it is the only legitimate approach to constitutional interpretation because (they say) it is the only approach that accords to the Constitution an objectively identifiable fixed meaning and, in so doing, prevents the Justices from imposing their personal policy preferences under the guise of constitutional interpretation. Yet the dueling opinions in *Heller* demonstrate why originalism fails to live up to its promise.

The 27 words of the Second Amendment provoked over 100 pages of interpretive analysis, and led two incredibly intelligent, historically well-versed, and widely respected Justices to diametrically different interpretations. And this should not be surprising. Most constitutional provisions are written at a very high level of generality—such as "Equal Protection" or "Due Process"—that give few hints about their "original" meaning as applied to concrete circumstances. And even those—such as the Second Amendment—that seem to speak at a higher level of specificity often are susceptible to multiple (and irreconcilable) interpretations. (The language of the Amendment, with its prefatory and operative clauses, is particularly obscure.) Add to these textual ambiguities the historical ambiguities that originalism invites—Would a "reasonable person" in 1791 have understood the first half of the Second Amendment to qualify the second half? Even assuming we can find enough evidence of such understanding, what if reasonable people in 1791 (like reasonable people today) disagreed about the meaning of the Amendment?—and originalism rarely produces meaning any more determinate than any other approach to constitutional interpretation.

If originalism is unlikely (at least in difficult cases, which, after all, are the only ones that end up seeing the light of day in a courtroom) to produce determinate meaning, then originalists' claims about how it constrains judges begin to fall apart. A judge seeking the original meaning of the Second Amendment can focus either on early militia provisions in state Declarations of Rights (as did Justice Stevens) or instead on the even-earlier English Bill of Rights or the writings of Blackstone (as did Justice Scalia); on contemporaneous dictionary definitions (as did Justice Scalia) or instead on contemporaneous state militia laws that used similar words (as did Justice Stevens). A judge can read early state constitutional provisions referring explicitly to the right to bear arms for self-defense either to confirm (as did Justice Scalia) or to refute (as did Justice Stevens) the view that the Second Amendment similarly protects such a right. And although there is no obvious reason to doubt the sincerity with which the Justices approached the question, one cannot ignore that the Justices widely viewed as the most conservative sided with the view preferred by political conservatives and that the more liberal Justices sided with the view preferred by political liberals. Originalism, it seems, is not nearly as constraining as its proponents claim.

Legal scholars have long debated the original meaning of the Second Amendment. But historians recognize that any such question is not susceptible to one authoritative answer; the Constitution, after all, was ratified by collective decision-making (in each state, no less), which reflected a dizzying array of (often dueling) intentions, expectations, hopes, and fears. One can debate whether the majority or the dissent had the better of the arguments. But it is time that we stopped pretending that this particular approach to constitutional interpretation is any better than others at establishing rules for judges to do what they must: to exercise judgment.

PART II

The Federal Courts

Article III of the Constitution delineates the limits of the "judicial Power" and vests that power in the Supreme Court and "in such inferior Courts as the Congress may from time to time ordain and establish." It further provides that those courts will be staffed by judges who "hold their Offices during good Behaviour" and whose compensation "shall not be diminished during their Continuance in Office." In other words, federal judges enjoy life tenure and protection from certain forms of political retribution for their decisions. Indeed, the only method specified for removal of a federal judge is conviction after impeachment, which requires a super-majority vote of the Senate. See U.S. Const., art. II, § 4; art. I, § 3, cl. 6.

U.S. Constitution, Article III, Section 1

The judicial Power of the United States, shall be vested in one supreme Court, and in such inferior Courts as the Congress may from time to time ordain and establish. The Judges, both of the supreme and inferior Courts, shall hold their Offices during good Behaviour, and shall, at stated Times, receive for their Services, a Compensation, which shall not be diminished during their Continuance in Office.

Judicial independence was thought necessary to check overreaching by the political branches; after all, judges who are immune from majoritarian pressures perhaps can be expected to protect individual rights against majoritarian incursion. But Anti-Federalist opponents of the Constitution attacked the proposed allocation of judicial power to an independent judiciary as constituting a threat to the authority of the states and to democracy itself. "Brutus," an influential critic, charged that the "real effect" of the federal system of government would "be brought home to the feelings of the people, through the medium of the judicial power." Because federal judges would be "totally independent, both of the people

> **FYI**
>
> Brutus is thought to be the pseudonym for Judge Robert Yates. Yates had been one of the delegates to the Constitutional Convention from New York, but he left the Convention before its conclusion because he believed (with some justification) that the delegates were exceeding their authority by proposing a new constitution instead of merely amending the Articles of Confederation. After the Convention, he devoted efforts to opposing ratification. Writing as Brutus, he sparred with Alexander Hamilton, his former colleague at the Convention, who argued for ratification.

and the legislature," judicial overreaching could not be "corrected by any power above them"—a situation that, he argued, was "altogether unprecedented in a free country." *Essays of Brutus No. 11*, New York Journal (Jan. 31, 1788).

Alexander Hamilton responded to these criticisms by noting the important limits on the power of the judiciary. The federal judiciary, he argued, "from the nature of its functions, will always be the least dangerous to the political rights of the Constitution; because it will be least in a capacity to annoy or injure them." Unlike the Executive, who "holds the sword of the community," and Congress, which "commands the purse" and "prescribes the rules by which the duties and rights of every citizen are to be regulated," the judiciary "has no influence over either the sword or the purse; no direction either of the strength or of the wealth of the society; and can take no active resolution whatever. It may truly be said to have neither FORCE nor WILL, but merely judgment; and must ultimately depend upon the aid of the executive arm even for the efficacy of its judgments." The Federalist No. 78.

These competing positions continue to have resonance today. As we will see, judicial power often is an important antidote to overreaching by the political branches, particularly to actions that burden the rights of minorities. And it is important to note that the term "minorities" includes not just racial minorities, holders of unpopular views, criminal defendants, and adherents to non-mainstream religions, but also members of other groups that are not always protected by majoritarian politics, such as farmers, gun owners, and property owners. But when the courts exercise their power to invalidate decisions that are the product of democratic action, they arguably act anti-democratically. This "counter-majoritarian difficulty" has long plagued the exercise of judicial power in the United States. See Alexander Bickel, *The Least Dangerous Branch* (2d ed. 1986). As we progress through the materials in this part, these competing elements of judicial power will never be far from the surface.

CHAPTER 2

Judicial Power

The most important—and controversial—power that the federal courts exercise is the power of judicial review. We take up that topic in Section A. We then turn in Section B to obstacles to the exercise of this power. These obstacles include the political question doctrine, the requirement of a case or controversy before a federal court can exercise jurisdiction, the requirement that litigants have "standing" to present issues in court, and the power of Congress to control certain aspects of federal court jurisdiction.

> **Definition**
>
> "Jurisdiction" is "a court's power to decide a case or issue a decree." *Black's Law Dictionary* (10th ed. 2014). Article III of the Constitution defines the jurisdiction of the federal courts.

A. JUDICIAL REVIEW

In November 1800, Thomas Jefferson received more votes in the presidential election than John Adams, the incumbent. Because no candidate received a majority of the electoral votes, however, the power to decide the election passed to the House of Representatives. In January 1801, President Adams nominated John Marshall, the Secretary of State, to serve as Chief Justice of the Supreme Court. He was confirmed by the Senate and took the oath of office on February 4, 1801. He continued to serve simultaneously as Secretary of State. On February 17, the House of Representatives chose Thomas Jefferson, a Republican, as President. He would not be sworn in as President, however, until March 4, and in late February the Federalist Congress created many new judgeships in an attempt to maintain control of the federal judiciary.

Pursuant to an Act passed on February 27, President Adams on March 2 nominated 42 judges—including William Marbury, who was nominated to be a Justice of the Peace in the District of Columbia. The Senate confirmed them on March 3, Adams's last day in office. Marshall, in his capacity as Secretary of State, signed and sealed the commissions of the judges but was unable to effect delivery

> **FYI**
>
> The election of 1800 revealed a defect in the Constitution's mechanism for selecting a President. Article II, § 1, cl. 3 provided that each elector would vote for two persons, and (if one candidate had the majority of electoral votes) the winner would become President and the candidate with the second-most electoral votes would become Vice President. Although Jefferson's Republican party had planned to have one elector withhold a vote for Aaron Burr (the candidate they hoped would become Vice President) in order to ensure that Jefferson would have the most votes, Jefferson and Burr ended up tied, and neither had a majority. The lame-duck, Federalist-controlled Congress came close to awarding the Presidency to Adams, but they eventually relented. The Twelfth Amendment, ratified in 1804, addressed the problem.

of all of them by the end of the day. (John Marshall's brother James Marshall personally set out from the State Department on March 3 to deliver commissions to judges in the District of Columbia, but he could not cover the distance in time and returned the undelivered commissions to the State Department. See Jean E. Smith, *John Marshall: Definer of a Nation* 317–18 (1996).) On March 4, Marshall, as Chief Justice, administered the oath of office to President Jefferson, who did not deliver the remaining commissions and treated them as legally void. Jefferson subsequently appointed James Madison as Secretary of State.

Republicans responded swiftly to the Federalist attempts to entrench themselves in the judiciary. Republicans in Congress repealed a statute that the lame-duck Federalists had passed creating more federal judgeships; limited the Supreme Court, which was composed entirely of Federalist appointees, to one sitting per year; and impeached and removed John Pickering, a Federalist district judge in New Hampshire. They also hinted that the Justices on the Supreme Court would be next. (Indeed, in 1805, not long after the decision in *Marbury*, the House impeached Federalist Supreme Court Justice Samuel Chase, although the Senate did not convict him.) This was the context in which the Supreme Court decided *Marbury v. Madison.*

Chief Justice John Marshall (1755–1835)
Library of Congress

Marbury v. Madison

5 U.S. (1 Cranch) 137 (1803)

Marshall, C.J., announced the opinion of the Court:

At the last term on the affidavits then read and filed with the clerk, a rule was granted in this case, requiring the Secretary of State to show cause why a mandamus should not issue, directing him to deliver to William Marbury his commission as a justice of the peace for the county of Washington, in the District of Columbia. No cause has been shown, and the present motion is for a mandamus.

Definition

"Mandamus" is Latin for "We command." A writ of mandamus is an order to an executive, administrative, or judicial officer commanding the performance of a particular act required by law.

In the order in which the court has viewed this subject, the following questions have been considered and decided. 1st. Has the applicant a right to the commission he demands? 2d. If he has a right, and that right has been violated, do the laws of his country afford him a remedy? 3d. If they do afford him a remedy, is it a *mandamus* issuing from this court?

The first object of inquiry is, 1st. Has the applicant a right to the commission he demands? His right originates in an Act of Congress passed in February 1801, concerning the District of Columbia. * * * In order to determine whether he is entitled to this commission, it becomes necessary to enquire whether he has been appointed to the office. For if he has been appointed, the law continues him in office for five years, and he is entitled to the possession of those evidences of office, which, being completed, became his property.

FYI

Chief Justice Marshall is speaking somewhat euphemistically in saying that no cause was shown. Neither Secretary of State Madison nor anyone else from the Jefferson Administration had appeared to respond to the Court's order to show cause.

[The constitutional power of appointment] has been exercised when the last act, required from the person possessing the power, has been performed. This last act is the signature [by the President] of the commission. * * * The commission being signed, the subsequent duty of the Secretary of State is prescribed by law, and not to be guided by the will of the President. He is to affix the seal of the United States to the commission, and is to record it. * * * The transmission of the commission, is a practice directed by convenience, but not by law. It cannot therefore be necessary to constitute the appointment which must precede it, and which is the mere act of the President.

It is therefore decidedly the opinion of the court, that when a commission has been signed by the President, the appointment is made; and that the commission is complete, when the seal of the United States has been affixed to it by the Secretary of State. * * * Mr. Marbury, then, since his commission was signed by the President, and sealed by the Secretary of State, was appointed; and as the law creating the office, gave the officer a right to hold for five years, independent of the executive, the appointment was not revocable; but vested in the officer legal rights, which are protected by the laws of this country. To withhold his commission, therefore, is an act deemed by the court not warranted by law, but violative of a vested legal right.

This brings us to the second inquiry; which is: If he has a right, and that right has been violated, do the laws of this country afford him a remedy? The very essence of civil liberty certainly consists in the right of every individual to claim the protection of the laws, whenever he receives an injury. One of the first duties of government is to afford that protection. * * * The government of the United States has been emphatically termed a government of laws, and not of men. It will certainly cease to deserve this high appellation, if the laws furnish no remedy for the violation of a vested legal right. If this obloquy is to be cast on the jurisprudence of our country, it must arise from the peculiar character of the case.

It behooves us then to enquire whether there be in its composition any ingredient which shall exempt it from legal investigation, or exclude the injured party from legal redress. Is it in the nature of the transaction? Is the act of delivering or withholding a commission to be considered as a mere political act, belonging to the executive department alone, for the performance of which, entire confidence is placed by our constitution in the supreme executive; and for any misconduct respecting which, the injured individual has no remedy. That there may be such cases is not to be questioned; but that every act of duty, to be performed in any of the great departments of government, constitutes such a case, is not to be admitted.

Make the Connection

The Court suggests that certain government actions are only "politically examinable." What sorts of actions fall into this category? We will consider this question, and the "political question doctrine," later in this chapter.

It follows then that the question, whether the legality of an act of the head of a department be examinable in a court of justice or not, must always depend on the nature of that act. * * * [W]here the heads of departments are the political or confidential agents of the executive, merely to execute the will of the President, or rather to act in cases in which the executive possesses a constitutional or legal discretion, nothing can be more perfectly clear than that their acts are only politically examinable. But where a specific duty is assigned by law, and individual rights depend upon the performance of that duty, it seems equally clear that the individual who considers himself injured, has a right to resort to the laws of his country for a remedy. [It] is then the opinion of the court, [that Marbury has a] right to the commission; a refusal to deliver which, is a plain violation of that right, for which the laws of his country afford him a remedy.

It remains to be inquired whether, [thirdly, he] is entitled to the remedy for which he applies. This depends on, 1st. The nature of the writ applied for; and 2d. The power of this court.

1st. The nature of the writ. * * * This writ, if awarded, would be directed to an officer of government, and its mandate to him would be, to use the words of Blackstone, "to do a particular thing therein specified, which appertains to his office and duty and which the court has previously determined, or at least supposes, to be consonant to right and justice." Or, in the words of Lord Mansfield, the applicant, in this case, has a right to execute an office of public concern, and is kept out of possession of that right. These circumstances certainly concur in this case.

> **Take Note**
>
> Chief Justice Marshall was fully aware that President Jefferson was likely to ignore, and to direct Madison to ignore, any judicial order commanding the delivery of Marbury's commission. How might this knowledge have affected Marshall's resolution of the case?

Still, to render the mandamus a proper remedy, the officer to whom it is to be directed, must be one to whom, on legal principles, such writ may be directed. * * * The intimate political relation, subsisting between the President of the United States and the heads of departments, necessarily renders any legal investigation of the acts of one of those high officers peculiarly irksome, as well as delicate; and excites some hesitation with respect to the propriety of entering into such investigation.

Impressions are often received without much reflection or examination, and it is not wonderful that in such a case as this, the assertion, by an individual, of his legal claims in a court of justice, to which claims it is the duty of that court to attend, should at first view be considered by some, as an attempt to intrude into the cabinet, and to intermeddle with the prerogatives of the executive.

It is scarcely necessary for the court to disclaim all pretensions to such a jurisdiction. An extravagance, so absurd and excessive, could not have been entertained for a moment. The province of the court is, solely, to decide on the rights of individuals, not to enquire how the executive, or executive officers, perform duties in which they have a discretion. Questions, in their nature political, or which are, by the constitution and laws, submitted to the executive, can never be made in this court.

But [when the head of a department] is directed by law to do a certain act affecting the absolute rights of individuals, in the performance of which he is not placed under the particular direction of the President, and the performance of which, the President cannot lawfully forbid, * * * it is not perceived on what ground the courts of the country are further excused from the duty of giving judgment.

> **Take Note**
>
> In this paragraph, Chief Justice Marshall is citing § 13 of the Judiciary Act of 1789. Notice that he addresses the question of the Court's own jurisdiction only after considering both whether Marbury has a right to his commission and whether the Jefferson Administration is obligated to deliver it. Typically, however, courts address jurisdictional questions before proceeding to the merits. Was it appropriate for Marshall to proceed in this fashion? Why do you suppose that he left the jurisdictional question for last?

This, then, is a plain case for a mandamus, either to deliver the commission, or a copy of it from the record; and it only remains to be inquired: Whether it can issue from this court. The act to establish the judicial courts of the United States authorizes the Supreme Court "to issue writs of mandamus, in cases warranted by the principles and usages of law, to any courts appointed, or persons holding office, under the authority of the United States."

The secretary of state, being a person holding an office under the authority of the United States, is precisely within the letter of the description; and if this court is not authorized to issue a writ of mandamus to such an officer, it must be because the law is unconstitutional, and therefore absolutely incapable of conferring the authority, and assigning the duties which its words purport to confer and assign.

The constitution [in Article III, § 1] vests the whole judicial power of the United States in one Supreme Court, and such inferior courts as congress shall, from time to time, ordain and establish. This power is expressly extended to all cases arising under the laws of the United States; and consequently, in some form, may be exercised over the present case; because the right claimed is given by a law of the United States.

In the distribution of this power it is declared [in Article III, § 2, cl. 2] that "the Supreme Court shall have original jurisdiction in all cases affecting ambassadors, other public ministers and consuls, and those in which a state shall be a party. In all other cases, the supreme court shall have appellate jurisdiction." [It] has been insisted, at the bar, that as the original grant of jurisdiction, to the supreme and inferior courts, is general, and the clause, assigning original jurisdiction to the Supreme Court, contains no negative or restrictive words; the power remains to the legislature, to assign original jurisdiction to that court in other cases than those specified in the article which has been recited; provided those cases belong to the judicial power of the United States.

> **Definition**
>
> "Original jurisdiction" is a "court's power to hear and decide a matter before any other court can review the matter"; appellate jurisdiction is the "power of a court to review and revise a lower court's decision." *Black's Law Dictionary* (10th ed. 2014). Note that the terms "ambassadors, other public ministers, and consuls" refer to different classes of diplomats from foreign countries. See *Black's Law Dictionary* (10th ed. 2014). These terms would not cover Madison in his role as the U.S. Secretary of State or Marbury in his hoped-for role as a Justice of the Peace.

If it had been intended to leave it in the discretion of the legislature to apportion the judicial power between the supreme and inferior courts according to the will of that body, it would certainly have been useless to have proceeded further than to have defined the judicial power, and the tribunals in which it should be vested. The subsequent part of the section is mere surplusage, is entirely without meaning, if such is to be the construction. * * * It cannot be presumed that any clause in the constitution is intended to be without effect; and therefore such a construction is inadmissible, unless the words require it.

When an instrument organizing fundamentally a judicial system, divides it into one supreme, and so many inferior courts as the legislature may ordain and establish; then enumerates its powers, and proceeds so far to distribute them, as to define the jurisdiction of the Supreme Court by declaring the cases in which it shall take original jurisdiction, and that in others it shall take appellate jurisdiction; the plain import of the words seems to be, that in one class of cases its jurisdiction is original, and not appellate; in the other it is appellate, and not original. If any other construction would render the clause inoperative, that is an additional reason for rejecting such other construction, and for adhering to their obvious meaning.

To enable this court then to issue a mandamus, it must be shown to be an exercise of appellate jurisdiction, or to be necessary to enable them to exercise appellate jurisdiction. It is the essential criterion of appellate jurisdiction, that it revises and corrects the proceedings in a cause already instituted, and does not create that cause. Although, therefore, a mandamus may be directed to courts, yet to issue such a writ to an officer for the delivery of a paper, is in effect the same as to sustain an original action for that paper, and therefore seems not to belong to appellate, but to original jurisdiction. Neither is it necessary in such a case as this, to enable the court to exercise its appellate jurisdiction.

The authority, therefore, given to the Supreme Court, by the act establishing the judicial courts of the United States, to issue writs of mandamus to public officers, appears not to be warranted by the Constitution; and it becomes necessary to enquire whether a jurisdiction, so conferred, can be exercised.

The question, whether an act, repugnant to the constitution, can become the law of the land, is a question deeply interesting to the United States; but, happily, not of an intricacy proportioned to its interest. It seems only necessary to recognize certain principles, supposed to have been long and well established, to decide it.

That the people have an original right to establish, for their future government, such principles as, in their opinion, shall most conduce to their own happiness, is the basis on which the whole American fabric has been erected. The exercise of this original right is a very great exertion; nor can it, nor ought it to be, frequently repeated. The principles, therefore, so established, are deemed fundamental. And as the authority, from which they proceed, is supreme, and can seldom act, they are designed to be permanent.

This original and supreme will organizes the government, and assigns, to different departments, their respective powers. It may either stop here; or establish certain limits not to be transcended by those departments. The government of the United States is of the latter description. The powers of the legislature are defined, and limited; and that those limits may not be mistaken, or forgotten, the constitution is written. To what purpose are powers limited, and to what purpose is that limitation committed to writing, if these limits may, at any time, be passed by those intended to be restrained? The distinction, between a government with limited and unlimited powers, is abolished, if those limits do not confine the persons on whom they are imposed, and if acts prohibited and acts allowed, are of equal obligation. It is a proposition too plain to be contested, that the Constitution controls any legislative act repugnant to it; or, that the legislature may alter the Constitution by an ordinary act.

Between these alternatives there is no middle ground. The constitution is either a superior, paramount law, unchangeable by ordinary means, or it is on a level with ordinary legislative acts, and like other acts, is alterable when the legislature shall please to alter it. If the former part of the alternative be true, then a legislative act contrary to the Constitution is not law: if the latter part be true, then written Constitutions are absurd attempts, on the part of the people, to limit a power in its own nature illimitable.

Certainly all those who have framed written constitutions contemplate them as forming the fundamental and paramount law of the nation, and consequently the theory of every such government must be, that an act of the legislature, repugnant to the constitution, is void. This theory is essentially attached to a written constitution, and is consequently to be considered, by this court, as one of the fundamental principles of our society.

If an act of the legislature, repugnant to the constitution, is void, does it, notwithstanding its invalidity, bind the courts, and oblige them to give it effect? Or, in other words, though it be not law, does it constitute a rule as operative as if it was a law? This would be to overthrow in fact what was established in theory; and would seem, at first view, an absurdity too gross to be insisted on. It shall, however, receive a more attentive consideration.

It is emphatically the province and duty of the judicial department to say what the law is. Those who apply the rule to particular cases, must of necessity expound and interpret that rule. If two laws conflict with each other, the courts must decide on the operation of each. * * * This is of the very essence of judicial duty. If then the courts are to regard the Constitution; and the Constitution is superior to any ordinary act of the legislature; the Constitution, and not such ordinary act, must govern the case to which they both apply. Those then who controvert the principle that the Constitution is to be considered, in court, as a paramount law, are reduced to the necessity of maintaining that courts must close their eyes on the Constitution, and see only the law.

This doctrine would subvert the very foundation of all written constitutions. It would declare that an act, which, according to the principles and theory of our government, is entirely void; is yet, in practice, completely obligatory. It would declare, that if the legislature shall do what is expressly forbidden, such act, notwithstanding the express prohibition, is in reality effectual. It would be giving to the legislature a practical and real omnipotence, with the same breath which professes to restrict their powers within narrow limits. It is prescribing limits, and declaring that those limits may be passed at pleasure.

That it thus reduces to nothing what we have deemed the greatest improvement on political institutions—a written constitution—would of itself be sufficient, in America, where written constitutions have been viewed with so much reverence, for rejecting the construction. But the peculiar expressions of the Constitution of the United States furnish additional arguments in favour of its rejection.

The judicial power of the United States is extended to all cases arising under the Constitution. Could it be the intention of those who gave this power, to say that, in using it, the Constitution should not be looked into? That a case arising under the Constitution should be decided without examining the instrument under which it arises? This is too extravagant to be maintained. In some cases then, the Constitution must be looked into by the judges. And if they can open it at all, what part of it are they forbidden to read, or to obey?

There are many other parts of the Constitution which serve to illustrate this subject. It is declared that "no tax or duty shall be laid on articles exported from any state." Suppose a duty on the export of cotton, of tobacco, or of flour; and a suit instituted to recover it. Ought judgment to be rendered in such a case? Ought the judges to close their eyes on the constitution, and only see the law?

The Constitution declares that "no bill of attainder or *ex post facto* law shall be passed." If, however, such a bill should be passed and a person should be prosecuted under it; must the court condemn to death those victims whom the constitution endeavors to preserve?

"No person," says the Constitution, "shall be convicted of treason unless on the testimony of two witnesses to the same overt act, or on confession in open court." Here the language of the Constitution is addressed especially to the courts. It prescribes, directly for them, a rule of evidence not to be departed from. If the legislature should change that rule, and declare *one* witness, or a confession *out of* court, sufficient for conviction, must the constitutional principle yield to the legislative act?

From these, and many other selections which might be made, it is apparent, that the framers of the Constitution contemplated that instrument, as a rule for the government of *courts,* as well as of the legislature. [Why] otherwise does it direct the judges to take an oath to support it? This oath certainly applies, in an especial manner, to their conduct in their official character.

Take Note

Does the Constitution require any other government actors to take an oath to support the Constitution? If so, what does this suggest about Marshall's argument?

How immoral to impose it on them, if they were to be used as the instruments, and the knowing instruments, for violating what they swear to support! Why does a judge swear to discharge his duties agreeably to the Constitution of the United States, if that constitution forms no rule for his government? If it is closed upon him, and cannot be inspected by him? If such be the real state of things, this is worse than solemn mockery. To prescribe, or to take this oath, becomes equally a crime.

It is also not entirely unworthy of observation, that in declaring what shall be the *supreme* law of the land, the *Constitution* itself is first mentioned; and not the laws of the United States generally, but those only which shall be made in *pursuance* of the constitution, have that rank.

Thus, the particular phraseology of the Constitution of the United States confirms and strengthens the principle, supposed to be essential to all written constitutions, that a law repugnant to the constitution is void; and that *courts,* as well as other departments, are bound by that instrument.

The rule must be discharged.

POINTS FOR DISCUSSION

a. The Judiciary Act of 1789

Section 13 of the Judiciary Act of 1789—the provision at issue in *Marbury*—delineated the jurisdiction of the Supreme Court. After conferring original jurisdiction on the Court over cases involving states and ambassadors, the section stated: "The Supreme Court shall also have appellate jurisdiction from the circuit courts and courts of the several states, in the cases herein after specially provided for; and shall have power to issue writs of prohibition to the district courts, when proceeding as courts of admiralty and maritime jurisdiction, and writs of mandamus, in cases warranted by the principles and usages of law, to any courts appointed, or persons holding office, under the authority of the United States." 1 Stat. 73. In light of the clauses that immediately preceded the clause granting authority to the Court to issue writs of mandamus, do you find convincing the Court's conclusion that the Act authorized the Supreme Court to exercise *original* jurisdiction over suits seeking writs of mandamus against federal officers?

b. Article III

Article III, § 2, cl. 2 provides: "In all Cases involving Ambassadors, other public Ministers and Counsuls, and those in which a State shall be Party, the Supreme Court shall have original Jurisdiction. In all other Cases before mentioned [in clause 1], the supreme Court shall have appellate Jurisdiction * * *." The Court concluded, in effect, that this provision creates mutually exclusive categories of original and appellate jurisdiction, such that Congress lacks power to confer original jurisdiction over cases that fall within the Supreme Court's appellate jurisdiction, and vice versa. Is this the only plausible interpretation of the provision? In light of the language of the provision—that the Court "shall" have original jurisdiction over some cases and "shall" have appellate jurisdiction over others—is it the most compelling interpretation? What other meanings can the word "shall" connote? In answering these questions, consider that 20 years after the decision in *Marbury*, the Court—in an opinion by Chief Justice Marshall—held that Congress may authorize the Court to exercise appellate jurisdiction over a case involving a State, even though such cases plainly fall within the Court's original jurisdiction as defined in *Marbury*. *Cohens v. Virginia*, 19 U.S. (6 Wheat.) 264, 399–400 (1821).

c. Arguments for and Against Judicial Review of Federal Statutes

The Court concluded that it has authority to determine whether a federal statute is inconsistent with the Constitution and thus void. What specific reasons did it give for this conclusion? Are these reasons based on the text of the Constitution, on the original intent or understanding of the Constitution, or on policy or other considerations?

The Court's assertion that "all those who have framed written constitutions contemplate them as forming the fundamental and paramount law of the nation, and * * * an act of the legislature, repugnant to the constitution, is void" is consistent with views expressed by Alexander Hamilton in the Federalist Papers. In The Federalist No. 78, Hamilton wrote:

> The complete independence of the courts of justice is peculiarly essential in a limited Constitution. By a limited Constitution, I understand one which contains certain specified exceptions to the legislative authority; such, for instance, as that it shall pass no bills of attainder, no ex-post-facto laws, and the like. Limitations of this kind can be preserved in practice no other way than through the medium of courts of justice, whose duty it must be to declare all acts contrary to the manifest tenor of the Constitution void. Without this, all the reservations of particular rights or privileges would amount to nothing.

Historians debate, however, whether this view of the Constitution was widely shared at the time of ratification.

In any event, it is worth noting that Chief Justice Marshall did not consider any possible counterarguments. Are there any arguments against judicial review of federal statutes? For example, is it relevant that there is no clause in the Constitution that says that courts may invalidate federal statutes, even though there is a provision—the Supremacy Clause in Article VI—that says that state judges may not enforce unconstitutional state laws? Is it worth noting that the Court's opinion cites no precedent to support its reasoning? Should it matter that Article I, § 7 says that a bill passed by the House and Senate and signed by the President is "a law" without qualification (i.e., without saying that it is "a law if the courts say it is constitutional")? With respect to this last point, consider that many of the Members of the Congress that enacted the Judiciary Act not only had taken an oath to support the Constitution, but also had served at the Constitutional Convention or in the state ratifying conventions. (Oliver Ellsworth, the principal drafter of the Judiciary Act, was a central figure at the former and an important figure at the Connecticut ratifying convention.) Do you suppose that they thought that section 13 of the Judiciary Act was constitutional? Why is the Court's interpretation of the Constitution superior to Congress's interpretation?

In light of this discussion, notice finally that Chief Justice Marshall stated that the central question in the case was "whether an act, repugnant to the constitution, can become the law of the land." He concluded, perhaps not surprisingly, that the answer must be "no." Was there really any debate about this proposition? Was the question that the Court answered really the central question in the case?

d. The Constitution and Ordinary Law

It is deeply ingrained in our social and political conscience—at least in part because of the conclusion in *Marbury v. Madison*—that statutes that conflict with the Constitution are void. But at least theoretically, statutes enacted today reflect the current democratic consensus. Why should we be deprived of the right to decide for ourselves, through democratic means, how to govern ourselves—and be so deprived, moreover, by un-elected judges enforcing a charter that represents the judgments of people who are long dead and gone? Even assuming that Chief Justice Marshall asked and answered the right question in *Marbury*, is it so clear that the Court should invalidate democratically enacted statutes on the ground that they are inconsistent with the Constitution? Why is the Constitution binding on us today?

e. Who Won in *Marbury*?

Who "won" in *Marbury*? Did Jefferson and Madison win? After all, the import of the holding—that the Court lacked jurisdiction to grant Marbury's petition—was that the Court could not order them to deliver Marbury's commission. In fact, Marbury never received his commission, even though according to the Court he had a right to it. But Jefferson and Madison's success came at a high price. They were also told by the Court that in one of their very first acts in office they had violated Marbury's vested legal rights. And the Federalists, who at the time controlled the federal courts, gained or solidified the power of judicial review. Was this a Pyrrhic victory?

MARTIN V. HUNTER'S LESSEE

14 U.S. (1 Wheat.) 304 (1816)

[This case concerned a long-running dispute over a huge piece of land in Virginia that formerly was owned by Lord Fairfax, a British loyalist. The State of Virginia claimed that it had lawfully seized Fairfax's land prior to the Treaty of Paris in 1783, which ended the Revolutionary War. Virginia subsequently granted parcels of the land to some of its citizens, including Hunter. Martin claimed ownership of the same parcel of land, tracing his claim to a devise from Fairfax in 1781. Martin claimed that Fairfax's lands had been protected from seizure by the Treaty of Paris in 1783 and by the Jay Treaty of 1794.

Hunter filed a lawsuit in Virginia state court in 1791. The litigation itself was on hold for about 20 years, during which time John Marshall and his brother James contracted to purchase a large part of the Fairfax estate from Fairfax's heirs. The Virginia Court of Appeals (the highest court in the state) first ruled in the case in 1810, upholding Virginia's earlier seizure of Fairfax's land and thus ruling in favor of Hunter. The United States Supreme Court reversed that judgment in *Fairfax's Devisee v. Hunter's Lessee*, 11 U.S. (7 Cranch) 603 (1813), and "instructed" and "commanded" the Virginia judges to enter judgment for Martin.

On remand, the Virginia Court of Appeals refused to enter judgment for Martin. It concluded that "the appellate power of the Supreme Court of the United States does not extend to this court," and that section 25 of the Judiciary Act of 1789, which authorized Supreme Court review of final decisions of the highest state courts rejecting claims, such as Martin's, based on federal law, thus was unconstitutional. The Virginia Court suggested that if Congress wanted to ensure United States Supreme Court review of all issues of federal law, it could create more inferior federal courts and confer on them jurisdiction over all issues arising under federal law. The Supreme Court reviewed that judgment in the opinion that follows.]

STORY, J., delivered the opinion of the court.

The third article of the constitution is that which must principally attract our attention. * * * The language of the article throughout is manifestly designed to be mandatory upon the legislature. * * * The judicial power of the United States *shall be vested* (not may be vested) in one supreme court, and in such inferior courts as congress may, from time to time, ordain and establish. Could congress have lawfully refused to create a supreme court, or to vest in it the constitutional jurisdiction?

The judicial power must [be] vested in some court, by congress; and to suppose that it was not an obligation binding on them, but might, at their pleasure, be omitted or declined, is to suppose that, under the sanction of the constitution, they might defeat the constitution itself; a construction which would lead to such a result cannot be sound.

If, then, it is a duty of congress to vest the judicial power of the United States, it is a duty to vest the *whole judicial power.* The language, if imperative as to one part, is imperative as to all. If it were otherwise, this anomaly would exist, that congress might successively refuse to vest the jurisdiction in any one class of cases enumerated in the constitution, and thereby defeat the jurisdiction as to all; for the constitution has not singled out any class on which congress are bound to act in preference to others.

FYI

Martin is the most significant case decided by the Marshall Court that Chief Justice Marshall did not write. He recused himself because of his claim to some of the Fairfax lands, which gave him an obvious stake in the outcome. Justice Joseph Story (1779–1845) was a great jurist in his own right. He became a Supreme Court Justice at age 32 and served on the Court for 34 years. Story was also a professor of law at Harvard and wrote a highly influential treatise, *Commentaries on the Constitution of the United States* (1833). This treatise, which the Supreme Court has cited in over 200 cases, is available online https://www.google.com/books/edition/Commentaries_on_the_Constitution_of_the/qAO3x-GN2rsC.

This leads us to the consideration of the great question as to the nature and extent of the appellate jurisdiction of the United States. * * * As [the] appellate jurisdiction is not limited as to the supreme court, and as to this court it may be exercised in all other cases than those of which it has original cognizance, what is there to restrain its exercise over state tribunals in the enumerated cases? The appellate power is not limited by the terms of the third article to any particular courts. The words are, "the judicial power (which includes appellate power) shall extend *to all cases*," &c., and "in all other cases before mentioned the supreme court shall have appellate jurisdiction." It is the *case*, then, and not *the court*, that gives the jurisdiction. If the judicial power extends to the case, it will be in vain to search in the letter of the constitution for any qualification as to the tribunal where it depends.

If the constitution meant to limit the appellate jurisdiction to cases pending in the courts of the United States, it would necessarily follow that the jurisdiction of these courts would, in all the cases enumerated in the constitution, be exclusive of state tribunals. How otherwise could the jurisdiction extend to *all* cases arising under the constitution, laws, and treaties of the United States, or *to all cases* of admiralty and maritime jurisdiction? If some of these cases might be entertained by state tribunals, and no appellate jurisdiction as to them should exist, then the appellate power would not extend to *all*, but to *some*, cases.

On the other hand, if [a] discretion be vested in congress to establish, or not to establish, inferior courts at their own pleasure, and congress should not establish such courts, the appellate jurisdiction of the supreme Court would have nothing to act upon, unless it could act upon cases pending in the state courts.

But it is plain that the framers of the constitution did contemplate that cases within the judicial cognizance of the United States not only might but would arise in the state courts, in the exercise of their ordinary jurisdiction. With this view the sixth article declares, that "this constitution, and the laws of the United States which shall be made in pursuance thereof, and all treaties made, or which shall be made, under the authority of the United States, shall be the supreme law of the land, and the judges in every state shall be bound thereby, any thing in the constitution or laws of any state to the contrary notwithstanding."

It must, therefore, be conceded that the constitution not only contemplated, but meant to provide for cases within the scope of the judicial power of the United States, which might yet depend before state tribunals. It was foreseen that in the exercise of their ordinary jurisdiction, state courts would incidentally take cognizance of cases arising under the constitution, the laws, and treaties of the United States. Yet to all these cases the judicial power, by the very terms of the constitution, is to extend. It cannot extend by original jurisdiction if that was already rightfully and exclusively attached in the state courts, which (as has been already shown) may occur; it must, therefore, extend by appellate jurisdiction, or not at all. It would seem to follow that the appellate power of the United States must, in such cases, extend to state tribunals; and if in such cases, there is no reason why it should not equally attach upon all others within the purview of the constitution.

It has been argued that such an appellate jurisdiction over state courts is inconsistent with the genius of our governments, and the spirit of the constitution.

That the latter was never designed to act upon state sovereignties, but only upon the people, and that if the power exists, it will materially impair the sovereignty of the states, and the independence of their courts. We cannot yield to the force of this reasoning; it assumes principles which we cannot admit, and draws conclusions to which we do not yield our assent.

It is a mistake that the constitution was not designed to operate upon states, in their corporate capacities. It is crowded with provisions which restrain or annul the sovereignty of the states in some of the highest branches of their prerogatives. * * * Nor can such a right be deemed to impair the independence of state judges. It is assuming the very ground in controversy to assert that they possess an absolute independence of the United States. In respect to the powers granted to the United States, they are not independent; they are expressly bound to obedience by the letter of the constitution; and if they should unintentionally transcend their authority, or misconstrue the constitution, there is no more reason for giving their judgments an absolute and irresistible force, than for giving it to the acts of the other co-ordinate departments of state sovereignty.

The argument urged from the possibility of the abuse of the revising power, is equally unsatisfactory. It is always a doubtful course, to argue against the use or existence of a power, from the possibility of its abuse. * * * From the very nature of things, the absolute right of decision, in the last resort, must rest somewhere—wherever it may be vested it is susceptible of abuse.

It is further argued, that no great public mischief can result from a construction which shall limit the appellate power of the United States to cases in their own courts: first, because state judges are bound by an oath to support the constitution of the United States, and must be presumed to be men of learning and integrity; and, secondly, because congress must have an unquestionable right to remove all cases within the scope of the judicial power from the state courts to the courts of the United States, at any time before final judgment, though not after final judgment. [A]dmitting that the judges of the state courts are, and always will be, of as much learning, integrity, and wisdom, as those of the courts of the United States, (which we very cheerfully admit) [does] not aid the argument. It is manifest that the constitution has proceeded upon a theory of its own, [presuming] (whether rightly or wrongly we do not inquire) that state attachments, state prejudices, state jealousies, and state interests, might some times obstruct, or

> **Food for Thought**
>
> Can you think of any provisions of the Constitution that appear to presume that state judges might at times be biased in some way in the performance of their duties?

control, or be supposed to obstruct or control, the regular administration of justice.

A motive of another kind, perfectly compatible with the most sincere respect for state tribunals, might induce the grant of appellate power over their decisions. That motive is the importance, and even necessity of *uniformity* of decisions throughout the whole United States, upon all subjects within the purview of the constitution. Judges of equal learning and integrity, in different states, might differently interpret a statute, or a treaty of the United States, or even the constitution itself: If there were no revising authority to control these jarring and discordant judgments, and harmonize them into uniformity, the laws, the treaties, and the constitution of the United States would be different in different states, and might, perhaps, never have precisely the same construction, obligation, or efficacy, in any two states. The public mischiefs that would attend such a state of things would be truly deplorable; and it cannot be believed that they could have escaped the enlightened convention which formed the constitution.

The remedy, too, of removal of suits would be utterly inadequate to the purposes of the constitution, if it could act only on the parties, and not upon the state courts. * * * If state courts should deny the constitutionality of the authority to remove suits from their cognizance, in what manner could they be compelled to relinquish the jurisdiction?

On the whole, the court are of opinion, that the appellate power of the United States does extend to cases pending in the state courts; and that the 25th section of the judiciary act, which authorizes the exercise of this jurisdiction in the specified cases, by a writ of error, is supported by the letter and spirit of the constitution.

It is the opinion of the whole court, that the judgment of the court of appeals of Virginia, rendered on the mandate in this cause, be reversed * * *.

POINTS FOR DISCUSSION

a. Text and History

Delegates at the Constitutional Convention were divided over whether to create lower federal courts. Some argued that the Constitution itself should create not only a Supreme Court but also inferior federal courts, to ensure a neutral forum for the assertion of federal rights. Others argued that the existing state courts would be adequate fora. The provision in Article III authorizing, but not requiring, Congress to create inferior federal courts was a compromise between the competing positions. What does the compromise reflect about the Framers' likely expectations about the

Supreme Court's power to review state-court judgments? In addition, Article VI provides that "the Judges in every State shall be bound" by federal law, "any Thing in the Constitution or Laws of any State to the Contrary notwithstanding." Does this provision help Justice Story's reasoning?

b. State Court Hostility to Federal Law

Justice Story suggested that the Constitution presupposes the possibility of hostility by state court judges to federal law or claims arising under federal law. Is this a realistic fear? If so, why might we expect such hostility? And if it made sense to fear it in 1789 (or 1816), does it make sense to fear it today?

Chief Justice Marshall did not participate in the decision in *Martin*. But five years later, in *Cohens v. Virginia*, 19 U.S. (6 Wheat.) 264, 399–400 (1821), Marshall addressed the constitutionality of section 25 of the Judiciary Act in a case in which one of the parties was a state. Virginia argued (among other things) that the provision in Article III conferring original jurisdiction on the Supreme Court in cases "in which a State shall be a Party" precluded the Supreme Court from exercising appellate jurisdiction in the case. (Recall that the Court in *Marbury* had concluded that the categories of original and appellate jurisdiction in Article III were mutually exclusive.) The Court rejected Virginia's argument. Echoing Justice Story's opinion in *Martin*, the Court concluded that "the judicial power, as originally given, extends to all cases arising under the constitution or a law of the United States, whoever may be the parties." (Chief Justice Marshall concluded that the discussion in *Marbury*—which, of course, he had written—about the Court's appellate jurisdiction was unpersuasive dicta.) Marshall also agreed with Story that state courts might exhibit hostility to federal law: "It would be hazarding too much to assert, that the judicatures of the States will be exempt from the prejudices by which the legislatures and people are influenced, and will constitute perfectly impartial tribunals. In many States the judges are dependent for office and for salary on the will of the legislature. * * * When we observe the importance which that constitution attaches to the independence of judges, we are the less inclined to suppose that it can have intended to leave these constitutional questions to tribunals where this independence may not exist * * *. There is certainly nothing in the circumstances under which our constitution was formed; nothing in the history of the times, which would justify the opinion that the confidence reposed in the States was so implicit as to leave in them and their tribunals the power of resisting or defeating, in the form of law, the legitimate measures of the Union."

c. Uniformity

Justice Story also reasoned that Supreme Court review of state court judgments was necessary to ensure the uniformity of federal law. Why isn't removal to federal court of cases involving questions of federal law a sufficient response to the concern about uniformity?

Together, *Marbury* and *Martin* stand for the proposition that the Court has the power of judicial review, which it can exercise in cases arising in state and federal court and in cases involving the constitutionality of state or federal laws. These undoubtedly are profoundly important propositions in our system of government. But just how profound turns on the scope of the power of judicial review. Did the Court in *Marbury* hold that judicial interpretations of the Constitution are binding on all actors subject to the provisions of the Constitution? Or did the Court in *Marbury* simply hold that judicial review is the mere consequence of a court's obligation to decide cases that come before it in accordance with the governing law, including the Constitution? If this is the case, then judicial interpretations of the Constitution would be binding on the parties to the litigation that produced the interpretation, but perhaps on no one else.

Perhaps because of the delicacy of the Court's role in a democratic society—and because of the controversy that surrounds so many of the Court's important decisions—many prominent voices have long urged that only the latter, more narrow account of the power of judicial review is correct. Abraham Lincoln, for example, argued that "the candid citizen must confess that if the policy of the Government upon vital questions affecting the whole people is to be irrevocably fixed by decisions of the Supreme Court, the instant they are made in ordinary litigation between parties in personal actions, the people will have ceased to be their own rulers, having to that extent practically resigned their Government into the hands of that eminent tribunal." First Inaugural Address, March 4, 1861. The Court finally took the opportunity in the case that follows to address the question of the scope of *Marbury*'s holding.

COOPER V. AARON

358 U.S. 1 (1958)

Opinion of the Court by THE CHIEF JUSTICE, MR. JUSTICE BLACK, MR. JUSTICE FRANKFURTER, MR. JUSTICE DOUGLAS, MR. JUSTICE BURTON, MR. JUSTICE CLARK, MR. JUSTICE HARLAN, MR. JUSTICE BRENNAN, and MR. JUSTICE WHITTAKER.

> **Take Note**
>
> The opinion of the Court was not announced either by one Justice or "per curiam," which means "by the Court." The Court took the highly unusual step of issuing a jointly signed opinion. Why would the Court do so in this case?

As this case reaches us it raises questions of the highest importance to the maintenance of our federal system of government. It necessarily involves a claim by the Governor and Legislature of a State that there is no duty on state officials to obey federal court orders resting on this Court's considered interpretation of the United States Constitution. Specifically it involves actions by the Governor and Legislature of Arkansas upon the premise that they are not bound by our holding in *Brown v. Board of Education*, 347 U.S. 483 (1954), [that] the Fourteenth Amendment forbids States to use their governmental powers to bar children on racial grounds from attending schools where there is state participation through any arrangement, management, funds or property. We are urged to uphold a suspension of the Little Rock School Board's plan to do away with segregated public schools in Little Rock until state laws and efforts to upset and nullify our holding in *Brown* have been further challenged and tested in the courts. We reject these contentions.

[Shortly after the decision in *Brown*, the Little Rock District School Board adopted a desegregation plan.] While the School Board was thus going forward with its preparation for desegregating the Little Rock school system, other state authorities, in contrast, were actively pursuing a program designed to perpetuate in Arkansas the system of racial segregation which this Court had held violated the Fourteenth Amendment. [The Arkansas state Constitution was amended to command the state legislature to oppose "in every Constitutional manner the unconstitutional desegregation decisions of the United States Supreme Court," and the legislature responded by enacting laws relieving school children from compulsory attendance at racially mixed schools. Although the Little Rock School Board continued with preparations to implement the first phase of a desegregation program, which entailed the enrollment of nine African-American children at Central High School, a school with more than two thousand students, the Governor of Arkansas dispatched units of the Arkansas National Guard to Central High School the day before the students arrived and placed the school "off limits" to the black students. Every school day for the next three weeks, members of the Guard, acting pursuant to the Governor's order, stood shoulder to shoulder at the school grounds and forcibly prevented the black students from entering.]

FYI

The Court issued two decisions in *Brown v. Board of Education;* the second, known as *Brown II*, ordered desegregation "with all deliberate speed." The litigation that followed directly involved lower federal courts around the country in overseeing desegregation plans. We will consider *Brown* and this line of cases in Volume 2.

[After intervention of the Attorney General of the United States, the District Court overseeing the implementation of the desegregation plan enjoined] the Governor and the officers of the Guard from preventing the attendance of Negro children at Central High School, and from otherwise obstructing or interfering with the orders of the court in connection with the plan. The National Guard was then withdrawn from the school. [The next school day the children] entered the high school [under] the protection of the Little Rock Police Department and members of the Arkansas State Police[, but] the officers caused the children to be removed from the school during the morning because they had difficulty controlling a large and demonstrating crowd which had gathered at the high school. [Two days later], however, the President of the United States dispatched federal troops to Central High School and admission of the Negro students to the school was thereby effected. Regular army troops continued at the high school until November 27, 1957. They were then replaced by federalized National Guardsmen who remained throughout the balance of the school year. Eight of the Negro students remained in attendance at the school throughout the school year.

> **Definition**
>
> The verb "enjoin" means "legally prohibit or restrain by injunction." An "injunction" is a "court order commanding or preventing an action." *Black's Law Dictionary* (10th ed. 2014).

[On] February 20, 1958, the School Board and the Superintendent of Schools filed a petition in the District Court seeking a postponement of their program for desegregation. Their position in essence was that because of extreme public hostility, which they stated had been engendered largely by the official attitudes and actions of the Governor and the Legislature, the maintenance of a sound educational program at Central High School, with the Negro students in attendance, would be impossible. The Board therefore proposed that the Negro students already admitted to the school be withdrawn and sent to segregated schools, and that all further steps to carry out the Board's desegregation program be postponed for a period later suggested by the Board to be two and one-half years. After a hearing the District Court granted the relief requested by the Board [finding that] the past year at Central High School had been attended by conditions of "chaos, bedlam and turmoil" [and] that there were "repeated incidents of more or less serious violence directed against the Negro students and their property." [The court of appeals reversed.]

In affirming the judgment of the Court of Appeals which reversed the District Court we have accepted without reservation the position of the School Board, the Superintendent of Schools, and their counsel that they displayed entire good faith in the conduct of these proceedings and in dealing with the unfortunate and distressing sequence of events which has been outlined. We likewise have accepted the findings of the District Court as to the conditions at Central High School during the 1957–1958 school year, and also the findings that the educational progress of all the students, white and colored, of that school has suffered and will continue to suffer if the conditions which prevailed last year are permitted to continue.

The significance of these findings, however, is to be considered in light of the fact, indisputably revealed by the record before us, that the conditions they depict are directly traceable to the actions of legislators and executive officials of the State of Arkansas, taken in their official capacities, which reflect their own determination to resist this Court's decision in the *Brown* case and which have brought about violent resistance to that decision in Arkansas. * * * One may well sympathize with the position of the Board in the face of the frustrating conditions which have confronted it, but, regardless of the Board's good faith, the actions of the other state agencies responsible for those conditions compel us to reject the Board's legal position.

[T]he constitutional rights of children not to be discriminated against in school admission on grounds of race or color declared by this Court in the *Brown* case can neither be nullified openly and directly by state legislators or state executive or judicial officers, nor nullified indirectly by them through evasive schemes for segregation whether attempted "ingeniously or ingenuously."

What has been said, in the light of the facts developed, is enough to dispose of the case. However, we should answer the premise of the actions of the Governor and Legislature that they are not bound by our holding in the *Brown* case. * * * Article VI of the Constitution makes the Constitution the "supreme Law of the Land." In 1803, Chief Justice Marshall, speaking for a unanimous Court, referring to the Constitution as "the fundamental and paramount law of the nation," declared in the notable case of *Marbury v. Madison* that "It is emphatically the province and duty of the judicial department to say what the law is." This decision declared the basic principle that the federal judiciary is supreme in the exposition of the law of the Constitution, and that principle has ever since been respected by this Court and the Country as a permanent and indispensable feature of our constitutional system. It follows that the interpretation of the Fourteenth Amendment enunciated by this Court in the *Brown* case is the supreme law of the land, and Art. VI of the Constitution makes it of binding effect on the States "any Thing in the Constitution or Laws of any State to the Contrary notwithstanding." Every state legislator and executive and judicial officer is solemnly committed by oath taken pursuant to Art. VI, cl. 3 "to support this Constitution."

No state legislator or executive or judicial officer can war against the Constitution without violating his undertaking to support it. * * * A Governor who asserts a power to nullify a federal court order is similarly restrained. If he had such power, said Chief Justice Hughes, in 1932, also for a unanimous Court, "it is manifest that the fiat of a state Governor, and not the Constitution of the United States, would be the supreme law of the land; that the restrictions of the Federal Constitution upon the exercise of state power would be but impotent phrases."

The basic decision in *Brown* was unanimously reached by this Court only after the case had been briefed and twice argued and the issues had been given the most serious consideration. Since the first *Brown* opinion three new Justices have come to the Court. They are at one with the Justices still on the Court who participated in that basic decision as to its correctness, and that decision is now unanimously reaffirmed. The principles announced in that decision and the obedience of the States to them, according to the command of the Constitution, are indispensable for the protection of the freedoms guaranteed by our fundamental charter for all of us. Our constitutional ideal of equal justice under law is thus made a living truth.

POINTS FOR DISCUSSION

a. Implications of Judicial Supremacy

The Court in *Cooper* emphatically rejected the view that government officials may ignore the Supreme Court's interpretation of the Constitution if they were not parties to the litigation that produced the interpretation. According to the decision in *Cooper*, it is not simply the "Constitution," but rather the Court's interpretation of the Constitution, that is the "supreme Law of the Land." In one sense, there is great appeal to this proposition. If political figures could ignore the Court and substitute their own interpretations of the Constitution, then the meaning of the Constitution would be left to the political process, and the courts' ability to protect individual rights against majoritarian incursion would be substantially diminished. The circumstances in *Cooper*—which led the Court firmly to insist that state-sanctioned racial segregation was intolerable—are perhaps the perfect example of the appeal of this view of judicial power.

But the principle of judicial supremacy might also lead, in at least some cases, to the entrenchment of deeply troubling views about constitutional meaning. President

Lincoln offered his view of judicial supremacy, with which we introduced the decision in *Cooper*, in response to the Supreme Court's decision in *Dred Scott v. Sandford*, 60 U.S. (19 How.) 393 (1857), which held that persons of African descent could not become citizens of the United States, and that Congress lacked power to prohibit slavery in territories of the United States. Judicial supremacy is significantly less appealing when one considers that it applies to all judicial interpretations of the Constitution.

In light of this tension, was the Court's decision in *Cooper* correct?

b. Judicial Supremacy and Congress

Cooper was decided against the backdrop of state resistance to Supreme Court interpretations of the Constitution. Is the binding force of the Court's interpretations any different when it is Congress, rather than a state or state official, that disagrees? In *Dickerson v. United States*, 530 U.S. 428 (2000), the Court considered the constitutionality of 18 U.S.C. § 3501, which purported to overrule the requirement announced in *Miranda v. Arizona*, 384 U.S. 436 (1966), that certain warnings must be given to a suspect subject to custodial interrogation in order to permit subsequent admission of the suspect's statements as evidence. The Court concluded that Congress "may not legislatively supersede our decisions interpreting and applying the Constitution." Because the Court concluded that in *Miranda* it had announced a "constitutional rule" rather than "merely exercised its supervisory authority to regulate evidence in the absence of congressional direction," the Court invalidated the statute. Justice Scalia, joined by Justice Thomas, dissented, concluding that the Court in *Miranda* had not in fact announced a constitutional rule.

c. Historical Responses to Judicial Supremacy

Judicial supremacy is not absolute. On the contrary, history has shown that there are at least two possible, but limited, ways to undo constitutional decisions by the Supreme Court.

One method to negate the Court's decisions is to amend the Constitution, under the procedures in Article V, to say the opposite of what the Supreme Court previously interpreted the Constitution to mean. The Constitution has been amended to overturn at least four Supreme Court decisions in this manner: the Eleventh Amendment overruled *Chisholm v. Georgia*, 2 U.S. (2 Dall.) 419 (1793) (concerning federal court jurisdiction over state governments); the Thirteenth and Fourteenth Amendments overruled *Dred Scott v. Sandford*, 60 U.S. (19 How.) 393 (1856) (described above); the Sixteenth Amendment overruled *Pollock v. Farmers' Loan & Trust Co.*, 158 U.S. 601 (1895) (concerning income taxes); and the Twenty-Sixth Amendment overruled *Oregon v. Mitchell*, 400 U.S. 112 (1970) (concerning the voting age).

Consider, for example, the *Dred Scott* case. How does the first sentence of the 14th Amendment affect *Dred Scott*'s holding that persons of African ancestry cannot be citizens? How does the 13th Amendment affect *Dred Scott*'s holding that Congress cannot prohibit slavery in federal territories? Does the possibility of amending the Constitution eliminate all concerns about judicial supremacy?

The other way to undo constitutional decisions is to replace justices, when they retire, with justices who hold different views and who are willing to overturn precedents that they consider incorrect. We will see a famous example in Chapter 3 when we consider how changes in Court personnel during the 1930s led to the overturning of numerous cases that had limited federal power. But altering the membership of the Supreme Court to affect the outcome of cases is not easy for two reasons. First, replacing the personnel of the Supreme Court generally cannot happen quickly, because the justices have life tenure. Should the Constitution be amended to address this difficulty? See Steven G. Calabresi, *Term Limits for the Supreme Court: Life Tenure Reconsidered*, 29 Harv. J.L. & Pub. Pol'y 769 (2006) (arguing for term limits in part because of the difficulty of overturning Supreme Court decisions by amending the Constitution). Second, political obstacles may prevent the nomination and confirmation of justices who disagree with precedent. Consider, for example, the opposition to judicial nominees who would overturn the Supreme Court's decisions concerning abortion.

Notice in the last paragraph of the *Cooper v. Aaron* opinion that the Court mentions the change in its membership since the *Brown* decision. Why do you think that the Court raised this topic?

d. Modern Challenges to Judicial Supremacy

Notwithstanding the decisions in *Martin* and *Cooper*—and powerful arguments, based on text, history, and structure, that the Court has authority to review state court judgments and declare actions by the States unconstitutional—attacks on the Court's power of judicial review have been a constant refrain throughout American history. From the Virginia and Kentucky Resolutions of 1798—legislative resolutions drafted by James Madison and Thomas Jefferson that argued that the states are entitled to ignore federal laws or actions that they believe exceed the federal government's constitutional authority—to the Nullification Crisis of the 1830s—in which John C. Calhoun and South Carolina similarly asserted such a right—to the Civil Rights struggles of the 1950s and '60s, such attacks have been commonplace. For a modern example, consider the following.

Perspective and Analysis

In 2004, the Alabama Supreme Court, relying on the United States Supreme Court's decision in *Roper v. Simmons*, 543 U.S. 551 (2005), vacated the death sentence imposed on Renaldo Adams, who had been convicted of rape and murder. In *Roper*, the Supreme Court held that it violates the Eighth Amendment's prohibition on "cruel and unusual punishment" to execute a person who committed a crime while still a minor. Tom Parker, an Associate Justice on the Alabama Supreme Court who had recused himself from the case, responded with this editorial:

> [M]y fellow Alabama justices freed Adams from death row not because of any error of our courts but because they chose to passively accommodate—rather than actively resist—the unconstitutional opinion of five liberal justices on the U.S. Supreme Court. Those liberal justices * * * based their ruling [in *Roper*] not on the original intent or actual language of the United States Constitution but on foreign law, including United Nations treaties. * * * The proper response to such blatant judicial tyranny would have been for the Alabama Supreme Court to decline to follow *Roper* in the *Adams* case. * * * State supreme courts may decline to follow bad U.S. Supreme Court precedents because those decisions bind only the parties to the particular case. Judges * * * should not follow obviously wrong decisions simply because they are "precedents." After all, a judge takes an oath to support the constitution—not to automatically follow activist justices who believe their own devolving standards of decency trump the text of the constitution.

Tom Parker, Op-Ed: Alabama Justices Surrender to Judicial Activism, *Birmingham News*, January 1, 2005, p. 4B.

POINTS FOR DISCUSSION

a. The Binding Force of Precedent

Is Justice Parker's discussion of the precedential effect of Supreme Court decisions interpreting the Constitution consistent with the view expressed in *Cooper*? If not, is his view nevertheless convincing? To what extent does this reasoning echo Chief Justice Marshall's reasoning in *Marbury*? To what extent does it conflict with it?

b. Reliance on "Foreign" Law in Interpreting the Constitution

As Justice Parker suggests in his article, the majority in the decision in *Roper* cited some foreign-law sources in reaching its conclusion about the meaning of the Eighth Amendment. We will explore the validity of this approach in Volume 2, when we consider *Lawrence v. Texas*.

B. OBSTACLES TO JUDICIAL REVIEW

Although the Supreme Court has held that courts generally have the power of judicial review, litigants face at least four important obstacles in attempting to persuade courts to strike down legislation or executive actions as unconstitutional. First, the Supreme Court has said that some issues are not "justiciable"—that is, capable of being resolved by the courts—because they present "political questions" that only the political branches (Congress and the President) may resolve. Second, long-standing practice holds that federal courts cannot give legal advice or make abstract decisions, but instead may decide only actual "cases and controversies." The timing also might be incorrect; federal courts generally cannot decide cases or controversies before they are ripe or after they have become moot. Third, federal courts will entertain claims only by persons who have "standing" to present them because they have something at stake in the litigation. Fourth, Congress can limit federal court jurisdiction by statute and thus constrain the ability of federal courts to engage in judicial review. In reading this material, consider not only what the legal rules are, but also where the rules come from, and how they affect constitutional litigation.

1. The Political Question Doctrine

In *Marbury*, the Court stated that "where the heads of departments are the political or confidential agents of the executive, merely to execute the will of the President, or rather to act in cases in which the executive possesses a constitutional or legal discretion, nothing can be more perfectly clear than that their acts are only politically examinable." The Court, of course, concluded that *Marbury* did not involve such actions. But the Court's statement gave rise to cases in which the Court declined to review challenged government actions, on the ground that the cases involved "political questions" that were outside of the province of the judicial power. The following case addresses how a court should decide whether a political question is presented in any given case.

BAKER V. CARR

369 U.S. 186 (1962)

MR. JUSTICE BRENNAN delivered the opinion of the Court.

[The plaintiffs were Tennessee voters who claimed that the apportionment of the state legislature violated their rights under the Equal Protection Clause. Although Tennessee law allocated legislative representation among its counties according to the total number of qualified voters who resided in each county, the state legislature had not reapportioned—that is, redrawn legislative district lines—in over 60 years. The plaintiffs, who lived in areas of the state that had experienced significant growth in population, claimed that the state's failure to reapportion had, in light of these substantial demographic changes, resulted in the "debasement of their votes." They sought an injunction requiring either "reapportionment by mathematical application of the Tennessee constitutional formulae to the most recent Federal Census figures" or elections conducted at large. The district court held that the suit presented a "political question" and was therefore nonjusticiable.]

> **FYI**
>
> The Supreme Court during the tenure of Chief Justice Earl Warren is remembered for opinions in many important civil rights cases, including *Brown v. Board of Education*, 347 U.S. 483 (1954), which held that racial segregation in public schools is unconstitutional. But Chief Justice Warren considered *Baker v. Carr* the Supreme Court's most important decision during his time on the Court. No other decision had as immediate or profound an effect on democracy. Within one year of the decision, litigants were challenging the apportionment of representation in 34 states. For many interesting facts about the case, see Stephen Ansolabehere & Samuel Issacharoff, *The Story of Baker v. Carr*, in *Constitutional Law Stories* 297 (Michael C. Dorf ed., 2004).

We hold that this challenge to an apportionment presents no nonjusticiable "political question." Of course the mere fact that the suit seeks protection of a political right does not mean it presents a political question. * * * Rather, it is argued that apportionment cases * * * can involve no federal constitutional right except one resting on the guaranty of a republican form of government[, Art. IV., § 4,] and that complaints based on that clause have been held to present political questions which are nonjusticiable. [B]ecause there appears to be some uncertainty as to why those cases did present political questions, and specifically as to whether this apportionment case is like those cases, we deem it necessary first to consider the contours of the "political question" doctrine.

> **FYI**
>
> Article IV, § 4 provides in relevant part: "The United States shall guarantee to every State in this Union a Republican Form of Government * * *." What is a "Republican" form of government? If it means government by representatives selected by the people, isn't this provision arguably violated by a representative system in which some voters' votes are worth substantially less than others'?

Our discussion * * * requires review of a number of political question cases, in order to expose the attributes of the doctrine—attributes which, in various settings, diverge, combine, appear, and disappear in seeming disorderliness. * * * That review reveals that * * * it is the relationship between the judiciary and the coordinate branches of the Federal Government, and not the federal judiciary's relationship to the States, which gives rise to the "political question."

Deciding whether a matter has in any measure been committed by the Constitution to another branch of government, or whether the action of that branch exceeds whatever authority has been committed, is itself a delicate exercise in constitutional interpretation, and is a responsibility of this Court as ultimate interpreter of the Constitution. [It] is apparent [from our cases] that several formulations which vary slightly according to the settings in which the questions arise may describe a political question, although each has one or more elements which identify it as essentially a function of the separation of powers. Prominent on the surface of any case held to involve a political question is found a textually demonstrable constitutional commitment of the issue to a coordinate political department; or a lack of judicially discoverable and manageable standards for resolving it; or the impossibility of deciding without an initial policy determination of a kind clearly for nonjudicial discretion; or the impossibility of a court's undertaking independent resolution without expressing lack of the respect due coordinate branches of government; or an unusual need for unquestioning adherence to a political decision already made; or the potentiality of embarrassment from multifarious pronouncements by various departments on one question. * * * The cases we have reviewed show the necessity for discriminating inquiry into the precise facts and posture of the particular case, and the impossibility of resolution by any semantic cataloguing.

But it is argued that this case shares the characteristics of * * * cases concerning the Constitution's guaranty * * * of a republican form of government. [Our review demonstrates] that Guaranty Clause claims involve those elements which define a "political question," and for that reason and no other, they are nonjusticiable. In particular, [the] nonjusticiability of such claims has nothing to do with their touching upon matters of state governmental organization. [Instead, the Court has found that] the Guaranty Clause is not a repository of judicially manageable standards * * * for invalidating state action.

We come, finally, to the ultimate inquiry[:] whether our precedents as to what constitutes a nonjusticiable "political question" bring the case before us under the umbrella of that doctrine. A natural beginning is to note whether any of the common characteristics which we have been able to identify and label descriptively are present. We find none: The question here is the consistency of state action with the Federal Constitution. We have no question decided, or to be decided, by a political branch of government coequal with this Court. Nor do we risk embarrassment of our government abroad, or grave disturbance at home if we take issue with Tennessee as to the constitutionality of her action here challenged. Nor need the appellants, in order to succeed in this action, ask the Court to enter upon policy determinations for which judicially manageable standards are lacking. Judicial standards under the Equal Protection Clause are well developed and familiar, and it has been open to courts since the enactment of the Fourteenth Amendment to determine, if on the particular facts they must, that a discrimination reflects no policy, but simply arbitrary and capricious action. This case does, in one sense, involve the allocation of political power within a State, and the appellants might conceivably have added a claim under the Guaranty Clause. Of course, as we have seen, any reliance on that clause would be futile. But because any reliance on the Guaranty Clause could not have succeeded it does not follow that appellants may not be heard on the equal protection claim which in fact they tender. True, it must be clear that the Fourteenth Amendment claim is not so enmeshed with those political question elements which render Guaranty Clause claims nonjusticiable as actually to present a political question itself. But we have found that not to be the case here. * * * The right asserted is within the reach of judicial protection under the Fourteenth Amendment.

MR. JUSTICE FRANKFURTER, whom MR. JUSTICE HARLAN joins, dissenting.

[The] Court's authority—possessed of neither the purse nor the sword—ultimately rests on sustained public confidence in its moral sanction. Such feeling must be nourished by the Court's complete detachment, in fact and in appearance, from political entanglements and by abstention from injecting itself into the clash of political forces in political settlements. * * * Even assuming the indispensable intellectual disinterestedness on the part of judges in such matters, they do not have accepted legal standards or criteria or even reliable analogies to draw upon for making judicial judgments. To charge courts with the task of accommodating the incommensurable factors of policy that underlie these mathematical puzzles is to attribute, however flatteringly, omnicompetence to judges.

The present case involves all of the elements that have made the Guarantee Clause cases non-justiciable. It is, in effect, a Guarantee Clause claim masquerading under a different label. But it cannot make the case more fit for judicial action that appellants invoke the Fourteenth Amendment rather than Art. IV, § 4, where, in fact, the gist of their complaint is the same—unless it can be found that the Fourteenth Amendment speaks with greater particularity to their situation.

Appellants invoke the right to vote and to have their votes counted. But * * * [t]alk of "debasement" or "dilution" is circular talk. One cannot speak of "debasement" or "dilution" of the value of a vote until there is first defined a standard of reference as to what a vote should be worth. What is actually asked of the Court in this case is to choose among competing bases of representation—ultimately, really, among competing theories of political philosophy—in order to establish an appropriate frame of government for the State of Tennessee and thereby for all the States of the Union.

Apportionment, by its character, is a subject of extraordinary complexity, involving—even after the fundamental theoretical issues concerning what is to be represented in a representative legislature have been fought out or compromised—considerations of geography, demography, electoral convenience, economic and social cohesions or divergences among particular local groups, communications, the practical effects of political institutions like the lobby and the city machine, ancient traditions and ties of settled usage, respect for proven incumbents of long experience and senior status, mathematical mechanics, censuses compiling relevant data, and a host of others. Legislative responses throughout the country to the reapportionment demands of the 1960 Census have glaringly confirmed that these are not factors that lend themselves to evaluations of a nature that are the staple of judicial determinations or for which judges are equipped to adjudicate by legal training or experience or native wit. And this is the more so true because in every strand of this complicated, intricate web of values meet the contending forces of partisan politics. The practical significance of apportionment is that the next election results may differ because of it. Apportionment battles are overwhelmingly party or intra-party contests. It will add a virulent source of friction and tension in federal-state relations to embroil the federal judiciary in them.

POINTS FOR DISCUSSION

a. Factors for Determining When a Question Is a Political Question

The Court in *Baker* offered a list of factors to consider in deciding whether a case presents a political question. Which of these factors did Justice Frankfurter, in dissent, believe required the Court to decline to resolve the plaintiffs' claims?

b. Applying the Factors

The Court held that because judicial standards under the Equal Protection Clause of the Fourteenth Amendment were "well developed and familiar," there were judicially manageable standards to govern the resolution of plaintiffs' apportionment claims. What were those judicially manageable standards? If they were well developed and familiar, why didn't the Court identify them in its opinion?

Is it likely that the Court will encounter difficulty in applying the *Baker* factors? Consider *Powell v. McCormack*, 395 U.S. 486 (1969), which involved a claim by Congressman Adam Clayton Powell that the House of Representatives had improperly refused to seat him after he was elected. After a House committee determined that Powell had presented false travel vouchers in seeking reimbursement for official travel and that he had used government funds to make illegal payments to his wife, the full House refused to seat Powell. The defendants urged the Court to dismiss the suit under the political question doctrine, arguing that Article I, § 5, which provides that each House of Congress "shall be the Judge of the Qualifications of its Members," was a textual commitment to the House of the power to decide whether a Member was ethically qualified to sit in the House. The Court rejected the defendants' claims and found the question justiciable. The Court noted that Article I, § 2, cl. 1 lists the "qualifications"—age, citizenship, and residence—to which section 5 refers, and that Powell had plainly satisfied them. The Court concluded that Article I, § 5 was at most a "textually demonstrable commitment to Congress to judge only the qualifications expressly set forth" in Article I, § 2, cl. 1.

> **Make the Connection**
>
> We will consider the right to vote, and standards for apportionment claims that the Court subsequently announced in *Reynolds v. Sims*, 377 U.S. 533 (1964), in Volume 2.

If the defendants were correct that Article I, § 5 was a textual commitment to the House to decide on a Member's qualifications, would it have meant that the Court could not decide a claim that the House had refused to seat Powell, who was 59 years old at the time, on the ground that he did not meet the Constitution's age requirements for Members of the House? If the House had refused to seat him because of his race? Does Article I, § 5, cl. 2, which provides that "Each House may * * *, with the Concurrence of two thirds, expel a Member," shed any light on defendants' position in *Powell*? (Although a majority of the House voted to refuse to seat Powell, the vote fell short of the two-thirds required for expulsion.)

NIXON V. UNITED STATES

506 U.S. 224 (1993)

CHIEF JUSTICE REHNQUIST delivered the opinion of the Court.

Petitioner Walter L. Nixon, Jr., asks this Court to decide whether Senate Rule XI, which allows a committee of Senators to hear evidence against an individual who has been impeached and to report that evidence to the full Senate, violates the Impeachment Trial Clause, Art. I, § 3, cl. 6. That Clause provides that the "Senate shall have the sole Power to try all Impeachments." But before we reach the merits of such a claim, we must decide whether it is "justiciable," that is, whether it is a claim that may be resolved by the courts. We conclude that it is not.

Nixon, a former Chief Judge of the United States District Court for the Southern District of Mississippi, was convicted by a jury of two counts of making false statements before a federal grand jury and sentenced to prison. The grand jury investigation stemmed from reports that Nixon had accepted a gratuity from a Mississippi businessman in exchange for asking a local district attorney to halt the prosecution of the businessman's son. Because Nixon refused to resign from his office as a United States District Judge, he continued to collect his judicial salary while serving out his prison sentence. On May 10, 1989, the House of Representatives adopted three articles of impeachment for high crimes and misdemeanors. The first two articles charged Nixon with giving false testimony before the grand jury and the third article charged him with bringing disrepute on the Federal Judiciary.

After the House presented the articles to the Senate, the Senate voted to invoke its own Impeachment Rule XI, under which the presiding officer appoints a committee of Senators to "receive evidence and take testimony." The Senate committee held four days of hearings, during which 10 witnesses, including Nixon, testified. Pursuant to Rule XI, the committee presented the full Senate with a complete transcript of the proceeding and a Report stating the uncontested facts and summarizing the evidence on the contested facts. Nixon and the House impeachment managers submitted extensive final briefs to the full Senate and delivered arguments from the Senate floor during the three hours set aside for oral argument in front of that body. Nixon himself gave a personal appeal, and several Senators posed questions directly to both parties. The Senate voted by more than the constitutionally required two-thirds majority to convict Nixon on the first two articles. The presiding officer then entered judgment removing Nixon from his office as United States District Judge.

Nixon thereafter commenced the present suit, arguing that Senate Rule XI violates the constitutional grant of authority to the Senate to "try" all impeachments because it prohibits the whole Senate from taking part in the evidentiary hearings. Nixon sought a declaratory judgment that his impeachment conviction was void and that his judicial salary and privileges should be reinstated.

A controversy is nonjusticiable—*i.e.*, involves a political question—where there is "a textually demonstrable constitutional commitment of the issue to a coordinate political department; or a lack of judicially discoverable and manageable standards for resolving it." *Baker v. Carr*. But the courts must, in the first instance, interpret the text in question and determine whether and to what extent the issue is textually committed. [T]he concept of a textual commitment to a coordinate political department is not completely separate from the concept of a lack of judicially discoverable and manageable standards for resolving it; the lack of judicially manageable standards may strengthen the conclusion that there is a textually demonstrable commitment to a coordinate branch.

Petitioner argues that the word "try" in the first sentence [of Art. I, § 3, cl. 6] imposes by implication [a] requirement on the Senate in that the proceedings must be in the nature of a judicial trial. From there petitioner goes on to argue that this limitation precludes the Senate from delegating to a select committee the task of hearing the testimony

Food for Thought

Judge Nixon was impeached in part for "bringing disrepute on the Federal Judiciary." Is this a valid ground for impeachment? Does the language of Article II, § 4 shed any light on that question? Is the validity of a decision by the House to impeach itself a political question? In 1970, Congressman Gerald Ford proposed the impeachment of Justice William Douglas for failing to meet the standard of "good behavior" required by Article III, § 1. Ford accused Justice Douglas of declining to disqualify himself in a case in which Justice Douglas allegedly had a monetary conflict of interest, of writing a book containing "a distorted diatribe against the government of the United States," and of engaging in other specific instances of bad conduct. Although Ford strongly emphasized that it would be wrong to remove a Supreme Court Justice "for his ideology or past decisions," Ford had difficulty defining exactly when "something less than a criminal act" constitutes an impeachable offense. "The only honest answer," Ford concluded, "is that an impeachable offense is whatever a majority of the House of Representatives considers [it] to be at a given moment in history." Remarks by Rep. Gerald R. Ford (R-Mich.), Republican Leader, prepared for delivery on the Floor of the U. S. House of Representatives on April 15, 1970. Is there a better definition of what constitutes an impeachable offense?

of witnesses * * *. Petitioner concludes from this that courts may review whether or not the Senate "tried" him before convicting him.

There are several difficulties with this position * * *. The word "try," both in 1787 and later, has considerably broader meanings than those to which petitioner would limit it. * * * Based on the variety of definitions, [we] cannot say that the Framers used the word "try" as an implied limitation on the method by which the Senate might proceed in trying impeachments. * * * The conclusion that the use of the word "try" in the first sentence of the Impeachment Trial Clause lacks sufficient precision to afford any judicially manageable standard of review of the Senate's actions is fortified by the existence of the three very specific requirements that the Constitution does impose on the Senate when trying impeachments: The Members must be under oath, a two-thirds vote is required to convict, and the Chief Justice presides when the President is tried. These limitations are quite precise, and their nature suggests that the Framers did not intend to impose additional limitations on the form of the Senate proceedings by the use of the word "try" in the first sentence.

Petitioner devotes only two pages in his brief to negating the significance of the word "sole" in the first sentence of Clause 6. * * * We think that the word "sole" is of considerable significance. Indeed, the word "sole" appears only one other time in the Constitution—with respect to the House of Representatives' "sole Power of Impeachment." Art. I, § 2, cl. 5. The commonsense meaning of the word "sole" is that the Senate alone shall have authority to determine whether an individual should be acquitted or convicted. * * * Petitioner [argues] that even if significance be attributed to the word "sole" in the first sentence of the Clause, the authority granted is to the Senate, and this means that "the Senate—not the courts, not a lay jury, not a Senate Committee—shall try impeachments." It would be possible to read the first sentence of the Clause this way, but it is not a natural reading. Petitioner's interpretation would bring into judicial purview not merely the sort of claim made by petitioner, but other similar claims based on the conclusion that the word "Senate" has imposed by implication limitations on procedures which the Senate might adopt. Such limitations would be inconsistent with the construction of the Clause as a whole, which, as we have noted, sets out three express limitations in separate sentences.

The history and contemporary understanding of the impeachment provisions support our reading of the constitutional language. The parties do not offer evidence of a single word in the history of the Constitutional Convention or in contemporary commentary that even alludes to the possibility of judicial review in the context of the impeachment powers. * * * Despite [proposals to place the power of impeachment with the federal judiciary], the Convention ultimately decided that the Senate would have "the sole Power to try all Impeachments." The Supreme Court was not the proper body because the Framers [doubted whether the Court] "would possess the degree of credit and authority" to carry out its judgment if it conflicted with the accusation brought by the Legislature—the people's representative. *See* The Federalist No. 65, at 441 (J. Cooke ed. 1961) (Hamilton). [In addition,] judicial review would be inconsistent with the Framers' insistence that our system be one of checks and balances. In our constitutional system, impeachment was designed to be the *only* check on the Judicial Branch by the Legislature. * * * Nixon's argument would place final reviewing authority with respect to impeachments in the hands of the same body that the impeachment process is meant to regulate.

Nevertheless, Nixon argues that judicial review is necessary in order to place a check on the Legislature. * * * The Framers anticipated this objection and created two constitutional safeguards to keep the Senate in check. The first safeguard is that the whole of the impeachment power is divided between the two legislative bodies, with the House given the right to accuse and the Senate given the right to judge. * * * The second safeguard is the two-thirds supermajority vote requirement.

In addition to the textual commitment argument, we are persuaded that the lack of finality and the difficulty of fashioning relief counsel against justiciability. * * * This lack of finality would manifest itself most dramatically if the President were impeached. The legitimacy of any successor, and hence his effectiveness, would be impaired severely, not merely while the judicial process was running its course, but during any retrial that a differently constituted Senate might conduct if its first judgment of conviction were invalidated. Equally uncertain is the question of what relief a court may give other than simply setting aside the judgment of conviction. Could it order the reinstatement of a convicted federal judge, or order Congress to create an additional judgeship if the seat had been filled in the interim?

[W]e conclude * * * that the word "try" in the Impeachment Trial Clause does not provide an identifiable textual limit on the authority which is committed to the Senate.

JUSTICE STEVENS, concurring.

For me, the debate about the strength of the inferences to be drawn from the use of the words "sole" and "try" is far less significant than the central fact that the Framers decided to assign the impeachment power to the Legislative

Branch. The disposition of the impeachment of Samuel Chase in 1805 demonstrated that the Senate is fully conscious of the profound importance of that assignment, and nothing in the subsequent history of the Senate's exercise of this extraordinary power suggests otherwise.

> **FYI**
>
> Justice Chase, a Federalist appointed to the Court by President Washington, was impeached by the House of Representatives for demonstrating political bias on the bench. Although the Senate was controlled by Jeffersonian Republicans, the Senate acquitted Chase of all charges, and he served on the Court until his death.

Respect for a coordinate branch of the Government forecloses any assumption that improbable hypotheticals like those mentioned by * * * Justice SOUTER will ever occur. Accordingly, the wise policy of judicial restraint, coupled with the potential anomalies associated with a contrary view, provide a sufficient justification for my agreement with the [Court].

JUSTICE WHITE, with whom JUSTICE BLACKMUN joins, concurring in the judgment.

The Court is of the view that the Constitution forbids us even to consider [Nixon's] contention. I find no such prohibition and would therefore reach the merits of the claim. I concur in the judgment because the Senate fulfilled its constitutional obligation to "try" petitioner.

[The] issue in the political question doctrine is *not* whether the constitutional text commits exclusive responsibility for a particular governmental function to one of the political branches. There are numerous instances of this sort of textual commitment, *e.g.*, Art. I, § 8, and it is not thought that disputes implicating these provisions are nonjusticiable. Rather, the issue is whether the Constitution has given one of the political branches final responsibility for interpreting the scope and nature of such a power.

> **Take Note**
>
> Justice Stevens wrote a "concurring" opinion, while Justice White wrote an opinion "concurring in the judgment." Both agreed with the majority that the lower court's decision should be affirmed. By concurring, Justice Stevens indicated that he also agreed with the majority's reasoning. By concurring only in the judgment, Justice White indicated that he did not agree with the majority's reasoning but did agree with the result.

The significance of the Constitution's use of the term "sole" lies not in the infrequency with which the term appears, but in the fact that it appears exactly twice, in parallel provisions concerning impeachment. That the word "sole" is found only in the House and Senate Impeachment Clauses demonstrates that its purpose is to emphasize the distinct role of each in the impeachment process.

* * * While the majority is thus right to interpret the term "sole" to indicate that the Senate ought to "function independently and without assistance or interference," it wrongly identifies the Judiciary, rather than the House, as the source of potential interference with which the Framers were concerned when they employed the term "sole."

In essence, the majority suggests that the Framers conferred upon Congress a potential tool of legislative dominance yet at the same time rendered Congress' exercise of that power one of the very few areas of legislative authority immune from any judicial review. * * * In a truly balanced system, impeachments tried by the Senate would serve as a means of controlling the largely unaccountable Judiciary, even as judicial review would ensure that the Senate adhered to a minimal set of procedural standards in conducting impeachment trials.

The majority also contends that the term "try" does not present a judicially manageable standard. [T]he term "try" is hardly so elusive as the majority would have it. Were the Senate, for example, to adopt the practice of automatically entering a judgment of conviction whenever articles of impeachment were delivered from the House, it is quite clear that the Senate will have failed to "try" impeachments. Indeed in this respect, "try" presents no greater, and perhaps fewer, interpretive difficulties than some other constitutional standards that have been found amenable to familiar techniques of judicial construction, including, for example, "Commerce [among] the several States" and "due process of law." The majority's conclusion that "try" is incapable of meaningful judicial construction is not without irony. One might think that if any class of concepts would fall within the definitional abilities of the Judiciary, it would be that class having to do with procedural justice.

[T]extual and historical evidence reveals that the Impeachment Trial Clause was not meant to bind the hands of the Senate beyond establishing a set of minimal procedures. Without identifying the exact contours of these procedures, it is sufficient to say that the Senate's use of a factfinding committee under Rule XI is entirely compatible with the Constitution's command that the Senate "try all impeachments." Petitioner's challenge to his conviction must therefore fail.

JUSTICE SOUTER, concurring in the judgment.

I agree with the Court that this case presents a nonjusticiable political question. Because my analysis differs somewhat from the Court's, however, I concur in its judgment by this separate opinion. [T]he political question doctrine is "essentially a function of the separation of powers," existing to restrain courts "from inappropriate interference in the business of the other branches of

Government," and deriving in large part from prudential concerns about the respect we owe the political departments. Not all interference is inappropriate or disrespectful, however, and application of the doctrine ultimately turns, as Learned Hand put it, on "how importunately the occasion demands an answer."

This occasion does not demand an answer. * * * It seems fair to conclude that the [Impeachment Trial] Clause contemplates that the Senate may determine, within broad boundaries, such subsidiary issues as the procedures for receipt and consideration of evidence necessary to satisfy its duty to "try" impeachments. Other significant considerations confirm a conclusion that this case presents a nonjusticiable political question: the "unusual need for unquestioning adherence to a political decision already made," as well as "the potentiality of embarrassment from multifarious pronouncements by various departments on one question." *Baker*. As the Court observes, judicial review of an impeachment trial would under the best of circumstances entail significant disruption of government.

One can, nevertheless, envision different and unusual circumstances that might justify a more searching review of impeachment proceedings. If the Senate were to act in a manner seriously threatening the integrity of its results, convicting, say, upon a coin toss, or upon a summary determination that an officer of the United States was simply "a bad guy," judicial interference might well be appropriate. In such circumstances, the Senate's action might be so far beyond the scope of its constitutional authority, and the consequent impact on the Republic so great, as to merit a judicial response despite the prudential concerns that would ordinarily counsel silence.

POINTS FOR DISCUSSION

a. Textual Commitment

What is the meaning of Article I, § 3, cl. 6's conferral on the Senate of the "sole Power to try all Impeachments"? If Congress had explicitly been granted the "sole Power" to regulate commerce among the states—a topic we will take up in Chapters 3 and 4—would a claim that Congress had exceeded its power to regulate interstate commerce be a non-justiciable political question?

b. Judicially Manageable Standards

Should the Court have been able to develop judicially manageable standards to apply the constitutional requirement that the Senate "try" all impeachments? Does that term provide less guidance than other constitutional provisions that the Court has concluded are justiciable? Is "try" more ambiguous and amorphous than, say, "due process," "equal protection," "cruel and unusual," or "freedom of speech"?

c. The Political Question Factors

Dean Erwin Chemerinsky, a prominent constitutional scholar, argues that the factors listed in *Baker v. Carr* "seem useless" for determining whether an issue is a political question. He explains: "[T]here is no place in the Constitution where the text states that the legislature or executive should decide whether a particular action constitutes a constitutional violation. The Constitution does not mention judicial review, much less limit it by creating 'textually demonstrable commitments' to other branches of government. Similarly, most important constitutional provisions are written in broad, open-textured language and certainly do not include 'judicially discoverable and manageable standards.' * * * As such, it hardly is surprising that the doctrine is described as confusing and unsatisfactory." Erwin Chemerinsky, *Constitutional Law: Principles and Policies* 131 (3d ed. 2006). Is this criticism valid? If so, how should the courts determine what is a political question? Or should the courts simply decide that no issues are political questions?

2. The Requirement of "Case" or "Controversy"

Article III, § 2 specifies the jurisdiction of the federal courts. In reading this provision, notice two things. First, the provision gives federal courts jurisdiction over various kinds of "cases" and "controversies." Second, the provision does not give federal courts jurisdiction over anything other than "cases" and "controversies."

U.S. Constitution, Article III, Section 2

Clause 1. The judicial Power shall extend to all Cases, in Law and Equity, arising under this Constitution, the Laws of the United States, and Treaties made, or which shall be made, under their Authority;—to all Cases affecting Ambassadors, other public Ministers and Consuls;—to all Cases of admiralty and maritime Jurisdiction;—to Controversies to which the United States shall be a Party;—to Controversies between two or more States;—between a State and Citizens of another State;—between Citizens of different States;—between Citizens of the same State claiming Lands under Grants of different States, and between a State, or the Citizens thereof, and foreign States, Citizens or Subjects.

Clause 2. In all Cases affecting Ambassadors, other public Ministers and Consuls, and those in which a State shall be Party, the supreme Court shall have original Jurisdiction. In all the other Cases before mentioned, the supreme Court shall have appellate Jurisdiction, both as to Law and Fact, with such Exceptions, and under such Regulations as the Congress shall make.

On the basis of these two points, as the following case will show, the Supreme Court has concluded that the federal courts may decide only cases and controversies. But those terms are not easily defined.

MUSKRAT V. UNITED STATES

219 U.S. 346 (1911)

DAY, J. delivered the opinion of the court:

[In the 1800s, the United States "reserved" millions of acres of land for the Cherokee Nation. This land mostly was held in common by the Cherokee Nation and was not owned by individual citizens of the Cherokee Nation. In 1902, Congress enacted legislation allotting to each citizen of the Cherokee Nation a portion of the reserved property. In 1904 and 1906, Congress enacted legislation that increased the number of persons who would have claims to the property. Some citizens of Cherokee Nation believed that the 1904 and 1906 enacments would diminish the allotments to which they were entitled under the 1902 legislation. In 1907, Congress enacted a statute that authorized a discrete class of persons who had interests in the land pursuant to the original 1902 law to "institute their suits in the court of claims to determine the validity of any acts of Congress passed since [the] act of [1902]." The 1907 Act conferred jurisdiction "upon the court of claims, with the right of appeal, by either party, to the Supreme Court of the United States, to hear, determine, and adjudicate each of said suits." The 1907 Act further provided that "[t]he suits brought hereunder shall be brought * * * against the United States as a party defendant, and, for the speedy disposition of the questions involved, preference shall be given to the same by said courts, and by the Attorney General, who is hereby charged with the defense of said suits." The plaintiffs filed suit pursuant to the 1907 Act.]

The first question in these cases, as in others, involves the jurisdiction of the court to entertain the proceeding, and that depends upon whether the jurisdiction conferred is within the power of Congress, having in view the limitations of the judicial power, as established by [Article III of] the Constitution of the United States.

Food for Thought

Should the Justices even have answered Jefferson's request? After all, in answering, didn't they essentially create law—about the propriety of advisory opinions—even though there was no justiciable case or controversy presented to them? Is it proper to cite the decision as precedent?

It will serve to elucidate the nature and extent of the judicial power thus conferred by the Constitution to note certain instances in which this court has had occasion to examine and define the same. * * * In 1793, by direction of the President, Secretary of State Jefferson addressed to the justices of the Supreme Court a communication soliciting their views upon the question whether their advice to the Executive would be available in the solution of important questions of the construction of treaties, laws of nations and laws of the land, which the Secretary said were often presented under circumstances which "do not give a cognizance of them to the tribunals of the country." [Chief] Justice Jay and his associates answered to President Washington that, in consideration of the lines of separation drawn by the Constitution between the three departments of government, and being judges of a court of last resort, afforded strong arguments against the propriety of extrajudically deciding the questions alluded to, and expressing the view that the power given by the Constitution to the President, of calling on heads of departments for opinions, "seems to have been purposely, as well as expressly, united to the executive departments."

"Judicial power * * * is the power of a court to decide and pronounce a judgment and carry it into effect between persons and parties who bring a case before it for decision." [By] the express terms of the Constitution, the exercise of the judicial power is limited to "cases" and "controversies." Beyond this it does not extend, and unless it is asserted in a case or controversy within the meaning of the Constitution, the power to exercise it is nowhere conferred. A "case" was defined by Mr. Chief Justice Marshall as early as the leading case of *Marbury v. Madison* to be a suit instituted according to the regular course of judicial procedure. * * * "The term 'controversies,' if distinguishable at all from 'cases,' is so in that it is less comprehensive than the latter, and includes only suits of a civil nature." * * * The term [case] implies the existence of present or possible adverse parties, whose contentions are submitted to the court for adjudication.

[T]he object and purpose of [this] suit is wholly comprised in the determination of the constitutional validity of certain acts of Congress * * *. Is such a determination within the judicial power conferred by the Constitution, as the same has been interpreted and defined in the authoritative decisions to which we have referred? We think it is not. That judicial power * * * is the right to determine actual controversies arising between adverse litigants, duly instituted in courts of proper jurisdiction. The right to declare a law unconstitutional arises because an act of Congress relied upon by one or the other of such parties in determining their rights is in conflict with the fundamental law. The exercise of this, the most important and delicate duty of this court, is not given to it as a body with revisory power over the action of Congress, but because the rights of the litigants in justiciable controversies require the court to choose between the fundamental law and a law purporting to be enacted within constitutional authority, but in fact beyond the power delegated to the legislative branch of the government.

This attempt to obtain a judicial declaration of the validity of the act of Congress is not presented in a "case" or "controversy," to which, under the Constitution of the United States, the judicial power alone extends. It is true the United States is made a defendant to this action, but it has no interest adverse to the claimants. The object is not to assert a property right as against the government, or to demand compensation for alleged wrongs because of action upon its part. The whole purpose of the law is to determine the constitutional validity of this class of legislation, in a suit not arising between parties concerning a property right necessarily involved in the decision in question, but in a proceeding against the government in its sovereign capacity, and concerning which the only judgment required is to settle the doubtful character of the legislation in question. [W]e think the Congress, in the act of March 1, 1907, exceeded the limitations of legislative authority, so far as it required of this court action not judicial in its nature within the meaning of the Constitution.

> **Take Note**
>
> What does the Court mean by an "adverse" interest? Doesn't the United States have an interest in defending the constitutionality of its laws? Indeed, doesn't the Executive Branch have a duty to defend Acts of Congress when they are challenged? See Article II, § 3 (stating that the President "shall take Care that the Laws be faithfully executed * * *").

The questions involved in this proceeding as to the validity of the legislation may arise in suits between individuals, and when they do and are properly brought before this court for consideration they, of course, must be determined in the exercise of its judicial functions.

POINTS FOR DISCUSSION

a. The Ban on Advisory Opinions

Since the Court's refusal in 1793 to answer Secretary of State Jefferson's legal query about the United States' legal obligations to Britain and France during the war between those two nations, the Court has declined to provide "advisory opinions"—that is, opinions about the proper resolution of abstract legal questions that are presented in a setting divorced from an actual dispute between adverse parties. What is the rationale for the ban on advisory opinions? Does this ban come at a cost?

Note that the "case or controversy" requirement of Article III does not apply to state courts. Some state courts, like the Massachusetts Supreme Judicial Court, do issue advisory opinions—even on questions of federal constitutional law. See, e.g.,

Opinion of the Justices to the Governor, 298 N.E.2d 840 (Mass. 1973) (advisory opinion that proposed legislation to restrict busing of children to desegregate schools would violate the Constitution).

b. The Claims in *Muskrat*

The plaintiffs in *Muskrat* asserted that their interests in Cherokee lands had been adversely affected by the statutes that they challenged. Even assuming a ban on advisory opinions, why weren't those claims justiciable? Is it because the United States, the defendant in their suits, had no interest adverse to the plaintiffs' interests? If suits against the United States were not proper, how could the plaintiffs have obtained a resolution of their claims about the validity of the enlargement of the class of persons entitled to the Cherokee lands?

c. Declaratory Judgment Actions

In most lawsuits, the plaintiff asks the court to award money damages to remedy an injury that the defendant has caused or to issue an injunction to prevent the defendant from causing an injury. But in some cases, the plaintiff only asks the court to decide and declare whether the defendant is violating the law without asking the court to provide any other remedy. The Declaratory Judgment Act, 28 U.S.C. § 2201, authorizes federal courts to "declare the rights and other legal relations of any interested party seeking such declaration, whether or not further relief is or could be sought." Are declaratory judgment actions consistent with the case and controversy requirement as applied in Muskrat? The Court has upheld the Act, holding that federal courts may issue declaratory judgments as long as there is an actual dispute between adverse litigants. See *Aetna Life Insu. Co. v. Haworth*, 300 U.S. 227 (1937).

d. Ripeness and Mootness

An action filed in federal court not only must have the proper hallmarks of adversity, but also must be filed and litigated at a time that ensures that the case or controversy between the parties is sufficiently live. First, the federal courts will not consider cases that are not yet "ripe"—that is, that have not yet developed into actual controversies. If the head of a federal agency announces at a press conference that the agency is merely considering proposing a rule to establish fuel-efficiency standards for automobiles, for example, a suit filed that day by car manufacturers challenging the agency's action likely will be dismissed because the agency has not yet acted and thus the plaintiffs have not yet been harmed. When the injury asserted by the plaintiffs is wholly speculative, the claim likely will be dismissed under the ripeness doctrine. For example, in *Anderson v. Green*, 513 U.S. 557 (1995) (per curiam), the Supreme Court dismissed a challenge to a California statute limiting welfare benefits. The Court held that the challenge was not ripe because the California statute would not take effect until the federal government issued a waiver, which had not happened. Until the waiver was issued, the Court explained, "any future injury was purely conjectural." *Id.* at 559.

Second, the federal courts generally will not consider claims that are "moot"—that is, claims in which the parties no longer have any meaningful and concrete stake. For example, a suit by a person detained by the government seeking to force the government to release him likely will be rendered moot upon his release. The plaintiff's desire to learn whether his prior detention was lawful is not alone sufficient to give the plaintiff a concrete stake in the outcome of the suit, because the relief that he seeks has already been granted. (If, on the other hand, the plaintiff seeks damages for the prior unlawful detention, his suit likely would not be moot.) See, e.g., *United States Parole Comm'n v. Geraghty*, 445 U.S. 388, 397 (1980) (explaining that the "requisite personal interest * * * must continue throughout" the litigation's existence).

In other words, suits filed too early—and thus lacking the requisite ripeness—and suits resolved too late—and thus lacking the requisite concrete stake in the relief sought—are generally not justiciable in federal court. Ripeness and mootness doctrines are both intended to effectuate the case and controversy requirement. See *Abbott Laboratories v. Gardner*, 387 U.S. 136 (1967) (stating that the basic rationale of ripeness doctrine is "to prevent the courts, through avoidance of premature adjudication, from entangling themselves in abstract disagreements"); *Hall v. Beals*, 396 U.S. 45 (1969) (explaining that mootness doctrine effectuates the ban on advisory opinions).

3. Standing

Many people may be interested in knowing whether a government action is constitutional, but only some of them can bring a lawsuit in federal court. The Supreme Court has said that only litigants who have "standing" may enforce constitutional provisions. According to the Court, a plaintiff must satisfy three requirements:

> (1) [I]njury in fact, by which we mean an invasion of a legally protected interest that is (a) concrete and particularized, and (b) actual or imminent, not conjectural or hypothetical; (2) a causal relationship between the injury and the challenged conduct, by which we mean that the injury fairly can be traced to the challenged action of the defendant, and has not resulted from the independent action of some third party not before the court; and (3) a likelihood that the injury will be redressed by a favorable decision, by which we mean that the prospect of obtaining relief from the injury as a result of a favorable ruling is not too

speculative. These elements are the irreducible minimum, required by the Constitution.

Northeastern Florida Chapter of Associated General Contractors v. City of Jacksonville, 508 U.S. 656, 663–664 (1993) (internal quotation marks and citations omitted).

In reading the following cases, consider whether these requirements are met, how insisting on these factors affects the availability of judicial review, and what justifications the Supreme Court might have for requiring standing.

ALLEN V. WRIGHT

468 U.S. 737 (1984)

JUSTICE O'CONNOR delivered the opinion of the Court.

Parents of black public school children allege in this nation-wide class action that the Internal Revenue Service (IRS) has not adopted sufficient standards and procedures to fulfill its obligation to deny tax-exempt status to racially discriminatory private schools. * * * The issue before us is whether plaintiffs have standing to bring this suit. We hold that they do not.

> **Definition**
>
> A "class action" is a "lawsuit in which the court authorizes a single person or a small group of people to represent the interests of a larger group." *Black's Law Dictionary* (10th ed. 2014).

The IRS denies tax-exempt [status] to racially discriminatory private schools. * * * To carry out this policy, the IRS has established guidelines and procedures for determining whether a particular school is in fact racially nondiscriminatory. * * * In 1976 respondents challenged these guidelines and procedures in a suit [in federal court]. The plaintiffs named in the complaint are parents of black children who, at the time the complaint was filed, were attending public schools in seven States in school districts undergoing desegregation.

> **FYI**
>
> There are two related benefits to tax-exempt status under the tax code. First, the tax-exempt institution does not have to pay taxes on income. Second, contributions to the tax-exempt institution are deductible by the persons making the contribution—which means that persons are more likely to make such contributions (because they are relatively cheaper) and thus that the tax-exempt organization is more likely to receive charitable contributions.

Respondents allege in their complaint that many racially segregated private schools * * * receive tax exemptions, [and that] some of the tax-exempt racially segregated private schools created or expanded in desegregating districts in fact have racially discriminatory policies.

Respondents allege that the IRS grant of tax exemptions to such racially discriminatory schools is unlawful.

Respondents do not allege that their children have been the victims of discriminatory exclusion from the schools whose tax exemptions they challenge as unlawful. Indeed, they have not alleged at any stage of this litigation that their children have ever applied or would ever apply to any private school. Rather, respondents claim a direct injury from the mere fact of the challenged Government conduct and * * * injury to their children's opportunity to receive a desegregated education. * * * Respondents * * * ask for a declaratory judgment that the challenged IRS tax-exemption practices are unlawful [and] an injunction requiring the IRS to deny tax exemptions to a considerably broader class of private schools than the class of racially discriminatory private schools. * * * In May 1977 the District Court permitted intervention as a defendant by petitioner Allen, the head of one of the private school systems identified in the complaint.

Article III of the Constitution confines the federal courts to adjudicating actual "cases" and "controversies." * * * The several doctrines that have grown up to elaborate that requirement are "founded in concern about the proper—and properly limited—role of the courts in a democratic society." *Warth v. Seldin*, 422 U.S. 490, 498 (1975). The Article III doctrine that requires a litigant to have "standing" to invoke the power of a federal court is perhaps the most important of these doctrines. "In essence the question of standing is whether the litigant is entitled to have the court decide the merits of the dispute or of particular issues." *Warth*. Standing doctrine embraces several judicially self-imposed limits on the exercise of federal jurisdiction, such as the general prohibition on a litigant's raising another person's legal rights, the rule barring adjudication of generalized grievances more appropriately addressed in the representative branches, and the requirement that a plaintiff's complaint fall within the zone of interests protected by the law invoked. The requirement of standing, however, has a core component derived directly from the Constitution. A plaintiff must allege personal injury fairly traceable to the defendant's allegedly unlawful conduct and likely to be redressed by the requested relief.

> **Take Note**
>
> The Court is reviewing the district court's grant of the defendant's motion to dismiss the plaintiffs' complaint without holding a trial. Because the district court resolved this case at the threshold, it did not consider the merits of the plaintiffs' claims. Is it problematic that claims that might have had substantial legal merit will not be resolved on the merits? Must a challenge to a plaintiff's standing be raised at the threshold of a suit?

Like the prudential component, the constitutional component of standing doctrine incorporates concepts concededly not susceptible of precise definition. The injury alleged must be, for example, "distinct and palpable" and not "abstract" or "conjectural" or "hypothetical." The injury must be "fairly" traceable to the challenged action, and relief from the injury must be "likely" to follow from a favorable decision. These terms cannot be defined so as to make application of the constitutional standing requirement a mechanical exercise.

Typically, [the] standing inquiry requires careful judicial examination of a complaint's allegations to ascertain whether the particular plaintiff is entitled to an adjudication of the particular claims asserted. [The question of standing] must be answered by reference to the Art. III notion that federal courts may exercise power only "in the last resort, and as a necessity," and only when adjudication is "consistent with a system of separated powers and [the dispute is one] traditionally thought to be capable of resolution through the judicial process." *Flast v. Cohen*, 392 U.S. 83, 97 (1968).

Respondents allege two injuries in their complaint to support their standing to bring this lawsuit. First, they say that they are harmed directly by the mere fact of Government financial aid to discriminatory private schools. Second, they say that the federal tax exemptions to racially discriminatory private schools in their communities impair their ability to have their public schools desegregated. We conclude that neither suffices to support respondents' standing. The first fails under clear precedents of this Court because it does not constitute judicially cognizable injury. The second fails because the alleged injury is not fairly traceable to the assertedly unlawful conduct of the IRS.[19]

Respondents' first claim of injury can be interpreted in two ways. It might be a claim simply to have the Government avoid the violation of law alleged in respondents' complaint. Alternatively, it might be a claim of stigmatic injury, or denigration, suffered by all members of a racial group when the Government discriminates on the basis of race. Under neither interpretation is this claim of injury judicially cognizable.

---

[19] The "fairly traceable" and "redressability" components of the constitutional standing inquiry were initially articulated by this Court as two facets of a single causation requirement. To the extent there is a difference, it is that the former examines the causal connection between the assertedly unlawful conduct and the alleged injury, whereas the latter examines the causal connection between the alleged injury and the judicial relief requested. Cases such as this, in which the relief requested goes well beyond the violation of law alleged, illustrate why it is important to keep the inquiries separate if the "redressability" component is to focus on the requested relief. Even if the relief respondents request might have a substantial effect on the desegregation of public schools, whatever deficiencies exist in the opportunities for desegregated education for respondents' children might not be traceable to IRS violations of law—grants of tax exemptions to racially discriminatory schools in respondents' communities.

This Court has repeatedly held that an asserted right to have the Government act in accordance with law is not sufficient, standing alone, to confer jurisdiction on a federal court. * * * "[A]ssertion of a right to a particular kind of Government conduct, which the Government has violated by acting differently, cannot alone satisfy the requirements of Art. III without draining those requirements of meaning." *Valley Forge Christian College v. Americans United for Separation of Church and State, Inc.*, 454 U.S. 464, 483 (1982). Respondents here have no standing to complain simply that their Government is violating the law.

Food for Thought

The Court seems to be suggesting that disputes by persons who simply disagree with the government's choices should be resolved in the political, rather than the judicial, arena. But aren't the plaintiffs in this case contending that the very question that they raise—whether the IRS is properly following the law as mandated by Congress—has already been decided by Congress in the political arena?

Neither do they have standing to litigate their claims based on the stigmatizing injury often caused by racial discrimination. There can be no doubt that this sort of noneconomic injury is one of the most serious consequences of discriminatory government action and is sufficient in some circumstances to support standing. Our cases make clear, however, that such injury accords a basis for standing only to "those persons who are personally denied equal treatment" by the challenged discriminatory conduct.

The consequences of recognizing respondents' standing on the basis of their first claim of injury illustrate why our cases plainly hold that such injury is not judicially cognizable. If the abstract stigmatic injury were cognizable, standing would extend nationwide to all members of the particular racial groups against which the Government was alleged to be discriminating by its grant of a tax exemption to a racially discriminatory school, regardless of the location of that school. * * * A black person in Hawaii could challenge the grant of a tax exemption to a racially discriminatory school in Maine. Recognition of standing in such circumstances would transform the federal courts into "no more than a vehicle for the vindication of the value interests of concerned bystanders." *United States v. SCRAP*, 412 U.S. 669, 687 (1973). Constitutional limits on the role of the federal courts preclude such a transformation.

It is in their complaint's second claim of injury that respondents allege harm to a concrete, personal interest that can support standing in some circumstances. The injury they identify—their children's diminished ability to receive an education in a racially integrated school—is, beyond any doubt, not only judicially cognizable but * * * one of the most serious injuries recognized in our legal system. Despite the constitutional importance of curing the injury alleged by respondents, however, [it] cannot support standing because the injury alleged is not fairly traceable to the Government conduct respondents challenge as unlawful.

The illegal conduct challenged by respondents is the IRS's grant of tax exemptions to some racially discriminatory schools. The line of causation between that conduct and desegregation of respondents' schools is attenuated at best. * * * It is, first, uncertain how many racially discriminatory private schools are in fact receiving tax exemptions. Moreover, it is entirely speculative, as respondents themselves conceded in the Court of Appeals, whether withdrawal of a tax exemption from any particular school would lead the school to change its policies. It is just as speculative whether any given parent of a child attending such a private school would decide to transfer the child to public school as a result of any changes in educational or financial policy made by the private school once it was threatened with loss of tax-exempt status. It is also pure speculation whether, in a particular community, a large enough number of the numerous relevant school officials and parents would reach decisions that collectively would have a significant impact on the racial composition of the public schools.

The links in the chain of causation between the challenged Government conduct and the asserted injury are far too weak for the chain as a whole to sustain respondents' standing. * * * "Carried to its logical end, [respondents'] approach would have the federal courts as virtually continuing monitors of the wisdom and soundness of Executive action; such a role is appropriate for the Congress acting through its committees and the 'power of the purse'; it is not the role of the judiciary, absent actual present or immediately threatened injury resulting from unlawful governmental action." *Laird v. Tatum*, 408 U.S. 1, 15 (1972). When transported into the Art. III context, that principle, grounded as it is in the idea of separation of powers, counsels against recognizing standing in a case brought, not to enforce specific legal obligations whose violation works a direct harm, but to seek a restructuring of the apparatus established by the Executive Branch to fulfill its legal duties. The Constitution, after all, assigns to the Executive Branch, and not to the Judicial Branch, the duty to "take Care that the Laws be faithfully executed." U.S. Const., Art. II, § 3. We could not recognize respondents' standing in this case without running afoul of that structural principle.

JUSTICE STEVENS, with whom JUSTICE BLACKMUN joins, dissenting.

Respondents, the parents of black school-children, have alleged that their children are unable to attend fully desegregated schools because large numbers of white children in the areas in which respondents reside attend private schools which do not admit minority children. The Court [and I] agree that this is an adequate allegation of "injury in fact." * * * This kind of injury may be actionable whether it is caused by the exclusion of black children from public schools or by an official policy of encouraging white children to attend nonpublic schools. A subsidy for the withdrawal of a white child can have the same effect as a penalty for admitting a black child. * * * The critical question in these cases, therefore, is whether respondents have alleged that the Government has created that kind of subsidy.

"Both tax exemptions and tax deductibility are a form of subsidy * * *. A tax exemption has much the same effect as a cash grant to the organization of the amount of tax it would have to pay on its income. Deductible contributions are similar to cash grants of the amount of a portion of the individual's contributions." *Regan v. Taxation With Representation of Washington*, 461 U.S. 540, 544 (1983). The purpose of this scheme, like the purpose of any subsidy, is to promote the activity subsidized * * *. If the granting of preferential tax treatment would "encourage" private segregated schools to conduct their "charitable" activities, it must follow that the withdrawal of the treatment would "discourage" them * * *.

This causation analysis is nothing more than a restatement of elementary economics: when something becomes more expensive, less of it will be purchased. [The tax-exemption provisions] are premised on that recognition. If racially discriminatory private schools lose the "cash grants" that flow from the operation of the statutes, the education they provide will become more expensive and hence less of their services will be purchased. Conversely, maintenance of these tax benefits makes an education in segregated private schools relatively more attractive, by decreasing its cost. Accordingly, without tax-exempt status, private schools will either not be competitive in terms of cost, or have to change their admissions policies, hence reducing their competitiveness for parents seeking "a racially segregated alternative" to public schools, which is what respondents have alleged many white parents in desegregating school districts seek. In either event the process of desegregation will be advanced * * *. Thus, the laws of economics, not to mention the laws of Congress embodied in [the tax code], compel the conclusion that the injury respondents have alleged—the increased segregation of their children's schools because of the ready availability of private schools that admit whites only—will be redressed if these schools' operations are inhibited through the denial of preferential tax treatment.

The Court could mean one of three things by its invocation of the separation of powers. First, it could simply be expressing the idea that if the plaintiff lacks

Art. III standing to bring a lawsuit, then there is no "case or controversy" within the meaning of Art. III and hence the matter is not within the area of responsibility assigned to the Judiciary by the Constitution. * * * While there can be no quarrel with this proposition, in itself it provides no guidance for determining if the injury respondents have alleged is fairly traceable to the conduct they have challenged. Second, the Court could be saying that it will require a more direct causal connection when it is troubled by the separation of powers implications of the case before it. That approach confuses the standing doctrine with the justiciability of the issues that respondents seek to raise. The purpose of the standing inquiry is to measure the plaintiff's stake in the outcome, not whether a court has the authority to provide it with the outcome it seeks. Third, the Court could be saying that it will not treat as legally cognizable injuries that stem from an administrative decision concerning how enforcement resources will be allocated. * * * However, as the Court also recognizes, this principle does not apply when suit is brought "to enforce specific legal obligations whose violation works a direct harm." * * * Here, respondents contend that the IRS is violating a specific constitutional limitation on its enforcement discretion. There is a solid basis for that contention.

Deciding whether the Treasury has violated a specific legal limitation on its enforcement discretion does not intrude upon the prerogatives of the Executive, for in so deciding we are merely saying "what the law is." Surely the question whether the Constitution or the Code limits enforcement discretion is one within the Judiciary's competence * * *.

POINTS FOR DISCUSSION

a. Why Standing?

What is the objective of enforcing a standing requirement? Is it to ensure that the plaintiff has a sufficient stake in the outcome so that there will be adversity between the parties and thus the issues and arguments will be fully developed in the litigation? If so, is there reason to think that the parents who filed the suit in *Allen* had a sufficient stake in the outcome? Is the objective to enforce separation-of-powers norms by ensuring that courts do not micromanage the decisions of the Executive Branch? If so, is it problematic that a different plaintiff—for example, the headmaster of a private school that does not discriminate on the basis of race but that must compete for students with tax-exempt schools that do—would have standing to assert the identical challenge to the federal regulation that the plaintiffs in *Allen* attempted unsuccessfully to assert? In reaching the merits in such a suit, wouldn't the Court be acting as the monitor of "the wisdom and soundness of Executive action"?

b. Which Plaintiffs?

If the IRS had been aggressive in denying tax-exempt status to private schools that discriminate on the basis of race, there is little doubt that the headmaster of such a school would have had standing to challenge, under the principles announced in Allen, the legality of the IRS's policy. Cf. *Bob Jones University v. United States*, 461 U.S. 574, 579 (1983) (holding that non-profit private university that prescribed and enforced racially discriminatory admission standards did not qualify as a tax-exempt organization under the Internal Revenue Code). Doesn't this suggest that the Court is more willing to entertain suits challenging over-regulation than it is to entertain suits challenging under-regulation? If Congress has ordered more aggressive regulation, as the plaintiffs in Allen alleged it had done, then why shouldn't the Court enforce that legislative judgment as willingly as it would enforce a legislative decision for the government to do less?

c. Precedent

In *Regents of the University of California v. Bakke*, 438 U.S. 265 (1978), the plaintiff, a white man, challenged an affirmative action plan at the University of California at Davis's medical school. Under that plan, the school "reserved" sixteen places in the entering class of 100 for "disadvantaged minority students." Bakke's application for admission was rejected, even though he had stronger quantitative credentials than some of the students who had been admitted for the "reserved" places. The facts showed, however, that even if there had been no affirmative action plan Bakke would not have been admitted, because there were many more than sixteen other white applicants who had been denied but who had better credentials than did Bakke. The Court concluded that Bakke had standing because he had been denied the opportunity "to compete for all 100 places in the class."

> **Make the Connection**
>
> We will consider the Court's decision in *Bakke*, and the subject of affirmative action, in Volume 2.

Was the Court's conclusion in *Allen* that the plaintiffs lacked standing consistent with the Court's decision in *Bakke* that the plaintiff had standing? After *Allen*, the Court has continued to follow the *Bakke* approach to standing for plaintiffs challenging government affirmative action programs. See *Northeastern Florida Chapter of Associated General Contractors v. City of Jacksonville*, 508 U.S. 656, 666 (1993).

Perspective and Analysis

The Court's standing doctrine has provoked a significant amount of scholarly attention. Consider the following reaction to the decision in *Allen* by a commentator (and federal judge) closely associated with the law and economics school of legal analysis:

> [I]t is hard to take seriously the claim that enforcement of legal rules does not affect bystanders. The rule against murder is designed to prevent other people from slaying me, as well as others, and I suffer an injury if the police announce that they will no longer enforce that rule in my neighborhood. * * * Only a judge who secretly believes that the law does not influence behavior would find no injury in fact. * * * The same reasoning establishes injury in fact when the government declines to enforce a law that was designed in part for my benefit.

Frank H. Easterbrook, *Foreword: The Court and the Economic System*, 98 Harv. L. Rev. 4, 40 (1984).

LUJAN V. DEFENDERS OF WILDLIFE

504 U.S. 555 (1992)

JUSTICE SCALIA delivered the opinion of the Court with respect to Parts I, II, III-A, and IV, and an opinion with respect to Part III-B, in which THE CHIEF JUSTICE, JUSTICE WHITE, and JUSTICE THOMAS join.

I.

The [Endangered Species Act of 1973 (ESA)] seeks to protect species of animals against threats to their continuing existence caused by man. The ESA instructs the Secretary of the Interior to promulgate by regulation a list of those species which are either endangered or threatened under enumerated criteria, and to define the critical habitat of these species. Section 7(a)(2) of the Act then provides, in pertinent part: "Each Federal agency shall, in consultation with and with the assistance of the Secretary [of the Interior], insure that any action authorized, funded, or carried out by such agency [is] not likely to jeopardize the continued existence of any endangered species or threatened species or result in the destruction or adverse modification of [critical] habitat[s] of such species * * *." [In 1986, the Fish and Wildlife Service and the National Marine Fisheries Service, on behalf of the Secretary of the Interior and the Secretary of Commerce respectively, promulgated a joint regulation] interpreting § 7(a)(2) to require consultation only for actions taken in the United States or on the high seas * * *. Shortly thereafter, respondents, organizations dedicated to wildlife conservation and other environmental causes, filed this action against the Secretary of the Interior, seeking a declaratory judgment that the [regulation] is in error as to the geographic scope of § 7(a)(2) and an injunction requiring the Secretary to promulgate a new regulation restoring the initial interpretation.

II.

Over the years, our cases have established that the irreducible constitutional minimum of standing contains three elements. First, the plaintiff must have suffered an "injury in fact"—an invasion of a legally protected interest which is (a) concrete and particularized, and (b) "actual or imminent, not 'conjectural' or 'hypothetical.' " Second, there must be a causal connection between the injury and the conduct complained of—the injury has to be "fairly [traceable] to the challenged action of the defendant, and not [the result of] the independent action of some third party not before the court." Third, it must be "likely," as opposed to merely "speculative," that the injury will be "redressed by a favorable decision."

When the suit is one challenging the legality of government action or inaction, the nature and extent of facts that must be averred (at the summary judgment stage) or proved (at the trial stage) in order to establish standing depends considerably upon whether the plaintiff is himself an object of the action (or forgone action) at issue. If he is, there is ordinarily little question that the action or inaction has caused him injury, and that a judgment preventing or requiring the action will redress it. When, however, as in this case, a plaintiff's asserted injury arises from the government's allegedly unlawful regulation (or lack of regulation) of *someone else,* much more is needed. In that circumstance, causation and redressability ordinarily hinge on the response of the regulated (or regulable) third party to the government action or inaction—and perhaps on the response of others as well. * * * Thus, when the plaintiff is not himself the object of the government action or inaction he challenges, standing is not precluded, but it is ordinarily "substantially more difficult" to establish. *Allen v. Wright*, 468 U.S. 737 (1984).

Take Note

The Court says here that persons directly regulated by the government are much more likely to be able to establish standing to challenge the regulation than are persons who are beneficiaries of the government's regulation of others. Why might this be so? Does this distinction presuppose some theory about what the government's proper regulatory role is—a theory that we might expect to find embodied in the very statutes on which plaintiffs such as those in *Lujan* rely?

III.

A.

Respondents' claim to injury is that the lack of consultation with respect to certain funded activities abroad "increas[es] the rate of extinction of endangered and threatened species." Of course, the desire to use or observe an animal species, even for purely esthetic purposes, is undeniably a cognizable interest for purpose of standing. See, e.g., *Sierra Club v. Morton,* 405 U.S. 727 (1972). "But the 'injury in fact' test requires more than an injury to a cognizable interest. It requires that the party seeking review be himself among the injured." *Id.* To survive the Secretary's summary judgment motion, respondents had to submit affidavits or other evidence showing, through specific facts, not only that listed species were in fact being threatened by funded activities abroad, but also that one or more of respondents' members would thereby be "directly" affected apart from their " 'special interest' in [the] subject."

Definition

An "affidavit" is a "voluntary declaration of facts written down and sworn to by a declarant." *Black's Law Dictionary* (10th ed. 2014).

[The] Court of Appeals focused on the affidavits of two Defenders' members—Joyce Kelly and Amy Skilbred. Ms. Kelly stated that she traveled to Egypt in 1986 and "observed the traditional habitat of the endangered nile crocodile there and intend[s] to do so again, and hope[s] to observe the crocodile directly." * * * Ms. Skilbred averred that she traveled to Sri Lanka in 1981 and "observed [the] habitat" of "endangered species such as the Asian elephant and the leopard" at what is now the site of [a] project funded by the Agency for International Development (AID), although she "was unable to see any of the endangered species." [She alleged that the project threatened endangered species, and that the threat] harmed her because she "intend[s] to return to Sri Lanka in the future and hope[s] to be more fortunate in spotting at least the endangered elephant and leopard." When Ms. Skilbred was asked at a subsequent deposition if and when she had any plans to return to Sri Lanka, she reiterated that "I intend to go back to Sri Lanka," but confessed that she had no current plans: "I don't know [when]. There is a civil war going on right now. * * * Not next year, I will say. In the future."

We shall assume for the sake of argument that these affidavits contain facts showing that certain agency-funded projects threaten listed species—though that is questionable. They plainly contain no facts, however, showing how damage to the species will produce "imminent" injury to Mses. Kelly and Skilbred. That the women "had visited" the areas of the projects before the projects commenced proves nothing. * * * And the affiants' profession of an "inten[t]" to return to the places they had visited before—where they will presumably, this time, be deprived of the opportunity to observe animals of the endangered species—is simply not enough. Such "some day" intentions—without any description of concrete plans, or indeed even any specification of *when* the some day will be—do not support a finding of the "actual or imminent" injury that our cases require.

> **Food for Thought**
>
> The dissent (below) suggests that the plaintiffs in *Lujan* have established injury in fact merely by purchasing plane tickets to visit the areas affected by the government-funded projects. If so, what is the point of insisting that they do so?

Besides relying upon the Kelly and Skilbred affidavits, respondents propose a series of novel standing theories. The first, inelegantly styled "ecosystem nexus," proposes that any person who uses *any part* of a "contiguous ecosystem" adversely affected by a funded activity has standing even if the activity is located a great distance away. [But] a plaintiff claiming injury from environmental damage must use the area affected by the challenged activity and not an area roughly "in the vicinity" of it. * * * To say that the Act protects ecosystems is not to say that the Act creates (if it were possible) rights of action in persons who have not been injured in fact, that is, persons who use portions of an ecosystem not perceptibly affected by the unlawful action in question.

Respondents' other theories are called, alas, the "animal nexus" approach, whereby anyone who has an interest in studying or seeing the endangered animals anywhere on the globe has standing; and the "vocational nexus" approach, under which anyone with a professional interest in such animals can sue. Under these theories, anyone who goes to see Asian elephants in the Bronx Zoo, and anyone who is a keeper of Asian elephants in the Bronx Zoo, has standing to sue because the Director of AID did not consult with the Secretary regarding the AID-funded project in Sri Lanka. This is beyond all reason. Standing is not "an ingenious academic exercise in the conceivable," but as we have said requires, at the summary judgment stage, a factual showing of perceptible harm. It is clear that the person who observes or works with a particular animal threatened by a federal decision is facing perceptible harm, since the very subject of his interest will no longer exist. It is even plausible—though it goes to the outermost limit of plausibility—to think that a person who observes or works with animals of a particular species in the very area of the world where that species is threatened by a federal decision is facing such harm, since some animals that might have been the subject of his interest will no longer exist. It goes beyond the limit, however, and into pure speculation and fantasy, to say that anyone who observes or works with an endangered species, anywhere in the world, is appreciably harmed by a single project affecting some portion of that species with which he has no more specific connection.

B.

Besides failing to show injury, respondents failed to demonstrate redressability. Instead of attacking the separate decisions to fund particular projects allegedly causing them harm, respondents chose to challenge a more generalized level of Government action (rules regarding consultation), the invalidation of which would affect all overseas projects. * * * Since the agencies funding the projects were not parties to the case, the District Court could accord relief only against the Secretary: He could be ordered to revise his regulation to require consultation for foreign projects. But this would not remedy respondents' alleged injury unless the funding agencies were bound by the Secretary's regulation, which is very much an open question. * * * The short of the matter is that redress of the only injury in fact respondents complain of requires action (termination of funding until consultation) by the individual funding agencies; and any relief the District Court could have provided in this suit against the Secretary was not likely to produce that action.

A further impediment to redressability is the fact that the agencies generally supply only a fraction of the funding for a foreign project. AID, for example, has provided less than 10% of the funding for the [Sri Lanka] project. Respondents have produced nothing to indicate that the projects they have named will either be suspended, or do less harm to listed species, if that fraction is eliminated. [I]t is entirely conjectural whether the nonagency activity that affects respondents will be altered or affected by the agency activity they seek to achieve.

IV.

The Court of Appeals found that respondents had standing for an additional reason: because they had suffered a "procedural injury." The so-called "citizen-suit" provision of the ESA provides, in pertinent part, that "any person may commence a civil suit on his own behalf [to] enjoin any person, including the United States and any other governmental instrumentality or agency [who] is alleged to be in violation of any provision of this chapter." * * * This is not a case where plaintiffs are seeking to enforce a procedural requirement the disregard of which could impair a separate concrete interest of theirs (*e.g.*, the procedural requirement for a hearing prior to denial of their license application, or the procedural requirement for an environmental impact statement before a federal facility is constructed next door to them). Nor is it simply a case where concrete injury has been suffered by many persons, as in mass fraud or mass tort situations. Nor, finally, is it the unusual case in which Congress has created a concrete private interest in the outcome of a suit against a private party for the government's benefit, by providing a cash bounty for the victorious plaintiff. Rather, the court held that the injury-in-fact requirement had been satisfied by congressional conferral upon *all* persons of an abstract, self-contained, noninstrumental "right" to have the Executive observe the procedures required by law. We reject this view.

Food for Thought

There is a long history of Congress's authorizing "private attorneys general" to file suits on behalf of the United States, with a bounty of part of the government's recovery as incentive for the suit. The False Claims Act, 31 U.S.C. §§ 3729–3733, for example, authorizes individuals to file suits on behalf of the United States against defendants who have defrauded the government and authorizes an award of up to 25% of the recovery for the private plaintiff. *Id.* § 3730(d). Can such statutory devices survive the Court's reasoning in this section of the opinion?

Whether the courts were to act on their own, or at the invitation of Congress, in ignoring the concrete injury requirement described in our cases, they would be discarding a principle fundamental to the separate and distinct constitutional role of the Third Branch—one of the essential elements that identifies those "Cases" and "Controversies" that are the business of the courts rather than of the political branches. "The province of the court," as Chief Justice Marshall said in *Marbury v. Madison* "is, solely, to decide on the rights of individuals." Vindicating the *public* interest (including the public interest in Government observance of the Constitution and laws) is the function of Congress and the Chief Executive. The question presented here is whether the public interest in proper administration of the laws (specifically, in agencies' observance of a particular, statutorily prescribed procedure) can be converted into an individual right by a statute that denominates it as such, and that permits all citizens (or, for that matter, a subclass of citizens who suffer no distinctive concrete harm) to sue. If the concrete injury requirement has the separation-of-powers significance we have always said, the answer must be obvious: To permit Congress to convert the undifferentiated public interest in executive officers' compliance with the law into an "individual right" vindicable in the courts is to permit Congress to transfer from the President to the courts the Chief Executive's most important constitutional duty, to "take Care that the Laws be faithfully executed." It would enable the courts, with the permission of Congress, "to assume a position of authority over the governmental acts of another and co-equal department," and to become "virtually continuing monitors of the wisdom and soundness of Executive action." *Allen.* We have always rejected that vision of our role. We hold that respondents lack standing to bring this action.

> **Make the Connection**
>
> We will consider the meaning of the "take Care" clause of Article II in Chapter 5.

JUSTICE KENNEDY, with whom JUSTICE SOUTER joins, concurring in part and concurring in the judgment.

Although I agree with the essential parts of the Court's analysis, I write separately to make several observations. While it may seem trivial to require that Mses. Kelly and Skilbred acquire airline tickets to the project sites or announce a date certain upon which they will return, this is not a case where it is reasonable to assume that the affiants will be using the sites on a regular basis, nor do the affiants claim to have visited the sites since the projects commenced. With respect to the Court's discussion of respondents' "ecosystem nexus," "animal nexus," and "vocational nexus" theories, I agree that on this record respondents' showing is insufficient to establish standing on any of these bases. I am not willing to foreclose the possibility, however, that in different circumstances a nexus theory similar to those proffered here might support a claim to standing. * * * In light of the conclusion that respondents have not demonstrated a concrete injury here sufficient to support standing under our precedents, I would not reach the issue of redressability that is discussed by the plurality in Part III-B.

I also join Part IV of the Court's opinion with the following observations. As Government programs and policies become more complex and farreaching, we must be sensitive to the articulation of new rights of action that do not have clear analogs in our common-law tradition. Modern litigation has progressed far from the paradigm of Marbury suing Madison to get his commission * * *. In my view, Congress has the power to define injuries and articulate chains of causation that will give rise to a case or controversy where none existed before, and I do not read the Court's opinion to suggest a contrary view. In exercising this power, however, Congress must at the very least identify the injury it seeks to vindicate and relate the injury to the class of persons entitled to bring suit. The citizen-suit provision of the Endangered Species Act does not meet these minimal requirements, because while the statute purports to confer a right on "any person [to enjoin] the United States and any other governmental instrumentality or agency [who] is alleged to be in violation of any provision of this chapter," it does not of its own force establish that there is an injury in "any person" by virtue of any "violation."

While it does not matter how many persons have been injured by the challenged action, the party bringing suit must show that the action injures him in a concrete and personal way. This requirement is not just an empty formality. It preserves the vitality of the adversarial process by assuring both that the parties before the court have an actual, as opposed to professed, stake in the outcome, and that "the legal questions presented [will] be resolved, not in the rarified atmosphere of a debating society, but in a concrete factual context conducive to a realistic appreciation of the consequences of judicial action." In addition, the requirement of concrete injury confines the Judicial Branch to its proper, limited role in the constitutional framework of Government.

JUSTICE BLACKMUN, with whom JUSTICE O'CONNOR joins, dissenting.

I think a reasonable finder of fact could conclude from the information in the affidavits and deposition testimony that either Kelly or Skilbred will soon return to the project sites, thereby satisfying the "actual or imminent" injury standard. * * * By requiring a "description of concrete plans" or "specification of *when* the some day [for a return visit] will be," the Court, in my view, demands what is likely an empty formality. No substantial barriers prevent Kelly or Skilbred from simply purchasing plane tickets to return to the Aswan and Mahaweli projects.

The Court [also] expresses concern that allowing judicial enforcement of "agencies' observance of a particular, statutorily prescribed procedure" would "transfer from the President to the courts the Chief Executive's most important constitutional duty, to 'take Care that the Laws be faithfully executed.' " In fact, the principal effect of foreclosing judicial enforcement of such procedures is to transfer power into the hands of the Executive at the expense—not of the courts—but of Congress, from which that power originates and emanates.

Under the Court's anachronistically formal view of the separation of powers, Congress legislates pure, substantive mandates and has no business structuring the procedural manner in which the Executive implements these mandates. * * * In complex regulatory areas, however, Congress often legislates, as it were, in procedural shades of gray. That is, it sets forth substantive policy goals and provides for their attainment by requiring Executive Branch officials to follow certain procedures, for example, in the form of reporting, consultation, and certification requirements.

The consultation requirement of § 7 of the Endangered Species Act is [an] action-forcing statute. Consultation is designed as an integral check on federal agency action, ensuring that such action does not go forward without full consideration of its effects on listed species. * * * Congress legislates in procedural shades of gray not to aggrandize its own power but to allow maximum Executive discretion in the attainment of Congress' legislative goals. * * * The Court never has questioned Congress' authority to impose such procedural constraints on Executive power. Just as Congress does not violate separation of powers by structuring the procedural manner in which the Executive shall carry out the laws, surely the federal courts do not violate separation of powers when, at the very instruction and command of Congress, they enforce these procedures.

[I] cannot join the Court on what amounts to a slash-and-burn expedition through the law of environmental standing. In my view, "[t]he very essence of civil liberty certainly consists in the right of every individual to claim the protection of the laws, whenever he receives an injury." *Marbury v. Madison.* I dissent.

POINTS FOR DISCUSSION

a. Injury in Fact

What criteria should the courts apply in deciding whether an alleged injury is a cognizable injury for purposes of Article III? If the point of the standing doctrine is to ensure that the plaintiff has the requisite stake in the outcome such that the suit is truly an adversarial contest between interested parties, are intangible, moral, or aesthetic injuries as cognizable as economic injuries?

b. Citizen-Suit Provisions

The Court held in *Lujan* that Congress cannot authorize a person to sue if that person has not suffered a cognizable injury, and thus that open-ended "citizen-suit provisions" are unconstitutional as applied to plaintiffs who have not actually suffered any cognizable injury. Justice Kennedy, however, stated in his concurring opinion that "Congress has the power to define injuries and articulate chains of causation that will give rise to a case or controversy where none existed before." Who gets to define "injury in fact"—Congress or the courts? In *Federal Election Commission v. Akins*, 524 U.S. 11 (1998), a divided Court held that voters who challenged a determination by the FEC that the American Israel Public Affairs Committee (AIPAC) was not a political committee subject to certain disclosure requirements under the Federal Election Campaign Act had standing. The Act authorizes "[a]ny person who believes a violation" of the Act has occurred to file a complaint with the FEC and to file a petition in federal court challenging the FEC's denial of such a complaint. 2 U.S.C.

§ 437g(a). The Court held that the plaintiffs' inability to obtain information about AIPAC's donors and campaign-related contributions and expenditures—information that "would help them (and others to whom they would communicate it) to evaluate candidates for public office, especially candidates who received assistance from AIPAC, and to evaluate the role that AIPAC's financial assistance might play in a specific election"—constituted a cognizable injury in fact. Is this decision consistent with *Lujan*?

Problem

Congress enacts a statute that requires the Nuclear Regulatory Commission (NRC) to "provide adequate training to managers of nuclear plants" in order to lower the risk of nuclear catastrophes. Residents who live near a nuclear power plant file suit against the NRC claiming that the agency failed adequately to train the plant's managers. The NRC moves to dismiss the suit for lack of standing. How should the Court rule?

Perspective and Analysis

What purpose is served by the various justiciability doctrines? Consider the following:

> [T]he intricate set of constraints that the Supreme Court has found to be implicit in the terse language of Article III do not serve any apparent purpose. * * * If we had no doctrines of justiciability whatsoever, the courts would still play only a proper, and properly limited, role in our democratic society, so long as they confined themselves to enforcing legal constraints on executive and congressional action. * * * [C]ourts should always permit actions *if Congress authorizes them.* * * * [D]emocracy requires courts to limit the substance of their rulings but does not imply a limit on the permitted modes of judicial proceeding.

Jonathan R. Siegel, *A Theory of Justiciability*, 86 Tex. L. Rev. 73 (2007). How might a supporter of justiciability requirements respond to Professor Siegel?

4. Congressional Control over Federal Court Jurisdiction

The barriers to the exercise of judicial power that we have considered so far—the political question doctrine, the case and controversy requirement, and standing—are all judicially developed doctrines based on interpretations of the Constitution. But sometimes the courts are disabled from action because Congress divests them of the power to act. Look carefully at the language of Article III. Section 1 does not require Congress to create lower federal courts, and Congress traditionally has defined the jurisdiction of the lower courts that it has created. In addition, section 2, clause 2 says that the Supreme Court has appellate jurisdiction subject to "such Exceptions, and under such Regulations as the Congress shall make." Well-known and largely uncontroversial examples of such exceptions or regulations are found in 28 U.S.C. §§ 1254 & 1257. In these statutes, Congress has specified that the Supreme Court generally has discretion to choose, by granting or denying certiorari, which appeals it will hear from lower federal courts and state courts. Most litigants, accordingly, do not have a right to a review of their cases on the merits by the Supreme Court. Congress thus has the power to limit opportunities for judicial review by restricting the jurisdiction of both the lower federal courts and the Supreme Court. Are there limits on Congress's power to strip the federal courts of jurisdiction?

> **Take Note**
>
> A "writ of certiorari" is a "writ issued by an appellate court, at its discretion, directing a lower court to deliver the record in the case for review." *Black's Law Dictionary* (10th ed. 2014). A litigant who wants the Supreme Court to review a lower court's decision files a petition for a writ of certiorari. The Supreme Court will grant the writ if four of the nine Justices think that the case warrants review.

EX PARTE MCCARDLE

74 U.S. 506 (1869)

[In the late 1860s, William McCardle published several editorials in the *Vicksburg Times* that sharply criticized federal military rule in the South during Reconstruction. (In one, for example, he called several military commanders "infamous, cowardly, and abandoned villains who, instead of wearing shoulder straps and ruling millions of people should have their heads shaved, their ears cropped, their foreheads branded, and their persons lodged in a penitentiary.") These editorials led to his arrest and detention by federal military officials, who convened a military commission to try him on charges that included impeding reconstruction and inciting insurrection. McCardle filed an action in federal court seeking a writ of habeas corpus, relying on a statute that Congress had enacted on

February 5, 1867, called the Habeas Corpus Act, which gave the federal courts jurisdiction over habeas petitions challenging confinement by state or federal officials in violation of federal law. (The Judiciary Act of 1789, which the Habeas Corpus Act did not purport to repeal, had authorized jurisdiction over habeas petitions only by those held by federal officials.) McCardle claimed that the Military Reconstruction Act, which authorized military rule in the South, was unconstitutional because it permitted the trial of civilians by military tribunals rather than regularly constituted courts. He also argued that the prosecution violated his rights under the First, Fifth, and Sixth Amendments.

> **Definition**
>
> *Habeas Corpus* literally means "you have the body." The writ of habeas corpus is an ancient writ from a court ordering the release of a person unlawfully held by the government.

The Habeas Corpus Act also authorized habeas petitioners to appeal lower-court judgments to the Supreme Court, and after the federal circuit court denied the writ, McCardle appealed to the Supreme Court. After the Supreme Court denied the government's motion to dismiss and held oral arguments on the merits of McCardle's petition, members of Congress became concerned that the Court might invalidate the Military Reconstruction Act. Congress responded by passing a bill repealing the portion of the Habeas Corpus Act that conferred on the Supreme Court appellate jurisdiction over cases involving petitions for habeas corpus. President Johnson, who was facing an impeachment trial in the Senate for his alleged obstruction of Reconstruction efforts, vetoed the bill, but Congress immediately overrode the veto, and the provision, known as the Repealer Act, became law on March 27, 1868. One year later, after arguments on the effect of the Repealer Act on the Court's jurisdiction, the Court issued the following opinion.]

CHIEF JUSTICE CHASE delivered the opinion of the court.

The first question necessarily is that of jurisdiction; for, if the act of March [27,] 1868, takes away the jurisdiction defined by the act of February [5], 1867, it is useless, if not improper, to enter into any discussion of other questions.

It is quite true, as was argued by the counsel for the petitioner, that the appellate jurisdiction of this court is not derived from acts of Congress. It is, strictly speaking, conferred by the Constitution. But it is conferred "with such exceptions and under such regulations as Congress shall make."

The exception to appellate jurisdiction in the case before us [is] not an inference from the affirmation of other appellate jurisdiction. It is made in terms. The provision of the act of 1867, affirming the appellate jurisdiction of this court in cases of habeas corpus is expressly repealed. It is hardly possible to imagine a plainer instance of positive exception. We are not at liberty to inquire into the motives of the legislature. We can only examine into its power under the Constitution; and the power to make exceptions to the appellate jurisdiction of this court is given by express words.

> **FYI**
>
> The Congressman who introduced the Repealer Act explained that the provision was intended to "sweep[ ] the [*McCardle*] case from the docket by taking away the jurisdiction of the court [to] prevent" the Court from determining "the invalidity and unconstitutionality of the reconstruction laws of Congress." Cong. Globe, 40th Cong., 2d Sess. 2062 (1868). Should this stated congressional motive have mattered?

What, then, is the effect of the repealing act upon the case before us? We cannot doubt as to this. Without jurisdiction the court cannot proceed at all in any cause. Jurisdiction is power to declare the law, and when it ceases to exist, the only function remaining to the court is that of announcing the fact and dismissing the cause. And this is not less clear upon authority than upon principle.

It is quite clear, therefore, that this court cannot proceed to pronounce judgment in this case, for it has no longer jurisdiction of the appeal; and judicial duty is not less fitly performed by declining ungranted jurisdiction than in exercising firmly that which the Constitution and the laws confer.

> **Take Note**
>
> What other source of jurisdiction is the Court referring to here? Had Congress actually stripped the Supreme Court of all jurisdiction to review habeas petitions?

Counsel seem to have supposed, if effect be given to the repealing act in question, that the whole appellate power of the court, in cases of habeas corpus, is denied. But this is an error. The act of 1868 does not except from that jurisdiction any cases but appeals from Circuit Courts under the act of 1867. It does not affect the jurisdiction which was previously exercised.

The appeal of the petitioner in this case must be dismissed for want of jurisdiction.

POINTS FOR DISCUSSION

a. The Exceptions Clause and the Supreme Court's Appellate Jurisdiction

Recall from our discussion of *Marbury v. Madison* that Article III confers on the Supreme Court appellate jurisdiction over most of the categories of cases within the judicial power. But the relevant provision states that in those cases the Supreme Court "shall have appellate jurisdiction, both as to Law and Fact, *with such Exceptions, and under such Regulations as the Congress shall make*" (emphasis added). What is the import of this language? The traditional view is that the Exceptions Clause confers on Congress plenary authority to deprive the Supreme Court of appellate jurisdiction—over either some class of cases or all cases otherwise within the federal judicial power. See, e.g., Herbert Wechsler, *The Courts and the Constitution*, 65 Colum. L. Rev. 1001 (1965). Subject to a very important caveat that we will discuss below, this appears to be the view that the Court in *McCardle* advanced.

Does this view mean that Congress could effectively achieve a de facto reversal of Supreme Court precedent with which it disagrees by stripping the Court of jurisdiction to hear cases of a certain type—for example, cases involving abortion, flag burning, or any other controversial practice? If so, is such a congressional power consistent with the broader notion of checks and balances that is central to the constitutional structure? Many commentators have concluded that Congress's power under the Exceptions Clause is implicitly limited. Henry Hart, for example, famously suggested that Congress might lack power under the Exceptions Clause to "destroy the essential role of the Supreme Court in the constitutional plan." Henry M. Hart, Jr., *The Power of Congress to Limit the Jurisdiction of the Federal Courts: An Exercise in Dialectic*, 66 Harv. L. Rev. 1362, 1365 (1953).

b. The Holding in *McCardle*

Did the Court in *McCardle* in fact adopt the view that Congress's power under the Exceptions Clause is plenary? The Court concluded by noting that the Repealer Act "did not except from [the Court's appellate] jurisdiction any cases but appeals from Circuit Courts under the act of 1867," and that it did "not affect the jurisdiction which was previously exercised." Indeed, one year after the decision in McCardle, the Court held in *Ex parte Yerger*, 75 U.S. (8 Wall.) 85 (1869), that it had jurisdiction to entertain "original" habeas petitions pursuant to the Judiciary Act of 1789, which the Repealer Act had not purported to disturb. In light of the existence of this alternative basis for Supreme Court jurisdiction, had Congress actually stripped the Court of jurisdiction? If not, what does that mean for the binding force of the Court's discussion of Congress's power to deprive the Court of appellate jurisdiction?

In 1996, the Court upheld restrictions on its power to review certain habeas decisions, reasoning that Congress had not purported to deprive the Court of its power under the Judiciary Act of 1789 to grant original habeas petitions. *Felker v. Turpin*, 518 U.S. 651 (1996). Should it matter that the Court has not granted such a petition since 1925?

William McCardle faced trial by military commission. In the Military Commissions Act of 2006, Congress authorized the use of military commissions to try "unlawful enemy combatants" suspected of war crimes arising out of the war on terror. One provision of this Act stated: "No court, justice, or judge shall have jurisdiction to hear or consider an application for a writ of habeas corpus filed by or on behalf of an alien detained by the United States who has been determined by the United States to have been properly detained as an enemy combatant or is awaiting such determination." 10 U.S.C. § 2241(e)(1). Is this provision constitutional? Might it matter that Congress has provided alternative means for detainees to challenge their confinement? In *Boumediene v. Bush*, 553 U.S. 723 (2008), the Court held that the provision was unconstitutional absent an express suspension of the writ of habeas corpus. We will explore this question in further detail in Chapter 5.

c. Congressional Control of the Jurisdiction of the Lower Federal Courts

Are there limits on Congress's power to control the jurisdiction of the *lower* federal courts? The conventional view is that there are no meaningful limits. After all, Article III does not even require Congress to create inferior courts; if Congress can refuse to create lower courts, then it should follow that Congress can create them but decline to confer the full range of Article III jurisdiction upon them. See *Sheldon v. Sill*, 49 U.S. (8 How.) 441 (1850). Indeed, that is what Congress effectively has done by imposing limits, for example, on the exercise of diversity jurisdiction. See 28 U.S.C. § 1332 (imposing amount-in-controversy requirement).

Over the years, however, many prominent commentators have taken issue with this view, arguing that Congress is required, at least under some circumstances, both to create lower federal courts and to confer upon them all, or at least some, of the judicial power. In *Martin v. Hunter's Lessee*, 1 Wheat. (14 U.S.) 304 (1816), for example, Justice Story reasoned that because the Supreme Court can have original jurisdiction in only two classes of cases, it "would seem * * * to follow that congress are bound to create some inferior courts, in which to vest all that jurisdiction which, under the constitution, is exclusively vested in the United States, and of which the supreme court cannot take original cognizance. They might establish one or more inferior courts; they might parcel out the jurisdiction among such courts, from time to time, at their own pleasure. But the whole judicial power of the United States should be, at all times, vested either in an original or appellate form, in some courts created under its authority." *Martin*, 14 U.S. (1 Wheat.) at 331; see also Akhil Reed Amar, *A Neo-Federalist View of Article III: Separating the Two Tiers of Federal Jurisdiction*, 65 B.U. L. Rev. 205, 206, 229–30 (1985); Lawrence Gene Sager, *Foreword: Constitutional Limitations on*

Congress' Authority to Regulate the Jurisdiction of the Federal Courts, 95 Harv. L. Rev. 17, 66 (1981).

Taken together, these arguments suggest that Congress very well might have authority to deprive the Supreme Court of at least some of its appellate jurisdiction and to deprive the lower federal courts of at least some of their original jurisdiction. But what if Congress attempts to divest *all* federal courts of jurisdiction, original and appellate, over particular types of cases?

Problem

In 2005, the House of Representatives passed the "Pledge Protection Act." The bill did not pass the Senate. The bill would have amended title 28 of the United States Code as follows, in relevant part:

Sec. 1632. Limitation on jurisdiction

(a) Except as provided in subsection (b), no court created by Act of Congress shall have any jurisdiction, and the Supreme Court shall have no appellate jurisdiction, to hear or decide any question pertaining to the interpretation of, or the validity under the Constitution of, the Pledge of Allegiance * * * or its recitation.

(b) The limitation in subsection (a) does not apply to (1) any court established by Congress under its power to make needful rules and regulation respecting the territory of the United States; or (2) the Superior Court of the District of Columbia or the District of Columbia Court of Appeals.

If the bill had been enacted into law, would it have been constitutional?

Executive Summary of This Chapter

The United States Supreme Court enjoys the power of judicial review—that is, the power to invalidate statutes that are unconstitutional. *Marbury v. Madison* (1803). This power includes the authority to review and invalidate state laws that are inconsistent with the Constitution. *Martin v. Hunter's Lessee* (1816).

Under the doctrine of **judicial supremacy**, decisions of the Court interpreting the Constitution are the "supreme Law of the Land" for purposes of Article VI of the Constitution, and therefore are binding on all state officers, *Cooper v. Aaron* (1958), and federal officers, *Dickerson v. United States* (2000).

Some constitutional questions are non-justiciable pursuant to the political question doctrine. Determining whether a political question exists in any given case requires consideration of several factors: (1) whether there is a textually demonstrable commitment in the Constitution of the issue to the President or Congress; (2) whether there are judicially discoverable and manageable standards for resolving the question; (3) whether resolution of the question calls for policy decisions inappropriate for judicial resolution; (4) whether resolution of the question will express a lack of due respect for other branches of government; (5) whether there is an unusual need for unquestioning adherence to a political decision that has already been made; and (6) whether there is the potential for embarrassment from inconsistent resolutions of the issue by the Court and one or more of the political branches. *Baker v. Carr* (1962).

Whether a state's legislative apportionment scheme violates the Equal Protection Clause is not a political question. *Baker v. Carr* (1962). Neither is a claim by a Member of Congress that he has been improperly excluded from his seat. *Powell v. McCormack* (1969). A claim that the Senate improperly delegated the task of "trying" an impeached federal judge, on the other hand, does present a political question. *Nixon v. United States* (1993).

The federal judicial power under Article III extends only to "Cases" and "Controversies." Accordingly, the Court lacks authority to issue advisory opinions about the proper resolution of abstract legal questions divorced from an actual dispute between adverse parties. In addition, the case or controversy requirement precludes Congress from conferring jurisdiction on the federal courts to decide abstract legal questions in suits that lack litigants with the requisite adversity of interests. *Muskrat v. United States* (1911).

The doctrines of ripeness and mootness also derive from the case or controversy requirement. A federal court will decline to resolve a controversy that is not ripe. A legal dispute is not ripe if it has not yet developed into an actual controversy, has not yet caused injury, or is otherwise asserted prematurely. *Anderson v. Green* (1995). A federal court will also generally decline to resolve a controversy that is moot. A controversy is moot if the parties no longer have any meaningful and concrete stake in its resolution. *United States Parole Comm'n v. Geraghty* (1980).

A federal court lacks authority to assert jurisdiction over a case in which the plaintiff or plaintiffs lack **standing**. In order to satisfy the requirements of Article III standing doctrine, a plaintiff must properly allege: (1) that he has suffered an "**injury in fact**"; (2) that the injury is **fairly traceable** to the challenged conduct; and (3) that the injury is **redressable** by a favorable decision. *Allen v. Wright* (1984).

To constitute a cognizable injury in fact, the plaintiff must assert something more than simply a "generalized grievance"—that is, a grievance that is widely shared and undifferentiated. *Allen v. Wright* (1984). In addition, the injury must be concrete and particularized, and actual or imminent, rather than speculative or conjectural. *Lujan v. Defenders of Wildlife* (1992). To satisfy the causation prongs of the test, the link between the challenged conduct and the alleged injury must not be unduly attenuated or speculative. *Allen v. Wright* (1984). Congress lacks power to authorize suits by persons who do not satisfy the test for Article III standing. *Lujan v. Defenders of Wildlife* (1992).

Congress has authority to deprive the lower federal courts of jurisdiction. *Sheldon v. Sill* (1850). Congress also has some authority pursuant to the Exceptions Clause of Article III to deprive the Supreme Court of appellate jurisdiction, *Ex parte McCardle* (1869), but the Supreme Court has never squarely decided whether Congress can completely deprive the Supreme Court of jurisdiction over a particular federal question. There might also be limits on Congress's power to strip all of the federal courts—lower courts and the Supreme Court—of jurisdiction over particular federal questions, but the question remains unresolved.

POINT-COUNTERPOINT

What is the role of the federal courts in our constitutional scheme?

POINT: PETER J. SMITH

The federal courts' essential functions are to protect individual rights from majoritarian incursion and to uphold the rule of law against government abuses of authority. When the government seeks to deprive an unpopular minority of the right to vote, for example, or seeks to suppress a citizen's ability to express an unpopular opinion, ordinary majoritarian politics by definition provide no means of redress. If we take seriously the notion that there are fundamental rights that are immune from governmental interference—a subject that we will take up in later chapters—then the federal courts, which are in very important ways independent from the political process, must stand open to vindicate those rights when they are threatened. At bottom, this is the most compelling justification for conferring the power of judicial review on the federal courts.

Of course, not all claims asserted in federal court seek to vindicate fundamental rights. Some claims seek to enforce against the government rights that are important simply by virtue of the fact that Congress has conferred them—such as the right to have clean water or air. When faced with such claims, the federal courts have an obligation to ensure that the government is following the rules that it has previously established for itself. After all, insisting that government officials follow the law ensures that we live under the rule of law, rather than the rule of men (or women) subject only to their own caprice, which is the conventional definition of tyranny.

If the federal courts are to fulfill these functions, then they must be generally open to the assertion of bona fide claims. Accordingly, we must be wary of barriers erected to limit the authority of the courts to intervene to protect individual rights or to uphold the rule of law. The maze of rules that we have seen in this part, however, has often frustrated the courts' ability to fulfill those functions. For example, it is difficult to resist the conclusion that the Court has deployed standing doctrine to keep from adjudication claims (or litigants) of which the Justices disapprove. (How else can we explain the fact that Allan Bakke, but not the plaintiffs in *Allen*, had standing to assert a race-based injury?) The political question doctrine, in theory a sensible idea, in practice lurks, because of its indeterminacy, as a tool for the Court to ratify problematic governmental decisions. And permitting Congress to divest the federal courts of jurisdiction over particular, disfavored issues—something that the Court has hinted, but fortunately never decided, that Congress could do—would strike at the core of the federal courts' essential function.

No one denies that the federal courts' role in our democratic society must be limited. But if we want to continue to have a Constitution that imposes meaningful limits on the authority of the political branches, then we must accept the power of judicial review and ensure that the courts can, in appropriate cases, exercise their authority to insist on the faithful and neutral application of the law.

COUNTERPOINT: GREGORY E. MAGGS

"A circumstance which crowns the defects of the Confederation," Alexander Hamilton wrote in *The Federalist Papers*, "[is] the want of a judiciary power." The Federalist No. 22. To remedy this deficiency of the Articles of Confederation, the Constitution prominently provided for "one supreme Court, and * * * such inferior Courts as the Congress may from time to time ordain and establish." U.S. Const. art. III, § 1. But what role were the new federal courts to have? This question does not have a single answer. The Framers envisioned several important functions.

Hamilton, for example, argued that the Supreme Court could promote uniform interpretations of federal law, something numerous state courts could not accomplish. The Federalist No. 22. With its original jurisdiction, the Supreme

Court also could quickly resolve sensitive cases involving ambassadors and states. The Federalist No. 81. Federal courts could serve as impartial tribunals in the "determination of controversies between different States and their citizens." The Federalist No. 80. And they would be a neutral forum for federal questions when "the prevalency of a local spirit may be found to disqualify the local [state] tribunals for the jurisdiction of national causes." The Federalist No. 81.

Hamilton advocated that federal courts should have the power of judicial review. The courts, he said, should exercise "a direct negative [on] State laws * * * as might be in manifest contravention of the articles of Union." The Federalist No. 80. And after observing that the Constitution "contains certain specified exceptions to the [federal] legislative authority; such, for instance, as that it shall pass no bills of attainder, no ex-post-facto laws, and the like," Hamilton also famously wrote: "Limitations of this kind can be preserved in practice no other way than through the medium of courts of justice, whose duty it must be to declare all acts contrary to the manifest tenor of the Constitution void." The Federalist No. 78.

But a role no one supposed the federal courts would assume is that of the inventor of new constitutional rights and the final arbiter of social policy. Hamilton said: "To avoid an arbitrary discretion in the courts, it is indispensable that they should be bound down by strict rules and precedents, which serve to define and point out their duty in every particular case that comes before them * * *." The Federalist No. 78. And yet, as we will see in subsequent chapters, the federal courts have strayed from this vision. We now have the peculiar situation where courts, rather than Congress or the state legislatures, decide on a clean slate the most contentious issues of our times: what the nation's abortion policies should be, how we fight our wars, the precise circumstances in which capital punishment may be imposed, whether adults may choose to end their lives, how states must accommodate homosexuality, and so forth. Someone has to decide these matters, but it seems awfully undemocratic and thoroughly inconsistent with the original vision to leave the choices to elite federal judges.

PART III

Federalism

One of the most important and divisive issues at the Constitutional Convention and subsequently in the ratification conventions was federalism: the relationship between the federal government and the states, and the relationship among the states. There was, to be sure, widespread agreement that the Articles of Confederation had created an unacceptably weak national government. Under the Articles, Congress lacked authority to impose taxes, and states often refused to contribute money when Congress requested it. Congress had no power to regulate commerce among the states, which enacted barriers to the importation of goods. And although the Articles conferred upon Congress power over foreign affairs, the power was ineffective because Congress was forced to rely on the states to implement its directives—there was, after all, no federal executive—and the states often refused to cooperate. Congress often had no choice but to sit idly by while the states fought among themselves, taxed and discriminated against goods produced in other states, and produced a deepening economic depression.

> **Make the Connection**
>
> We discussed the Articles of Confederation in Chapter 1.

Dissatisfaction with Congress's weakness under the Articles of Confederation was the impetus for the Constitutional Convention, but the proposed solution was not total consolidation of authority. On the one hand, the proposal that the Convention produced included some suggestions of very broad federal power. In addition to curing the most obvious defects of the Articles—such as conferring upon Congress the power to tax and the power to regulate interstate and foreign commerce—it authorized Congress to "make all Laws which shall be necessary and proper for carrying into Execution" not only the powers of Congress, but also "all other Powers vested by this Constitution in the Government of the United Sates, or in any Department or Officer thereof." Article I, § 8, cl. 18. It also provided that federal law "shall be the supreme Law of the Land * * *, any Thing in the Constitution or Laws of any State to the Contrary notwithstanding." Article VI, cl. 2. But the proposed Constitution also contained provisions that suggested important limits on the power of the federal government. The Constitution presupposed the continuing existence of the states, see Article IV, § 4, and entitled the states to equal representation in the Senate, Article I, § 3, cl. 1; Article V. More important, Congress's powers were enumerated, which suggested that Congress could not exercise powers not enumerated—a view confirmed upon the ratification of the Tenth Amendment, which provides, "The powers not delegated to the United States by the Constitution, nor prohibited by it to the States, are reserved to the States respectively, or to the people." Indeed, although the Constitution imposed some specific limits on the exercise of the states' power, see Article I, § 10, it did not purport to define the extent or scope of the power of the states.

Why Federalism?

The Constitution, in other words, obviously divides powers between the federal and state governments, but it doesn't give perfect guidance about where exactly the lines between competing sources of authority should be drawn. This ambiguity—particularly in the Constitution's application to modern problems—often leads to reliance, explicitly or implicitly, on arguments about the relative desirability of divided authority. What are the virtues of dividing authority between the states and the federal government in the first place? Conversely, what are the arguments in favor of consolidating power in one national government? Obviously, over the years many of the participants in these debates have had self-interested reasons to support one view or another. At the Convention, for example, the small states supported limits on federal authority to prevent dilution of their influence at the hands of the larger states. And individuals prosecuted for violating federal criminal statutes today have an obvious incentive to argue against the constitutional validity of the statutes under which they have been charged. Conversely, litigants relying on federal statutes that confer some benefit upon them can be expected to argue in favor of federal authority. But the arguments for and against the centralization of authority go beyond the mere self-interest of participants in the debates.

Proponents of de-centralization generally argue that such an approach better reflects the diversity of interests and preferences of individuals in different parts of the nation and encourages innovation in government, whereas centralization leads to one-size-fits-all decisions that stifle choice. See, e.g., Michael W. McConnell, *Federalism: Evaluating the Founders' Design*, 54 U. Chi. L. Rev. 1484 (1987). They also argue that dispersing government power is likely to protect individual liberty by limiting the power of any one government to act oppressively, see The Federalist No. 51, and that local officials are more likely than federal officials to be responsive to citizens, see The Federalist No. 45. Supporters of more robust centralized authority generally respond that centralization often is necessary to prevent individual states from imposing "externalities"—such as polluted air—on citizens of other states. See, e.g., David L. Shapiro, *Federalism: A Dialogue* (1995). James Madison argued, moreover, that the greatest threat to individual liberty comes from the tyranny of a majority faction, which is more likely to occur in a smaller, more homogenous political unit such as a state legislature. See The Federalist No. 10.

We would not presume to resolve a controversy as intractable as this one, but these arguments about the value of federalism are never far from the surface in the cases that follow. We begin our consideration of federalism with the powers of Congress. We will turn in Chapter 4 to the limits that the Constitution imposes on state power.

CHAPTER 3

Federal Legislative Power

A. EXPRESS AND IMPLIED FEDERAL POWERS

During the ratification debates, Anti-Federalist opponents of the Constitution argued that it would create an unduly powerful national government that would threaten both the separate existence of the states and the individual liberties over which the Revolution had been fought. Federalist supporters of the Constitution responded by arguing that such threats were illusory, because the national government would be authorized to exercise only those powers delegated "by positive grant expressed in the instrument of the union"—that is, only those powers enumerated in the Constitution. James Wilson, *Speech at the Pennsylvania Statehouse*, reprinted in 13 Merrill Jensen, John Kaminski, and Gaspare Saladino, *The Documentary History of the Ratification of the Constitution* 344 (1976); see also The Federalist No. 45 (James Madison) ("The powers delegated by the proposed Constitution to the federal government are few and defined. Those which are to remain in the State governments are numerous and indefinite."). The implications of this theory of enumeration, however, turned at least in part on how expansively or restrictively the powers actually enumerated would be construed.

To understand this debate, look carefully at Article I, section 8. This section enumerates the powers of Congress. The first 17 clauses grant Congress power to impose taxes, spend money, regulate commerce, set immigration standards, raise an Army and Navy, and so forth. All of these powers seem very important. But notice that these powers are stated in quite broad terms and do not specify many details. For example, clause 7 says that Congress may "establish Post Offices," but it does not say anything about procuring mail trucks, selling postage stamps, or hiring postal workers. Despite this omission, no one doubts that Congress may provide for these things. One reason for this conclusion is that clause 18 (the "Necessary and Proper Clause" or so-called "sweeping clause") grants Congress the power "[t]o make all Laws which shall be necessary and proper for carrying into Execution the foregoing Powers * * *." Perhaps the reasonable implication of Congress's power to establish post offices is the related power to authorize the use of mail trucks, postage stamps, and postal workers; in any event, such incidents, simply put, are necessary and proper for carrying into execution the power to establish post offices.

A significant question is how broadly or how narrowly courts should read the Necessary and Proper Clause. A broad reading would enable Congress to exercise many implied powers that are not expressly stated. A narrow reading, by contrast, would confine Congress more closely to its express powers. The case that follows, one of the most famous in all of American constitutional law, takes up that question.

McCulloch v. Maryland

17 U.S. (4 Wheat.) 316 (1819)

[In 1791, a debate arose about whether Congress had the power to charter a bank. President Washington sought advice from Alexander Hamilton, his Secretary of the Treasury, and Thomas Jefferson, his Secretary of State. Hamilton argued that Congress had the power, and Jefferson disagreed. Ultimately, Congress passed a bill chartering the Bank of the United States as a corporation, and President Washington signed the bill into law. The Bank was owned by private investors and largely dealt with commercial customers. Like other financial institutions, the Bank could make loans and it could take deposits (which it promised to repay by issuing promissory notes). But the Bank also had a special relationship with the federal government. The Treasury deposited funds in the Bank, and the Bank stood ready to make loans to the United States in times of need. Because of the Bank's large size, its policies on making and calling loans could have a substantial effect on the national economy. The charter of the Bank expired in 1811, but fiscal challenges led to pressure on Congress to create a new national bank. In 1816, Congress passed a bill creating the Second Bank of the United States, and President Madison,

Definition

Businesses, banks, universities, hospitals, and many other entities are typically organized as corporations. This means that they have their own legal identities that are distinct from the people who own them or who work for them. For example, a corporation can enter into contracts, acquire and own property, and incur liability just like a real person. If investors want to start a corporation, they must obtain a corporate charter from the government, usually by paying a small fee and meeting various organizational requirements. Most corporate charters are issued at the state level. But the federal government also issues charters. Examples include Amtrak, the George Washington University, and Sallie Mae.

who years earlier had argued that Congress lacked the power to create a national bank, signed the bill.

The Bank established branches in many states, including Maryland. In 1818, a nationwide financial panic led the Bank to call in loans, which exacerbated the economic depression that the country was already experiencing. Public anger mounted against the Bank, which was also accused of mismanagement and corruption. Maryland responded by imposing a tax on all banks operating in the state that were "not chartered by the Legislature." The law required unchartered banks either to issue bank notes only on stamped paper provided by the state for a fee for each issuance or to pay an annual lump sum of $15,000. The law imposed on the officers of banks that failed to comply a penalty of $500 for each offense, and made the penalties enforceable in an "action of debt," which could be maintained by any person who discovered non-compliance with the law. (The law authorized the plaintiff in such an action to recover half of the penalty as a bounty for bringing the suit.)

John James filed this action of debt on behalf of Maryland against James McCulloch, the Cashier of the Baltimore branch of the Bank of the United States. (As Cashier, McCulloch effectively ran the branch. He had also been accused of complicity in financial improprieties at the Bank.) McCulloch conceded that the Bank was operating without a charter from the state of Maryland and that the Bank had issued notes without complying with the Maryland law. The Maryland Court of Appeals ruled in favor of the state.]

CHIEF JUSTICE MARSHALL delivered the opinion of the Court.

In the case now to be determined, [Maryland], a sovereign state, denies the obligation of a law enacted by the legislature of the Union, and the [plaintiff in error] contests the validity of an act which has been passed by the legislature of that state. * * * The first question made in the cause is—has congress power to incorporate a bank? [T]his can scarcely be considered as an open question, entirely unprejudiced by the former proceedings of the nation respecting it. The principle now contested was introduced at a very early period of our history, has been recognized by many successive legislatures, and has been acted upon by the judicial department, in cases of peculiar delicacy, as a law of undoubted obligation.

> **Food for Thought**
>
> In light of *Marbury v. Madison*, should the fact that Congress has asserted a particular power be treated as evidence that the Constitution in fact confers that power upon Congress?

It will not be denied, that a bold and daring usurpation might be resisted, after an acquiescence still longer and more complete than this. But * * * [a]n exposition of the constitution, deliberately established by legislative acts, on the faith of which an immense property has been advanced, ought not to be lightly disregarded. The power now contested was exercised by the first congress elected under the present constitution. The bill for incorporating the Bank of the United States did not steal upon an unsuspecting legislature, and pass unobserved. Its principle was completely understood, and was opposed with equal zeal and ability. After being resisted, first, in the fair and open field of debate, and afterwards, in the executive cabinet, with as much persevering talent as any measure has ever experienced, and being supported by arguments which convinced minds as pure and as intelligent as this country can boast, it became a law. The original act was permitted to expire; but a short experience of the embarrassments to which the refusal to revive it exposed the government, convinced those who were most prejudiced against the measure of its necessity, and induced the passage of the present law.

> **FYI**
>
> The Court was aware of the earlier debate over the constitutionality of the Bank, and that Madison had changed his view and signed a bill to charter the Bank. Madison stated at the time that the question of Congress's power to create the Bank was "precluded in my judgment by repeated recognitions under varied circumstances of the validity of such an institution in acts of the legislative, executive, and judicial branches of Government."

It would require no ordinary share of intrepidity, to assert that a measure adopted under these circumstances, was a bold and plain usurpation, to which the constitution gave no countenance. These observations belong to the cause; but they are not made under the impression, that, were the question entirely new, the law would be found irreconcilable with the constitution.

In discussing this question, the counsel for the state of Maryland [urge the Court to consider the Constitution] not as emanating from the people, but as the act of sovereign and independent states. The powers of the general government, it has been said, are delegated by the states, who alone are truly sovereign; and must be exercised in subordination to the states, who alone possess supreme dominion. It would be difficult to sustain this proposition. The convention which framed the constitution was indeed elected by the state legislatures. But the instrument * * * was submitted to the *people*. They acted upon it in the only manner in which they can act safely, effectively and wisely, on such a subject, by assembling in convention. It is true, they assembled in their several states—and where else should they have assembled? No political dreamer was ever wild enough to think of breaking down the lines which separate the states, and of compounding the American people into one common mass. Of consequence, when they act, they act in their states. But the measures they adopt do not, on that account, cease to be the measures of the people themselves, or become the measures of the state governments.

From these conventions, the constitution derives its whole authority. The government proceeds directly from the people; is "ordained and established" in the name of the people. * * * The assent of the states, in their sovereign capacity, is implied, in calling a convention, and thus submitting that instrument to the people. But the people were at perfect liberty to accept or reject it; and their act was final. It required not the affirmance, and could not be negatived, by the state governments. The constitution, when thus adopted, was of complete obligation, and bound the state sovereignties. The government of the Union, then (whatever may be the influence of this fact on the case), is, emphatically and truly, a government of the people. In form, and in substance, it emanates from them. Its powers are granted by them, and are to be exercised directly on them, and for their benefit.

> **Food for Thought**
>
> Referring to the Preamble, Patrick Henry, a prominent opponent of the proposed Constitution, asked at the Virginia ratifying convention, "who authorized them to speak the language of, We, the People, instead of We, the States? States are the characteristics, and the soul of a confederation. If the States be not the agents of this compact, it must be one great consolidated National Government of the people of all the States." For Henry, this was a reason to oppose ratification, but of course he did not ultimately prevail in his argument. Given this history of debate, do you find the Court's view of the nature of sovereignty under the Constitution convincing?

This government is acknowledged by all to be one of enumerated powers. * * * If any one proposition could command the universal assent of mankind, we might expect it would be this—that the government of the Union, though limited in its powers, is supreme within its sphere of action.

> **Take Note**
>
> The Articles of Confederation provided that each state "retains" every power "not expressly granted." The Court interprets the text of the Constitution in light of its contrast with the Articles of Confederation. Is this a sensible approach to interpretation?

Among the enumerated powers, we do not find that of establishing a bank or creating a corporation. But there is no phrase in the instrument which, like the articles of confederation, excludes incidental or implied powers; and which requires that everything granted shall be expressly and minutely described. Even the 10th amendment, which was framed for the purpose of quieting the excessive jealousies which had been excited, omits the word "expressly," and declares only that the powers "not delegated to the United States, nor prohibited to the states, are reserved to the states or to the people;" thus leaving the question, whether the particular power which may become the subject of contest has been delegated to the one government, or prohibited to the other, to depend on a fair construction of the whole instrument. The men who drew and adopted this amendment had experienced the embarrassments resulting from the insertion of this word in the articles of confederation, and probably omitted it, to avoid those embarrassments.

A constitution, to contain an accurate detail of all the subdivisions of which its great powers will admit, and of all the means by which they may be carried into execution, would partake of the prolixity of a legal code, and could scarcely be embraced by the human mind. It would, probably, never be understood by the public. Its nature, therefore, requires that only its great outlines should be marked, its important objects designated, and the minor ingredients which compose those objects be deduced from the nature of the objects themselves. That this idea was entertained by the framers of the American constitution, is not only to be inferred from the nature of the instrument, but from the language. Why else were some of the limitations, found in the 9th section of the 1st article, introduced? It is also, in some degree, warranted by their having omitted to use any restrictive term which might prevent its receiving a fair and just interpretation. In considering this question, then, we must never forget that it is a *constitution* we are expounding.

FYI

Justice Frankfurter called the statement at the end of this paragraph—"we must never forget, this is a constitution we are expounding"—the "single most important utterance in the literature of constitutional law." Felix Frankfurter, *John Marshall and the Judicial Function*, 69 Harv. L. Rev. 217, 218–19 (1955). What does the statement mean, and what does it suggest about the proper way to interpret the Constitution? In this opinion, is Chief Justice Marshall "expounding" the federal powers or "expanding" them?

Although, among the enumerated powers of government, we do not find the word "bank" or "incorporation," we find the great powers to lay and collect taxes; to borrow money; to regulate commerce; to declare and conduct a war; and to raise and support armies and navies. The sword and the purse, all the external relations, and no inconsiderable portion of the industry of the nation, are entrusted to its government. It can never be pretended that these vast powers draw after them others of inferior importance, merely because they are inferior. Such an idea can never be advanced. But it may with great reason be contended that a government, entrusted with such ample powers, on the due execution of which the happiness and prosperity of the nation so vitally depends, must also be entrusted with ample means for their execution. The power being given, it is the interest of the nation to facilitate its execution. It can never be their interest, and cannot be presumed to have been their intention, to clog and embarrass its execution, by withholding the most appropriate means. * * * Can we adopt that construction (unless the words imperiously require it), which would impute to the framers of that instrument, when granting these powers for the public good, the intention of impeding their exercise, by withholding a choice of means? If, indeed, such be the mandate of the constitution, we have only to obey; but that instrument does not profess to enumerate the means by which the powers it confers may be executed; nor does it prohibit the creation of a corporation, if the existence of such a being be essential to the beneficial exercise of those powers. It is, then, the subject of fair inquiry, how far such means may be employed.

[Maryland argues that] the power of creating a corporation is one appertaining to sovereignty, and is not expressly conferred on congress. * * * [But] the government which has a right to do an act, and has imposed on it the duty of performing that act, must, according to the dictates of reason, be allowed to select the means * * *. The power of creating a corporation, though appertaining to sovereignty, is not like the power of making war, or levying taxes, or of regulating commerce, a great substantive and independent power, which cannot be implied as incidental to other powers, or used as a means of executing them. It is never the end for which other powers are exercised, but a means by which other objects are accomplished. * * * No sufficient reason is, therefore, perceived, why it may not pass as incidental to those powers which are expressly given, if it be a direct mode of executing them.

But the constitution of the United States has not left the right of congress to employ the necessary means, for the execution of the powers conferred on the government, to general reasoning. To its enumeration of powers is added, that of making "all laws which shall be necessary and proper, for carrying into execution the foregoing powers, and all other powers vested by this constitution, in the government of the United States, or in any department thereof." The counsel for the state of Maryland have urged various arguments, to prove that this clause, though, in terms, a grant of power, is not so, in effect; but is really restrictive of the general right, which might otherwise be implied, of selecting means for executing the enumerated powers. * * * Congress is not empowered by it to make all laws, which may have relation to the powers conferred on the government, but such only as may be "*necessary and proper*" for carrying them into execution. The word "*necessary*" is considered as controlling the whole sentence, and as limiting the right to pass laws for the execution of the granted powers, to such as are indispensable, and without which the power would be nugatory. That it excludes the choice of means, and leaves to congress, in each case, that only which is most direct and simple.

Is it true that this is the sense in which the word "necessary" is always used? Does it always import an absolute physical necessity, so strong that one thing to which another may be termed necessary, cannot exist without that other? We think it does not. [W]e find that it frequently imports no more than that one thing is convenient, or useful, or essential to another. To employ the means necessary to an end, is generally understood as employing any means calculated to produce the end, and not as being confined to those single means, without which the end would be entirely unattainable. * * * It is essential to just construction that many words which import something excessive should be understood in a more mitigated sense—in that sense which common usage justifies. The word "necessary" * * * admits of all degrees of comparison; and is often connected with other words, which increase or diminish the impression the mind receives of the urgency it imports. A thing may be necessary, very necessary, absolutely or indispensably necessary. To no mind would the same idea be conveyed by these several phrases. The comment on the word is well illustrated by * * * the 10th section of the 1st article of the constitution. It is, we think, impossible to compare the sentence which prohibits a state from laying "imposts, or duties on imports or exports, except what may be *absolutely* necessary for executing its inspection laws," with that which authorizes congress "to make all laws which shall be necessary and proper for carrying into execution" the powers of the general government, without feeling a conviction that the convention understood itself to change materially the meaning of the word "necessary" by prefixing the word "absolutely." This word, then, like others, is used in various senses; and, in its construction, the subject, the context, the intention of the person using them, are all to be taken into view.

Let this be done in the case under consideration. The subject is the execution of those great powers on which the welfare of a nation essentially depends. It must have been the intention of those who gave these powers, to insure, so far as human prudence could insure, their beneficial execution. This could not be done by confiding the choice of means to such narrow limits as not to leave it in the power of congress to adopt any which might be appropriate, and which were conducive to the end. This provision is made in a constitution, intended to endure for ages to come, and consequently, to be adapted to the various *crises* of human affairs. To have prescribed the means by which government should, in all future time, execute its powers, would have been to change, entirely, the character of the instrument, and give it the properties of a legal code. It would have been an unwise attempt to provide, by immutable rules, for exigencies which, if foreseen at all, must have been seen dimly, and which can be best provided for as they occur. To have declared that the best means shall not be used, but those alone, without which the power given would be nugatory, would have been to deprive the legislature of the capacity to avail itself of experience, to exercise its reason, and to accommodate its legislation to circumstances.

If we apply this principle of construction to any of the powers of the government, we shall find it so pernicious in its operation that we shall be compelled to discard it. * * * Take, for example, the power "to establish post-offices and post-roads." This power is executed by the single act of making the establishment. But, from this has been inferred the power and duty of carrying the mail along the post-road, from one post-office to another. And from this implied power, has again been inferred the right to punish those who steal letters from the post-office, or rob the mail. It may be said, with some plausibility, that the right to carry the mail, and to punish those who rob it, is not indispensably necessary to the establishment of a post-office and post-road. This right is indeed essential to the beneficial exercise of the power, but not indispensably necessary to its existence. * * * If the word "necessary" means "needful," "requisite," "essential," "conducive to," in order to let in the power of punishment for the infraction of law; why is it not equally comprehensive, when required to authorize the use of means which facilitate the execution of the powers of government, without the infliction of punishment?

In ascertaining the sense in which the word "necessary" is used in this clause of the constitution, we may derive some aid from that with which it is associated. Congress shall have power "to make all laws which shall be necessary *and proper* to carry into execution" the powers of the government. If the word "necessary" was used in that strict and rigorous sense for which the counsel for the state of Maryland contend, it would be an extraordinary departure from the usual course of the human mind, as exhibited in composition, to add a word, the only possible effect of which is, to qualify that strict and rigorous meaning; to present to the mind the idea of some choice of means of legislation, not strained and compressed within the narrow limits for which gentlemen contend.

But the argument which most conclusively demonstrates the error of the construction contended for by the counsel for the state of Maryland is founded on the intention of the convention, as manifested in the whole clause. * * * 1st. The clause is placed among the powers of congress, not among the limitations on those powers. 2d. Its terms purport to enlarge, not to diminish the powers vested in the government. It purports to be an additional power, not a restriction on those already granted. No reason has been, or can be assigned, for thus concealing an intention to narrow the discretion of the national legislature, under words which purport to enlarge it.

The result of the most careful and attentive consideration bestowed upon this clause is, that if it does not enlarge, it cannot be construed to restrain the powers of congress, or to impair the right of the legislature to exercise its best judgment in the selection of measures to carry into execution the constitutional powers of the government. If no other motive for its insertion can be suggested, a sufficient one is found in the desire to remove all doubts respecting the right to legislate on that vast mass of incidental powers which must be involved in the constitution, if that instrument be not a splendid bauble.

We admit, as all must admit, that the powers of the government are limited, and that its limits are not to be transcended. But we think the sound construction of the constitution must allow to the national legislature that discretion, with respect to the means by which the powers it confers are to be carried into execution, which will enable that body to perform the high duties assigned to it, in the manner most beneficial to the people. Let the end be legitimate, let it be within the scope of the constitution, and all means which are appropriate, which are plainly adapted to that end, which are not prohibited, but consist with the letter and spirit of the constitution, are constitutional.

Take Note

The last sentence of this paragraph is often quoted as the holding of *McCulloch v. Maryland.* A "holding" is a "court's determination of a matter of law pivotal to its decision." *Black's Law Dictionary* (10th ed. 2014). What exactly does the Court's holding in *McCulloch* mean?

If a corporation may be employed, indiscriminately with other means, to carry into execution the powers of the government, no particular reason can be assigned for excluding the use of a bank, if required for its fiscal operations. To use one, must be within the discretion of congress, if it be an appropriate mode of executing the powers of government. That it is a convenient, a useful, and essential instrument in the prosecution of its fiscal operations, is not now a subject of controversy. All those who have been concerned in the administration of our finances, have concurred in representing its importance and necessity; and so strongly have they been felt, that statesmen of the first class, whose previous opinions against it had been confirmed by every circumstance which can fix the human judgment, have yielded those opinions to the exigencies of the nation. * * * The time has passed away, when it can be necessary to enter into any discussion, in order to prove the importance of this instrument, as a means to effect the legitimate objects of the government.

But were its necessity less apparent, none can deny its being an appropriate measure; and if it is, the decree of its necessity, as has been very justly observed, is to be discussed in another place. Should congress, in the execution of its powers, adopt measures which are prohibited by the constitution; or should congress, under the pretext of executing its powers, pass laws for the accomplishment of objects not entrusted to the government; it would become the painful duty of this tribunal, should a case requiring such a decision come before it, to say that such an act was not the law of the land. But where the law is not prohibited, and is really calculated to effect any of the objects entrusted to the government, to undertake here to inquire into the degree of its necessity would be to pass the line which circumscribes the judicial department, and to tread on legislative ground. This court disclaims all pretensions to such a power.

> **Take Note**
>
> How does a Court determine whether Congress has enacted a particular statute in an attempt to accomplish "objects not entrusted to the government"? Should the Court determine Congress's motive in enacting the statute? If so, how can a Court determine the motive of a body composed of hundreds of individuals, each with his or her own particular (and perhaps complex) motives?

It being the opinion of the court, that the act incorporating the bank is constitutional; and that the power of establishing a branch in the state of Maryland might be properly exercised by the bank itself, we proceed to inquire—

2. Whether the state of Maryland may, without violating the constitution, tax that branch? That the power of taxation is one of vital importance; that it is retained by the states; that it is not abridged by the grant of a similar power to the government of the Union; that it is to be concurrently exercised by the two governments—are truths which have never been denied. But such is the paramount character of the constitution, that its capacity to withdraw any subject from the action of even this power is admitted. The states are expressly forbidden to lay any duties on imports or exports, except what may be absolutely necessary for executing their inspection laws. If the obligation of this prohibition must be conceded—if it may restrain a state from the exercise of its taxing power on imports and exports—the same paramount character would seem to restrain, as it certainly may restrain, a state from such other exercise of this power, as is in its nature incompatible with, and repugnant to, the constitutional laws of the Union. A law, absolutely repugnant to another, as entirely repeals that other as if express terms of repeal were used.

On this ground, the counsel for the bank place its claim to be exempted from the power of a state to tax its operations. There is no express provision for the case, but the claim has been sustained on a principle which so entirely pervades the constitution, is so intermixed with the materials which compose it, so interwoven with its web, so blended with its texture, as to be incapable of being separated from it, without rending it into shreds. This great principle is that the constitution and the laws made in pursuance thereof are supreme; that they control the constitution and laws of the respective states, and cannot be controlled by them. From this, which may be almost termed an axiom, other propositions are deduced as corollaries * * *. These are, 1st. That a power to create implies a power to preserve; 2d. That a power to destroy, if wielded by a different hand, is hostile to, and incompatible with these powers to create and to preserve; 3d. That where this repugnancy exists, that authority which is supreme must control, not yield to that over which it is supreme.

> **Food for Thought**
>
> Does the inclusion in Article I, section 10 of a specific limitation on some forms of state taxation help Marshall's argument, or undermine it? And is his argument here consistent with his argument in the prior section of the opinion about the import of express limitations in the text of the Constitution?

It is admitted, that the power of taxing the people and their property, is essential to the very existence of government, and may be legitimately exercised on the objects to which it is applicable, to the utmost extent to which the government may choose to carry it. The only security against the abuse of this power is found in the structure of the government itself. In imposing a tax, the legislature acts upon its constituents. This is, in general, a sufficient security against erroneous and oppressive taxation.

The people of a state, therefore, give to their government a right of taxing themselves and their property, and as the exigencies of government cannot be limited, they prescribe no limits to the exercise of this right, resting confidently on the interest of the legislator, and on the influence of the constituent over their representative, to guard them against its abuse. But the means employed by the government of the Union have no such security, nor is the right of a state to tax them sustained by the same theory. Those means are not given by the people of a particular state, not given by the constituents of the legislature, which claim the right to tax them, but by the people of all the states. They are given by all, for the benefit of all—and upon theory, should be subjected to that government only which belongs to all.

We are not driven to the perplexing inquiry, so unfit for the judicial department, what degree of taxation is the legitimate use, and what degree may amount to the abuse of the power. The attempt to use it on the means employed by the government of the Union, in pursuance of the constitution, is itself an abuse, because it is the usurpation of a power which the people of a single state cannot give. We find, then, on just theory, a total failure of this original right to tax the means employed by the government of the Union, for the execution of its powers. The right never existed, and the question whether it has been surrendered, cannot arise.

But, waiving this theory for the present, let us resume the inquiry, whether this power can be exercised by the respective states, consistently with a fair construction of the constitution? That the power to tax involves the power to destroy; that the power to destroy may defeat and render useless the power to create; that there is a plain repugnance in conferring on one government a power to control the constitutional measures of another, which other, with respect to those very measures, is declared to be supreme over that which exerts the control, are propositions not to be denied. But all inconsistencies are to be reconciled by the magic of the word *confidence*. Taxation, it is said, does not necessarily and unavoidably destroy. To carry it to the excess of destruction, would be an abuse, to presume which, would banish that confidence which is essential to all government. But is this a case of confidence? Would the people of any one state trust those of another with a power to control the most insignificant operations of their state government? We know they would not. Why, then, should we suppose, that the people of any one state should be willing to trust those of another with a power to control the operations of a government to which they have confided their most important and most valuable interests? In the legislature of the Union alone, are all represented. The legislature of the Union alone, therefore, can be trusted by the people with the power of controlling measures which concern all, in the confidence that it will not be abused. This, then, is not a case of confidence, and we must consider it is as it really is.

Make the Connection

The Court reasons that when Congress acts, it necessarily represents the views of all of the people in all of the several States. Doesn't this argument suggest that there is no need for the Courts to police federal statutes for compliance with federalism norms?

If we apply the principle for which the state of Maryland contends, to the constitution, generally, we shall find it capable of changing totally the character of that instrument. * * * If the states may tax one instrument, employed by the government in the execution of its powers, they may tax any and every other instrument. They may tax the mail; they may tax the mint; they may tax patent-rights; they may tax the papers of the custom-house; they may tax judicial process; they may tax all the means employed by the government, to an excess which would defeat all the ends of government. This was not intended by the American people. They did not design to make their government dependent on the states.

It has also been insisted, that, as the power of taxation in the general and state governments is acknowledged to be concurrent, every argument which would sustain the right of the general government to tax banks chartered by the states will equally sustain the right of the states to tax banks chartered by the general government. But the two cases are not on the same reason. The people of all the states have created the general government, and have conferred upon it the general power of taxation. The people of all the states, and the states themselves, are represented in congress, and, by their representatives, exercise this power. When they tax the chartered institutions of the states, they tax their constituents; and these taxes must be uniform. But when a state taxes the operations of the government of the United States, it acts upon institutions created, not by their own constituents, but by people over whom they claim no control. It acts upon the measures of a government created by others as well as themselves, for the benefit of others in common with themselves. The difference is that which always exists, and always must exist, between the action of the whole on a part, and the action of a part on the whole—between the laws of a government declared to be supreme, and those of a government which, when in opposition to those laws, is not supreme. But if the full application of this argument could be admitted, it might bring into question the right of congress to tax the state banks, and could not prove the rights of the states to tax the Bank of the United States.

[T]he states have no power, by taxation or otherwise, to retard, impede, burden, or in any manner control, the operations of the constitutional laws enacted by congress to carry into execution the powers vested in the general government. This is, we think, the unavoidable consequence of that supremacy which the constitution has declared. [T]his is a tax on the operations of the bank, and is, consequently, a tax on the operation of an instrument employed by the government of the Union to carry its powers into execution. Such a tax must be unconstitutional.

POINTS FOR DISCUSSION

a. We the People v. We the States

There is little doubt that the Framers believed deeply in the concept of popular sovereignty. But did they conceive of a single, undifferentiated national polity, as perhaps is indicated by the opening phrase of the Preamble, "We the People of the United States"? Or did they instead view the states as the proper repositories of popular sovereignty, as indicated by the requirement that the Constitution—and any subsequent Amendments—be ratified in three-fourths of the states? What are the implications of preferring one view over the other?

b. Implied Powers

Before even referring to the Necessary and Proper Clause, Chief Justice Marshall reasoned that Congress's enumerated powers were properly interpreted to imply subsidiary powers. What are the implications of this reasoning on the theory that Congress is limited to the powers enumerated in the text? What would be the implications of accepting Maryland's arguments against the existence of implied congressional powers?

c. Implied from What?

From which enumerated power is the authority to create a bank implied? Does Marshall answer this seemingly essential question? If not, what does that mean for his arguments?

d. "The Sweeping Clause"

The question presented in *McCulloch* was not new. Anti-Federalist opponents of the Constitution had trained much of their fire on the Necessary and Proper Clause, which they called the "sweeping clause," arguing that it would authorize the federal government to do almost anything. The first important test of the Clause's meaning came in 1791, when, at the urging of Secretary of the Treasury Alexander Hamilton, Congress enacted a bill creating the First Bank of the United States. Washington sought the views of Hamilton and Thomas Jefferson, who was Secretary of State, about the bill's constitutionality. In a now-famous opinion, Jefferson argued that the bill was unconstitutional. He began by noting that the power to incorporate a bank did not fall within any of the "powers especially enumerated" in Article I. In his view, the power to "lay taxes for the purpose of paying the debts of the United States" did not authorize the bill because "no debt is paid by this bill, nor any tax laid;" the power to "borrow money" did not authorize it because the bill "neither borrows money nor ensures the borrowing it;" and the power to regulate commerce did not authorize it because to "make a thing which may be bought and sold, is not to prescribe regulations for buying and selling." Jefferson then turned to the Necessary and Proper Clause:

> The [general] phrase is, "to make all laws necessary and proper for carrying into execution the enumerated powers." But they can all be carried into execution without a bank. A bank therefore is not necessary, and consequently not authorized by this phrase. It has been urged that a bank will give great facility or convenience in the collection of taxes. Suppose this were true: yet the Constitution allows only the means which are "necessary," not those which are merely "convenient" for effecting the enumerated powers. If such a latitude of construction be allowed to this phrase as to give any non-enumerated power, it will go to everyone, for there is not one which ingenuity may not torture into a convenience in some instance or other, to some one of so long a list of enumerated powers. It would swallow up all the delegated powers, and reduce the whole to one power * * *. Therefore it was that the Constitution restrained them to the necessary means, that is to say, to those means without which the grant of power would be nugatory. * * * Perhaps, indeed, bank bills may be a more convenient vehicle * * *. But a little difference in the degree of convenience cannot constitute the necessity which the Constitution makes the ground for assuming any non-enumerated power.

A few years later, shortly before he became President, Jefferson criticized the view of the Necessary and Proper Clause that Chief Justice Marshall would later advance. Responding to a federal bill to charter a mining company, Jefferson mocked: "Congress are authorized to defend the nation. Ships are necessary for defence; copper is necessary for ships; mines, necessary for copper; a company necessary to work the mines; and who can doubt this reasoning who has ever played at 'This is the House that Jack Built'? Under such a process of filiation of necessities the sweeping clause makes clean work." 10 *The Writings of Thomas Jefferson* 165 (Lipscomb & Bergh, eds. 1904). Jefferson clearly believed, at least at the time, that such arguments impermissibly expanded the powers of the federal government. Under Jefferson's view, what would the Necessary and Proper Clause mean? And how would the courts go about enforcing the limits that such a view would entail?

e. Types of Arguments About Constitutional Meaning

> **Make the Connection**
>
> We discussed theories of interpreting the Constitution in Chapter 1.

Chief Justice Marshall's opinion in *McCulloch* is a classic compendium of the various forms of constitutional arguments. Can you identify points that he makes based on constitutional text? Constitutional structure? History? Original Meaning? Political

Theory? Pragmatic considerations? Are arguments of these sorts of equal value in interpreting the Constitution?

UNITED STATES V. COMSTOCK

560 U.S. 126 (2010)

JUSTICE BREYER delivered the opinion of the court.

[This case began when the United States instituted civil commitment proceedings against the five respondents. Three of the respondents had pleaded guilty to possession of child pornography, one had pleaded guilty to sexual abuse of a minor, and one had been charged with aggravated sexual abuse of a minor, but had been found mentally incompetent to stand trial. The United States alleged that each respondent was about to be released from federal custody, that each had engaged in sexually violent conduct or child molestation in the past, and that each suffered from a mental illness that made him sexually dangerous to others.]

The federal statute before us allows a district court to order the civil commitment of an individual who is currently "in the custody of the [Federal] Bureau of Prisons," 18 U.S.C. § 4248, if that individual (1) has previously "engaged or attempted to engage in sexually violent conduct or child molestation," (2) currently "suffers from a serious mental illness, abnormality, or disorder," and (3) "as a result of" that mental illness, abnormality, or disorder is "sexually dangerous to others," in that "he would have serious difficulty in refraining from sexually violent conduct or child molestation if released." §§ 4247(a)(5)–(6).

Confinement in the federal facility will last until either (1) the person's mental condition improves to the point where he is no longer dangerous (with or without appropriate ongoing treatment), in which case he will be released; or (2) a State assumes responsibility for his custody, care, and treatment, in which case he will be transferred to the custody of that State. §§ 4248(d)(1)–(2). The statute establishes a system for ongoing psychiatric and judicial review of the individual's case, including judicial hearings at the request of the confined person at six-month intervals. §§ 4247(e)(1)(B), (h).

In November and December 2006, the Government instituted proceedings [under § 4248] in the Federal District Court for the Eastern District of North Carolina against the five respondents in this case. * * * Each of the five respondents moved to dismiss the civil-commitment proceeding on constitutional grounds.

The question presented is whether the Necessary and Proper Clause, Art. I, § 8, cl. 18, grants Congress authority sufficient to enact the statute before us. In resolving that question, we assume, but we do not decide, that other provisions of the Constitution—such as the Due Process Clause—do not prohibit civil commitment in these circumstances. *Cf. Addington v. Texas*, 441 U.S. 418 (1979). In other words, we assume for argument's sake that the Federal Constitution would permit a State to enact this statute, and we ask solely whether the Federal Government, exercising its enumerated powers, may enact such a statute as well. On that assumption, we conclude that the Constitution grants Congress legislative power sufficient to enact § 4248. We base this conclusion on five considerations, taken together.

First, the Necessary and Proper Clause grants Congress broad authority to enact federal legislation. Nearly 200 years ago, this Court stated that the Federal "[G]overnment is acknowledged by all to be one of enumerated powers," *McCulloch v. Maryland*, 4 Wheat. 316, 405 (1819), which means that "[e]very law enacted by Congress must be based on one or more of" those powers, *United States v. Morrison*, 529 U.S. 598, 607 (2000). But, at the same time, "a government, entrusted with such" powers "must also be entrusted with ample means for their execution." *McCulloch*, 4 Wheat., at 408. Accordingly, the Necessary and Proper Clause makes clear that the Constitution's grants of specific federal legislative authority are accompanied by broad power to enact laws that are "convenient, or useful" or "conducive" to the authority's "beneficial exercise." Chief Justice Marshall emphasized that the word "necessary" does not mean "absolutely necessary." In language that has come to define the scope of the Necessary and Proper Clause, he wrote: "Let the end be legitimate, let it be within the scope of the constitution, and all means which are appropriate, which are plainly adapted to that end, which are not prohibited, but consist with the letter and spirit of the constitution, are constitutional." We have since made clear that, in determining whether the Necessary and Proper Clause grants Congress the legislative authority to enact a particular federal statute, we look to see whether the statute constitutes a means that is rationally related to the implementation of a constitutionally enumerated power. *Sabri v. United States*, 541 U.S. 600, 605 (2004).

Thus, the Constitution, which nowhere speaks explicitly about the creation of federal crimes beyond those related to "counterfeiting," "treason," or "Piracies and Felonies committed on the high Seas" or "against the Law of Nations," Art. I, § 8, cls. 6, 10; Art. III, § 3, nonetheless grants Congress broad authority to create such crimes. See *McCulloch*, 4 Wheat., at 416 ("All admit that the government may, legitimately, punish any violation of its laws; and yet, this is not among the enumerated powers of Congress"). And Congress routinely exercises its authority to enact criminal laws in furtherance of, for example, its enumerated powers to regulate interstate and foreign commerce, to enforce civil rights, to spend funds for the general welfare, to establish federal courts, to establish post offices, to regulate bankruptcy, to regulate naturalization, and so forth.

Similarly, Congress, in order to help ensure the enforcement of federal criminal laws enacted in furtherance of its enumerated powers, "can cause a prison to be erected at any place within the jurisdiction of the United States, and direct that all persons sentenced to imprisonment under the laws of the United States shall be confined there." *Ex parte Karstendick*, 93 U.S. 396, 400 (1876). * * * Neither Congress' power to criminalize conduct, nor its power to imprison individuals who engage in that conduct, nor its power to enact laws governing prisons and prisoners, is explicitly mentioned in the Constitution. But Congress nonetheless possesses broad authority to do each of those things in the course of "carrying into Execution" the enumerated powers "vested by" the "Constitution in the Government of the United States," Art. I, § 8, cl. 18—authority granted by the Necessary and Proper Clause.

Second, the civil-commitment statute before us constitutes a modest addition to a set of federal prison-related mental-health statutes that have existed for many decades. We recognize that even a longstanding history of related federal action does not demonstrate a statute's constitutionality. See, *e.g.*, *Walz v. Tax Comm'n of City of New York*, 397 U.S. 664, 678 (1970). A history of involvement, however, can nonetheless be "helpful in reviewing the substance of a congressional statutory scheme," *Gonzales v. Raich*, 545 U.S. 1, 21 (2005), and, in particular, the reasonableness of the relation between the new statute and pre-existing federal interests.

Here, Congress has long been involved in the delivery of mental health care to federal prisoners, and has long provided for their civil commitment. In 1855 it established Saint Elizabeth's Hospital in the District of Columbia to provide treatment to "the insane of the army and navy . . . and of the District of Columbia." Act of Mar. 3, 1855, 10 Stat. 682; 39 Stat. 309. In 1857 it provided for confinement at Saint Elizabeth's of any person within the District of Columbia who had been "charged with [a] crime" and who was "insane" or later became "insane during the continuance of his or her sentence in the United States penitentiary." Act of Feb. 7, 1857, §§ 5–6, 11 Stat. 158. In 1874, expanding the geographic scope of its statutes, Congress provided for civil commitment in federal facilities (or in state facilities if a State so agreed) of "*all* persons who have been or shall be convicted of *any* offense in any court of the United States" and who are or "shall become" insane "during the term of their imprisonment." Act of June 23, 1874, ch. 465, 18 Stat. 251 (emphasis added). And in 1882 Congress provided for similar commitment of those "charged" with federal offenses who become "insane" while in the "custody" of the United States. Act of Aug. 7, 1882, 22 Stat. 330 (emphasis added). Thus, over the span of three decades, Congress created a national, federal civil-commitment program under which any person who was either charged with or convicted of any federal offense in any federal court could be confined in a federal mental institution. [In 1948 and 1949, Congress] provided for the civil commitment of individuals who are, or who become, mentally incompetent at any time after their arrest and before the expiration of their federal sentence, 18 U.S.C. §§ 4241, 4244, 4247–4248, [and in] 1984 Congress modified these basic statutes [before enacting the particular statute here at issue in 2006.]

Third, Congress reasonably extended its longstanding civil-commitment system to cover mentally ill and sexually dangerous persons who are already in federal custody, even if doing so detains them beyond the termination of their criminal sentence. For one thing, the Federal Government is the custodian of its prisoners. As federal custodian, it has the constitutional power to act in order to protect nearby (and other) communities from the danger federal prisoners may pose. Indeed, at common law, one "who takes charge of a third person" is "under a duty to exercise reasonable care to control" that person to prevent him from causing reasonably foreseeable "bodily harm to others." Restatement (Second) of Torts § 319, p. 129 (1963–1964). If a federal prisoner is infected with a communicable disease that threatens others, surely it would be "necessary and proper" for the Federal Government to take action, pursuant to its role as federal custodian, to refuse (at least until the threat diminishes) to release that individual among the general public, where he might infect others (even if not threatening an interstate epidemic, cf. Art. I, § 8, cl. 3). And if confinement of such an individual is a "necessary and proper" thing to do, then how could it not be similarly "necessary and proper" to confine an individual whose mental illness threatens others to the same degree?

Fourth, the statute properly accounts for state interests. Respondents and the dissent contend that § 4248 violates the Tenth Amendment because it "invades the province of state sovereignty" in an area typically left to state control. *New York v. United States*, 505 U.S. 144, 155 (1992). But the Tenth Amendment's text is clear: "The powers *not delegated to the United States* by the Constitution, nor prohibited by it to the States, are reserved to the States respectively, or to the people." (Emphasis added.) The powers "delegated to the United States by the Constitution" include those specifically enumerated powers listed in Article I along with the implementation authority granted by the Necessary and Proper

Clause. Virtually by definition, these powers are not powers that the Constitution "reserved to the States."

Fifth, the links between § 4248 and an enumerated Article I power are not too attenuated. * * * [T]he same enumerated power that justifies the creation of a federal criminal statute, and that justifies the additional implied federal powers that the dissent considers legitimate, justifies civil commitment under § 4248 as well. Thus, we must reject respondents' argument that the Necessary and Proper Clause permits no more than a single step between an enumerated power and an Act of Congress.

Taken together, these [five] considerations lead us to conclude that the statute is a "necessary and proper" means of exercising the federal authority that permits Congress to create federal criminal laws, to punish their violation, to imprison violators, to provide appropriately for those imprisoned, and to maintain the security of those who are not imprisoned but who may be affected by the federal imprisonment of others. The Constitution consequently authorizes Congress to enact the statute.

> **Take Note**
>
> Why did the Court take these five considerations into account? Is this list of considerations based on the text of the Constitution or on precedent? Did the Court identify these considerations by looking at sources that might show the original meaning of the Constitution? Or did the Court simply select them in an effort to create a reasonable way of deciding Necessary and Proper Clause cases? Are they all relevant? Can you think of additional relevant considerations?

JUSTICE ALITO, concurring in the judgment.

I entirely agree with the dissent that "[t]he Necessary and Proper Clause empowers Congress to enact only those laws that 'carr[y] into Execution' one or more of the federal powers enumerated in the Constitution," but § 4248 satisfies that requirement because it is a necessary and proper means of carrying into execution the enumerated powers that support the federal criminal statutes under which the affected prisoners were convicted. The Necessary and Proper Clause provides the constitutional authority for most federal criminal statutes. In other words, most federal criminal statutes rest upon a congressional judgment that, in order to execute one or more of the powers conferred on Congress, it is necessary and proper to criminalize certain conduct, and in order to do that it is obviously necessary and proper to provide for the operation of a federal criminal justice system and a federal prison system.

The only additional question presented here is whether, in order to carry into execution the enumerated powers on which the federal criminal laws rest, it is also necessary and proper for Congress to protect the public from dangers created by the federal criminal justice and prison systems. In my view, the answer to that question is "yes." Just as it is necessary and proper for Congress to provide for the apprehension of escaped federal prisoners, it is necessary and proper for Congress to provide for the civil commitment of dangerous federal prisoners who would otherwise escape civil commitment as a result of federal imprisonment.

This is not a case in which it is merely possible for a court to think of a rational basis on which Congress might have perceived an attenuated link between the powers underlying the federal criminal statutes and the challenged civil commitment provision. Here, there is a substantial link to Congress' constitutional powers. For this reason, I concur in the judgment that Congress had the constitutional authority to enact 18 U.S.C. § 4248.

[JUSTICE KENNEDY's opinion concurring in the judgment is omitted.]

JUSTICE THOMAS, with whom JUSTICE SCALIA joins * * *, dissenting.

No enumerated power in Article I, § 8, expressly delegates to Congress the power to enact a civil-commitment regime for sexually dangerous persons, nor does any other provision in the Constitution vest Congress or the other branches of the Federal Government with such a power. Accordingly, § 4248 can be a valid exercise of congressional authority only if it is "necessary and proper for carrying into Execution" one or more of those federal powers actually enumerated in the Constitution.

Section 4248 does not fall within any of those powers. The Government identifies no specific enumerated power or powers as a constitutional predicate for § 4248, and none are readily discernable. Indeed, not even the Commerce Clause—the enumerated power this Court has interpreted most expansively, see, *e.g.*, *NLRB v. Jones & Laughlin Steel Corp.*, 301 U.S. 1, 37 (1937)—can justify federal civil detention of sex offenders. Under the Court's precedents, Congress may not regulate noneconomic activity (such as sexual violence) based solely on the effect such activity may have, in individual cases or in the aggregate, on interstate commerce. *United States v. Morrison*, 529 U.S. 598, 617–618 (2000); *United States v. Lopez*, 514 U.S. 549, 563–567 (1995). That limitation forecloses any claim that § 4248 carries into execution Congress' Commerce Clause power, and the Government has never argued otherwise.

Make the Connection

We will consider Congress's power under the Commerce Clause, and the Court's decisions in *Morrison* and *Lopez*, later in this chapter.

To be sure, protecting society from violent sexual offenders is certainly an important end. Sexual abuse is a despicable act with untold consequences for the victim personally and society generally. But the Constitution does not vest in Congress the authority to protect society from every bad act that might befall it.

The Court observes that Congress has the undisputed authority to "criminalize conduct" that interferes with enumerated powers; to "imprison individuals who engage in that conduct"; to "enact laws governing [those] prisons"; and to serve as a "custodian of its prisoners." From this, the Court assumes that § 4248 must also be a valid exercise of congressional power because it is "reasonably adapted" to *those* exercises of Congress' incidental—and thus unenumerated—authorities. But that is not the question. The Necessary and Proper Clause does not provide Congress with authority to enact any law simply because it furthers *other laws* Congress has enacted in the exercise of its incidental authority; the Clause plainly requires a showing that every federal statute "carr[ies] into Execution" one or more of the Federal Government's *enumerated powers*.*

Federal laws that criminalize conduct that interferes with enumerated powers, establish prisons for those who engage in that conduct, and set rules for the care and treatment of prisoners awaiting trial or serving a criminal sentence satisfy this test because each helps to "carr[y] into Execution" the enumerated powers that justify a criminal defendant's arrest or conviction. * * * Civil detention under § 4248, on the other hand, lacks any such connection to an enumerated power.

[T]he Court finally concludes that the civil detention of a "sexually dangerous person" under § 4248 carries into execution the enumerated power that justified that person's arrest or conviction in the first place. [But § 4248] does not require a federal court to find any connection between the reasons supporting civil commitment and the enumerated power with which that person's criminal conduct interfered. * * * [Section] 4248 permits the term of federal civil commitment to continue beyond the date on which a convicted prisoner's sentence expires or the date on which the statute of limitations on an untried defendant's crime has run, [authorizing] federal custody over a person at a time when the Government would lack jurisdiction to detain him for violating a criminal law that executes an enumerated power. [And] the definition of a "sexually dangerous person" relevant to § 4248 does not require the court to find that the person is likely to violate a law executing an enumerated power in the future. In sum, the enumerated powers that justify a criminal defendant's arrest or conviction cannot justify his subsequent civil detention under § 4248.

* Justice Scalia did not join this paragraph or the one that follows.—*Eds.*

POINTS FOR DISCUSSION

a. Necessary and Proper for What?

Article I, § 8, clause 18 grants Congress the power "[t]o make all Laws which shall be necessary and proper for carrying into Execution the foregoing Powers [i.e., the powers expressly enumerated in Art. I, § 8, clauses 1–17], and all other Powers vested by this Constitution." Which, if any, of Congress's granted constitutional powers is the statute at issue necessary and proper for carrying into execution? Is it the Commerce Power? If so, why? Why didn't the Court specify one such enumerated power? If Congress can use the Necessary and Proper Clause to enact a law merely because it is incidental to other federal laws, what would be an example of a law that falls beyond the scope of the Necessary and Proper Clause?

b. Weighing the Factors

The Court listed five considerations to take into account when applying the Necessary and Proper Clause. In this case, all of the considerations appeared to point in the same direction. How would the case have come out if some of the considerations weighed against federal power? For example, what would be the result if there were no long history of federal involvement in this arena or no attempt to accommodate state interests?

c. Drawing Lines

The dissent reasoned that some federal laws governing the treatment of prisoners properly carry into execution the enumerated power that justified the prisoners' conviction in the first place, but that the law at issue in *Comstock* did not. If the Court adopted the dissent's approach, how would it decide which laws are incidental to enumerated powers and which are merely incidental to laws that are themselves incidental to enumerated powers?

B. THE COMMERCE POWER

McCulloch demonstrates that federal power can be either express or implied—and that the same is true of limits on state power, a subject that we will revisit in Chapter 4. The Constitution, after all, does not expressly confer upon Congress the power to create a Bank of the United States, but the Court in *McCulloch* concluded that such a power is fairly implied from other grants of power in Article I.

Even when the Constitution expressly confers power on Congress, questions arise about the scope and extent of that power. Although there are 17 clauses in Article I, section 8 conferring specific powers on Congress—in addition to the Necessary and Proper Clause, which was an important focus of the Court's decision in *McCulloch*—the one that historically has been the most important is the Commerce Clause.

> **U.S. Constitution, Article I, Section 8, Clause 3**
>
> The Congress shall have Power * * * To regulate Commerce with foreign Nations, and among the several States, and with the Indian Tribes.

Under the Articles of Confederation, the states engaged in bitter trade wars, imposing tariffs on each other's goods. These trade battles worsened an already fragile economy, but Congress was largely powerless to act. There was widespread agreement that Congress ought to have the power to protect the national market, and the Framers responded by including the Commerce Clause in the new Constitution.

One consequence of this history is that there has long been substantial support for the view that the states should be disabled from protectionist actions that resemble the trade wars under the Articles of Confederation. We will take up this topic in Chapter 4 when we consider the so-called Dormant Commerce Clause Doctrine. But first, we consider Congress's affirmative power to act pursuant to the Commerce Clause. As we will see, this clause has served as the basis for the vast majority of federal laws enacted in the last 120 years. During that time—indeed, since the ratification of the Constitution—the nature of commerce has changed dramatically, and the nature of the national market that was a central concern of the Framers has changed and expanded, as well.

Over the years, the Court has had many opportunities to consider the extent of the Commerce Power. Current law holds that Congress may regulate not only interstate commerce itself, but also the channels and instrumentalities of interstate commerce and intrastate economic activities that in the aggregate have a substantial effect on interstate commerce. How did this doctrine develop? We start at the beginning.

1. The Early View

The Marshall Court did not have many opportunities to consider the scope of Congress's power to regulate pursuant to the Commerce Clause. The case that follows provided Chief Justice Marshall with his first meaningful opportunity to opine on the scope of Congress's power to regulate interstate commerce.

GIBBONS V. OGDEN

22 U.S. (9 Wheat.) 1 (1824)

[The New York legislature in 1808 granted an exclusive right to Robert Livingston and Robert Fulton to operate steamboats in New York waters. Livingston and Fulton in turn licensed Ogden to operate a ferry between New York City and Elizabethtown, New Jersey. Gibbons, who originally had been Ogden's partner, began to operate a steamboat in competition with Ogden's service. Ogden sued Gibbons, relying on his monopoly under New York state law. Gibbons responded by demonstrating that he had been granted a license to operate ferries as "vessels to be employed in the coasting trade" pursuant to a 1793 federal statute. If the federal license meant that Gibbons was free to steam from state to state, it would have been impossible for a court to give effect both to Ogden's monopoly rights under the New York law and to Gibbons's rights under federal law. Gibbons argued that Ogden's exclusive right under New York law was preempted by the federal statute pursuant to the Supremacy Clause of Article VI. The New York courts sided with Ogden and enjoined Gibbons from operating his ferries in New York waters, and Gibbons appealed to the Supreme Court.]

> **Make the Connection**
>
> We will consider Congress's power to preempt state law—and the Court's role in determining when Congress has in fact preempted state law—in Chapter 4.

MR. CHIEF JUSTICE MARSHALL delivered the opinion of the Court:

The appellant contends that this decree is erroneous, because the laws which purport to give the exclusive privilege it sustains are repugnant to the constitution and laws of the United States. They are said to be repugnant [t]o that clause in the constitution which authorizes Congress to regulate commerce.

The words are, "Congress shall have power to regulate commerce with foreign nations, and among the several States, and with the Indian tribes." The subject to be regulated is commerce; and our constitution being * * * one of enumeration, and not of definition, to ascertain the extent of the power, it becomes necessary to settle the meaning of the word. The counsel for the appellee would limit it to traffic, to buying and selling, or the interchange of commodities, and do not admit that it comprehends navigation. This would restrict a general term, applicable to many objects, to one of its significations. Commerce, undoubtedly, is traffic, but it is something more: it is intercourse. It describes the commercial intercourse between nations, and parts of nations, in all its branches, and is regulated by prescribing rules for carrying on that intercourse. * * * All America understands, and has uniformly understood, the word "commerce," to comprehend navigation. It was so understood, and must have been so understood, when the constitution was framed. The power over commerce, including navigation, was one of the primary objects for which the people of America adopted their government, and must have been contemplated in forming it. The convention must have used the word in that sense, because all have understood it in that sense; and the attempt to restrict it comes too late.

> **Food for Thought**
>
> The Court relies both on the original understanding of the word "commerce" and the original intent of those who drafted and ratified the Constitution. Does this suggest that the meaning of the word "commerce" is frozen at its meaning in 1789? What would that view mean for Congress's power to adapt to changes in the nature of commerce and the American economy?

[A]dditional confirmation is, we think, furnished by the words of the instrument itself. The 9th section of the 1st article declares that "no preference shall be given, by any regulation of commerce or revenue, to the ports of one State over those of another." [T]he most obvious preference which can be given to one port over another, in regulating commerce, relates to navigation. But the subsequent part of the sentence is still more explicit. It is, "nor shall vessels bound to or from one State, be obliged to enter, clear, or pay duties, in another." These words have a direct reference to navigation. * * * The word used in the constitution, then, comprehends, and has been always understood to comprehend, navigation within its meaning; and a power to regulate navigation, is as expressly granted, as if that term had been added to the word "commerce."

Navigation is included in commerce

The subject to which the power is * * * applied, is to commerce "among the several States." The word "among" means intermingled with. A thing which is among others is intermingled with them. Commerce among the States cannot stop at the external boundary line of each State, but may be introduced into the interior.

It is not intended to say that these words comprehend that commerce, which is completely internal, which is carried on between man and man in a State, or between different parts of the same State, and which does not extend to or affect other States. Such a power would be inconvenient, and is certainly unnecessary.

Comprehensive as the word "among" is, it may very properly be restricted to that commerce which concerns more States than one. The phrase is not one which would probably have been selected to indicate the completely interior traffic of a State, because it is not an apt phrase for that purpose; and the enumeration of the particular classes of commerce, to which the power was to be extended, would not have been made, had the intention been to extend the power to every description. The enumeration presupposes something not enumerated; and that something, if we regard the language or the subject of the sentence, must be the exclusively internal commerce of a State. The genius and character of the whole government seem to be that its action is to be applied to all the external concerns of the nation, and to those internal concerns which affect the States generally; but not to those which are completely within a particular State, which do not affect other States, and with which it is not necessary to interfere, for the purpose of executing some of the general powers of the government. The completely internal commerce of a State, then, may be considered as reserved for the State itself.

We are now arrived at the inquiry—What is this power? It is the power to regulate; that is, to prescribe the rule by which commerce is to be governed. This power, like all others vested in Congress, is complete in itself, may be exercised to its utmost extent, and acknowledges no limitations, other than are prescribed in the constitution. * * * [T]he sovereignty of Congress, though limited to specified objects, is plenary as to those objects * * *. The wisdom and the discretion of Congress, their identity with the people, and the influence which their constituents possess at elections, are, in this, as in many other instances, as that, for example, of declaring war, the sole restraints on which they have relied, to secure them from its abuse. They are the restraints on which the people must often [rely] solely, in all representative governments.

> **Take Note**
>
> The Court declares that Congress's power to regulate is "plenary." "Plenary" means "completed" or "unqualified." This means that Congress can impose any kind of regulation that it chooses—prohibitions, taxes, quality standards, and so forth. As we see more cases in this chapter, consider whether the Court has in fact treated this power as plenary.

The power of Congress, then, comprehends navigation, within the limits of every State in the Union; so far as that navigation may be, in any manner, connected with "commerce with foreign nations, or among the several States, or with the Indian tribes." It may, of consequence, pass the jurisdictional line of New York, and act upon the very waters to which the prohibition now under consideration applies.

[The Court's discussion of the argument that the Commerce Clause prevents states from acting, even in the absence of federal legislation, to regulate commerce is discussed in Chapter 4.]

[I]n exercising the power of regulating their own purely internal affairs, whether of trading or police, the States may sometimes enact laws, the validity of which depends on their interfering with, and being contrary to, an act of Congress passed in pursuance of the constitution. [Accordingly,] the Court will enter upon the inquiry, whether the laws of New York, as expounded by the highest tribunal of that State, have, in their application to this case, come into collision with an act of Congress, and deprived a citizen of a right to which that act entitles him. Should this collision exist, * * * the acts of New York must yield to the law of Congress; and the decision sustaining the privilege they confer, against a right given by a law of the Union, must be erroneous.

[The federal statute pursuant to which Gibbons received his license] demonstrates the opinion of Congress that steam boats may be enrolled and licensed, in common with vessels using sails. They are, of course, entitled to the same privileges, and can no more be restrained from navigating waters, and entering ports which are free to such vessels, than if they were wafted on their voyage by the winds, instead of being propelled by the agency of fire. The one element may be as legitimately used as the other, for every commercial purpose authorized by the laws of the Union; and the act of a State inhibiting the use of either to any vessel having a license under the act of Congress, comes, we think, in direct collision with that act.

MR. JUSTICE JOHNSON[, concurring:]

For a century the States had submitted, with murmurs, to the commercial restrictions imposed by the parent State; and now, finding themselves in the unlimited possession of those powers over their own commerce, which they had so long been deprived of, and so earnestly coveted, that selfish principle which, well controlled, is so salutary, and which, unrestricted, is so unjust and tyrannical, guided by inexperience and jealousy, began to show itself in iniquitous laws and impolitic measures, from which grew up a conflict of commercial regulations, destructive to the harmony of the States, and fatal to their commercial interests abroad. This was the immediate cause that led to the forming of a convention.

FYI

Justice Johnson was President Jefferson's first appointment to the Court. Yet his view of federal power arguably was even broader than that advanced by Marshall, a Federalist and a nationalist until the end.

The history of the times will, therefore, sustain the opinion, that the grant of power over commerce, if intended to be commensurate with the evils existing, and the purpose of remedying those evils, could be only commensurate with the power of the States over the subject. And this opinion is supported by a very remarkable evidence of the general understanding of the whole American people, when the grant was made. * * * The power of a sovereign state over commerce * * * amounts to nothing more than a power to limit and restrain it at pleasure.

POINTS FOR DISCUSSION

a. Questions the Court Answers

The Court answers three questions about Article I, § 8, cl. 3: (1) What does "commerce" mean? Is it just buying and selling or is it something else? (2) What is commerce "among the several states"? Is it only shipping goods from one state to another or is it something more? (3) What is the power to "regulate"? Can Congress impose any kind of restriction or requirement on commerce among the states or is its power subject to limitations?

b. Political Safeguards of Federalism

Chief Justice Marshall stated that "[t]he wisdom and the discretion of Congress, their identity with the people, and the influence which their constituents possess at elections, are * * * the sole restraints on which [the people] have relied, to secure them from its abuse." Taken to its logical extreme, doesn't this argument suggest that the Court should *never* invalidate an Act of Congress on the ground that it is inconsistent with federalism norms? Or is Chief Justice Marshall saying only that, if Congress has the power to regulate a subject, its power is plenary as to that subject?

c. Express and Implied Limitations on State Power

In *Gibbons*, the Court was confronted with conflicting claims of right, one arising under federal law and the other arising under state law. The Court concluded that the federal statute preempted the state law. In light of the history on which Justice Johnson relied, should the states be disabled from regulating interstate commerce even in the absence of affirmative legislation from Congress? We will consider that question in Chapter 4.

2. The Middle Years: Uncertainty and a Restrictive View

In the first half of the nineteenth century, the Court had few occasions to construe the scope of Congress's power to regulate commerce, because Congress rarely exercised that power. And the cases during that time that did involve the Commerce Clause generally involved challenges to state, rather than federal, action, pursuant to the Dormant Commerce Clause Doctrine, which we will consider in Chapter 4. In the second half of the nineteenth century, however, the effects of industrialization led to several federal legislative responses. Congress regulated railroads, which were rapidly expanding across the continent, and attempted to regulate monopolies and unreasonable restraints of trade. Those efforts at regulation were challenged by parties on whom they imposed burdens, and the Court's responses were not entirely consistent. In some cases, such as the *E.C. Knight* case that follows, the Court offered a restrictive reading of Congress's power. In others—such as the *Shreveport Rate Case*, below—the Court construed Congress's power to regulate interstate commerce broadly.

UNITED STATES V. E.C. KNIGHT CO.

156 U.S. 1 (1895)

MR. CHIEF JUSTICE FULLER * * * delivered the opinion of the Court.

By the purchase of the stock of the four Philadelphia refineries with shares of its own stock the American Sugar Refining Company acquired nearly complete control of the manufacture of refined sugar within the United States. The bill charged that the contracts under which these purchases were made constituted combinations in restraint of trade * * * contrary to the [federal Sherman Antitrust Act]. The fundamental question is whether, conceding that the existence of a monopoly in manufacture is established by the evidence, that monopoly can be directly suppressed under the act of congress in the mode attempted by this bill. * * * That which belongs to commerce is within the jurisdiction of the United States, but that which does not belong to commerce is within the jurisdiction of the police power of the state.

> **FYI**
>
> The Sherman Antitrust Act prohibits "[e]very contract, combination in the form of trust or otherwise, or conspiracy, in restraint of trade or commerce among the several States, or with foreign nations," 15 U.S.C. § 1, and prohibits attempts "to monopolize any part of the trade or commerce among the several States, or with foreign nations," 15 U.S.C. § 2.

Are Monopolies considered commerce?

The argument is that the power to control the manufacture of refined sugar is a monopoly over a necessary of life, to the enjoyment of which by a large part of the population of the United States interstate commerce is indispensable, and that, therefore, the general government, in the exercise of the power to regulate commerce, may repress such monopoly directly, and set aside the instruments which have created it. But this argument cannot be confined to necessaries of life merely, and must include all articles of general consumption. Doubtless the power to control the manufacture of a given thing involves, in a certain sense, the control of its disposition, but this is a secondary, and not the primary, sense; and, although the exercise of that power may result in bringing the operation of commerce into play, it does not control it, and affects it only incidentally and indirectly. Commerce succeeds to manufacture, and is not a part of it.

It will be perceived how far-reaching the proposition is that the power of dealing with a monopoly directly may be exercised by the general government whenever interstate or international commerce may be ultimately affected. * * * [I]f the national power extends to all contracts and combinations in manufacture, agriculture, mining, and other productive industries, whose ultimate result may affect external commerce, comparatively little of business operations and affairs would be left for state control.

It was in the light of well-settled principles that the [Sherman Act] was framed. * * * [W]hat the law struck at was combinations, contracts, and conspiracies to monopolize trade and commerce among the several states or with foreign nations; but the contracts and acts of the defendants related exclusively to the acquisition of the Philadelphia refineries and the business of sugar refining in Pennsylvania, and bore no direct relation to commerce between the states or with foreign nations. The object was manifestly private gain in the manufacture of the commodity, but not through the control of interstate or foreign commerce. * * * There was nothing in the proofs to indicate any intention to put a restraint upon trade or commerce, and the fact, as we have seen, that trade or commerce might be indirectly affected, was not enough to entitle complainants to a decree.

Food for Thought

Why do you suppose the American Sugar Refining Company sought to acquire all other sugar refiners in the United States? Should it have been difficult to adduce proof of the defendant's "intention to put a restraint upon trade or commerce"? What effect should evidence of such an intention have on the Court's analysis?

The circuit court declined * * * to grant the relief prayed, and dismissed the bill. [Affirmed.]

MR. JUSTICE HARLAN, dissenting.

Any combination * * * that disturbs or unreasonably obstructs freedom in buying and selling articles manufactured to be sold to persons in other states, or to be carried to other states—a freedom that cannot exist if the right to buy and sell is fettered by unlawful restraints that crush out competition—affects, not incidentally, but directly, the people of all the states; and the remedy for such an evil is found only in the exercise of powers confided to a government which, this court has said, was the government of all, exercising powers delegated by all, representing all, acting for all.

[T]he act of 1890 * * * does not strike at the manufacture simply of articles that are legitimate or recognized subjects of commerce, but at combinations that unduly restrain, because they monopolize, the buying and selling of articles which are to go into interstate commerce.

[The Court's] view of the scope of the act leaves the public, so far as national power is concerned, entirely at the mercy of combinations which arbitrarily control the prices of articles purchased to be transported from one state to another state. I cannot assent to that view. In my judgment, the general government is not placed by the constitution in such a condition of helplessness that it must fold its arms and remain inactive while capital combines, under the name of a corporation, to destroy competition, not in one state only, but throughout the entire country, in the buying and selling of articles—especially the necessaries of life—that go into commerce among the states. The doctrine of the autonomy of the states cannot properly be invoked to justify a denial of power in the national government to meet such an emergency, involving, as it does, that freedom of commercial intercourse among the states which the constitution sought to attain.

POINTS FOR DISCUSSION

a. The Constitution and Statutory Interpretation

Did the Court hold that the Sherman Antitrust Act was unconstitutional? Or did it hold that Congress did not purport to reach the type of conduct that gave rise to the United States' claims against the American Sugar Refining Company? If the latter, what role did the Court's interpretation of the Constitution play in interpreting the scope of the statute? Do you think that Congress meant to regulate the type of conduct in which the defendant was accused of engaging?

b. Precedent

Is it possible to reconcile the decision in *E.C. Knight* with Chief Justice Marshall's statement in *Gibbons* that Congress has power to regulate commerce that "concerns more States than one"?

SHREVEPORT RATE CASE

234 U.S. 342 (1914)

MR. JUSTICE HUGHES delivered the opinion of the court:

[The Interstate Commerce Commission established rates for transporting goods by rail from Shreveport, Louisiana, to various stops in Texas. The Commission then ordered several railroads to cease charging rates for transporting goods within Texas that were disproportionately lower than the prevailing rates for the transportation of goods between points in Texas and Shreveport. (The railroads had been charging more for shorter trips from points in Texas to Shreveport than they had been charging for longer trips entirely in Texas.) The ICC concluded that such rates "unjustly discriminated in favor of traffic within the state of Texas, and against similar traffic between Louisiana and Texas." Three railroads filed suit to set aside the Commission's order.]

[Congress's] authority, extending to these interstate carriers as instruments of interstate commerce, necessarily embraces the right to control their operations in all matters having such a close and substantial relation to interstate traffic that the control is essential or appropriate to the security of that traffic, to the efficiency of the interstate service, and to the maintenance of conditions under which interstate commerce may be conducted upon fair terms and without molestation or hindrance. As it is competent for Congress to legislate to these ends, unquestionably it may seek their attainment by requiring that the agencies of interstate commerce shall not be used in such manner as to cripple, retard, or destroy it. The fact that carriers are instruments of intrastate commerce, as well as of interstate commerce, does not derogate from the complete and paramount authority of Congress over the latter, or preclude the Federal power from being exerted to prevent the intrastate operations of such carriers from being made a means of injury to that which has been confided to Federal care. Wherever the interstate and intrastate transactions of carriers are so related that the government of the one involves the control of the other, it is Congress, and not the state, that is entitled to prescribe the final and dominant rule, for otherwise Congress would be denied the exercise of its constitutional authority, and the state, and not the nation, would be supreme within the national field.

> **Make the Connection**
>
> The ICC was exercising power that Congress delegated to it to regulate rates for shipping by rail. The suit thus involved whether the power that Congress delegated was within Congress's power under the Commerce Clause. We will consider Congress's power to delegate decision-making authority to agencies in Chapter 6. We will also consider state attempts to regulate interstate rail traffic, in the *Wabash* case, in Chapter 4.

Congress has the Authority in this situation

Congress, in the exercise of its paramount power, may prevent the common instrumentalities of interstate and intrastate commercial intercourse from being used in their intrastate operations to the injury of interstate commerce. This is not to say that Congress possesses the authority to regulate the internal commerce of a state, as such, but that it does possess the power to foster and protect interstate commerce, and to take all measures necessary or appropriate to that end, although intrastate transactions of interstate carriers may thereby be controlled.

> **Food for Thought**
>
> In what way did the comparatively lower rates for intrastate shipping affect the *interstate* shipping market? In light of those effects, did it make sense to conclude that Congress was protecting the interstate market by regulating rates in the intrastate market?

This principle is applicable here. We find no reason to doubt that Congress is entitled to keep the highways of interstate communication open to interstate traffic upon fair and equal terms. * * * It is immaterial, so far as the protecting power of Congress is concerned, that the discrimination arises from intrastate rates as compared with interstate rates. The use of the instrument of interstate commerce in a discriminatory manner so as to inflict injury upon that commerce, or some part thereof, furnishes abundant ground for Federal intervention.

POINTS FOR DISCUSSION

a. Precedent

Is the holding in the *Shreveport Rate Case* reconcilable with the decision in *E.C. Knight*? If Congress has the "power to foster and protect interstate commerce," why doesn't it have the power to prevent monopolization that will affect the prices of goods sold interstate? Conversely, if Congress does not have authority to regulate manufacturing, on the theory that manufacturing is not "commerce" and affects commerce only indirectly, then why does it have authority to regulate intrastate shipping? Is the transportation of goods by railroad "commerce" in a way that manufacturing is not?

b. Textual Sources of Authority

Is the Court relying only on the Commerce Clause in reaching its conclusion in the *Shreveport Rate Case*? Or is it implicitly relying on the Necessary and Proper Clause, as well? Recall that the Court in *McCulloch* held that the Necessary and Proper Clause authorizes Congress to enact measures "plainly adapted" to the effectuation of ends legitimately sought pursuant to Congress's other affirmative powers. What is the relevance of the Necessary and Proper Clause in cases involving Congress's power to regulate interstate commerce?

The view of the Court in *E.C. Knight*—that Congress has power only to regulate commerce narrowly defined, and not the effects of local activity on interstate commerce—could not for long coexist peacefully with the view of the Court in the *Shreveport Rate Case*, under which Congress has authority to regulate intrastate matters that have such a "close and substantial relation to interstate traffic that the control is essential or appropriate to the security of that traffic, to the efficiency of interstate service, and to the maintenance of conditions under which interstate commerce may be conducted upon fair terms and without molestation or hindrance." But at least for a time, the Court unpredictably vacillated between *E.C. Knight*'s formal view of commerce and the *Shreveport Rate*

Case's more flexible effects test. The Court also sometimes upheld legislation on the ground that Congress may regulate local activities that are part of a larger "current of commerce among the States." *Swift & Co. v. United States*, 196 U.S. 375 (1905) (upholding an injunction under the Sherman Act against price fixing by local meat sellers); *Stafford v. Wallace*, 258 U.S. 495 (1922) (holding that the Packers and Stockyards Act of 1921 could constitutionally be applied to local dealers)

But the doctrine was even more confused than that. In the late nineteenth and early twentieth century, Congress enacted a series of statutes that regulated interstate shipments and transactions—that is, something like the "commerce" to which the Court in *E.C. Knight* had limited Congress's power—but that clearly appeared motivated as much by social and moral concerns as by economic concerns. The Court was often divided in its responses to such statutes. Consider the case that follows.

CHAMPION V. AMES

188 U.S. 321 (1903)

MR. JUSTICE HARLAN delivered the opinion of the court:

[The appellant was indicted for conspiring to violate an 1895 federal statute criminalizing the interstate transportation of lottery tickets, by arranging for the shipment of lottery tickets from Texas to California. He sought a writ of habeas corpus on the ground that the 1895 Act was unconstitutional.]

The appellant insists that the carrying of lottery tickets from one state to another state by an express company engaged in carrying freight and packages from state to state, although such tickets may be contained in a box or package, does not constitute, and cannot by any act of Congress be legally made to constitute, commerce among the states within the meaning of the [Commerce Clause]. * * * We are of opinion that lottery tickets are subjects of traffic, and therefore are subjects of commerce, and the regulation of the carriage of such tickets from state to state, at least by independent carriers, is a regulation of commerce among the several states.

But it is said that the statute in question does not regulate the carrying of lottery tickets from state to state, but by punishing those who cause them to be so carried Congress in effect prohibits such carrying; that in respect of the carrying from one state to another of articles or things that are, in fact, or according to usage in business, the subjects of commerce, the authority given Congress was not to *prohibit*, but only to *regulate*. * * * If lottery traffic, *carried on through interstate commerce*, is a matter of which Congress may take cognizance and over which its power may be exerted, can it be possible that it must tolerate the traffic, and simply regulate the manner in which it may be carried on? Or may not Congress, for the protection of the people of all the states, and under the power to regulate interstate commerce, devise such means, within the scope of the Constitution, and not prohibited by it, as will drive that traffic out of commerce among the states?

If a state, when considering legislation for the suppression of lotteries within its own limits, may properly take into view the evils that inhere in the raising of money, in that mode, why may not Congress, invested with the power to regulate commerce among the several states, provide that such commerce shall not be polluted by the carrying of lottery tickets from one state to another? In this connection it must not be forgotten that the power of Congress to regulate commerce among the states is plenary, is complete in itself, and is subject to no limitations except such as may be found in the Constitution. * * * If it be said that [the Act] is inconsistent with the 10th Amendment, [the] answer is that the power to regulate commerce among the states has been expressly delegated to Congress.

Besides, Congress, by that act, does not assume to interfere with traffic or commerce in lottery tickets carried on exclusively within the limits of any state, but has in view only commerce of that kind among the several states. It has not assumed to interfere with the completely internal affairs of any state, and has only legislated in respect of a matter which concerns the people of the United States. As a state may, for the purpose of guarding the morals of its own people, forbid all sales of lottery tickets within its limits, so Congress, for the purpose of guarding the people of the United States against the "widespread pestilence of lotteries" and to protect the commerce which concerns all the states, may prohibit the carrying of lottery tickets from one state to another. In legislating upon the subject of the traffic in lottery tickets, as carried on through interstate commerce, Congress only supplemented the action of those states—perhaps all of them—which, for the protection of the public morals, prohibit the drawing of lotteries, as well as the sale or circulation of lottery tickets, within their respective limits. It said, in effect, that it would not permit the declared policy of the states, which sought to protect their people against the mischiefs of the lottery business, to be overthrown or disregarded by the agency of interstate commerce. We should hesitate long before adjudging that an evil of such appalling character, carried on through interstate commerce, cannot be met and crushed by the only power competent to that end. We say competent to that end, because Congress alone has the power to occupy, by legislation, the whole field of interstate commerce.

It is said, however, that if, in order to suppress lotteries carried on through interstate commerce, Congress may exclude lottery tickets from such commerce, that principle leads necessarily to the conclusion that Congress may arbitrarily exclude from commerce among the states any article, commodity, or thing, of whatever kind or nature, or however useful or valuable, which it may choose, no matter with what motive, to declare shall not be carried from one state to another. It will be time enough to consider the constitutionality of such legislation when we must do so. The present case does not require the court to declare the full extent of the power that Congress may exercise in the regulation of commerce among the states. * * * It would not be difficult to imagine legislation that would be justly liable to such an objection as that stated, and be hostile to the objects for the accomplishment of which Congress was invested with the general power to regulate commerce among the several states. But, as often said, the possible abuse of a power is not an argument against its existence. [Affirmed.]

MR. CHIEF JUSTICE FULLER, with whom concur MR. JUSTICE BREWER, MR. JUSTICE SHIRAS, and MR. JUSTICE PECKHAM, dissenting:

> **FYI**
>
> The federal statute was entitled "An Act for the Suppression of Lottery Traffic through National and Interstate Commerce and the Postal Service, Subject to the Jurisdiction and Laws of the United States."

That the purpose of Congress in this enactment was the suppression of lotteries cannot reasonably be denied. That purpose is avowed in the title of the act, and is its natural and reasonable effect, and by that its validity must be tested. It is urged [that] because Congress is empowered to regulate commerce between the several states, it, therefore, may suppress lotteries by prohibiting the carriage of lottery matter. Congress may, indeed, make all laws necessary and proper for carrying the powers granted to it into execution, and doubtless an act prohibiting the carriage of lottery matter would be necessary and proper to the execution of a power to suppress lotteries; but that power belongs to the states and not to Congress. To hold that Congress has general police power would be to hold that it may accomplish objects not [entrusted] to the general government, and to defeat the operation of the 10th Amendment.

POINTS FOR DISCUSSION

a. Commerce "Among the States"

The federal statute at issue in *Champion* prohibited, among other things, the mere interstate transportation of lottery tickets by mail, even if the tickets were not sold across state lines. Is there an argument that such acts do not constitute commerce, even under the *E.C. Knight* Court's conception of the term? Or should it be enough that the regulated activity spanned state lines?

b. Federal Objectives

Recall that in *McCulloch* the Court declared, "should congress, under the pretext of executing its powers, pass laws for the accomplishment of objects not entrusted to the government; it would become the painful duty of this tribunal, should a case requiring such a decision come before it, to say that such an act was not the law of the land." Does this mean that when Congress invokes the commerce power in an attempt to regulate some local matter, the Court should invalidate the regulation? Should Congress's motives matter in deciding whether it has properly invoked its power under the Commerce Clause? The Court in *Champion* seemed to conclude that it was of no moment that Congress apparently enacted the statute to protect the people "against the widespread pestilence of lotteries," because the statute, in prohibiting an article from interstate commerce, regulated interstate transactions, a matter always within Congress's competence.

Champion v. Ames was one of a series of cases in which the Court upheld Congress's authority to regulate interstate transactions as a means of achieving social and moral objectives. Following this approach, for example, the Court upheld a statute that prohibited from interstate commerce food and drug items that contained a "deleterious" ingredient, *Hipolite Egg Co. v. United States*, 220 U.S. 45 (1911), and a statute prohibiting the transportation in interstate commerce of women for immoral purposes, *Hoke v. United States*, 227 U.S. 308 (1913). But the Court's decisions did not apply this principle uniformly, and the Court soon moved towards a more narrow and formal view of Congress's power under the Commerce Clause. Consider the cases that follow.

HAMMER V. DAGENHART

247 U.S. 251 (1918)

MR. JUSTICE DAY delivered the opinion of the Court.

A bill was filed in the United States District Court for the Western District of North Carolina by a father in his own behalf and as next friend of his two minor sons, one under the age of fourteen years and the other between the ages of fourteen and sixteen years, employ[ees] in a cotton mill at Charlotte, North Carolina, to enjoin the enforcement of the act of Congress intended to prevent interstate commerce in the products of child labor. [The law prohibited the transportation in interstate commerce of goods produced in factories that employed (1) children under fourteen years old or (2) children between fourteen and sixteen years old (a) at night, (b) for more than eight hours per day, or (c) for more than six days per week.]

[I]t is insisted that adjudged cases in this court establish the doctrine that the power to regulate given to Congress incidentally includes the authority to prohibit the movement of ordinary commodities * * *. The cases demonstrate the contrary. They rest upon the character of the particular subjects dealt with and the fact that the scope of governmental authority, state or national, possessed over them is such that the authority to prohibit is as to them but the exertion of the power to regulate. [In *Champion*, *Hipolite Egg*, and *Hoke*,] the use of interstate transportation was necessary to the accomplishment of harmful results. In other words, although the power over interstate transportation was to regulate, that could only be accomplished by prohibiting the use of the facilities of interstate commerce to effect the evil intended.

This element is wanting in the present case. The thing intended to be accomplished by this statute is the denial of the facilities of interstate commerce to those manufacturers in the states who employ children within the prohibited ages. The act in its effect does not regulate transportation among the states, but aims to standardize the ages at which children may be employed in mining and manufacturing within the states. The goods shipped are of themselves harmless. * * * When offered for shipment, and before transportation begins, the labor of their production is over, and the mere fact that they were intended for interstate commerce transportation does not make their production subject to federal control under the commerce power.

Take Note

Under the *E.C. Knight* conception of commerce, manufacturing and other "local" activities were not within Congress's power to regulate, even if they had significant "indirect" effects on commerce. But the statute at issue in *Hammer* regulated the interstate shipment of goods, which would appear to constitute interstate commerce even within the *E.C. Knight* view. Is the Court applying the *E.C. Knight* test—which, we have seen, was a relatively narrow view of Congress's power—or some other, even more restrictive, test?

The making of goods and the mining of coal are not commerce, nor does the fact that these things are to be afterwards shipped, or used in interstate commerce, make their production a part thereof. [T]he production of articles, intended for interstate commerce, is a matter of local regulation. * * * If it were otherwise, all manufacture intended for interstate shipment would be brought under federal control to the practical exclusion of the authority of the states, a result certainly not contemplated by the framers of the Constitution when they vested in Congress the authority to regulate commerce among the States.

It is further contended that the authority of Congress may be exerted to control interstate commerce in the shipment of child-made goods because of the effect of the circulation of such goods in other states where the evil of this class of labor has been recognized by local legislation, and the right to thus employ child labor has been more rigorously restrained than in the state of production. In other words, that the unfair competition, thus engendered, may be controlled by closing the channels of interstate commerce to manufacturers in those states where the local laws do not meet what Congress deems to be the more just standard of other states.

There is no power vested in Congress to require the states to exercise their police power so as to prevent possible unfair competition. Many causes may co-operate to give one state, by reason of local laws or conditions, an economic advantage over others. The commerce clause was not intended to give to Congress a general authority to equalize such conditions. * * * The grant of authority over a purely federal matter was not intended to destroy the local power always existing and carefully reserved to the states in the Tenth Amendment to the Constitution.

To sustain this statute would not be in our judgment a recognition of the lawful exertion of congressional authority over interstate commerce, but would sanction an invasion by the federal power of the control of a matter purely local in its character, and over which no authority has been delegated to Congress in conferring the power to regulate commerce among the states. * * * Thus the act in a two-fold sense is repugnant to the Constitution. It not only transcends the authority delegated to Congress over commerce but also exerts a power as to a purely local matter to which the federal authority does not extend. The far reaching result of upholding the act cannot be more plainly indicated than by pointing out that if Congress can thus regulate matters entrusted to local authority by prohibition of the movement of commodities in interstate commerce, all freedom of commerce will be at an end, and the power of the states over local matters may be eliminated, and thus our system of government be practically destroyed. [For] these reasons we hold that this law exceeds the constitutional authority of Congress.

MR. JUSTICE HOLMES, [joined by MR. JUSTICE MCKENNA, MR. JUSTICE BRANDEIS, and MR. JUSTICE CLARKE,] dissenting.

[I]f an act is within the powers specifically conferred upon Congress, it seems to me that it is not made any less constitutional because of the indirect effects that it may have, however obvious it may be that it will have those effects, and that we are not at liberty upon such grounds to hold it void. * * * The statute confines itself to prohibiting the carriage of certain goods in interstate or foreign commerce. Congress is given power to regulate such commerce in unqualified terms. [A] law is not beyond the regulative power of Congress merely because it prohibits certain transportation out and out. *Champion v. Ames.*

The question then is narrowed to whether the exercise of its otherwise constitutional power by Congress can be pronounced unconstitutional because of its possible reaction upon the conduct of the States in a matter upon which I have admitted that they are free from direct control. [T]he power to regulate commerce and other constitutional powers could not be cut down or qualified by the fact that it might interfere with the carrying out of the domestic policy of any State.

The notion that prohibition is any less prohibition when applied to things now thought evil I do not understand. But if there is any matter upon which civilized countries have agreed[,] it is the evil of premature and excessive child labor. I should have thought that if we were to introduce our own moral conceptions where in my opinion they do not belong, this was preeminently a case for upholding the exercise of all its powers by the United States. But I had thought that the propriety of the exercise of a power admitted to exist in some cases was for the consideration of Congress alone and that this Court always had disavowed the right to intrude its judgment upon questions of policy or morals. It is not for this Court to pronounce when prohibition is necessary to regulation if it ever may be necessary—to say that it is permissible as against strong drink but not as against the product of ruined lives. * * * The national welfare as understood by Congress may require a different attitude within its sphere from that of some self-seeking State. It seems to me entirely constitutional for Congress to enforce its understanding by all the means at its command.

POINTS FOR DISCUSSION

a. Precedent

The federal statute at issue in *Hammer* prohibited the interstate shipment of goods produced with child labor. In *Champion v. Ames*, the Court had sustained Congress's power to regulate the interstate shipment of goods even though Congress's apparent motive was to enforce its own social and moral views. Yet the Court in *Hammer* appears to have held that Congress cannot regulate even *inter*state commerce if the effect of that regulation is to control *intra*state activity. Why didn't the Court feel bound by *Champion* and related cases? Is the ground on which the Court distinguished those cases convincing?

b. "Two-Fold" Repugnancy

The Court stated that the act "in a two-fold sense is repugnant to the Constitution" because it both exceeded Congress's power under the Commerce

Clause and regulated a matter "purely local in character." Are these different grounds for unconstitutionality? If the Tenth Amendment is the basis for the latter form of repugnancy, does the Court's view represent a sensible interpretation of the Tenth Amendment?

President Franklin Delano Roosevelt (1882–1945)
Library of Congress

Hammer reveals that the Court in the first third of the twentieth century was increasingly emboldened in enforcing or perhaps imposing limits on Congress's power to regulate the economy. But at the same time that the Court was settling on a restrictive test for federal power, large majorities of voters in the country were beginning to look to the federal government to address serious economic problems. In the 1930s, the nation was in the worst economic depression in its history; over 30 million Americans—25 percent of the population—had no source of income at all. Franklin D. Roosevelt was elected President after promising to solve the economic crisis with strong national regulation of the marketplace. Roosevelt proposed the "New Deal," which would use federal law to restrain what he viewed as abusive labor practices and other excesses of big businesses. He also promised to promote healthy competition, to protect consumer and employee health, safety, and morality, and to create a social safety net. A sympathetic Congress enacted dozens of federal statutes to regulate numerous aspects of the national economy.

The Court initially responded to these aggressive assertions of federal authority by invalidating the statutes that came before it. In *Panama Refining Co. v. Ryan*, 293 U.S. 388 (1935), the Supreme Court struck down orders issued under the National Industrial Recovery Act of 1933 that sought to prohibit interstate and foreign trade in petroleum goods produced in excess of state quotas. In *Railroad Retirement Board v. Alton Railroad Co.*, 295 U.S. 330 (1935), the Court held that the Commerce Clause did not permit Congress to create a compulsory retirement and

> **Make the Connection**
>
> We will consider Congress's power to delegate decision-making authority, and the non-delegation doctrine specifically, in Chapter 6.

pension plan for all carriers subject to the Interstate Commerce Act. In *A.L.A. Schechter Poultry Corp. v. United States*, 295 U.S. 495 (1935), the Court struck down the National Industrial Recovery Act of 1933 (NIRA), which authorized the President to issue "codes of fair competition for * * * trade or industry." These codes, which were industry-specific and which the President typically issued after consultation with trade associations in the relevant industries, generally regulated employee wages and hours and identified and prohibited unfair trade practices. The Court concluded both that the Act unconstitutionally delegated legislative power and that the Act's authorization of regulation of employee wages and hours exceeded Congress's power under the Commerce Clause. In *United States v. Butler*, 297 U.S. 1 (1936), the Court struck down provisions in the Agricultural Adjustment Act of 1933 that conditionally spent money on farmers if they would limit their production. In *Carter v. Carter Coal Co.*, 298 U.S. 238 (1936), which we consider below, the Court held unconstitutional provisions in the Bituminous Coal Conservation Act of 1935 regulating wages of coal miners and other matters. In other cases, the Supreme Court struck down provisions of the Federal Farm Bankruptcy Act of 1934, see *Louisville Joint Stock Land Bank v. Radford*, 295 U.S. 555 (1935), and the Railroad Retirement Act of 1934, see Alton Railroad Co.

Congress and the President believed that these federal laws were crucial for relieving terrible economic conditions during the Great Depression, and they had enacted them with great popular support. The Supreme Court's decisions were thus highly frustrating and controversial. Never before had so many federal laws in short order been struck down as unconstitutional. The following case is illustrative of the others decided during this period.

CARTER V. CARTER COAL CO.

298 U.S. 238 (1936)

MR. JUSTICE SUTHERLAND delivered the opinion of the Court.

[President Roosevelt asked Congress to enact a regulatory scheme for the coal industry. Congress responded by enacting the Bituminous Coal Conservation Act of 1935. James W. Carter, a shareholder of the Carter Coal Co., immediately challenged the law on the ground, among others, that it exceeded Congress's power under the Commerce Clause. The statute created a Commission in the Department of Interior that was authorized to create a code applicable to the coal industry that would regulate the maximum hours and minimum wages of workers in coal mines and establish minimum prices for the sale of coal. The statute also conferred collective bargaining rights on coal workers. To ensure compliance, the statute provided that any coal company that refused to comply with the code would have to pay a substantial tax. Unlike the statute at issue in *Hammer*, the statute at issue in *Carter Coal* did not purport to regulate the interstate shipment of a particular good or type of goods. Instead, the Bituminous Coal Conservation Act regulated labor practices in a particular industry.]

That commodities produced or manufactured within a state are intended to be sold or transported outside the state does not render their production or manufacture subject to federal regulation under the commerce clause. * * * One who produces or manufactures a commodity, subsequently sold and shipped by him in interstate commerce, whether such sale and shipment were originally intended or not, has engaged in two distinct and separate activities. So far as he produces or manufactures a commodity, his business is purely local. So far as he sells and ships, or contracts to sell and ship, the commodity to customers in another state, he engages in interstate commerce. In respect of the former, he is subject only to regulation by the state; in respect of the latter, to regulation only by the federal government. Production is not commerce; but a step in preparation for commerce.

The employment of men, the fixing of their wages, hours of labor, and working conditions, the bargaining in respect of these things—whether carried on separately or collectively—each and all constitute intercourse for the purposes of production, not of trade. * * * [T]he effect of the labor provisions of the act, including those in respect of minimum wages, wage agreements, collective bargaining, and the Labor Board and its powers, primarily falls upon production and not upon commerce; and confirms the further resulting conclusion that production is a purely local activity. It follows that none of these essential antecedents of production constitutes a transaction in or forms any part of interstate commerce.

That the production of every commodity intended for interstate sale and transportation has some effect upon interstate commerce may be, if it has not already been, freely granted; and we are brought to the final and decisive inquiry, whether here that effect is direct * * * or indirect. The distinction is not formal, but substantial in the highest degree. Whether the effect of a given activity or condition is direct or indirect is not always easy to determine. The word "direct" implies that the activity or condition invoked or blamed shall operate proximately—not mediately, remotely, or collaterally—to produce the effect. It connotes the absence of an efficient intervening agency or condition. And the extent of the effect bears no logical relation to its character. The distinction between a direct and an indirect effect turns, not upon the magnitude of either the cause or the effect, but entirely upon the manner in which the effect has been brought about. If the production by one man of a single ton of coal intended for interstate sale and shipment, and actually so sold and shipped, affects interstate commerce indirectly, the effect does not become direct by multiplying the tonnage, or increasing the number of men employed, or adding to the expense or complexities of the business, or by all combined.

The relation of employer and employee is a local relation. * * * The wages are paid for the doing of local work. Working conditions are obviously local conditions. The employees are not engaged in or about commerce, but exclusively in producing a commodity. And the controversies and evils, which it is the object of the act to regulate and minimize, are local controversies and evils affecting local work undertaken to accomplish that local result. Such effect as they may have upon commerce, however extensive it may be, is secondary and indirect. An increase in the greatness of the effect adds to its importance. It does not alter its character.

JUSTICE CARDOZO, joined by JUSTICE BRANDEIS and JUSTICE STONE, dissenting.

To regulate the price for [interstate] transactions is to regulate commerce itself, and not alone its antecedent conditions or its ultimate consequences. Regulation of prices being an exercise of the commerce power in respect of interstate transactions, the question remains whether it comes within that power as applied to intrastate sales where interstate prices are directly or intimately affected. Mining and agriculture and manufacture are not interstate commerce considered by themselves, yet their relation to that commerce may be such that for the protection of the one there is need to regulate the other. Sometimes it is said that the relation must be "direct" to bring that power into play. In many circumstances such a description will be sufficiently precise to meet the needs of the occasion. But a great principle of constitutional law is not susceptible of comprehensive statement in an adjective. The underlying thought is merely this, that "the law is not indifferent to considerations of degree." At times * * * the waves of causation will have radiated so far that their undulatory motion, if discernible at all, will be too faint or obscure, too broken by cross-currents, to be heeded by the law. * * * Perhaps, if one group of adjectives is to be chosen in preference to another, "intimate" and "remote" will be found to be as good as any. At all events, "direct" and "indirect," even if accepted as sufficient, must not be read too narrowly. A survey of the cases shows that the words have been interpreted with suppleness of adaptation and flexibility of meaning. The power is as broad as the need that evokes it. * * * [T]he prices for intrastate sales of coal have so inescapable a relation to those for interstate sales that a system of regulation for transactions of the one class is necessary to give adequate protection to the system of regulation adopted for the other.

POINTS FOR DISCUSSION

a. Direct and Indirect Effects

The Court held that Congress has power to regulate only an intrastate activity's direct effects on interstate commerce. How should a Court decide whether effects are indirect? Does a statute guaranteeing the right of labor unions representing workers at large factories to strike regulate an activity with a direct effect or an indirect effect on interstate commerce?

b. Precedent

In *McCulloch*, the Court stated that where a law "is really calculated to effect any of the objects entrusted to the government, to undertake [to] inquire into the degree of its necessity would be to pass the line which circumscribes the judicial department, and to tread on legislative ground." Is the Court's approach in *Carter Coal* consistent with *McCulloch*? Was the statute challenged in *Carter Coal* "really calculated to effect" an object entrusted to the federal government? Was the Court's tolerance only for laws that regulate the "direct" effects of local activity on interstate commerce consistent with *McCulloch*'s deference to legislative judgments?

After the decision in *Carter Coal*, it seemed likely that the Court would strike down the central legislative measures of the New Deal—in particular, the National Labor Relations Act, which regulated the relationship between unions and management, and the Social Security Act—at the first opportunity. The Court's boldness in invalidating federal efforts to regulate the economy coincided with the Court's aggressiveness in striking down *state* laws regulating the workplace, the latter on the ground that they interfered with an unwritten freedom of contract protected by the Due Process Clause of the Fourteenth Amendment. (We will consider that line of cases, exemplified by the Court's decision in *Lochner v. New York*, in Volume 2.)

In response, shortly after his re-election in 1936, President Roosevelt announced his "Court-packing plan." Arguing that the Justices were too "aged and infirm," "laboring under a heavy burden," and generally out of touch with the complexities of the modern world, Roosevelt proposed adding a new seat on the Court for every Justice over age 70 who stayed on the bench, until the Court included fifteen members. Message to Congress (Feb. 5, 1937). At the time, six of the Justices—including the Justices who most consistently supported a restrictive

> **Make the Connection**
>
> We discussed ways in which Congress can control judicial decision-making in Chapter 2, when we considered Congress's power to control the jurisdiction of the federal courts. Is there any express or implicit constitutional prohibition on a plan to increase the size of the Supreme Court? What about a plan to decrease the size of the Supreme Court? Would it matter if Congress's motive were to respond to an increase in the federal courts' docket? Or if Congress's motive were to work a *de facto* reversal of unpopular Supreme Court precedent?

view of federal power—were over 70 years old. Roosevelt argued to the nation that we must "save the Constitution from the Court and the Court from itself." President Roosevelt's Fireside Chat on Reorganization of the Judiciary, (March 9, 1937).

Although Congress was controlled by Democrats sympathetic to President Roosevelt, the Senate, after lively debate, rejected a bill based on Roosevelt's proposal. By that point, however, there were already signs that the Court was changing course—as illustrated by the decision in *NLRB v. Jones & Laughlin Steel Corp.*, below, and *West Coast Hotel Co. v. Parrish*, which we take up in Volume 2. In those cases, Justice Roberts, who previously had voted with the Court's conservative majority, voted to uphold government claims of power. There is debate over whether Roberts's change of heart—the famous "switch in time that saved the Nine"—was in response to Roosevelt's Court-packing plan or instead was because of a change of mind independent of political pressure.

> **For More Information**
>
> For more information on the Court-Packing Plan and the "switch in time," see Michael Ariens, *A Thrice-Told Tale, or Felix the Cat*, 107 Harv. L. Rev. 620 (1994); Richard D. Friedman, *Switching Time and Other Thought Experiments: The Hughes Court and Constitutional Transformation*, 142 U. Pa. L. Rev. 1891 (1994).

But regardless of the cause, the Court began to chart a new approach that was highly deferential to the assertion of federal authority under the Commerce Clause.

3. The New Deal and Beyond: An Expansive View

NLRB v. Jones & Laughlin Steel Corp.

301 U.S. 1 (1937)

Mr. Chief Justice Hughes delivered the opinion of the Court.

In a proceeding under the National Labor Relations Act of 1935 the National Labor Relations Board found that the respondent, Jones & Laughlin Steel Corporation, had violated the act by * * * discriminating against members of the union with regard to hire and tenure of employment, and [by] coercing and intimidating its employees in order to interfere with their self-organization. The [NLRB] ordered the corporation to cease and desist from such discrimination and coercion [and] to offer reinstatement [to discharged employees].

[Jones & Laughlin manufactured iron and steel in plants in Pennsylvania and was the fourth largest producer of steel in the United States. With its nineteen subsidiaries, it owned and operated mines, lake and river transportation facilities, and terminal railroads located at its manufacturing plants. It owned or controlled mines in Michigan, Minnesota, Pennsylvania, and West Virginia, operated ships and railroads for the interstate transportation of raw materials, and maintained warehouses in Illinois, Michigan, Ohio, and Tennessee. It also operated steel fabricating shops in New York and Louisiana and owned or controlled stores and warehouses around the country and maintained sales offices in twenty United States cities.]

We think it clear that the [Act] may be construed so as to operate within the sphere of constitutional authority. The jurisdiction conferred upon the Board, and invoked in this instance, is found in section 10(a), which provides: "The Board is empowered * * * to prevent any person from engaging in any unfair labor practice * * * affecting commerce." * * * It is a familiar principle that acts which directly burden or obstruct interstate or foreign commerce, or its free flow, are within the reach of the congressional power. Acts having that effect are not rendered immune because they grow out of labor disputes. It is the effect upon commerce, not the source of the injury, which is the criterion. Whether or not particular action does affect commerce in such a close and intimate fashion as to be subject to federal control, and hence to lie within the authority conferred upon the Board, is left by the statute to be determined as individual cases arise.

Respondent * * * rests upon the proposition that manufacturing in itself is not commerce. * * * Although activities may be intrastate in character when separately considered, if they have such a close and substantial relation to interstate commerce that their control is essential or appropriate to protect that commerce from burdens and obstructions, Congress cannot be denied the power to exercise that control. Undoubtedly the scope of this power must be considered in the light of our dual system of government and may not be extended so as to embrace effects upon interstate commerce so indirect and remote that to embrace them, in view of our complex society, would effectually obliterate the distinction between what is national and what is local and create a completely centralized government. The question is necessarily one of degree.

That intrastate activities, by reason of close and intimate relation to interstate commerce, may fall within federal control is demonstrated in the case of carriers who are engaged in both interstate and intrastate transportation. *Shreveport Rate Case.* The close and intimate effect which brings the subject within the reach of federal power may be due to activities in relation to productive industry although the industry when separately viewed is local.

[T]he fact that the employees here concerned were engaged in production is not determinative. The question remains as to the effect upon interstate commerce of the labor practice involved. In [*Schechter*] we found that the effect there was so remote as to be beyond the federal power. To find "immediacy or directness" there was to find it "almost everywhere," a result inconsistent with the maintenance of our federal system. In [*Carter Coal*], the Court was of the opinion that the provisions of the statute relating to production were invalid upon several grounds [including] improper delegation of legislative power [and a violation of] due process. These cases are not controlling here.

FYI

In sections of the opinion not included in this casebook, the Court in *Carter Coal* concluded that the Bituminous Coal Conservation Act improperly delegated legislative authority and violated the Due Process Clause of the Fifth Amendment, subjects that we will consider in Chapter 6 and Volume 2, respectively. But in light of the section of the opinion in that case that is reproduced here, is it fair for the Court in *Jones & Laughlin* to suggest that the case's discussion of Congress's power under the Commerce Clause is not controlling?

[The] stoppage of [respondent's] operations by industrial strife would have a most serious effect upon interstate commerce. In view of respondent's far-flung activities, it is idle to say that the effect would be indirect or remote. It is obvious that it would be immediate and might be catastrophic. * * * When industries organize themselves on a national scale, making their relation to interstate commerce the dominant factor in their activities, how can it be maintained that their industrial labor relations constitute a forbidden field into which Congress may not enter when it is necessary to protect interstate commerce from the paralyzing consequences of industrial war? We have often said that interstate commerce itself is a practical conception. It is equally true that interferences with that commerce must be appraised by a judgment that does not ignore actual experience.

The steel industry is one of the great basic industries of the United States, with ramifying activities affecting interstate commerce at every point. [Respondent's enterprise] presents in a most striking way the close and intimate relation which a manufacturing industry may have to interstate commerce and we have no doubt that Congress had constitutional authority to safeguard the right of respondent's employees to self-organization and freedom in the choice of representatives for collective bargaining.

Practice Pointer

It is no coincidence that the first case under the NLRA to make it to the Court was an action against a giant steel conglomerate. The lawyers at the agency clearly concluded that there was a substantially better chance of prevailing on their constitutional defense of the statute if they sought to apply to it an employer whose activities so obviously affected interstate commerce.

MR. JUSTICE MCREYNOLDS, joined by JUSTICE VAN DEVANTER, JUSTICE SUTHERLAND, and JUSTICE BUTLER, dissenting.

Manifestly [the Court's] view of congressional power would extend it into almost every field of human industry. Any effect on interstate commerce by the discharge of employees shown here would be indirect and remote in the highest degree, as consideration of the facts will show. The immediate effect in the factory may be to create discontent among all those employed and a strike may follow, which, in turn, may result in reducing production, which ultimately may reduce the volume of goods moving in interstate commerce. By this chain of indirect and progressively remote events we finally reach the evil with which it is said the legislation under consideration undertakes to deal. A more remote and indirect interference with interstate commerce or a more definite invasion of the powers reserved to the states is difficult, if not impossible, to imagine. * * * Almost anything—marriage, birth, death—may in some fashion affect commerce. * * * It seems clear to us that Congress has transcended the powers granted.

UNITED STATES V. DARBY

312 U.S. 100 (1941)

MR. JUSTICE STONE delivered the opinion of the Court.

[Appellee was a lumber manufacturer in Georgia who was indicted for violating the Fair Labor Standards Act of 1938. The indictment charged that appellee shipped lumber in interstate commerce to customers outside the state, and that in the production of that lumber appellee employed workmen at less than the prescribed minimum wage or more than the prescribed maximum hours without payment to them of any wage for overtime. The indictment also charged that appellee employed workmen in the production of lumber for interstate commerce at wages below the minimum wage or for more than the maximum hours per week without payment to them of the prescribed overtime wage. The district court quashed the indictment.]

> **Take Note**
>
> The federal government generally cannot prosecute a defendant unless a grand jury indicts (i.e., formally charges) the defendant after finding sufficient evidence to believe that the defendant committed a crime. In this case, a grand jury indicted Darby for violating the Fair Labor Standards Act. Darby asked the District Court to quash the indictment (i.e., dismiss the charges). The District Court granted the request. The government appealed, making the government the "appellant" and Darby the "appellee."

The prohibition of shipment of the proscribed goods in interstate commerce. Section 15(a)(1) [of the FLSA] prohibits * * * the shipment in interstate commerce of goods produced for interstate commerce by employees whose wages and hours of employment do not conform to the requirements of the Act. * * * While manufacture is not of itself interstate commerce[,] the shipment of manufactured goods interstate is such commerce and the prohibition of such shipment by Congress is indubitably a regulation of the commerce. The power to regulate commerce is the power "to prescribe the rule by which commerce is to be governed." *Gibbons.* It extends not only to those regulations which aid, foster and protect the commerce, but embraces those which prohibit it.

But it is said that * * * while the prohibition is nominally a regulation of the commerce its motive or purpose is regulation of wages and hours of persons engaged in manufacture, the control of which has been reserved to the states and upon which Georgia and some of the states of destination have placed no restriction * * *. The power of Congress over interstate commerce * * * is not a forbidden invasion of state power merely because either its motive or its consequence is to restrict the use of articles of commerce within the states of destination * * *. The motive and purpose of a regulation of interstate commerce are matters for the legislative judgment upon the exercise of which the Constitution places no restriction and over which the courts are given no control. * * * [W]e conclude that the prohibition of the shipment interstate of goods produced under the forbidden substandard labor conditions is within the constitutional authority of Congress.

In the more than a century which has elapsed since the decision of *Gibbons v. Ogden*, these principles of constitutional interpretation have been so long and repeatedly recognized by this Court as applicable to the Commerce Clause, that there would be little occasion for repeating them now were it not for the decision of this Court twenty-two years ago in *Hammer v. Dagenhart.* * * * The reasoning and conclusion of the Court's opinion there cannot be reconciled with the conclusion which we have reached, that the power of Congress under the Commerce Clause is plenary to exclude any article from interstate commerce subject only to the specific prohibitions of the Constitution. * * * The distinction on which the decision was rested that Congressional power to prohibit interstate commerce is limited to articles which in themselves have some harmful or deleterious property—a distinction which was novel when made and unsupported by any provision of the Constitution—has long since been abandoned. The thesis of the opinion that the motive of the prohibition or its effect to control in some measure the use or production within the states of the article thus excluded from the commerce can operate to deprive the regulation of its constitutional authority has long since ceased to have force. * * * The conclusion is inescapable that *Hammer v. Dagenhart* was a departure from the principles which have prevailed in the interpretation of the commerce clause both before and since the decision and that such vitality, as a precedent, as it then had has long since been exhausted. It should be and now is overruled.

Validity of the wage and hour requirements. Section 15(a)(2) * * * require[s] employers to conform to the wage and hour provisions with respect to all employees engaged in the production of goods for interstate commerce. * * * The power of Congress over interstate commerce is not confined to the regulation of commerce among the states. It extends to those activities intrastate which so affect interstate commerce or the exercise of the power of Congress over it as to make regulation of them appropriate means to the attainment of a legitimate end, the exercise of the granted power of Congress to regulate interstate commerce. *McCulloch.* * * * Congress * * * may choose the means reasonably adapted to the attainment of the permitted end, even though they involve control of intrastate activities. [The Court has sustained congressional] regulation of intrastate transactions which are so commingled with or related to interstate commerce that all must be regulated if the interstate commerce is to be effectively

Take Note

In this paragraph, the Supreme Court adopts two important principles regarding Congress's power to regulate commerce. The first principle (sometimes called the "affectation" or "effects" principle) is that Congress can regulate not only interstate commerce itself, but also intrastate activities that substantially *affect* commerce. The second principle (sometimes called the "aggregation" principle) is that an activity's effect on commerce is determined not by looking at the effect of a single instance of the activity but instead by looking at the effect of the activity when undertaken by everyone across the whole country.

controlled. [*Shreveport Rate Case.*] * * * The means adopted by § 15(a)(2) for the protection of interstate commerce by the suppression of the production of the condemned goods for interstate commerce is so related to the commerce and so affects it as to be within the reach of the commerce power. Congress * * * recognized that in present day industry, competition by a small part may affect the whole and that the total effect of the competition of many small producers may be great.

So far as *Carter Coal* is inconsistent with this conclusion, its doctrine is limited in principle by the decisions [such as *Jones & Laughlin,*] which we follow.

Our conclusion is unaffected by the Tenth Amendment which provides: "The powers not delegated to the United States by the Constitution, nor prohibited by it to the States, are reserved to the States respectively, or to the people." The amendment states but a truism that all is retained which has not been surrendered. There is nothing in the history of its adoption to suggest that it was more than declaratory of the relationship between the national and state governments as it had been established by the Constitution before the amendment or that its purpose was other than to allay fears that the new national government might seek to exercise powers not granted, and that the states might not be able to exercise fully their reserved powers.

> **Take Note**
>
> What does the Court mean when it says the Tenth Amendment merely states a "truism"? And of what part of the Constitution is the principle stated in the Tenth Amendment merely declaratory?

Reversed.

POINTS FOR DISCUSSION

a. More Switches in Time

The Court decided *Jones & Laughlin* in 1937 by a slim 5–4 majority. Yet *Darby,* which was decided only four years later, was unanimous. What do you suppose accounts for the sudden consensus on the Court?

b. "Constitutional Moments"

Article V provides the procedure for amending the Constitution, which requires ratification by the legislatures of (or conventions in) three-quarters of the states. Perhaps because the threshold for amendment is so high, the Constitution has been amended very few times in American history. Of the 27 amendments, ten were ratified together as the Bill of Rights (and an eleventh, which was proposed with the original ten, was ratified years later as the Twenty-Seventh Amendment); three were ratified as part of the process of Reconstruction; and two—the Eighteenth and Twenty-First Amendments, relating to prohibition—cancel each other out.

Is it possible for the Constitution to be amended outside of the formal procedures identified in Article V? Bruce Ackerman has argued that the political consensus that produced the New Deal—and the Court's ratification of Congress's authority to enact it—amounted to a "constitutional moment" that effectively inaugurated a new constitutional regime. See Bruce Ackerman, *We the People: Foundations* (1991). Even assuming that the Constitution can be changed in this manner, do the New Deal cases obviously depart from the principles that the Court had early on established to delimit Congress's power under the Commerce Clause?

c. The "Affectation Doctrine" or the "Effects Test"

The Court stated that Congress may regulate not only interstate commerce itself, but also "those activities intrastate which so affect interstate commerce or the exercise of the power of Congress over it as to make regulation of them appropriate means to a legitimate end." Subsequent cases have sometimes referred to the principle that Congress may regulate intrastate activities that affect interstate commerce as the "affectation doctrine," see, e.g., *Prudential Ins. Co. v. Benjamin*, 328 U.S. 408, 423 (1946), which we consider in Chapter 4, or the "effects test," see, e.g., *United States v. Lopez*, 514 U.S. 549 (1995), which we consider later in this chapter.

WICKARD V. FILBURN

317 U.S. 111 (1942)

MR. JUSTICE JACKSON delivered the opinion of the Court.

[Filburn sought to enjoin enforcement of a $117 penalty imposed under the Agricultural Adjustment Act of 1938 upon that part of his 1941 wheat crop that was in excess of the marketing quota established for his farm. Pursuant to the Act, the Secretary of Agriculture had established quotas for individual farms in order to "control the volume moving in interstate and foreign commerce in order to avoid surpluses and shortages and the consequent abnormally low or high wheat prices and obstructions to commerce." Filburn's allotment for 1941 was 223 bushels, but he exceeded that quota by 239 bushels. Filburn used the wheat that he grew on his farm to feed livestock, to seed his new crops, to make flour for consumption at home, and to sell on the market. Filburn argued that he intended to use some of the excess for personal consumption, and he challenged the Act as applied to wheat that he produced for personal consumption.]

> **FYI**
>
> Roscoe Filburn's farm had been in his family for five generations. Proud of his self-sufficiency, Filburn boasted that he had never had to work for another man. When Filburn planted his crop in the spring of 1941, the penalty for exceeding the production quota was merely 15 cents per bushel, and many farmers planted more than they were allowed. Secretary of Agriculture Claude Wickard even made a radio address encouraging farmers to grow more wheat to "provide insurance against food shortages" as World War II was being fought in Europe. But at the end of May 1941, with the crops in the ground, the federal government more than tripled the penalty, raising it to 49 cents. Incensed by the unfairness of this surprise move, Filburn argued that the increased penalty violated due process—and prevailed at trial. The Commerce Clause issue arose only on appeal. For many interesting facts about the case, see Jim Chen, "The Story of Wickard v. Filburn: Agriculture, Aggregation, and Congressional Power over Commerce," in *Constitutional Law Stories* 83 (Michael C. Dorf ed., 2004).

The question would merit little consideration since our decision in *Darby*, sustaining the federal power to regulate production of goods for commerce[,] except for the fact that this Act extends federal regulation to production not intended in any part for commerce but wholly for consumption on the farm. * * * Appellee says that this is a regulation of production and consumption of wheat [and that the effects of such activities] upon interstate commerce are at most "indirect." * * * [But once] an economic measure of the reach of the power granted to Congress in the Commerce Clause is accepted, questions of federal power cannot be decided simply by finding the activity in question to be "production" nor can consideration of its economic effects be foreclosed by calling them "indirect." * * * That an activity is of local character may help in a doubtful case to determine whether Congress intended to reach it. * * * But even if appellee's activity be local and though it may not be regarded as commerce, it may still, whatever its nature, be reached by Congress if it exerts a substantial economic effect on interstate commerce and this irrespective of whether such effect is what might at some earlier time have been defined as "direct" or "indirect."

Commerce among the states in wheat is large and important. Although wheat is raised in every state but one, production in most states is not equal to consumption. [Some states produce more wheat than is needed in the state, and others produce less than is needed to satisfy in-state demand.] The decline in the export trade has left a large surplus in production which in connection with an abnormally large supply of wheat and other grains in recent years caused congestion in a number of markets; tied up railroad cars; and caused elevators in some instances to turn away grains, and railroads to institute embargoes to prevent further congestion. In the absence of regulation the price of wheat in the United States would be much affected by world conditions. During 1941 producers who cooperated with the Agricultural Adjustment program received an average price on the farm of about $1.16 a bushel as compared with the world market price of 40 cents a bushel.

The maintenance by government regulation of a price for wheat undoubtedly can be accomplished as effectively by sustaining or increasing the demand as by limiting the supply. The effect of the statute before us is to restrict the amount which may be produced for market and the extent as well to which one may forestall resort to the market by producing to meet his own needs. That appellee's own contribution to the demand for wheat may be trivial by itself is not enough to remove him from the scope of federal regulation where, as here, his contribution, taken together with that of many others similarly situated, is far from trivial.

It is well established by decisions of this Court that the power to regulate commerce includes the power to regulate the prices at which commodities in that commerce are dealt in and practices affecting such prices. One of the primary purposes of the Act in question was to increase the market price of wheat and to that end to limit the volume thereof that could affect the market. It can hardly be denied that a factor of such volume and variability as home-consumed wheat would have a substantial influence on price and market conditions. This may arise because being in marketable condition such wheat overhangs the market and if induced by rising prices tends to flow into the market and check price increases. But if we assume that it is never marketed, it supplies a need of the man who grew it which would otherwise be reflected by purchases in the open market. Home-grown wheat in this sense competes with wheat in commerce. The stimulation of commerce is a use of the regulatory function quite as definitely as prohibitions or restrictions thereon. This record leaves us in no doubt that Congress may properly have considered that wheat consumed on the farm where grown if wholly outside the scheme of regulation would have a substantial effect in defeating and obstructing its purpose to stimulate trade therein at increased prices.

It is said, however, that this Act, forcing some farmers into the market to buy what they could provide for themselves, is an unfair promotion of the markets and prices of specializing wheat growers. It is of the essence of regulation that it lays a restraining hand on the self-interest of the regulated and that advantages from the regulation commonly fall to others. The conflicts of economic interest between the regulated and those who advantage by it are wisely left under our system to resolution by the Congress under its more flexible and responsible legislative process. Such conflicts rarely lend themselves to judicial determination.

And with the wisdom, workability, or fairness, of the plan of regulation we have nothing to do.

POINTS FOR DISCUSSION

a. The Aggregation Principle

Filburn's use of 239 bushels of home-grown wheat obviously did not have any discernable impact on the two-billion bushel interstate market for wheat. The Court, however, viewed Filburn's activity "taken together with that of many others similarly situated"—that is, the Court aggregated the effect on interstate commerce of all potential local use of home-grown wheat in excess of the statutory quota. If the Court instead had held that the Act could not be applied to Filburn's use of the wheat, on the ground that his use itself had no meaningful impact on interstate commerce, what would that have meant for the quota scheme as a whole?

b. The Rational-Basis Test

Wickard is emblematic of the "rational-basis" approach to reviewing exercises of the Commerce power, under which the Court asks whether Congress had a rational basis for concluding that the regulated conduct, when viewed in the aggregate, has a substantial effect on interstate commerce. Applying the aggregation principle and the rational-basis test, is there any local, intrastate conduct that is not within Congress's power to regulate?

Some students react to *Wickard v. Filburn* with surprise and skepticism. They wonder how the federal government can properly be called a government of limited powers if Congress can regulate how much wheat a person grows on his own property for his own consumption. As we will see shortly, some Justices have questioned whether the Supreme Court made a wrong turn by interpreting the Commerce power to allow Congress to regulate intrastate economic activities so long as in the aggregate those activities may affect interstate commerce. But before passing final judgment on the effects test and the aggregation principle, consider some of what Congress has accomplished with these broad powers.

In 1964, Congress enacted the Civil Rights Act, a sweeping law that sought to prohibit discrimination in several settings. Title II of the Act prohibited discrimination on the basis of "race, color, religion, or national origin" in places of "public accommodation." Title II specified that the facilities to which the prohibition applied included inns, hotels, motels, restaurants, cafeterias, lunch rooms, lunch counters, theaters, concert halls, and sports arenas. It further defined places of public accommodation as places whose "operations affect commerce," which included places that "offer[ ] to serve interstate travelers" or places where "a substantial portion of the food [served] has moved in commerce."

The Act thus applied to many private—that is, non-state—actors. Because the Court has long interpreted the Fourteenth Amendment to apply only to state action, in enacting the Civil Rights Act Congress relied on its authority under the Commerce Clause. The Court upheld Title II of the Civil Rights Act in the two cases that follow.

Make the Connection

We consider the Fourteenth Amendment, Congress's power to enforce the Fourteenth Amendment, and the "state action" doctrine in Volume 2.

HEART OF ATLANTA MOTEL, INC. v. UNITED STATES

379 U.S. 241 (1964)

MR. JUSTICE CLARK delivered the opinion of the Court.

Appellant owns and operates the Heart of Atlanta Motel which has 216 rooms available to transient guests [and which is] readily accessible to interstate highways * * *. Appellant solicits patronage from outside the State of Georgia through various national advertising media, including magazines of national circulation; it maintains over 50 billboards and highway signs within the State, soliciting patronage for the motel; it accepts convention trade from outside Georgia and approximately 75% of its registered guests are from out of State. Prior to passage of [Title II of the Civil Rights Act of 1964] the motel had followed a practice of refusing to rent rooms to Negroes, and it alleged that it intended to continue to do so. In an effort to perpetuate that policy this suit was filed.

While the Act as adopted carried no congressional findings the record of its passage through each house is replete with evidence of the burdens that discrimination by race or color places upon interstate commerce. [The] testimony included the fact that our people have become increasingly mobile with millions of people of all races traveling from State to State; that Negroes in particular have been the subject of discrimination in transient accommodations, having to travel great distances to secure the same; that often they have been unable to obtain accommodations and have had to call upon friends to put them up overnight; and that these conditions had become so acute as

Food for Thought

The Court appears to rely heavily on evidence in the legislative record that Congress amassed in the course of enacting the statute. Given the standard that the Court applied in *Jones & Laughlin*, *Darby*, and *Wickard* for reviewing exercises of the commerce power, would it have mattered if Congress had not held any hearings or adduced any evidence before enacting the statutes?

to require the listing of available lodging for Negroes in a special guidebook which was itself "dramatic testimony to the difficulties" Negroes encounter in travel. These exclusionary practices were found to be nationwide * * *. This testimony indicated a qualitative as well as quantitative effect on interstate travel by Negroes. The former was the obvious impairment of the Negro traveler's pleasure and convenience that resulted when he continually was uncertain of finding lodging. As for the latter, there was evidence that this uncertainty stemming from racial discrimination had the effect of discouraging travel on the part of a substantial portion of the Negro community. [T]he voluminous testimony presents overwhelming evidence that discrimination by hotels and motels impedes interstate travel.

In framing Title II of this Act Congress was * * * dealing with what it considered a moral problem. But that fact does not detract from the overwhelming evidence of the disruptive effect that racial discrimination has had on commercial intercourse. It was this burden which empowered Congress to enact appropriate legislation, and, given this basis for the exercise of its power, Congress was not restricted by the fact that the particular obstruction to interstate commerce with which it was dealing was also deemed a moral and social wrong.

It is said that the operation of the motel here is of a purely local character. But, assuming this to be true, * * * the power of Congress to promote interstate commerce also includes the power to regulate the local incidents thereof, including local activities in both the States of origin and destination, which might have a substantial and harmful effect upon that commerce. One need only examine the evidence which we have discussed above to see that Congress may—as it has—prohibit racial discrimination by motels serving travelers, however "local" their operations may appear.

How obstructions in commerce may be removed—what means are to be employed—is within the sound and exclusive discretion of the Congress. It is subject only to one caveat—that the means chosen by it must be reasonably adapted to the end permitted by the Constitution. We cannot say that its choice here was not so adapted.

[The concurring opinions of JUSTICES BLACK, DOUGLAS, and GOLDBERG are reprinted below, after the Court's opinion in *Katzenbach v. McClung*.]

KATZENBACH V. MCCLUNG

379 U.S. 294 (1964)

MR. JUSTICE CLARK delivered the opinion of the Court.

Ollie's Barbecue is a family-owned restaurant in Birmingham, Alabama, specializing in barbecued meats and homemade pies, with a seating capacity of 220 customers. It is located on a state highway 11 blocks from an interstate one and a somewhat greater distance from railroad and bus stations. The restaurant caters to a family and white-collar trade with a take-out service for Negroes. It employs 36 persons, two-thirds of whom are Negroes.

In the 12 months preceding the passage of the Act, the restaurant purchased locally approximately $150,000 worth of food, $69,683 or 46% of which was meat that it bought from a local supplier who had procured it from outside the State. The District Court expressly found that a substantial portion of the food served in the restaurant had moved in interstate commerce. The restaurant has refused to serve Negroes in its dining accommodations since its original opening in 1927, and since July 2, 1964, it has been operating in violation of the Act. The court below concluded that if it were required to serve Negroes it would lose a substantial amount of business.

[The relevant provisions of Title II] place any "restaurant * * * principally engaged in selling food for consumption on the premises" under the Act [if] "a substantial portion of the food which it serves * * * has moved in commerce." Ollie's Barbecue admits that it is covered by these provisions of the Act. * * * There is no claim that interstate travelers frequented the restaurant. The sole question, therefore, narrows down to whether Title II, as applied to a restaurant annually receiving about $70,000 worth of food which has moved in commerce, is a valid exercise of the power of Congress.

The [legislative] record is replete with testimony of the burdens placed on interstate commerce by racial discrimination in restaurants. A comparison of per capita spending by Negroes in restaurants, theaters, and like establishments indicated less spending, after discounting income differences, in areas where discrimination is widely practiced. This condition, which was especially aggravated in the South, was attributed * * * to racial

> **Take Note**
>
> The Court in *McClung* considered an "as-applied" challenge to Title II of the Civil Rights Act—that is, a claim that the statute could not constitutionally be applied in this fashion, even if Congress generally had power to regulate others subject to the statute. If the Court had concluded that the statute was unconstitutional as applied to Ollie's Barbeque, then what would have been the implications for the constitutionality of the statute as applied in other contexts?

segregation. This diminutive spending springing from a refusal to serve Negroes and their total loss as customers has, regardless of the absence of direct evidence, a close connection to interstate commerce. The fewer customers a restaurant enjoys the less food it sells and consequently the less it buys. * * * In addition, there were many references to discriminatory situations causing wide unrest and having a depressant effect on general business conditions in the respective communities. Moreover there was an impressive array of testimony that discrimination in restaurants had a direct and highly restrictive effect upon interstate travel by Negroes[, for] one can hardly travel without eating. Likewise, it was said, that discrimination deterred professional, as well as skilled, people from moving into areas where such practices occurred and thereby caused industry to be reluctant to establish there.

We believe that this testimony afforded ample basis for the conclusion that established restaurants in such areas sold less interstate goods because of the discrimination, that interstate travel was obstructed directly by it, that business in general suffered and that many new businesses refrained from establishing there as a result of it. It goes without saying that, viewed in isolation, the volume of food purchased by Ollie's Barbecue from sources supplied from out of state was insignificant when compared with the total foodstuffs moving in commerce. But, [as we held in] *Wickard*, "[that] contribution, taken together with that of many others similarly situated, is far from trivial."

Appellees * * * object to the omission of a provision for a case-by-case determination—judicial or administrative—that racial discrimination in a particular restaurant affects commerce. But * * * Congress has determined for itself that refusals of service to Negroes have imposed burdens both upon the interstate flow of food and upon the movement of products generally. Of course, the mere fact that Congress has said when particular activity shall be deemed to affect commerce does not preclude further examination by this Court. But where we find that the legislators, in light of the facts and testimony before them, have a rational basis for finding a chosen regulatory scheme necessary to the protection of commerce, our investigation is at an end. The only remaining question—one answered in the affirmative by the court below—is whether the particular restaurant either serves or offers to serve interstate travelers or serves food a substantial portion of which has moved in interstate commerce. The Civil Rights Act of 1964, as here applied, we find to be plainly appropriate in the resolution of what the Congress found to be a national commercial problem of the first magnitude.

[The following opinions apply as well to *Heart of Atlanta Motel*, above.]

MR. JUSTICE BLACK, concurring.

I recognize that every remote, possible, speculative effect on commerce should not be accepted as an adequate constitutional ground to uproot and throw into the discard all our traditional distinctions between what is purely local, and therefore controlled by state laws, and what affects the national interest and is therefore subject to control by federal laws. I recognize too that some isolated and remote lunchroom which sells only to local people and buys almost all its supplies in the locality may possibly be beyond the reach of the power of Congress to regulate commerce, just as such an establishment is not covered by the present Act.

> **Food for Thought**
>
> Applying the majority's approach, would a restaurant that "sells only to local people and buys almost all its supplies in the locality" really be beyond Congress's power to regulate? Wouldn't the effects on spending by black customers and on interstate travel by black people be similar to those that the Court details with respect to restaurants that discriminate and that receive some percentage of their food from out of state?

But in deciding the constitutional power of Congress in cases like the two before us we do not consider the effect on interstate commerce of only one isolated, individual, local event, without regard to the fact that this single local event when added to many others of a similar nature may impose a burden on interstate commerce by reducing its volume or distorting its flow.

MR. JUSTICE DOUGLAS, concurring.

[T]he result reached by the Court is for me much more obvious as a protective measure under the Fourteenth Amendment than under the Commerce Clause. For the former deals with the constitutional status of the individual[,] not with the impact on commerce of local activities or vice versa. A decision based on the Fourteenth Amendment would have a more settling effect, making unnecessary litigation over whether a particular restaurant or inn is within the commerce definitions of the Act or whether a particular customer is an interstate traveler. Under my construction, the Act would apply to all customers in all the enumerated places of public accommodation. And that construction would put an end to all obstructionist strategies and finally close one door on a bitter chapter in American history.

MR. JUSTICE GOLDBERG, concurring.

The primary purpose of the Civil Rights Act of 1964 * * * is the vindication of human dignity and not mere economics. [In my view,] § 1 of the Fourteenth Amendment guarantees to all Americans the constitutional right "to be treated as equal members of the community with respect to public accommodations," and

* * * "Congress has authority under § 5 of the Fourteenth Amendment, or under the Commerce Clause, to implement [those] rights * * *."

POINTS FOR DISCUSSION

a. Food That Has "Moved in Commerce"

On what theory of the Commerce Clause is Congress permitted to regulate a restaurant that serves food that itself has moved in interstate commerce? Can Congress criminalize the theft of a car on the theory that the car's muffler moved in interstate commerce before it was installed on the car? In light of today's economy, if Congress can regulate on this theory, is there anything that it can't regulate?

Or is the point that Congress can regulate local conduct on the theory that such conduct, when viewed in the aggregate, affects interstate commerce? If that is the theory on which the Court upheld Congress's assertion of power, then wouldn't the statute be constitutional even if there were no requirement that the restaurant serve food that has moved in interstate commerce?

b. Congressional Findings

What level of deference should the Court accord to "findings" that Congress makes in support of the enactment of a statute? On some accounts, because the courts are limited to the actual cases or controversies presented to them, Congress, which can hear wide-ranging testimony, is a better fact-finder than the courts. See, e.g., Lon Fuller, *The Forms and Limits of Adjudication*, 92 Harv. L. Rev. 353, 394–96 (1978). But can't Congress essentially "find" anything it wants? Can't Members of Congress simply stack the evidence presented in the fact-finding process to preordain the conclusion that they prefer?

c. An Odd Way of Looking at Things?

Under the effects test, Congress may regulate almost any subject, so long as Congress can link the activity somehow to commerce. But attempting to link all subjects of regulation to commerce causes Congress and the Supreme Court to look at social problems in an odd way—a way that perhaps only lawyers understand. Notice that in the last sentence of the majority opinion in *McClung*, the Court said that Congress may forbid racial discrimination in restaurants because this discrimination is a "national commercial problem of the first magnitude." Is that how you would have described the problem of racial discrimination before you started reading this chapter of the casebook? ("Hey, Ollie, stop that! You might affect interstate commerce!") Would the Constitution be improved by adding a provision that would allow Congress to ban racial discrimination in a more straightforward way? Does it include such a provision?

d. The Civil Rights Struggle and the Constitution

Congress enacted the Civil Rights Act ten years after the Court's decision in *Brown v. Board of Education*, which declared racial segregation in public schools unconstitutional. (We consider *Brown* in Volume 2.) As we saw in *Cooper v. Aaron* in Chapter 2, *Brown* was met in the South with fierce resistance, and public and private discrimination on the basis of race continued. Notwithstanding the willingness of several Justices in *Heart of Atlanta Motel* and *McClung* to revisit the Court's precedents, the Court had long read the Fourteenth Amendment's Equal Protection Clause to prohibit only discrimination by state, rather than private, actors. The Court thus relied in those cases on Congress's power under the Commerce Clause. Yet if Congress's power under the Commerce Clause extends to prohibiting local discrimination by private actors, then it is difficult to conceive of any limits on Congress's Commerce power. Would it have been feasible in the 1960s to amend the Constitution to authorize Congress to prohibit discrimination by private actors? If not, what does that suggest about the propriety of stretching the Commerce power to embrace the Civil Rights Act?

4. Recent Cases: New Limits—or Old?

From 1937 to 1995, the Court did not invalidate any federal laws on the ground that they exceeded Congress's power under the Commerce Clause. During that time, as evidenced by the decisions in *Wickard*, *Heart of Atlanta Motel*, and *McClung*, the Court suggested that its role in enforcing federalism-based limits on federal power was sharply circumscribed. (During that time, even the occasional suggestions to the contrary—such as the Court's decision in *National League of Cities v. Usery*, which we will consider later in this chapter—were quickly disavowed.) A generation of students learned that there were virtually no—and perhaps actually no—limits on Congress's power to regulate pursuant to the Commerce Clause. In 1995, however, the Court invalidated a federal law on the ground that it exceeded Congress's power under the Commerce Clause.

UNITED STATES V. LOPEZ

514 U.S. 549 (1995)

CHIEF JUSTICE REHNQUIST delivered the opinion of the Court.

In the Gun-Free School Zones Act of 1990, [Pub. L. 101–647, sec. 1702, 104 Stat. 4789, 4844 (1990) (codified, as amended, at 18 U.S.C. § 922(q)),] Congress made it a federal offense "for any individual knowingly to possess a firearm at a place that the individual knows, or has reasonable cause to believe, is a school zone." [The statute defined "school zone" as "in, or on the grounds of, a public,

Take Note

Possession of a gun near a school was illegal under Texas law, as well. What does this suggest about the necessity of the federal statute at issue in this case? Should the content of state law be relevant to determining the scope of Congress's power under the Commerce Clause?

parochial or private school" or "within a distance of 1,000 feet from the grounds of a public, parochial or private school."] On March 10, 1992, respondent, who was then a 12th-grade student, arrived at Edison High School in San Antonio, Texas, carrying a concealed .38-caliber handgun and five bullets. He was arrested and charged under Texas law with firearm possession on school premises.

The next day, the state charges were dismissed after federal agents charged respondent by complaint with violating the Gun-Free School Zones Act of 1990. [Respondent moved to dismiss his federal indictment. The District Court denied the motion, and respondent was convicted and sentenced to six months' imprisonment and two years' supervised release.]

Practice Pointer

Some of the Commerce Clause challenges that we have seen so far were filed as declaratory judgment actions by parties who sought to avoid the requirements of federal law. The respondent in this case, in contrast, raised his constitutional challenge as a defense to prosecution for violation of the federal law. Do you think that the procedural posture in which the challenge was raised in this case was likely to make the Court more sympathetic to the respondent's claims, or less?

We start with first principles. The Constitution creates a Federal Government of enumerated powers. As James Madison wrote: "The powers delegated by the proposed Constitution to the federal government are few and defined. Those which are to remain in the State governments are numerous and indefinite." The Federalist No. 45. * * * *Jones & Laughlin Steel, Darby,* and *Wickard* ushered in an era of Commerce Clause jurisprudence that greatly expanded the previously defined authority of Congress under that Clause. In part, this was a recognition of the great changes that had occurred in the way business was carried on in this country. Enterprises that had once been local or at most regional in nature had become national in scope. But the doctrinal change also reflected a view that earlier Commerce Clause cases artificially had constrained the authority of Congress to regulate interstate commerce. But even these modern-era precedents which have expanded congressional power under the Commerce Clause confirm that this power is subject to outer limits. [T]he Court has heeded [those warnings] and undertaken to decide whether a rational basis existed for concluding that a regulated activity sufficiently affected interstate commerce.

Consistent with this structure, we have identified three broad categories of activity that Congress may regulate under its commerce power. First, Congress may regulate the use of the channels of interstate commerce. [See *Darby*; *Heart of Atlanta Motel*.] Second, Congress is empowered to regulate and protect the instrumentalities of interstate commerce, or persons or things in interstate commerce, even though the threat may come only from intrastate activities. [*Shreveport Rate Case*.] Finally, Congress' commerce authority includes the power to regulate those activities having a substantial relation to interstate commerce, *i.e.*, those activities that substantially affect interstate commerce. [*Jones & Laughlin*.]

We now turn to consider the power of Congress, in the light of this framework, to enact § 922(q). The first two categories of authority may be quickly disposed of: § 922(q) is not a regulation of the use of the channels of interstate commerce, nor is it an attempt to prohibit the interstate transportation of a commodity through the channels of commerce; nor can § 922(q) be justified as a regulation by which Congress has sought to protect an instrumentality of interstate commerce or a thing in interstate commerce. Thus, if § 922(q) is to be sustained, it must be under the third category as a regulation of an activity that substantially affects interstate commerce.

First, we have upheld a wide variety of congressional Acts regulating intrastate economic activity where we have concluded that the activity substantially affected interstate commerce. * * * Where economic activity substantially affects interstate commerce, legislation regulating that activity will be sustained. Even *Wickard*, which is perhaps the most far reaching example of Commerce Clause authority over intrastate activity, involved economic activity in a way that the possession of a gun in a school zone does not. Section 922(q) is a criminal statute that by its terms has nothing to do with "commerce" or any sort of economic enterprise, however broadly one might define those terms. Section 922(q) is not an essential part of a larger regulation of economic activity, in which the regulatory scheme could be undercut unless the intrastate activity were regulated. It cannot, therefore, be sustained under our cases upholding regulations of activities that arise out of or are connected with a commercial transaction, which viewed in the aggregate, substantially affects interstate commerce.

Second, § 922(q) contains no jurisdictional element which would ensure, through case-by-case inquiry, that the firearm possession in question affects interstate commerce. * * *

Take Note

When the Court says that the statute contains no "jurisdictional element," it means that the statute requires no express link to interstate commerce. For example, the statute does not limit its application to guns that were produced for an interstate market, guns that were shipped in interstate commerce, or guns that somehow affect interstate commerce.

We agree with the Government that Congress normally is not required to make formal findings as to the substantial burdens that an activity has on interstate commerce. But to the extent that congressional findings would enable us to evaluate the legislative judgment that the activity in question substantially affected interstate commerce, even though no such substantial effect was visible to the naked eye, they are lacking here.

The Government's essential contention, *in fine*, is that we may determine here that § 922(q) is valid because possession of a firearm in a local school zone does indeed substantially affect interstate commerce. The Government argues that possession of a firearm in a school zone may result in violent crime and that violent crime can be expected to affect the functioning of the national economy in two ways. First, the costs of violent crime are substantial, and, through the mechanism of insurance, those costs are spread throughout the population. Second, violent crime reduces the willingness of individuals to travel to areas within the country that are perceived to be unsafe. The Government also argues that the presence of guns in schools poses a substantial threat to the educational process by threatening the learning environment. A handicapped educational process, in turn, will result in a less productive citizenry. That, in turn, would have an adverse effect on the Nation's economic well-being. As a result, the Government argues that Congress could rationally have concluded that § 922(q) substantially affects interstate commerce.

We pause to consider the implications of the Government's arguments. The Government admits, under its "costs of crime" reasoning, that Congress could regulate not only all violent crime, but all activities that might lead to violent crime, regardless of how tenuously they relate to interstate commerce. Similarly, under the Government's "national productivity" reasoning, Congress could regulate any activity that it found was related to the economic productivity of individual citizens: family law (including marriage, divorce, and child custody), for example. Under the theories that the Government presents in support of § 922(q), it is difficult to perceive any limitation on federal power, even in areas such as criminal law enforcement or education where States historically have been sovereign. Thus, if we were to accept the Government's arguments, we are hard pressed to posit any activity by an individual that Congress is without power to regulate.

> **Take Note**
>
> Is the relationship between the regulated conduct and interstate commerce in this case any more attenuated than the relationship between the conduct at issue in *Heart of Atlanta Motel* and *McClung* and interstate commerce?

Although Justice BREYER argues that acceptance of the Government's rationales would not authorize a general federal police power, he is unable to identify any activity that the States may regulate but Congress may not. * * * Justice BREYER focuses, for the most part, on the threat that firearm possession in and near schools poses to the educational process and the potential economic consequences flowing from that threat. Specifically, the dissent reasons that (1) gun-related violence is a serious problem; (2) that problem, in turn, has an adverse effect on classroom learning; and (3) that adverse effect on classroom learning, in turn, represents a substantial threat to trade and commerce. This analysis would be equally applicable, if not more so, to subjects such as family law and direct regulation of education.

Justice BREYER rejects our reading of precedent and argues that "Congress could rationally conclude that schools fall on the commercial side of the line." [D]epending on the level of generality, any activity can be looked upon as commercial. Under the dissent's rationale, Congress could just as easily look at child rearing as "fall[ing] on the commercial side of the line" because it provides a "valuable service—namely, to equip [children] with the skills they need to survive in life and, more specifically, in the workplace." We do not doubt that Congress has authority under the Commerce Clause to regulate numerous commercial activities that substantially affect interstate commerce and also affect the educational process. That authority, though broad, does not include the authority to regulate each and every aspect of local schools.

> **Take Note**
>
> Did the Court invalidate the Gun-Free School Zones Act as applied to the respondent? Or did it strike down the statute "on its face"—that is, as unconstitutional in all (or substantially all) of its applications, and thus categorically beyond Congress's power to enact in its present form?

The possession of a gun in a local school zone is in no sense an economic activity that might, through repetition elsewhere, substantially affect any sort of interstate commerce. To uphold the Government's contentions here, we would have to pile inference upon inference in a manner that would bid fair to convert congressional authority under the Commerce Clause to a general police power of the sort retained by the States. Admittedly, some of our prior cases have taken long steps down that road, giving great deference to congressional action. [W]e decline here to proceed any further. To do so would require us to conclude that the Constitution's enumeration of powers does not presuppose something not enumerated, and that there never will be a distinction between what is truly national and what is truly local. This we are unwilling to do.

JUSTICE KENNEDY, with whom JUSTICE O'CONNOR joins, concurring.

The history of the judicial struggle to interpret the Commerce Clause during the transition from the economic system the Founders knew to the single, national market still emergent in our own era counsels great restraint before the Court determines that the Clause is insufficient to support an exercise of the national power. * * * *Stare decisis* operates with great force in counseling us not to call in question the essential principles now in place respecting the congressional power to regulate transactions of a commercial nature. That fundamental restraint on our power forecloses us from reverting to an understanding of commerce that would serve only an 18th-century economy, dependent then upon production and trading practices that had changed but little over the preceding centuries; it also mandates against returning to the time when congressional authority to regulate undoubted commercial activities was limited by a judicial determination that those matters had an insufficient connection to an interstate system. Congress can regulate in the commercial sphere on the assumption that we have a single market and a unified purpose to build a stable national economy.

> **Definition**
>
> "*Stare decisis*" is a doctrine "under which a court must follow earlier judicial decisions when the same points arise again in litigation." *Black's Law Dictionary* (10th ed. 2014).

It does not follow, however, that in every instance the Court lacks the authority and responsibility to review congressional attempts to alter the federal balance. This case requires us to consider our place in the design of the Government and to appreciate the significance of federalism in the whole structure of the Constitution. Of the various structural elements in the Constitution, separation of powers, checks and balances, judicial review, and federalism, only concerning the last does there seem to be much uncertainty respecting the existence, and the content, of standards that allow the Judiciary to play a significant role in maintaining the design contemplated by the Framers. * * * There is irony in this, because of the four structural elements in the Constitution just mentioned, federalism was the unique contribution of the Framers to political science and political theory. Though on the surface the idea may seem counterintuitive, it was the insight of the Framers that freedom was enhanced by the creation of two governments, not one.

The theory that two governments accord more liberty than one requires for its realization two distinct and discernable lines of political accountability: one between the citizens and the Federal Government; the second between the citizens and the States. * * * Were the Federal Government to take over the regulation of entire areas of traditional state concern, areas having nothing to do with the regulation of commercial activities, the boundaries between the spheres of federal and state authority would blur and political responsibility would become illusory. The resultant inability to hold either branch of the government answerable to the citizens is more dangerous even than devolving too much authority to the remote central power.

Although it is the obligation of all officers of the Government to respect the constitutional design, the federal balance is too essential a part of our constitutional structure and plays too vital a role in securing freedom for us to admit inability to intervene when one or the other level of Government has tipped the scales too far.

JUSTICE THOMAS, concurring.

[O]ur case law has drifted far from the original understanding of the Commerce Clause. In a future case, we ought to temper our Commerce Clause jurisprudence in a manner that both makes sense of our more recent case law and is more faithful to the original understanding of that Clause. * * * In an appropriate case, I believe that we must further reconsider our "substantial effects" test with an eye toward constructing a standard that reflects the text and history of the Commerce Clause without totally rejecting our more recent Commerce Clause jurisprudence.

At the time the original Constitution was ratified, "commerce" consisted of selling, buying, and bartering, as well as transporting for these purposes. See 1 S. Johnson, A Dictionary of the English Language 361 (4th ed. 1773) (defining commerce as "Intercour[s]e; exchange of one thing for another; interchange of any thing; trade; traffick"); N. Bailey, An Universal Etymological English Dictionary (26th ed. 1789) ("trade or traffic"); T. Sheridan, A Complete Dictionary of the English Language (6th ed. 1796) ("Exchange of one thing for another; trade, traffick"). This understanding finds support in the etymology of the word, which literally means "with merchandise." See 3 Oxford English Dictionary 552 (2d ed. 1989) (com-"with"; merci-"merchandise"). In fact, when Federalists and Anti-Federalists discussed the Commerce Clause during the ratification period, they often used trade (in its selling/bartering sense) and commerce interchangeably. See The Federalist No. 4 (J. Jay) (asserting that countries will cultivate our friendship when our "trade" is prudently regulated by Federal Government); *id.*, No. 7 (A. Hamilton) (discussing "competitions of commerce" between States resulting from state "regulations of trade"); *id.*, No. 40

> **Take Note**
>
> Is Justice Thomas proposing the conceptual test for commerce that the Court followed in *E.C. Knight, Hammer, and Carter Coal*? Is his definition of commerce consistent with the test for commerce that the Court suggested in *Gibbons*? If not, does this undermine Justice Thomas's claims about the original understanding of the term "commerce"?

(J. Madison) (asserting that it was an "acknowledged object of the Convention . . . that the regulation of trade should be submitted to the general government"); Lee, Letters of a Federal Farmer No. 5, in Pamphlets on the Constitution of the United States 319 (P. Ford ed. 1888); Smith, An Address to the People of the State of New York, in id., at 107.

The Constitution not only uses the word "commerce" in a narrower sense than our case law might suggest, it also does not support the proposition that Congress has authority over all activities that "substantially affect" interstate commerce. [O]n this Court's understanding of congressional power, many of Congress' other enumerated powers under Art. I, § 8, are wholly superfluous. After all, if Congress may regulate all matters that substantially affect commerce, there is no need for the Constitution to specify that Congress may enact bankruptcy laws, or coin money and fix the standard of weights and measures, or punish counterfeiters of United States coin and securities. * * * Put simply, much if not all of Art. I, § 8 (including portions of the Commerce Clause itself), would be surplusage if Congress had been given authority over matters that substantially affect interstate commerce. An interpretation of cl. 3 that makes the rest of § 8 superfluous simply cannot be correct.

My review of the case law indicates that the substantial effects test is but an innovation of the 20th century. * * * If anything, the "wrong turn" was the Court's dramatic departure in the 1930s from a century and a half of precedent. Apart from its recent vintage and its corresponding lack of any grounding in the original understanding of the Constitution, the substantial effects test suffers from the further flaw that it appears to grant Congress a police power over the Nation. When asked at oral argument if there were *any* limits to the Commerce Clause, the Government was at a loss for words. Likewise, the principal dissent insists that there are limits, but it cannot muster even one example.

If we wish to be true to a Constitution that does not cede a police power to the Federal Government, our Commerce Clause's boundaries simply cannot be "defined" as being "commensurate with the national needs" or self-consciously intended to let the Federal Government "defend itself against economic forces that Congress decrees inimical or destructive of the national economy." See *post*,

BREYER, J., dissenting. Such a formulation of federal power is no test at all: It is a blank check.

JUSTICE STEVENS, dissenting.

Guns are both articles of commerce and articles that can be used to restrain commerce. Their possession is the consequence, either directly or indirectly, of commercial activity. In my judgment, Congress' power to regulate commerce in firearms includes the power to prohibit possession of guns at any location because of their potentially harmful use; it necessarily follows that Congress may also prohibit their possession in particular markets. The market for the possession of handguns by school-age children is, distressingly, substantial. Whether or not the national interest in eliminating that market would have justified federal legislation in 1789, it surely does today.

JUSTICE SOUTER, dissenting.

In judicial review under the Commerce Clause, [the rational-basis test] reflects our respect for the institutional competence of the Congress on a subject expressly assigned to it by the Constitution and our appreciation of the legitimacy that comes from Congress's political accountability in dealing with matters open to a wide range of possible choices.

It was not ever thus, however, as even a brief overview of Commerce Clause history during the past century reminds us. The modern respect for the competence and primacy of Congress in matters affecting commerce developed only after one of this Court's most chastening experiences, when it perforce repudiated an earlier and untenably expansive conception of judicial review in derogation of congressional commerce power. [The] period from the turn of the century to 1937 is better noted for a series of cases applying highly formalistic notions of "commerce" to invalidate federal social and economic legislation. These restrictive views of commerce subject to congressional power complemented the Court's activism in limiting the enforceable scope of state economic regulation.

It is most familiar history that during this same period the Court routinely invalidated state social and economic legislation under an expansive conception of Fourteenth Amendment substantive due process. [U]nder each conception of judicial review the Court's character for the first third of the century showed itself in exacting

Make the Connection

We consider the cases to which Justice Souter alludes—in particular, the *Lochner* decision—and "substantive due process" in Volume 2.

judicial scrutiny of a legislature's choice of economic ends and of the legislative means selected to reach them.

It was not merely coincidental, then, that sea changes in the Court's conceptions of its authority under the Due Process and Commerce Clauses occurred virtually together, in 1937. * * * There is today, however, a backward glance at both the old pitfalls, as the Court treats deference under the rationality rule as subject to gradation according to the commercial or noncommercial nature of the immediate subject of the challenged regulation. The distinction between what is patently commercial and what is not looks much like the old distinction between what directly affects commerce and what touches it only indirectly. And the act of calibrating the level of deference by drawing a line between what is patently commercial and what is less purely so will probably resemble the process of deciding how much interference with contractual freedom was fatal. Thus, it seems fair to ask whether the step taken by the Court today does anything but portend a return to the untenable jurisprudence from which the Court extricated itself almost 60 years ago. The answer is not reassuring.

JUSTICE BREYER, with whom JUSTICE STEVENS, JUSTICE SOUTER, and JUSTICE GINSBURG join, dissenting.

[W]e must ask whether Congress could have had a *rational basis* for finding a significant (or substantial) connection between gun-related school violence and interstate commerce. * * * Congress could reasonably have found the empirical connection that its law, implicitly or explicitly, asserts.

For one thing, reports, hearings, and other readily available literature make clear that the problem of guns in and around schools is widespread and extremely serious. * * * Congress could therefore have found a substantial educational problem—teachers unable to teach, students unable to learn—and concluded that guns near schools contribute substantially to the size and scope of that problem. Having found that guns in schools significantly undermine the quality of education in our Nation's classrooms, Congress could also have found, given the effect of education upon interstate and foreign commerce, that gun-related violence in and around schools is a commercial, as well as a human, problem. Education, although far more than a matter of economics, has long been inextricably intertwined with the Nation's economy.

The economic links I have just sketched seem fairly obvious. Why then is it not equally obvious, in light of those links, that a widespread, serious, and substantial physical threat to teaching and learning *also* substantially threatens the commerce to which that teaching and learning is inextricably tied? * * * At the very least, Congress could rationally have concluded that the links are "substantial."

[A] holding that the particular statute before us falls within the commerce power would not expand the scope of that Clause. Rather, it simply would apply preexisting law to changing economic circumstances. It would recognize that, in today's economic world, gun-related violence near the classroom makes a significant difference to our economic, as well as our social, well-being.

The majority's holding * * * creates three serious legal problems. First, the majority's holding runs contrary to modern Supreme Court cases that have upheld congressional actions despite connections to interstate or foreign commerce that are less significant than the effect of school violence. * * * The second legal problem the Court creates comes from its apparent belief that it can reconcile its holding with earlier cases by making a critical distinction between "commercial" and noncommercial "transaction[s]." The majority clearly cannot intend such a distinction to focus narrowly on an act of gun possession standing by itself, for such a reading could not be reconciled with [*McClung*, because in that case] the specific transaction (the race-based exclusion * * *) was not itself "commercial." And, if the majority instead means to distinguish generally among broad categories of activities, differentiating what is educational from what is commercial, then, as a practical matter, the line becomes almost impossible to draw. Schools that teach reading, writing, mathematics, and related basic skills serve *both* social and commercial purposes, and one cannot easily separate the one from the other.

The third legal problem created by the Court's holding is that it threatens legal uncertainty in an area of law that, until this case, seemed reasonably well settled. Congress has enacted many statutes (more than 100 sections of the United States Code), including criminal statutes (at least 25 sections), that use the words "affecting commerce" to define their scope, and other statutes that contain no jurisdictional language at all. * * * [T]he legal uncertainty now created will restrict Congress' ability to enact criminal laws aimed at criminal behavior that, considered problem by problem rather than instance by instance, seriously threatens the economic, as well as social, well-being of Americans.

POINTS FOR DISCUSSION

a. Economic Activity

The Court in *Lopez* suggested that Congress has authority to regulate local activity on the theory that, in the aggregate, it substantially affects interstate commerce only if the activity is "economic" in nature. How should a Court determine whether an activity is economic? *Wickard* involved regulation of the cultivation and consumption of home-grown wheat. Were those economic activities? What about the discrimination at issue in *Heart of Atlanta Motel* and *McClung*?

b. Changes in the Nature of "Commerce"

The majority in *Lopez* acknowledged that the Court's view of permissible subjects for regulation under the Commerce Clause has changed as the nature of the interstate market has changed, but insisted that some semblance of the original understanding—that there are limits to Congress's power—must be preserved. Justice Thomas asserted that the meaning of the term "commerce" should be fixed according to the view of that term in 1789. And the dissenters asserted that as the world has changed, so must the scope of Congress's power to regulate commerce, defined in light of modern circumstances—even if this means, in practice, that Congress has virtually limitless power. Which of these views makes the most sense? Is it possible to be faithful to the "original meaning" of the Constitution and still conclude that Congress's power to regulate today is broader than it was in 1789?

c. Precedent and Original Meaning

In a footnote in his separate opinion, Justice Thomas said: "Although I might be willing to return to the original understanding, I recognize that many believe that it is too late in the day to undertake a fundamental reexamination of the past 60 years. Consideration of *stare decisis* and reliance interests may convince us that we cannot wipe the slate clean." Would it be appropriate, if more Justices were willing, to overrule 60 years worth of cases if they are inconsistent with the Constitution's original meaning? Not even self-professed originalists agree on this question. Compare Gary Lawson, The *Constitutional Case Against Precedent,* 17 Harv. J.L. & Publ. Pol'y 23 (1994) (arguing that it is unconstitutional for the Court to follow precedent that deviates from the Constitution's original, objective meaning), with Robert Bork, *The Tempting of America: The Political Seduction of the Law* 155–59 (1990) (arguing that some decisions are "so thoroughly embedded in our national life that [they] should not be overruled").

d. The Gun-Free School Zones Act Amended

To address the constitutional problem with the Gun-Free School Zones Act, Congress amended the statute to add a jurisdictional element. As amended, the statute now provides: "It shall be unlawful for any individual knowingly to possess a firearm that has moved in or that otherwise affects interstate or foreign commerce at a place that the individual knows, or has reasonable cause to believe, is a school zone." 18 U.S.C. § 922(q). Federal courts have upheld the statute as amended. See, e.g., *United States v. Dorsey*, 418 F.3d 1038, 1046 (9th Cir. 2005). Are these decisions consistent with Lopez? If so, how important was the Lopez decision in light of these subsequent developments?

Problem

Congress enacts the "Dead-Beat Parent Act of 2020." It provides in relevant part: "The failure to pay child support in compliance with a state-court order shall be punishable by a fine of not more than $10,000 and imprisonment of not more than 2 years." Dennis Dilbert, a California resident, is indicted under the Act for failing to pay child support to his former spouse, who also lives, with the couple's children, in California. He has moved to quash the indictment on the ground that the Act exceeds Congress's power. How should the court rule? Could the statute be amended to remove doubts about its constitutionality without significantly changing its substance?

UNITED STATES V. MORRISON

529 U.S. 598 (2000)

CHIEF JUSTICE REHNQUIST delivered the opinion of the Court.

In these cases we consider the constitutionality of 42 U.S.C. § 13981, which provides a federal civil remedy for the victims of gender-motivated violence. * * * Petitioner Christy Brzonkala enrolled at [Virginia Tech, where she] met respondents Antonio Morrison and James Crawford, who were both students and members of its varsity football team. Brzonkala alleges that, within 30 minutes of meeting [them], they assaulted and repeatedly raped her. * * * In early 1995, Brzonkala filed a complaint against respondents under Virginia Tech's Sexual Assault Policy. After the hearing, Virginia Tech's Judicial Committee found * * * Morrison guilty of sexual assault and sentenced him to immediate suspension for two semesters. * * * Morrison appealed his second conviction through the university's administrative system. On August 21, 1995, Virginia Tech's [provost] set aside Morrison's punishment[, concluding that it was "excessive." As a result, Brzonkala] dropped out of the university. In December 1995, Brzonkala sued Morrison, Crawford, and Virginia Tech [alleging] that Morrison's and Crawford's attack violated § 13981 * * *. Morrison and Crawford moved to dismiss this complaint on the [ground] that § 13981's civil remedy is unconstitutional.

Section 13981 was part of the Violence Against Women Act of 1994. [Subsection (b)] states that "all persons within the United States shall have the right to be free from crimes of violence motivated by gender," [and subsection (c)] declares: "A person (including a person who acts under color of any statute, ordinance, regulation, custom, or usage of any State) who commits a crime of violence motivated by gender and thus deprives another of the right declared in subsection (b) of this section shall be liable to the party injured, in an action for the recovery of compensatory and punitive damages, injunctive and declaratory relief, and such other relief as a court may deem appropriate."

Petitioners * * * seek to sustain § 13981 as a regulation of activity that substantially affects interstate commerce. Given § 13981's focus on gender-motivated violence wherever it occurs (rather than violence directed at the instrumentalities of interstate commerce, interstate markets, or things or persons in interstate commerce), we agree that this is the proper inquiry. *Lopez* * * * provides the proper framework for conducting the required analysis of § 13981.

Gender-motivated crimes of violence are not, in any sense of the phrase, economic activity. While we need not adopt a categorical rule against aggregating the effects of any noneconomic activity in order to decide these cases, thus far in our Nation's history our cases have upheld Commerce Clause regulation of intrastate activity only where that activity is economic in nature.

Like the Gun-Free School Zones Act at issue in *Lopez*, § 13981 contains no jurisdictional element establishing that the federal cause of action is in pursuance of Congress' power to regulate interstate commerce. * * * Congress elected to cast § 13981's remedy over a wider, and more purely intrastate, body of violent crime.

In contrast with the lack of congressional findings that we faced in *Lopez*, § 13981 *is* supported by numerous findings regarding the serious impact that gender-motivated violence has on victims and their families. But the existence of congressional findings is not sufficient, by itself, to sustain the constitutionality of Commerce Clause legislation. * * * In these cases, Congress' findings are substantially weakened by the fact that they rely so heavily on a method of reasoning that we have already rejected as unworkable if we are to maintain the Constitution's enumeration of powers. Congress found that gender-motivated violence affects interstate commerce "by deterring potential victims from traveling interstate, from engaging in employment in interstate business, and from transacting with business, and in places involved in interstate commerce; by diminishing national productivity, increasing medical and other costs, and decreasing the supply of and the demand for interstate products."

Food for Thought

Is it realistic to fear that Congress will, if the prospect of judicial invalidation is substantially diminished, attempt comprehensively to regulate family law and violent crime? What might prevent Congress from doing so? What role should such considerations play in determining the consistency of federal law with federalism norms?

The reasoning that petitioners advance seeks to follow the but-for causal chain from the initial occurrence of violent crime (the suppression of which has always been the prime object of the States' police power) to every attenuated effect upon interstate commerce. If accepted, petitioners' reasoning would allow Congress to regulate any crime as long as the nationwide, aggregated impact of that crime has substantial effects on employment, production, transit, or consumption. Indeed, if Congress may regulate gender-motivated violence, it would be able to regulate murder or any other type of violence since gender-motivated violence, as a subset of all violent crime, is certain to have lesser economic impacts than the larger class of which it is a part. Petitioners' reasoning, moreover, will not limit Congress to regulating violence but may, as we suggested in *Lopez*, be applied equally as well to family law and other areas of traditional state regulation since the aggregate effect of marriage, divorce, and childrearing on the national economy is undoubtedly significant. Under our written Constitution, however, the limitation of congressional authority is not solely a matter of legislative grace.

> **Take Note**
>
> The phrase "but-for causal chain" refers to matters linked together by a "but-for cause." A "but-for cause" is a "cause without which [an] event could not have occurred." *Black's Law Dictionary* (10th ed. 2014). For example, a driver's negligence would be the "but-for cause" of an accident if the accident would not have occurred but for (i.e., without) the driver's carelessness.

We accordingly reject the argument that Congress may regulate noneconomic, violent criminal conduct based solely on that conduct's aggregate effect on interstate commerce. * * * The regulation and punishment of intrastate violence that is not directed at the instrumentalities, channels, or goods involved in interstate commerce has always been the province of the States. Indeed, we can think of no better example of the police power, which the Founders denied the National Government and reposed in the States, than the suppression of violent crime and vindication of its victims.

> **Make the Connection**
>
> The Court also held, in a portion of the opinion that we consider in Volume 2, that Congress's power to enforce the Fourteenth Amendment did not authorize it to enact the Violence Against Women Act.

If the allegations here are true, no civilized system of justice could fail to provide [Brzonkala] a remedy for the conduct of respondent Morrison. But under our federal system that remedy must be provided by the Commonwealth of Virginia, and not by the United States.

State issue not federal

JUSTICE THOMAS, concurring.

[T]he very notion of a "substantial effects" test under the Commerce Clause is inconsistent with the original understanding of Congress' powers and with this Court's early Commerce Clause cases. * * * Until this Court replaces its existing Commerce Clause jurisprudence with a standard more consistent with the original understanding, we will continue to see Congress appropriating state police powers under the guise of regulating commerce.

JUSTICE SOUTER, with whom JUSTICE STEVENS, JUSTICE GINSBURG, and JUSTICE BREYER join, dissenting.

Our cases, which remain at least nominally undisturbed, stand for the following propositions. Congress has the power to legislate with regard to activity that, in the aggregate, has a substantial effect on interstate commerce. The fact of such a substantial effect is not an issue for the courts in the first instance, but for the Congress, whose institutional capacity for gathering evidence and taking testimony far exceeds ours. By passing legislation, Congress indicates its conclusion, whether explicitly or not, that facts support its exercise of the commerce power. The business of the courts is to review the congressional assessment, not for soundness but simply for the rationality of concluding that a jurisdictional basis exists in fact. Any explicit findings that Congress chooses to make, though not dispositive of the question of rationality, may advance judicial review by identifying factual authority on which Congress relied. Applying those propositions in these cases can lead to only one conclusion.

One obvious difference from *Lopez* is the mountain of data assembled by Congress, here showing the effects of violence against women on interstate commerce. Passage of the Act in 1994 was preceded by four years of hearings, which included testimony from physicians and law professors; from survivors of rape and domestic violence; and from representatives of state law enforcement and private business. The record includes reports on gender bias from task forces in 21 States, and we have the benefit of specific factual findings in the eight separate Reports issued by Congress and its committees over the long course leading to enactment.

Congress thereby explicitly stated the predicate for the exercise of its Commerce Clause power. Is its conclusion irrational in view of the data amassed? [T]he sufficiency of the evidence before Congress to provide a rational basis for the finding cannot seriously be questioned. Indeed, the legislative record here is far more voluminous than the record compiled by Congress and found sufficient in two prior cases upholding Title II of the Civil Rights Act of 1964 against Commerce Clause challenges. *Heart of Atlanta Motel*; *McClung*.

The Act would have passed muster at any time between *Wickard* in 1942 and *Lopez* in 1995 * * *. The fact that the Act does not pass muster before the Court today is therefore proof, to a degree that *Lopez* was not, that the Court's nominal adherence to the substantial effects test is merely that. Although a new jurisprudence has not emerged with any distinctness, it is clear that some congressional conclusions about obviously substantial, cumulative effects on commerce are being assigned lesser values than the once-stable doctrine would assign them. These devaluations are accomplished not by any express repudiation of the substantial effects test or its application through the aggregation of individual conduct, but by supplanting rational basis scrutiny with a new criterion of review.

The premise that the enumeration of powers implies that other powers are withheld is sound; the conclusion that some particular categories of subject matter are therefore presumptively beyond the reach of the commerce power is, however, a non sequitur. * * * [H]istory has shown that categorical exclusions have proven as unworkable in practice as they are unsupportable in theory. [See, *e.g.*, *E.C. Knight*, *Hammer*, *Schechter Poultry*, *Carter Coal*.] Why is the majority tempted to reject the lesson so painfully learned in 1937? An answer emerges from contrasting *Wickard* with [*Carter Coal*.] * * * The Court in *Carter Coal* was still trying to create a laissez-faire world out of the 20th-century economy, and formalistic commercial distinctions were thought to be useful instruments in achieving that object. The Court in *Wickard* knew it could not do any such thing and in the aftermath of the New Deal had long since stopped attempting the impossible.

If we now ask why the formalistic economic/noneconomic distinction might matter today, after its rejection in *Wickard*, the answer is not that the majority fails to see causal connections in an integrated economic world. The answer is that in the minds of the majority there is a new animating theory that makes categorical formalism seem useful again. Just as the old formalism had value in the service of an economic conception, the new one is useful in serving a conception of federalism. It is the instrument by which assertions of national power are to be limited in favor of preserving a supposedly discernible, proper sphere of state autonomy to legislate or refrain from legislating as the individual States see fit. [But as] with "conflicts of economic interest," so with supposed conflicts of sovereign political interests implicated by the Commerce Clause: the Constitution remits them to politics.

Today's majority * * * finds no significance whatever in the state support for the Act based upon the States' acknowledged failure to deal adequately with gender-based violence in state courts, and the belief of their own law enforcement agencies that national action is essential. The National Association of Attorneys General supported the Act unanimously, and Attorneys General from 38 States urged Congress to enact the Civil Rights Remedy, representing that "the current system for dealing with violence against women is inadequate." * * * Thirty-six [States] have filed an *amicus* brief in support of petitioners in these cases, and only one State has taken respondents' side. It is, then, not the least irony of these cases that the States will be forced to enjoy the new federalism whether they want it or not.

JUSTICE BREYER, with whom JUSTICE STEVENS joins, and with whom JUSTICE SOUTER and JUSTICE GINSBURG join as to Part I-A, dissenting.

The "economic/noneconomic" distinction is not easy to apply. Does the local street corner mugger engage in "economic" activity or "noneconomic" activity when he mugs for money? Would evidence that desire for economic domination underlies many brutal crimes against women save the present statute? * * * [C]an Congress simply rewrite the present law and limit its application to restaurants, hotels, perhaps universities, and other places of public accommodation? Given the latter exception, can Congress save the present law by including it, or much of it, in a broader "Safe Transport" or "Workplace Safety" act?

More important, why should we give critical constitutional importance to the economic, or noneconomic, nature of an interstate-commerce-affecting *cause*? If chemical emanations through indirect environmental change cause identical, severe commercial harm outside a State, why should it matter whether local factories or home fireplaces release them? * * * Nothing in the Constitution's language, or that of earlier cases prior to *Lopez*, explains why the Court should ignore one highly relevant characteristic of an interstate-commerce-affecting cause (how "local" it is), while placing critical constitutional weight upon a different, less obviously relevant, feature (how "economic" it is).

Most importantly, the Court's complex rules seem unlikely to help secure the very object that they seek, namely, the protection of "areas of traditional state regulation" from federal intrusion. * * * [I]n a world where most everyday products or their component parts cross interstate boundaries, Congress will frequently find it possible to redraft a statute using language that ties the regulation to the interstate movement of some relevant object, thereby regulating local criminal activity or, for that matter, family affairs. Although this possibility does not give the Federal Government the power to regulate everything, it means that any substantive limitation will apply randomly in terms of the interests the majority seeks to protect. * * * Complex Commerce Clause rules creating fine distinctions that achieve only random results do little to further the important federalist interests that called them into being. That is why modern (pre-*Lopez*) case law rejected them.

We live in a Nation knit together by two centuries of scientific, technological, commercial, and environmental change. Those changes, taken together, mean that virtually every kind of activity, no matter how local, genuinely can affect commerce, or its conditions, outside the State—at least when considered in the aggregate. And that fact makes it close to impossible for courts to develop meaningful subject-matter categories that would exclude some kinds of local activities from ordinary Commerce Clause "aggregation" rules without, at the same time, depriving Congress of the power to regulate activities that have a genuine and important effect upon interstate commerce. Since judges cannot change the world, the "defect" means that, within the bounds of the rational, Congress, not the courts, must remain primarily responsible for striking the appropriate state/federal balance. Congress is institutionally motivated to do so. Its Members represent state and local district interests. They consider the views of state and local officials when they legislate, and they have even developed formal procedures to ensure that such consideration takes place.

POINTS FOR DISCUSSION

a. Institutional Roles

The majority in *Morrison* insisted on preserving a meaningful role for the Court in policing the boundaries between federal and state authority, whereas the dissenting Justices argued for substantial—and virtually complete—deference to Congress's judgment about the limits of its own power. What are the most compelling arguments for these contrasting views of the Court's and Congress's institutional roles?

b. State Support

Justice Souter argued that it is ironic for the Court to invalidate on federalism grounds a federal statute that officials from the states overwhelmingly supported and defended. Should state support be relevant to the Court's analysis of the constitutionality of a federal statute? Can the states "waive" a federalism challenge by supporting the enactment of a federal statute? What if officials from all 50 states, rather than simply a majority, had demonstrably supported the enactment (and constitutionality) of the Violence Against Women Act?

GONZALES V. RAICH

545 U.S. 1 (2005)

JUSTICE STEVENS delivered the opinion of the Court.

California is one of at least nine States that authorize the use of marijuana for medicinal purposes. The question presented in this case is whether the power vested in Congress by Article I, § 8, of the Constitution "[t]o make all Laws which shall be necessary and proper for carrying into Execution" its authority to "regulate Commerce with foreign Nations, and among the several States" includes the power to prohibit the local cultivation and use of marijuana in compliance with California law.

In 1996, California voters passed Proposition 215, now codified as the Compassionate Use Act of 1996. * * * The Act creates an exemption from criminal prosecution for physicians, as well as for patients and primary caregivers, who possess or cultivate marijuana for medicinal purposes with the recommendation or approval of a physician. Respondents Angel Raich and Diane Monson are California residents who suffer from a variety of serious medical conditions and have sought to avail themselves of medical marijuana pursuant to the terms of the Compassionate Use Act. * * * [They] thereafter brought this action * * * seeking injunctive and declaratory relief prohibiting the enforcement of the federal Controlled Substances Act (CSA) to the extent it prevents them from possessing, obtaining, or manufacturing cannabis for their personal medical use. [Under the CSA, the manufacture, distribution, or possession of marijuana is a federal criminal offense. The district court denied respondents' motion for a preliminary injunction, but the court of appeals reversed and ordered the district court to enter a preliminary injunction, concluding that respondents had demonstrated a strong likelihood of success on their claim that Congress lacked power under the Commerce Clause to regulate their activities.]

> **Definition**
>
> A "preliminary injunction" is a "temporary injunction issued before or during trial to prevent an irreparable injury from occurring before the court has a chance to decide the case." *Black's Law Dictionary* (10th ed. 2014).

Respondents in this case do not dispute that passage of the CSA * * * was well within Congress' commerce power. * * * Rather, [they] argue that the CSA's categorical prohibition of the manufacture and possession of marijuana as applied to the intrastate manufacture and possession of marijuana for medical purposes pursuant to California law exceeds Congress' authority under the Commerce Clause.

Our case law firmly establishes Congress' power to regulate purely local activities that are part of an economic "class of activities" that have a substantial effect on interstate commerce. * * * [*Wickard*] establishes that Congress can regulate purely intrastate activity that is not itself "commercial," in that it is not produced for sale, if it concludes that failure to regulate that class of activity would undercut the regulation of the interstate market in that commodity. The similarities between this case and *Wickard* are striking. Like the farmer in *Wickard,* respondents are cultivating, for home consumption, a fungible commodity for which there is an established, albeit illegal, interstate market. Just as the Agricultural Adjustment Act was designed "to control the volume [of wheat] moving in interstate and foreign commerce in order to avoid surpluses" and consequently control the market price, a primary purpose of the CSA is to control the supply and demand of controlled substances in both lawful and unlawful drug markets. In *Wickard,* we had no difficulty concluding that Congress had a rational basis for believing that, when viewed in the aggregate, leaving home-consumed wheat outside the regulatory scheme would have a substantial influence on price and market conditions. Here too, Congress had a rational basis for concluding that leaving home-consumed marijuana outside federal control would similarly affect price and market conditions.

More concretely, one concern prompting inclusion of wheat grown for home consumption in the 1938 Act was that rising market prices could draw such wheat into the interstate market, resulting in lower market prices. The parallel concern making it appropriate to include marijuana grown for home consumption in the CSA is the likelihood that the high demand in the interstate market will draw such marijuana into that market. While the diversion of homegrown wheat tended to frustrate the federal interest in stabilizing prices by regulating the volume of commercial transactions in the interstate market, the diversion of homegrown marijuana tends to frustrate the federal interest in eliminating commercial transactions in the interstate market in their entirety. In both cases, the regulation is squarely within Congress' commerce power because production of the commodity meant for home consumption, be it wheat or marijuana, has a substantial effect on supply and demand in the national market for that commodity.

Congress did not make a specific finding that the intrastate cultivation and possession of marijuana for medical purposes based on the recommendation of a physician would substantially affect the larger interstate marijuana market. [But] we have never required Congress to make particularized findings in order to legislate. While congressional findings are certainly helpful in reviewing the substance of a congressional statutory scheme, particularly when the connection to commerce is not self-evident, * * * the absence of particularized findings does not call into question Congress' authority to legislate.

> **Food for Thought**
>
> Would it make sense to require congressional findings about the relationship between interstate commerce and the particular conduct at issue? Is it reasonable to expect that Congress would make findings about any possible conduct that might be embraced by the prohibition in the statute? Or is the point that the likely failure of Congress to do so suggests something about the breadth of the statute in the first place?

We need not determine whether respondents' activities, taken in the aggregate, substantially affect interstate commerce in fact, but only whether a "rational basis" exists for so concluding. Given the enforcement difficulties that attend distinguishing between marijuana cultivated locally and marijuana grown elsewhere, and concerns about diversion into illicit channels, we have no difficulty concluding that Congress had a rational basis for believing that failure to regulate the intrastate manufacture and possession of marijuana would leave a gaping hole in the CSA. * * * That the regulation ensnares some purely intrastate activity is of no moment. As we have done many times before, we refuse to excise individual components of that larger scheme.

[R]espondents rely heavily on * * * *Lopez* and *Morrison.* As an initial matter, the statutory challenges at issue in those cases were markedly different from the challenge respondents pursue in the case at hand. Here, respondents ask us to excise individual applications of a concededly valid statutory scheme. In contrast, in both *Lopez* and *Morrison,* the parties asserted that a particular statute or provision fell outside Congress' commerce power in its entirety. [W]e have often reiterated that "[w]here the class of activities is regulated and that class is within the reach of federal power, the courts have no power 'to excise, as trivial, individual instances' of the class."

At issue in *Lopez* was the validity of * * * a brief, single-subject statute making it a crime for an individual to possess a gun in a school zone. The Act did not regulate any economic activity and did not contain any requirement that the possession of a gun have any connection to past interstate activity or a predictable impact on future commercial activity. * * * [The CSA is] a lengthy and detailed statute creating a comprehensive framework for regulating the production, distribution, and possession of five classes of "controlled substances." Our opinion in *Lopez* casts no doubt on the validity of such a program.

Unlike those at issue in *Lopez* and *Morrison,* the activities regulated by the CSA are quintessentially economic. * * * The CSA is a statute that regulates the production, distribution, and consumption of commodities for which there is an established, and lucrative, interstate market. Prohibiting the intrastate possession or manufacture of an article of commerce is a rational (and commonly utilized) means of regulating commerce in that product. Because the CSA is a statute that directly regulates economic, commercial activity, our opinion in *Morrison* casts no doubt on its constitutionality.

The Court of Appeals was able to conclude otherwise only by isolating a "separate and distinct" class of activities that it held to be beyond the reach of federal power, defined as "the intrastate, noncommercial cultivation, possession and use of marijuana for personal medical purposes on the advice of a physician and in accordance with state law." 352 F.3d, at 1229. The question, however, is whether Congress' [decision] to include this narrower "class of activities" within the larger regulatory scheme [was] constitutionally deficient. We have no difficulty concluding that Congress acted rationally in determining that none of the characteristics making up the purported class, whether viewed individually or in the aggregate, compelled an exemption from the CSA; rather, the subdivided class of activities defined by the Court of Appeals was an essential part of the larger regulatory scheme.

More fundamentally, if, as the principal dissent contends, the personal cultivation, possession, and use of marijuana for medicinal purposes is beyond the "outer limits of Congress' Commerce Clause authority," it must also be true that such personal use of marijuana (or any other homegrown drug) for *recreational* purposes is also beyond those "outer limits," whether or not a State elects to authorize or even regulate such use. * * * One need not have a degree in economics to understand why a nationwide exemption for the vast quantity of marijuana (or other drugs) locally cultivated for personal use (which presumably would include use by friends, neighbors, and family members) may have a substantial impact on the interstate market for this extraordinarily popular substance. The congressional judgment that an exemption for such a significant segment of the total market would undermine the orderly enforcement of the entire regulatory scheme * * * is not only rational, but "visible to the naked eye" under any commonsense appraisal of the probable consequences of such an open-ended exemption.

The exemption for cultivation by patients and caregivers can only increase the supply of marijuana in the California market. The likelihood that all such production will promptly terminate when patients recover or will precisely match the patients' medical needs during their convalescence seems remote; whereas the danger that excesses will satisfy some of the admittedly enormous demand for recreational use seems obvious. Moreover, that the national and international narcotics trade has thrived in the face of vigorous criminal enforcement efforts suggests that no small number of unscrupulous people will make use of the California exemptions to serve their commercial ends whenever it is feasible to do so. * * * Congress could have rationally concluded that the aggregate impact on the national market of all the transactions exempted from federal supervision is unquestionably substantial.

JUSTICE SCALIA, concurring in the judgment.

[U]nlike the channels, instrumentalities, and agents of interstate commerce, activities that substantially affect interstate commerce are not themselves part of interstate commerce, and thus the power to regulate them cannot come from the Commerce Clause alone. Rather, * * * Congress's regulatory authority over intrastate activities that are not themselves part of interstate commerce (including activities that have a substantial effect on interstate commerce) derives from the Necessary and Proper Clause.

And the * * * authority to enact laws necessary and proper for the regulation of interstate commerce is not limited to laws governing intrastate activities that substantially affect interstate commerce. Where necessary to make a regulation of interstate commerce effective, Congress may regulate even those intrastate activities that do not themselves substantially affect interstate commerce. * * * Moreover, * * * Congress may regulate even noneconomic local activity if that regulation is a necessary part of a more general regulation of interstate commerce. The relevant question is simply whether the means chosen are "reasonably adapted" to the attainment of a legitimate end under the commerce power.

Today's principal dissent objects that, by permitting Congress to regulate activities necessary to effective interstate regulation, the Court reduces *Lopez* and *Morrison* to "little more than a drafting guide." Unlike the power to regulate activities that have a substantial effect on interstate commerce, the power to enact laws enabling effective regulation of interstate commerce can only be exercised in conjunction with congressional regulation of an interstate market, and it extends only to those measures necessary to make the interstate regulation effective. Neither [*Lopez* nor *Morrison*] involved the power of Congress to exert control over intrastate activities in connection with a more comprehensive scheme of regulation.

In the CSA, Congress has undertaken to extinguish the interstate market in Schedule I controlled substances, including marijuana. The Commerce Clause unquestionably permits this. * * * To effectuate its objective, Congress has prohibited almost all intrastate activities related to [marijuana]—both economic activities (manufacture, distribution, possession with the intent to distribute) and noneconomic activities (simple possession). That simple possession is a noneconomic activity is immaterial to whether it can be prohibited as a necessary part of a larger regulation. Rather, Congress's authority to enact all of these prohibitions of intrastate controlled-substance activities depends only upon whether they are appropriate means of achieving the legitimate end of eradicating [those] substances from interstate commerce.

By this measure, I think the regulation must be sustained. * * * Drugs like marijuana are fungible commodities. [M]arijuana that is grown at home and possessed for personal use is never more than an instant from the interstate market—and this is so whether or not the possession is for medicinal use or lawful use under the laws of a particular State.

Take Note

Justice Scalia joined the majority in *Lopez* and *Morrison*, as did Justice Kennedy, who did not write separately in *Raich*. The other Justices in the majority in *Lopez* and *Morrison* dissented in *Raich*, and the dissenters from *Lopez* and *Morrison* were in the majority in *Raich*. Does Justice Scalia's opinion (which Justice Kennedy did not join) provide a convincing reason to treat the cases differently?

JUSTICE O'CONNOR, with whom THE CHIEF JUSTICE and JUSTICE THOMAS join as to all but Part III, dissenting.

One of federalism's chief virtues [is] that it promotes innovation by allowing for the possibility that "a single courageous State may, if its citizens choose, serve as a laboratory; and try novel social and economic experiments without risk to the rest of the country." *New State Ice Co. v. Liebmann,* 285 U.S. 262, 311 (1932) (Brandeis, J., dissenting). This case exemplifies the role of States as laboratories. [California] has come to its own conclusion about the difficult and sensitive question of whether marijuana should be available to relieve severe pain and suffering. Today the Court sanctions an application of the federal Controlled Substances Act that extinguishes that experiment, without any proof that the personal cultivation, possession, and use of marijuana for medicinal purposes, if economic activity in the first place, has a substantial effect on interstate commerce and is therefore an appropriate subject of federal regulation. In so doing, the Court announces a rule that gives Congress a perverse incentive to legislate broadly pursuant to the Commerce Clause—nestling questionable assertions of its authority into comprehensive regulatory schemes—rather than with precision. That rule and the result it produces in this case are irreconcilable with our decisions in *Lopez* and *Morrison.*

I. Our decision [in *Lopez*] about whether gun possession in school zones substantially affected interstate commerce turned on four considerations. First, we observed that our "substantial effects" cases generally have upheld federal regulation of economic activity that affected interstate commerce, but that [the Gun-Free School Zones Act] was a criminal statute having "nothing to do with 'commerce' or any sort of economic enterprise." * * * Second, we noted that the statute contained no express jurisdictional requirement establishing its connection to interstate commerce. Third, we found telling the absence of legislative findings about the regulated conduct's impact on interstate commerce. * * * Finally, we rejected as too attenuated the Government's argument that firearm possession in school zones could result in violent crime which in turn could adversely affect the national economy. * * * Later in *Morrison,* we relied on the same four considerations * * *. In my view, the case before us is materially indistinguishable from *Lopez* and *Morrison* when the same considerations are taken into account.

II. [T]he Court appears to reason that the placement of local activity in a comprehensive scheme confirms that it is essential to that scheme. If the Court is right, then *Lopez* stands for nothing more than a drafting guide: Congress should have described the relevant crime as "transfer or possession of a firearm anywhere in the nation"—thus including commercial and noncommercial activity, and clearly encompassing some activity with assuredly substantial effect on interstate commerce. Had it done so, the majority hints, we would have sustained its authority to regulate possession of firearms in school zones. Furthermore, today's decision suggests we would readily sustain a congressional decision to attach the regulation of intrastate activity to a pre-existing comprehensive (or even not-so-comprehensive) scheme. If so, the Court invites increased federal regulation of local activity even if, as it suggests, Congress would not enact a *new* interstate scheme exclusively for the sake of reaching intrastate activity.

> **Food for Thought**
>
> Justice O'Connor asserts that the Court's conclusion will encourage Congress to enact broad, comprehensive regulatory schemes in order to reach more particularized and localized forms of activity. Is this a realistic threat? What might limit Congress's willingness or ability to do so?

The hard work for courts [is] to identify objective markers for confining the analysis in Commerce Clause cases. * * * A number of objective markers are available to confine the scope of constitutional review here. [M]edical and nonmedical (*i.e.,* recreational) uses of drugs are realistically distinct and can be segregated.

Moreover, * * * it is relevant that this case involves the interplay of federal and state regulation in areas of criminal law and social policy, where "States lay claim by right of history and expertise." To ascertain whether Congress' encroachment is constitutionally justified in this case, then, I would focus here on the personal cultivation, possession, and use of marijuana for medicinal purposes.

> **Take Note**
>
> Do you agree that defining the regulated conduct as the local possession of marijuana for medicinal purposes pursuant to a doctor's order in compliance with state law is an "objective" way to apply the *Lopez* and *Morrison* tests? Doesn't defining the regulated conduct that way effectively pre-ordain the conclusion that Congress lacks the power asserted? Conversely, doesn't the majority's approach—to define the regulated conduct as the unlawful sale of marijuana in an established market—virtually pre-ordain the opposite conclusion? How should the Court address this problem of level of generality?

Having thus defined the relevant conduct, we must determine whether, under our precedents, the conduct is economic and, in the aggregate, substantially affects interstate commerce. * * * The Court's definition of economic activity is breathtaking. It defines as economic any activity involving the production, distribution, and consumption of commodities. [T]he Court's definition of economic activity for purposes of Commerce Clause jurisprudence threatens to sweep all of productive human activity into federal regulatory reach. * * * It will not do to say that Congress may regulate noncommercial activity simply because it may have an effect on the demand for commercial goods, or because the noncommercial endeavor can, in some sense, substitute for commercial activity. Most commercial goods or services have some sort of privately producible analogue. Home care substitutes for daycare. Charades games substitute for movie tickets. * * * To draw the line wherever private activity affects the demand for market goods is to draw no line at all, and to declare everything economic. We have already rejected the result that would follow—a federal police power.

The homegrown cultivation and personal possession and use of marijuana for medicinal purposes has no apparent commercial character. * * * *Lopez* makes clear that possession is not itself commercial activity. And respondents have not come into possession by means of any commercial transaction; they have simply grown, in their own homes, marijuana for their own use, without acquiring, buying, selling, or bartering a thing of value. * * * Even assuming that economic activity is at issue in this case, [t]here is simply no evidence that homegrown medicinal marijuana users constitute, in the aggregate, a sizable enough class to have a discernable, let alone substantial, impact on the national illicit drug market—or otherwise to threaten the CSA regime.

III. If I were a California citizen, I would not have voted for the medical marijuana ballot initiative; if I were a California legislator I would not have supported the Compassionate Use Act. But whatever the wisdom of California's experiment with medical marijuana, the federalism principles that have driven our Commerce Clause cases require that room for experiment be protected in this case. For these reasons I dissent.

JUSTICE THOMAS, dissenting.

[N]o evidence from the founding suggests that "commerce" included the mere possession of a good or some purely personal activity that did not involve trade or exchange for value. In the early days of the Republic, it would have been unthinkable that Congress could prohibit the local cultivation, possession, and consumption of marijuana.

We normally presume that States enforce their own laws, and there is no reason to depart from that presumption here. * * * But even assuming that States' controls allow some seepage of medical marijuana into the illicit drug market, there is a multibillion-dollar interstate market for marijuana. It is difficult to see how this vast market could be affected by diverted medical cannabis, let alone in a way that makes regulating intrastate medical marijuana obviously essential to controlling the interstate drug market. * * * Congress' goal of curtailing the interstate drug trade would not plainly be thwarted if it could not apply the CSA to patients like Monson and Raich. That is, unless Congress' aim is really to exercise police power of the sort reserved to the States in order to eliminate even the intrastate possession and use of marijuana.

The majority's treatment of the substantial effects test is malleable, because the majority expands the relevant conduct. By defining the class at a high level of generality (as the intrastate manufacture and possession of marijuana), the majority overlooks that individuals authorized by state law to manufacture and possess medical marijuana exert no demonstrable effect on the interstate drug market. [T]he majority defines economic activity in the broadest possible terms * * *. This carves out a vast swath of activities that are subject to federal regulation. If the majority is to be taken seriously, the Federal Government may now regulate quilting bees, clothes drives, and potluck suppers throughout the 50 States.

The majority's opinion only illustrates the steady drift away from the text of the Commerce Clause. There is an inexorable expansion from "commerce" to "commercial" and "economic" activity, and finally to all "production, distribution, and consumption" of goods or services for which there is an "established interstate market." Federal power expands, but never contracts, with each new locution. The majority is not interpreting the Commerce Clause, but rewriting it. * * * One searches the Court's opinion in vain for any hint of what aspect of American life is reserved to the States. * * * Our federalist system, properly understood, allows California and a growing number of other States to decide for themselves how to safeguard the health and welfare of their citizens.

POINTS FOR DISCUSSION

a. As-Applied v. Facial Challenges

The plaintiffs in *Raich* raised an "as-applied" challenge to the CSA—that is, they argued that it was unconstitutional as applied to their conduct—and the court rejected their challenge. In *Lopez*, in contrast, the Court struck down the statute there at issue "on its face"—that is, it held that the statute was unconstitutional in its entirety, and should be declared unconstitutional in all applications. In other contexts, it is generally substantially more difficult to prevail on a facial challenge than it is to prevail on an as-applied challenge. (We will see examples when we turn to the First Amendment in Volume 2.) The implication of the decisions in *Raich* and *Lopez*, however, is that it might be easier in Commerce Clause cases to prevail on a facial challenge—at least if Congress has not created a comprehensive scheme of regulation. Does this approach make sense?

b. Comprehensive Schemes

Central to the Court's conclusion in *Raich* was that the ban on local cultivation and possession was essential to the more comprehensive scheme of regulation under the CSA. Does this mean that federal statutes enacted pursuant to the commerce power are more likely to survive scrutiny if they sweep broadly—regulating a larger range of conduct, including more local conduct—rather than narrowly? If so, does this make sense from a federalism standpoint?

NATIONAL FEDERATION OF INDEPENDENT BUSINESS V. SEBELIUS

567 U.S. 519 (2012)

[The Patient Protection and Affordable Care Act of 2010 ("Affordable Care Act" or "ACA"), Pub. L. No. 111–148, 124 Stat 119 (2010), is a complicated law containing hundreds of provisions that aim to make health care in the United States less expensive and more accessible. Shortly after enactment of the law, twenty-six states and several private litigants challenged its constitutionality.

Portions of the lengthy Supreme Court decision in the case appear in three parts of this book. This portion is about whether Congress had power under the Commerce Clause and Necessary and Proper Clause to enact a provision of the Act informally known as the "individual mandate." Chief Justice Roberts described the individual mandate as follows:

> The individual mandate requires most Americans to maintain "minimum essential" health insurance coverage. 26 U.S.C. § 5000A. The mandate does not apply to some individuals, such as prisoners and undocumented aliens. § 5000A(d). Many individuals will receive the required coverage through their employer, or from a government program such as Medicaid or Medicare. See § 5000A(f). But for individuals who are not exempt and do not receive health insurance through a third party, the means of satisfying the requirement is to purchase insurance from a private company.
>
> Beginning in 2014, those who do not comply with the mandate must make a "[s]hared responsibility payment" to the Federal Government. § 5000A(b)(1). That payment, which the Act describes as a "penalty," is calculated as a percentage of household income, subject to a floor based on a specified dollar amount and a ceiling based on the average annual premium the individual would have to pay for qualifying private health insurance. § 5000A(c). In 2016, for example, the penalty will be 2.5 percent of an individual's household income, but no less than $695 and no more than the average yearly premium for insurance that covers 60 percent of the cost of 10 specified services (e.g., prescription drugs and hospitalization). *Ibid.*; 42 U.S.C. § 18022. The Act provides that the penalty will be paid to the Internal Revenue Service with an individual's taxes, and "shall be assessed and collected in the same manner" as tax penalties, such as the penalty for claiming too large an income tax refund. 26 U.S.C. § 5000A(g)(1). The Act, however, bars the IRS from using several of its normal enforcement tools, such as criminal prosecutions and levies. § 5000A(g)(2). And some individuals who are subject to the mandate are nonetheless exempt from the penalty—for example, those with income below a certain threshold and members of Indian tribes. § 5000A(e).

As the excerpts below show, five Justices (expressing their views in three opinions) concluded that Congress did not have power under the Commerce Clause and Necessary and Proper Clause to enact the individual mandate, while four Justices (in another opinion) concluded that Congress did have this power.

The excerpts from opinions below are in the order that they appear in the published decision.]

[Opinion of CHIEF JUSTICE ROBERTS.]

The Government's first argument is that the individual mandate is a valid exercise of Congress's power under the Commerce Clause and the Necessary and Proper Clause. According to the Government, the health care market is characterized by a significant cost-shifting problem. Everyone will eventually need health care at a time and to an extent they cannot predict, but if they do not have insurance, they often will not be able to pay for it. Because state and federal laws nonetheless require hospitals to provide a certain degree of care to individuals without regard to their ability to pay, see, *e.g.*, 42 U.S.C. § 1395dd; Fla. Stat. Ann. § 395.1041, hospitals end up receiving compensation for only a portion of the services they provide. To recoup the losses, hospitals pass on the cost to insurers through higher rates, and insurers, in turn, pass on the cost to policy holders in the form of higher premiums. Congress estimated that the cost of uncompensated care raises family health insurance premiums, on average, by over $1,000 per year.

In the Affordable Care Act, Congress addressed the problem of those who cannot obtain insurance coverage because of preexisting conditions or other health issues. It did so through the Act's "guaranteed-issue" and "community-rating" provisions. These provisions together prohibit insurance companies from denying coverage to those with such conditions or charging unhealthy individuals higher premiums than healthy individuals.

The guaranteed-issue and community-rating reforms do not, however, address the issue of healthy individuals who choose not to purchase insurance to cover potential health care needs. In fact, the reforms sharply exacerbate that problem, by providing an incentive for individuals to delay purchasing health insurance until they become sick, relying on the promise of guaranteed and affordable coverage. The reforms also threaten to impose massive new costs on insurers, who are required to accept unhealthy individuals but prohibited from charging them rates necessary to pay for their coverage. This will lead insurers to significantly increase premiums on everyone.

The individual mandate was Congress's solution to these problems. By requiring that individuals purchase health insurance, the mandate prevents cost-shifting by those who would otherwise go without it. In addition, the mandate forces into the insurance risk pool more healthy individuals, whose premiums on average will be higher than their health care expenses. This allows insurers to subsidize the costs of covering the unhealthy individuals the reforms require them to accept. * * *

The Government contends that the individual mandate is within Congress's power because the failure to purchase insurance "has a substantial and deleterious effect on interstate commerce" by creating the cost-shifting problem. The path of our Commerce Clause decisions has not always run smooth, see *United States v. Lopez,* 514 U.S. 549, 552–559 (1995), but it is now well established that Congress has broad authority under the Clause. We have recognized, for example, that "[t]he power of Congress over interstate commerce is not confined to the regulation of commerce among the states," but extends to activities that "have a substantial effect on interstate commerce." *United States v. Darby,* 312 U.S. 100, 118–119 (1941). Congress's power, moreover, is not limited to regulation of an activity that by itself substantially affects interstate commerce, but also extends to activities that do so only when aggregated with similar activities of others. See *Wickard v. Filburn,* 317 U.S. 111, 127–128 (1942).

Given its expansive scope, it is no surprise that Congress has employed the commerce power in a wide variety of ways to address the pressing needs of the time. But Congress has never attempted to rely on that power to compel individuals not engaged in commerce to purchase an unwanted product. * * *

The Constitution grants Congress the power to "*regulate* Commerce." Art. I, § 8, cl. 3 (emphasis added). The power to *regulate* commerce presupposes the existence of commercial activity to be regulated. If the power to "regulate" something included the power to create it, many of the provisions in the Constitution would be superfluous. For example, the Constitution gives Congress the power to "coin Money," in addition to the power to "regulate the Value thereof." *Id.,* cl. 5. And it gives Congress the power to "raise and support Armies" and to "provide and maintain a Navy," in addition to the power to "make Rules for the Government and Regulation of the land and naval Forces." *Id.,* cls. 12–14. If the power to regulate the armed forces or the value of money included the power to bring the subject of the regulation into existence, the specific grant of such powers would have been unnecessary. The language of the Constitution reflects the natural understanding that the power to regulate assumes there is already something to be regulated.

Our precedent also reflects this understanding. As expansive as our cases construing the scope of the commerce power have been, they all have one thing in common: They uniformly describe the power as reaching "activity." It is nearly impossible to avoid the word when quoting them. See, *e.g., Lopez, supra,* at 560 ("Where economic activity substantially affects interstate commerce, legislation regulating that activity will be sustained"); *Wickard, supra,* at 125 ("[E]ven if appellee's activity be local and though it may not be regarded as commerce, it may still, whatever its nature, be reached by Congress if it exerts a substantial economic effect on interstate commerce"); *NLRB v. Jones & Laughlin Steel Corp.,* 301 U.S. 1, 37 (1937) ("Although activities may be intrastate in character when separately considered, if they have such a close and substantial relation to interstate commerce that their control is essential or appropriate to protect that commerce from burdens and obstructions, Congress cannot be denied the power to exercise that control").

The individual mandate, however, does not regulate existing commercial activity. It instead compels individuals to *become* active in commerce by purchasing a product, on the ground that their failure to do so affects interstate commerce. Construing the Commerce Clause to permit Congress to regulate individuals precisely *because* they are doing nothing would open a new and potentially vast domain to congressional authority. Every day individuals do not do an infinite number of things. In some cases they decide not to do something; in others they simply fail to do it. Allowing Congress to justify federal regulation by pointing to the effect of inaction on commerce would bring countless decisions an individual could *potentially* make within the scope of federal regulation, and—under the Government's theory—empower Congress to make those decisions for him.

Applying the Government's logic to the familiar case of *Wickard v. Filburn* shows how far that logic would carry us from the notion of a government of limited powers. In *Wickard,* the Court famously upheld a federal penalty imposed on a farmer for growing wheat for consumption on his own farm. That amount of wheat caused the farmer to exceed his quota under a program designed to support the price of wheat by limiting supply. The Court rejected the farmer's argument that growing wheat for home consumption was beyond the reach of the commerce power. It did so on the ground that the farmer's decision to grow wheat for his own use allowed him to avoid purchasing wheat in the market. That decision, when considered in the aggregate along with similar decisions of others, would have had a substantial effect on the interstate market for wheat.

Wickard has long been regarded as "perhaps the most far reaching example of Commerce Clause authority over intrastate activity," *Lopez,* 514 U.S., at 560, but the Government's theory in this case would go much further. Under *Wickard* it is within Congress's power to regulate the market for wheat by supporting its price. But price can be supported by increasing demand as well as by decreasing supply. The aggregated decisions of some consumers not to purchase wheat have a substantial effect on the price of wheat, just as decisions not to purchase health insurance have on the price of insurance. Congress can therefore command that those not buying wheat do so, just as it argues here that it may command that those not buying health insurance do so. The farmer in *Wickard* was at least actively engaged in the production of wheat, and the Government could regulate that activity because of its effect on commerce. The Government's theory here would effectively override that limitation, by establishing that individuals may be regulated under the Commerce Clause whenever enough of them are not doing something the Government would have them do.

Indeed, the Government's logic would justify a mandatory purchase to solve almost any problem. To consider a different example in the health care market, many Americans do not eat a balanced diet. That group makes up a larger percentage of the total population than those without health insurance. See, *e.g.*, Dept. of Agriculture and Dept. of Health and Human Services, Dietary Guidelines for Americans 1 (2010). The failure of that group to have a healthy diet increases health care costs, to a greater extent than the failure of the uninsured to purchase insurance, Those increased costs are borne in part by other Americans who must pay more, just as the uninsured shift costs to the insured. Congress addressed the insurance problem by ordering everyone to buy insurance. Under the Government's theory, Congress could address the diet problem by ordering everyone to buy vegetables.

That is not the country the Framers of our Constitution envisioned. James Madison explained that the Commerce Clause was "an addition which few oppose and from which no apprehensions are entertained." The Federalist No. 45, at 293. While Congress's authority under the Commerce Clause has of course expanded with the growth of the national economy, our cases have "always recognized that the power to regulate commerce, though broad indeed, has limits." *Maryland v. Wirtz*, 392 U.S. 183, 196 (1968). The Government's theory would erode those limits, permitting Congress to reach beyond the natural extent of its authority, "everywhere extending the sphere of its activity and drawing all power into its impetuous vortex." The Federalist No. 48, at 309 (J. Madison). Congress already enjoys vast power to regulate much of what we do. Accepting the Government's theory would give Congress the same license to regulate what we do not do, fundamentally changing the relation between the citizen and the Federal Government.

Food for Thought

Is it true that upholding the individual mandate would effectively remove all limitations on the Commerce Power? Could Congress enact the laws at issue in *United States v. Lopez* or *United States v. Morrison* under the theory advanced by the government here?

The Government sees things differently. It argues that because sickness and injury are unpredictable but unavoidable, "the uninsured as a class are active in the market for health care, which they regularly seek and obtain." The individual mandate "merely regulates how individuals finance and pay for that active participation—requiring that they do so through insurance, rather than through attempted self-insurance with the back-stop of shifting costs to others."

Everyone will likely participate in the markets for food, clothing, transportation, shelter, or energy; that does not authorize Congress to direct them to purchase particular products in those or other markets today. The Commerce Clause is not a general license to regulate an individual from cradle to grave, simply because he will predictably engage in particular transactions. Any police power to regulate individuals as such, as opposed to their activities, remains vested in the States.

The Government argues that the individual mandate can be sustained as a sort of exception to this rule, because health insurance is a unique product. According to the Government, upholding the individual mandate would not justify mandatory purchases of items such as cars or broccoli because, as the Government puts it, "[h]ealth insurance is not purchased for its own sake like a car or broccoli; it is a means of financing health-care consumption and covering universal risks." But cars and broccoli are no more purchased for their "own sake" than health insurance. They are purchased to cover the need for transportation and food. * * * The individual mandate forces individuals into commerce precisely because they elected to refrain from commercial activity. Such a law cannot be sustained under a clause authorizing Congress to "regulate Commerce."

The Government next contends that Congress has the power under the Necessary and Proper Clause to enact the individual mandate because the mandate is an "integral part of a comprehensive scheme of economic regulation"—the guaranteed-issue and community-rating insurance reforms. * * *

As our jurisprudence under the Necessary and Proper Clause has developed, we have been very deferential to Congress's determination that a regulation is "necessary." We have thus upheld laws that are " 'convenient, or useful' or 'conducive' to the authority's 'beneficial exercise.' " *United States v. Comstock*, 130 S.Ct. 1949, 1965 (2010) (quoting *McCulloch v. Maryland*, 17 U.S. (4 Wheat.) 316, 413, 418 (1819). But we have also carried out our responsibility to declare unconstitutional those laws that undermine the structure of government established by the Constitution. Such laws, which are not "consist[ent] with the letter and spirit of the constitution," *McCulloch, supra,* at 421, are not "*proper* [means] for carrying into Execution" Congress's enumerated powers. Rather, they are, "in the words of The Federalist, 'merely acts of usurpation' which 'deserve to be treated as such.' " *Printz v. United States,* 521 U.S. 898, 924 (1997) (alterations omitted) (quoting The Federalist No. 33, at 204 (A. Hamilton)).

Applying these principles, the individual mandate cannot be sustained under the Necessary and Proper Clause as an essential component of the insurance reforms. Each of our prior cases upholding laws under that Clause involved exercises of authority derivative of, and in service to, a granted power. For example, we have upheld provisions permitting continued confinement of those *already in federal custody* when they could not be safely released, *Comstock, supra,* at 1954–1955; criminalizing bribes involving organizations *receiving federal funds, Sabri v. United States,* 541 U.S. 600, 602, 605 (2004); and tolling state statutes of limitations while cases are *pending in federal court, Jinks v. Richland County,* 538 U.S. 456, 459, 462 (2003). The individual mandate, by contrast, vests Congress with the extraordinary ability to create the necessary predicate to the exercise of an enumerated power.

The Government relies primarily on our decision in *Gonzales v. Raich,* 545 U.S. 1 (2005). In *Raich,* we considered "comprehensive legislation to regulate the interstate market" in marijuana. Certain individuals sought an exemption from that regulation on the ground that they engaged in only intrastate possession and consumption. We denied any exemption, on the ground that marijuana is a fungible commodity, so that any marijuana could be readily diverted into the interstate market. Congress's attempt to regulate the interstate market for marijuana would therefore have been substantially undercut if it could not also regulate intrastate possession and consumption. Accordingly, we recognized that "Congress was acting well within its authority" under the Necessary and Proper Clause even though its "regulation ensnare[d] some purely intrastate activity." *Raich* thus did not involve the exercise of any "great substantive and independent power," *McCulloch, supra,* at 411, of the sort at issue here. Instead, it concerned only the constitutionality of "individual *applications* of a concededly valid statutory scheme." *Raich, supra,* at 23 (emphasis added).

Just as the individual mandate cannot be sustained as a law regulating the substantial effects of the failure to purchase health insurance, neither can it be upheld as a "necessary and proper" component of the insurance reforms. The commerce power thus does not authorize the mandate.

> **Take Note**
>
> Each of the opinions in this case claims that its interpretation of the Commerce Clause is consistent with the original meaning of that Clause. What evidence does each opinion cite in support of its claim? Which opinion is most persuasive on this point? Does any opinion question the idea that the Court must interpret the Commerce Clause in accordance with its original meaning?

[Opinion of JUSTICE GINSBURG, joined by JUSTICE BREYER, JUSTICE KAGAN, and JUSTICE SOTOMAYOR.]

Consistent with the Framers' intent, we have repeatedly emphasized that Congress' authority under the Commerce Clause is dependent upon "practical" considerations, including "actual experience." *NLRB v. Jones & Laughlin Steel Corp.,* 301 U.S. 1, 41–42 (1937). We afford Congress the leeway "to undertake to solve national problems directly and realistically." *American Power & Light Co. v. SEC,* 329 U.S. 90, 103 (1946).

Until today, this Court's pragmatic approach to judging whether Congress validly exercised its commerce power was guided by two familiar principles. First, Congress has the power to regulate economic activities "that substantially affect interstate commerce." *Gonzales v. Raich,* 545 U.S. 1, 17 (2005). This capacious power extends even to local activities that, viewed in the aggregate, have a substantial impact on interstate commerce. See *ibid.*

Second, we owe a large measure of respect to Congress when it frames and enacts economic and social legislation. See *Raich,* 545 U.S., at 17; *Hodel v. Indiana,* 452 U.S. 314, 326 (1981) ("This [C]ourt will certainly not substitute its judgment for that of Congress unless the relation of the subject to interstate commerce and its effect upon it are clearly non-existent." (internal quotation marks omitted)). When appraising such legislation, we ask only (1) whether Congress had a "rational basis" for concluding that the regulated activity substantially affects interstate commerce, and (2) whether there is a "reasonable connection between the regulatory means selected and the asserted ends." *Id.,* at 323–324. In answering these questions, we presume the statute under review is constitutional and may strike it down only on a "plain showing" that Congress acted irrationally. *United States v. Morrison,* 529 U.S. 598, 607 (2000).

Straightforward application of these principles would require the Court to hold that the minimum coverage provision is proper Commerce Clause legislation. Beyond dispute, Congress had a rational basis for concluding that the uninsured, as a class, substantially affect interstate commerce. Those without insurance consume billions of dollars of health-care products and services each year. Those goods are produced, sold, and delivered largely by national and regional companies who routinely transact business across state lines. The uninsured also cross state lines to receive care. Some have medical emergencies while away from home. Others, when sick, go to a neighboring State that provides better care for those who have not prepaid for care.

Not only do those without insurance consume a large amount of health care each year; critically, [their] inability to pay for a significant portion of that consumption drives up market prices, foists costs on other consumers, and reduces market efficiency and stability. Given these far-reaching effects on interstate commerce, the decision to forgo insurance is hardly inconsequential or equivalent to "doing nothing"; it is, instead, an economic decision Congress has the authority to address under the Commerce Clause.

The minimum coverage provision, furthermore, bears a "reasonable connection" to Congress' goal of protecting the health-care market from the disruption caused by individuals who fail to obtain insurance. By requiring those who do not carry insurance to pay a toll, the minimum coverage provision gives individuals a strong incentive to insure. This incentive, Congress had good reason to believe, would reduce the number of uninsured and, correspondingly, mitigate the adverse impact the uninsured have on the national health-care market.

Congress also acted reasonably in requiring uninsured individuals, whether sick or healthy, either to obtain insurance or to pay the specified penalty. As earlier observed, because every person is at risk of needing care at any moment, all those who lack insurance, regardless of their current health status, adversely affect the price of health care and health insurance. Moreover, an insurance-purchase requirement limited to those in need of immediate care simply could not work. Insurance companies would either charge these individuals prohibitively expensive premiums, or, if community-rating regulations were in place, close up shop.

"[W]here we find that the legislators . . . have a rational basis for finding a chosen regulatory scheme necessary to the protection of commerce, our investigation is at an end." *Katzenbach v. McClung*, 379 U.S. 294, 303–304 (1964). Congress' enactment of the minimum coverage provision, which addresses a specific interstate problem in a practical, experience-informed manner, easily meets this criterion.

Rather than evaluating the constitutionality of the minimum coverage provision in the manner established by our precedents, the CHIEF JUSTICE relies on a newly minted constitutional doctrine. The commerce power does not, the CHIEF JUSTICE announces, permit Congress to "compe[l] individuals to become active in commerce by purchasing a product."

The CHIEF JUSTICE's novel constraint on Congress' commerce power gains no force from our precedent and for that reason alone warrants disapprobation. But even assuming, for the moment, that Congress lacks authority under the Commerce Clause to "compel individuals not engaged in commerce to purchase an unwanted product," such a limitation would be inapplicable here. Everyone will, at some point, consume health-care products and services. Thus, if the CHIEF JUSTICE is correct that an insurance-purchase requirement can be applied only to those who "actively" consume health care, the minimum coverage provision fits the bill.

For [these reasons], the minimum coverage provision is valid Commerce Clause legislation. When viewed as a component of the entire ACA, the provision's constitutionality becomes even plainer.

The Necessary and Proper Clause "empowers Congress to enact laws in effectuation of its [commerce] powe[r] that are not within its authority to enact in isolation." *Gonzales v. Raich*, 545 U.S. 1, 39 (2005) (SCALIA, J., concurring in judgment). * * * [O]ne of Congress' goals in enacting the Affordable Care Act was to eliminate the insurance industry's practice of charging higher prices or denying coverage to individuals with preexisting medical conditions. The commerce power allows Congress to ban this practice, a point no one disputes. See *United States v. South-Eastern Underwriters Assn.*, 322 U.S. 533, 545, 552–553 (1944) (Congress may regulate "the methods by which interstate insurance companies do business.").

Congress knew, however, that simply barring insurance companies from relying on an applicant's medical history would not work in practice. Without the individual mandate, Congress learned, guaranteed-issue and community-rating requirements would trigger an adverse-selection death-spiral in the health-insurance market: Insurance premiums would skyrocket, the number of uninsured would increase, and insurance companies would exit the market. When complemented by an insurance mandate, on the other hand, guaranteed issue and community rating would work as intended, increasing access to insurance and reducing uncompensated care. The minimum coverage provision is thus an "essential par[t] of a larger regulation of economic activity"; without the provision, "the regulatory scheme [w]ould be undercut." *Raich*, 545 U.S., at 24–25. Put differently, the minimum coverage provision, together with the guaranteed-issue and community-rating requirements, is " 'reasonably adapted' to the attainment of a legitimate end under the commerce power": the elimination of pricing and sales practices that take an applicant's medical history into account.

[Opinion of JUSTICE SCALIA, JUSTICE KENNEDY, JUSTICE THOMAS, and JUSTICE ALITO.]

What is absolutely clear, affirmed by the text of the 1789 Constitution, by the Tenth Amendment ratified in 1791, and by innumerable cases of ours in the 220 years since, is that there are structural limits upon federal power—upon what it can prescribe with respect to private conduct, and upon what it can impose upon the sovereign States. Whatever may be the conceptual limits upon the Commerce Clause and upon the power to tax and spend, they cannot be such as will enable the Federal Government to regulate all private conduct and to compel the States to function as administrators of federal programs.

Take Note

These four Justices issued a "joint opinion." In most cases, one Justice writes and issues an opinion that other Justices join in support. But in some cases, multiple Justices will co-author a joint opinion, as was done here. Why might the Justices decide to collaborate in jointly writing and issuing an opinion?

That clear principle carries the day here. The striking case of *Wickard v. Filburn,* 317 U.S. 111 (1942), which held that the economic activity of growing wheat, even for one's own consumption, affected commerce sufficiently that it could be regulated, always has been regarded as the *ne plus ultra* of expansive Commerce Clause jurisprudence. To go beyond that, and to say the failure to grow wheat (which is not an economic activity, or any activity at all) nonetheless affects commerce and therefore can be federally regulated, is to make mere breathing in and out the basis for federal prescription and to extend federal power to virtually all human activity.

Definition

Ne plus ultra (Latin: no more beyond) means the highest point.

Article I, § 8, of the Constitution gives Congress the power to "regulate Commerce . . . among the several States." The Individual Mandate in the Act commands that every "applicable individual shall for each month beginning after 2013 ensure that the individual, and any dependent of the individual who is an applicable individual, is covered under minimum essential coverage." 26 U.S.C. § 5000A(a) (2006 ed., Supp. IV). If this provision "regulates" anything, it is the *failure* to maintain minimum essential coverage. One might argue that it regulates that failure by requiring it to be accompanied by payment of a penalty. But that failure—that abstention from commerce—is not "Commerce." To be sure, *purchasing* insurance *is* "Commerce"; but one does not regulate commerce that does not exist by compelling its existence.

In *Gibbons v. Ogden,* 9 Wheat. 1, 196 (1824), Chief Justice Marshall wrote that the power to regulate commerce is the power "to prescribe the rule by which commerce is to be governed." That understanding is consistent with the original meaning of "regulate" at the time of the Constitution's ratification, when "to regulate" meant "[t]o adjust by rule, method or established mode," 2 N. Webster, An American Dictionary of the English Language (1828); "[t]o adjust by rule or method," 2 S. Johnson, A Dictionary of the English Language (7th ed. 1785); "[t]o adjust, to direct according to rule," 2 J. Ash, New and Complete Dictionary of the English Language (1775); "to put in order, set to rights, govern or keep in order," T. Dyche & W. Pardon, *A New General English Dictionary* (16th ed. 1777). It can mean to direct the manner of something but not to direct that something come into being. There is no instance in which this Court or Congress (or anyone else, to our knowledge) has used "regulate" in that peculiar fashion.

We do not doubt that the buying and selling of health insurance contracts is commerce generally subject to federal regulation. But when Congress provides that (nearly) all citizens must buy an insurance contract, it goes beyond "adjust[ing] by rule or method" or "direct[ing] according to rule"; it directs the creation of commerce.

In response, the Government offers two theories as to why the Individual Mandate is nevertheless constitutional. Neither theory suffices to sustain its validity.

The Government presents the Individual Mandate as a unique feature of a complicated regulatory scheme governing many parties with countervailing incentives that must be carefully balanced. Congress has imposed an extensive set of regulations on the health insurance industry, and compliance with those regulations will likely cost the industry a great deal. If the industry does not respond by increasing premiums, it is not likely to survive. And if the industry does increase premiums, then there is a serious risk that its products—insurance plans—will become economically undesirable for many and prohibitively expensive for the rest.

At the outer edge of the commerce power, this Court has insisted on careful scrutiny of regulations that do not act directly on an interstate market or its participants. * * * In *United States v. Lopez,* 514 U.S. 549 (1995), we held that Congress could not, as a means of fostering an educated interstate labor market through the protection of schools, ban the possession of a firearm within a school zone. And in *United States v. Morrison,* 529 U.S. 598 (2000), we held that Congress could not, in an effort to ensure the full participation of women in the interstate economy, subject private individuals and companies to suit for gender-motivated violent torts. The lesson of these cases is that the Commerce Clause, even when supplemented by the Necessary and Proper Clause, is not *carte blanche* for doing whatever will help achieve the ends Congress seeks by the regulation of commerce. And [these] cases show that the scope of the Necessary and Proper Clause is exceeded not only when the congressional action directly violates the sovereignty of the States but also when it violates the background principle of enumerated (and hence limited) federal power.

The case upon which the Government principally relies to sustain the Individual Mandate under the Necessary and Proper Clause is *Gonzales v. Raich,* 545 U.S. 1 (2005). That case held that Congress could, in an effort to restrain the interstate market in marijuana, ban the local cultivation and possession of that drug. *Raich* is no precedent for what Congress has done here. That case's prohibition of growing (cf. *Wickard,* 317 U.S. 111), and of possession (cf. innumerable federal statutes) did not represent the expansion of the federal power to direct into a broad new field. The mandating of economic activity does, and since it is a field so limitless that it converts the Commerce Clause into a general authority to direct the economy, that mandating is not "consist[ent] with the letter and spirit of the constitution." *McCulloch v. Maryland,* 4 Wheat. 316, 421 (1819).

More over, *Raich* is far different from the Individual Mandate in another respect. The Court's opinion in *Raich* pointed out that the growing and possession prohibitions were the only practicable way of enabling the prohibition of interstate traffic in marijuana to be effectively enforced. Intrastate marijuana could no more be distinguished from interstate marijuana than, for example, endangered-species trophies obtained before the species was federally protected can be distinguished from trophies obtained afterwards—which made it necessary and proper to prohibit the sale of all such trophies, see *Andrus v. Allard,* 444 U.S. 51 (1979).

With the present statute, by contrast, there are many ways other than this unprecedented Individual Mandate by which the regulatory scheme's goals of reducing insurance premiums and ensuring the profitability of insurers could be achieved. For instance, those who did not purchase insurance could be subjected to a surcharge when they do enter the health insurance system. Or they could be denied a full income tax credit given to those who do purchase the insurance.

The Government was invited, at oral argument, to suggest what federal controls over private conduct (other than those explicitly prohibited by the Bill of Rights or other constitutional controls) could *not* be justified as necessary and proper for the carrying out of a general regulatory scheme. It was unable to name any. As we said at the outset, whereas the precise scope of the Commerce Clause and the Necessary and Proper Clause is uncertain, the proposition that the Federal Government cannot do everything is a fundamental precept. See *Lopez*, 514 U.S., at 564 ("[I]f we were to accept the Government's arguments, we are hard pressed to posit any activity by an individual that Congress is without power to regulate"). Section 5000A is defeated by that proposition.

> **Practice Pointer**
>
> Was the Government counsel simply unprepared or did the Government have no reasonable answer? If you were representing the Government, and had been asked this question at oral argument, what answer might you have given?

The Government's second theory in support of the Individual Mandate is that § 5000A is valid because it is actually a "regulat[ion of] activities having a substantial relation to interstate commerce, . . . *i.e.*, . . . activities that substantially affect interstate commerce." *Id.*, at 558–559. This argument takes a few different forms, but the basic idea is that § 5000A regulates "the way in which individuals finance their participation in the health-*care* market." That is, the provision directs the manner in which individuals purchase health care services and related goods (directing that they be purchased through insurance) and is therefore a straightforward exercise of the commerce power.

The primary problem with this argument is that § 5000A does not apply only to persons who purchase all, or most, or even any, of the health care services or goods that the mandated insurance covers. Indeed, the main objection many have to the Mandate is that they have no intention of purchasing most or even any of such goods or services and thus no need to buy insurance for those purchases. The Government responds that the health-care market involves "essentially universal participation." The principal difficulty with this response is that it is, in the only relevant sense, not true. It is true enough that everyone consumes "health care," if the term is taken to include the purchase of a bottle of aspirin. But the health care "market" that is the object of the Individual Mandate not only includes but principally consists of goods and services that the young people primarily affected by the Mandate *do not purchase*. They are quite simply not participants in that market, and cannot be made so (and thereby subjected to regulation) by the simple device of defining participants to include all those who will, later in their lifetime, probably purchase the goods or services covered by the mandated insurance. Such a definition of market participants is unprecedented, and were it to be a premise for the exercise of national power, it would have no principled limits.

The Affordable Care Act seeks to achieve "near-universal" health insurance coverage. § 18091(2)(D) (2006 ed., Supp. IV). The two pillars of the Act are the Individual Mandate and the expansion of coverage under Medicaid.* In our view, both these central provisions of the Act—the Individual Mandate and Medicaid Expansion—are invalid. It follows, as some of the parties urge, that all other provisions of the Act must fall as well.

[Opinion of JUSTICE THOMAS]

The joint dissent and the CHIEF JUSTICE correctly apply our precedents to conclude that the Individual Mandate is beyond the power granted to Congress under the Commerce Clause and the Necessary and Proper Clause. Under those precedents, Congress may regulate "economic activity [that] substantially affects interstate commerce." *United States v. Lopez,* 514 U.S. 549, 560 (1995). I adhere to my view that "the very notion of a 'substantial effects' test under the Commerce Clause is inconsistent with the original understanding of Congress' powers and with this Court's early Commerce Clause cases." *United States v. Morrison,* 529 U.S. 598, 627 (2000) (THOMAS, J., concurring). As I have explained, the Court's continued use of that test "has encouraged the Federal Government to persist in its view that the Commerce Clause has virtually no limits." *Morrison, supra,* at 627. The Government's unprecedented claim in this suit that it may regulate not only economic activity but also *inactivity* that substantially affects interstate commerce is a case in point.

POINTS FOR DISCUSSION

a. Test for What Congress Can Regulate Under the Commerce Clause

Five Justices agreed that Congress does not have power under the Commerce Clause to enact the individual mandate. How did Chief Justice Roberts's opinion differ from the joint opinion of Justice Scalia, Kennedy, Thomas, and Alito? Is it possible to identify a test for what Congress can regulate under the Commerce Clause?

b. Holding or Dicta?

In another portion of the case, a majority of the Justices concluded that Congress could use its powers of taxation to enact "the shared responsibility payment" provision, a provision requiring payment of money by those who do not purchase insurance in accordance with the individual mandate. Does upholding "the shared

* The portion of the joint opinion addressing the Medicaid expansion is included in the section of the casebook addressing Congress's power to spend for the general welfare.—*Eds.*

responsibility payment" mean that the Court's discussion of the Commerce Power is unnecessary for resolving the case?

C. THE TAXING POWER

Although the Commerce Clause has been the basis for a significant number of statutes over the last 70 years, it is not Congress's only meaningful power. Article I, § 8, which enumerates the powers of Congress, also confers on Congress the power to tax and spend, powers that Congress has used frequently to achieve its regulatory objectives. We address Congress's power to tax first, and then turn to Congress's spending power.

U.S. Constitution, Article I, Section 8, Clause 1

The Congress shall have Power To lay and collect Taxes, Duties, Imposts and Excises, to pay the Debts and provide for the common Defence and general Welfare of the United States; but all Duties, Imposts and Excises shall be uniform throughout the United States * * *.

Article I, section 8, clause 1 gives Congress a general power to impose taxes. This power is subject to several limitations. Duties, imposts, and excises must be uniform throughout the United States. See Art. I, § 8, cl. 1. Any "direct tax" other than an income tax—a complex subject addressed in the excerpt from *NFIB v. Sebelius* in this section below—must be laid in proportion to the population of each state. See *id.* § 9, cl. 4. In addition, Congress cannot impose duties on exports, cannot impose duties on shipment from one state to another, and cannot give preference to any port over another. See *id.* cls. 5 & 6. Noticeably absent from this list of limitation is any requirement that taxes must be limited to interstate activities. The taxation power differs from the commerce power in this important respect.

Taxes serve multiple functions. First, they raise revenue for the government. Second, by raising the cost of certain forms of behavior, they create disincentives to engage in that behavior—and incentives to engage in other, comparatively cheaper, behavior.

When a tax is particularly successful at the second function, it is little different in practice and effect from direct regulation of the behavior at issue. Assuming that there are limits on Congress's power to regulate certain forms of conduct pursuant to the Commerce Clause, can Congress circumvent those limits by reliance on its power to tax?

CHILD LABOR TAX CASE

259 U.S. 20 (1922)

MR. CHIEF JUSTICE TAFT delivered the opinion of the Court.

This case presents the question of the constitutional validity of the Child Labor Tax Law. [Pursuant to that Act, the United States assessed Drexel Furniture Company $6,312.79—10 per cent of its net profits for 1919—for employing in its factory a boy under 14 years of age.] The company paid the tax under protest, and, after rejection of its claim for a refund, brought this suit.

> **Make the Connection**
>
> The Court decided this case only four years after its decision in *Hammer v. Dagenhart*, which held that Congress lacks power pursuant to the Commerce Clause to regulate the practice of child labor.

The law is attacked on the ground that it is a regulation of the employment of child labor in the states—an exclusively state function under the federal Constitution and within the reservations of the Tenth Amendment. It is defended on the ground that it is a mere excise tax levied by the Congress of the United States under its broad power of taxation conferred by section 8, article 1, of the federal Constitution.

> **Definition**
>
> An "excise tax" is a tax on the manufacture, sale, or use of goods, or on the carrying on of some specified activity.

We must construe the law and interpret the intent and meaning of Congress from the language of the act. * * * Does this law impose a tax with only that incidental restraint and regulation which a tax must inevitably involve? Or does it regulate by the use of the so-called tax as a penalty? [The tax] provides a heavy exaction for a departure from a detailed and specified course of conduct in business. That course of business is that employers shall employ in mines and quarries, children of an age greater than 16 years; in mills and factories, children of an age greater than 14 years, and shall prevent children of less than 16 years in mills and factories from working more than 8 hours a day or 6 days in the week. If an employer departs from this prescribed course of business, he is to pay to the government one-tenth of his entire net income in the business for a full year. The amount is not to be proportioned in any degree to the extent or frequency of the departures, but is to be paid by the employer in full measure whether he employs 500 children for a year, or employs only one for a day. [I]t is only where he knowingly departs from the prescribed course that payment is to be exacted. Scienters are associated with penalties, not with taxes. The employer's factory is to be subject to inspection at any time not only by the taxing officers of the Treasury, the Department normally charged with the collection of taxes, but also by the Secretary of Labor and his subordinates, whose normal function is the advancement and protection of the welfare of the workers. In the light of these features of the act, a court must be blind not to see that the so-called tax is imposed to stop the employment of children within the age limits prescribed. Its prohibitory and regulatory effect and purpose are palpable. All others can see and understand this. How can we properly shut our minds to it?

Definition

"Scienter" is a "degree of knowledge that makes a person legally responsible for the consequences of his or her act or omission." *Black's Law Dictionary* (10th ed. 2014).

Out of a proper respect for the acts of a co-ordinate branch of the government, this court has gone far to sustain taxing acts as such, even though there has been ground for suspecting, from the weight of the tax, it was intended to destroy its subject. But in the act before us the presumption of validity cannot prevail, because the proof of the contrary is found on the very face of its provisions. Grant the validity of this law, and all that Congress would need to do, hereafter, in seeking to take over to its control any one of the great number of subjects * * * reserved to [the states] by the Tenth Amendment, would be to enact a detailed measure of complete regulation of the subject and enforce it by a so-called tax upon departures from it. To give such magic to the word "tax" would be to break down all constitutional limitation of the powers of Congress and completely wipe out the sovereignty of the states.

The difference between a tax and a penalty is sometimes difficult to define, and yet the consequences of the distinction in the required method of their collection often are important. Where the sovereign enacting the law has power to impose both tax and penalty, the difference between revenue production and mere regulation may be immaterial, but not so when one sovereign can impose a tax only, and the power of regulation rests in another. Taxes are occasionally imposed in the discretion of the Legislature on proper subjects with the primary motive of obtaining revenue from them and with the incidental motive of discouraging them by making their continuance onerous. They do not lose their character as taxes because of the incidental motive. But there comes a time in the extension of the penalizing features of the so-called tax when it loses its character as such and becomes a mere penalty, with

Food for Thought

It is notoriously difficult to determine the purpose or motive of a collective body such as a legislature, in which each member who voted for a proposal may have had individualized—and complex—reasons for doing so. See Frank H. Easterbrook, *Statutes' Domains*, 50 U. Chi. L. Rev. 533, 547–48 (1983). Should the Court consider Congress's purpose or motive here?

the characteristics of regulation and punishment. Such is the case in the law before us. Although Congress does not invalidate the contract of employment or expressly declare that the employment within the mentioned ages is illegal, it does exhibit its intent practically to achieve the latter result by adopting the criteria of wrongdoing and imposing its principal consequence on those who transgress its standard.

The case before us cannot be distinguished from that of *Hammer v. Dagenhart*. * * * The congressional power over interstate commerce is, within its proper scope, just as complete and unlimited as the congressional power to tax, and the legislative motive in its exercise is just as free from judicial suspicion and inquiry. Yet when Congress threatened to stop interstate commerce in ordinary and necessary commodities, unobjectionable as subjects of transportation, and to deny the same to the people of a state in order to coerce them into compliance with Congress' regulation of state concerns, the court said this was not in fact regulation of interstate commerce, but rather that of state concerns and was invalid. So here the so-called tax is a penalty to coerce people of a state to act as Congress wishes them to act in respect of a matter completely the business of the state government under the federal Constitution. This case requires as did [*Hammer*] the application of the principle announced [in *McCulloch*]: "Should Congress, * * * under the pretext of executing its powers, pass laws for the accomplishment of objects not entrusted to the government; it would become the painful duty of this tribunal * * * to say that such an act was not the law of the land."

For the reasons given, we must hold the Child Labor Tax Law invalid * * *.

POINTS FOR DISCUSSION

a. The Scope of the Taxing Power

If Congress has power pursuant to the Commerce Clause to regulate a particular activity, does it have power to impose a tax on that activity, even if the tax amounts to a "penalty"? Notice that the Court decided the *Child Labor Tax Case* only a few years after it decided *Hammer v. Dagenhart*, which considered the constitutionality of a federal law prohibiting the transportation in interstate commerce of goods produced in factories that used child labor. When the Court subsequently overruled *Hammer*, did it also overrule the *Child Labor Tax Case* sub silentio?

b. Taxes v. Penalties

What criteria should a court apply to determine whether a tax is a revenue-raising measure with an incidental motive to regulate or instead a penalty that constitutes impermissible regulation? Don't all taxes seek both to raise revenue and affect private choices?

There is currently a federal tax on the purchase of gasoline. Suppose that Congress today raised that tax $0.50 per gallon. Would the increase be a "penalty" or simply a "tax"? Would the answer be different if the tax before the increase took effect were already $2.00 per gallon? Given the scope of the Commerce Clause, does the answer to this question matter for the tax's constitutionality?

UNITED STATES V. KAHRIGER

345 U.S. 22 (1953)

MR. JUSTICE REED delivered the opinion of the Court.

The issue raised by this appeal is the constitutionality of the occupational tax provisions of the Revenue Act of 1951, which levy a tax on persons engaged in the business of accepting wagers, and require such persons to register with the Collector of Internal Revenue. The unconstitutionality of the tax is asserted on two grounds. First, it is said that Congress, under the pretense of exercising its power to tax has attempted to penalize illegal intrastate gambling through the regulatory features of the Act, and has thus infringed the police power which is reserved to the states. Secondly, it is urged that the registration provisions of the tax violate the privilege against self-incrimination and are arbitrary and vague, contrary to the guarantees of the Fifth Amendment.

[Respondent Joseph Kahriger was charged with violating the Act on grounds that he was in the business of accepting wagers and that he willfully failed to register for and pay the occupational tax in question. Kahriger presumably did not register because his gambling activities were illegal under state law and he did not want to call attention to himself.]

The substance of respondent's position with respect to the Tenth Amendment is that Congress has chosen to tax a specified business which is not within its power to regulate. * * * Appellee would have us say that because there is legislative history indicating a congressional motive to suppress wagering, this tax is not a proper exercise of such taxing power. * * * [But we have upheld other taxes even though the] intent to curtail and hinder [was] manifest. [The] tax is [not] invalid [simply] because the revenue obtained is negligible. Appellee * * * argues that the sole purpose of the statute is to penalize

Take Note

Isn't it fair to assume that the tax invalidated in the *Child Labor Tax Case* also raised revenue for the government? (Indeed, the plaintiff in that case had been assessed several thousand dollars in taxes.) If so, can the *Child Labor Tax Case* be distinguished from this case? Does the Court even attempt to distinguish it?

only illegal gambling in the states through the guise of a tax measure. [T]he instant tax has a regulatory effect. But regardless of its regulatory effect, the wagering tax produces revenue. As such it [is similar to other taxes that] we have found valid.

Where federal legislation has rested on other congressional powers, such as the Necessary and Proper Clause or the Commerce Clause, this Court has generally sustained the statutes, despite their effect on matters ordinarily considered state concern. * * * Where Congress has employed the taxing clause a greater variation in the decisions has resulted. * * * It is hard to understand why the power to tax should raise more doubts because of indirect effects than other federal powers.

Penalty provisions in tax statutes added for breach of a regulation concerning activities in themselves subject only to state regulation have caused this Court to declare the enactments invalid. *Child Labor Tax Case.* Unless there are provisions, extraneous to any tax need, courts are without authority to limit the exercise of the taxing power. All the provisions of this excise are adapted to the collection of a valid tax.

[In an omitted portion of the opinion, the Court held that applying the registration provisions to Kahriger did not violate the privilege against self incrimination.]

MR. JUSTICE JACKSON, concurring.

I concur in the judgment and opinion of the Court, but with such doubt that if the minority agreed upon an opinion which did not impair legitimate use of the taxing power I probably would join it. But we deal here with important and contrasting values in our scheme of government, and it is important that neither be allowed to destroy the other. Of course, all taxation has a tendency proportioned to its burdensomeness to discourage the activity taxed. One cannot formulate a revenue-raising plan that would not have economic and social consequences. Congress may and should place the burden of taxes where it will least handicap desirable activities and bear most heavily on useless or harmful ones. If Congress may tax one citizen to the point of discouragement for making an honest living, it is hard to say that it may not do the same to another just because he makes a sinister living.

But here is a purported tax law which * * * lays no tax except on specified gamblers whose calling in most states is illegal. It requires this group to step forward and identify themselves, not because they like others have income, but because of its source. This is difficult to regard as a rational or good-faith revenue measure, despite the deference that is due Congress. On the contrary, it seems to be a plan to tax out of existence the professional gambler whom it has been found impossible to prosecute out of existence.

It will be a sad day for the revenues if the good will of the people toward their taxing system is frittered away in efforts to accomplish by taxation moral reforms that cannot be accomplished by direct legislation. But the evil that can come from this statute will probably soon make itself manifest to Congress. The evil of a judicial decision impairing the legitimate taxing power by extreme constitutional interpretations might not be transient.

Even though this statute approaches the fair limits of constitutionality, I join the decision of the Court.

Make the Connection

Recall that in the second half of the decision in *McCulloch v. Maryland*, the Court suggested that politics is the only protection for citizens subject to a tax imposed by a government whose representatives they get to choose. Is Justice Jackson, notwithstanding his concerns about the tax in this case, effectively adopting that view?

MR. JUSTICE FRANKFURTER, dissenting.

Congress may make an oblique use of the taxing power in relation to activities with which Congress may deal directly, as for instance, commerce between the States. * * * However, when oblique use is made of the taxing power as to matters which substantively are not within the powers delegated to Congress, the Court cannot shut its eyes to what is obviously, because designedly, an attempt to control conduct which the Constitution left to the responsibility of the States, merely because Congress wrapped the legislation in the verbal cellophane of a revenue measure. [T]he context of the circumstances which brought forth this enactment * * * emphatically supports what was revealed on the floor of Congress, namely, that what was formally a means of raising revenue for the Federal Government was essentially an effort to check if not to stamp out professional gambling.

POINTS FOR DISCUSSION

a. Precedent

Did the Court in *Kahriger* overrule the *Child Labor Tax Case*? It noted that "[p]enalty provisions in tax statutes added for breach of a regulation concerning activities in themselves subject only to state regulation have caused this Court to declare the enactments invalid," but it also suggested that such provisions are unconstitutional only if they are "extraneous to any tax need"—that is, only if they do not produce any revenue. Is it possible to conceive of a tax that is imposed for the "breach" of a federal regulation and that is entirely "extraneous to any tax need"?

b. Current Law

Since the decision in *Kahriger*, the Court has not invalidated a federal tax on the ground that it exceeds Congress's power to tax. Do you suppose that this is because of the test for the taxing power announced in *Kahriger*, the modern scope of Congress's power under the Commerce Clause, or both? Consider the case that follows.

NATIONAL FEDERATION OF INDEPENDENT BUSINESS V. SEBELIUS

567 U.S. 519 (2012)

[The Patient Protection and Affordable Care Act of 2010 ("Affordable Care Act" or "ACA"), Pub. L. No. 111–148, 124 Stat 119 (2010), is a complicated law containing hundreds of provisions that aim to make health care in the United States less expensive and more accessible. Shortly after enactment of the law, twenty-six states and several private litigants challenged its constitutionality. Portions of the lengthy Supreme Court decision in the case appear in three parts of this book. The excerpts below from opinions in the case consider whether Congress properly used its power to impose taxes to enact what the Court informally called the "shared responsibility payment" provision of the Act. Chief Justice Roberts explained the shared responsibility payment provision as follows:

> The individual mandate requires most Americans to maintain "minimum essential" health insurance coverage. 26 U.S.C. § 5000A. The mandate does not apply to some individuals, such as prisoners and undocumented aliens. § 5000A(d). Many individuals will receive the required coverage through their employer, or from a government program such as Medicaid or Medicare. See § 5000A(f). But for individuals who are not exempt and do not receive health insurance through a third party, the means of satisfying the requirement is to purchase insurance from a private company.
>
> Beginning in 2014, those who do not comply with the mandate must make a "[s]hared responsibility payment" to the Federal Government. § 5000A(b)(1). That payment, which the Act describes as a "penalty," is calculated as a percentage of household income, subject to a floor based on a specified dollar amount and a ceiling based on the average annual premium the individual would have to pay for qualifying private health insurance. § 5000A(c). In 2016, for example, the penalty will be 2.5 percent of an individual's household income, but no less than $695 and no more than the average yearly premium for insurance that covers 60

percent of the cost of 10 specified services (*e.g.*, prescription drugs and hospitalization). *Ibid.*; 42 U.S.C. § 18022. The Act provides that the penalty will be paid to the Internal Revenue Service with an individual's taxes, and "shall be assessed and collected in the same manner" as tax penalties, such as the penalty for claiming too large an income tax refund. 26 U.S.C. § 5000A(g)(1). The Act, however, bars the IRS from using several of its normal enforcement tools, such as criminal prosecutions and levies. § 5000A(g)(2). And some individuals who are subject to the mandate are nonetheless exempt from the penalty—for example, those with income below a certain threshold and members of Indian tribes. § 5000A(e).

Five members of the Court concluded that the Shared Responsibility Payment was a constitutional exercise of Congress's taxation power, while the other four members disagreed.]

> **Take Note**
>
> The Court concludes that the Shared Responsibility Payment is a tax for constitutional purposes and thus a valid exercise of Congress's taxing power. The dissent concludes that the provision is a penalty (and not a tax) and is therefore unconstitutional. Why does the constitutionality of the Shared Responsibility Payment turn on whether it is a tax? What grounds do the two opinions use for deciding how to characterize the Shared Responsibility Payment? Why do they disagree?

[Opinion of the Court, delivered by CHIEF JUSTICE ROBERTS, and joined by JUSTICES BREYER, GINSBURG, SOTOMAYOR, and KAGAN.]

The exaction the Affordable Care Act imposes on those without health insurance looks like a tax in many respects. The "[s]hared responsibility payment," as the statute entitles it, is paid into the Treasury by "taxpayer[s]" when they file their tax returns. 26 U.S.C. § 5000A(b). It does not apply to individuals who do not pay federal income taxes because their household income is less than the filing threshold in the Internal Revenue Code. § 5000A(e)(2). For taxpayers who do owe the payment, its amount is determined by such familiar factors as taxable income, number of dependents, and joint filing status. The requirement to pay is found in the Internal Revenue Code and enforced by the IRS, which—as we previously explained—must assess and collect it "in the same manner as taxes." This process yields the essential feature of any tax: it produces at least some revenue for the Government. *United States v. Kahriger*, 345 U.S. 22, 28, n. 4 (1953). Indeed, the payment is expected to raise about $4 billion per year by 2017.

It is of course true that the Act describes the payment as a "penalty," not a "tax." But [that] does not determine whether the payment may be viewed as an exercise of Congress's taxing power. * * * We have * * * held that exactions not labeled taxes nonetheless were authorized by Congress's power to tax. In the License Tax Cases, 5 Wall. (72 U.S.) 462 (1866), for example, we held that federal licenses to sell liquor and lottery tickets—for which the licensee had to pay a fee—could be sustained as exercises of the taxing power. *Id.* at 471. And in *New York v. United States*, 505 U.S. 144 (1992), we upheld as a tax a "surcharge" on out-of-state nuclear waste shipments, a portion of which was paid to the Federal Treasury. *Id.* at 171. We thus ask whether the shared responsibility payment falls within Congress's taxing power, "[d]isregarding the designation of the exaction, and viewing its substance and application." *United States v. Constantine,* 296 U.S. 287, 294 (1935).

Our cases confirm this functional approach. For example, in *Bailey v. Drexel Furniture Co. (Child Labor Tax Case)*, 259 U.S. 20 (1922), we focused on three practical characteristics of the so-called tax on employing child laborers that convinced us the "tax" was actually a penalty. First, the tax imposed an exceedingly heavy burden—10 percent of a company's net income—on those who employed children, no matter how small their infraction. Second, it imposed that exaction only on those who knowingly employed underage laborers. Such scienter requirements are typical of punitive statutes, because Congress often wishes to punish only those who intentionally break the law. Third, this "tax" was enforced in part by the Department of Labor, an agency responsible for punishing violations of labor laws, not collecting revenue. *Id.*, at 36–37.

The same analysis here suggests that the shared responsibility payment may for constitutional purposes be considered a tax, not a penalty: First, for most Americans the amount due will be far less than the price of insurance, and, by statute, it can never be more. It may often be a reasonable financial decision to make the payment rather than purchase insurance, unlike the "prohibitory" financial punishment in *Drexel Furniture.* Second, the individual mandate contains no scienter requirement. Third, the payment is collected solely by the IRS through the normal means of taxation—except that the Service is *not* allowed to use those means most suggestive of a punitive sanction, such as criminal prosecution. See § 5000A(g)(2). The reasons the Court in *Drexel Furniture* held that what was called a "tax" there was a penalty support the conclusion that what is called a "penalty" here may be viewed as a tax.

None of this is to say that the payment is not intended to affect individual conduct. Although the payment will raise considerable revenue, it is plainly designed to expand health insurance coverage. But taxes that seek to influence conduct are nothing new. Some of our earliest federal taxes sought to deter the purchase of imported manufactured goods in order to foster the growth of domestic industry. See W. Brownlee, Federal Taxation in America 22 (2d ed. 2004); cf. 2 J. Story, Commentaries on the Constitution of the United States § 962, p. 434 (1833) ("the taxing power is often, very often, applied for other purposes, than revenue"). Today, federal and state taxes can compose more than half the retail price of cigarettes, not just to raise more money, but to encourage people to quit smoking. And we have upheld such obviously regulatory measures as taxes on selling marijuana and sawed-off shotguns. See *United States v. Sanchez*, 340 U.S. 42, 44–45 (1950); *Sonzinsky v. United States*, 300 U.S. 506, 513 (1937). Indeed, "[e]very tax is in some measure regulatory. To some extent it interposes an economic impediment to the activity taxed as compared with others not taxed." *Sonzinsky, supra*, at 513. That § 5000A seeks to shape decisions about whether to buy health insurance does not mean that it cannot be a valid exercise of the taxing power.

In distinguishing penalties from taxes, this Court has explained that "if the concept of penalty means anything, it means punishment for an unlawful act or omission." *United States v. Reorganized CF & I Fabricators of Utah, Inc.*, 518 U.S. 213, 224 (1996); see also *United States v. La Franca*, 282 U.S. 568, 572 (1931) ("[A] penalty, as the word is here used, is an exaction imposed by statute as punishment for an unlawful act"). While the individual mandate clearly aims to induce the purchase of health insurance, it need not be read to declare that failing to do so is unlawful. Neither the Act nor any other law attaches negative legal consequences to not buying health insurance, beyond requiring a payment to the IRS. The Government agrees with that reading, confirming that if someone chooses to pay rather than obtain health insurance, they have fully complied with the law.

Indeed, it is estimated that four million people each year will choose to pay the IRS rather than buy insurance. We would expect Congress to be troubled by that prospect if such conduct were unlawful. That Congress apparently regards such extensive failure to comply with the mandate as tolerable suggests that Congress did not think it was creating four million outlaws. It suggests instead that the shared responsibility payment merely imposes a tax citizens may lawfully choose to pay in lieu of buying health insurance.

Even if the taxing power enables Congress to impose a tax on not obtaining health insurance, any tax must still comply with other requirements in the Constitution. Plaintiffs argue that the shared responsibility payment does not do so, citing Article I, § 9, clause 4. That clause provides: "No Capitation, or other direct, Tax shall be laid, unless in Proportion to the Census or Enumeration herein before directed to be taken." This requirement means that any "direct Tax" must be apportioned so that each State pays in proportion to its population. According to the plaintiffs, if the individual mandate imposes a tax, it is a direct tax, and it is unconstitutional because Congress made no effort to apportion it among the States.

> **Take Note**
>
> Having concluded that the Shared Responsibility Payment is a tax for constitutional purposes, the majority next had to decide whether it was a "direct" tax. Why is this inquiry necessary? Notice that the Court does not cite any recent precedents on the issue. Why might there be no recent precedents on the issue of what is a direct tax?

Even when the Direct Tax Clause was written it was unclear what else, other than a capitation (also known as a "head tax" or a "poll tax"), might be a direct tax. See *Springer v. United States,* 102 U.S. 586, 596–598 (1881). Soon after the framing, Congress passed a tax on ownership of carriages, over James Madison's objection that it was an unapportioned direct tax. *Id.,* at 597. This Court upheld the tax, in part reasoning that apportioning such a tax would make little sense, because it would have required taxing carriage owners at dramatically different rates depending on how many carriages were in their home State. See *Hylton v. United States,* 3 Dall. (3 U.S.) 171, 174 (1796) (opinion of Chase, J.). The Court was unanimous, and those Justices who wrote opinions either directly asserted or strongly suggested that only two forms of taxation were direct: capitations and land taxes. See *id.,* at 175; *id.,* at 177 (opinion of Paterson, J.); *id.,* at 183 (opinion of Iredell, J.).

That narrow view of what a direct tax might be persisted for a century. In 1880, for example, we explained that "*direct taxes,* within the meaning of the Constitution, are only capitation taxes, as expressed in that instrument, and taxes on real estate." *Springer, supra,* at 602. In 1895, we expanded our interpretation to include taxes on personal property and income from personal property, in the course of striking down aspects of the federal income tax. *Pollock v. Farmers' Loan & Trust Co.,* 158 U.S. 601, 618 (1895). That result was overturned by the Sixteenth Amendment, although we continued to consider taxes on personal property to be direct taxes. See *Eisner v. Macomber,* 252 U.S. 189, 218–219 (1920).

A tax on going without health insurance does not fall within any recognized category of direct tax. It is not a capitation. Capitations are taxes paid by every person, "without regard to property, profession, or *any other circumstance*." *Hylton, supra,* at 175 (opinion of Chase, J.) (emphasis altered). The whole point of the shared responsibility payment is that it is triggered by specific circumstances—earning a certain amount of income but not obtaining health insurance. The payment is also plainly not a tax on the ownership of land or personal property. The shared responsibility payment is thus not a direct tax that must be apportioned among the several States.

There may, however, be a more fundamental objection to a tax on those who lack health insurance. Even if only a tax, the payment under § 5000A(b) remains a burden that the Federal Government imposes for an omission, not an act. If it is troubling to interpret the Commerce Clause as authorizing Congress to regulate those who abstain from commerce, perhaps it should be similarly troubling to permit Congress to impose a tax for not doing something.

Take Note

The final issue was whether Congress has the power to tax "inactivity" even if it cannot regulate inactivity under the Commerce Clause. Why does the Court decide that taxation is different from regulating commerce?

Three considerations allay this concern. First, and most importantly, it is abundantly clear the Constitution does not guarantee that individuals may avoid taxation through inactivity. A capitation, after all, is a tax that everyone must pay simply for existing, and capitations are expressly contemplated by the Constitution. The Court today holds that our Constitution protects us from federal regulation under the Commerce Clause so long as we abstain from the regulated activity. But from its creation, the Constitution has made no such promise with respect to taxes. See Letter from Benjamin Franklin to M. Le Roy (Nov. 13, 1789) ("Our new Constitution is now established . . . but in this world nothing can be said to be certain, except death and taxes").

Second, Congress's ability to use its taxing power to influence conduct is not without limits. A few of our cases policed these limits aggressively, invalidating punitive exactions obviously designed to regulate behavior otherwise regarded at the time as beyond federal authority. See, *e.g., United States v. Butler,* 297 U.S. 1 (1936); *Drexel Furniture,* 259 U.S. at 20. More often and more recently we have declined to closely examine the regulatory motive or effect of revenue-raising measures. See *Kahriger,* 345 U.S., at 27–31 (collecting cases). We have nonetheless maintained that " 'there comes a time in the extension of the penalizing features of the so-called tax when it loses its character as such and becomes a mere penalty with the characteristics of regulation and punishment.' " *Department of Revenue of*

Montana v. Kurth Ranch, 511 U.S. 767, 779 (1994) (quoting *Drexel Furniture, supra,* at 38).

We have already explained that the shared responsibility payment's practical characteristics pass muster as a tax under our narrowest interpretations of the taxing power. Because the tax at hand is within even those strict limits, we need not here decide the precise point at which an exaction becomes so punitive that the taxing power does not authorize it.

Third, although the breadth of Congress's power to tax is greater than its power to regulate commerce, the taxing power does not give Congress the same degree of control over individual behavior. Once we recognize that Congress may regulate a particular decision under the Commerce Clause, the Federal Government can bring its full weight to bear. Congress may simply command individuals to do as it directs. An individual who disobeys may be subjected to criminal sanctions. Those sanctions can include not only fines and imprisonment, but all the attendant consequences of being branded a criminal: deprivation of otherwise protected civil rights, such as the right to bear arms or vote in elections; loss of employment opportunities; social stigma; and severe disabilities in other controversies, such as custody or immigration disputes.

By contrast, Congress's authority under the taxing power is limited to requiring an individual to pay money into the Federal Treasury, no more. If a tax is properly paid, the Government has no power to compel or punish individuals subject to it. We do not make light of the severe burden that taxation—especially taxation motivated by a regulatory purpose—can impose. But imposition of a tax nonetheless leaves an individual with a lawful choice to do or not do a certain act, so long as he is willing to pay a tax levied on that choice.

The Affordable Care Act's requirement that certain individuals pay a financial penalty for not obtaining health insurance may reasonably be characterized as a tax. Because the Constitution permits such a tax, it is not our role to forbid it, or to pass upon its wisdom or fairness.

JUSTICE SCALIA, JUSTICE KENNEDY, JUSTICE THOMAS, and JUSTICE ALITO, dissenting.

Our cases establish a clear line between a tax and a penalty: " '[A] tax is an enforced contribution to provide for the support of government; a penalty . . . is an exaction imposed by statute as punishment for an unlawful act.' " *United States v. Reorganized CF & I Fabricators of Utah, Inc.,* 518 U.S. 213, 224 (1996) (quoting *United States v. La Franca,* 282 U.S. 568, 572 (1931)). In a few cases, this Court has held that a "tax" imposed upon private conduct was so onerous as to be in effect a penalty. But we have never held—*never*—that a penalty imposed for violation of the law was so trivial as to be in effect a tax. We have never held that *any* exaction imposed for violation of the law is an exercise of Congress' taxing power—even when the statute *calls* it a tax, much less when (as here) the statute repeatedly calls it a penalty. When an act "adopt[s] the criteria of wrongdoing" and then imposes a monetary penalty as the "principal consequence on those who transgress its standard," it creates a regulatory penalty, not a tax. *Child Labor Tax Case*, 259 U.S. 20, 38 (1922).

Take Note

What does the dissent say is the test for deciding whether a law is a tax or a penalty? Does the majority announce a different test?

So the question is, quite simply, whether the exaction here is imposed for violation of the law. It unquestionably is. The minimum-coverage provision is found in 26 U.S.C. § 5000A, entitled "*Requirement* to maintain minimum essential coverage." (Emphasis added.) It commands that every "applicable individual *shall* . . . ensure that the individual . . . is covered under minimum essential coverage." *Ibid.* (emphasis added). And the immediately following provision states that, "[i]f . . . an applicable individual . . . fails to meet the *requirement* of subsection (a) . . . there is hereby imposed . . . a *penalty*." § 5000A(b) (emphasis added). And several of Congress' legislative "findings" with regard to § 5000A confirm that it sets forth a legal requirement and constitutes the assertion of regulatory power, not mere taxing power. See 42 U.S.C. § 18091(2)(A) ("The requirement regulates activity . . ."); § 18091(2)(C) ("The requirement . . . will add millions of new consumers to the health insurance market . . ."); § 18091(2)(D) ("The requirement achieves near-universal coverage").

That § 5000A imposes not a simple tax but a mandate to which a penalty is attached is demonstrated by the fact that some are exempt from the tax who are not exempt from the mandate—a distinction that would make no sense if the mandate were not a mandate. Section 5000A(d) exempts three classes of people from the definition of "applicable individual" subject to the minimum coverage requirement: Those with religious objections or who participate in a "health care sharing ministry," § 5000A(d)(2); those who are "not lawfully present" in the United States, § 5000A(d)(3); and those who are incarcerated, § 5000A(d)(4). Section 5000A(e) then creates a separate set of exemptions, excusing from liability for the penalty certain individuals who are subject to the minimum coverage requirement: Those who cannot afford coverage, § 5000A(e)(1); who earn too little income to require filing a tax return, § 5000A(e)(2); who are members of an Indian tribe, § 5000A(e)(3); who experience only short gaps in coverage, § 5000A(e)(4); and who, in the judgment of the Secretary of Health and Human

Services, "have suffered a hardship with respect to the capability to obtain coverage," § 5000A(e)(5). If § 5000A were a tax, these two classes of exemption would make no sense; there being no requirement, *all* the exemptions would attach to the penalty (renamed tax) alone.

In the face of all these indications of a regulatory requirement accompanied by a penalty, the Solicitor General assures us that "neither the Treasury Department nor the Department of Health and Human Services interprets Section 5000A as imposing a legal obligation," Petitioners' Minimum Coverage Brief 61, and that "[i]f [those subject to the Act] pay the tax penalty, they're in compliance with the law," Tr. of Oral Arg. 50 (Mar. 26, 2012). These self-serving litigating positions are entitled to no weight. What counts is what the statute says, and that is entirely clear.

Against the mountain of evidence that the minimum coverage requirement is what the statute calls it—a requirement—and that the penalty for its violation is what the statute calls it—a penalty—the Government brings forward the flimsiest of indications to the contrary. It notes that "[t]he minimum coverage provision amends the Internal Revenue Code to provide that a non-exempted individual . . . will owe a monetary penalty, in addition to the income tax itself," and that "[t]he [Internal Revenue Service (IRS)] will assess and collect the penalty in the same manner as assessable penalties under the Internal Revenue Code." Petitioners' Minimum Coverage Brief 53. The manner of collection could perhaps suggest a tax if IRS penalty-collection were unheard-of or rare. It is not. See, *e.g.*, 26 U.S.C. § 527(j) (2006 ed.) (IRS-collectible penalty for failure to make campaign-finance disclosures); § 5761(c) (IRS-collectible penalty for domestic sales of tobacco products labeled for export); § 9707 (IRS-collectible penalty for failure to make required health-insurance premium payments on behalf of mining employees). In *Reorganized CF & I Fabricators of Utah, Inc.*, 518 U.S. 213 (1996), we held that an exaction not only *enforced* by the Commissioner of Internal Revenue but even *called* a "tax" was in fact a penalty. "[I]f the concept of penalty means anything," we said, "it means punishment for an unlawful act or omission." *Id.*, at 224. See also *Lipke v. Lederer*, 259 U.S. 557 (1922) (same). Moreover, while the penalty is assessed and collected by the IRS, § 5000A is administered both by that agency and by the Department of Health and Human Services (and also the Secretary of Veteran Affairs), which is responsible for defining its substantive scope—a feature that would be quite extraordinary for taxes.

The Government points out that "[t]he amount of the penalty will be calculated as a percentage of household income for federal income tax purposes, subject to a floor and [a] ca[p]," and that individuals who earn so little money that they "are not required to file income tax returns for the taxable year are not subject to the penalty" (though they are, as we discussed earlier, subject to the mandate). Petitioners' Minimum Coverage Brief 12, 53. But varying a penalty according to ability to pay is an utterly familiar practice. See, *e.g.*, 33 U.S.C. § 1319(d) (2006 ed., Supp. IV) ("In determining the amount of a civil penalty the court shall consider . . . the economic impact of the penalty on the violator").

The last of the feeble arguments in favor of petitioners that we will address is the contention that what this statute repeatedly calls a penalty is in fact a tax because it contains no scienter requirement. The *presence* of such a requirement suggests a penalty—though one can imagine a tax imposed only on willful action; but the *absence* of such a requirement does not suggest a tax. Penalties for absolute-liability offenses are commonplace. And where a statute is silent as to scienter, we traditionally presume a *mens rea* requirement if the statute imposes a "severe penalty." *Staples v. United States,* 511 U.S. 600, 618 (1994). Since we have an entire jurisprudence addressing when it is that a scienter requirement should be inferred from a penalty, it is quite illogical to suggest that a penalty is not a penalty for want of an express scienter requirement.

And the nail in the coffin is that the mandate and penalty are located in Title I of the Act, its operative core, rather than where a tax would be found—in Title IX, containing the Act's "Revenue Provisions." In sum, "the terms of [the] act rende[r] it unavoidable," *Parsons v. Bedford,* 3 Pet. (28 U.S.) 433, 448 (1830), that Congress imposed a regulatory penalty, not a tax.

For all these reasons, to say that the Individual Mandate merely imposes a tax is not to interpret the statute but to rewrite it. Judicial tax-writing is particularly troubling. Taxes have never been popular, see, *e.g.*, Stamp Act of 1765, and in part for that reason, the Constitution requires tax increases to originate in the House of Representatives. See Art. I, § 7, cl. 1. That is to say, they must originate in the legislative body most accountable to the people, where legislators must weigh the need for the tax against the terrible price they might pay at their next election, which is never more than two years off. The Federalist No. 58 "defend[ed] the decision to give the origination power to the House on the ground that the Chamber that is more accountable to the people should have the primary role in raising revenue." *United States v. Munoz-Flores,* 495 U.S. 385, 395 (1990). We have no doubt that Congress knew precisely what it was doing when it rejected an earlier version of this legislation that imposed a tax instead of a requirement-with-penalty. See Affordable Health Care for America Act, H.R. 3962, 111th Cong., 1st Sess., § 501 (2009); America's Healthy Future Act of 2009, S. 1796, 111th Cong., 1st Sess., § 1301. Imposing a tax through judicial legislation inverts the constitutional scheme, and places the power to tax in the branch of government least accountable to the citizenry.

POINTS FOR DISCUSSION

a. Constitutional Law, Statutory Interpretation, or Both?

Is the dispute in this part of the case about the scope of the taxing power, about how to interpret 26 U.S.C. § 5000A, or about both? Do the majority and dissent disagree about the scope of Congress's power to tax? Does either side reject the Penalty Doctrine established in the *Child Labor Tax Case,* 259 U.S. 20, 38 (1922), and subsequently limited by the Doctrine of Objective Constitutionality established in *United States v. Kahriger,* 345 U.S. 22 (1953)?

b. Capitation or Direct Tax

Is there a counter argument to the majority's conclusion that the Shared Responsibility Payment is not a capitation or a direct tax? The Brief of the Tax Foundation as Amicus Curiae In Support of Respondents asserted:

> Assuming arguendo that the Government's characterization of the mandate as a tax is correct, it would operate as a levy on individuals and not their incomes. The mandate penalty in 2016, for example, is imposed either in the amount of $695 per uninsured adult, or at the rate of 2.5 percent of the uninsured taxpayer's income in excess of the filing threshold (in 2010, $9,350), whichever is greater. See 26 U.S.C. § 5000A(c). Although the latter calculation could conceivably be considered a tax on income, the former direct amount cannot be. If it is a tax, it is a capitation tax, levied directly on the individual. Because its collection is not apportioned according to state population, its operation would violate U.S. Const, art. I, § 9, cl. 4.

Department of Health & Human Servs. v. Florida, 2012 WL 523361, *17–18 (U.S.) (Brief of the Tax Foundation as Amicus Curiae In Support of Respondents).

D. THE SPENDING POWER

Given that Congress has the power to tax, it is not surprising that it also has the power to spend the money that it raises through taxation. Article I, § 8, cl. 1 authorizes Congress "to pay the Debts and provide for the common Defence and general Welfare of the United States." As the following cases will show, the Supreme Court has held that Congress has broad discretion to use the spending power. It can authorize any spending that is necessary and proper for carrying out its express powers under Article, I, § 8, such as building post offices or raising an Army and a Navy. Congress can also spend money on matters unrelated to its express powers so long as the spending promotes the general welfare—a subject that is almost entirely within the discretion of Congress. A more complicated question is whether Congress can attach conditions to spending and thus achieve goals that it cannot achieve directly through the exercise of the commerce power. Does it matter whether Congress is granting money to private actors or instead to the state governments? The cases that follow grapple with those questions.

UNITED STATES V. BUTLER

297 U.S. 1 (1936)

MR. JUSTICE ROBERTS delivered the opinion of the Court.

In this case we must determine whether certain provisions of the Agricultural Adjustment Act [of] 1933 conflict with the Federal Constitution. [In order to achieve the Act's stated purpose of stabilizing prices for agricultural commodities, the Act empowered the Secretary of Agriculture to pay farmers to reduce the number of acres dedicated to production for market. The Act further provided that the Secretary would obtain revenue for such payments by taxing processors of the particular agricultural commodity whose production the Secretary sought to limit. After the Secretary decided to stabilize cotton prices, the United States sought to impose a tax on the Hoosac Mills Corporation. The receivers of the company challenged the tax and the statutory scheme that authorized it.]

Take Note

Justice Roberts is the Justice who "switched" his vote on the scope of federal power in 1937, one year after the decision in *Butler* (and *Carter Coal*). As you read his opinion here, consider whether it gives any hints of the switch to come.

It is not contended that [Article I, § 8, cl. 1] grants power to regulate agricultural production upon the theory that such legislation would promote the general welfare. The government concedes that the phrase "to provide for the general welfare" qualifies the power "to lay and collect taxes." The view that the clause grants power to provide for the general welfare, independently of the taxing power, has never been authoritatively accepted. Mr. Justice Story points out that, if it were adopted, "it is obvious that under color of the generality of the words, to 'provide for the common defence and general welfare,' the government of the United States is, in reality, a government of general and unlimited powers, notwithstanding the subsequent enumeration of specific powers." The true construction undoubtedly is that the only thing granted is the power to tax for the purpose of providing funds for payment of the nation's debts and making provision for the general welfare.

Nevertheless, the government asserts that warrant is found in this clause for the adoption of the Agricultural Adjustment Act. * * * Since the foundation of the nation, sharp differences of opinion have persisted as to the true interpretation of the phrase ["to provide for the general Welfare of the United States."] Madison asserted it amounted to no more than a reference to the other powers enumerated in the subsequent clauses of the same section; that, as the United States is a government of limited and enumerated powers, the grant of power to tax and spend for the general national welfare must be confined to the enumerated legislative fields committed to the Congress. In this view the phrase is mere tautology, for taxation and appropriation are or may be necessary incidents of the exercise of any of the enumerated legislative powers. Hamilton, on the other hand, maintained the clause confers a power separate and distinct from those later enumerated, is not restricted in meaning by the grant of them, and Congress consequently has a substantive power to tax and to appropriate, limited only by the requirement that it shall be exercised to provide for the general welfare of the United States. Each contention has had the support of those whose views are entitled to weight.

Food for Thought

The disagreement between Madison and Hamilton about the scope of the spending power is one of a few prominent disagreements between the two principal authors of the Federalist Papers, which are widely regarded as having provided the most cogent arguments in favor of ratification of the Constitution. Are such disagreements problematic for the theory of originalism, which holds that the Constitution's meaning is fixed according to the original meaning of its text? Is there any other method of interpreting the Constitution which involves fewer ambiguities or differences of opinion?

[We] conclude that the reading advocated by [Hamilton] is the correct one. While, therefore, the power to tax is not unlimited, its confines are set in the clause which confers it, and not in those of section 8 which bestow and define the legislative powers of the Congress. It results that the power of Congress to authorize expenditure of public moneys for public purposes is not limited by the direct grants of legislative power found in the Constitution.

We are not now required to ascertain the scope of the phrase "general welfare of the United States" or to determine whether an appropriation in aid of agriculture falls within it. Wholly apart from that question, another principle embedded in our Constitution prohibits the enforcement of the Agricultural Adjustment Act. The act invades the reserved rights of the states. It is a statutory plan to regulate and control agricultural production, a matter beyond the powers delegated to the federal government. The tax, the appropriation of the funds raised, and the direction for their disbursement are but parts of the plan. They are but means to an unconstitutional end.

From the accepted doctrine that the United States is a government of delegated powers, it follows that those not expressly granted, or reasonably to be implied from such as are conferred, are reserved to the states or to the people. To forestall any suggestion to the contrary, the Tenth Amendment was adopted. The same proposition, otherwise stated, is that powers not granted are prohibited. None to regulate agricultural production is given, and therefore legislation by Congress for that purpose is forbidden.

The government asserts that [the plan] is constitutionally sound because the end is accomplished by voluntary co-operation. [But the] regulation is not in fact voluntary. The farmer, of course, may refuse to comply, but the price of such refusal is the loss of benefits. * * * This is coercion by economic pressure. The asserted power of choice is illusory. But if the plan were one for purely voluntary co-operation it would stand no better so far as federal power is concerned. At best, it is a scheme for purchasing with federal funds submission to federal regulation of a subject reserved to the states. * * * [C]ontracts for the reduction of acreage and the control of production are outside the range of [federal] power. * * * The Congress cannot invade state jurisdiction to compel individual action; no more can it purchase such action.

MR. JUSTICE STONE, [joined by MR. JUSTICE BRANDEIS and MR. JUSTICE CARDOZO,] dissenting.

The suggestion of coercion finds no support in the record or in any data showing the actual operation of the act. Threat of loss, not hope of gain, is the essence of economic coercion.

It is upon the contention that state power is infringed by purchased regulation of agricultural production that chief reliance is placed. * * * The Constitution requires that public funds shall be spent for a defined purpose, the promotion of the general welfare. * * * Expenditures would fail of their purpose and thus lose their constitutional sanction if the terms of payment were not such that by their influence on the action of the recipients the permitted end would be attained. * * * Congress may not command that the science of agriculture be taught in state universities. But if it would aid the teaching of that science by grants to state institutions, it is appropriate, if not necessary, that the grant be on the condition that it be used for the intended purpose. * * * It is a contradiction in terms to say that there is power to spend for the national welfare, while rejecting any power to impose conditions reasonably adapted to the attainment of the end which alone would justify the expenditure.

The limitation now sanctioned must lead to absurd consequences. The government may give seeds to farmers, but may not condition the gift upon their being planted in places where they are most needed or even planted at all. The government may give money to the unemployed, but may not ask that those who get it shall give labor in return, or even use it to support their families. * * * If the expenditure is for a national public purpose, that purpose will not be thwarted because payment is on condition which will advance that purpose.

The power to tax and spend is not without constitutional restraints. One restriction is that the purpose must be truly national. Another is that it may not be used to coerce action left to state control. Another is the conscience and patriotism of Congress and the Executive. [But] interpretation of our great charter of government which proceeds on any assumption that the responsibility for the preservation of our institutions is the exclusive concern of any one of the three branches of government * * * is far more likely, in the long run, "to obliterate the constituent members" of "an indestructible union of indestructible states" than the frank recognition that language, even of a constitution, may mean what it says: that the power to tax and spend includes the power to relieve a nationwide economic maladjustment by conditional gifts of money.

POINTS FOR DISCUSSION

a. Competing Views of the General Welfare Clause

As a textual matter, there are three potential interpretations of the General Welfare Clause. First, one could read the clause as a grant of authority that is separate from the preceding provision that confers the power to tax—in effect, to read, "Congress shall have Power To . . . provide for the common Defence and general Welfare of the United States." Under this reading, Congress would have the power to pass virtually any regulation, subject only to the requirement that the regulation be in the general welfare. If this reading were correct, then limits on Congress's other powers would be irrelevant.

Second, one could read the General Welfare Clause simply as a shorthand reference to the enumerated powers that follow in Article I, § 8. Under this view, which James Madison advanced, Congress would have power to tax or spend only when it is acting legitimately pursuant to one of its other enumerated powers. If this reading were correct, then Congress would have no authority to spend beyond that which it is already authorized to do pursuant to its other enumerated powers in conjunction with the Necessary and Proper Clause. On this view, the General Welfare Clause would simply confirm that one of the permissible means of effectuating the enumerated powers is the expenditure of money.

Third, one could read the General Welfare Clause to permit Congress to spend for the general welfare even if Congress could not achieve its desired objective pursuant to its other enumerated powers. This view, which Alexander Hamilton advanced, mediates between the broad implications of the first view and the constraining implications of the Madisonian view. On this view, Congress's power to spend would be broader than its power to regulate pursuant to its other enumerated powers.

The Court in *Butler* stated that the Hamiltonian view was the correct interpretation of the General Welfare Clause. Did the Court properly apply that view to the federal spending program challenged in the case?

b. The New Deal and Federal Spending Programs

Butler was one of several cases—many of which we have already seen—in which the Court invalidated federal enactments that were part of the New Deal. But just as the Court began in 1937 to recognize broader federal authority under the Commerce Clause and broader governmental power to regulate social and economic matters—a topic we consider in Volume 2—the Court began that year to uphold federal spending programs, as well. In *Charles C. Steward Machine Co. v. Davis,* 301 U.S. 548 (1937), the Court upheld, in a 5–4 decision, the unemployment compensation provisions of the Social Security Act, which had been a centerpiece of the New Deal legislative program. The challenged provision imposed a payroll tax on employers but provided a rebate to employers who contributed to a state unemployment compensation fund. The Court acknowledged that "every rebate from a tax when conditioned upon conduct is in some measure a temptation. But to hold that motive or temptation is equivalent to coercion is to plunge the law in endless difficulties." And in *Helvering v. Davis*, 301 U.S. 619 (1937), the Court upheld, in a 7–2 decision, the old-age benefits provisions of the Social Security Act, which imposed a tax on employees to fund payments to older citizens. The Court noted that the discretion to draw the line between matters of local and general welfare "belongs to Congress, unless the choice is clearly wrong, a display of arbitrary power."

The Court's view of Congress's spending power in the modern era has been similarly broad, as the following case demonstrates.

South Dakota v. Dole

483 U.S. 203 (1987)

Chief Justice Rehnquist delivered the opinion of the Court.

Petitioner South Dakota permits persons 19 years of age or older to purchase beer containing up to 3.2% alcohol. In 1984 Congress enacted 23 U.S.C. § 158, which directs the Secretary of Transportation to withhold a percentage of federal highway funds otherwise allocable from States "in which the purchase or public possession [of] any alcoholic beverage by a person who is less than twenty-one years of age is lawful." The State sued * * * seeking a declaratory judgment that § 158 violates the constitutional limitations on congressional exercise of the spending power and violates the Twenty-first Amendment to the United States Constitution.

> **FYI**
>
> The Twenty-First Amendment, which repealed Prohibition, provides in relevant part: "The transportation or importation into any State, Territory, or possession of the United States for delivery or use therein of intoxicating liquors, in violation of the laws thereof, is hereby prohibited." One reading of this language—though certainly not the only plausible one—is that the States' control over the lawfulness of the sale or possession of alcohol is plenary, notwithstanding Congress's affirmative powers. But see *Granholm v. Heald*, 544 U.S. 460 (2005).

In this Court, the parties direct most of their efforts to defining the proper scope of the Twenty-first Amendment[,] the bounds of which have escaped precise definition. Despite the extended treatment of the question by the parties, however, we need not decide in this case whether that Amendment would prohibit an attempt by Congress to legislate directly a national minimum drinking age. Here, Congress has acted indirectly under its spending power to encourage uniformity in the States' drinking ages. [W]e find this legislative effort within constitutional bounds even if Congress may not regulate drinking ages directly.

Incident to [the spending] power, Congress may attach conditions on the receipt of federal funds * * *. The breadth of this power was made clear in *Butler*, where the Court [determined that] objectives not thought to be within Article I's "enumerated legislative fields" may nevertheless be attained through the use of the spending power and the conditional grant of federal funds.

The spending power is of course not unlimited, but is instead subject to several general restrictions articulated in our cases. The first of these limitations is derived from the language of the Constitution itself: the exercise of the spending power must be in pursuit of "the general welfare." In considering whether a particular expenditure is intended to serve general public purposes, courts should defer substantially to the judgment of Congress. Second, we have required that if Congress desires to condition the States' receipt of federal funds, it "must do so unambiguously, enabling the States to exercise their choice knowingly, cognizant of the consequences of their participation." Third, our cases have suggested (without significant elaboration) that conditions on federal grants might be illegitimate if they are unrelated "to the federal interest in particular national projects or programs." Finally, we have noted that other constitutional provisions may provide an independent bar to the conditional grant of federal funds.

We can readily conclude that the provision is designed to serve the general welfare * * *. Congress found that the differing drinking ages in the States created particular incentives for young persons to combine their desire to drink with their ability to drive, and that this interstate problem required a national solution. * * * The conditions upon which States receive the funds, moreover, could not be more clearly stated by Congress. And * * * the condition imposed by Congress is directly related to one of the main purposes for which highway funds are expended—safe interstate travel. * * * [T]he lack of uniformity in the States' drinking ages create[s] "an incentive to drink and drive" because "young persons commute to border States where the drinking age is lower." By enacting § 158, Congress conditioned the receipt of federal funds in a way reasonably calculated to address this particular impediment to a purpose for which the funds are expended.

Food for Thought

What is the point of the "germaneness" requirement? If the Hamiltonian view of the spending power is correct, then the consequence is that Congress may achieve pursuant to the spending power objectives that it could not achieve directly pursuant to the commerce power. If this is true, then why does it matter whether the condition imposed on the receipt of funds is related to the purpose for which the funds are granted?

The remaining question about the validity of § 158—and the basic point of disagreement between the parties—is whether the Twenty-first Amendment constitutes an "independent constitutional bar" to the conditional grant of federal funds. * * * [T]he "independent constitutional bar" limitation on the spending power is not, as petitioner suggests, a prohibition on the indirect achievement of objectives which Congress is not empowered to achieve directly. Instead, we think that the language in our earlier opinions stands for the unexceptionable proposition that the power may not be used to induce the States to engage in activities that would themselves be unconstitutional. Thus, for example, a grant of federal funds conditioned on invidiously discriminatory state action or the infliction of cruel and unusual punishment would be an illegitimate exercise of the

Congress' broad spending power. But no such claim can be or is made here. Were South Dakota to succumb to the blandishments offered by Congress and raise its drinking age to 21, the State's action in so doing would not violate the constitutional rights of anyone.

Our decisions have recognized that in some circumstances the financial inducement offered by Congress might be so coercive as to pass the point at which "pressure turns into compulsion." *Steward Machine*. Here, however, Congress has directed only that a State desiring to establish a minimum drinking age lower than 21 lose a relatively small percentage of certain federal highway funds. Petitioner contends that the coercive nature of this program is evident from the degree of success it has achieved. We cannot conclude, however, that a conditional grant of federal money of this sort is unconstitutional simply by reason of its success in achieving the congressional objective. When we consider * * * that all South Dakota would lose if she adheres to her chosen course as to a suitable minimum drinking age is 5% of the funds otherwise obtainable under specified highway grant programs, the argument as to coercion is shown to be more rhetoric than fact.

Here Congress has offered relatively mild encouragement to the States to enact higher minimum drinking ages than they would otherwise choose. But the enactment of such laws remains the prerogative of the States not merely in theory but in fact. Even if Congress might lack the power to impose a national minimum drinking age directly, we conclude that encouragement to state action found in § 158 is a valid use of the spending power.

JUSTICE BRENNAN, dissenting.

[R]egulation of the minimum age of purchasers of liquor falls squarely within the ambit of those powers reserved to the States by the Twenty-first Amendment. Since States possess this constitutional power, Congress cannot condition a federal grant in a manner that abridges this right. The Amendment, itself, strikes the proper balance between federal and state authority.

JUSTICE O'CONNOR, dissenting.

My disagreement with the Court * * * on the spending power issue * * * is a disagreement about the application of a principle rather than a disagreement on the principle itself. * * * In my view, establishment of a minimum drinking age of 21 is not sufficiently related to interstate highway construction to justify so conditioning funds appropriated for that purpose.

[I]f the purpose of § 158 is to deter drunken driving, it is far too over and under-inclusive. It is over-inclusive because it stops teenagers from drinking even when they are not about to drive on interstate highways. It is under-inclusive because teenagers pose only a small part of the drunken driving problem in this Nation. When Congress appropriates money to build a highway, it is entitled to insist that the highway be a safe one. But it is not entitled to insist as a condition of the use of highway funds that the State impose or change regulations in other areas of the State's social and economic life because of an attenuated or tangential relationship to highway use or safety. Indeed, if the rule were otherwise, the Congress could effectively regulate almost any area of a State's social, political, or economic life on the theory that use of the interstate transportation system is somehow enhanced.

"Congress has no power under the Spending Clause to impose requirements on a grant that go beyond specifying how the money should be spent. A requirement that is not such a specification is not a condition, but a regulation, which is valid only if it falls within one of Congress' delegated regulatory powers." [Br. for the National Conf. of State Legislatures as *Amicus Curiae.*] This approach harks back to *Butler.* * * * The *Butler* Court saw the Agricultural Adjustment Act for what it was—an exercise of regulatory, not spending, power. The error in *Butler* was not the Court's conclusion that the Act was essentially regulatory, but rather its crabbed view of the extent of Congress' regulatory power under the Commerce Clause. The Agricultural Adjustment Act was regulatory but it was regulation that today would likely be considered within Congress' commerce power. *Wickard.*

> **Take Note**
>
> Justice O'Connor reasoned that Congress should be permitted to impose conditions on a state's receipt of funds only if the condition dictates how the granted funds may be spent. In light of this position, would you say that her disagreement with the Court was over the "application of a principle rather than a disagreement on the principle itself"?

If the spending power is to be limited only by Congress' notion of the general welfare, the reality, given the vast financial resources of the Federal Government, is that the Spending Clause gives "power to the Congress to tear down the barriers, to invade the states' jurisdiction, and to become a parliament of the whole people, subject to no restrictions save such as are self-imposed." *Butler.*

POINTS FOR DISCUSSION

a. Conditioned Spending

The statute in *Dole*, unlike the statute in *Butler*, involved a grant of funds to the states, rather than to private persons. When Congress grants funds to the states with conditions attached, Congress seeks to encourage—or perhaps force—the states to regulate pursuant to federal directives. Should such grants to the states be viewed as presumptively more constitutionally suspect than conditional grants to private persons?

b. The Limits on the Spending Power

The Court in *Dole* articulated five requirements for the exercise of the spending power: (1) Congress must act in pursuit of the general welfare; (2) any conditions on the states' receipt of federal funds must be imposed unambiguously; (3) the conditions imposed on the receipt of funds must be germane to the purposes for which Congress approved the grant; (4) the condition cannot require action that would violate some other constitutional provision; and (5) Congress cannot offer the states financial inducements that amount to coercion. Given the Court's application of these requirements, are there meaningful limits on Congress's power to achieve its regulatory objectives through the exercise of the spending power? Can you think of examples of laws that would violate each of these requirements? Why has the Court permitted Congress such broad leeway to act pursuant to the spending power while imposing more limits on Congress's power to act pursuant to the Commerce Clause? Consider the case that follows.

NATIONAL FEDERATION OF INDEPENDENT BUSINESS V. SEBELIUS

567 U.S. 519 (2012)

[The Patient Protection and Affordable Care Act of 2010 ("Affordable Care Act" or "ACA"), Pub. L. No. 111–148, 124 Stat 119 (2010), is a complicated law containing hundreds of provisions that aim to make health care in the United States less expensive and more accessible. Shortly after enactment of the law, twenty-six states and several private litigants challenged its constitutionality. Portions of the lengthy Supreme Court decision in the case appear in three parts of this book. This portion considers whether Congress properly used the Spending Clause to induce states to participate in what the Supreme Court informally called the "Medicaid expansion." Chief Justice Roberts's opinion explained the Medicaid expansion briefly as follows:

> The second provision of the Affordable Care Act directly challenged here is the Medicaid expansion. Enacted in 1965, Medicaid offers federal funding to States to assist pregnant women, children, needy families, the blind, the elderly, and the disabled in obtaining medical care. See 42 U.S.C. § 1396a(a)(10). In order to receive that funding, States must comply with federal criteria governing matters such as who receives care

> and what services are provided at what cost. By 1982 every State had chosen to participate in Medicaid. Federal funds received through the Medicaid program have become a substantial part of state budgets, now constituting over 10 percent of most States' total revenue.
>
> The Affordable Care Act expands the scope of the Medicaid program and increases the number of individuals the States must cover. For example, the Act requires state programs to provide Medicaid coverage to adults with incomes up to 133 percent of the federal poverty level, whereas many States now cover adults with children only if their income is considerably lower, and do not cover childless adults at all. See § 1396a(a)(10)(A)(i)(VIII). The Act increases federal funding to cover the States' costs in expanding Medicaid coverage, although States will bear a portion of the costs on their own. § 1396d(y)(1). If a State does not comply with the Act's new coverage requirements, it may lose not only the federal funding for those requirements, but all of its federal Medicaid funds. See § 1396c.

Two opinions in the case concluded that the Medicaid Expansion was unconstitutional. One of these opinions was written by Chief Justice Roberts and joined by Justices Breyer and Kagan. The other opinion was jointly written by Justices Scalia, Kennedy, Thomas, and Alito. Justice Ginsburg wrote a third opinion, joined by Justice Sotomayor, in which she concluded that the Medicaid expansion is constitutional. The relevant portions of these three lengthy opinions are excerpted below in the order in which they appear in the published decision.]

[Opinion of CHIEF JUSTICE ROBERTS, joined by JUSTICE BREYER and JUSTICE KAGAN.]

The States also contend that the Medicaid expansion exceeds Congress's authority under the Spending Clause. They claim that Congress is coercing the States to adopt the changes it wants by threatening to withhold all of a State's Medicaid grants, unless the State accepts the new expanded funding and complies with the conditions that come with it. This, they argue, violates the basic principle that the "Federal Government may not compel the States to enact or administer a federal regulatory program." *New York v. United States,* 505 U.S. 144, 188 (1992).

There is no doubt that the Act dramatically increases state obligations under Medicaid. The current Medicaid program requires States to cover only certain discrete categories of needy individuals—pregnant women, children, needy families, the blind, the elderly, and the disabled. There is no mandatory coverage for most childless adults, and the States typically do not offer any such coverage.

The States also enjoy considerable flexibility with respect to the coverage levels for parents of needy families. On average States cover only those unemployed parents who make less than 37 percent of the federal poverty level, and only those employed parents who make less than 63 percent of the poverty line.

The Medicaid provisions of the Affordable Care Act, in contrast, require States to expand their Medicaid programs by 2014 to cover *all* individuals under the age of 65 with incomes below 133 percent of the federal poverty line. The Act also establishes a new "[e]ssential health benefits" package, which States must provide to all new Medicaid recipients—a level sufficient to satisfy a recipient's obligations under the individual mandate. The Affordable Care Act provides that the Federal Government will pay 100 percent of the costs of covering these newly eligible individuals through 2016. In the following years, the federal payment level gradually decreases, to a minimum of 90 percent. In light of the expansion in coverage mandated by the Act, the Federal Government estimates that its Medicaid spending will increase by approximately $100 billion per year, nearly 40 percent above current levels.

The Spending Clause grants Congress the power "to pay the Debts and provide for the . . . general Welfare of the United States." U.S. Const., Art. I, § 8, cl. 1. We have long recognized that Congress may use this power to grant federal funds to the States, and may condition such a grant upon the States' "taking certain actions that Congress could not require them to take." *College Savings Bank v. Florida Prepaid Postsecondary Educ. Expense Bd.,* 527 U.S. 666, 686 (1999). Such measures "encourage a State to regulate in a particular way, [and] influenc[e] a State's policy choices." *New York*, supra, at 166. The conditions imposed by Congress ensure that the funds are used by the States to "provide for the . . . general Welfare" in the manner Congress intended.

As our decision in *Charles C. Steward Mach. Co. v. Davis,* 301 U.S. 548 (1937), confirms, Congress may attach appropriate conditions to federal taxing and spending programs to preserve its control over the use of federal funds. In the typical case we look to the States to defend their prerogatives by adopting "the simple expedient of not yielding" to federal blandishments when they do not want to embrace the federal policies as their own. *Massachusetts v. Mellon,* 262 U.S. 447, 482 (1923). The States are separate and independent sovereigns. Sometimes they have to act like it.

The States, however, argue that the Medicaid expansion is far from the typical case. They object that Congress has "crossed the line distinguishing encouragement from coercion," *New York*, *supra*, at 175, in the way it has structured the funding: Instead of simply refusing to grant the new funds to States that will not accept the new conditions, Congress has also threatened to withhold those States' existing Medicaid funds. The States claim that this threat serves no purpose other than to force unwilling States to sign up for the dramatic expansion in health care coverage effected by the Act.

Given the nature of the threat and the programs at issue here, we must agree. We have upheld Congress's authority to condition the receipt of funds on the States' complying with restrictions on the use of those funds, because that is the means by which Congress ensures that the funds are spent according to its view of the "general Welfare." Conditions that do not here govern the use of the funds, however, cannot be justified on that basis. When, for example, such conditions take the form of threats to terminate other significant independent grants, the conditions are properly viewed as a means of pressuring the States to accept policy changes.

In *South Dakota v. Dole*, 483 U.S. 203 (1987), we considered a challenge to a federal law that threatened to withhold five percent of a State's federal highway funds if the State did not raise its drinking age to 21. The Court found that the condition was "directly related to one of the main purposes for which highway funds are expended—safe interstate travel." *Id.* at 208. At the same time, the condition was not a restriction on how the highway funds—set aside for specific highway improvement and maintenance efforts—were to be used.

We accordingly asked whether "the financial inducement offered by Congress" was "so coercive as to pass the point at which 'pressure turns into compulsion.' " *Id.*, at 211 (quoting *Steward Machine*, *supra*, at 590). By "financial inducement" the Court meant the threat of losing five percent of highway funds; no new money was offered to the States to raise their drinking ages. We found that the inducement was not impermissibly coercive, because Congress was offering only "relatively mild encouragement to the States." *Dole*, 483 U.S., at 211. We observed that "all South Dakota would lose if she adheres to her chosen course as to a suitable minimum drinking age is 5%" of her highway funds. *Ibid.* In fact, the federal funds at stake constituted less than half of one percent of South Dakota's budget at the time. In consequence, "we conclude[d] that [the] encouragement to state action [was] a valid use of the spending power." 483 U.S., at 212. Whether to accept the drinking age change "remain[ed] the prerogative of the States not merely in theory but in fact." *Id.*, at 211–212.

In this case, the financial "inducement" Congress has chosen is much more than "relatively mild encouragement"—it is a gun to the head. Section 1396c of the Medicaid Act provides that if a State's Medicaid plan does not comply with the Act's requirements, the Secretary of Health and Human Services may declare that "further payments will not be made to the State." 42 U.S.C. § 1396c. A State that opts out of the Affordable Care Act's expansion in health care coverage thus stands to lose not merely "a relatively small percentage" of its existing Medicaid funding, but *all* of it. *Dole, supra,* at 211. Medicaid spending accounts for over 20 percent of the average State's total budget, with federal funds covering 50 to 83 percent of those costs. The Federal Government estimates that it will pay out approximately $3.3 trillion between 2010 and 2019 in order to cover the costs of *pre*-expansion Medicaid. In addition, the States have developed intricate statutory and administrative regimes over the course of many decades to implement their objectives under existing Medicaid. It is easy to see how the *Dole* Court could conclude that the threatened loss of less than half of one percent of South Dakota's budget left that State with a "prerogative" to reject Congress's desired policy, "not merely in theory but in fact." 483 U.S., at 211–212. The threatened loss of over 10 percent of a State's overall budget, in contrast, is economic dragooning that leaves the States with no real option but to acquiesce in the Medicaid expansion.

Here, the Government claims that the Medicaid expansion is properly viewed merely as a modification of the existing program because the States agreed that Congress could change the terms of Medicaid when they signed on in the first place. The Government observes that the Social Security Act, which includes the original Medicaid provisions, contains a clause expressly reserving "[t]he right to alter, amend, or repeal any provision" of that statute. 42 U.S.C. § 1304. So it does. But "if Congress intends to impose a condition on the grant of federal moneys, it must do so unambiguously." *Pennhurst State School and Hospital v. Halderman,* 451 U.S. 1, 17 (1981). A State confronted with statutory language reserving the right to "alter" or "amend" the pertinent provisions of the Social Security Act might reasonably assume that Congress was entitled to make adjustments to the Medicaid program as it developed. Congress has in fact done so, sometimes conditioning only the new funding, other times both old and new. See, *e.g.,* Social Security Amendments of 1972, 86 Stat. 1381–1382, 1465 (extending Medicaid eligibility, but partly conditioning only the new funding); Omnibus Budget Reconciliation Act of 1990, § 4601, 104 Stat. 1388–166 (extending eligibility, and conditioning old and new funds).

The Medicaid expansion, however, accomplishes a shift in kind, not merely degree. The original program was designed to cover medical services for four particular categories of the needy: the disabled, the blind, the elderly, and needy families with dependent children. See 42 U.S.C. § 1396a(a)(10). Previous amendments to Medicaid eligibility merely altered and expanded the boundaries of these categories. Under the Affordable Care Act, Medicaid is transformed into a program to meet the health care needs of the entire nonelderly population with income below 133 percent of the poverty level. It is no longer a program to care for the neediest among us, but rather an element of a comprehensive national plan to provide universal health insurance coverage.

The Court in *Steward Machine* did not attempt to "fix the outermost line" where persuasion gives way to coercion. 301 U.S., at 591. The Court found it "[e]nough for present purposes that wherever the line may be, this statute is within it." *Ibid.* We have no need to fix a line either. It is enough for today that wherever that line may be, this statute is surely beyond it. Congress may not simply "conscript state [agencies] into the national bureaucratic army," *FERC v. Mississippi*, 456 U.S. 742, 775 (1982) (O'Connor, J., concurring in judgment in part and dissenting in part), and that is what it is attempting to do with the Medicaid expansion.

> **Take Note**
>
> Why is the court unable to "fix a line" where persuasion becomes coercion? How is Congress to know whether major new conditional spending programs are constitutional?

Nothing in our opinion precludes Congress from offering funds under the Affordable Care Act to expand the availability of health care, and requiring that States accepting such funds comply with the conditions on their use. What Congress is not free to do is to penalize States that choose not to participate in that new program by taking away their existing Medicaid funding. Section 1396c gives the Secretary of Health and Human Services the authority to do just that. It allows her to withhold *all* "further [Medicaid] payments . . . to the State" if she determines that the State is out of compliance with any Medicaid requirement, including those contained in the expansion. 42 U.S.C. § 1396c. In light of the Court's holding, the Secretary cannot apply § 1396c to withdraw existing Medicaid funds for failure to comply with the requirements set out in the expansion.

That fully remedies the constitutional violation we have identified. The chapter of the United States Code that contains § 1396c includes a severability clause confirming that we need go no further. That clause specifies that "[i]f any provision of this chapter, or the application thereof to any person or circumstance, is held invalid, the remainder of the chapter, and the application of such provision to other persons or circumstances shall not be affected thereby." § 1303. Today's holding does not affect the continued application of § 1396c to the existing Medicaid program. Nor does it affect the Secretary's ability to withdraw funds provided under the Affordable Care Act if a State that has chosen to participate in the expansion fails to comply with the requirements of that Act.

[Opinion of JUSTICE GINSBURG, joined by JUSTICE SOTOMAYOR.]

Congress' authority to condition the use of federal funds is not confined to spending programs as first launched. The legislature may, and often does, amend the law, imposing new conditions grant recipients henceforth must meet in order to continue receiving funds. Yes, there are federalism-based limits on the use of Congress' conditional spending power. In the leading decision in this area, *South Dakota v. Dole,* 483 U.S. 203 (1987), the Court identified four criteria. The conditions placed on federal grants to States must (a) promote the "general welfare," (b) "unambiguously" inform States what is demanded of them, (c) be germane "to the federal interest in particular national projects or programs," and (d) not "induce the States to engage in activities that would themselves be unconstitutional." *Id.*, at 207–208, 210 (internal quotation marks omitted).

The Court in *Dole* mentioned, but did not adopt, a further limitation, one hypothetically raised a half-century earlier: In "some circumstances," Congress might be prohibited from offering a "financial inducement . . . so coercive as to pass the point at which 'pressure turns into compulsion.' " *Id.,* at 211 (quoting *Steward Machine Co. v. Davis,* 301 U.S. 548, 590 (1937)). Prior to today's decision, however, the Court has never ruled that the terms of any grant crossed the indistinct line between temptation and coercion.

This case does not present the concerns that led the Court in *Dole* even to consider the prospect of coercion. In *Dole*, the condition—set 21 as the minimum drinking age—did not tell the States how to use funds Congress provided for highway construction. Further, in view of the Twenty-First Amendment, it was an open question whether Congress could directly impose a national minimum drinking age.

The ACA, in contrast, relates solely to the federally funded Medicaid program; if States choose not to comply, Congress has not threatened to withhold funds earmarked for any other program. Nor does the ACA use Medicaid funding to induce States to take action Congress itself could not undertake. The Federal Government undoubtedly could operate its own health-care program for poor persons, just as it operates Medicare for seniors' health care.

> **Take Note**
>
> What distinction does Justice Ginsburg see between this case and *South Dakota v. Dole,* and why does Justice Ginsburg conclude that this distinction makes a difference? Does Justice Ginsburg dispute the conclusion that the ACA is coercive?

That is what makes this such a simple case, and the Court's decision so unsettling. Congress, aiming to assist the needy, has appropriated federal money to subsidize state health-insurance programs that meet federal standards. The principal standard the ACA sets is that the state program cover adults earning no more than 133% of the federal poverty line. Enforcing that prescription ensures that federal funds will be spent on health care for the poor in furtherance of Congress' present perception of the general welfare.

The starting premise on which THE CHIEF JUSTICE's coercion analysis rests is that the ACA did not really "extend" Medicaid; instead, Congress created an entirely new program to co-exist with the old. THE CHIEF JUSTICE calls the ACA new, but in truth, it simply reaches more of America's poor than Congress originally covered.

Medicaid was created to enable States to provide medical assistance to "needy persons." By bringing health care within the reach of a larger population of Americans unable to afford it, the Medicaid expansion is an extension of that basic aim. * * * To the four categories of beneficiaries for whom coverage became mandatory in 1965, and the three mandatory classes added in the late 1980s, the ACA adds an eighth: individuals under 65 with incomes not exceeding 133% of the federal poverty level.

Congress has broad authority to construct or adjust spending programs to meet its contemporary understanding of "the general Welfare." Courts owe a large measure of respect to Congress' characterization of the grant programs it establishes. Even if courts were inclined to second-guess Congress' conception of the character of its legislation, how would reviewing judges divine whether an Act of Congress, purporting to amend a law, is in reality not an amendment, but a new creation? At what point does an extension become so large that it "transforms" the basic law?

Consider also that Congress could have repealed Medicaid. Thereafter, Congress could have enacted Medicaid II, a new program combining the pre-2010 coverage with the expanded coverage required by the ACA. By what right does a court stop Congress from building up without first tearing down?

THE CHIEF JUSTICE [holds] that the Constitution precludes the Secretary from withholding "existing" Medicaid funds based on States' refusal to comply with the expanded Medicaid program. For the foregoing reasons, I disagree that any such withholding would violate the Spending Clause. * * * But in view of THE CHIEF JUSTICE's disposition, I agree with him that the Medicaid Act's severability clause determines the appropriate remedy. That clause provides that "[i]f any provision of [the Medicaid Act], or the application thereof to any person or circumstance, is held invalid, the remainder of the chapter, and the application of such provision to other persons or circumstances shall not be affected thereby." 42 U.S.C. § 1303.

[Joint opinion of JUSTICE SCALIA, KENNEDY, THOMAS, and ALITO.]

Once it is recognized that spending-power legislation cannot coerce state participation, two questions remain: (1) What is the meaning of coercion in this context? (2) Is the ACA's expanded Medicaid coverage coercive? We now turn to those questions.

The answer to the first of these questions—the meaning of coercion in the present context—is straightforward. As we have explained, the legitimacy of attaching conditions to federal grants to the States depends on the voluntariness of the States' choice to accept or decline the offered package. Therefore, if States really have no choice other than to accept the package, the offer is coercive, and the conditions cannot be sustained under the spending power. And as our decision in *South Dakota v. Dole* makes clear, theoretical voluntariness is not enough.

The Federal Government's argument in this case at best pays lip service to the anticoercion principle. The Federal Government suggests that it is sufficient if States are "free, *as a matter of law,* to turn down" federal funds. Brief for Respondents in No. 11–400, p. 17 (emphasis added); see also *id.*, at 25. According to the Federal Government, neither the amount of the offered federal funds nor the amount of the federal taxes extracted from the taxpayers of a State to pay for the program in question is relevant in determining whether there is impermissible coercion. *Id.*, at 41–46.

This argument ignores reality. When a heavy federal tax is levied to support a federal program that offers large grants to the States, States may, as a practical matter, be unable to refuse to participate in the federal program and to substitute a state alternative. Even if a State believes that the federal program is ineffective and inefficient, withdrawal would likely force the State to impose a huge tax increase on its residents, and this new state tax would come on top of the federal taxes already paid by residents to support subsidies to participating States.

Acceptance of the Federal Government's interpretation of the anticoercion rule would permit Congress to dictate policy in areas traditionally governed primarily at the state or local level. Suppose, for example, that Congress enacted legislation offering each State a grant equal to the State's entire annual expenditures for primary and secondary education. Suppose also that this funding came with conditions governing such things as school curriculum, the hiring and tenure of teachers, the drawing of school districts, the length and hours of the school day, the school calendar, a dress code for students, and rules for student discipline. *As a matter of law,* a State could turn down that offer, but if it did so, its residents would not only be required to pay the federal taxes needed to support this expensive new program, but they would also be forced to pay an equivalent amount in state taxes. And if the State gave in to the federal law, the State and its subdivisions would surrender their traditional authority in the field of education. Asked at oral argument whether such a law would be allowed under the spending power, the Solicitor General responded that it would. Tr. of Oral Arg. 44–45 (Mar. 28, 2012).

Whether federal spending legislation crosses the line from enticement to coercion is often difficult to determine, and courts should not conclude that legislation is unconstitutional on this ground unless the coercive nature of an offer is unmistakably clear. In this case, however, there can be no doubt. In structuring the ACA, Congress unambiguously signaled its belief that every State would have no real choice but to go along with the Medicaid Expansion. If the anticoercion rule does not apply in this case, then there is no such rule.

Medicaid has long been the largest federal program of grants to the States. * * * The States devote a larger percentage of their budgets to Medicaid than to any other item. * * * A State forced out of the Medicaid program would face burdens in addition to the loss of federal Medicaid funding. For example, a nonparticipating State might be found to be ineligible for other major federal funding sources, such as Temporary Assistance for Needy Families (TANF), which is premised on the expectation that States will participate in Medicaid. See 42 U.S.C. § 602(a)(3) (2006 ed.) (requiring that certain beneficiaries of TANF funds be "eligible for medical assistance under the State['s Medicaid] plan"). And withdrawal or expulsion from the Medicaid program would not relieve a State's hospitals of their obligation under federal law to provide care for patients who are unable to pay for medical services. The Emergency Medical Treatment and Active Labor Act, § 1395dd, requires hospitals that receive any federal funding to provide stabilization care for indigent patients but does not offer federal funding to assist facilities in carrying out its mandate. Many of these patients are now covered by Medicaid. If providers could not look to the Medicaid program to pay for this care, they would find it exceedingly difficult to comply with federal law unless they were given substantial state support. See, *e.g.,* Brief for Economists as *Amici Curiae* in No 11–400, p. 11. For these reasons, the offer that the ACA makes to the States—go along with a dramatic expansion of Medicaid or potentially lose all federal Medicaid funding—is quite unlike anything that we have seen in a prior spending-power case.

If Congress had thought that States might actually refuse to go along with the expansion of Medicaid, Congress would surely have devised a backup scheme so that the most vulnerable groups in our society, those previously eligible for Medicaid, would not be left out in the cold. But nowhere in the over 900-page Act is such a scheme to be found. By contrast, because Congress thought that some States might decline federal funding for the operation of a "health benefit exchange," Congress provided a backup scheme; if a State declines to participate in the operation of an exchange, the Federal Government will step in and operate an exchange in that State. See 42 U.S.C. § 18041(c)(1). Likewise, knowing that States would not necessarily provide affordable health insurance for aliens lawfully present in the United States—because Medicaid does not require States to provide such coverage—Congress extended the availability of the new federal insurance subsidies to all aliens. See 26 U.S.C. § 36B(c)(1)(B)(ii) (excepting from the income limit individuals who are "not eligible for the medicaid program . . . by reason of [their] alien status"). Congress did not make these subsidies available for citizens with incomes below the poverty level because Congress obviously assumed that they would be covered by Medicaid. If Congress had contemplated that some of these citizens would be left without Medicaid coverage as a result of a State's withdrawal or expulsion from the program, Congress surely would have made them eligible for the tax subsidies provided for low-income aliens.

These features of the ACA convey an unmistakable message: Congress never dreamed that any State would refuse to go along with the expansion of Medicaid. Congress well understood that refusal was not a practical option.

The Federal Government does not dispute the inference that Congress anticipated 100% state participation, but it argues that this assumption was based on the fact that ACA's offer was an "exceedingly generous" gift. * * * This characterization of the ACA's offer raises obvious questions. If that offer is "exceedingly generous," as the Federal Government maintains, why have more than half the States brought this lawsuit, contending that the offer is coercive? And why did Congress find it necessary to threaten that any State refusing to accept this "exceedingly generous" gift would risk losing all Medicaid funds? Congress could have made just the *new* funding provided under the ACA contingent on acceptance of the terms of the Medicaid Expansion. Congress took such an approach in some earlier amendments to Medicaid, separating new coverage requirements and funding from the rest of the program so that only new funding was conditioned on new eligibility extensions. See, *e.g.,* Social Security Amendments of 1972, 86 Stat. 1465.

In sum, it is perfectly clear from the goal and structure of the ACA that the offer of the Medicaid Expansion was one that Congress understood no State could refuse. The Medicaid Expansion therefore exceeds Congress' spending power and cannot be implemented.

POINTS FOR DISCUSSION

a. Differences Among the Opinions

How do the three opinions differ from each other? Does this case have a clear holding? Why might the Chief Justice and Justices Breyer and Kagan have decided not to join the joint opinion by Justices Scalia, Kennedy, Thomas, and Alito?

b. Modification v. Repeal

Does Congress have power to repeal the current Medicaid regime? If Congress could and did repeal the current Medicaid Act, could Congress sometime later enact a new law that creates a program that makes federal funds available only for states that provide coverage for both Medicaid's original beneficiaries and those covered by the Medicaid expansion in the Affordable Care Act? If so, then how could the Medicaid Expansion be unconstitutional?

c. Remedy

Chief Justice Roberts concluded that the constitutional defect in the Medicaid Expansion could be cured by construing the statute to prevent the Secretary from withholding funds from the traditional Medicaid Program in response to a state's failure to comply with the requirements of the Medicaid Expansion. The joint dissent responded by accusing Chief Justice Roberts of "rewriting the Medicaid Expansion." Do you agree that the Chief Justice impermissibly rewrote the statute in order to render it constitutional?

E. THE WAR AND TREATY POWERS

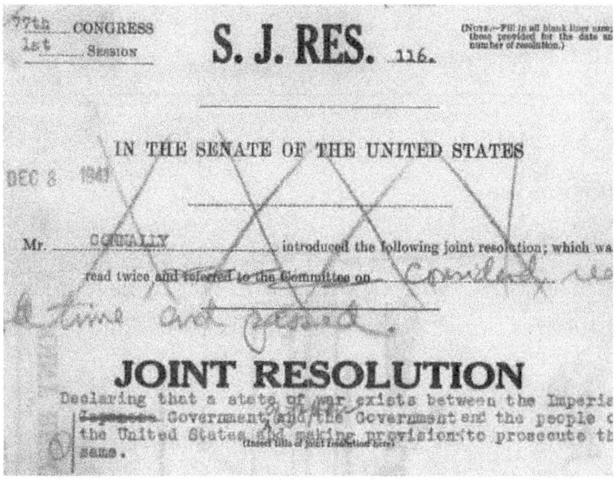
77th CONGRESS
1st SESSION
S. J. RES. 116.

IN THE SENATE OF THE UNITED STATES

DEC 8 1941

Mr. CONNALLY introduced the following joint resolution; which was read twice and referred to the Committee on

JOINT RESOLUTION

Declaring that a state of war exists between the Imperial Japanese Government and the Government and the people of the United States and making provision to prosecute the same.

Senate Joint Resolution 116 (Dec. 8, 1942), "Declaring that a state of war exists between the Imperial Government of Japan and the Government and the people of the United States and making provision to prosecute the same."
U.S. Senate

Article I, § 8 gives Congress the power to declare war, to raise and support armies, to provide and maintain a navy, and to make rules for the regulation of those forces. In addition, Article II, § 2 makes the President the Commander in Chief of the Armed Forces and gives the President the authority to make treaties, subject to the consent of two-thirds of the Senate. Do these powers, particularly when viewed in conjunction with the Necessary and Proper Clause, authorize Congress to legislate on any matter arguably related to war and foreign relations? Consider the two cases that follow.

WOODS V. CLOYD W. MILLER CO.

333 U.S. 138 (1948)

MR. JUSTICE DOUGLAS delivered the opinion of the Court.

The case is here on a direct appeal [from] a judgment of the District Court holding unconstitutional Title II of the Housing and Rent Act of 1947. [The Act made it unlawful "to offer, solicit, demand, accept, or receive any rent for the use or occupancy of any controlled housing accommodations in excess of the maximum rent" prescribed by an agency pursuant to authority under the Act and the Emergency Price Control Act of 1942.] The Act became effective on July 1, 1947, and the following day the appellee demanded of its tenants increases of 40% and 60% for rental accommodations in the Cleveland Defense-Rental Area, and admitted violation of the Act and regulations adopted pursuant thereto. Appellant thereupon instituted this proceeding to enjoin the violations.

The District Court was of the view that the authority of Congress to regulate rents by virtue of the war power ended with the Presidential Proclamation terminating hostilities on December 31, 1946, since that proclamation inaugurated "peace-in-fact" though it did not mark termination of the war. It also concluded that even if the war power continues, Congress did not act under it because it did not say so, and only if Congress says so, or enacts provisions so implying, can it be held that Congress intended to exercise such power.

> **FYI**
>
> Germany and Japan surrendered in 1945, and President Truman in December 1946 proclaimed the "end of hostilities." On December 31, 1946, however, President Truman declared that "a state of war still exists." 12 Fed.Reg. 1. In addition, on July 25, 1947, upon approving a joint resolution terminating various war statutes, President Truman issued a statement declaring that the "emergencies declared by the President on September 8, 1939, and May 27, 1941, and the state of war continue to exist."

We conclude, in the first place, that the war power sustains this legislation. The Court said in *Hamilton v. Kentucky Distilleries and Warehouse Co.*, 251 U.S. 146, 161 (1919), that the war power includes the power "to remedy the evils which have arisen from its rise and progress" and continues for the duration of that emergency. Whatever may be the consequences when war is officially terminated, the war power does not necessarily end with the cessation of hostilities. * * * In *Hamilton* and *Ruppert v. Caffey*, 251 U.S. 264 (1920), prohibition laws which were enacted after the Armistice in World War I were sustained as exercises of the war power because they conserved manpower and increased efficiency of production in the critical days during the period of demobilization, and helped to husband the supply of grains and cereals depleted by the war effort. Those cases followed the reasoning of *Stewart v. Kahn*, 11 Wall. 493 (1870), which held that Congress had the power to toll the statute of limitations of the States during the period when the process of their courts was not available to litigants due to the conditions obtaining in the Civil War.

The constitutional validity of the present legislation follows a fortiori from those cases. The legislative history of the present Act makes abundantly clear that there has not yet been eliminated the deficit in housing which in considerable measure was caused by the heavy demobilization of veterans and by the cessation or reduction in residential construction during the period of hostilities due to the allocation of building materials to military projects. Since the war effort contributed heavily to that deficit, Congress has the power even after the cessation of hostilities to act to control the forces that a short supply of the needed article created. If that were not true, the Necessary and Proper Clause would be drastically limited in its application to the several war powers. [Such a limit] would render Congress powerless to remedy conditions the creation of which necessarily followed from the mobilization of men and materials for successful prosecution of the war. So to read the Constitution would be to make it self-defeating.

We recognize the force of the argument that the effects of war under modern conditions may be felt in the economy for years and years, and that if the war power can be used in days of peace to treat all the wounds which war inflicts on our society, it may not only swallow up all other powers of Congress but largely obliterate the Ninth and the Tenth Amendments as well. There are no such implications in today's decision. We deal here with the consequences of a housing deficit greatly intensified during the period of hostilities by the war effort. Any power, of course, can be abused. But we cannot assume that Congress is not alert to its constitutional responsibilities.

The question of the constitutionality of action taken by Congress does not depend on recitals of the power which it undertakes to exercise. Here it is plain from the legislative history that Congress was invoking its war power to cope with a current condition of which the war was a direct and immediate cause. Its judgment on that score is entitled to the respect granted like legislation enacted pursuant to the police power.

Reversed.

MR. JUSTICE JACKSON, concurring.

I agree with the result in this case, but the arguments that have been addressed to us lead me to utter more explicit misgivings about war powers than the Court has done. The Government asserts no constitutional basis for this legislation other than this vague, undefined and undefinable "war power."

No one will question that this power is the most dangerous one to free government in the whole catalogue of powers. It usually is invoked in haste and excitement when calm legislative consideration of constitutional limitation is difficult. It is executed in a time of patriotic fervor that makes moderation unpopular. And, worst of all, it is interpreted by the Judges under the influence of the same passions and pressures. Always, as in this case, the Government urges hasty decision to forestall some emergency or serve some purpose and pleads that paralysis will result if its claims to power are denied or their confirmation delayed. Particularly when the war power is invoked to do things to the liberties of people, or to their property or economy that only indirectly affect conduct of the war and do not relate to the management of the war itself, the constitutional basis should be scrutinized with care.

I think we can hardly deny that the war power is as valid a ground for federal rent control now as it has been at any time. We still are technically in a state of war. I would not be willing to hold that war powers may be indefinitely prolonged merely by keeping legally alive a state of war that had in fact ended. I cannot accept the argument that war powers last as long as the effects and consequences of war for if so they are permanent—as permanent as the war debts. But I find no reason to conclude that we could find fairly that the present state of war is merely technical. We have armies abroad exercising our war power and have made no peace terms with our allies not to mention our principal enemies. I think the conclusion that the war power has been applicable during the lifetime of this legislation is unavoidable.

MISSOURI V. HOLLAND

252 U.S. 416 (1920)

MR. JUSTICE HOLMES delivered the opinion of the Court.

This is a bill in equity brought by the State of Missouri to prevent a game warden of the United States from attempting to enforce the Migratory Bird Treaty Act of July 3, 1918 * * *. The ground of the bill is that the statute is an unconstitutional interference with the rights reserved to the States by the Tenth Amendment * * *.

On December 8, 1916, a treaty between the United States and Great Britain was proclaimed by the President. It recited that many species of birds in their annual migrations traversed many parts of the United States and of Canada, that they were of great value as a source of food and in destroying insects injurious to vegetation, but were in danger of extermination through lack of adequate protection. It therefore provided for specified closed seasons and protection in other forms, and agreed that the two powers would take or propose to their lawmaking bodies the necessary measures for carrying the treaty out. The [1918 Act], entitled an act to give effect to the convention, prohibited the killing, capturing or selling any of the migratory birds included in the terms of the treaty except as permitted by regulations compatible with those terms, to be made by the Secretary of Agriculture.

To answer this question it is not enough to refer to the Tenth Amendment, reserving the powers not delegated to the United States, because by Article II, Section 2, the power to make treaties is delegated expressly, and by Article VI treaties made under the authority of the United States, along with the Constitution and laws of the United States made in pursuance thereof, are declared the supreme law of the land. If the treaty is valid there can be no dispute about the validity of the statute under Article 1, Section 8, as a necessary and proper means to execute the powers of the Government. The language of the Constitution as to the supremacy of treaties being general, the question before us is narrowed to an inquiry into the ground upon which the present supposed exception is placed.

It is said that a treaty cannot be valid if it infringes the Constitution, that there are limits, therefore, to the treaty-making power, and that one such limit is that what an act of Congress could not do unaided, in derogation of the powers reserved to the States, a treaty cannot do. An earlier act of Congress that attempted by itself and not in pursuance of a treaty to regulate the killing of migratory birds within the States had been held bad in the District Court. *United States v. Shauver*, 214 Fed. 154; *United States v. McCullagh*, 221 Fed. 288.

Food for Thought

What are the "formal acts" that the Constitution prescribes for the creation of a binding treaty? Is it possible that there are no constraints on the treaty power other than compliance with those requirements? Would a treaty be valid if it were inconsistent with the First Amendment or some other protection for individual rights? If not, should federalism-based limits on the government's power be treated any differently?

Whether the two cases cited were decided rightly or not they cannot be accepted as a test of the treaty power. Acts of Congress are the supreme law of the land only when made in pursuance of the Constitution, while treaties are declared to be so when made under the authority of the United States. It is open to question whether the authority of the United States means more than the formal acts prescribed to make the convention.

We do not mean to imply that there are no qualifications to the treaty-making power; but they must be ascertained in a different way. It is obvious that there may be matters of the sharpest exigency for the national well being that an act of Congress could not deal with but that a treaty followed by such an act could, and it is not lightly to be assumed that, in matters requiring national action, "a power which must belong to and somewhere reside in every civilized government" is not to be found. *Andrews v. Andrews*, 188 U.S. 14, 33 (1903). * * * [W]e may add that when we are dealing with words that also are a constituent act, like the Constitution of the United States, we must realize that they have called into life a being the development of which could not have been foreseen completely by the most gifted of its begetters. It was enough for them to realize or to hope that they had created an organism; it has taken a century and has cost their successors much sweat and blood to prove that they created a nation. The case before us must be considered in the light of our whole experience and not merely in that of what was said a hundred years ago. The treaty in question does not contravene any prohibitory words to be found in the Constitution. The only question is whether it is forbidden by some invisible radiation from the general terms of the Tenth Amendment. We must consider what this country has become in deciding what that amendment has reserved.

The State as we have intimated founds its claim of exclusive authority upon an assertion of title to migratory birds, an assertion that is embodied in statute. No doubt it is true that as between a State and its inhabitants the State may regulate the killing and sale of such birds, but it does not follow that its authority is exclusive of paramount powers. * * * Here a national interest of very nearly the first magnitude is involved. It can be protected only by national action in concert with that of another power. The subject matter is only transitorily within the State and has no permanent habitat therein. But for the treaty and the statute there soon might be no birds for any powers to deal with. We see nothing in the Constitution that compels the Government to sit by while a food supply is cut off and the protectors of our forests and our crops are destroyed. It is not sufficient to rely upon the States. The reliance is vain, and were it otherwise, the question is whether the United States is forbidden to act. We are of opinion that the treaty and statute must be upheld.

MR. JUSTICE VAN DEVANTER and MR. JUSTICE PITNEY dissent.

POINTS FOR DISCUSSION

a. The War Power

Article I enumerates several powers related to matters of war. Do those grants of specific authority imply a more general "war power"? What limits might apply to the exercise of such a power? If Congress enjoys such a power after it formally declares war, at what point after the end of a war does the power cease to authorize broad action? Does the power authorize the same sorts of actions when the United States becomes involved in a military conflict without a formal declaration of war, as it has several times in the last half century?

b. The Treaty Power

Article VI provides that treaties made under the authority of the United States, along with the Constitution and statutes "made in pursuance thereof," are the "supreme Law of the Land." Can treaties validly regulate matters that Congress could not regulate pursuant to its other affirmative sources of authority, such as the Commerce Clause? Congress often passes legislation to implement treaties, acting pursuant to the Treaty Power and the Necessary and Proper Clause. Doesn't the Court's decision in *Missouri v. Holland* effectively permit Congress to use this approach to enact laws that would otherwise be inconsistent with federalism norms? Is there a realistic threat that Congress will do so?

In *Bond v. United States*, 572 U.S. 844 (2014), the Court held that a federal statute that implemented a chemical weapons treaty by imposing criminal penalties for possessing and using a chemical weapon did not reach the petitioner's attempt to injure her husband's lover with chemicals. The Court accordingly did not address the government's contention that the statute was a necessary and proper means of executing the power to make treaties. In his concurrence in the judgment, Justice Scalia, joined in relevant part by Justice Thomas, asserted that the Court's approach in *Missouri v. Holland* was inconsistent with the Constitution's text and structure and an unwarranted "loophole" to the principle that Congress does not enjoy limitless power. Justice Thomas, joined in relevant part by Justices Scalia and Alito, also wrote separately to make clear his view that to interpret the Treaty Power to extend "to every conceivable domestic subject matter—even matters without any nexus to foreign relations—would destroy the basic constitutional distinction between domestic and foreign powers," and would impermissibly give the federal government a " 'police power' over all aspects of American life." Should the Court read the Treaty Power and the Necessary and Proper Clause to permit Congress to regulate domestic matters that it otherwise could not regulate pursuant to its other enumerated powers?

F. STATE IMMUNITY FROM FEDERAL REGULATION

The cases that we have considered thus far on the scope of Congress's power have mostly addressed Congress's power to regulate private—that is, non-state—conduct. Indeed, the central question for the exercise of Congress's affirmative powers under Article I has been whether Congress has authority to regulate localized conduct on the theory that the conduct has a sufficient relationship to matters expressly within Congress's competence. Should the question of the scope of Congress's power be answered differently when Congress seeks to regulate state, rather than private, action? (The decision in *South Dakota v. Dole* arguably was an introduction to this question.) We will put to one side for now Congress's power to force state action when acting pursuant to its authority to enforce the Reconstruction Amendments (i.e., the 13th–15th Amendments), which contain explicit limits on the power of the states.

> **Make the Connection**
>
> We consider Congress's power to enforce the Reconstruction Amendments in Volume 2.

We are concerned here with instances in which Congress seeks to exercise its Article I powers to regulate the states, either in the same fashion that it regulates private actors or in a fashion unique to state actors. Are the states immune from all forms of federal regulation? Are they immune from any forms of federal regulation? In the last few decades, the Court has struggled with this question, as the cases that follow will demonstrate.

Three key principles have emerged. First, when acting pursuant to its powers under Article I, Congress may regulate the states in the same fashion that it regulates private actors. See *Garcia v. San Antonio Metropolitan Transit Authority*, 469 U.S. 528 (1985). For example, the federal law that prevents private employers from engaging in age discrimination can be applied to state agencies without violating the Constitution. See *E.E.O.C. v. Kentucky Ret. Sys.*, 16 F. App'x 443, 450 (6th Cir. 2001). Second, Congress cannot compel a state to enact legislation. For example, while Congress can use financial incentives to induce a state to enact a law setting the minimum age for drinking alcohol, *South Dakota v. Dole*, 483 U.S. 203 (1987), Congress cannot require a state to enact such a law. Finally, Congress cannot require state officials to implement or administer federal laws. *Printz v. United States*, 521 U.S. 898 (1997). For example, Congress cannot compel municipal authorities to enforce the federal immigration laws, although state law may require them to do so. See *City of El Cenizo, Texas v. Texas*, 890 F.3d 164, 178 (5th Cir. 2018). We explore these principles in the cases that follow.

NATIONAL LEAGUE OF CITIES V. USERY

426 U.S. 833 (1976)

MR. JUSTICE REHNQUIST delivered the opinion of the Court.

The original Fair Labor Standards Act[, which required employers covered by the Act to pay their employees a minimum hourly wage and time and a half for overtime,] specifically excluded the States and their political subdivisions from its coverage. In 1974, however, Congress * * * extended the minimum wage and maximum hour provisions to almost all public employees employed by the States and by their various political subdivisions.

> **Make the Connection**
>
> Recall that the Court upheld the validity of the wage and hour provisions of the FLSA in *Darby*.

It is one thing to recognize the authority of Congress to enact laws regulating individual businesses necessarily subject to the dual sovereignty of the government of the Nation and of the State in which they reside. It is quite another to uphold a similar exercise of congressional authority directed, not to private citizens, but to the States as States. [T]here are attributes of sovereignty attaching to every state government which may not be impaired by Congress * * *.

Quite apart from the substantial costs imposed [by the minimum-wage and overtime provisions] upon the States and their political subdivisions, the Act displaces state policies regarding the manner in which they will structure delivery of those governmental services which their citizens require. The Act * * * directly supplants the considered policy choices of the States' elected officials and administrators as to how they wish to structure pay scales in state employment. The State might wish to employ persons with little or no training, or those who wish to work on a casual basis, or those who for some other reason do not possess minimum employment requirements, and pay them less than the federally prescribed minimum wage. * * * But the Act would forbid such choices by the States. The only "discretion" left to them under the Act is either to attempt to increase their revenue to meet the additional financial burden imposed upon them by paying congressionally prescribed wages to their existing complement of employees, or to reduce that complement to a number which can be paid the federal minimum wage without increasing revenue.

> **Food for Thought**
>
> Doesn't every employer subject to the FLSA face the same dilemma that the Court says the states will face? Of course, private employers cannot raise taxes to pay for higher wages, but they can raise the price of the goods or services that they provide. Is there something about the public context that makes congressional imposition of such a choice on the states impermissible?

[The challenged] provisions will impermissibly interfere with the integral governmental functions of [States and their political subdivisions]. [T]heir application will * * * significantly alter or displace the States' abilities to structure employer-employee relationships in such areas as fire prevention, police protection, sanitation, public health, and parks and recreation. These activities are typical of those performed by state and local governments in discharging their dual functions of administering the public law and furnishing public services. Indeed, it is functions such as these which governments are created to provide, services such as these which the States have traditionally afforded their citizens. If Congress may withdraw from the States the authority to make those fundamental employment decisions upon which their systems for performance of these functions must rest, we think there would be little left of the States' "separate and independent existence." * * * We hold that insofar as the challenged amendments operate to directly displace the States' freedom to structure integral operations in areas of traditional governmental functions, they are not within the authority granted Congress by Art. I, § 8, cl. 3.

MR. JUSTICE BLACKMUN, concurring.

Although I am not untroubled by certain possible implications of the Court's opinion[,] I do not read the opinion so despairingly as does my Brother BRENNAN. * * * I may misinterpret the Court's opinion, but it seems to me that it adopts a balancing approach, and does not outlaw federal power in areas such as environmental protection, where the federal interest is demonstrably greater and where state facility compliance with imposed federal standards would be essential. With this understanding on my part of the Court's opinion, I join it.

> **Take Note**
>
> Justice Blackmun provided the fifth vote for the Court's decision to invalidate the FLSA as it applied to these public employers, but his view of Congress's power to regulate the States appears different from the majority's. Under such circumstances, what is the precedential force of Justice Rehnquist's opinion? Of Justice Blackmun's?

MR. JUSTICE BRENNAN, with whom MR. JUSTICE WHITE and MR. JUSTICE MARSHALL join, dissenting.

The Court * * * repudiate[s] principles governing judicial interpretation of our Constitution settled since the time of Mr. Chief Justice John Marshall, discarding his postulate that the Constitution contemplates that restraints upon exercise by Congress of its plenary commerce power lie in the political process and not in the judicial process.

My Brethren * * * have today manufactured an abstraction without substance, founded neither in the words of the Constitution nor on precedent. An abstraction having such profoundly pernicious consequences is not made less so by characterizing the 1974 amendments as legislation directed against the "States Qua States." * * * [M]y Brethren are also repudiating the long line of our precedents holding that a judicial finding that Congress has not unreasonably regulated a subject matter of "commerce" brings to an end the judicial role. [*McCulloch*.]

Today's repudiation of this unbroken line of precedents * * * can only be regarded as a transparent cover for invalidating a congressional judgment with which they disagree. The only analysis even remotely resembling that adopted today is found in a line of opinions dealing with the Commerce Clause and the Tenth Amendment that ultimately provoked a constitutional crisis for the Court in the 1930s. E.g., *Carter Coal*; *Butler*; *Hammer*.

MR. JUSTICE STEVENS, dissenting.

[T]he Federal Government's power over the labor market is adequate to embrace these employees. Since I am unable to identify a limitation on that federal power that would not also invalidate federal regulation of state activities that I consider unquestionably permissible, I am persuaded that this statute is valid.

GARCIA V. SAN ANTONIO METROPOLITAN TRANSIT AUTHORITY

469 U.S. 528 (1985)

JUSTICE BLACKMUN delivered the opinion of the Court.

[As explained in the previous case, *National League of Cities v. Usery* (1976), the Fair Labor Standards Act (FLSA) requires certain employers to pay their employees a minimum hourly rate and also an "overtime" wage for hours worked in excess of 40 hours a week. When the San Antonio Metropolitan Transit Authority refused to pay overtime wages to bus driver Joe G. Garcia and other employees, they sued the Transit Authority to enforce the Act. The Transit Authority argued that it was a state governmental entity engaged in a traditional governmental function (i.e., operating the city's mass transit system) and was thus constitutionally immune from the requirements of the Act.]

In the present cases, a Federal District Court concluded that municipal ownership and operation of a mass-transit system is a traditional governmental function and thus * * * is exempt from the obligations imposed by the FLSA. * * * [T]he attempt to draw the boundaries of state regulatory immunity in terms of "traditional governmental function" is not only unworkable but is also inconsistent with established principles of federalism and, indeed, with those very federalism principles on which *National League of Cities* purported to rest. That case, accordingly, is overruled.

Any rule of state immunity that looks to the "traditional," "integral," or "necessary" nature of governmental functions inevitably invites an unelected federal judiciary to make decisions about which state policies it favors and which ones it dislikes. We therefore now reject, as unsound in principle and unworkable in practice, a rule of state immunity from federal regulation that turns on a judicial appraisal of whether a particular governmental function is "integral" or "traditional." Any such rule leads to inconsistent results at the same time that it disserves principles of democratic self-governance, and it breeds inconsistency precisely because it is divorced from those principles. If there are to be limits on the Federal Government's power to interfere with state functions—as undoubtedly there are—we must look elsewhere to find them.

We doubt that courts ultimately can identify principled constitutional limitations on the scope of Congress' Commerce Clause powers over the States merely by relying on *a priori* definitions of state sovereignty. * * * Apart from the limitation on federal authority inherent in the delegated nature of Congress' Article I powers, the principal means chosen by the Framers to ensure the role of the States in the federal system lies in the structure of the Federal Government itself. It is no novelty to observe that the composition of the Federal Government was designed in large part to protect the States from overreaching by Congress. The Framers thus gave the States a role in the selection both of the Executive and the Legislative Branches of the Federal Government. The States were vested with indirect influence over the House of Representatives and the Presidency by their control of electoral qualifications and their role in Presidential elections. U.S. Const., Art. I, § 2, and Art. II, § 1. They were given more direct influence in the Senate, where each State received equal representation and each Senator was to be selected by the legislature of his State. Art. I, § 3. The significance attached to the States' equal representation in the Senate is underscored by the prohibition of any constitutional amendment divesting a State of equal representation without the State's consent. Art. V.

In short, the Framers chose to rely on a federal system in which special restraints on federal power over the States inhered principally in the workings of the National Government itself, rather than in discrete limitations on the objects of federal authority. State sovereign interests, then, are more properly protected by procedural safeguards inherent in the structure of the federal system than by judicially created limitations on federal power. * * * We realize that changes in the structure of the Federal Government have taken place since 1789, not the least of which has been the substitution of popular election of Senators by the adoption of the Seventeenth Amendment in 1913, and that these changes may work to alter the influence of the States in the federal political process. Nonetheless, against this background, we are convinced that the fundamental limitation that the constitutional scheme imposes on the Commerce Clause to protect the "States as States" is one of process rather than one of result. Any substantive restraint on the exercise of Commerce Clause powers must find its justification in the procedural nature of this basic limitation, and it must be tailored to compensate

> **Food for Thought**
>
> Does the conclusion that the courts should decline to enforce state-autonomy-based limitations against congressional exercises of authority necessarily follow from the premise that the Framers sought to create a governmental structure to minimize the risk of federal overreaching? Isn't it possible that there are both structural protections against federal overreaching and judicially enforceable ones? See, e.g., Bradford R. Clark, *Putting the Safeguards Back Into the Political Safeguards of Federalism*, 80 Tex. L. Rev. 327 (2001).

for possible failings in the national political process rather than to dictate a "sacred province of state autonomy."

Congress' action in affording SAMTA employees the protections of the wage and hour provisions of the FLSA contravened no affirmative limit on Congress' power under the Commerce Clause. * * * [T]he principal and basic limit on the federal commerce power is that inherent in all congressional action—the built-in restraints that our system provides through state participation in federal governmental action.

We do not lightly overrule recent precedent. We have not hesitated, however, when it has become apparent that a prior decision has departed from a proper understanding of congressional power under the Commerce Clause. See *Darby*. Due respect for the reach of congressional power within the federal system mandates that we do so now. *National League of Cities v. Usery* is overruled.

JUSTICE POWELL, with whom THE CHIEF JUSTICE, JUSTICE REHNQUIST, and JUSTICE O'CONNOR join, dissenting.

A unique feature of the United States is the *federal* system of government guaranteed by the Constitution and implicit in the very name of our country. Despite some genuflecting in the Court's opinion to the concept of federalism, today's decision effectively reduces the Tenth Amendment to meaningless rhetoric when Congress acts pursuant to the Commerce Clause.

[According to the Court,] the extent to which the States may exercise their authority, when Congress purports to act under the Commerce Clause, henceforth is to be determined from time to time by political decisions made by members of the Federal Government, decisions the Court says will not be subject to judicial review. I note that it does not seem to have occurred to the Court that *it*—an unelected majority of five Justices—today rejects almost 200 years of the understanding of the constitutional status of federalism.

Members of Congress are elected from the various States, but once in office they are Members of the Federal Government. Although the States participate in the Electoral College, this is hardly a reason to view the President as a representative of the States' interest against federal encroachment.[9] * * * The fact

---

[9] At one time in our history, the view that the structure of the Federal Government sufficed to protect the States might have had a somewhat more practical, although not a more logical, basis. Professor Wechsler, whose seminal article in 1954 proposed the view adopted by the Court today, predicated his argument on assumptions that simply do not accord with current reality. * * * The adoption of the Seventeenth Amendment (providing for direct election of Senators), the weakening of political parties on the local level, and the rise of national media, among other things, have made Congress increasingly less representative of state and local interests, and more likely to be responsive to the demands of various national constituencies. * * *

that Congress generally does not transgress constitutional limits on its power to reach state activities does not make judicial review any less necessary to rectify the cases in which it does do so. The States' role in our system of government is a matter of constitutional law, not of legislative grace.

[The Court's holding] is inconsistent with the fundamental principles of our constitutional system. At least since *Marbury*, it has been the settled province of the federal judiciary "to say what the law is" with respect to the constitutionality of Acts of Congress. * * * In our federal system, the States have a major role that cannot be pre-empted by the National Government. [T]he States' ratification of the Constitution was predicated on this understanding of federalism. Indeed, the Tenth Amendment was adopted specifically to ensure that the important role promised the States by the proponents of the Constitution was realized. * * * [B]y usurping functions traditionally performed by the States, federal overreaching under the Commerce Clause undermines the constitutionally mandated balance of power between the States and the Federal Government, a balance designed to protect our fundamental liberties.

> **Take Note**
>
> Justice Powell appears to suggest that the Tenth Amendment sometimes deprives Congress of the power to regulate, even though Congress might otherwise have affirmative power under the Commerce Clause to regulate the matters in question. Is this view of the Tenth Amendment consistent with the view of the Tenth Amendment that the Court advanced in *Darby*?

JUSTICE REHNQUIST, dissenting.

I join both Justice POWELL's and Justice O'CONNOR's thoughtful dissents. [U]nder any one of [their] approaches the judgment in these cases should be affirmed, and I do not think it incumbent on those of us in dissent to spell out further the fine points of a principle that will, I am confident, in time again command the support of a majority of this Court.

> **Take Note**
>
> Justice Rehnquist predicted that the Court would, at some point in the future, begin to protect state sovereignty more aggressively. One year after the decision in *Garcia*, Justice Rehnquist became Chief Justice. After completing the materials in this chapter, consider whether his prediction has come true.

JUSTICE O'CONNOR, with whom JUSTICE POWELL and JUSTICE REHNQUIST join, dissenting.

Incidental to [the] expansion of the commerce power, Congress has been given an ability it lacked prior to the emergence of an integrated national economy. Because virtually every *state* activity, like virtually every activity of a private individual, arguably "affects" interstate commerce, Congress can now supplant the States from the significant sphere of activities envisioned for them by the Framers.

The last two decades have seen an unprecedented growth of federal regulatory activity. * * * The political process has not protected against these encroachments on state activities, even though they directly impinge on a State's ability to make and enforce its laws. With the abandonment of *National League of Cities,* all that stands between the remaining essentials of state sovereignty and Congress is the latter's underdeveloped capacity for self-restraint.

The problems of federalism in an integrated national economy are capable of more responsible resolution than holding that the States as States retain no status apart from that which Congress chooses to let them retain. The proper resolution, I suggest, lies in weighing state autonomy as a factor in the balance when interpreting the means by which Congress can exercise its authority on the States as States.

It has been difficult for this Court to craft bright lines defining the scope of the state autonomy protected by *National League of Cities.* Such difficulty is to be expected whenever constitutional concerns as important as federalism and the effectiveness of the commerce power come into conflict. * * * I would not shirk the duty * * *.

POINTS FOR DISCUSSION

a. The Political Safeguards of Federalism

The Court's conclusion in *Garcia* represents an embrace of the "political safeguards of federalism" as the principal—and perhaps the only—limit on Congress's ability to regulate the states. On this theory, the states' essential role in the selection of the President and the composition of Congress provide adequate protection for the states' interests from federal interference. But state legislatures no longer select Senators, and although the Electoral College in theory provides an important role for the states in the election of the President, all states now award electoral votes based on the outcome of the popular vote in the state. Does this suggest that the political safeguards cannot be expected to function as well today as the Framers perhaps originally believed? Or can we expect national decisions about whether to regulate state institutions to reflect the proper operation of those safeguards? Should we be concerned that, in effect, citizens from states that supply a majority of both houses of Congress can force regulation of dissenting states, whose citizens oppose the federal choice? Or is that just a natural by-product of majoritarian rule?

b. Means Restrictions on the Exercise of Federal Power

Notice that there was no dispute in *Garcia* that Congress has power pursuant to the Commerce Clause to regulate the wages and hours of employees. See *Darby*. Should that be the end of the matter? Sometimes it is clear that it cannot be the end of the matter. For example, even though Congress has power to regulate wages, it is clear that it could not enact a statute providing that only registered Democrats are guaranteed a minimum wage; such a statute would violate the First Amendment, even though it would regulate a subject—employee wages—that otherwise is within the commerce power. If the Court recognizes that other provisions of the Constitution limit the manner in which Congress may exercise its power under the Commerce Clause, then why shouldn't it recognize the same for the Tenth Amendment? Are there any important differences for these purposes between the Tenth Amendment and the other rights-granting provisions in the Bill of Rights?

NEW YORK V. UNITED STATES

505 U.S. 144 (1992)

JUSTICE O'CONNOR delivered the opinion of the Court.

In these cases, we address the constitutionality of three provisions of the Low-Level Radioactive Waste Policy Amendments Act of 1985. * * * We conclude that while Congress has substantial power under the Constitution to encourage the States to provide for the disposal of the radioactive waste generated within their borders, the Constitution does not confer upon Congress the ability simply to compel the States to do so.

We live in a world full of low level radioactive waste. Radioactive material is present in luminous watch dials, smoke alarms, measurement devices, medical fluids, research materials, and the protective gear and construction materials used by workers at nuclear power plants. * * * The waste must be isolated from humans for long periods of time, often for hundreds of years. Millions of cubic feet of low level radioactive waste must be disposed of each year. * * * [S]ince 1979 only three disposal sites—those in Nevada, Washington, and South Carolina—have been in operation. Waste generated in the rest of the country must be shipped to one of these three sites for disposal. * * * In 1979, both the Washington and Nevada sites were forced to shut down temporarily, leaving South Carolina to shoulder the responsibility of storing low level radioactive waste produced in every part of the country. The Governor of South Carolina, understandably perturbed, ordered a 50% reduction in the quantity of waste accepted at the Barnwell site. The Governors of Washington and Nevada announced plans to shut their sites permanently.

Faced with the possibility that the Nation would be left with no disposal sites for low level radioactive waste, Congress responded by enacting [the statute at issue here.] The Act provides three types of incentives to encourage the States to comply with their statutory obligation to provide for the disposal of waste generated within their borders. [The "monetary incentives" permitted states with disposal sites to levy a surcharge on the disposal of waste received from other states. The "access incentives" permitted states with disposal sites to increase the cost of access to their sites and then to deny access entirely to waste generated in states that failed to meet a federal deadline for the establishment of disposal sites of their own. And the "take title" provision required states that failed by a particular date to dispose of all waste generated within their borders to take title to the waste and, if the states failed to take possession of the waste, to face liability for all damages incurred by waste generators as a consequence of that failure.] New York * * * has identified five potential sites [for disposal facilities, in two counties.] Residents of the two counties oppose the State's choice of location. [The] State of New York and the two counties * * * filed this suit against the United States in 1990.

[Federalism] questions can be viewed in either of two ways. In some cases the Court has inquired whether an Act of Congress is authorized by one of the powers delegated to Congress in Article I of the Constitution. In other cases the Court has sought to determine whether an Act of Congress invades the province of state sovereignty reserved by the Tenth Amendment. In a case like [this], involving the division of authority between federal and state governments, the two inquiries are mirror images of each other. If a power is delegated to Congress in the Constitution, the Tenth Amendment expressly disclaims any reservation of that power to the States; if a power is an attribute of state sovereignty reserved by the Tenth Amendment, it is necessarily a power the Constitution has not conferred on Congress.

It is in this sense that the Tenth Amendment "states but a truism that all is retained which has not been surrendered." *Darby.* * * * The Tenth Amendment thus directs us to determine, as in this case, whether an incident of state sovereignty is protected by a limitation on an Article I power. * * * In the end, just as a cup may be half empty or half full, it makes no difference whether one views the question at issue in these cases as one of ascertaining the limits of the power delegated to the Federal Government under the affirmative provisions of the Constitution or one of discerning the core of sovereignty retained by the States under the Tenth Amendment. Either way, we must determine whether any of the three challenged provisions of the [Act] oversteps the boundary between federal and state authority.

Petitioners do not contend that Congress lacks the power to regulate the disposal of low level radioactive waste, [and they] do not dispute that under the Supremacy Clause Congress could, if it wished, pre-empt state radioactive waste regulation. Petitioners contend only that the Tenth Amendment limits the power of Congress to regulate in the way it has chosen.

Most of our recent cases interpreting the Tenth Amendment have concerned the authority of Congress to subject state governments to generally applicable laws. [See *National League of Cities v. Usery*; *Garcia v. San Antonio Metro. Transit Auth.*] [T]his is not a case in which Congress has subjected a State to the same legislation applicable to private parties. This litigation instead concerns the circumstances under which Congress may use the States as implements of regulation; that is, whether Congress may direct or otherwise motivate the States to regulate in a particular field or a particular way.

As an initial matter, Congress may not simply "commandee[r] the legislative processes of the States by directly compelling them to enact and enforce a federal regulatory program." *Hodel v. Virginia Surface Mining & Reclamation Assn.*, 452 U.S. 264, 288 (1981). * * * While Congress has substantial powers to govern the Nation directly, including in areas of intimate concern to the States, the Constitution has never been understood to confer upon Congress the ability to require the States to govern according to Congress' instructions. Indeed, the question whether the Constitution should permit Congress to employ state governments as regulatory agencies was a topic of lively debate among the Framers. Under the Articles of Confederation, Congress lacked the authority in most respects to govern the people directly. * * * The inadequacy of this governmental structure was responsible in part for the Constitutional Convention. Alexander Hamilton observed: "The great and radical vice in the construction of the existing Confederation is in the principle of LEGISLATION for STATES or GOVERNMENTS, in their CORPORATE or COLLECTIVE CAPACITIES, and as contra-distinguished from the INDIVIDUALS of whom they consist." The Federalist No. 15. As Hamilton saw it, "we must extend the authority of the Union to the persons of the citizens—the only proper objects of government."

The Convention generated a great number of proposals for the structure of the new Government, but two quickly took center stage. Under the Virginia Plan, as first introduced by Edmund Randolph, Congress would exercise legislative authority directly upon individuals, without employing the States as intermediaries. Under the New Jersey Plan, as first introduced by William

Paterson, Congress would continue to require the approval of the States before legislating, as it had under the Articles of Confederation. * * * In the end, the Convention opted for a Constitution in which Congress would exercise its legislative authority directly over individuals rather than over States. * * * In providing for a stronger central government, therefore, the Framers explicitly chose a Constitution that confers upon Congress the power to regulate individuals, not States.

This is not to say that Congress lacks the ability to encourage a State to regulate in a particular way, or that Congress may not hold out incentives to the States as a method of influencing a State's policy choices. * * * First, under Congress' spending power, "Congress may attach conditions on the receipt of federal funds." *South Dakota v. Dole*, 483 U.S. 203, 206 (1987). * * * Second, where Congress has the authority to regulate private activity under the Commerce Clause, we have recognized Congress' power to offer States the choice of regulating that activity according to federal standards or having state law pre-empted by federal regulation. *Hodel v. Virginia Surface Mining & Reclamation Assn., Inc.* 452 U.S. 264, 288 (1981).

By either of these methods, * * * the residents of the State retain the ultimate decision as to whether or not the State will comply. If a State's citizens view federal policy as sufficiently contrary to local interests, they may elect to decline a federal grant. If state residents would prefer their government to devote its attention and resources to problems other than those deemed important by Congress, they may choose to have the Federal Government rather than the State bear the expense of a federally mandated regulatory program, and they may continue to supplement that program to the extent state law is not pre-empted. Where Congress encourages state regulation rather than compelling it, state governments remain responsive to the local electorate's preferences; state officials remain accountable to the people.

Make the Connection

Under the "Dormant Commerce Clause Doctrine," states generally do not have power to burden or discriminate against interstate commerce. If this is true, then how can Congress authorize them to discriminate without violating the Constitution? We will take up this question in Chapter 4.

By contrast, where the Federal Government compels States to regulate, the accountability of both state and federal officials is diminished. If the citizens of New York, for example, do not consider that making provision for the disposal of radioactive waste is in their best interest, they may elect state officials who share their view. That view can always be pre-empted under the Supremacy Clause if it is contrary to the national view, but in such a case it is the Federal Government that makes the decision in full view of the public, and it will be federal officials that suffer the consequences if the decision turns out to be detrimental or unpopular. But where the Federal Government directs the States to regulate, it may be state officials who will bear the brunt of public disapproval, while the federal officials who devised the regulatory program may remain insulated from the electoral ramifications of their decision. Accountability is thus diminished when, due to federal coercion, elected state officials cannot regulate in accordance with the views of the local electorate in matters not pre-empted by federal regulation.

[The monetary incentives are a permissible combination of] an unexceptionable exercise of Congress' power to authorize the States to burden interstate commerce[, a] federal tax on interstate commerce, [and a] conditional exercise of Congress' authority under the Spending Clause. [The access incentives are valid because they are within Congress's power] to authorize the States to discriminate against interstate commerce [and Congress's power to] offer States the choice of regulating that activity according to federal standards or having state law pre-empted by federal regulation.

The take title provision is of a different character. * * * In this provision, Congress has crossed the line distinguishing encouragement from coercion. * * * The take title provision offers state governments a "choice" of either accepting ownership of waste or regulating according to the instructions of Congress. * * * [T]he Constitution would not permit Congress simply to transfer radioactive waste from generators to state governments. Such a forced transfer, standing alone, would in principle be no different than a congressionally compelled subsidy from state governments to radioactive waste producers. The same is true of the provision requiring the States to become liable for the generators' damages. * * * Either type of federal action would "commandeer" state governments into the service of federal regulatory purposes, and would for this reason be inconsistent with the Constitution's division of authority between federal and state governments. [T]he second alternative held out to state governments—regulating pursuant to Congress' direction—would, standing alone, present a simple command to state governments to implement legislation enacted by Congress. As we have seen, the Constitution does not empower Congress to subject state governments to this type of instruction. Because [both options are beyond the authority of Congress to offer,] it follows that Congress lacks the power to offer the States a choice between the two.

Respondents note that the Act embodies a bargain among the sited and unsited States, a compromise to which New York was a willing participant and from which New York has reaped much benefit. [But the] Constitution does not protect the sovereignty of States for the benefit of the States or state governments as abstract political entities, or even for the benefit of the public officials governing the States. To the contrary, the Constitution divides authority between federal and state governments for the protection of individuals. Where Congress exceeds its authority relative to the States, therefore, the departure from the constitutional plan cannot be ratified by the "consent" of state officials.

States are not mere political subdivisions of the United States. State governments are neither regional offices nor administrative agencies of the Federal Government. The positions occupied by state officials appear nowhere on the Federal Government's most detailed organizational chart. * * * The Federal Government may not compel the States to enact or administer a federal regulatory program.

JUSTICE WHITE, with whom JUSTICE BLACKMUN and JUSTICE STEVENS join, concurring in part and dissenting in part.

Ultimately, I suppose, the entire structure of our federal constitutional government can be traced to an interest in establishing checks and balances to prevent the exercise of tyranny against individuals. But these fears seem extremely far distant to me in a situation such as this. We face a crisis of national proportions in the disposal of low-level radioactive waste, and Congress has acceded to the wishes of the States by permitting local decisionmaking rather than imposing a solution from Washington. New York itself participated and supported passage of this legislation at both the gubernatorial and federal representative levels, and then enacted state laws specifically to comply with the deadlines and timetables agreed upon by the States in the 1985 Act. For me, the Court's civics lecture has a decidedly hollow ring at a time when action, rather than rhetoric, is needed to solve a national problem.

> **Take Note**
>
> Justice White reasons that the Court's holding will force Congress to regulate directly matters that it had attempted to leave, at least in part, to the discretion of state officials. Assuming Congress continues to believe that a national solution is needed to the problem of disposal of radioactive waste, what options are available to it after the decision in *New York*? Are those options more or less solicitous of state autonomy?

The ultimate irony of the decision today is that in its formalistically rigid obeisance to "federalism," the Court gives Congress fewer incentives to defer to the wishes of state officials in achieving local solutions to local problems. This legislation was a classic example of Congress acting as arbiter among the States in their attempts to accept responsibility for managing a problem of grave import. The States urged the National Legislature not to impose from Washington a solution to the country's low-level radioactive waste management problems. Instead, they sought a reasonable level of local and regional autonomy * * *. By invalidating the measure designed to ensure compliance for recalcitrant States, such as New York, the Court upsets the delicate compromise achieved among the States and forces Congress to erect several additional formalistic hurdles to clear before achieving exactly the same objective.

JUSTICE STEVENS, concurring in part and dissenting in part.

Under the Articles of Confederation, the Federal Government had the power to issue commands to the States. Because that indirect exercise of federal power proved ineffective, the Framers of the Constitution empowered the Federal Government to exercise legislative authority directly over individuals within the States, even though that direct authority constituted a greater intrusion on state sovereignty. Nothing in that history suggests that the Federal Government may not also impose its will upon the several States as it did under the Articles. The Constitution enhanced, rather than diminished, the power of the Federal Government.

POINTS FOR DISCUSSION

a. The Tenth Amendment

The Court stated that "if a power is an attribute of state sovereignty reserved by the Tenth Amendment, it is necessarily a power the Constitution has not conferred on Congress." Is this consistent with the view of the Tenth Amendment advanced by the Court in *Darby*? In *Garcia*? If not, is it nevertheless a more sensible view?

b. Political Accountability

Do you agree that voters might be uncertain whom to blame if the federal government requires the state to open a radioactive waste dump? Wouldn't state officials be likely to proclaim—loudly and publicly—that the dump is there only because the federal government required it? Or is the problem that federal law didn't specify *where* in the state the dump should go, thus leaving the decision to state officials, who likely would be blamed for that decision? Would it help if Congress not only directed the state to create a dump, but also mandated where in the state the dump should go? Can you see why Congress would be unlikely to do that?

c. Means and Ends

The Court held that Congress could not require the state to take title to the waste, but it upheld Congress's power to attach conditions to the receipt of federal funds to encourage the state to provide for the disposal of radioactive waste. Given the wide scope of Congress's power pursuant to the General Welfare Clause, what is the point of the limitation announced in *New York v. United States*? If Congress can achieve all of its goals simply by offering money and attaching specific conditions, does the rule of *New York* provide any meaningful protection for state autonomy?

d. Basis for the Decision

How would you characterize the basis of the Court's decision? Is the Court relying on evidence of the original meaning, on precedent, or just on considerations of policy? For a textual argument that states have some immunity from federal regulation because the term "state" in the Constitution means "sovereign state," see Michael B. Rappaport, *Reconciling Textualism and Federalism: The Proper Textual Basis of the Supreme Court's Tenth and Eleventh Amendment Decisions*, 93 Nw. U. L. Rev. 819 (1999). Is that a satisfying basis for the decision?

PRINTZ V. UNITED STATES

521 U.S. 898 (1997)

JUSTICE SCALIA delivered the opinion of the Court.

The [Brady Handgun Violence Prevention Act] requires the Attorney General to establish a national instant background-check system by November 30, 1998, and immediately puts in place certain interim provisions until that system becomes operative. Under the interim provisions, a firearms dealer who proposes to transfer a handgun must [obtain information from the transferee and provide that information to] the "chief law enforcement officer" (CLEO) of the transferee's residence. * * * When a CLEO receives the required notice of a proposed transfer from the firearms dealer, the CLEO must "make a reasonable effort to ascertain within 5 business days whether receipt or possession would be in violation of the law, including research in whatever State and local recordkeeping systems are available and in a national system designated by the Attorney General." The Act does not require the CLEO to take any particular action if he determines that a pending transaction would be unlawful; he may notify the firearms dealer to that effect, but is not required to do so. If, however, the CLEO notifies a gun dealer that a prospective purchaser is ineligible to receive a handgun, he must, upon request, provide the would-be purchaser with a written statement of the reasons for that determination. Moreover, if the CLEO does not discover any basis for objecting to the sale, he must destroy any records in his possession relating to the transfer, including his copy of the Brady Form. [A]ny person who "knowingly violates [this provision] shall be [fined], imprisoned for not more than 1 year, or both." Petitioners Jay Printz and Richard Mack, the CLEOs for Ravalli County, Montana, and Graham County, Arizona, respectively, filed separate actions challenging the constitutionality of the Brady Act's interim provisions.

From the description set forth above, it is apparent that the Brady Act purports to direct state law enforcement officers to participate, albeit only temporarily, in the administration of a federally enacted regulatory scheme. * * * Petitioners here object to being pressed into federal service, and contend that congressional action compelling state officers to execute federal laws is unconstitutional. Because there is no constitutional text speaking to this precise question, the answer to the CLEOs' challenge must be sought in historical understanding and practice, in the structure of the Constitution, and in the jurisprudence of this Court.

Petitioners contend that compelled enlistment of state executive officers for the administration of federal programs is, until very recent years at least, unprecedented. The Government contends, to the contrary, that "the earliest Congresses enacted statutes that required the participation of state officials in the implementation of federal laws." [E]arly congressional enactments "provide contemporaneous and weighty evidence of the Constitution's meaning." [Those statutes] required state courts to record applications for citizenship, to transmit abstracts of citizenship applications and other naturalization records to the Secretary of State, and to register aliens seeking naturalization and issue certificates of registry. * * * These early laws establish, at most, that the Constitution was originally understood to permit imposition of an obligation on state *judges* to enforce federal prescriptions * * *. [W]e do not think the early statutes imposing obligations on state courts imply a power of Congress to impress the state executive into its service. Indeed, it can be argued that the numerousness of these statutes, contrasted with the utter lack of statutes imposing obligations on the States' executive (notwithstanding the attractiveness of that course to Congress), suggests an assumed *absence* of such power.

> **FYI**
>
> The Supremacy Clause of Article VI provides that state judges are "bound" by federal law. Does this suggest that Congress's power to require state judges to enforce federal law is different from its power to require state executive officials to implement federal law?

In addition to early legislation, the Government also appeals to other sources we have usually regarded as indicative of the original understanding of the Constitution. It points to portions of The Federalist [that suggest that Congress would rely on state officers to collect federal taxes.] But none of these statements necessarily implies—what is the critical point here—that Congress could impose these responsibilities *without the consent of the States*. They appear to rest on the natural assumption that the States would consent to allowing their officials to assist the Federal Government. The Federalist [No. 27 states that] "the legislatures, courts, and magistrates, of the [States] will be incorporated into the operations of the national government *as far as its just and constitutional authority extends;* and will be rendered auxiliary to the enforcement of its laws." [Justice Souter concludes that this demonstrates that the Constitution originally was understood to confer on the federal government the authority asserted in the Brady Act. But this reading] makes state *legislatures* subject to federal direction[, contrary to our holding in *New York v. United States*.] These problems are avoided, of course, if the calculatedly vague consequences the passage recites are taken to refer to nothing more (or less) than the duty owed to the National Government, on the part of *all* state officials, to enact, enforce, and interpret state law in such fashion as not to obstruct the operation of federal law.

The constitutional practice we have examined above tends to negate the existence of the congressional power asserted here, but is not conclusive. We turn next to consideration of the structure of the Constitution * * *. It is incontestible that the Constitution established a system of "dual sovereignty." Although the States surrendered many of their powers to the new Federal Government, they retained "a residuary and inviolable sovereignty." The Federalist No. 39. This is reflected throughout the Constitution's text * * *. The Framers' experience under the Articles of Confederation had persuaded them that using the States as the instruments of federal governance was both ineffectual and provocative of federal-state conflict. [They] rejected the concept of a central government that would act upon and through the States, and instead designed a system in which the State and Federal Governments would exercise concurrent authority over the people * * *. The power of the Federal Government would be augmented immeasurably if it were able to impress into its service—and at no cost to itself—the police officers of the 50 States.

Food for Thought

Can you identify provisions of the Constitution that confirm the structural principle on which Justice Scalia relies?

[F]ederal control of state officers * * * would also have an effect upon * * * the separation and equilibration of powers between the three branches of the Federal Government itself. The Constitution does not leave to speculation who is to administer the laws enacted by Congress; the President, it says, "shall take Care that the Laws be faithfully executed," Art. II, § 3, personally and through officers whom he appoints * * *. The Brady Act effectively transfers this responsibility to thousands of CLEOs in the 50 States, who are left to implement the program without meaningful Presidential control * * *. The insistence of the Framers upon unity in the Federal Executive—to ensure both vigor and accountability—is well known. That unity would be shattered, and the power of the President would be subject to reduction, if Congress could act as effectively without the President as with him, by simply requiring state officers to execute its laws.

Finally, and most conclusively in the present litigation, we turn to the prior jurisprudence of this Court. * * * The Government contends that [u]nlike the "take title" provisions invalidated in [*New York v. United States*,] the background-check provision of the Brady Act does not require state legislative or executive officials to make policy, but instead issues a final directive to state CLEOs. * * * Executive action that has utterly no policymaking component is rare, particularly at an executive level as high as a jurisdiction's chief law enforcement officer. Is it really true that there is no policymaking involved in deciding, for example, what "reasonable efforts" shall be expended to conduct a background check? * * * It is quite impossible [to] draw the Government's proposed line at "no policymaking," and we would have to fall back upon a line of "not too much policymaking." How much is too much is not likely to be answered precisely; and an imprecise barrier against federal intrusion upon state authority is not likely to be an effective one.

Make the Connection

This question of executive authority to exercise policy discretion arises as well when Congress delegates authority to Executive officials. We will discuss Congress's power to do so in Chapter 6.

Even assuming, moreover, that the Brady Act leaves no "policymaking" discretion with the States, we fail to see how that improves rather than worsens the intrusion upon state sovereignty. Preservation of the States as independent and autonomous political entities is arguably less undermined by requiring them to make policy in certain fields than * * * by "reducing them to puppets of a ventriloquist Congress." It is an essential attribute of the States' retained sovereignty that they remain independent and autonomous within their proper sphere of authority.

The Government also maintains that requiring state officers to perform discrete, ministerial tasks specified by Congress does not violate the principle of *New York* because it does not diminish the accountability of state or federal officials. This argument fails even on its own terms. By forcing state governments to absorb the financial burden of implementing a federal regulatory program, Members of Congress can take credit for "solving" problems without having to ask their constituents to pay for the solutions with higher federal taxes. And even when the States are not forced to absorb the costs of implementing a federal program, they are still put in the position of taking the blame for its burdensomeness and for its defects. Under the present law, for example, it will be the CLEO and not some federal official who stands between the gun purchaser and immediate possession of his gun. And it will likely be the CLEO, not some federal official, who will be blamed for any error (even one in the designated federal database) that causes a purchaser to be mistakenly rejected.

Finally, the Government [argues that the Brady Act] places a minimal and only temporary burden upon state officers. There is considerable disagreement over the extent of the burden, but we need not pause over that detail. [The extent of the burden] might be relevant if we were evaluating whether the incidental application to the States of a federal law of general applicability excessively interfered with the functioning of state governments. But where, as here, it is the whole *object* of the law to direct the functioning of the state executive, and hence to compromise the structural framework of dual sovereignty, such a "balancing" analysis is inappropriate. It is the very *principle* of separate state sovereignty that such a law offends, and no comparative assessment of the various interests can overcome that fundamental defect.

We held in *New York* that Congress cannot compel the States to enact or enforce a federal regulatory program. Today we hold that Congress cannot circumvent that prohibition by conscripting the State's officers directly. The Federal Government may neither issue directives requiring the States to address particular problems, nor command the States' officers, or those of their political subdivisions, to administer or enforce a federal regulatory program. It matters not whether policymaking is involved, and no case-by-case weighing of the burdens or benefits is necessary; such commands are fundamentally incompatible with our constitutional system of dual sovereignty.

JUSTICE O'CONNOR, concurring.

[T]he Court appropriately refrains from deciding whether other purely ministerial reporting requirements imposed by Congress on state and local authorities pursuant to its Commerce Clause powers are similarly invalid. The provisions invalidated here, however, which directly compel state officials to administer a federal regulatory program, utterly fail to adhere to the design and structure of our constitutional scheme.

JUSTICE THOMAS, concurring.

[T]he Federal Government's authority under the Commerce Clause * * * does not extend to the regulation of wholly *intra* state, point-of-sale transactions. Absent the underlying authority to regulate the intrastate transfer of firearms, Congress surely lacks the corollary power to impress state law enforcement officers into administering and enforcing such regulations. * * * Even if we construe Congress' authority to regulate interstate commerce to encompass those intrastate transactions that "substantially affect" interstate commerce, I question whether Congress can regulate the particular transactions at issue here. * * * The Second Amendment * * * provides: "A well regulated Militia, being necessary to the security of a free State, the right of the people to keep and bear arms, shall not be infringed." [If] the Second Amendment is read to confer a *personal* right to "keep and bear arms," a colorable argument exists that the Federal Government's regulatory scheme, at least as it pertains to the purely intrastate sale or possession of firearms, runs afoul of that Amendment's protections. As the parties did not raise this argument, however, we need not consider it here.

For More Information

The claim that the Second Amendment does not confer a "personal" right to bear arms is based on the argument that the opening clauses of the text—which provide, "A well regulated Militia, being necessary to the security of a free State"—modify the grant of the "right of the people to keep and bear Arms." After years of uncertainty, the Court held in 2008 that the Amendment does indeed protect an individual right to bear arms, unconnected to service in a state militia. See *District of Columbia v. Heller*, 554 U.S. 570 (2008), which we considered in Chapter 1.

JUSTICE STEVENS, with whom JUSTICE SOUTER, JUSTICE GINSBURG, and JUSTICE BREYER join, dissenting.

There is not a clause, sentence, or paragraph in the entire text of the Constitution of the United States that supports the proposition that a local police officer can ignore a command contained in a statute enacted by Congress pursuant to an express delegation of power enumerated in Article I. Under the Articles of Confederation the National Government had the power to issue commands to the several sovereign States, but it had no authority to govern individuals directly. Thus, it raised an army and financed its operations by issuing requisitions to the constituent members of the Confederacy, rather than by creating federal agencies to draft soldiers or to impose taxes.

That method of governing proved to be unacceptable, not because it demeaned the sovereign character of the several States, but rather because it was cumbersome and inefficient. * * * The basic change in the character of the government that the Framers conceived was designed to enhance the power of the national government, not to provide some new, unmentioned immunity for state officers. * * * Alexander Hamilton explained that "we must *extend* the authority of the Union to the persons of the citizens." The Federalist No. 15. Indeed, the historical materials strongly suggest that the founders intended to enhance the capacity of the Federal Government by empowering it—as a part of the new authority to make demands directly on individual citizens—to act through local officials. * * * Opponents of the Constitution had repeatedly expressed fears that the new Federal Government's ability to impose taxes directly on the citizenry would result in an overbearing presence of federal tax collectors in the States. Federalists rejoined that this problem would not arise because, as Hamilton explained, "the United States will make use of the State officers and State regulations for collecting" certain taxes. [The Federalist] No. 36. Similarly, Madison made clear that the new central Government's power to raise taxes directly from the citizenry would "not be resorted to, except for supplemental purposes of revenue, and that the eventual collection, under the immediate authority of the Union, will generally be made by the officers appointed by the several States." The Federalist No. 45.

Bereft of support in the history of the founding, the Court rests its conclusion on the claim that there is little evidence the National Government actually exercised such a power in the early years of the Republic. [But] we have never suggested that the failure of the early Congresses to address the scope of federal power in a particular area or to exercise a particular authority was an argument against its existence. That position, if correct, would undermine most of our post-New Deal Commerce Clause jurisprudence. * * * More importantly, the fact that Congress did elect to rely on state judges and the clerks of state courts to perform a variety of executive functions is surely evidence of a contemporary understanding that their status as state officials did not immunize them from federal service. * * * The majority's insistence that this evidence of federal enlistment of state officials to serve executive functions is irrelevant simply because the assistance of "judges" was at issue rests on empty formalistic reasoning of the highest order.

Perversely, the majority's rule seems more likely to damage than to preserve the safeguards against tyranny provided by the existence of vital state governments. By limiting the ability of the Federal Government to enlist state officials in the implementation of its programs, the Court creates incentives for the National Government to aggrandize itself. In the name of State's rights, the majority would have the Federal Government create vast national bureaucracies to implement its policies. This is exactly the sort of thing that the early Federalists promised would not occur, in part as a result of the National Government's ability to rely on the magistracy of the States.

JUSTICE SOUTER, dissenting.

In deciding these cases, which I have found closer than I had anticipated, it is The Federalist that finally determines my position. * * * Hamilton in No. 27 first notes that because the new Constitution would authorize the National Government to bind individuals directly through national law, it could "employ the ordinary magistracy of each [State] in the execution of its laws." Were he to stop here, he would not necessarily be speaking of anything beyond the possibility of cooperative arrangements by agreement. But he then addresses the combined effect of the proposed Supremacy Clause, Art. VI, cl. 2, and state officers' oath requirement, Art. VI, cl. 3, and he states that "the Legislatures, Courts and Magistrates of the respective members will be incorporated into the operations of the national government, *as far as its just and constitutional authority extends;* and will be rendered auxiliary to the enforcement of its laws." The natural reading of this language is not merely that the officers of the various branches of state governments may be employed in the performance of national functions; Hamilton says that the state governmental machinery "will be incorporated" into the Nation's operation, and because the "auxiliary" status of the state officials will occur because they are "bound by the sanctity of an oath," I take him to mean that their auxiliary functions will be the products of their obligations thus undertaken to support federal law, not of their own, or the States', unfettered choices. Madison in No. 44 supports this reading [by arguing] that national officials "will have no agency in carrying the State Constitutions into effect. The members and officers of the State Governments, on the contrary, will have an essential agency in giving effect to the Federal Constitution." [This view is confirmed by The Federalist Nos. 36 and 45, which anticipated state collection of federal revenue.]

To be sure, it does not follow that any conceivable requirement may be imposed on any state official. I continue to agree, for example, that Congress may not require a state legislature to enact a regulatory scheme and that *New York v. United States* was rightly decided; after all, the essence of legislative power, within the limits of legislative jurisdiction, is a discretion not subject to command.[1] But insofar as national law would require nothing from a state officer inconsistent with the power proper to his branch of tripartite state government, * * * I suppose that the reach of federal law as Hamilton described it would not be exceeded.

---

1 The core power of an executive officer is to enforce a law in accordance with its terms; that is why a state executive "auxiliary" may be told what result to bring about. The core power of a legislator acting within the legislature's subject-matter jurisdiction is to make a discretionary decision on what the law should be; that is why a legislator may not be legally ordered to exercise discretion a particular way without damaging the legislative power as such.

JUSTICE BREYER, with whom JUSTICE STEVENS joins, dissenting.

[T]he United States is not the only nation that seeks to reconcile the practical need for a central authority with the democratic virtues of more local control. At least some other countries, facing the same basic problem, have found that local control is better maintained through application of a principle that is the direct opposite of the principle the majority derives from the silence of our Constitution. The federal systems of Switzerland, Germany, and the European Union, for example, all provide that constituent states, not federal bureaucracies, will themselves implement many of the laws, rules, regulations, or decrees enacted by the central "federal" body. They do so in part because they believe that such a system interferes less, not more, with the independent authority of the "state," member nation, or other subsidiary government, and helps to safeguard individual liberty as well.

> **Food for Thought**
>
> What is the relevance of foreign law in determining the meaning of the United States Constitution? Does Justice Breyer treat the experience of other countries as an authoritative source of meaning for the United States Constitution? We will consider this question when we discuss *Lawrence v. Texas* in Volume 2.

Of course, we are interpreting our own Constitution, not those of other nations, and there may be relevant political and structural differences between their systems and our own. But their experience may nonetheless cast an empirical light on the consequences of different solutions to a common legal problem—in this case the problem of reconciling central authority with the need to preserve the liberty-enhancing autonomy of a smaller constituent governmental entity. And that experience here offers empirical confirmation of the implied answer to a question Justice STEVENS asks: Why, or how, would what the majority sees as a constitutional alternative—the creation of a new federal gun-law bureaucracy, or the expansion of an existing federal bureaucracy—better promote either state sovereignty or individual liberty? As comparative experience suggests, there is no need to interpret the Constitution as containing an absolute principle forbidding the assignment of virtually any federal duty to any state official.

POINTS FOR DISCUSSION

a. The Dog That Didn't Bark

In reaching the conclusion that Congress lacks the power to direct state and local executive officials to enforce federal law, the Court relied on the absence of any early statutes imposing such obligations on such officials. Even assuming that actions by the early Congresses should be treated as evidence of constitutional meaning, should *inaction* by the early Congresses be treated as evidence of the original understanding of Congress's power? What else, aside from a congressional belief that it lacked the power in question, might explain Congress's failure to enact any such statutes in the early years of the Republic?

b. Implementation v. Compliance

The Court held in *Garcia* that Congress has power to require states to pay their employees a minimum wage according to federal standards. The Court held in *Printz* that Congress lacks power to require state executive officials to implement federal law. Is it possible to reconcile these two decisions? In order to comply with the federal minimum wage law, aren't state officials who oversee payroll matters for the state required to take actions—such as keeping track of overtime hours and preparing and issuing paychecks—to conform to federal requirements?

Is there a meaningful difference between complying with federal law—which is what Congress can force state officials to do—and implementing federal law—which Congress cannot force state officials to do? One way to distinguish between the two types of actions is by noting that when Congress directs state officials to implement federal law, it is in effect requiring state officials to enforce federal law against third parties. See *South Carolina v. Baker*, 485 U.S. 505 (1988) (holding that Congress had power to impose federal income tax on interest from bearer bonds issued by states, even though the tax in effect forced states to issue registered (and thus tax-exempt) bonds, because Congress did not "seek to control or influence the manner in which states regulate private parties"). In contrast, when Congress requires a state to pay its employees a federal minimum wage, it is regulating the states directly in the same manner that it regulates private parties—in this example, private employers. Does that mean that the crucial difference is whether Congress imposes requirements that it imposes on the states on similarly situated private parties, as well? See *Reno v. Condon*, 528 U.S. 141 (2000) (upholding the Driver's Privacy Protection Act, which restricted the states' ability to sell personal information that they collected on drivers, because the statute did "not require the States in their sovereign capacity to regulate their own citizens").

Problem

Congress enacts legislation creating the "Federal Missing Children Database," which seeks to maintain information on children reported missing, in order to facilitate cooperative efforts to locate the children. In enacting the statute, Congress finds that abducted children often are transported across state lines, and that state law enforcement efforts to locate missing children often have been hampered by the lack of ready access to information about children missing in other states. The statute directs the Attorney General of the United States to maintain a database of information about children reported missing anywhere in the United States and to share the information in the database with state law enforcement officials. The statute also directs state law enforcement officials to report to the Attorney General (1) any report of a missing child, and (2) information about the missing child's physical appearance, birthday, and immediate family. A local sheriff objects to the reporting requirement. How should the court rule?

G. STATE SOVEREIGN IMMUNITY AS A LIMIT ON FEDERAL POWER

New York and *Printz* held that the states enjoy immunity from some forms of federal regulation. But they did not purport to overrule *Garcia*, which held that Congress can impose on the states substantive requirements similar to those that it imposes on private actors, such as the obligation to pay a minimum wage to employees. When Congress imposes such obligations, it often also provides for a private right of action to enforce the obligation. Accordingly, employees in private industry may sue their employers to recover wages unlawfully withheld. May Congress authorize similar remedies against the states for violation of statutory obligations that are otherwise validly imposed?

The Eleventh Amendment provides one possible answer.

U.S. Constitution, Amendment XI

The Judicial power of the United States shall not be construed to extend to any suit in law or equity, commenced or prosecuted against one of the United States by Citizens of another State, or by Citizens or Subjects of any Foreign State.

Recall that as originally written, Article III extended the judicial power to "Controversies * * * between a State and Citizens of another State" and "between a State, or the Citizens thereof, and foreign States, Citizens or Subjects." By its terms, the Eleventh Amendment appears to remove these controversies from Article III's enumeration of the federal judicial power. How far does this language reach?

It is universally understood that the Eleventh Amendment was proposed and ratified in response to the Court's early decision in *Chisholm v. Georgia*, 2 U.S. (2.

Dall.) 419 (1793), which read Article III literally to permit a state-law suit for damages by a citizen of South Carolina against the state of Georgia. But from there the disagreements begin. Consider the case that follows.

ALDEN V. MAINE

527 U.S. 706 (1999)

JUSTICE KENNEDY delivered the opinion of the Court.

[Petitioners, a group of probation officers, originally filed suit in federal court against their employer, the State of Maine, alleging that the State had violated the overtime provisions of the Fair Labor Standards Act of 1938 (FLSA), 29 U.S.C. § 201 et *seq.*, and seeking compensation and liquidated damages. The district court dismissed the suit, holding that Maine enjoyed sovereign immunity from such a suit in federal court under the Eleventh Amendment.] Petitioners then filed the same action in state court. The state trial court dismissed the suit on the basis of sovereign immunity, and the Maine Supreme Judicial Court affirmed. * * * We hold that the powers delegated to Congress under Article I of the United States Constitution do not include the power to subject nonconsenting States to private suits for damages in state courts.

The Eleventh Amendment makes explicit reference to the States' immunity from suits "commenced or prosecuted against one of the United States by Citizens of another State, or by Citizens or Subjects of any Foreign State." U.S. Const., Amdt. 11. We have, as a result, sometimes referred to the States' immunity from suit as "Eleventh Amendment immunity." The phrase is convenient shorthand but something of a misnomer, for the sovereign immunity of the States neither derives from, nor is limited by, the terms of the Eleventh Amendment. Rather, as the Constitution's structure, its history, and the authoritative interpretations by this Court make clear, the States' immunity from suit is a fundamental aspect of the sovereignty which the States enjoyed before the ratification of the Constitution, and which they retain today (either literally or by virtue of their admission into the Union upon an equal footing with the other States) except as altered by the plan of the Convention or certain constitutional Amendments.

The generation that designed and adopted our federal system considered immunity from private suits central to sovereign dignity. When the Constitution was ratified, it was well established in English law that the Crown could not be sued without consent in its own courts. * * * Although the American people had rejected other aspects of English political theory, the doctrine that a sovereign could not be sued without its consent was universal in the States when the Constitution was drafted and ratified.

The ratification debates, furthermore, underscored the importance of the States' sovereign immunity to the American people. Grave concerns were raised by the provisions of Article III, which extended the federal judicial power to controversies between States and citizens of other States or foreign nations. * * * The leading advocates of the Constitution assured the people in no uncertain terms that the Constitution would not strip the States of sovereign immunity. One assurance was contained in The Federalist No. 81, written by Alexander Hamilton: "It is inherent in the nature of sovereignty not to be amenable to the suit of an individual *without its consent.* This is the general sense and the general practice of mankind; and the exemption, as one of the attributes of sovereignty, is now enjoyed by the government of every State in the Union. Unless, therefore, there is a surrender of this immunity in the plan of the convention, it will remain with the States and the danger intimated must be merely ideal." At the Virginia ratifying convention, James Madison echoed this theme: "Its jurisdiction in controversies between a state and citizens of another state is much objected to, and perhaps without reason. It is not in the power of individuals to call any state into court. * * * It appears to me that this [clause] can have no operation but this—to give a citizen a right to be heard in the federal courts; and if a state should condescend to be a party, this court may take cognizance of it." 3 Debates on the Federal Constitution 533 (J. Elliot 2d ed. 1854).

Although the state conventions which addressed the issue of sovereign immunity in their formal ratification documents sought to clarify the point by constitutional amendment, they made clear that they, like Hamilton [and] Madison, [understood] the Constitution as drafted to preserve the States' immunity from private suits. The Rhode Island Convention thus proclaimed that "[i]t is declared by the Convention, that the judicial power of the United States, in cases in which a state may be a party, does not extend to criminal prosecutions, or to authorize any suit by any person against a state." 1 *id.,* at 336. The convention sought, in addition, an express amendment "to remove all doubts or controversies respecting the same."

Despite the persuasive assurances of the Constitution's leading advocates and the expressed understanding of the only state conventions to address the issue in explicit terms, this Court held, just five years after the Constitution was adopted, that Article III authorized a private citizen of another State to sue the State of Georgia without its consent. *Chisholm v. Georgia*, 2 U.S. (2 Dall.) 419 (1793). Each of the four Justices who concurred in the judgment issued a separate opinion. The common theme of the opinions was that the case fell within the literal text of Article III, which by its terms granted jurisdiction over controversies "between a

State and Citizens of another State," and "between a State, or the Citizens thereof, and foreign States, Citizens, or Subjects." U.S. Const., Art. III, § 2. * * * Two Justices also argued that sovereign immunity was inconsistent with the principle of popular sovereignty established by the Constitution, 2 Dall., at 454–458 (Wilson, J.); *id.,* at 470–472 (Jay, C. J.).

The Court's decision "fell upon the country with a profound shock." * * * The States, in particular, responded with outrage to the decision. * * * An initial proposal to amend the Constitution was introduced in the House of Representatives the day after *Chisholm* was announced; the proposal adopted as the Eleventh Amendment was introduced in the Senate promptly following an intervening recess. Congress turned to the latter proposal with great dispatch; little more than two months after its introduction it had been endorsed by both Houses and forwarded to the States.

The text and history of the Eleventh Amendment [suggest] that Congress acted not to change but to restore the original constitutional design. By its terms, [the] Eleventh Amendment did not redefine the federal judicial power but instead overruled the Court. * * * Congress chose not to enact language codifying the traditional understanding of sovereign immunity but rather to address the specific provisions of the Constitution that had raised concerns during the ratification debates and formed the basis of the *Chisholm* decision. * * * The [most] natural inference is that the Constitution was understood, in light of its history and structure, to preserve the States' traditional immunity from private suits. As the Amendment clarified the only provisions of the Constitution that anyone had suggested might support a contrary understanding, there was no reason to draft with a broader brush.

As a consequence, we have looked to "history and experience, and the established order of things," rather than "[a]dhering to the mere letter" of the Eleventh Amendment, in determining the scope of the States' constitutional immunity from suit. Following this approach, the Court has upheld States' assertions of sovereign immunity in various contexts falling outside the literal text of the Eleventh Amendment. In *Hans v. Louisiana,* 134 U.S. 1 (1890), the Court held that sovereign immunity barred a citizen from suing his own State under the federal-question head of jurisdiction [notwithstanding] the petitioner's argument that the Eleventh Amendment, by its terms, applied only to suits brought by citizens of other States. * * * Later decisions rejected similar requests to conform the principle of sovereign immunity to the strict language of the Eleventh Amendment in holding that nonconsenting States are immune from suits brought by federal corporations, *Smith v. Reeves,* 178 U.S. 436 (1900), foreign nations,

Principality of Monaco v. Mississippi, 292 U.S. 313 (1934), or Indian tribes, *Blatchford v. Native Village of Noatak*, 501 U.S. 775 (1991), and in concluding that sovereign immunity is a defense to suits in admiralty, though the text of the Eleventh Amendment addresses only suits "in law or equity," *Ex parte New York*, 256 U.S. 490 (1921). These holdings reflect a settled doctrinal understanding [that the] Eleventh Amendment confirmed, rather than established, sovereign immunity as a constitutional principle; it follows that the scope of the States' immunity from suit is demarcated not by the text of the Amendment alone but by fundamental postulates implicit in the constitutional design.

In this case we must determine whether Congress has the power, under Article I, to subject nonconsenting States to private suits in their *own* courts. As the foregoing discussion makes clear, the fact that the Eleventh Amendment by its terms limits only "[t]he Judicial power of the United States" does not resolve the question. While the constitutional principle of sovereign immunity does pose a bar to federal jurisdiction over suits against nonconsenting States, this is not the only structural basis of sovereign immunity implicit in the constitutional design. Rather, "[t]here is also the postulate that States of the Union, still possessing attributes of sovereignty, shall be immune from suits, without their consent, save where there has been 'a surrender of this immunity in the plan of the convention.' " *Principality of Monaco,* 292 U.S., at 322–323 (quoting The Federalist No. 81). In exercising its Article I powers Congress may subject the States to private suits in their own courts only if there is "compelling evidence" that the States were required to surrender this power to Congress pursuant to the constitutional design.

The Constitution, by delegating to Congress the power to establish the supreme law of the land when acting within its enumerated powers, does not foreclose a State from asserting immunity to claims arising under federal law merely because that law derives not from the State itself but from the national power. * * * We reject any contention that substantive federal law by its own force necessarily overrides the sovereign immunity of the States. When a State asserts its immunity to suit, the question is not the primacy of federal law but the implementation of the law in a manner consistent with the constitutional sovereignty of the States.

Nor can we conclude that the specific Article I powers delegated to Congress necessarily include, by virtue of the Necessary and Proper Clause or otherwise, the incidental authority to subject the States to private suits as a means of achieving objectives otherwise within the scope of the enumerated powers. * * * Although the sovereign immunity of the States derives at least in part from the common-law tradition, the structure and history of the Constitution make clear that the immunity exists today by constitutional design.

Although the Constitution grants broad powers to Congress, our federalism requires that Congress treat the States in a manner consistent with their status as residuary sovereigns and joint participants in the governance of the Nation. The principle of sovereign immunity preserved by constitutional design "[accords] the States the respect owed them as members of the federation." * * * Underlying constitutional form are considerations of great substance. Private suits against nonconsenting States—especially suits for money damages—may threaten the financial integrity of the States. [A]n unlimited congressional power to authorize suits in state court to levy upon the treasuries of the States for compensatory damages, attorney's fees, and even punitive damages could create staggering burdens, giving Congress a power and a leverage over the States that is not contemplated by our constitutional design.

The constitutional privilege of a State to assert its sovereign immunity in its own courts does not confer upon the State a concomitant right to disregard the Constitution or valid federal law. The States and their officers are bound by obligations imposed by the Constitution and by federal statutes that comport with the constitutional design. We are unwilling to assume the States will refuse to honor the Constitution or obey the binding laws of the United States.

Sovereign immunity, moreover, does not bar all judicial review of state compliance with the Constitution and valid federal law. [S]overeign immunity bars suits only in the absence of consent. Many States, on their own initiative, have enacted statutes consenting to a wide variety of suits. Nor, subject to constitutional limitations, does the Federal Government lack the authority or means to seek the States' voluntary consent to private suits. *Cf. South Dakota v. Dole*, 483 U.S. 203 (1987). [In addition, in] ratifying the Constitution, the States consented to suits brought by other States or by the Federal Government. * * * [Moreover, we] have held also that in adopting the Fourteenth Amendment, the people required the States to surrender a portion of the sovereignty that had been preserved to them by the original Constitution, so that Congress may authorize private suits against nonconsenting States pursuant to its § 5 enforcement power. *Fitzpatrick v. Bitzer*, 427 U.S. 445 (1976). [T]he principle of sovereign immunity [bars] suits against States but not lesser entities [such as] municipal corporations. Nor does sovereign

> **Make the Connection**
>
> We considered Congress's powers to grant funds to the states with strings attached earlier in this chapter. We consider Congress's power under Section 5 of the Fourteenth Amendment in Volume 2.

immunity bar [certain] actions against state officers for injunctive or declaratory relief. *Ex parte Young*, 209 U.S. 123 (1908). * * *

When Congress legislates in matters affecting the States, it may not treat these sovereign entities as mere prefectures or corporations. Congress must accord States the esteem due to them as joint participants in a federal system, one beginning with the premise of sovereignty in both the central Government and the separate States. Congress has ample means to ensure compliance with valid federal laws, but it must respect the sovereignty of the States. [*Affirmed.*]

JUSTICE SOUTER, with whom JUSTICE STEVENS, JUSTICE GINSBURG, and JUSTICE BREYER join, dissenting.

The Court rests its decision principally on the claim that immunity from suit was "a fundamental aspect of the sovereignty which the States enjoyed before the ratification of the Constitution," an aspect which the Court understands to have survived the ratification of the Constitution in 1788 and to have been "confirm[ed]" and given constitutional status by the adoption of the Tenth Amendment in 1791. If the Court truly means by "sovereign immunity" what that term meant at common law, its argument would be insupportable. While sovereign immunity entered many new state legal systems as a part of the common law selectively received from England, it was not understood to be indefeasible or to have been given any such status by the new National Constitution, which did not mention it. Had the question been posed, state sovereign immunity could not have been thought to shield a State from suit under federal law on a subject committed to national jurisdiction by Article I of the Constitution. Congress exercising its conceded Article I power may unquestionably abrogate such immunity. [I]t is fair to read [the Court's] references to a "fundamental aspect" of state sovereignty as referring not to a prerogative inherited from the Crown, but to a conception necessarily implied by statehood itself. The conception is thus not one of common law so much as of natural law, a universally applicable proposition discoverable by reason.

The Court's principal rationale for today's result, then, turns on history: was the natural law conception of sovereign immunity as inherent in any notion of an independent State widely held in the United States in the period preceding the ratification of 1788 (or the adoption of the Tenth Amendment in 1791)? The answer is certainly no. There is almost no evidence that the generation of the Framers thought sovereign immunity was fundamental in the sense of being unalterable. Whether one looks at the period before the framing, to the ratification controversies, or to the early republican era, the evidence is the same. Some Framers thought sovereign immunity was an obsolete royal prerogative inapplicable in a republic; some thought sovereign immunity was a common law power defeasible, like other common law rights, by statute; and perhaps a few thought, in keeping with a natural law view distinct from the common law conception, that immunity was inherent in a sovereign because the body that made a law could not logically be bound by it. Natural law thinking on the part of a doubtful few will not, however, support the Court's position.

The only arguable support for the Court's absolutist view that I have found among the leading participants in the debate surrounding ratification was [Hamilton's statement in The Federalist No. 81,] where he described the sovereign immunity of the States in language suggesting principles associated with natural law. [T]he thrust of his argument was that sovereign immunity was "inherent in the nature of sovereignty." * * * [Hamilton's statement] stands in contrast to formulations indicating no particular position on the natural-law-versus-common-law origin, to the more widespread view that sovereign immunity derived from common law, and to the more radical stance that the sovereignty of the people made sovereign immunity out of place in the United States.

In the Virginia ratifying convention, Madison was among those who debated sovereign immunity in terms of the result it produced, not its theoretical underpinnings. [But there] was no unanimity among the Virginians either on state- or federal-court immunity, however, for Edmund Randolph anticipated the position he would later espouse as plaintiff's counsel in *Chisholm v. Georgia*, 2 Dall. 419 (1793). He [argued that] the Constitution permitted suit against a State in federal court: "I think, whatever the law of nations may say, that any doubt respecting the construction that a state may be plaintiff, and not defendant, is taken away by the words *where a state shall be a party*." 3 Elliot's Debates 573. Randolph clearly believed that the Constitution both could, and in fact by its language did, trump any inherent immunity enjoyed by the States.

At the furthest extreme from Hamilton, James Wilson made several comments in the Pennsylvania Convention that suggested his hostility to any idea of state sovereign immunity. [He argued that] "the government of each state ought to be subordinate to the government of the United States." Wilson was also pointed in commenting on federal jurisdiction over cases between a State and citizens of another State: "When a citizen has a controversy with another state, there ought to be a tribunal where both parties may stand on a just and equal footing." Finally, Wilson laid out his view that sovereignty was in fact not located in the States at all: "Upon what principle is it contended that the sovereign power resides in the state governments? [M]y position is, that the sovereignty resides in the people; they have not parted with it; they have only dispensed such portions of the power as were conceived necessary for the public welfare." While this statement did not specifically address sovereign immunity, it expressed the major premise of what would later become Justice Wilson's position in *Chisholm:* that because the people, and not the States, are sovereign, sovereign immunity has no applicability to the States.

FYI

Edmund Randolph and James Wilson were both important figures at the Constitutional Convention and in the subsequent campaign to ratify the Constitution. Randolph proposed the "Virginia Plan," which was drafted by James Madison and which became the basis of the proposal ultimately adopted at the convention, but he refused to sign the final document, concerned that it lacked sufficient checks and balances. However, he supported ratification, and he later served as the first Attorney General of the United States. Wilson had signed the Declaration of Independence, during the ratification battles he gave an important speech laying out the theory of enumeration, and he subsequently served on the Supreme Court.

From a canvass of this spectrum of opinion expressed at the ratifying conventions, one thing is certain. No one was espousing an indefeasible, natural law view of sovereign immunity. The controversy over the enforceability of state debts subject to state law produced emphatic support for sovereign immunity from eminences as great as Madison and Marshall, but neither of them indicated adherence to any immunity conception outside the common law.

At the close of the ratification debates, the issue of the sovereign immunity of the States under Article III had not been definitively resolved, and in some instances the indeterminacy led the ratification conventions to respond in ways that point to the range of thinking about the doctrine. [T]he state ratifying conventions' felt need for clarification on the question of state suability demonstrates that uncertainty surrounded the matter even at the moment of ratification. This uncertainty set the stage for the divergent views expressed in *Chisholm.*

If the natural law conception of sovereign immunity as an inherent characteristic of sovereignty enjoyed by the States had been broadly accepted at the time of the founding, one would expect to find it reflected somewhere in the five opinions delivered by the Court in *Chisholm*. Yet that view did not appear in any of them. * * * Not even Justice Iredell, who alone among the Justices thought that a State could not be sued in federal court, echoed Hamilton or hinted at a constitutionally immutable immunity doctrine. * * * This dearth of support makes it very implausible for today's Court to argue that a substantial (let alone a dominant) body of thought at the time of the framing understood sovereign immunity to be an inherent right of statehood, adopted or confirmed by the Tenth Amendment.

The Court [also relies on] a structural basis in the Constitution's creation of a federal system. [But the] Court's argument that state-court sovereign immunity on federal questions is inherent in the very concept of federal structure is demonstrably mistaken. * * * The State of Maine is not sovereign with respect to the national objectives of the FLSA. It is not the authority that promulgated the FLSA, on which the right of action in this case depends. That authority is the United States acting through the Congress, whose legislative power under Article I of the Constitution to extend FLSA coverage to state employees has already been decided, see *Garcia v. San Antonio Metropolitan Transit Authority*, and is not contested here.

It is symptomatic of the weakness of the structural notion proffered by the Court that it seeks to buttress the argument by relying on "the dignity and respect afforded a State, which the immunity is designed to protect." [T]he Court calls "immunity from private suits central to sovereign dignity" and assumes that this "dignity" is a quality easily translated from the person of the King to the participatory abstraction of a republican State. * * * The thoroughly anomalous character of this appeal to dignity is obvious from a reading of Blackstone's description of royal dignity, which he sets out as a premise of his discussion of sovereignty: "Under every monarchical establishment, it is necessary to distinguish the prince from his subjects. [The] law therefore ascribes to the king [certain] attributes of a great and transcendent nature; by which the people are led to consider him in the light of a superior being, and to pay him that awful respect, which may enable him with greater ease to carry on the business of government." It would be hard to imagine anything more inimical to the republican conception, which rests on the understanding of its citizens precisely that the government is not above them, but of them, its actions being governed by law just like their own.

Whatever justification there may be for an American government's immunity from private suit, it is not dignity.

[T]here is much irony in the Court's profession that it grounds its opinion on a deeply rooted historical tradition of sovereign immunity, when the Court abandons a principle nearly as inveterate, and much closer to the hearts of the Framers: that where there is a right, there must be a remedy. [*Marbury v. Madison*, 1 Cranch 137 (1803).] It will not do for the Court to respond that a remedy was never available where the right in question was against the sovereign. A State is not the sovereign when a federal claim is pressed against it * * *. Before us, Maine has not claimed that petitioners are not covered by the FLSA, but only that it is protected from suit. * * * Why the State of Maine has not rendered this case unnecessary by paying damages to petitioners under the FLSA of its own free will remains unclear to me.

POINTS FOR DISCUSSION

a. Constitutional Text and Structural Implications

The Court concluded in *Alden* that the states' immunity from suit derives not from the Eleventh Amendment, but instead from background constitutional postulates and structural implications of the federal system. On this view, what role does the Eleventh Amendment play? Does it add anything to the Constitution? We have already seen examples of the Court's relying on structural implications, but in most cases—such as in *McCulloch* and *Printz*—those implications have not run directly counter to constitutional text. Does the Eleventh Amendment's explicit focus on suits in *federal court* make the Court's analysis in *Alden* problematic?

> **Take Note**
>
> Article III, section 2, says that the judicial power of the United States extends to "cases . . . arising under this Constitution, the laws of the United States, and treaties" and "controversies . . . between a state and citizens of another state." The former is called "federal question" jurisdiction, and the latter is called "diversity" jurisdiction. A historically important constitutional question has been whether the federal courts can exercise these types of jurisdiction in cases in which state governments are parties.

Consider the disagreement between Chief Justice Rehnquist (for the Court) and Justice Souter (in dissent) in *Seminole Tribe of Fla. v. Florida*, 517 U.S. 44 (1996), which held that Congress lacks power under Article I to subject the states to private suits for damages in federal court. Chief Justice Rehnquist's opinion declined to rest on "a mere literal application of the words of § 2 of Article III," and instead focused on "postulates" "[b]ehind the words" of the Eleventh Amendment. Chief Justice Rehnquist thus criticized Justice Souter's dissenting opinion, which offered a "lengthy analysis of the text of the Eleventh Amendment," for being "directed at a straw man." Justice Souter responded by stating that "plain text is the Man of Steel in a confrontation with 'background principle[s]' and 'postulates which limit and control.' " Did the Court in *Alden* offer a different response to Justice Souter's criticism?

A conclusion that the Eleventh Amendment defines the full extent of constitutionally protected sovereign immunity would require the abandonment of a significant number of Supreme Court decisions. The suit that the Court permitted in *Chisholm* arose under state law; the plaintiff sought to recover a debt that he claimed the state owed him for goods that he had previously provided the state. One view of the Eleventh Amendment, accordingly, is that it simply deprived the federal courts of jurisdiction over suits arising under state law by citizens of one state against another state. (Indeed, many commentators have advanced this view. See, *e.g.*, William A. Fletcher, *A Historical Interpretation of the Eleventh Amendment: A Narrow Construction of an Affirmative Grant of Jurisdiction Rather Than a Prohibition Against Jurisdiction*, 35 Stan. L. Rev. 1033 (1983).) But at least since the late nineteenth century, the Court has advanced a much more robust view of the scope of state sovereign immunity.

In *Hans v. Louisiana*, 134 U.S. 1 (1890), the Court held that the Eleventh Amendment barred a federal-question suit by a citizen against his own state. And the Court has held that the Eleventh Amendment also bars suits against states in federal court by foreign nations, *Principality of Monaco v. Mississippi*, 292 U.S. 313 (1934), and Indian tribes, *Blatchford v. Native Village of Noatak*, 501 U.S. 775 (1991), notwithstanding the express language of the Amendment. The Court's view in *Alden*—which further extended the states' immunity to suits in state court—helped to free these decisions of the weight of the Eleventh Amendment. But in so doing, the Court effectively had to conclude that the Eleventh Amendment is constitutional surplusage. Do you find this approach convincing?

b. Sovereign Immunity and Political Theory

The doctrine of sovereign immunity derives from the notion that the "King can do no wrong," and thus cannot be subjected to suit for alleged wrongs. Given this historical pedigree, does the doctrine have any place in our constitutional system? Is it consistent with the foundational notion of popular sovereignty? Does it matter whether the doctrine is invoked to bar suits by the state's own citizens or instead citizens of other states (or countries)? If so, why?

c. State Immunity and Congressional Power

Even if the states presumptively enjoy sovereign immunity from private suits, is it clear that Congress lacks power to subject them to such suits as a remedy for state violation of requirements that Congress has otherwise validly imposed? As noted in *Alden*, the Court has held that Congress may authorize private suits for damages against the states pursuant to its authority to enforce the Fourteenth Amendment. That Amendment, after all, was designed to limit the power of the states, and thus effectively altered the federal-state balance, at least with respect to matters addressed by the substantive provisions of the Amendment. Can Congress also rely on its powers under Article I to subject the states to suit for violation of federal law enacted pursuant to those powers?

In *Pennsylvania v. Union Gas*, 491 U.S. 1 (1989), a plurality of the Court held that Congress can invoke its powers under Article I to "abrogate" the states' immunity from suit. Seven years later, however, the Court overruled *Union Gas* in *Seminole Tribe of Florida v. Florida*, 517 U.S. 44 (1996), which held (in a 5–4 decision) that Congress lacks power under Article I to subject the states to suit for violation of otherwise validly imposed federal requirements. Under current law, therefore, Congress may override the states' sovereign immunity (in federal and, presumably, state court) only when it acts properly to enforce the Fourteenth Amendment, a power that the Court has construed increasingly narrowly, see *Board of Trustees of Univ. of Alabama v. Garrett*, 531 U.S. 356 (2001) (holding that Congress did not have authority under Section 5 of the Fourteenth Amendment to subject the states to suit for violation of the Americans with Disabilities Act).

d. *National League of Cities* Redux?

Recall that the Court in *Garcia* overruled the prior decision in *National League of Cities*, which had held that Congress lacks authority pursuant to the Commerce Clause to regulate the states in the same fashion that it regulates private actors. The practical effect of the Court's decisions in *Seminole Tribe* and *Alden*, however, is that Congress cannot authorize a state employee to sue the state for damages when it fails to comply with the requirements of the Fair Labor Standards Act. Do those cases effectively overrule *Garcia*?

Executive Summary of This Chapter

Congress is limited to those powers enumerated in the Constitution. The enumerated powers, however, and the **Necessary and Proper Clause** imply the existence of subsidiary powers. Accordingly, Congress may seek to achieve any end that is legitimate under its express powers as long as its chosen means are reasonably adapted to achieving that end. *McCulloch v. Maryland* (1819). The Constitution also imposes some implied limits on the powers of the states, which lack power to tax instrumentalities of the federal government.

Under the **Commerce Clause**, Congress may regulate (1) interstate commerce, which is commerce that concerns more than one state; (2) the use of the "channels" of commerce, such as roads and navigable waters; (3) the "instrumentalities" of commerce, or persons or things in interstate commerce;

and (4) intrastate "economic" activity that Congress might rationally believe **substantially affects** interstate commerce. *Gibbons v. Ogden* (1824); *United States v. Lopez* (1995).

Congress's power to regulate subjects within the scope of the Commerce Clause is plenary. *Gibbons v. Ogden* (1824). In reviewing legislation enacted under the Commerce Clause, courts will not consider: (1) whether the actual purpose of the legislation is to regulate interstate commerce, *United States v. Darby* (1941); or (2) the wisdom, workability, or fairness of the legislation, *Wickard v. Filburn* (1942). Congress's plenary power to regulate commerce, however, does not enable Congress to create commerce by compelling individuals to purchase an unwanted product. *NFIB v. Sebelius* (2012).

When determining whether the local activity that Congress seeks to regulate has the requisite connection to interstate commerce, the Court considers all of the regulated activity in the aggregate. *Wickard v. Filburn* (1942). Congress generally lacks authority to regulate local, non-economic conduct on the theory that, in the aggregate, the activity has a substantial effect on interstate commerce. *United States v. Morrison* (2000). In determining whether the local activity that Congress seeks to regulate is "economic" in nature, the Court sometimes considers other conduct for which the activity can serve as a substitute, *Gonzales v. Raich* (2005); *Wickard v. Filburn* (1942), and at other times appears to apply a more stringent test, *United States v. Morrison* (2000).

When Congress seeks to regulate local, non-economic conduct, the Court will consider congressional findings about the connection between the regulated conduct and interstate commerce, and whether the statute contains a "jurisdictional element," such as a provision limiting the statute to conduct "affecting commerce," *NLRB v. Jones & Laughlin Steel Corp.* (1937). It is not clear, however, whether findings and a jurisdictional element can save such a statute. By contrast, when Congress creates a comprehensive scheme that directly regulates economic, commercial activity, the Court will not, in an as-applied challenge, excise individual applications of the scheme even when it applies to local, non-economic conduct. *Gonzales v. Raich* (2005).

Congress has the **power to tax and spend for the general welfare**. Although Congress cannot rely on its power to tax when it seeks to regulate—by imposing a tax as a "penalty"—conduct not otherwise within the reach of Congress's affirmative powers, *Child Labor Tax Case* (1922), the Court will invalidate a tax on this ground only if it is "extraneous to any tax need"—that is, effectively, only if it does not produce any revenue, *United States v. Kahriger* (1953); *NFIB v. Sebelius* (2012). "Direct taxes" must be apportioned so that each state pays in proportion to its population. U.S. Const. art. I, § 2, cl. 3; *id.* § 9, cl. 4. Direct taxes include taxes on the ownership of land or personal property. But a tax on "going without health insurance" is not a direct tax. *NFIB v. Sebelius* (2012).

Pursuant to its power to spend for the general welfare, Congress may seek to accomplish objectives that it could not otherwise reach pursuant to its other enumerated powers. *United States v. Butler* (1936). Congress may also seek to accomplish its objectives by imposing conditions upon the receipt of federal funds by the states, as long as certain requirements are met: (1) the exercise of the spending power must be in pursuit of "the general welfare" (though the Court defers substantially to the judgment of Congress in this regard); (2) conditions imposed upon the states' receipt of federal funds must be unambiguous; (3) the conditions must be related to the federal interest in the spending program; (4) the conditions must not violate any independent constitutional bar; and (5) the financial inducement offered by Congress must not be so coercive as to pass the point at which "pressure turns into compulsion." *South Dakota v. Dole* (1987). With respect to element (5) of this test, a threatened loss of over 10 percent of a State's overall budget is an example of "economic dragooning that leaves the States with no real option but to acquiesce." *NFIB v. Sebelius* (2012).

Congress's "**war power**" includes the authority to regulate "the evils which have arisen from [a war's] rise and progress," even if the war itself has already ended. *Woods v. Cloyd M. Miller Co.* (1948). The "**treaty power**," which derives from the authority of the President to make treaties subject to the consent of two-thirds of the Senate and from treaties' status under the Supremacy Clause, authorizes Congress to regulate matters that might otherwise be beyond the scope of federal power. *Missouri v. Holland* (1920).

When Congress acts pursuant to its powers under Article I, it may regulate the states in the same fashion that it regulates private actors. Accordingly, Congress has authority to require the states to pay their employees a minimum wage. *Garcia v. San Antonio Metropolitan Transit Authority* (1985). However, Congress cannot compel a state to enact or administer a federal regulatory program. *New York v. United States* (1992); *Printz v. United States* (1997).

Even though Congress has authority under Article I to regulate the states, it may not invoke those powers to subject the states to private suits for damages without their consent in federal court, *Seminole Tribe of Florida v. Florida* (1996), or state court, *Alden v. Maine* (1999), because of **state sovereign immunity.**

POINT-COUNTERPOINT

Was the expansion of federal powers inevitable? Is it defensible?

POINT: GREGORY E. MAGGS

Congress's powers have increased in three ways since 1789. First, several amendments to the Constitution have added federal powers. The Thirteenth, Fourteenth, and Fifteenth Amendments, for instance, now empower Congress to enforce their prohibitions on slavery, the denial of Due Process and Equal Protection, and voting discrimination. The Sixteenth Amendment now empowers Congress to impose income taxes. The Nineteenth, Twenty-Third, Twenty-Fourth, and Twenty-Sixth Amendments also grant new powers. Adding these powers might not have been inevitable; history could have turned out differently. But certainly the United States would be very different without them. In any event, the process by which these powers were added is clearly defensible. All were adopted according to the amendment procedures in Article V.

Second, changed circumstances have made some grants of power in the Constitution more significant. The Spending Power in Article I, § 8 provides one example. Over time the United States' revenue and credit have grown so much that the government now can spend $2.5 trillion per year, wildly more than it could have done in 1789. Congress's power to raise an Army and a Navy has become more significant now that the United States has the money, technology, and manpower to field the most powerful military forces in the world. Likewise, the power to regulate foreign commerce has taken on more importance now that the United States imports $2.3 trillion of goods and services annually. Similar conclusions hold true for many of Congress's other powers. The expansion of federal powers in this manner is also defensible. The Constitution's grants of power are written without qualification, and surely no one thought in 1789 that economic and other conditions would remain static. The original understanding and hope was that our nation would expand, prosper, and become more powerful.

Third, federal powers have expanded—at least in a practical sense—because the Supreme Court has allowed Congress to enact legislation that exceeds any powers granted in the Constitution. Most significantly, the Supreme Court has revised its interpretation of the Commerce Clause to allow Congress to regulate matters that are, quite simply, not "commerce * * * among the several states": wages and hours, production of farm products, etc. Given overwhelming popular demand for federal regulation of these matters, it is perhaps understandable that Congress would attempt to push the bounds of its powers. But the manner of achieving this third type of expansion was neither inevitable nor defensible. If Congress and the people believed that the federal government needed more power, they could have amended the Constitution to grant it, as they have done many times in the past.

Perhaps the harm has not been so significant because Congress generally has enacted popular legislation. But by allowing Congress to skip the amendment process, the Supreme Court has undercut the doctrines of limited powers and judicial review. These doctrines are meant to prevent tyranny, and they should not be weakened when alternatives are so readily available.

COUNTERPOINT: PETER J. SMITH

In 1789, most commerce in the United States was local. There were few reliable means of interstate transportation, and technology for the production of goods was rudimentary. Accordingly, the typical American used and consumed goods that were produced close to home—if not at home itself. Without nationwide (let alone global) economic integration, activity in one area of the country had little meaningful impact on activity elsewhere in the country. Congress thus rarely had occasion to exercise its power to regulate interstate commerce.

Then the world changed. Railroads facilitated the interstate transportation of goods, and new technology dramatically improved production and distribution. Formerly diffuse markets became linked. Wealth spread, but so did the problems that inevitably attend economic progress. And economic integration meant not only that the rising tide would lift many boats, but also that economic trouble could quickly spread far and wide. In this new world, which even the most forward-thinking of the Framers could not possibly have anticipated, activity in one part of the country had meaningful effects even in the most remote areas of the country. Patchwork regulation—if it occurred at all, in light of local pressures to attract jobs—was likely to produce as many negative systemic consequences as positive ones.

These changes alone were enough to lead many to conclude that federal regulation was necessary. And the Great Depression, which caused economic dislocation, unemployment, and general misery on a vast and unprecedented scale, convinced many of the remaining doubters. Economists, of course, continue to disagree about the wisdom of regulation of markets and industry, but that course tends to be popular whenever the market's failures stand in starkest relief—as they did in the 1930s. It thus was inevitable that Congress would assert the authority to regulate more expansively than it ever had before.

Judicial validation of Congress's expansive assertion of authority is fully justified, for at least three reasons. First, the original meaning of Congress's commerce power (not to mention its power under the Necessary and Proper Clause), when viewed at the appropriate level of generality, is entirely consistent with the modern understanding of the scope of Congress's authority. There is no more reason to think that the Framers sought to freeze into the word "commerce" the economic realities of 1789 than there is to think that they sought to freeze into the word "speech" in the First Amendment the limited modes of communication that existed in 1791. Just as no one would seriously contend that political films or webcasts do not count as protected "speech" simply because they did not exist two hundred years ago, we should not confine Congress's power to activity that would have been understood as "commerce," narrowly defined, two hundred years ago. As the world—and, with it, the nature of economic activity—has changed, so necessarily has Congress's power to regulate interstate commerce.

Second, a more restrictive reading of Congress's authority inevitably would require courts to make inherently policy-laden judgments about the propriety of economic regulation in particular circumstances. As we will see in Volume 2, such an approach is fundamentally inconsistent with the judicial role.

Third, whereas there is considerable need for a judicial role to protect individual rights—because majoritarian political institutions by definition cannot always be trusted to protect minority rights—the need for judicial intervention to protect federalism values is small. Structural features of the Constitution—equal representation in the Senate, for example, and statewide, at-large elections for Senators—mean that there is a built-in check on excessive federal overreaching. And even if the "political safeguards of federalism" do not function perfectly due to changes to the original structural arrangement, they still appear to have some constraining effect. (Consider the presidential campaign of 1980 and the congressional campaign of 1994, both of which saw the election of candidates who pledged to devolve power to the states.)

The cost of judicial intervention, on the other hand, can be great: the invalidation of popular (and at least sometimes desirable) legislation, solely in the name of some amorphous concept of states' rights, a concept that (we must acknowledge) was also deployed cynically to defend slavery and to obstruct the civil rights movement of the twentieth century. The Court's interpretation of the Commerce Clause did not usurp the amendment process. It merely recognized that the Constitution was designed to adapt to change.

CHAPTER 4

Limitations on State Power

INTRODUCTION

This chapter covers four important constitutional limitations on state power that concern the role of the states in our federal system. The first limitation addresses the relationship of federal law to state law. As we will see, under the Supremacy Clause in Article VI, federal legislation may "preempt" or supersede state law. The second limitation relates to the power of states to regulate subjects that Congress also may regulate. Specifically, under the so-called "Dormant Commerce Clause Doctrine" (sometimes called the "Negative Commerce Clause Doctrine"), the Supreme Court has held that the grant of power to Congress to regulate interstate commerce implicitly restricts the power of the states to regulate commerce in several ways. The third limitation pertains to relations between states and citizens of other states. The Privileges and Immunities Clause in Article IV prevents states from engaging in certain types of discrimination against residents of other states. The fourth limitation concerns state attempts to regulate Congress by setting qualifications for members of the House and Senate.

These four limitations are by no means the only restrictions that the Constitution places on state law. On the contrary, Article I, § 10 bars the states from entering foreign treaties, coining money, and enacting bills of attainder, ex post facto laws, or laws impairing the obligation of contracts. The same provision says that states, without the consent of Congress, may not impose tariffs on imports or exports, keep troops and ships of war, or enter into compacts with other states. In addition, the Fourteenth Amendment prohibits states from denying any person equal protection or due process of law. The guarantee of due process of law is extremely important because the Supreme Court has held that it includes many of the limitations on governmental action found in the Bill of Rights. Other constitutional amendments impose further limitations on state law.

We will consider many of these additional restrictions on state power in subsequent chapters.

A. PREEMPTION OF STATE LAW BY FEDERAL LAW

The Supremacy Clause in Article VI makes federal law "supreme" over state laws. As a result, federal law—including federal statutes, federal treaties, and the Constitution—sometimes will supplant state law that otherwise would apply to a particular situation. The courts describe the displacement of state constitutions, statutes, regulations, and common law rules by federal law as "federal preemption of state law."

U.S. Constitution, Article VI, Clause 2

"This Constitution, and the Laws of the United States which shall be made in Pursuance thereof; and all Treaties made, or which shall be made, under the Authority of the United States, shall be the supreme Law of the Land."

This part of the chapter addresses preemption of state laws by federal legislation. Federal legislative preemption is clearly the most common constitutional ground upon which state laws are judicially invalidated. In 2017, for example, more than 4300 reported cases concerned federal preemption of state laws. As both Congress and the states enact new legislation, even more preemption cases may arise in the future.

Federal legislative preemption comes in two basic forms: "express preemption" and "implied preemption." Express preemption occurs when Congress expressly displaces state regulation of a particular subject. For example, a provision of the Federal Cigarette Labeling and Advertising Act provides that "[n]o requirement or prohibition based on smoking and health shall be imposed under State law with respect to the advertising or promotion of any cigarettes the packages of which are [lawfully] labeled." But Congress need not directly address the preemptive effect of its laws in order for a court to find preemption; a court can also find that Congress has impliedly preempted state law. Implied preemption, in turn, comes in two basic forms: "conflict preemption" and "field preemption." Conflict preemption occurs (1) when "compliance with both federal and state regulations is a physical impossibility," *Florida Lime & Avocado Growers, Inc. v. Paul,* 373 U.S. 132, 142–143 (1963), or (2) when state law "stands as an obstacle to the accomplishment and execution of the full purposes and objectives of Congress," *Hines v. Davidowitz,* 312 U.S. 52, 67 (1941). For example, for many years, federal law has required cigarette cartons to contain a label warning consumers of the dangers of tobacco. Even absent any express provision about the effect on state law, the federal law would preempt a state law that attempted to prohibit cigarette cartons from including a warning label, because a cigarette manufacturer could not comply with both the federal and state laws. In addition, the federal law would preempt a state law requiring cigarette cartons to have a label saying: "Don't believe the federal warning label. Smoking is good for you." Although a cigarette manufacturer could comply with the federal law and this hypothetical state law by including both the federal and state labels on each cigarette carton, a court surely would find that the state law undercuts the objective of the federal law (i.e., ensuring that smokers understand the risk of cigarettes). *Cf. Hines*, 312 U.S. at 52 (federal alien registration statute preempted a more burdensome Pennsylvania alien registration statute because the state law posed an obstacle to the federal goal of requiring registration while otherwise preserving aliens' civil liberties).

Field preemption happens when Congress chooses to regulate a subject exclusively by federal law. As the Supreme Court has said, in some instances a "scheme of federal regulation may be so pervasive as to make reasonable the inference that Congress left no room for the States to supplement it." *Rice v. Santa Fe Elevator Corp.*, 331 U.S. 218, 230 (1947). When field preemption occurs, no state laws may apply to the subject, even if the state laws do not directly conflict with the specific requirements of federal law. For example, Congress at one time preempted all state regulation of any type of signal carried by cable television systems. See *Capital Cities Cable, Inc. v. Crisp*, 467 U.S. 691, 698–99 (1984). Field preemption is rarer than conflict preemption. Usually, Congress attempts to regulate only certain aspects of a subject, while leaving additional, non-conflicting regulation to the states.

SILKWOOD V. KERR-MCGEE CORP.

464 U.S. 238 (1984)

JUSTICE WHITE delivered the opinion of the Court.

This case requires us to determine whether a state-authorized award of punitive damages arising out of the escape of plutonium from a federally-licensed nuclear facility is preempted either because it falls within that forbidden field or because it conflicts with some other aspect of the Atomic Energy Act.

Karen Silkwood was a laboratory analyst for Kerr-McGee at its Cimmaron plant near Crescent, Oklahoma. The plant fabricated plutonium fuel pins for use as reactor fuel in nuclear power plants. Accordingly, the plant was subject to licensing and regulation by the Nuclear Regulatory Commission (NRC) pursuant to the Atomic Energy Act, 42 U.S.C. §§ 2011–2284 (1976 ed. and Supp. V).

During a three-day period of November 1974, Silkwood was contaminated by plutonium from the Cimmaron plant. On November 5, Silkwood was grinding and polishing plutonium samples, utilizing glove boxes designed for that purpose. In accordance with established procedures, she checked her hands for contamination when she withdrew them from the glove box. * * * A monitoring device revealed contamination on Silkwood's left hand, right wrist, upper arm, neck, hair, and nostrils. She was immediately decontaminated, and at the end of her shift, the monitors detected no contamination. * * * The next day, Silkwood arrived at the plant and began doing paperwork in the laboratory. Upon leaving the laboratory, Silkwood monitored herself and again discovered surface contamination. Once again, she was decontaminated.

On the third day, November 7, Silkwood was monitored upon her arrival at the plant. High levels of contamination were detected. Four urine samples and one fecal sample submitted that morning were also highly contaminated. Suspecting that the contamination had spread to areas outside the plant, the company directed a decontamination squad to accompany Silkwood to her apartment. Silkwood's roommate, who was also an employee at the plant, was * * * also contaminated, although to a lesser degree than Silkwood. The squad then monitored the apartment, finding contamination in several rooms, with especially high levels in the bathroom, the kitchen, and Silkwood's bedroom.

> **FYI**
>
> In 1983, Hollywood made a movie about Karen Silkwood's experience called *Silkwood.* Starring Meryl Streep, Kurt Russell, and Cher, the film was nominated for 5 Oscars. Generations of students have rented this film while studying constitutional law.

The contamination level in Silkwood's apartment was such that many of her personal belongings had to be destroyed. Silkwood herself was sent to the Los Alamos Scientific Laboratory to determine the extent of contamination in her vital body organs. She returned to work on November 13. That night, she was killed in an unrelated automobile accident.

Bill Silkwood, Karen's father, brought the present diversity action in his capacity as administrator of her estate. The action was based on common law tort principles under Oklahoma law and was designed to recover for the contamination injuries to Karen's person and property. * * *

The jury returned a verdict in favor of Silkwood, finding actual damages of $505,000 ($500,000 for personal injuries and $5,000 for property damage) and punitive damages of $10,000,000. [The Court of Appeals reversed the $500,000 award for personal injuries because the Oklahoma workers' compensation law did not permit this recovery. The Court of Appeals further held that federal laws regulating the Kerr-McGee facility preempted state tort law, barring recovery of punitive damages.]

> **Definition**
>
> "Punitive damages" are damages "awarded in addition to actual damages when the defendant acted with recklessness, malice, or deceit." *Black's Law Dictionary* (10th ed. 2014).

As we recently observed in *Pacific Gas & Electric Co. v. State Energy Resources Conservation & Development Comm'n,* 461 U.S. 190 (1983), state law can be preempted in either of two general ways. If Congress evidences an intent to occupy a given field, any state law falling within that field is preempted. If Congress has not entirely displaced state regulation over the matter in question, state law is still preempted to the extent it actually conflicts with federal law, that is, when it is impossible to comply with both state and federal law, or where the state law stands as an obstacle to the accomplishment of the full purposes and objectives of Congress. Kerr-McGee contends that the award in this case is invalid under either analysis. We consider each of these contentions in turn.

> **Take Note**
>
> In this paragraph, the Court summarizes the different ways that federal law may impliedly preempt state law. The Supreme Court consistently uses this framework in federal preemption cases. Are the different types of preemption truly distinct, or is there often overlap between the two?

In *Pacific Gas & Electric,* an examination of the statutory scheme and legislative history of the Atomic Energy Act convinced us that "Congress . . . intended that the federal government regulate the radiological safety aspects involved . . . in the construction and operation of a nuclear plant." 461 U.S. at 205. Thus, we concluded that "the federal government has occupied the entire field of nuclear safety concerns, except the limited powers expressly ceded to the states." *Id.* at 211.

Kerr-McGee argues that our ruling in *Pacific Gas & Electric* is dispositive of the issue in this case. Noting that "regulation can be as effectively asserted through an award of damages as through some form of preventive relief," *San Diego Building Trades Council v. Garmon,* 359 U.S. 236, 247 (1959), Kerr-McGee submits that because the state-authorized award of punitive damages in this case punishes and deters conduct related to radiation hazards, it falls within the prohibited field. However, a review of the same legislative history which prompted our holding in *Pacific Gas & Electric,* coupled with an examination of Congress' actions with respect to other portions of the Atomic Energy Act, convinces us that the preempted field does not extend as far as Kerr-McGee would have it.

As we recounted in *Pacific Gas & Electric*, "[u]ntil 1954 [the] use, control and ownership of nuclear technology remained a federal monopoly." 461 U.S. at 206. In that year, Congress enacted legislation which provided for private involvement in the development of atomic energy. However, the federal government retained extensive control over the manner in which this development occurred. In particular, the Atomic Energy Commission (the predecessor of the NRC) was given "exclusive jurisdiction to license the transfer, delivery, receipt, acquisition, possession and use of nuclear materials." *Id.* at 207.

FYI

The Atomic Energy Commission (Commission or AEC) was a federal agency charged with nuclear regulation from 1946 to 1974. Its functions were later transferred to the Nuclear Regulatory Commission (NRC) and the Department of Energy.

In 1959 Congress amended the Atomic Energy Act in order to "clarify the respective responsibilities of the States and the Commission with respect to the regulation of byproduct, source, and special nuclear materials." 42 U.S.C. § 2021(a)(1). The Commission was authorized to turn some of its regulatory authority over to any state which would adopt a suitable regulatory program. However, the Commission was to retain exclusive regulatory authority over "the disposal of such . . . byproduct, source, or special nuclear material as the Commission determines . . . should, because of the hazards or potential hazards thereof, not be disposed of without a license from the Commission." 42 U.S.C. § 2021(c)(4). The states were therefore still precluded from regulating the safety aspects of these hazardous materials.

Congress' decision to prohibit the states from regulating the safety aspects of nuclear development was premised on its belief that the Commission was more qualified to determine what type of safety standards should be enacted in this complex area. As Congress was informed by the AEC, the 1959 legislation provided for continued federal control over the more hazardous materials because "the technical safety considerations are of such complexity that it is not likely that any State would be prepared to deal with them during the foreseeable future." H.R.Rep. No. 1125, 86th Cong., 1st Sess. 3 (1959). If there were nothing more, this concern over the states' inability to formulate effective standards and the foreclosure of the states from conditioning the operation of nuclear plants on compliance with state-imposed safety standards arguably would disallow resort to state-law remedies by those suffering injuries from radiation in a nuclear plant.

There is, however, ample evidence that Congress had no intention of forbidding the states from providing such remedies.

Indeed, there is no indication that Congress even seriously considered precluding the use of such remedies either when it enacted the Atomic Energy Act in 1954 or when it amended it in 1959. This silence takes on added significance in light of Congress' failure to provide any federal remedy for persons injured by such conduct. It is difficult to believe that Congress would, without comment, remove all means of judicial recourse for those injured by illegal conduct.

More importantly, the only congressional discussion concerning the relationship between the Atomic Energy Act and state tort remedies indicates that Congress assumed that such remedies would be available. After the 1954 law was enacted, private companies contemplating entry into the nuclear industry expressed concern over potentially bankrupting state-law suits arising out of a nuclear incident. As a result, in 1957 Congress passed the Price-Anderson Act, an amendment to the Atomic Energy Act. Pub.L. 85–256, 71 Stat. 576 (1957). That Act established an indemnification scheme under which operators of licensed nuclear facilities could be required to obtain up to $60 million in private financial protection against such suits. The government would then provide indemnification for the next $500 million of liability, and the resulting $560 million would be the limit of liability for any one nuclear incident.

Although the Price-Anderson Act does not apply to the present situation, the discussion preceding its enactment and subsequent amendment indicates that Congress assumed that persons injured by nuclear accidents were free to utilize existing state tort law remedies. The Joint Committee Report on the original version of the Price-Anderson Act explained the relationship between the Act and existing state tort law as follows:

> "Since the rights of third parties who are injured are established by State law, there is no interference with the State law until there is a likelihood that the damages exceed the amount of financial responsibility required together with the amount of the indemnity. At that point the Federal interference is limited to the prohibition of making payments through the state courts and to prorating the proceeds available."

S.Rep. No. 296, 85th Cong., 1st Sess. 9 (1957), U.S. Code Cong. & Admin. News 1957, pp. 1803, 1810.

Kerr-McGee focuses on the differences between compensatory and punitive damages awards and asserts that, at most, Congress intended to allow the former. This argument, however, is misdirected because our inquiry is not whether

Congress expressly allowed punitive damages awards. Punitive damages have long been a part of traditional state tort law. As we noted above, Congress assumed that traditional principles of state tort law would apply with full force unless they were expressly supplanted. Thus, it is Kerr-McGee's burden to show that Congress intended to preclude such awards. Yet, the company is unable to point to anything in the legislative history or in the regulations that indicates that punitive damages were not to be allowed. To the contrary, the regulations issued implementing the insurance provisions of the Price-Anderson Act themselves contemplate that punitive damages might be awarded under state law.

In sum, it is clear that in enacting and amending the Price-Anderson Act, Congress assumed that state-law remedies, in whatever form they might take, were available to those injured by nuclear incidents. This was so even though it was well aware of the NRC's exclusive authority to regulate safety matters. No doubt there is tension between the conclusion that safety regulation is the exclusive concern of the federal law and the conclusion that a state may nevertheless award damages based on its own law of liability. But as we understand what was done over the years in the legislation concerning nuclear energy, Congress intended to stand by both concepts and to tolerate whatever tension there was between them. We can do no less. It may be that the award of damages based on the state law of negligence or strict liability is regulatory in the sense that a nuclear plant will be threatened with damages liability if it does not conform to state standards, but that regulatory consequence was something that Congress was quite willing to accept.

> **Take Note**
>
> State tort law generally imposes liability for injuries caused by negligence, which is failure to exercise reasonable care. An example would be liability for an accident caused by careless driving. In special cases, state law also imposes "strict liability" for certain kinds of injuries, meaning that liability does not depend on the care or lack of care exercised. An example would be the liability of a manufacturer for a defective product.

The United States, as amicus curiae, contends that the award of punitive damages in this case is preempted because it conflicts with the federal remedial scheme, noting that the NRC is authorized to impose civil penalties on licensees when federal standards have been violated. However, the award of

> **Definition**
>
> The phrase *amicus curiae* means "friend of the court." The term refers to someone who is not a party to a lawsuit but whom a court allows to file a brief. The Supreme Court often invites the Solicitor General of the United States (a top-level Justice Department official) to file briefs as *amicus curiae* in cases concerning federal legislation when the United States is not a party.

punitive damages in the present case does not conflict with that scheme. Paying both federal fines and state-imposed punitive damages for the same incident would not appear to be physically impossible. Nor does exposure to punitive damages frustrate any purpose of the federal remedial scheme.

JUSTICE BLACKMUN, with whom JUSTICE MARSHALL joins, dissenting.

The principles set forth in *Pacific Gas* compel the conclusion that the punitive damages awarded in this case, and now upheld, are pre-empted. The prospect of paying a large fine—in this case a potential $10 million—for failure to operate a nuclear facility in a particular manner has an obvious effect on the safety precautions that nuclear licensees will follow. The Court does not dispute, moreover, that punitive damages are expressly designed for this purpose. Punitive damages are "private fines levied by civil juries." *Gertz v. Robert Welch, Inc.,* 418 U.S. 323, 350 (1974). * * *

JUSTICE POWELL, with whom THE CHIEF JUSTICE and JUSTICE BLACKMUN join, dissenting.

Where injury is sustained as a result of the operation of a nuclear facility, it is not contested that compensatory damages under state law properly may be awarded. Rather, in view of the purpose and effect of punitive damages, the question is whether such damages may be imposed not to compensate the injured citizen or her family but solely to punish and deter conduct at the nuclear facility.

We stated in *Pacific Gas* that "Congress has occupied entirely the field of nuclear safety concerns." On its face this is a holding that state action of any kind in this area is preempted, whether or not Congress has been silent on specific issues that may arise. * * *

Even if *Pacific Gas* had not been decided, I would find preemption of punitive damages awards because they conflict with the fundamental concept of comprehensive federal regulation of nuclear safety. See *Hines v. Davidowitz,* 312 U.S. 52, 67 (1941). * * * Congress has enacted detailed legislation and created a highly qualified administrative agency to promulgate and enforce regulations. * * * The effectiveness of the overall program requires that nuclear policy and regulation be insulated from *ad hoc,* uninformed and perhaps biased decision-making. It is reasonable for a nuclear facility to be held liable, even without fault on its part, to compensate for injury or loss occasioned by the operation of the facility. It is not reasonable to infer that Congress intended to allow juries of lay persons, selected essentially at random, to impose unfocused penalties solely for the purpose of punishment and some undefined deterrence. These purposes wisely have been left within the regulatory authority and discretion of the NRC.

POINTS FOR DISCUSSION

a. Field Preemption and Conflict Preemption

What kind of preemption did Kerr-McGee ask the Court to find in this case? What kind of preemption did the United States as *amicus curiae* ask the court to find? What kind of preemption did the dissent think existed? Why did the Court find neither kind of preemption?

b. Reason for Federal Preemption of State Law

What policy consideration may have justified inclusion of the Supremacy Clause in the Constitution? Some history may help in answering this question. When the states were deciding whether to ratify the Constitution, federal preemption was a major issue. Opponents of the Constitution argued that the Supremacy Clause made the federal government too powerful. But Alexander Hamilton argued in response that federal laws had to be supreme if they were to have any force. He wrote in Federalist No. 33: "[W]hat would they amount to, if they were not to be supreme? It is evident they would amount to nothing. A LAW by the very meaning of the term includes supremacy. It is a rule which those to whom it is prescribed are bound to observe." Can you explain Hamilton's argument? Why would a federal law "amount to nothing" if it were not supreme over state law?

c. Basic Policy Question Regarding Preemption

A leading commentator on Constitutional Law has concisely summarized the basic policy question regarding preemption as follows: "Ultimately, preemption doctrines are about allocating governing authority between federal and state governments. A broad view of preemption leaves less room for governance by state and local governments." Erwin Chemerinsky, *Constitutional Law: Principles and Policies* 287 (1997). In considering this policy question, note that the Supreme Court has announced the following principle: "In all pre-emption cases, and particularly in those [where] Congress has legislated * * * in a field which the States have traditionally occupied, we start with the assumption that the historic police powers of the States were not to be superseded by the Federal Act unless that was the clear and manifest purpose of Congress." *Medtronic, Inc. v. Lohr,* 518 U.S. 470, 485 (1996). What does this presumption regarding preemption say about the Court's position on the basic policy question?

Problem

This problem is based on *Arizona v. United States*, 567 U.S. 387 (2012), an important decision about state laws addressing immigration. Arizona enacted a statute that, among other things, made it a misdemeanor "for a person who is unlawfully present in the United States and who is an unauthorized alien to knowingly apply for work, solicit work in a public place or perform work as an employee or independent contractor in this state." Ariz. Rev. Stat. Ann. § 13–2928(C). Litigants argued that federal immigration law preempted this Arizona statute. Federal immigration law imposes civil penalties on aliens who unlawfully accept employment but does not impose criminal penalties.

1. May a state impose an additional sanction, such as a criminal penalty, for conduct separately prohibited by federal law? Contrast these three views from the Arizona decision, which struck down the Arizona law:

Justice KENNEDY (for the Court): "Congress decided it would be inappropriate to impose criminal penalties on aliens who seek or engage in unauthorized employment. It follows that a state law to the contrary is an obstacle to the regulatory system Congress chose."

Justice SCALIA (dissenting): "The laws under challenge here do not extend or revise federal immigration restrictions, but merely enforce those restrictions more effectively."

Justice ALITO (dissenting): "The Court gives short shrift to our presumption against pre-emption. * * * The one thing that is clear from the federal scheme is that Congress chose not to impose federal criminal penalties on aliens who seek or obtain unauthorized work. But that does not mean that Congress also chose to pre-empt state criminal penalties. The inference is plausible, but far from necessary."

Which view is most consistent with the analysis in *Silkwood v. Kerr-McGee*?

2. Should the Supreme Court decide preemption cases by considering the policies behind the federal laws or simply by examining the text of these laws? Justice Thomas, also dissenting, looked only for an express conflict, asserting that "the 'purposes and objectives' theory of implied pre-emption is inconsistent with the Constitution because it invites courts to engage in freewheeling speculation about congressional purpose." Is there a counter argument to this view?

Problem

Federal law authorizes the Secretary of Agriculture to "establish and maintain minimum standards of quality and maturity" for agricultural commodities. Each year, the Secretary has promulgated a regulation that forbids the picking and shipping of avocados before a certain date, to ensure quality and maturity. California law prohibits the sale of avocados that contain less than 8 percent oil. A trade group representing Florida avocado growers filed suit to enjoin enforcement of the California law against Florida avocados certified as mature under the federal regulations. How should the Court rule?

B. THE DORMANT COMMERCE CLAUSE DOCTRINE

As we saw in Chapter 3, Article I, § 8 of the Constitution grants a number of important powers to Congress. Congress can impose taxes, spend money, regulate commerce, create post offices, raise an army and navy, and so forth. We have already considered what Congress may do with these powers. A separate issue, examined here, is whether the mere grant of these powers to Congress divests the state governments of any powers. This question does not have a simple answer.

Some of the powers listed in Article I, § 8 belong exclusively to Congress. For example, Article I, § 8, clause 5 gives Congress the right to coin money, and Article I, § 10, clause 1 then says that the states may not coin money. Therefore, Congress may coin money but the states may not. But Congress and the states share other powers. For example, although Article I, § 8, clause 1 gives Congress the power to impose taxes and spend money, no one has ever thought that the states lost this power by ratifying the Constitution. On the contrary, although Congress raises revenue and spends money, the states have their own taxes, their own treasuries, and their own expenditures.

Make the Connection

Recall that the Court in *McCulloch* acknowledged that the states have concurrent power to tax, even though there may be some federalism-based limits on their ability to exercise that power.

Still other powers fall somewhere in between; they are neither exclusively federal nor equally shared between the federal and state governments. For example, Article I, § 8, clause 12 gives Congress the power to raise an Army. Article I, § 10, clause 3 then says that the states cannot keep troops "without the consent of Congress." In other words, states can have an armed force, but only if Congress allows it.

Into which of these different categories does the very important power of regulating commerce fall? It might seem that the power is concurrently enjoyed by the federal and state governments. We know from Chapter 3 that Congress has the power to regulate not only commerce itself, but also the instrumentalities and channels of commerce, and even intrastate economic activities that substantially affect interstate commerce. At the same time, no one doubts that the states also may regulate commerce.

But the answer is not so simple. Over time, the Supreme Court has said that the grant of power to Congress in Article I, § 8, clause 3 to regulate interstate commerce imposes several implicit restrictions on state regulations of commerce, all of which we will see in the cases below. The Court has struggled to define the precise contours of these limitations. At one time, the Court insisted that states cannot regulate subjects for which national uniformity is necessary; at another time, the Court held that although the states can enact laws that have only an "indirect" effect on interstate commerce, they lack power to enact laws that "directly" interfere with interstate commerce. As we saw in our unit on Congress's power under the Commerce Clause, the Court has abandoned the direct-effects test for allocating power between the states and the federal government, but the Court has never formally abandoned the "uniform national standards" test.

Under current doctrine, which we explore in detail below, a state cannot treat interstate commerce differently from intrastate commerce when there is a reasonable, nondiscriminatory, alternative way of furthering the state's legitimate interests. Legitimate local interests include protecting health and safety, conserving natural resources, and similar things, but do not include protecting local businesses from competition. In addition, a state cannot impose a burden on interstate commerce that is excessive in relation to legitimate local interests.

These limitations make up the so-called "Dormant Commerce Clause Doctrine" (also known as the "Negative Commerce Clause Doctrine"). The name of this doctrine has a simple explanation. A power of Congress is "dormant" if the power exists but is not being exercised. Under the Dormant Commerce Clause Doctrine, even if Congress has not attempted to regulate a particular aspect of commerce that Congress could regulate, Congress's dormant power has a "negative" implication: namely, that the states are subject to the implied limitations discussed above.

The traditional justification given for the Dormant Commerce Clause Doctrine is that the United States adopted the Constitution to address problems that had arisen under the Articles of Confederation. One of the major issues facing the Union in the 1780s was that individual states were enacting tariffs and regulations that inhibited interstate commerce. In Federalist No. 22, Alexander Hamilton explained that these burdensome state-law restrictions on trade were causing discord among the states and that the impediments to trade were likely to get worse unless they were addressed at the national level. Hamilton wrote: "The interfering and unneighbourly regulations of some states contrary to the true spirit of the Union, have in different instances given just cause of umbrage and complaint to others; and it is to be feared that examples of this nature, if not restrained by a national controul, would be multiplied and extended till they became * * * injurious impediments to the intercourse between the different parts of the confederacy."

Hamilton and other supporters of the Constitution clearly believed that including the Commerce Clause in Article I, § 8 would address this problem. The Supreme Court, accordingly, has concluded that the mere presence of the Commerce Clause in the Constitution may bar burdensome or discriminatory state commerce regulations. But critics of the Dormant Commerce Clause Doctrine have a different view. They believe that the Commerce Clause gives Congress the power to regulate interstate commerce, including the power to preempt state laws concerning commerce, but that Congress must exercise that power by enacting legislation before any preemption can occur. In their view, the Commerce Clause in its dormant state has no effect on state regulations. You will see this disagreement among the Justices in some of the cases included in this chapter.

1. Early Cases

Early suggestions that the grant of power to Congress to regulate commerce might limit state power to regulate commerce appeared first in *Gibbons v. Ogden*, the landmark case on the Commerce Clause included at the start of Chapter 3.

GIBBONS V. OGDEN

22 U.S. (9 Wheat.) 1, 190 (1824)

[Recall that Gibbons, the appellant, challenged the constitutionality of a New York law that would restrain him from offering steamboat service from New Jersey to New York. One of Gibbons's arguments was that the New York law was unconstitutional because the Constitution grants Congress the exclusive power to regulate interstate commerce. The Supreme Court found it unnecessary to decide this question because the Court concluded that a federal statute, the Federal Licensing Act, preempted the New York law. But the Court addressed the argument briefly as follows.]

The appellant * * * contends that full power to regulate a particular subject implies the whole power, and leaves no residuum; that a grant of the whole is incompatible with the existence of a right in another to any part of it.

FYI

Gibbons was represented by one of the greatest lawyers in American history, Daniel Webster (1782–1852). Webster served in Congress as a member of the House of Representatives from New Hampshire and later as a Senator from Massachusetts. He also was a Secretary of State. Webster argued several important Supreme Court cases, including *McCulloch v. Maryland* and *Gibbons v. Ogden*.

The grant of the power to lay and collect taxes is, like the power to regulate commerce, made in general terms, and has never been understood to interfere with the exercise of the same power by the State; and hence has been drawn an argument which has been applied to the question under consideration. But the two grants are not, it is conceived, similar in their terms or their nature. Although many of the powers formerly exercised by the States are transferred to the government of the Union, yet the State governments remain, and constitute a most important part of our system. The power of taxation is indispensable to their existence, and is a power which, in its own nature, is capable of residing in, and being exercised by, different authorities at the same time. * * * When * * * each government exercises the power of taxation, neither is exercising the power of the other. But, when a State proceeds to regulate commerce with foreign nations, or among the several States, it is exercising the very power that is granted to Congress, and is doing the very thing which Congress is authorized to do. There is no analogy, then, between the power of taxation and the power of regulating commerce.

Daniel Webster (1782–1852)
Library of Congress

In discussing the question, whether this power is still in the States, in the case under consideration, we may dismiss from it the inquiry, whether it is surrendered by the mere grant to Congress, or is retained until Congress shall exercise the power. We may dismiss that inquiry, because it has been exercised, and the regulations which Congress deemed it proper to make, are now in full operation.

The sole question is, can a State regulate commerce with foreign nations and among the States, while Congress is regulating it?

It is obvious, that the government of the Union, in the exercise of its express powers, that, for example, of regulating commerce with foreign nations and among the States, may use means that may also be employed by a State, in the exercise of its acknowledged powers; that, for example, of regulating commerce within the State. If Congress license vessels to sail from one port to another, in the same State, the act is supposed to be, necessarily, incidental to the power expressly granted to Congress, and implies no claim of a direct power to regulate the purely internal commerce of a State, or to act directly on its system of police. So, if a State, in passing laws on subjects acknowledged to be within its control, and with a view to those subjects, shall adopt a measure of the same character with one which Congress may adopt, it does not derive its authority from the particular power which has been granted, but from some other, which remains with the State, and may be executed by the same means. All experience shows, that the same measures, or measures scarcely distinguishable from each other, may flow from distinct powers; but this does not prove that the powers themselves are identical. Although the means used in their execution may sometimes approach each other so nearly as to be confounded, there are other situations in which they are sufficiently distinct to establish their individuality.

In our complex system, presenting the rare and difficult scheme of one general government, whose action extends over the whole, but which possesses only certain enumerated powers; and of numerous State governments, which retain and exercise all powers not delegated to the Union, contests respecting power must arise. Were it even otherwise, the measures taken by the respective governments to execute their acknowledged powers, would often be of the same description, and might, sometimes, interfere. This, however, does not prove that the one is exercising, or has a right to exercise, the powers of the other.

Take Note

The Supreme Court summarizes here what Gibbons argued about the effect of the Commerce Clause. What does the initial sentence of the paragraph mean? Does the Court agree or disagree with the argument?

It has been contended by the counsel for the appellant, that, as the word "to regulate" implies in its nature, full power over the thing to be regulated, it excludes, necessarily, the action of all others that would perform the same operation on the same thing. That regulation is designed for the entire result, applying to those parts which remain as they were, as well as to those which are altered. It produces a uniform whole, which is as much disturbed and deranged by changing what the regulating power designs to leave untouched, as that on which it has operated.

There is great force in this argument, and the Court is not satisfied that it has been refuted.

MR. JUSTICE JOHNSON.

The judgment entered by the Court in this cause, has my entire approbation; but having adopted my conclusions on views of the subject materially different from those of my brethren, I feel it incumbent on me to exhibit those views. I have, also, another inducement: in questions of great importance and great delicacy, I feel my duty to the public best discharged, by an effort to maintain my opinions in my own way.

In attempts to construe the Constitution, I have never found much benefit resulting from the inquiry, whether the whole, or any part of it, is to be construed strictly, or literally. The simple, classical, precise, yet comprehensive language, in which it is couched, leaves, at most, but very little latitude for construction; and when its intent and meaning is discovered, nothing remains but to execute the will of those who made it, in the best manner to effect the purposes intended. The great and paramount purpose, was to unite this mass of wealth and power, for the protection of the humblest individual; his rights, civil and political, his interests and prosperity, are the sole end; the rest are nothing but the means. But the principal of those means, one so essential as to approach nearer the characteristics of an end, was the independence and harmony of the States, that they may the better subserve the purposes of cherishing and protecting the respective families of this great republic.

If there was any one object riding over every other in the adoption of the constitution, it was to keep the commercial intercourse among the States free from all invidious and partial restraints. And I cannot overcome the conviction, that if the licensing act was repealed to-morrow, the rights of the appellant to a reversal of the decision complained of, would be as strong as it is under this license.

POINTS FOR DISCUSSION

a. Relationship of Preemption to the Dormant Commerce Clause Doctrine

The majority opinion exhibits the standard understanding of the relationship of statutory preemption to the Dormant Commerce Clause Doctrine. If Congress has enacted legislation that governs a particular issue, then the federal statute preempts any state laws, and there is no need to apply the Dormant Commerce Clause Doctrine.

b. Meaning of the Concurring Opinion

Although the majority of the Court in *Gibbons* found it unnecessary to decide whether the state law would have violated the Commerce Clause in the absence of federal legislation, Justice Johnson reached this issue in his concurrence. How did he justify his conclusion? What was his method of interpreting the Constitution?

c. The Police Power of the States

In *Willson v. Black-Bird Creek Co.*, 27 U.S. (2 Pet.) 245 (1829), Delaware enacted legislation authorizing the Black Bird Creek Company to construct a dam over a small river. After the dam was built, the owners of a sloop broke up the dam so that their vessel could navigate the river. When the Black Bird Creek Company sued the owners of the sloop for damages, the owners argued in defense that they were not liable because they had a federal right to use the river and Delaware could not abridge this right by authorizing the construction of the dam. Chief Justice John Marshall, writing for the court, rejected this argument. He said: "We do not think that the act [of Delaware] empowering the Black Bird Creek Marsh Company to place a dam across the creek, can, under all the circumstances of the case, be considered as repugnant to the power [of Congress] to regulate commerce in its dormant state, or as being in conflict with any law passed on the subject." The Dormant Commerce Clause Doctrine acquired its name from this statement; the word "dormant" means "asleep." Why would the federal power to regulate commerce be considered dormant in this case?

For some years after the *Willson* decision, the Supreme Court suggested that the states might have a "police power"—meaning a power to regulate for the protection of local health and safety—unaffected by the Commerce Clause. But this theory that the states had a separate sphere of legislative authority ultimately "did not prove to be a useful tool" for deciding cases. John E. Nowak & Ronald D. Rotunda, *Constitutional Law* 284 (5th ed. 1995). The Supreme Court instead adopted different limitations, discussed below, as it searched for the limitations that now make up the Dormant Commerce Clause Doctrine.

2. The "Uniform National Standard" Test

Two decades after the Supreme Court decided *Gibbons v. Ogden* and *Willson v. Black-Bird Creek*, the Court became more specific about the negative implications of the Commerce Clause. In *Cooley v. Board of Wardens*, 53 U.S. (12 How.) 299 (1851), reprinted below, the Court announced a situation in which the grant of power to Congress to regulate commerce would limit state laws: namely, when the states attempt to regulate a subject for which a uniform national standard is necessary. In *Cooley*, the Supreme Court ultimately concluded that a uniform national standard was not needed and therefore did not invalidate the state law at issue. But as you will see, the Court reached the opposite conclusion in the case that follows, *Wabash, St. L. & P. Ry. Co. v. Illinois*, 118 U.S. 557 (1886). Consider how the "uniform national standard" test came into being, and why the Court reached different conclusions about its application in the two cases.

COOLEY V. BOARD OF WARDENS

53 U.S. (12 How.) 299 (1851)

MR. JUSTICE CURTIS delivered the opinion of the Court.

[Aaron B. Cooley was the consignee of two vessels, the *Undine* and the *Consul*, both of which sailed from the Port of Philadelphia without engaging the services of a local pilot. One of the vessels was engaged in coastal trade, sailing from Philadelphia to New York. The Board of Wardens of the Port of Philadelphia brought an action of debt against Cooley to recover the fees for both vessels as provided under the state law described below.]

These cases are brought here by writs of error to the Supreme Court of the Commonwealth of Pennsylvania. They are actions to recover half pilotage fees under the 29th section of the act of the Legislature of Pennsylvania, passed on the second day of March, 1803. The plaintiff in error alleges that the highest court of the state has decided against a right * * * to be exempted from the payment of the sums of money demanded, pursuant to the State law above referred to, because that law contravenes several provisions of the Constitution of the United States.

> **Take Note**
>
> "Plaintiff in error" is an archaic term for "appellant."

The particular section of the state law drawn in question is as follows:

> "That every ship or vessel arriving from or bound to any foreign port or place, and every ship or vessel of the burden of seventy-five tons or more, sailing from or bound to any port not within the river Delaware, shall be obliged to receive a pilot. * * * And if the master of any such ship or vessel shall refuse or neglect to take a pilot, the master, owner or consignee of such vessel shall forfeit and pay * * * a sum equal to the half-pilotage of such ship or vessel * * *."

We think this particular regulation concerning half-pilotage fees, is an appropriate part of a general system of regulations of this subject. Testing it by the practice of commercial states and countries legislating on this subject, we find it has usually been deemed necessary to make similar provisions. Numerous laws of this kind are cited in the learned argument of the counsel for the defendant in error; and their fitness, as a part of the system of pilotage, in many places, may be inferred from their existence in so many different states and countries. Like other laws they are framed to meet the most usual cases * * *; they rest upon the propriety of securing lives and property exposed to the perils of a dangerous navigation, by taking on board a person peculiarly skilled to encounter or avoid them; upon the policy of discouraging the commanders of vessels from refusing to receive such persons on board at the proper times and places; and upon the expediency, and even intrinsic justice, of not suffering those who have incurred labor, and expense, and danger, to place themselves in a position to render important service generally necessary, to go unrewarded, because the master of a particular vessel either rashly refuses their proffered assistance, or, contrary to the general experience, does not need it. * * *

It remains to consider the objection, that it is repugnant to the third clause of the eighth section of the first article [of the Constitution]. * * * That the power to regulate commerce includes the regulation of navigation, we consider settled. And when we look to the nature of the service performed by pilots, to the relations which that service and its compensations bear to navigation between the several states, and between the ports of the United States and foreign countries, we are brought to the conclusion, that the regulation of the qualifications of pilots, of the modes and times of offering and rendering their services, of the responsibilities which shall rest upon them, of the powers they shall possess, of the compensation they may demand, and of the penalties by which their rights and duties may be enforced, do constitute regulations of navigation, and consequently of commerce, within the just meaning of this clause of the Constitution.

Make the Connection

Recall that the Court held in *Gibbons* that "commerce" includes navigation.

* * * [W]e are brought directly and unavoidably to the consideration of the question, whether the grant of the commercial power to Congress, did *per se* deprive the states of all power to regulate pilots. This question has never been decided by this court, nor, in our judgment, has any case depending upon all the considerations which must govern this one, come before this court. The grant of commercial power to Congress does not contain any terms which expressly exclude the states from exercising an authority over its subject-matter. If they are excluded it must be because the nature of the power, thus granted to Congress, requires that a similar authority should not exist in the states. If it were conceded on the one side, that the nature of this power, like that to legislate for the District

of Columbia, is absolutely and totally repugnant to the existence of similar power in the states, probably no one would deny that the grant of the power to Congress, as effectually and perfectly excludes the states from all future legislation on the subject, as if express words had been used to exclude them. And on the other hand, if it were admitted that the existence of this power in Congress, like the power of taxation, is compatible with the existence of a similar power in the states, then it would be in conformity with the contemporary exposition of the Constitution (The Federalist, No. 32), and with the judicial construction, given from time to time by this court, after the most deliberate consideration, to hold that the mere grant of such a power to Congress, did not imply a prohibition on the states to exercise the same power; that it is not the mere existence of such a power, but its exercise by Congress, which may be incompatible with the exercise of the same power by the states, and that the states may legislate in the absence of congressional regulations.

Either absolutely to affirm, or deny that the nature of this power requires exclusive legislation by Congress, is to lose sight of the nature of the subjects of this power, and to assert concerning all of them, what is really applicable but to a part. Whatever subjects of this power are in their nature national, or admit only of one uniform system, or plan of regulation, may justly be said to be of such a nature as to require exclusive legislation by Congress. That this cannot be affirmed of laws for the regulation of pilots and pilotage is plain. The act of 1789* contains a clear and authoritative declaration by the first Congress, that the nature of this subject is such, that until Congress should find it necessary to exert its power, it should be left to the legislation of the states; that it is local and not national; that it is likely to be the best provided for, not by one system, or plan of regulations, but by as many as the legislative discretion of the several states should deem applicable to the local peculiarities of the ports within their limits.

> **Take Note**
>
> Here is where the Court establishes the rule that the Commerce Clause prevents the states from regulating subjects that require a uniform national standard. What logic leads the Court to create this rule?

Viewed in this light, so much of this act of 1789 as declares that pilots shall continue to be regulated "by such laws as the states may respectively hereafter enact for that purpose," instead of being held to be inoperative, as an attempt to

* In 1789, Congress enacted a law saying "all pilots in the bays, inlets, rivers, harbors, and ports of the United States shall continue to be regulated in conformity with the existing laws of the states, respectively, wherein such pilots may be, or with such laws as the states may respectively hereafter enact for the purpose, until further legislative provision shall be made by Congress." This law did not apply to the present case because the Pennsylvania law was enacted after 1789. But the federal law did indicate that Congress was content to allow some state regulations to govern pilotage.—*Eds.*

confer on the states a power to legislate, of which the Constitution had deprived them, is allowed an appropriate and important signification. It manifests the understanding of Congress, at the outset of the government, that the nature of this subject is not such as to require its exclusive legislation. The practice of the states, and of the national government, has been in conformity with this declaration, from the origin of the national government to this time; and the nature of the subject when examined, is such as to leave no doubt of the superior fitness and propriety, not to say the absolute necessity, of different systems of regulation, drawn from local knowledge and experience, and conformed to local wants.

It is the opinion of a majority of the court that the mere grant to Congress of the power to regulate commerce, did not deprive the states of power to regulate pilots, and that although Congress has legislated on this subject, its legislation manifests an intention, with a single exception, not to regulate this subject, but to leave its regulation to the several states.

WABASH, ST. L. & P. RY. CO. V. ILLINOIS

118 U.S. 557 (1886)

MILLER, J.

This is a writ of error to the supreme court of Illinois. * * * The first count [charged] that the Wabash, St. Louis & Pacific Railway Company had, in violation of a statute of the state of Illinois, been guilty of an unjust discrimination in its rates or charges of toll and compensation for the transportation of freight. The specific allegation is that the railroad company charged Elder & McKinney for transporting 26,000 pounds of goods and chattels from Peoria, in the state of Illinois, to New York city, the sum of $39, being at the rate of 15 cents per hundred pounds for said car-load; and that on the same day they agreed to carry and transport for Isaac Bailey and F. O. Swannell another car-load of goods and chattels from Gilman, in the state of Illinois, to said city of New York, for which they charged the sum of $65, being at the rate of 25 cents per hundred pounds. * * * This freight being of the same class in both instances, and carried over the same road, except as to the difference in the distance, it is obvious that a discrimination against Bailey & Swannell was made in the charges against them, as compared with those against Elder & McKinney; and this is true whether we regard the charge for the whole distance from the terminal points in Illinois to New York city, or the proportionate charge for the haul within the state of Illinois.

The language of the statute which is supposed to be violated by this transaction is * * * that if any railroad corporation shall charge, collect, or receive, for the transportation of any passenger or freight of any description upon its railroad, for any distance within the state, the same or a greater amount of toll or compensation than is at the same time charged, collected, or received for the transportation in the same direction of any passenger or like quantity of freight of the same class over a greater distance of the same road, all such discriminating rates, charges, collections, or receipts, whether made directly or by means of rebate, drawback, or other shift or evasion, shall be deemed and taken against any such railroad corporation as *prima facie* evidence of unjust discrimination prohibited by the provisions of this act. * * *

FYI

The *Wabash* case had far-reaching consequences. Because the Supreme Court held that the states could not regulate interstate railway rates, the task was left to the federal government. But Congress thought that it would be too burdensome to enact legislation setting rates for every route in the entire country. Instead, Congress created the Interstate Commerce Commission and granted the Commission the authority to set rates. This was one of the first steps in the development of the modern administrative state, in which Congress creates administrative agencies that in turn promulgate legally binding regulations. See Paul Stephen Dempsey, *Rate Regulation and Antitrust Immunity in Transportation: The Genesis and Evolution of This Endangered Species*, 32 Am. U. L. Rev. 335, 341 (1983).

If the Illinois statute could be construed to apply exclusively to contracts for a carriage which begins and ends within the state, disconnected from a continuous transportation through or into other states, there does not seem to be any difficulty in holding it to be valid. For instance, a contract might be made to carry goods for a certain price from Cairo to Chicago, or from Chicago to Alton. The charges for these might be within the competency of the Illinois legislature to regulate. The reason for this is that both the charge and the actual transportation in such cases are exclusively confined to the limits of the territory of the state, and is not commerce among the states, or interstate commerce, but is exclusively commerce within the state. So far, therefore, as this class of transportation, as an element of commerce, is affected by the statute under consideration, it is not subject to the constitutional provision concerning commerce among the states. * * *

Definition

"Prima facie evidence" is evidence that is sufficient "to establish a fact or raise a presumption unless disproved or rebutted." *Black's Law Dictionary* (10th ed. 2014).

> **Food for Thought**
>
> Alton, Cairo, and Chicago are cities in the state of Illinois. Given the Court's modern interpretation of the scope of the Commerce Clause, is it clear that such intrastate rates would not be within Congress's power to regulate? Recall the *Shreveport Rate Case*, which we considered in Chapter 3.

The supreme court of Illinois does not place its judgment in the present case on the ground that the transportation and the charge are exclusively state commerce, but, conceding that it may be a case of commerce among the states, or interstate commerce, which congress would have the right to regulate if it had attempted to do so, argues that this statute of Illinois belongs to that class of commercial regulations which may be established by the laws of a state until congress shall have exercised its power on that subject * * *.

[There is a] class of regulations of commerce which, like pilotage, bridging navigable rivers, and many others, could be acted upon by the states, in the absence of any legislation by congress on the same subject. By the slightest attention to the matter, it will be readily seen that the circumstances under which a bridge may be authorized across a navigable stream within the limits of a state for the use of a public highway, and the local rules which shall govern the conduct of the pilots of each of the varying harbors of the coasts of the United States, depend upon principles far more limited in their application and importance than those which should regulate the transportation of persons and property across the half or the whole of the continent, over the territories of half a dozen states, through which they are carried without change of car or breaking bulk.

Of the justice or propriety of the principle which lies at the foundation of the Illinois statute it is not the province of this court to speak. As restricted to a transportation which begins and ends within the limits of the state, it may be very just and equitable, and it certainly is the province of the state legislature to determine that question; but when it is attempted to apply to transportation through an entire series of states a principle of this kind, and each one of the states shall attempt to establish its own rates of transportation, its own methods to prevent discrimination in rates, or to permit it, the deleterious influence upon the freedom of commerce among the states, and upon the transit of goods through those states, cannot be overestimated. That this species of regulation is one which must be, if established at all, of a general and national character, and cannot be safely and wisely remitted to local rules and local

> **Take Note**
>
> The Court concludes here that, if rates for interstate transportation of goods are to be regulated, they must be regulated by a uniform national standard. Why does the Court reach this conclusion?

regulations, we think is clear from what has already been said. And if it be a regulation of commerce, as we think we have demonstrated it is, and as the Illinois court concedes it to be, it must be of that national character; and the regulation can only appropriately exist by general rules and principles, which demand that it should be done by the congress of the United States under the commerce clause of the constitution.

The judgment of the supreme court of Illinois is therefore reversed, and the case remanded to that court for further proceedings in conformity with this opinion.

POINTS FOR DISCUSSION

a. Justifying the Court's Conclusion

Suppose a railroad wants to carry goods from New Jersey to Massachusetts. Suppose further that New Jersey law says that the railroad must charge a rate of 15¢ per hundred pounds for this interstate journey, but Massachusetts law says that the railroad may not charge a rate of more than 10¢ per hundred pounds for the journey. Does this hypothetical illustrate why, as the Court says in this case, state regulation of interstate transportation rates is "inappropriate" and that any regulation must be of "a general national character"?

b. Comparison

How does the regulation of railroad rates in this case differ from the regulation of ship pilotage in local harbors in *Cooley v. Board of Wardens*? Why did the Supreme Court think that a uniform national rule concerning piloting ships into harbors was not necessary, but that one for interstate railroad rates was necessary?

c. Wisdom of the State Law

Notice how the Court refuses to consider the "justice or propriety" of the Illinois law, but instead focuses only on whether the law concerns a matter for which uniform national regulation is required. Why is the wisdom of the state law not at issue? Is it possible to apply the uniform national standard test without any consideration of the wisdom of the state regulation at issue?

3. The "Discrimination Against Interstate Commerce" Test

In *Cooley v. Board of Wardens*, the Supreme Court developed the rule that states cannot regulate subjects for which a uniform national standard is necessary. The Court has never abandoned this rule, and it continues to cite *Cooley* in Dormant

Commerce Clause cases. In the second half of the Twentieth Century, however, the Court began to articulate other limitations imposed by the Dormant Commerce Clause Doctrine.

The first of these limitations is that a state may not engage in discrimination against interstate commerce unless necessary to further a legitimate state interest. The prohibition against discrimination applies to statutes that discriminate on their face or that have a discriminatory purpose or effect. The Supreme Court has said: "The commerce clause forbids discrimination, whether forthright or ingenious. In each case it is our duty to determine whether the statute under attack, whatever its name may be, will in its practical operation work discrimination against interstate commerce." *Best & Co. v. Maxwell,* 311 U.S. 454, 455–456 (1940). The prohibition against discrimination is strict, but not absolute. The Supreme Court has declared that "a State may validate a statute that discriminates against interstate commerce by showing that it advances a legitimate local purpose that cannot be adequately served by reasonable nondiscriminatory alternatives." *New Energy Co. v. Limbach*, 486 U.S. 269, 278 (1988).

As the following cases show, states have attempted to discriminate against interstate commerce in different ways. They may try, for example, to restrict imports and thus protect local producers from external competition. Or they may try to limit exports, preserving goods for local consumers. Either way, interstate commerce is treated differently from commerce wholly within the state. Once a court finds discrimination, it must consider the reason for the discrimination and whether the state could have found nondiscriminatory ways to protect its interests.

DEAN MILK CO. V. CITY OF MADISON, WISC.

340 U.S. 349 (1951)

MR. JUSTICE CLARK delivered the opinion of the Court.

This appeal challenges the constitutional validity of two sections of an ordinance of the City of Madison, Wisconsin, regulating the sale of milk and milk products within the municipality's jurisdiction. One section in issue makes it unlawful to sell any milk as pasteurized unless it has been processed and bottled at an approved pasteurization plant within a radius of five miles from the central square of Madison. Another section, which prohibits the sale of milk, or the importation, receipt or storage of milk for sale, in Madison unless from a source of supply possessing a permit issued after inspection by Madison officials, is attacked insofar as it expressly relieves municipal authorities from any duty to inspect farms located beyond twenty-five miles from the center of the city.

The area defined by the ordinance with respect to milk sources encompasses practically all of Dane County and includes some 500 farms which supply milk for Madison. Within the five-mile area for pasteurization are plants of five processors, only three of which are engaged in the general wholesale and retail trade in Madison. Inspection of these farms and plants is scheduled once every thirty days and is performed by two municipal inspectors, one of whom is full-time. The courts below found that the ordinance in question promotes convenient, economical and efficient plant inspection.

Appellant purchases and gathers milk from approximately 950 farms in northern Illinois and southern Wisconsin, none being within twenty-five miles of Madison. Its pasteurization plants are located at Chemung and Huntley, Illinois, about 65 and 85 miles respectively from Madison. Appellant was denied a license to sell its products within Madison solely because its pasteurization plants were more than five miles away.

It is conceded that the milk which appellant seeks to sell in Madison is supplied from farms and processed in plants licensed and inspected by public health authorities of Chicago, and is labeled "Grade A" under the Chicago ordinance which adopts the rating standards recommended by the United States Public Health Service. Both the Chicago and Madison ordinances, though not the sections of the latter here in issue, are largely patterned after the Model Milk Ordinance of the Public Health Service. However, Madison contends and we assume that in some particulars its ordinance is more rigorous than that of Chicago.

Upon these facts we find it necessary to determine only the issue raised under the Commerce Clause, for we agree with appellant that the ordinance imposes an undue burden on interstate commerce. [This] is not an instance in which an enactment falls because of federal legislation which, as a proper exercise of paramount national power over commerce, excludes measures which might otherwise be within the police power of the states. * * *

Nor can there be objection to the avowed purpose of this enactment. We assume that difficulties in sanitary regulation of milk and milk products originating in remote areas may present a situation in which "upon a consideration of all the relevant facts and circumstances it appears that the matter is one which may appropriately be regulated in the interest of

> **Make the Connection**
>
> Just as promoting safety is considered a legitimate interest in judging the constitutionality of discrimination against interstate commerce, so too is it seen as a legitimate state interest in evaluating burdens placed on interstate commerce, as we will see later in this chapter.

the safety, health and well-being of local communities * * *." *Parker v. Brown*, 317 U.S. 341, 362–363 (1943).

But this regulation, like the provision invalidated in *Baldwin v. G.A.F. Seelig, Inc.*, 294 U.S. 511 (1935), in practical effect excludes from distribution in Madison wholesome milk produced and pasteurized in Illinois. "The importer [may] keep his milk or drink it, but sell it he may not." *Id.* at 521. In thus erecting an economic barrier protecting a major local industry against competition from without the State, Madison plainly discriminates against interstate commerce.[4] This it cannot do, even in the exercise of its unquestioned power to protect the health and safety of its people, if reasonable nondiscriminatory alternatives, adequate to conserve legitimate local interests, are available. A different view, that the ordinance is valid simply because it professes to be a health measure, would mean that the Commerce Clause of itself imposes no limitations on state action other than those laid down by the Due Process Clause, save for the rare instance where a state artlessly discloses an avowed purpose to discriminate against interstate goods. Our issue then is whether the discrimination inherent in the Madison ordinance can be justified in view of the character of the local interests and the available methods of protecting them.

> **Take Note**
>
> In this passage, the Court expresses the rule for when a state law violates the Dormant Commerce Clause Doctrine because of discrimination against interstate commerce. Can you articulate what constitutes "discrimination" within the meaning of the rule?

It appears that reasonable and adequate alternatives are available. If the City of Madison prefers to rely upon its own officials for inspection of distant milk sources, such inspection is readily open to it without hardship for it could charge the actual and reasonable cost of such inspection to the importing producers and processors. Moreover, appellee Health Commissioner of Madison testified that as proponent of the local milk ordinance he had submitted the provisions here in controversy and an alternative proposal based on § 11 of the Model Milk Ordinance recommended by the United States Public Health Service. The model provision imposes no geographical limitation on location of milk sources and processing plants but excludes from the municipality milk not produced and pasteurized conformably to standards as high as those enforced by the receiving city. In implementing such an ordinance, the importing city obtains milk ratings based on uniform standards and established by health authorities in the jurisdiction where production and processing occur. The receiving city may

---

4 It is immaterial that Wisconsin milk from outside the Madison area is subjected to the same proscription as that moving in interstate commerce.

determine the extent of enforcement of sanitary standards in the exporting area by verifying the accuracy of safety ratings of specific plants or of the milkshed in the distant jurisdiction through the United States Public Health Service, which routinely and on request spot checks the local ratings. The Commissioner testified that Madison consumers "would be safeguarded adequately" under either proposal and that he had expressed no preference. The milk sanitarian of the Wisconsin State Board of Health testified that the State Health Department recommends the adoption of a provision based on the Model Ordinance. Both officials agreed that a local health officer would be justified in relying upon the evaluation by the Public Health Service of enforcement conditions in remote producing areas.

To permit Madison to adopt a regulation not essential for the protection of local health interests and placing a discriminatory burden on interstate commerce would invite a multiplication of preferential trade areas destructive of the very purpose of the Commerce Clause. Under the circumstances here presented, the regulation must yield to the principle that "one state in its dealings with another may not place itself in a position of economic isolation." *Baldwin v. G.A.F. Seeling, Inc.*, 294 U.S. at 527. * * * [W]e conclude that the judgment below sustaining the five-mile provision as to pasteurization must be reversed.

The Supreme Court of Wisconsin thought it unnecessary to pass upon the validity of the twenty-five-mile limitation, apparently in part for the reason that this issue was made academic by its decision upholding the five-mile section. In view of our conclusion as to the latter provision, a determination of appellant's contention as to the other section is now necessary. As to this issue, therefore, we vacate the judgment below and remand for further proceedings not inconsistent with the principles announced in this opinion. It is so ordered.

POINTS FOR DISCUSSION

a. Discrimination Against Interstate Commerce

The Madison ordinance does not say anything about excluding products from other states. But the Court says the law "in practical effect excludes from distribution in Madison wholesome milk produced and pasteurized in Illinois." Why doesn't it make a difference that the discrimination is implicit and not explicit? Also, why doesn't it matter, as the Court says in footnote 4, that the law also excludes milk from other parts of Wisconsin?

b. Legitimate State Interest

What was the city's interest in having the law? Did the Court think that the interest was legitimate? Is it possible to conceive of the city's interest as being illegitimate, given the purposes of the Dormant Commerce Clause Doctrine?

c. Less Discriminatory Alternatives

How could the city have accomplished its goal without discriminating against interstate commerce? Is the Court the most competent actor to decide whether less discriminatory alternatives are viable alternatives?

d. Purpose of Prohibiting Discrimination

The Court says that permitting Madison to place "a discriminatory burden on interstate commerce would invite a multiplication of preferential trade areas destructive of the very purpose of the Commerce Clause." Why would upholding the Madison law invite other obstacles to trade?

e. Historical Basis for the Dormant Commerce Clause Doctrine

Recall that one of the principal defects of the Articles of Confederation was that it effectively permitted the states to engage in economically disastrous protectionism (i.e. protection of local businesses from non-local competition), and that the inclusion of the Commerce Clause in the new Constitution was a response to this problem. Does this history justify judicial enforcement, even absent legislation from Congress, of a ban on state regulation that discriminates against interstate commerce?

HUGHES V. OKLAHOMA

441 U.S. 322 (1979)

MR. JUSTICE BRENNAN delivered the opinion of the Court.

The question presented for decision is whether Okl. Stat., Tit. 29, § 4–115(B) (Supp. 1978), violates the Commerce Clause, Art. I, § 8, cl. 3, of the United States Constitution, insofar as it provides that "[n]o person may transport or ship minnows for sale outside the state which were seined or procured within the waters of this state. . . ." The prohibition against transportation out of State for sale thus does not apply to hatchery-bred minnows, but only to "natural" minnows seined or procured from waters within the State.

> **FYI**
>
> A minnow is a small fish often used as bait for catching other fish. A seine is a kind of net placed vertically in the water to trap fish.

Section 4–115(B) is part of the Oklahoma Wildlife Conservation Code. Another provision of that Code requires that persons have a minnow dealer's license before they can lawfully seine or trap minnows within the State—except for their own use as bait—§ 4–116 (Supp. 1978), but no limit is imposed on the number of minnows a licensed dealer may take from state waters. Nor is there any regulation except § 4–115(B) concerning the disposition of lawfully acquired minnows; they may be sold within Oklahoma to any person and for any purpose, and may be taken out of the State for any purpose except sale.

Appellant William Hughes holds a Texas license to operate a commercial minnow business near Wichita Falls, Tex. An Oklahoma game ranger arrested him on a charge of violating § 4–115(B) by transporting from Oklahoma to Wichita Falls a load of natural minnows purchased from a minnow dealer licensed to do business in Oklahoma. Hughes' defense that § 4–115(B) was unconstitutional because it was repugnant to the Commerce Clause was rejected, and he was convicted and fined. * * *

Section 4–115(B) on its face discriminates against interstate commerce. It forbids the transportation of natural minnows out of the State for purposes of sale, and thus "overtly blocks the flow of interstate commerce at [the] State's borders." *Philadelphia v. New Jersey*, 437 U.S. 617 (1978). Such facial discrimination by itself may be a fatal defect, regardless of the State's purpose, because "the evil of protectionism can reside in legislative means as well as legislative ends." *Id.* at 626. At a minimum such facial discrimination invokes the strictest scrutiny of any purported legitimate local purpose and of the absence of nondiscriminatory alternatives.

> **FYI**
>
> *Facial discrimination* means discrimination that is apparent from the language of the statute. Some statutes discriminate on their face, while others are written in nondiscriminatory terms but are discriminatory in their effects.

Oklahoma argues that § 4–115(B) serves a legitimate local purpose in that it is "readily apparent as a conservation measure." The State's interest in maintaining the ecological balance in state waters by avoiding the removal of inordinate numbers of minnows may well qualify as a legitimate local purpose. We consider the States' interests in conservation and protection of wild animals as legitimate local purposes similar to the States' interests in protecting the health and safety of their citizens.

[But far] from choosing the least discriminatory alternative, Oklahoma has chosen to "conserve" its minnows in the way that most overtly discriminates against interstate commerce. The State places no limits on the numbers of minnows that can be taken by licensed minnow dealers; nor does it limit in any way how these minnows may be disposed of within the State. Yet it forbids the transportation of any commercially significant number of natural minnows out of the State for sale. Section 4–115(B) is certainly not a "last ditch" attempt at conservation after nondiscriminatory alternatives have proved unfeasible. It is rather a choice of the most discriminatory means even though nondiscriminatory alternatives would seem likely to fulfill the State's purported legitimate local purpose more effectively. We therefore hold that § 4–115(B) is repugnant to the Commerce Clause.

[Our decision] does not leave the States powerless to protect and conserve wild animal life within their borders. Today's decision makes clear, however, that States may promote this legitimate purpose only in ways consistent with the basic principle that "our economic unit is the Nation," *H.P. Hood & Sons, Inc. v. Du Mond*, 336 U.S. 525, 537 (1949), and that when a wild animal "becomes an article of commerce . . . its use cannot be limited to the citizens of one State to the exclusion of citizens of another State." *Geer v. Connecticut,* 161 U.S. 519, 538 (1896) (Field, J., dissenting). *Reversed.*

MR. JUSTICE REHNQUIST, with whom THE CHIEF JUSTICE joins, dissenting.

Contrary to the view of the Court, I do not think that Oklahoma's regulation of the commercial exploitation of natural minnows either discriminates against out-of-state enterprises in favor of local businesses or that it burdens the interstate commerce in minnows. At least, no such showing has been made on the record before us. This is not a case where a State's regulation permits residents to export naturally seined minnows but prohibits nonresidents from so doing. No person is allowed to export natural minnows for sale outside of Oklahoma; the statute is evenhanded in its application. The State has not used its power to protect its own citizens from outside competition. Nor is this a case where a State requires a nonresident business, as a condition to exporting minnows, to move a significant portion of its operations to the State or to use certain state resources in pursuit of its business for the benefit of the local economy. And, notwithstanding the Court's protestations to the contrary, Oklahoma has not blocked the flow of interstate commerce in minnows at the State's borders. Appellant, or anyone else, may freely export as many minnows as he wishes, so long as the minnows so transported are hatchery minnows and not naturally seined minnows. On this record, I simply fail to see how interstate commerce in minnows, the commodity at issue here, is impeded in the least by Oklahoma's regulatory scheme.

POINT FOR DISCUSSION

a. Discrimination

Why did the Court think that the law discriminated against interstate commerce? Why did the dissent think that the law did not? If the law was discriminatory, against whom or what did it discriminate?

b. Less Discriminatory Alternatives in Environmental Protection

Does this case limit how states may attempt to protect the environment? Or does it just invalidate the specific means chosen by Oklahoma? How, if at all, could the state have accomplished its goal of protecting minnows in a less discriminatory manner?

c. Importation of Minnows

In *Maine v. Taylor*, 477 U.S. 131 (1986), the Supreme Court upheld the conviction of a man who had violated a Maine statute prohibiting the importation of baitfish into Maine. The Court held that the state statute did not violate the Dormant Commerce Clause Doctrine. Even though the statute discriminated against interstate commerce, the state had a strong interest in protecting native fisheries from harms caused by non-native species. In addition, the Court concluded that the state could not further this interest through alternative non-discriminatory means. Why is this case different from *Hughes v. Oklahoma*? Why weren't non-discriminatory options available to Maine?

4. The "Excessive Burden on Interstate Commerce" Test

We have seen that the states may not discriminate against interstate commerce. But given the nature of commerce today, even state regulation that does not treat out-of-state interests differently from in-state interests has the potential to create effects on commerce outside the borders of the state imposing the regulation. Another limitation that the Court has developed, in a series of cases, is that states may not impose a burden on interstate commerce that is excessive in relation to legitimate local interests. In a frequently quoted portion of *Pike v. Bruce Church*, 397 U.S. 137, 142 (1970), the Supreme Court more formally stated the modern rule as follows:

> "Where [a state law] regulates evenhandedly to effectuate a legitimate local public interest, and its effects on interstate commerce are only incidental, it will be upheld unless the burden imposed on such commerce is clearly excessive in relation to the putative local benefits. If a legitimate local purpose is found, then the question becomes one of degree. And the extent of the burden that will be tolerated will of course

depend on the nature of the local interest involved, and on whether it could be promoted as well with a lesser impact on interstate activities."

For example, suppose that a state sets a speed limit of 45 miles an hour on all of its highways. Interstate truckers who feel this speed limit is too low might challenge the law under the *Pike* test. A court would have to ask why the state set the speed limit at 45 miles an hour, what kind of burden the law places on interstate commerce, and whether the burden is excessive in comparison to the state's interests in having the law.

Under this rule, legitimate local interests include protecting health and safety and conserving natural resources, but they do not include protecting local businesses from competition. This "excessive burden" rule did not reach its final form in a single case; rather, it took several decades for the rule to develop. In reading the following decisions, notice how the rule evolved and became more specific as the Supreme Court considered additional cases. Consider whether this rule is different from the "uniform national standards" test that we considered earlier in this chapter. Also consider why some members of the Supreme Court have felt uncomfortable in weighing the importance of state interests when applying the test.

SOUTH CAROLINA STATE HIGHWAY DEPT. V. BARNWELL BROS.

303 U.S. 177 (1938)

MR. JUSTICE STONE delivered the opinion of the Court.

Act No. 259 of the General Assembly of South Carolina, of April 28, 1933, prohibits use on the state highways of motor trucks and "semi-trailer motor trucks" whose width exceeds 90 inches, and whose weight including load exceeds 20,000 pounds. For purposes of the weight limitation, section 2 of the statute provides that a semitrailer motortruck, which is a motor propelled truck with a trailer whose front end is designed to be attached to and supported by the truck, shall be considered a single unit. The principal question for decision is whether these prohibitions impose an unconstitutional burden upon interstate commerce.

The District Court of three judges, after hearing evidence, ruled that the challenged provisions of the statute have not been superseded by the Federal Motor Carrier Act, and * * * that the challenged provisions, being an exercise of the state's power to regulate the use of its highways so as to protect them from injury and to insure their safe and economical use, do not violate the Fourteenth Amendment. But it held that the weight and width prohibitions place an unlawful burden on interstate motor traffic passing over specified highways of the state, which for the most part are of concrete or a concrete base surfaced with asphalt. It accordingly enjoined the enforcement of the weight provision against interstate motor carriers on the specified highway, and also the width limitation of 90 inches, except in the case of vehicles exceeding 96 inches in width. * * *

The trial court rested its decision that the statute unreasonably burdens interstate commerce, upon findings, not assailed here, that there is a large amount of motortruck traffic passing interstate in the southeastern part of the United States, which would normally pass over the highways of South Carolina, but which will be barred from the state by the challenged restrictions if enforced, and upon its conclusion that, when viewed in the light of their effect upon interstate commerce, these restrictions are unreasonable.

To reach this conclusion the court weighed conflicting evidence and made its own determinations as to the weight and width of motortrucks commonly used in interstate traffic and the capacity of the specified highways of the state to accommodate such traffic without injury to them or danger to their users. It found that interstate carriage by motortrucks has become a national industry; that from 85 to 90 per cent of the motor trucks used in interstate transportation are 96 inches wide and of a gross weight, when loaded, of more than 10 tons; that only four other states prescribe a gross load weight as low as 20,000 pounds; and that the American Association of State Highway Officials and the National Conference on Street and Highway Safety in the Department of Commerce have recommended for adoption weight and width limitations in which weight is limited to axle loads of 16,000 to 18,000 pounds and width is limited to 96 inches.

While the constitutional grant to Congress of power to regulate interstate commerce has been held to operate of its own force to curtail state power in some measure,[2] it did not forestall all state action affecting interstate commerce.

> **Food for Thought**
>
> Footnote 2 contains a famous and often-cited political theory for why the Dormant Commerce Clause Doctrine should allow some state regulation of commerce but not all regulation. What does the last sentence of the footnote mean?

Ever since *Willson v. Black-bird Creek Marsh Co.*, 27 U.S. (2 Pet.) 245 (1829), and *Cooley v.*

2 State regulations affecting interstate commerce, whose purpose or effect is to gain for those within the state an advantage at the expense of those without, or to burden those out of the state without any corresponding advantage to those within, have been thought to impinge upon the constitutional prohibition even though Congress has not acted. Underlying the stated rule has been the thought, often expressed in judicial opinion, that when the regulation is of such a character that its burden falls principally upon those without the state, legislative action is not likely to be subjected to those political restraints which are normally exerted on legislation where it affects adversely some interests within the state.

Board of Port Wardens, 53 U.S. (12 How.) 299 (1851), it has been recognized that there are matters of local concern, the regulation of which unavoidably involves some regulation of interstate commerce but which, because of their local character and their number and diversity, may never be fully dealt with by Congress. Notwithstanding the commerce clause, such regulation in the absence of congressional action has for the most part been left to the states by the decisions of this Court, subject to the other applicable constitutional restraints.

[T]he present case affords no occasion for saying that the bare possession of power by Congress to regulate the interstate traffic forces the states to conform to standards which Congress might, but has not adopted, or curtails their power to take measures to insure the safety and conservation of their highways which may be applied to like traffic moving intrastate. Few subjects of state regulation are so peculiarly of local concern as is the use of state highways. There are few, local regulation of which is so inseparable from a substantial effect on interstate commerce. Unlike the railroads, local highways are built, owned, and maintained by the state or its municipal subdivisions. The state has a primary and immediate concern in their safe and economical administration. The present regulations, or any others of like purpose, if they are to accomplish their end, must be applied alike to interstate and intrastate traffic both moving in large volume over the highways. The fact that they affect alike shippers in interstate and intrastate commerce in large number within as well as without the state is a safeguard against their abuse.

Congress, in the exercise of its plenary power to regulate interstate commerce, may determine whether the burdens imposed on it by state regulation, otherwise permissible, are too great, and may, by legislation designed to secure uniformity or in other respects to protect the national interest in the commerce, curtail to some extent the state's regulatory power. But that is a legislative, not a judicial, function, to be performed in the light of the congressional judgment of what is appropriate regulation of interstate commerce, and the extent to which, in that field, state power and local interests should be required to yield to the national authority and interest. In the absence of such legislation the judicial function, under the commerce clause, Const. art. 1, § 8, cl. 3, as well as the Fourteenth Amendment, stops with

Take Note

The Court says here that a state legislature may impose burdens on interstate commerce so long as it has "acted within its province" and the "means chosen" are reasonable. Modern cases do not follow this formulation of the rule. Instead, as explained above, they ask whether the burden on interstate commerce is excessive in comparison to legitimate local interests. Notice, however, that the Court's analysis here in fact is similar to the modern approach.

the inquiry whether the state Legislature in adopting regulations such as the present has acted within its province, and whether the means of regulation chosen are reasonably adapted to the end sought.

[In considering the challenged weight limitation, the district court relied on evidence that was] based on theoretical strength of concrete highways laid under ideal conditions, and none of it was based on an actual study of the highways of South Carolina or of the subgrade and other road building conditions which prevail there and which have a material bearing on the strength and durability of such highways. There is uncontradicted testimony that approximately 60 per cent. of the South Carolina standard paved highways in question were built without a longitudinal center joint which has since become standard practice, the portion of the concrete surface adjacent to the joint being strengthened by reinforcement or by increasing its thickness; and that owing to the distribution of the stresses on concrete roads when in use, those without a center joint have a tendency to develop irregular longitudinal cracks. As the concrete in the center of such roads is thinner than that at the edges, the result is that the highway is split into two irregular segments, each with a weak inner edge which, according to the expert testimony, is not capable of supporting indefinitely wheel loads in excess of 4,200 pounds.

These considerations, with the presumption of constitutionality, afford adequate support for the weight limitation without reference to other items of the testimony tending to support it. * * * The fact that many states have adopted a different standard is not persuasive. The conditions under which highways must be built in the several states, their construction, and the demands made upon them, are not uniform. The road building art, as the record shows, is far from having attained a scientific certainty and precision, and scientific precision is not the criterion for the exercise of the constitutional regulatory power of the states. The Legislature, being free to exercise its own judgment, is not bound by that of other Legislatures. It would hardly be contended that if all the states had adopted a single standard none, in the light of its own experience and in the exercise of its judgment upon all the complex elements which enter into the problem, could change it.

Only a word need be said as to the width limitation. While a large part of the highways in question are from 18 to 20 feet in width, approximately 100 miles are only 16 feet wide. On all the use of a 96-inch truck leaves but a narrow margin for passing. On the road 16 feet wide it leaves none. The 90-inch limitation has been in force in South Carolina since 1920, and the concrete highways which it has built appear to be adopted to vehicles of that width. The record shows without contradiction that the use of heavy loaded trucks on the highways tends to force other traffic off the concrete surface onto the shoulders of the road adjoining its edges, and to increase repair costs materially. It appears also that as the width of trucks is increased it obstructs the view of the highway, causing much inconvenience and increased hazard in its use. It plainly cannot be said that the width of trucks used on the highways in South Carolina is unrelated to their safety and cost of maintenance, or that a 90-inch width limitation, adopted to safeguard the highways of the state, is not within the range of the permissible legislative choice.

The regulatory measures taken by South Carolina are within its legislative power. * * * Reversed.

POINTS FOR DISCUSSION

a. The *Pike v. Bruce Church* Test

The Supreme Court decided this case before it established the modern formulation of the rule regarding excessive burdens, quoted above, from *Pike v. Bruce Church*, 397 U.S. 137 (1970). But the Court has said that even though *Barnwell Bros.* used a "less formalistic approach," the decision is a "classic case" consistent with the modern understanding of the Dormant Commerce Clause. *Arkansas Elec. Co-op. Corp. v. Arkansas Public Service Comm'n*, 461 U.S. 375, 393 (1983).

b. Legitimate Interests

Why did the Court think that South Carolina had a legitimate interest in regulating the weight and width of trucks using its highways? Even if South Carolina has a legitimate interest in regulating the weight and width of trucks, does that mean that the state may enact any regulation that it desires? Do you agree that state highways are "peculiarly of local concern" today?

SOUTHERN PACIFIC CO. V. STATE OF ARIZONA

325 U.S. 761 (1945)

MR. CHIEF JUSTICE STONE delivered the opinion of the Court.

The Arizona Train Limit Law of May 16, 1912, Arizona Code Ann., 1939, § 69–119, makes it unlawful for any person or corporation to operate within the state a railroad train of more than fourteen passenger or seventy freight cars, and authorizes the state to recover a money penalty for each violation of the Act. The questions for decision are whether Congress has, by legislative enactment, restricted the power of the states to regulate the length of interstate trains as a safety measure and, if not, whether the statute contravenes the commerce clause of the federal Constitution.

Congress, although asked to do so, has declined to pass legislation specifically limiting trains to seventy cars. We are therefore brought to appellant's principal contention, that the state statute contravenes the commerce clause of the Federal Constitution.

The findings show that the operation of long trains, that is trains of more than fourteen passenger and more than seventy freight cars, is standard practice over the main lines of the railroads of the United States, and that, if the length of trains is to be regulated at all, national uniformity in the regulation adopted, such as only Congress can prescribe, is practically indispensable to the operation of an efficient and economical national railway system. On many railroads passenger trains of more than fourteen cars and freight trains of more than seventy cars are operated, and on some systems freight trains are run ranging from one hundred and twenty-five to one hundred and sixty cars in length. Outside of Arizona, where the length of trains is not restricted, appellant runs a substantial proportion of long trains. In 1939 on its comparable route for through traffic through Utah and Nevada from 66 to 85% of its freight trains were over 70 cars in length and over 43% of its passenger trains included more than fourteen passenger cars.

In Arizona, approximately 93% of the freight traffic and 95% of the passenger traffic is interstate. Because of the Train Limit Law appellant is required to haul over 30% more trains in Arizona than would otherwise have been necessary. The record shows a definite relationship between operating costs and the length of trains, the increase in length resulting in a reduction of operating costs per car. The additional cost of operation of trains complying with the Train Limit Law in Arizona amounts for the two railroads traversing that state to about $1,000,000 a year. The reduction in train lengths also impedes efficient operation. More locomotives and more manpower are required; the necessary conversion and reconversion of train lengths at terminals and the delay caused by breaking up and remaking long trains upon entering and leaving the state in order to comply with the law, delays the traffic and diminishes its volume moved in a given time, especially when traffic is heavy.

At present the seventy freight car laws are enforced only in Arizona and Oklahoma, with a fourteen car passenger car limit in Arizona. The record here shows that the enforcement of the Arizona statute results in freight trains being broken up and reformed at the California border and in New Mexico, some distance from the Arizona line. Frequently it is not feasible to operate a newly assembled train from the New Mexico yard nearest to Arizona, with the result that the Arizona limitation governs the flow of traffic as far east as El Paso, Texas. For similar reasons the Arizona law often controls the length of passenger trains all the way from Los Angeles to El Paso.

If one state may regulate train lengths, so may all the others, and they need not prescribe the same maximum limitation. The practical effect of such regulation is to control train operations beyond the boundaries of the state exacting it because of the necessity of breaking up and reassembling long trains at the nearest terminal points before entering and after leaving the regulating state. The serious impediment to the free flow of commerce by the local regulation of train lengths and the practical necessity that such regulation, if any, must be prescribed by a single body having a nation-wide authority are apparent.

The trial court found that the Arizona law had no reasonable relation to safety, and made train operation more dangerous. Examination of the evidence and the detailed findings makes it clear that this conclusion was rested on facts found which indicate that such increased danger of accident and personal injury as may result from the greater length of trains is more than offset by the increase in the number of accidents resulting from the larger number of trains when train lengths are reduced. In considering the effect of the statute as a safety measure, therefore, the factor of controlling significance for present purposes is not whether there is basis for the conclusion of the Arizona Supreme Court that the increase in length of trains beyond the statutory maximum has an adverse effect upon safety of operation. The decisive question is whether in the circumstances the total effect of the law as a safety measure in reducing accidents and casualties is so slight or problematical as not to outweigh the national interest in keeping interstate commerce free from interferences which seriously impede it and subject it to local regulation which does not have a uniform effect on the interstate train journey which it interrupts.

> **Take Note**
>
> The Court announces that it will weigh the state's legitimate interests in enacting a law against the burden that the law places on interstate commerce. State laws that impose an excessive burden are unconstitutional. How exactly should a court go about balancing a state's interests in regulation against the burdens it imposes on commerce?

The principal source of danger of accident from increased length of trains is the resulting increase of "slack action" of the train. Slack action is the amount of free movement of one car before it transmits its motion to an adjoining coupled car. This free movement results from the fact that in railroad practice cars are loosely coupled, and the coupling is often combined with a stock-absorbing device, a "draft gear," which, under stress, substantially increases the free movement as the train is started or stopped. Loose coupling is necessary to enable the train to proceed freely around curves and is an aid in starting heavy trains, since the application of the locomotive power to the train operates on each car in the train successively, and the power is thus utilized to start only one car at a time.

As the trial court found, reduction of the length of trains also tends to increase the number of accidents because of the increase in the number of trains. The application of the Arizona law compelled appellant to operate 30.08%, or 4,304, more freight trains in 1938 than would otherwise have been necessary. And the record amply supports the trial court's conclusion that the frequency of accidents is closely related to the number of trains run. The number of accidents due to grade crossing collisions between trains and motor vehicles and pedestrians, and to collisions between trains, which are usually far more serious than those due to slack action, and accidents due to locomotive failures, in general vary with the number of trains. Increase in the number of trains results in more starts and stops, more "meets" and "passes," and more switching movements, all tending to increase the number of accidents not only to train operatives and other railroad employees, but to passengers and members of the public exposed to danger by train operations.

Here we conclude that the state does go too far. Its regulation of train lengths, admittedly obstructive to interstate train operation, and having a seriously adverse effect on transportation efficiency and economy, passes beyond what is plainly essential for safety since it does not appear that it will lessen rather than increase the danger of accident. Its attempted regulation of the operation of interstate trains cannot establish nation-wide control such as is essential to the maintenance of an efficient transportation system, which Congress alone can prescribe. The state interest cannot be preserved at the expense of the national interest by an enactment which regulates interstate train lengths without securing such control, which is a matter of national concern. To this the interest of the state here asserted is subordinate. Reversed.

MR. JUSTICE BLACK, dissenting.

[W]hether it is in the interest of society for the length of trains to be governmentally regulated is a matter of public policy. Someone must fix that policy—either the Congress, or the state, or the courts. A century and a half of constitutional history and government admonishes this

Food for Thought

Justice Hugo Black was an extremely influential member of the Court. Appointed in 1937, he supported a broad reading of Congress's commerce power. At the same time, Justice Black urged a narrow interpretation of the Dormant Commerce Clause Doctrine. See Earl M. Maltz, *The Impact of The Constitutional Revolution of 1937 on The Dormant Commerce Clause*, 19 Harv. J.L. & Pub. Pol'y 121, 129 (1995). Are these views consistent?

Court to leave that choice to the elected legislative representatives of the people themselves, where it properly belongs both on democratic principles and the requirements of efficient government.

POINTS FOR DISCUSSION

a. Understanding the Court's Reasoning

Why does the majority think that the state legislation goes too far? Is the majority saying that safety is not a legitimate state interest?

b. Political Theory

Recall what the Court said in footnote 2 of the *Barnwell Bros.* case: "when the regulation is of such a character that its burden falls principally upon those without the state, legislative action is not likely to be subjected to those political restraints which are normally exerted on legislation where it affects adversely some interests within the state." Does this case involve an example of such regulation?

c. Disagreement Between the Majority and the Dissent

Does Justice Black disagree with how the majority weighs the state's interest in safety or is he making a different point in his dissent? Is the reasoning of the majority or the dissent closer to the earlier Dormant Commerce Clause Doctrine cases in which the Court disclaimed any pretension to consider the wisdom of state laws?

d. Origin of the Balancing Test

In an omitted portion of the opinion, the Court cited Columbia University Professor Noel Dowling's influential article, *Interstate Commerce and State Power*, 27 Va. L. Rev. 1 (1940). In this article, Dowling argued against trying to decide whether a state law violates the Commerce Clause based on whether the state law has more than an "incidental" effect on interstate commerce. Instead, Dowling recommended weighing the state's interest in the law against the burden that it imposes on interstate commerce. See *id.* at 21–22. What might be a problem with a test that focuses only on whether a state law imposes more than an "incidental burden"? Is there anything problematic about weighing state interests?

e. The Scope of the Commerce Power

We saw in Chapter 3 that the Court has concluded that Congress has extensive power to regulate local activity on the theory that such activity, when viewed in the aggregate, has a substantial effect on interstate commerce. Given the scope of Congress's power under the Commerce Clause and the Necessary and Proper Clause, is it possible to conceive of a state regulation that does not impose at least some burden on interstate commerce? How does a Court decide whether such a burden is "excessive"?

As the preceding cases have shown, a court must determine whether a state law that burdens interstate commerce furthers a legitimate state interest, such as promoting safety. In making this determination, a question arises whether a court must consider any possible justification for the law or whether the court must look at the actual motivation of the state legislature in creating the law. This issue divided the Supreme Court in the following case.

KASSEL V. CONSOLIDATED FREIGHTWAYS CORP. OF DELAWARE

450 U.S. 662 (1981)

JUSTICE POWELL announced the judgment of the Court and delivered an opinion, in which JUSTICE WHITE, JUSTICE BLACKMUN, and JUSTICE STEVENS joined.

> **Take Note**
>
> Justice Powell's opinion received the support of only four Justices. It thus represents the views of only a plurality, not a majority, of the Court. The plurality and the concurrence reach the same conclusion, but they use different reasoning. What is the difference?

The State of Iowa * * * by statute restricts the length of vehicles that may use its highways. Unlike all other States in the West and Midwest, Iowa generally prohibits the use of 65-foot doubles within its borders. Instead, most truck combinations are restricted to 55 feet in length. Doubles, mobile homes, trucks carrying vehicles such as tractors and other farm equipment, and singles hauling livestock, are permitted to be as long as 60 feet. * * * Notwithstanding these restrictions, Iowa's statute permits cities abutting the state line by local ordinance to adopt the length limitations of the adjoining State. Where a city has exercised this option, otherwise oversized trucks are permitted within the city limits and in nearby commercial zones.[6]

Because of Iowa's statutory scheme, Consolidated cannot use its 65-foot doubles to move commodities through the State. * * * Consolidated filed this suit in the District Court averring that Iowa's statutory scheme unconstitutionally burdens interstate commerce. * * *

---

6 The Iowa Legislature in 1974 passed House Bill 671, which would have permitted 65-foot doubles. But Iowa Governor Ray vetoed the bill, noting that it "would benefit only a few Iowa-based companies while providing a great advantage for out-of-state trucking firms and competitors at the expense of our Iowa citizens." Governor's Veto Message of March 2, 1974, reprinted in App. 626. The "border-cities exemption" was passed by the General Assembly and signed by the Governor shortly thereafter. * * *

[R]egulations that touch upon safety—especially highway safety—are those that "the Court has been most reluctant to invalidate." But the incantation of a purpose to promote the public health or safety does not insulate a state law from Commerce Clause attack. Regulations designed for that salutary purpose nevertheless may further the purpose so marginally, and interfere with commerce so substantially, as to be invalid under the Commerce Clause.

The evidence [at trial] showed, and the District Court found, that the 65-foot double was at least the equal of the 55-foot single in the ability to brake, turn, and maneuver. * * * Consolidated, meanwhile, demonstrated that Iowa's law substantially burdens interstate commerce. Trucking companies that wish to continue to use 65-foot doubles must route them around Iowa or detach the trailers of the doubles and ship them through separately. Alternatively, trucking companies must use the smaller 55-foot singles or 60-foot doubles permitted under Iowa law. Each of these options engenders inefficiency and added expense.

In addition to increasing the costs of the trucking companies (and, indirectly, of the service to consumers), Iowa's law may aggravate, rather than ameliorate, the problem of highway accidents. Fifty-five foot singles carry less freight than 65-foot doubles. Either more small trucks must be used to carry the same quantity of goods through Iowa, or the same number of larger trucks must drive longer distances to bypass Iowa. In either case, [the] restriction requires more highway miles to be driven to transport the same quantity of goods. Other things being equal, accidents are proportional to distance traveled. Thus, if 65-foot doubles are as safe as 55-foot singles, Iowa's law tends to increase the number of accidents, and to shift the incidence of them from Iowa to other States.

Perhaps recognizing the weakness of the evidence supporting its safety argument, and the substantial burden on commerce that its regulations create, Iowa urges the Court simply to "defer" to the safety judgment of the State. It argues that the length of trucks is generally, although perhaps imprecisely, related to safety. The task of drawing a line is one that Iowa contends should be left to its legislature.

The Court normally does accord "special deference" to state highway safety regulations. This traditional deference "derives in part from the assumption that where such regulations do not discriminate on their face against interstate commerce, their burden usually falls on local economic interests as well as other States' economic interests, thus insuring that a State's own political processes will serve as a check against unduly burdensome regulations." Less deference to the legislative judgment is due, however, where the local regulation bears disproportionately on out-of-state residents and businesses. Such a disproportionate burden is apparent here. Iowa's scheme, although generally banning large doubles from the State, nevertheless has several exemptions that secure to Iowans many of the benefits of large trucks while shunting to neighboring States many of the costs associated with their use.

At the time of trial there were two particularly significant exemptions. First, singles hauling livestock or farm vehicles were permitted to be as long as 60 feet. As the Court of Appeals noted, this provision undoubtedly was helpful to local interests. Second, cities abutting other States were permitted to enact local ordinances adopting the larger length limitation of the neighboring State. This exemption offered the benefits of longer trucks to individuals and businesses in important border cities without burdening Iowa's highways with interstate through traffic.

It is thus far from clear that Iowa was motivated primarily by a judgment that 65-foot doubles are less safe than 55-foot singles. Rather, Iowa seems to have hoped to limit the use of its highways by deflecting some through traffic. [T]he statutory exemptions, their history, and the arguments Iowa has advanced in support of its law in this litigation, all suggest that the deference traditionally accorded a State's safety judgment is not warranted. The controlling factors thus are the findings of the District Court [with] respect to the relative safety of the types of trucks at issue, and the substantiality of the burden on interstate commerce. Because Iowa has imposed this burden without any significant countervailing safety interest, its statute violates the Commerce Clause.

JUSTICE BRENNAN, with whom JUSTICE MARSHALL joins, concurring in the judgment.

My Brothers POWELL and REHNQUIST make the mistake of disregarding the intention of Iowa's lawmakers and assuming that resolution of the case must hinge upon the argument offered by Iowa's attorneys: that 65-foot doubles are more dangerous than shorter trucks. They then canvass the factual record and findings of the courts below and reach opposite conclusions as to whether the evidence adequately supports that empirical judgment. I repeat: my Brothers POWELL and REHNQUIST have asked and answered the wrong question. For although Iowa's lawyers in this litigation have defended the truck-length regulation on the basis of the safety advantages of 55-foot singles and 60-foot doubles over 65-foot doubles, Iowa's actual rationale for maintaining the regulation had nothing to do with these purported differences. Rather, Iowa sought to discourage interstate truck traffic on Iowa's highways. Thus, the safety advantages and disadvantages of the types and lengths of trucks involved in this case are irrelevant to the decision.

The Iowa Legislature has consistently taken the position that size, weight, and speed restrictions on interstate traffic should be set in accordance with uniform national standards. * * * In 1974, the Iowa Legislature [voted] to increase the permissible length of trucks to conform to uniform standards then in effect in most other States. * * * But Governor Ray broke from prior state policy, and vetoed the legislation. [Governor Ray's] principal concern was that to allow 65-foot doubles would "basically ope[n] our state to literally thousands and thousands more trucks per year." This increase in interstate truck traffic would, in the Governor's estimation, greatly increase highway maintenance costs, which are borne by the citizens of the State, and increase the number of accidents and fatalities within the State. The legislative response was not to override the veto, but to accede to the Governor's action, and in accord with his basic premise, to enact a "border cities exemption." This permitted cities within border areas to allow 65-foot doubles while otherwise maintaining the 60-foot limit throughout the State to discourage interstate truck traffic. * * * The Governor admitted that he blocked legislative efforts to raise the length of trucks because the change "would benefit only a few Iowa-based companies while providing a great advantage for out-of-state trucking firms and competitors at the expense of our Iowa citizens."

Take Note

Did Justice Brennan conclude that the burdens imposed on interstate commerce by the challenged regulation outweigh the state's interests in enacting it? Or did he conclude that the regulation is defective for a different reason?

Iowa may not shunt off its fair share of the burden of maintaining interstate truck routes, nor may it create increased hazards on the highways of neighboring States in order to decrease the hazards on Iowa highways. Such an attempt has all the hallmarks of the "simple . . . protectionism" this Court has condemned in the economic area. *Philadelphia v. New Jersey*, 437 U.S. 617 (1978). Just as a State's attempt to avoid interstate competition in economic goods may damage the prosperity of the Nation as a whole, so Iowa's attempt to deflect interstate truck traffic has been found to make the Nation's highways as a whole more hazardous. That attempt should therefore be subject to "a virtually *per se* rule of invalidity."

JUSTICE REHNQUIST, with whom THE CHIEF JUSTICE and JUSTICE STEWART join, dissenting.

It is emphatically not our task to balance any incremental safety benefits from prohibiting 65-foot doubles as opposed to 60-foot doubles against the burden on interstate commerce. Lines drawn for safety purposes will rarely pass muster if the question is whether a slight increment can be permitted without sacrificing safety.

My Brother BRENNAN argues that the Court should consider only *the* purpose the Iowa legislators *actually* sought to achieve by the length limit, and not the purposes advanced by Iowa's lawyers in defense of the statute. This argument calls to mind what was said of the Roman Legions: that they may have lost battles, but they never lost a war, since they never let a war end until they had won it. The argument has been consistently rejected by the Court in other contexts, and Justice BRENNAN can cite no authority for the proposition that possible legislative purposes suggested by a State's lawyers should not be considered in Commerce Clause cases. The problems with a view such as that advanced in the opinion concurring in the judgment are apparent. To name just a few, it assumes that individual legislators are motivated by one discernible "actual" purpose, and ignores the fact that different legislators may vote for a single piece of legislation for widely different reasons. How, for example, would a court adhering to the views expressed in the opinion concurring in the judgment approach a statute, the legislative history of which indicated that 10 votes were based on safety considerations, 10 votes were based on protectionism, and the statute passed by a vote of 40–20? What would the *actual* purpose of the *legislature* have been in that case? This Court has wisely "never insisted that a legislative body articulate its reasons for enacting a statute." *United States R.R. Retirement Bd v. Fritz*, 449 U.S. 166, 179 (1980).

POINTS FOR DISCUSSION

a. Plurality, Concurrence in Judgment, and Dissent

Why did the plurality think the law was unconstitutional? Why did the concurring Justices reach the same conclusion? Why did the dissent think that both the majority and the concurring Justices were wrong?

b. Actual Motivation v. Putative Benefits

The members of the Court disagreed about whether they should consider only a state's actual interest in enacting a law or instead any putative possible benefits of the law. This case did not finally resolve that question, because there was no majority opinion, and only an opinion joined by five members of the Supreme Court can establish precedent of the Court. (Anyone citing Justice Powell's opinion should identify it as a plurality opinion; a plurality opinion carries less weight than a majority opinion, but perhaps more weight than a concurrence in the judgment that is not a plurality opinion.)

5. The Meaning of "Interstate Commerce"

We have seen that, under the Dormant Commerce Clause Doctrine, a state cannot generally discriminate against interstate commerce or impose an excessive burden on interstate commerce. Under these two limitations, questions sometimes arise about just what constitutes "interstate commerce." The question has taken on particular salience as the Court has expansively construed Congress's power to regulate interstate commerce. Does the term include the transportation of garbage? Does it embrace the operation of property for charitable purposes? For answers to these illustrative questions, consider the following cases.

CITY OF PHILADELPHIA V. NEW JERSEY

437 U.S. 617 (1978)

MR. JUSTICE STEWART delivered the opinion of the Court.

> **FYI**
>
> According to the briefs filed in the case, Philadelphia was transporting its waste to New Jersey because localities in Pennsylvania refused to take it. Rather than challenge local restrictions, Philadelphia chose to contest restrictions in New Jersey. In a turn of events, sometime after the case, New Jersey began transporting its waste to Pennsylvania, a practice which Pennsylvania was legally unable to stop.

A New Jersey law prohibits the importation of most "solid or liquid waste which originated or was collected outside the territorial limits of the State. . . ." In this case we are required to decide whether this statutory prohibition violates the Commerce Clause of the United States Constitution.

The statutory provision in question is ch. 363 of 1973 N.J. Laws, which took effect in early 1974. In pertinent part it provides:

> "No person shall bring into this State any solid or liquid waste which originated or was collected outside the territorial limits of the State, except garbage to be fed to swine in the State of New Jersey, until the commissioner [of the State Department of Environmental Protection] shall determine that such action can be permitted without endangering the public health, safety and welfare and has promulgated regulations permitting and regulating the treatment and disposal of such waste in this State."

As authorized by ch. 363, the Commissioner promulgated regulations permitting four categories of waste to enter the State. Apart from these narrow exceptions, however, New Jersey closed its borders to all waste from other States. * * * Immediately affected by these developments were the operators of private landfills in New Jersey, and several cities in other States that had agreements with these operators for waste disposal. They brought suit against New Jersey and its Department of Environmental Protection in state court, attacking the statute and regulations [under the Dormant Commerce Clause Doctrine].

Before it addressed the merits of the appellants' claim, the New Jersey Supreme Court questioned whether the interstate movement of those wastes banned by ch. 363 is "commerce" at all within the meaning of the Commerce Clause. Any doubts on that score should be laid to rest at the outset.

The state court expressed the view that there may be two definitions of "commerce" for constitutional purposes. When relied on "to support some exertion of federal control or regulation," the Commerce Clause permits "a very sweeping concept" of commerce. But when relied on "to strike down or restrict state legislation," that Clause and the term "commerce" have a "much more confined . . . reach."

The state court reached this conclusion in an attempt to reconcile modern Commerce Clause concepts with several old cases of this Court holding that States can prohibit the importation of some objects because they "are not legitimate subjects of trade and commerce." *Bowman v. Chicago & Northwestern R. Co.*, 125 U.S. 465, 489 (1888). These articles include items "which, on account of their existing condition, would bring in and spread disease, pestilence, and death, such as rags or other substances infected with the germs of yellow fever or the virus of small-pox, or cattle or meat or other provisions that are diseased or decayed, or otherwise, from their condition and quality, unfit for human use or consumption." *Ibid.* See also *Baldwin v. G. A. F. Seelig, Inc.*, 294 U.S. 511, 525 (1935), and cases cited therein. The state court found that ch. 363, as narrowed by the state regulations, banned only "those wastes which can[not] be put to effective use," and therefore those wastes were not commerce at all, unless "the mere transportation and disposal of valueless waste between states constitutes interstate commerce within the meaning of the constitutional provision."

We think the state court misread our cases, and thus erred in assuming that they require a two-tiered definition of commerce. In saying that innately harmful articles "are not legitimate subjects of trade and commerce," the *Bowman* Court was stating its conclusion, not the starting point of its reasoning. All objects of interstate trade merit Commerce Clause protection; none is excluded by definition at the outset. In *Bowman* and similar cases, the Court held simply that because

> **Take Note**
>
> The Court explains here what "interstate commerce" is for the purpose of the Dormant Commerce Clause Doctrine. Is the Court's definition of interstate commerce identical to the phrase's definition for purposes of determining Congress's power to regulate under the Commerce Clause?

the articles' worth in interstate commerce was far outweighed by the dangers inhering in their very movement, States could prohibit their transportation across state lines. Hence, we reject the state court's suggestion that the banning of "valueless" out-of-state wastes by ch. 363 implicates no constitutional protection. Just as Congress has power to regulate the interstate movement of these wastes, States are not free from constitutional scrutiny when they restrict that movement.

The crucial inquiry, therefore, must be directed to determining whether ch. 363 is basically a protectionist measure, or whether it can fairly be viewed as a law directed to legitimate local concerns, with effects upon interstate commerce that are only incidental.

The purpose of ch. 363 is set out in the statute itself as follows:

> "The Legislature finds and determines that . . . the volume of solid and liquid waste continues to rapidly increase, that the treatment and disposal of these wastes continues to pose an even greater threat to the quality of the environment of New Jersey, that the available and appropriate land fill sites within the State are being diminished, that the environment continues to be threatened by the treatment and disposal of waste which originated or was collected outside the State, and that the public health, safety and welfare require that the treatment and disposal within this State of all wastes generated outside of the State be prohibited."

Food for Thought

Garbage is different from the goods that the states sought to protect in other cases that we have seen in this chapter, in that, generally speaking, no one wants it. So what is the good—the "scarce natural resource"—that New Jersey sought to protect and that is at issue in this case?

The New Jersey law at issue in this case falls squarely within the area that the Commerce Clause puts off limits to state regulation. On its face, it imposes on out-of-state commercial interests the full burden of conserving the State's remaining landfill space. It is true that in our previous cases the scarce natural resource was itself the article of commerce, whereas here the scarce resource and the article of commerce are distinct. But that difference is without consequence. In both instances, the State has overtly moved to slow or freeze the flow of commerce for protectionist reasons. It does not matter that the State has shut the article of commerce inside the State in one case and outside the State in the other. What is crucial is the attempt by one State to isolate itself from a problem common to many by erecting a barrier against the movement of interstate trade.

Today, cities in Pennsylvania and New York find it expedient or necessary to send their waste into New Jersey for disposal, and New Jersey claims the right to close its borders to such traffic. Tomorrow, cities in New Jersey may find it expedient or necessary to send their waste into Pennsylvania or New York for disposal, and those States might then claim the right to close their borders. The Commerce Clause will protect New Jersey in the future, just as it protects her neighbors now, from efforts by one State to isolate itself in the stream of interstate commerce from a problem shared by all. * * * *Reversed.*

MR. JUSTICE REHNQUIST, with whom THE CHIEF JUSTICE joins, dissenting.

The Supreme Court of New Jersey expressly found that ch. 363 was passed "to preserve the health of New Jersey residents by keeping their exposure to solid waste and landfill areas to a minimum." The Court points to absolutely no evidence that would contradict this finding by the New Jersey Supreme Court. Because I find no basis for distinguishing the laws under challenge here from our past cases upholding state laws that prohibit the importation of items that could endanger the population of the State, I dissent.

POINTS FOR DISCUSSION

a. Meaning of Interstate Commerce

Why does the Court think that this case involves interstate commerce even if no one (by virtue of the New Jersey regulation) is buying or selling the trash? Does a broad reading of the term commerce transform the Dormant Commerce Clause Doctrine into a general anti-discrimination prohibition? Or is trash in fact considerably more "valuable" than New Jersey claimed?

b. Environmental Justice

One commentator criticizes this decision in terms of both constitutional law and environmental justice: "The constitutional critique of the Court's interstate waste decisions [is that there is] a political imbalance in the system: by pursuing a national, unfettered market above all else, the Court inappropriately diminishes state and local autonomy in confronting serious health and environmental concerns. The evolving theory of environmental justice urges us to recognize a social imbalance as well: this same commitment to an unfettered market in waste undercuts the ability of local residents to affect more equitable distribution patterns of migrating waste." Robert R.M. Verchick, *The Commerce Clause, Environmental Justice, And The Interstate Garbage Wars*, 70 S. Cal. L. Rev. 1239, 1289 (1997). How might the Court respond to this criticism?

The following case also concerns the definition of interstate commerce. Beyond this specific issue, however, the decision has become well known because the two dissenting opinions show that great disagreement has arisen in recent years about the scope and legitimacy of the Dormant Commerce Clause Doctrine.

CAMPS NEWFOUND/OWATONNA, INC. V. TOWN OF HARRISON

520 U.S. 564 (1997)

JUSTICE STEVENS delivered the opinion of the Court.

The question presented is whether an otherwise generally applicable state property tax violates the Commerce Clause of the United States Constitution, Art. I, § 8, cl. 3, because its exemption for property owned by charitable institutions excludes organizations operated principally for the benefit of nonresidents.

Petitioner is a Maine nonprofit corporation that operates a summer camp for the benefit of children of the Christian Science faith. The regimen at the camp includes supervised prayer, meditation, and church services designed to help the children grow spiritually and physically in accordance with the tenets of their religion. About 95 percent of the campers are not residents of Maine.

The camp is located in the town of Harrison (Town); it occupies 180 acres on the shores of a lake about 40 miles northwest of Portland. Petitioner's revenues include camper tuition averaging about $400 per week for each student, contributions from private donors, and income from a "modest endowment." In recent years, the camp has had an annual operating deficit of approximately $175,000. From 1989 to 1991, it paid over $20,000 in real estate and personal property taxes each year.

The Maine statute at issue provides a general exemption from real estate and personal property taxes for "benevolent and charitable institutions incorporated" in the State. With respect to institutions that are "in fact conducted or operated principally for the benefit of persons who are not residents of Maine," however, a charity may only qualify for a more limited tax benefit, and then only if the weekly charge for services provided does not exceed $30 per person. * * * Because most of the campers come from out of State, petitioner could not qualify for a complete exemption. And, since the weekly tuition was roughly $400, petitioner was ineligible for any charitable tax exemption at all.

This case involves an issue that we have not previously addressed—the disparate real estate tax treatment of a nonprofit service provider based on the residence of the consumers that it serves. The Town argues that our dormant

Commerce Clause jurisprudence is wholly inapplicable to this case, because interstate commerce is not implicated here and Congress has no power to enact a tax on real estate. * * *

We are unpersuaded by the Town's argument that the dormant Commerce Clause is inapplicable here, either because campers are not "articles of commerce," or, more generally, because the camp's "product is delivered and 'consumed' entirely within Maine." Even though petitioner's camp does not make a profit, it is unquestionably engaged in commerce, not only as a purchaser, see *Katzenbach v. McClung,* 379 U.S. 294, 300–301 (1964); *United States v. Lopez,* 514 U.S. 549, 558 (1995), but also as a provider of goods and services. It markets those services, together with an opportunity to enjoy the natural beauty of an inland lake in Maine, to campers who are attracted to its facility from all parts of the Nation. The record reflects that petitioner "advertises for campers in [out-of-state] periodicals . . . and sends its Executive Director annually on camper recruiting trips across the country." Petitioner's efforts are quite successful; 95 percent of its campers come from out of State. The attendance of these campers necessarily generates the transportation of persons across state lines that has long been recognized as a form of "commerce."

Summer camps are comparable to hotels that offer their guests goods and services that are consumed locally. In *Heart of Atlanta Motel, Inc. v. United States,* 379 U.S. 241 (1964), we recognized that interstate commerce is substantially affected by the activities of a hotel that "solicits patronage from outside the State of Georgia through various national advertising media, including magazines of national circulation." *Id.* at 243. In that case, we held that commerce was substantially affected by private race discrimination that limited access to the hotel and thereby impeded interstate commerce in the form of travel. *Id.* Official discrimination that limits the access of nonresidents to summer camps creates a similar impediment. Even when business activities are purely local, if "it is interstate commerce that feels the pinch, it does not matter how local the operation which applies the squeeze." *Heart of Atlanta* (quoting *United States v. Women's Sportswear Mfrs. Assn.,* 336 U.S. 460, 464 (1949)).

> **Take Note**
>
> In this passage, the Court explains why this case involves interstate commerce. Must Congress have had power to enact a regulation similar to the challenged state regulation in order for the state regulation to be vulnerable under the Dormant Commerce Clause Doctrine? If not, why is the state regulation problematic?

Although *Heart of Atlanta* involved Congress' affirmative Commerce Clause powers, its reasoning is applicable here. As we stated in *Hughes v. Oklahoma,* 441

U.S. 322 (1979): "The definition of 'commerce' is the same when relied on to strike down or restrict state legislation as when relied on to support some exertion of federal control or regulation." *Id.,* at 326, n. 2. * * *

There is no question that were this statute targeted at profit-making entities, it would violate the dormant Commerce Clause. "State laws discriminating against interstate commerce on their face are 'virtually *per se* invalid.' " *Fulton Corp. v. Faulkner,* 516 U.S. 325, 331 (1996) (quoting *Oregon Waste Systems, Inc. v. Department of Environmental Quality of Ore.,* 511 U.S. 93 (1994)). It is not necessary to look beyond the text of this statute to determine that it discriminates against interstate commerce. The Maine law expressly distinguishes between entities that serve a principally interstate clientele and those that primarily serve an intrastate market, singling out camps that serve mostly in-staters for beneficial tax treatment, and penalizing those camps that do a principally interstate business. As a practical matter, the statute encourages affected entities to limit their out-of-state clientele, and penalizes the principally nonresident customers of businesses catering to a primarily interstate market.

Food for Thought

In what way does the challenged tax provision, which applies only to in-state businesses, penalize the non-resident customers of the camp and other similar businesses?

We see no reason why the nonprofit character of an enterprise should exclude it from the coverage of either the affirmative or the negative aspect of the Commerce Clause. There are a number of lines of commerce in which both for-profit and nonprofit entities participate. Some educational institutions, some hospitals, some child care facilities, some research organizations, and some museums generate significant earnings; and some are operated by not-for-profit corporations.

For purposes of Commerce Clause analysis, any categorical distinction between the activities of profit-making enterprises and not-for-profit entities is therefore wholly illusory. Entities in both categories are major participants in interstate markets. And, although the summer camp involved in this case may have a relatively insignificant impact on the commerce of the entire Nation, the interstate commercial activities of nonprofit entities as a class are unquestionably significant. See *Wickard v. Filburn,* 317 U.S. 111, 127–128 (1942); *Lopez,* 514 U.S. at 556, 559–560.

JUSTICE SCALIA, with whom THE CHIEF JUSTICE, JUSTICE THOMAS, and JUSTICE GINSBURG join, dissenting.

Facially discriminatory or not, the exemption is no more an artifice of economic protectionism than any state law which dispenses public assistance only to the State's residents. Our cases have always recognized the legitimacy of limiting state-provided welfare benefits to bona fide residents. * * * If [a] State that provides social services directly may limit its largesse to its own residents, I see no reason why a State that chooses to provide some of its social services indirectly—by compensating or subsidizing private charitable providers—cannot be similarly restrictive.

JUSTICE THOMAS, with whom JUSTICE SCALIA joins, and with whom THE CHIEF JUSTICE joins [in relevant part], dissenting.

The negative Commerce Clause has no basis in the text of the Constitution, makes little sense, and has proved virtually unworkable in application. In one fashion or another, every Member of the current Court and a goodly number of our predecessors have at least recognized these problems, if not been troubled by them. Because the expansion effected by today's holding further undermines the delicate balance in what we have termed "Our Federalism," *Younger v. Harris,* 401 U.S. 37, 44 (1971), I think it worth revisiting the underlying justifications for our involvement in the negative aspects of the Commerce Clause, and the compelling arguments demonstrating why those justifications are illusory.

To cover its exercise of judicial power in an area for which there is no textual basis, the Court has historically offered two different theories in support of its negative Commerce Clause jurisprudence. The first theory posited was that the Commerce Clause itself constituted an *exclusive* grant of power to Congress. The "exclusivity" rationale was likely wrong from the outset, however. See, *e.g.,* The Federalist No. 32 * * * (A. Hamilton) ("[N]otwithstanding the affirmative grants of general authorities, there has been the most pointed care in those cases where it was deemed improper that the like authorities should reside in the states, to insert negative clauses prohibiting the exercise of them by the states"). It was seriously questioned even in early cases. See, *e.g., Southern Pacific Co. v. Arizona ex rel. Sullivan,* 325 U.S. 761, 766–767 (1945) ("Ever since *Willson v. Black-Bird Creek Marsh Co.*, 27 U.S. (2 Pet.) 245 (1829), and *Cooley v. Board of Wardens*, 53 U.S. (12 How.) 299 (1851), it has been recognized that, in the absence of conflicting legislation by Congress, there is a residuum of power in the state to make laws governing matters of local concern which nevertheless in some measure affect interstate commerce or even, to some extent, regulate it").

The second theory offered to justify creation of a negative Commerce Clause is that Congress, by its silence, pre-empts state legislation. In other words, we presumed that congressional "inaction" was "equivalent to a declaration that inter-State commerce shall be free and untrammelled." *Welton v. Missouri,* 91 U.S. 275, 282 (1876). To the extent that the "pre-emption-by-silence" rationale ever made sense, it, too, has long since been rejected by this Court in virtually every analogous area of the law.

Moreover, our negative Commerce Clause jurisprudence has taken us well beyond the invalidation of obviously discriminatory taxes on interstate commerce. We have used the Clause to make policy-laden judgments that we are ill equipped and arguably unauthorized to make. * * *

> **Make the Connection**
>
> The Court often considers governmental interests and the availability of other regulatory choices when it addresses challenges under the Due Process Clause, the Equal Protection Clause, and the First Amendment, topics that we will consider in Volume 2. Is it more problematic for judges to apply such scrutiny when the Dormant Commerce Clause Doctrine is at issue?

Any test that requires us to assess (1) whether a particular statute serves a "legitimate" local public interest; (2) whether the effects of the statute on interstate commerce are merely "incidental" or "clearly excessive in relation to the putative benefits"; (3) the "nature" of the local interest; and (4) whether there are alternative means of furthering the local interest that have a "lesser impact" on interstate commerce, and even then makes the question "one of degree," surely invites us, if not compels us, to function more as legislators than as judges.

In my view, none of this policy-laden decision making is proper. Rather, the Court should confine itself to interpreting the text of the Constitution * * *.

POINTS FOR DISCUSSION

a. Subsidies

Does this case mean that state governments cannot give any benefits or subsidies to state residents (while withholding them from out-of-state residents) if the subsidy might affect interstate commerce? In *West Lynn Creamery, Inc. v. Healy*, 512 U.S. 186 (1994), the Court invalidated a Massachusetts law that imposed a tax on all sales of milk to Massachusetts retailers but then rebated the proceeds of the tax to Massachusetts dairy farmers, even though two-thirds of milk sold in Massachusetts came from outside the state. The Court acknowledged that a "pure subsidy funded out of general revenue ordinarily imposes no burden on interstate commerce, but merely assists local business," but it invalidated the Massachusetts law because "a State may not benefit in-state economic interests by burdening out-of-state competitors." Don't all subsidies limited to in-state businesses effectively burden out-of-state competitors by lowering the cost of goods or services for in-state businesses?

In contrast, consider *State Commercial Fisheries Entry Com'n v. Carlson*, 65 P.3d 851 (Alaska 2003), which involved a challenge by out-of-state commercial fishermen to an Alaska law that charged them three times as much for commercial fishing licenses as it did in-state residents. The Alaska Supreme Court upheld the Alaska law, distinguishing *Camps NewFound* as follows:

> In *Camps Newfound*, the United States Supreme Court struck down a local Maine property tax exemption for a charitable camp that primarily served [out-of-state] residents. A Maine town had attempted to argue that the business of the camp did not involve articles of commerce because the services of the camp were "delivered and 'consumed' entirely within Maine." The Court noted that "[t]he attendance of these campers necessarily generates the transportation of persons across state lines that has long been recognized as a form of 'commerce.' " We find there to be no direct analogy between the campers in *Camps Newfound* and the movement of commercial fishers into Alaska. The Court in *Camps Newfound* drew a comparison of the summer camps to hotels. This comparison indicates a sufficient distinction from commercial fishing licenses and permits to allay concerns about the constitutionality of the fee differential.

Id. at 862 (footnotes omitted). Is this distinction convincing? Can you think of any other ground that might justify a state's charging out-of-state commercial fishermen more money for their licenses?

b. Policy Judgments

Is Justice Thomas correct in saying that the Dormant Commerce Clause Doctrine requires the courts to make policy-laden judgments? What would happen if the Supreme Court abandoned the Dormant Commerce Clause Doctrine?

c. Text, History, and Structure

Justice Thomas asserts that the Dormant Commerce Clause Doctrine is illegitimate because (1) it is not based on constitutional text and (2) no theory justifies the doctrine absent a textual basis. Does Justice Thomas apply the same approach to interpreting the Constitution here as he does in cases involving limits on Congress's power? Should historical understandings of the nature of the commerce power be relevant to determining whether it disables the states from acting, even if those understandings are not explicit in the text? And does Justice Thomas acknowledge the political process argument, which we saw advanced in footnote 2 in the *Barnwell Bros.* opinion, for the Dormant Commerce Clause Doctrine?

6. The Market-Participant Exception

The Supreme Court has recognized a "market-participant" exception to the Dormant Commerce Clause Doctrine. The exception applies when a state government acts like a private business, buying or selling goods or services in the market. Just as the courts would not scrutinize a business's decisions about whom to buy from or sell to, the Supreme Court has said that courts should not limit a state government's market activities, even if the state government favors in-state buyers or sellers. The market participation exception, as the Court has said, "differentiates between a State's acting in its distinctive governmental capacity, and a State's acting in the more general capacity of a market participant; only the former is subject to the limitations of the negative Commerce Clause." *New Energy Co. of Indiana v. Limbach*, 486 U.S. 269, 277 (1988).

SOUTH-CENTRAL TIMBER DEVELOPMENT, INC. V. WUNNICKE

467 U.S. 82 (1984)

JUSTICE WHITE announced the judgment of the Court and delivered the opinion of the Court with respect to Parts I and II, and an opinion with respect to Parts III and IV, in which JUSTICE BRENNAN, JUSTICE BLACKMUN, and JUSTICE STEVENS joined.

We granted certiorari in this case to review a decision of the Court of Appeals for the Ninth Circuit that held that Alaska's requirement that timber taken from state lands be processed within the State prior to export was "implicitly authorized" by Congress and therefore does not violate the Commerce Clause. We hold that it was not authorized and reverse the judgment of the Court of Appeals.

I

In September 1980, the Alaska Department of Natural Resources published a notice that it would sell approximately 49 million board-feet of timber in the area of Icy Cape, Alaska, on October 23, 1980. The notice of sale, the prospectus, and the proposed contract for the sale all provided, pursuant to 11 Alaska Admin.Code § 76.130 (1974), that "[p]rimary manufacture within the State of Alaska will be required as a special provision of the contract." Under the primary-manufacture requirement, the successful bidder must partially process the timber prior to shipping it outside of the State. The requirement is imposed by contract and does not limit the export of unprocessed timber not owned by the State. The stated purpose of the requirement is to "protect existing industries, provide for the establishment of new industries, derive revenue from all timber resources, and manage the State's forests on a sustained yield basis." When it imposes the requirement, the State charges a significantly lower price for the timber than it otherwise would.

The major method of complying with the primary-manufacture requirement is to convert the logs into cants, which are logs slabbed on at least one side. In order to satisfy the Alaska requirement, cants must be either sawed to a maximum thickness of 12 inches or squared on four sides along their entire length.

> **FYI**
>
> Logs are *slabbed* by sawing one side lengthwise to form a square edge.

Petitioner, South-Central Timber Development, Inc., is an Alaska corporation engaged in the business of purchasing standing timber, logging the timber, and shipping the logs into foreign commerce, almost exclusively to Japan. It does not operate a mill in Alaska and customarily sells unprocessed logs. When it learned that the primary-manufacture requirement was to be imposed on the Icy Cape sale, it brought an action in Federal District Court seeking an injunction, arguing that the requirement violated the negative implications of the Commerce Clause.

II

[The Court held that Congress had not authorized the state regulation.]

III

> **Make the Connection**
>
> The possibility that Congress may consent to state discrimination against interstate commerce is addressed in the next section of this chapter.

We now turn to the issues left unresolved by the Court of Appeals. The first of these issues is whether Alaska's restrictions on export of unprocessed timber from state-owned lands are exempt from Commerce Clause scrutiny under the "market-participant doctrine."

Our cases make clear that if a State is acting as a market participant, rather than as a market regulator, the dormant Commerce Clause places no limitation on its activities. The precise contours of the market-participant doctrine have yet to be established, however, the doctrine having been applied in only three cases of this Court to date.

The first of the cases, *Hughes v. Alexandria Scrap Corp.*, 426 U.S. 794 (1976), involved a Maryland program designed to reduce the number of junked automobiles in the State. A "bounty" was established on Maryland-licensed junk cars, and the State imposed more stringent documentation requirements on out-of-state scrap processors than on in-state ones. The Court rejected a Commerce Clause attack on the program, although it noted that under traditional Commerce Clause analysis the program might well be invalid because it had the effect of reducing the flow of goods in interstate commerce. The Court concluded that Maryland's action was not "the kind of action with which the Commerce Clause is concerned," because "[n]othing in the purposes animating the Commerce Clause prohibits a State, in the absence of congressional action, from participating in the market and exercising the right to favor its own citizens over others."

In *Reeves, Inc. v. Stake*, 447 U.S. 429 (1980), the Court upheld a South Dakota policy of restricting the sale of cement from a state-owned plant to state residents, declaring that "[t]he basic distinction drawn in *Alexandria Scrap* between States as market participants and States as market regulators makes good sense and sound law." The Court relied upon " 'the long recognized right of trader or manufacturer, engaged in an entirely private business, freely to exercise his own independent discretion as to parties with whom he will deal.' " *Id.*, at 438–439 (quoting *United States v. Colgate & Co.*, 250 U.S. 300, 307 (1919)). In essence, the Court recognized the principle that the Commerce Clause places no limitations on a State's refusal to deal with particular parties when it is participating in the interstate market in goods.

The most recent of this Court's cases developing the market-participant doctrine is *White v. Massachusetts Council of Construction Employers, Inc.*, 460 U.S. 204 (1983), in which the Court sustained against a Commerce Clause challenge an executive order of the Mayor of Boston that required all construction projects funded in whole or in part by city funds or city-administered funds to be performed by a work force of at least 50% city residents. The Court rejected the argument that the city was not entitled to the protection of the doctrine because the order had the effect of regulating employment contracts between public contractors and their employees. Recognizing that "there are some limits on a state or local government's ability to impose restrictions that reach beyond the immediate parties with which the government transacts business," the Court found it unnecessary to define those limits because "[e]veryone affected by the order [was], in a substantial if informal sense, 'working for the city.' " The fact that the employees were "working for the city" was "crucial" to the market-participant analysis in *White.*

The State of Alaska contends that its primary-manufacture requirement fits squarely within the market-participant doctrine, arguing that "Alaska's entry into the market may be viewed as precisely the same type of subsidy to local interests that the Court found unobjectionable in *Alexandria Scrap*." However, when

Maryland became involved in the scrap market it was as a purchaser of scrap; Alaska, on the other hand, participates in the timber market, but imposes conditions downstream in the timber-processing market. Alaska is not merely subsidizing local timber processing in an amount "roughly equal to the difference between the price the timber would fetch in the absence of such a requirement and the amount the state actually receives." If the State directly subsidized the timber-processing industry by such an amount, the purchaser would retain the option of taking advantage of the subsidy by processing timber in the State or forgoing the benefits of the subsidy and exporting unprocessed timber. Under the Alaska requirement, however, the choice is made for him: if he buys timber from the State he is not free to take the timber out of state prior to processing.

The State also would have us find *Reeves* controlling. * * * Although the Court in *Reeves* did strongly endorse the right of a State to deal with whomever it chooses when it participates in the market, it did not—and did not purport to—sanction the imposition of any terms that the State might desire. For example, the Court expressly noted in *Reeves* that "Commerce Clause scrutiny may well be more rigorous when a restraint on foreign commerce is alleged," that a natural resource "like coal, timber, wild game, or minerals" was not involved, but instead the cement was "the end product of a complex process whereby a costly physical plant and human labor act on raw materials," and that South Dakota did not bar resale of South Dakota cement to out-of-state purchasers. In this case, all three of the elements that were not present in *Reeves*—foreign commerce, a natural resource, and restrictions on resale—are present.

Finally, Alaska argues that since the Court in *White* upheld a requirement that reached beyond "the boundary of formal privity of contract," then, a fortiori, the primary-manufacture requirement is permissible, because the State is not regulating contracts for resale of timber or regulating the buying and selling of timber, but is instead "a seller of timber, pure and simple." Yet it is clear that the State is more than merely a seller of timber. In the commercial context, the seller usually has no say over, and no interest in, how the product is to be used after sale; in this case, however, payment for the timber does not end the obligations of the purchaser, for, despite the fact that the purchaser has taken delivery of the timber and has paid for it, he cannot do with it as he pleases. Instead, he is obligated to deal with a stranger to the contract after completion of the sale.

Definition

"Privity of contract" is the "relationship between the parties to a contract, allowing them to sue each other but preventing a third party from doing so." *Black's Law Dictionary* (10th ed. 2014)

That privity of contract is not always the outer boundary of permissible state activity does not necessarily mean that the Commerce Clause has no application within the boundary of formal privity. The market-participant doctrine permits a State to influence "a discrete, identifiable class of economic activity in which [it] is a major participant." *White*, 460 U.S., at 211, n. 7. Contrary to the State's contention, the doctrine is not carte blanche to impose any conditions that the State has the economic power to dictate, and does not validate any requirement merely because the State imposes it upon someone with whom it is in contractual privity.

The limit of the market-participant doctrine must be that it allows a State to impose burdens on commerce within the market in which it is a participant, but allows it to go no further. The State may not impose conditions, whether by statute, regulation, or contract, that have a substantial regulatory effect outside of that particular market. Unless the "market" is relatively narrowly defined, the doctrine has the potential of swallowing up the rule that States may not impose substantial burdens on interstate commerce even if they act with the permissible state purpose of fostering local industry.

IV

Finally, the State argues that even if we find that Congress did not authorize the processing restriction, and even if we conclude that its actions do not qualify for the market-participant exception, the restriction does not substantially burden interstate or foreign commerce under ordinary Commerce Clause principles. We need not labor long over that contention.

Take Note

Part IV is also a plurality opinion. Why did the other members of the Court consider it unnecessary to reach the question whether the Alaska law violated the Dormant Commerce Clause Doctrine?

Viewed as a naked restraint on export of unprocessed logs, there is little question that the processing requirement cannot survive scrutiny under the precedents of the Court. * * * Because of the protectionist nature of Alaska's local-processing requirement and the burden on commerce resulting therefrom, we conclude that it falls within the rule of virtual per se invalidity of laws that "bloc[k] the flow of interstate commerce at a State's borders." *City of Philadelphia v. New Jersey*, 437 U.S. 617, 624 (1978).

JUSTICE POWELL, with whom THE CHIEF JUSTICE joins, concurring in part and concurring in the judgment.

I join Parts I and II of Justice WHITE's opinion. I would remand the case to the Court of Appeals to allow that court to consider whether Alaska was acting as a "market participant" and whether Alaska's primary-manufacture requirement substantially burdened interstate commerce * * *.

JUSTICE REHNQUIST, with whom JUSTICE O'CONNOR joins, dissenting.

In my view, the line of distinction drawn in the plurality opinion between the State as market participant and the State as market regulator is both artificial and unconvincing. * * * The contractual term at issue here no more transforms Alaska's sale of timber into "regulation" of the processing industry than the resident-hiring preference imposed by the city of Boston in *White* constituted regulation of the construction industry. Alaska is merely paying the buyer of the timber indirectly, by means of a reduced price, to hire Alaska residents to process the timber. Under existing precedent, the State could accomplish that same result in any number of ways. For example, the State could choose to sell its timber only to those companies that maintain active primary-processing plants in Alaska. *Reeves, Inc. v. Stake*, 447 U.S. 429 (1980). Or the State could directly subsidize the primary-processing industry within the State. *Hughes v. Alexandria Scrap Corp.*, 426 U.S. 794 (1976). The State could even pay to have the logs processed and then enter the market only to sell processed logs. It seems to me unduly formalistic to conclude that the one path chosen by the State as best suited to promote its concerns is the path forbidden it by the Commerce Clause.

POINTS FOR DISCUSSION

a. Distinctions

How did the plurality opinion distinguish the *White*, *Reeves*, and *Hughes* cases? Why did the dissent find these distinctions unconvincing?

b. Dangers of the Market-Participant Exception

The plurality says: "Unless the 'market' is relatively narrowly defined, the [market-participant exception] has the potential of swallowing up the rule that States may not impose substantial burdens on interstate commerce even if they act with the permissible state purpose of fostering local industry." Can you think of examples that would illustrate this concern?

c. Alternatives

Is Justice Rehnquist correct that the state could accomplish its goal of supporting the Alaska timber-processing industry in several other permissible ways? If so, what does that suggest about the market-participant exception? About the Dormant Commerce Clause Doctrine more generally?

d. State Monopolies over an Industry

In some instances, state and local governments enact laws that favor themselves at the expense of all others. For example, laws may give a governmental unit a monopoly over certain kinds of goods or services, such as trash collection or mass transit. Because these laws exclude all businesses from competition, they necessarily exclude out-of-state businesses. As a result, the question arises whether these laws should be viewed as discriminating against interstate commerce. The market-participant exception does not apply in these cases because the government is not simply competing in the marketplace with other businesses, but instead has enacted laws that give it advantages. In *United Haulers Ass'n, Inc. v. Oneida-Herkimer Solid Waste Management Auth.*, 550 U.S. 330 (2007), the Court held that such arrangements "do not discriminate against interstate commerce for purposes of the Commerce Clause." The Court reasoned:

> "Compelling reasons justify treating these laws differently from laws favoring particular private businesses over their competitors. 'Conceptually, of course, any notion of discrimination assumes a comparison of substantially similar entities.' *General Motors Corp. v. Tracy,* 519 U.S. 278, 298 (1997). But States and municipalities are not private businesses—far from it. Unlike private enterprise, government is vested with the responsibility of protecting the health, safety, and welfare of its citizens. These important responsibilities set state and local government apart from a typical private business.
>
> Given these differences, it does not make sense to regard laws favoring local government and laws favoring private industry with equal skepticism. As our local processing cases demonstrate, when a law favors in-state business over out-of-state competition, rigorous scrutiny is appropriate because the law is often the product of 'simple economic protectionism.' *Wyoming v. Oklahoma,* 502 U.S. 437, 454 (1992). Laws favoring local government, by contrast, may be directed toward any number of legitimate goals unrelated to protectionism. * * *
>
> The contrary approach of treating public and private entities the same under the dormant Commerce Clause would lead to unprecedented and unbounded interference by the courts with state and local government. The

dormant Commerce Clause is not a roving license for federal courts to decide what activities are appropriate for state and local government to undertake, and what activities must be the province of private market competition."

Should the Court simply have concluded that the market-participant exception applies in these sorts of cases, and thus that it does not matter whether the laws discriminate against interstate commerce?

---

7. Congressional Consent

We now have seen several limitations that the Dormant Commerce Clause Doctrine imposes on the power of the states to regulate. The following decisions consider whether Congress may remove these limitations by legislation. In other words, may Congress authorize the states to pass legislation that otherwise would violate the Dormant Commerce Clause Doctrine? As you will see, the answer is yes, even though ordinarily Congress cannot authorize conduct that otherwise violates the Constitution. In reading the cases, consider why Congress has this power in the context of the Dormant Commerce Clause Doctrine.

PRUDENTIAL INS. CO. V. BENJAMIN

328 U.S. 408 (1946)

MR. JUSTICE RUTLEDGE delivered the opinion of the Court.

[In *Paul v. Virginia*, 75 U.S. (8 Wall.) 168, 183 (1869), the Supreme Court held that a Virginia statute that discriminated against out-of-state insurance companies did not violate the Dormant Commerce Clause Doctrine because "issuing a policy of insurance is not a transaction of commerce." But 75 years later, in *United States v. South-Eastern Underwriters Ass'n*, 322 U.S. 533 (1944), the Supreme Court held that Congress could regulate the business of insurance through the federal antitrust laws because insurance is a commercial enterprise and "[n]o commercial enterprise of any kind which conducts its activities across state lines [is] wholly beyond the regulatory power of Congress under the Commerce Clause." *Id.* at 553. The *South-Eastern Underwriters* decision created uncertainty about whether the reasoning in *Paul v. Virginia*—that issuing an insurance policy was not commerce—was still valid, and consequently doubt about whether the Dormant Commerce Clause Doctrine would apply to discriminatory state insurance laws. Congress partially responded to this concern by passing the McCarran Act, 59 Stat. 33, 34 (1945), which says that federal law generally will regulate insurance only "to the extent that such business is not regulated by State law." In this case,

Prudential Insurance Co., a business incorporated in New Jersey, challenged a South Carolina tax on "foreign" (i.e., out-of-state) insurance companies doing business in South Carolina. The case raised the question whether the McCarran Act was sufficient to make the South Carolina tax constitutional.]

The tax is laid on foreign insurance companies and must be paid annually as a condition of receiving a certificate of authority to carry on the business of insurance within the state. The exaction amounts to three per cent of the aggregate of premiums received from business done in South Carolina, without reference to its interstate or local character. No similar tax is required of South Carolina corporations.

Prudential insists that the tax discriminates against interstate commerce and in favor of local business, since it is laid only on foreign corporations and is measured by their gross receipts from premiums derived from business done in the state, regardless of its interstate or local character. Accordingly it says the tax cannot stand consistently with many decisions of this Court outlawing state taxes which discriminate against interstate commerce. South Carolina denies that the tax is discriminatory or has been affected by the *South-Eastern Underwriters* decision. But in any event it maintains that the tax is valid, more particularly in view of the McCarran Act, by which it is claimed Congress has consented to continuance of this form of taxation and thus has removed any possible constitutional objection which otherwise might exist. This Prudential asserts Congress has not done and could not do.

We are not required however to consider whether * * * the authorities on which Prudential chiefly relies would require invalidation of South Carolina's tax. For they are not on point. * * * [T]hey are the cases which from *Welton v. Missouri*, 91 U.S. 91 U.S. (1 Otto) 275 (1875), until now have outlawed state taxes found to discriminate against interstate commerce. No one of them involved a situation like that now here. In each the question of validity of the state taxing statute arose when Congress' power lay dormant. In none had Congress acted or purported to act, either by way of consenting to the state's tax or otherwise. Those cases therefore presented no question of the validity of such a tax where Congress had taken affirmative action consenting to it or purporting to give it validity. Nor, consequently, could they stand as controlling precedents for such a case.

This would seem so obvious as hardly to require further comment, except for the fact that Prudential has argued so earnestly to the contrary. Its position puts the McCarran Act to one side, either as not intended to have effect toward validating this sort of tax or, if construed otherwise, as constitutionally ineffective to do so. Those questions present the controlling issues in this case. But before we turn to them it will be helpful to note the exact effects of Prudential's argument.

Fundamentally it maintains that the commerce clause "of its own force" and without reference to any action by Congress, whether through its silence or otherwise, forbids discriminatory state taxation of interstate commerce. This is to say, in effect, that neither Congress acting affirmatively nor Congress and the states thus acting coordinately can validly impose any regulation which the Court has found or would find to be forbidden by the commerce clause, if laid only by state action taken while Congress' power lies dormant. In this view the limits of state power to regulate commerce in the absence of affirmative action by Congress are also the limits of Congress' permissible action in this respect, whether taken alone or in coordination with state legislation.

Merely to state the position in this way compels its rejection. So conceived, Congress' power over commerce would be nullified to a very large extent. For in all the variations of commerce clause theory it has never been the law that what the states may do in the regulation of commerce, Congress being silent, is the full measure of its power. Much less has this boundary been thought to confine what Congress and the states acting together may accomplish. So to regard the matter would invert the constitutional grant into a limitation upon the very power it confers.

The commerce clause is in no sense a limitation upon the power of Congress over interstate and foreign commerce. On the contrary, it is, as Marshall declared in *Gibbons v. Ogden*, a grant to Congress of plenary and supreme authority over those subjects. The only limitation it places upon Congress' power is in respect to what constitutes commerce, including whatever rightly may be found to affect it sufficiently to make Congressional regulation necessary or appropriate. This limitation, of course, is entirely distinct from the implied prohibition of the commerce clause. The one is concerned with defining commerce, with fixing the outer boundary of the field over which the authority granted shall govern. The other relates only to matters within the field of commerce, once this is defined, including whatever may fall within the "affectation" doctrine. The one limitation bounds the power of Congress. The other confines only the powers of the states. And the two areas are not coextensive. The distinction is not always clearly observed, for both questions may and indeed at times do arise in the same case and in close relationship. But to blur them, and thereby equate the implied prohibition with the affirmative endowment is altogether fallacious. There is no such equivalence.

It is not necessary to spend much time with interpreting the McCarran Act. Pertinently it is as follows:

> "Sec. 1. The Congress hereby declares that the continued regulation and taxation by the several States of the business of insurance is in the public interest, and that silence on the part of the Congress shall not be construed to impose any barrier to the regulation or taxation of such business by the several States.
>
> "Sec. 2. (a) The business of insurance, and every person engaged therein, shall be subject to the laws of the several States which relate to the regulation or taxation of such business.
>
> "(b) No Act of Congress shall be construed to invalidate, impair, or supersede any law enacted by any State for the purpose of regulating the business of insurance, or which imposes a fee or tax upon such business, unless such Act specifically relates to the business of insurance. * * *" 59 Stat. 34.

Two conclusions, corollary in character and important for this case, must be drawn from Congress' action and the circumstances in which it was taken. * * * Congress intended to declare, and in effect declared, that uniformity of regulation, and of state taxation, are not required in reference to the business of insurance, by the national public interest, except in the specific respects otherwise expressly provided for. This necessarily was a determination by Congress that state taxes, which in its silence might be held invalid as discriminatory, do not place on interstate insurance business a burden which it is unable generally to bear or should not bear in the competition with local business. Such taxes were not uncommon, among the states, and the statute clearly included South Carolina's tax now in issue.

In view of all these considerations, we would be going very far to rule that South Carolina no longer may collect her tax. To do so would flout the expressly declared policies of both Congress and the state. Moreover it would establish a ruling never heretofore made and in doing this would depart from the whole trend of decision in a great variety of situations most analogous to the one now presented. For, as we have already emphasized, the authorities most closely in point upon the problem are not, as appellant insists, those relating to discriminatory state taxes laid in the dormancy of Congress' power. They are rather the decisions which, in every instance thus far not later overturned, have sustained coordinated action taken by Congress and the states in the regulation of commerce.

POINTS FOR DISCUSSION

a. Can Congress Overrule the Supreme Court?

In discussing how Congress may authorize states to enact laws that otherwise would violate the Dormant Commerce Clause Doctrine, a leading commentator writes: "[T]his is one of the few areas where Congress has clear authority to overrule a Supreme Court decision interpreting the Constitution. If the Court deems a matter to violate the dormant commerce clause, Congress can respond by enacting a law approving the action, thereby effectively overruling the Supreme Court." Erwin Chemerinsky, *Constitutional Law: Principles and Policies* 449 (3d ed. 2006). Why can Congress overrule the Supreme Court in this area? Is this consistent with *Marbury v. Madison*?

b. Policy Considerations

Under what circumstances should Congress authorize states to discriminate against interstate commerce? Don't all discriminatory measures cause problems of the kind the Commerce Clause was designed to prevent?

c. Extent of Congress's Power

The Court cites the familiar rule that Congress has plenary power to regulate interstate commerce, meaning that Congress can regulate it in any otherwise constitutional way that it chooses. Congress therefore can authorize all of the states to discriminate in the insurance context. But under this theory, may Congress authorize some states to discriminate against interstate commerce but not others? For example, may Congress validly enact legislation saying that South Carolina may impose discriminatory taxes on out-of-state insurance companies but that North Carolina may not? See Thomas B. Colby, *Revitalizing the Forgotten Uniformity Constraint on the Commerce Power*, 91 Va. L. Rev. 249, 262 (2005)(recognizing that modern decisions permit Congress to discriminate among the states, but arguing that these decisions are "directly contrary both to the original intent of the Framers and to the once-settled general understanding of the scope of the commerce power").

C. PRIVILEGES AND IMMUNITIES CLAUSE

This chapter already has considered two limitations on state power: the Supremacy Clause and the Dormant Commerce Clause Doctrine. In this section, we consider a third limitation, the Privileges and Immunities Clause found in article IV, section 2, clause 1 of the Constitution.

U.S. Constitution, Article IV, Section 2, Clause 1

"The Citizens of each State shall be entitled to all Privileges and Immunities of Citizens in the several States."

The Supreme Court's cases have established four important principles with respect to the Privileges and Immunities Clause. First, the clause is an anti-discrimination measure that limits the ability of states to treat citizens of other states differently from the state's own citizens. As the Supreme Court has said, the Privileges and Immunities Clause protects the citizens of each state because it "inhibits discriminating legislation against them by other States." *Paul v. Virginia*, 75 U.S. (8 Wall.) 168, 180 (1869).

FYI

In establishing these principles, the Supreme Court sometimes has looked to the Articles of Confederation, which contained a similar but more detailed anti-discrimination provision. Article IV of the Articles of Confederation said: "The better to secure and perpetuate mutual friendship and intercourse among the people of the different States in this Union, the free inhabitants of each of these States, paupers, vagabonds, and fugitives from justice excepted, shall be entitled to all privileges and immunities of free citizens in the several States; and the people of each State shall have free ingress and regress to and from any other State, and shall enjoy therein all the privileges of trade and commerce, subject to the same duties, impositions, and restrictions as the inhabitants thereof respectively, provided that such restrictions shall not extend so far as to prevent the removal of property imported into any State, to any other State, of which the owner is an inhabitant; provided also that no imposition, duties or restriction shall be laid by any State, on the property of the United States, or either of them."

Second, the Privileges and Immunities Clause limits discrimination only with respect to rights that are "fundamental to the promotion of interstate harmony." *Supreme Court of New Hampshire v. Piper*, 470 U.S. 274, 279 (U.S. 1985). These rights include important things, such as obtaining employment, *Hicklin v. Orbeck*, 437 U.S. 518 (1978), or obtaining medical services, *Doe v. Bolton*, 410 U.S. 179, 200 (1973). But the anti-discrimination privilege does not extend to less essential matters. States, for example, may discriminate against out-of-state residents in issuing recreational hunting licenses, *Baldwin v. Fish and Game Commission of Montana*, 436 U.S. 371 (1978), or even offering admissions to a state university, *Rosenstock v. Board of Governors of University of North Carolina*, 423 F. Supp. 1321 (D.C.N.C. 1976). The courts continue to develop the distinction between rights fundamental to the promotion of interstate harmony and other rights as they consider additional cases.

Third, the Privileges and Immunities Clause may allow a state to discriminate against non-residents, even with respect to certain very important rights, if the state has a "substantial reason" for the discrimination. *Saenz v. Roe*, 526 U.S. 489, 502 (1999). For example, as the Court has said, "no one would suggest that the Privileges and Immunities Clause requires a State to open its polls to a person who declines to assert that the State is the only one where he claims a right to vote." *Baldwin*, 436 U.S. at 383.

Fourth, the term "citizen" has a specific meaning. The term refers to United States citizens, a group that does not include aliens or corporations. See *Zobel v. Williams*, 457 U.S. 55, 74 (1982) (O'Connor, J., concurring). And in determining whether a person is a "citizen" of a particular state, "it is now established that the terms 'citizen' and 'resident' are essentially interchangeable, for purposes of analysis of most cases under the Privileges and Immunities Clause." *Hicklin*, 437 U.S. at 524.

Finally, note that there is another clause in the Constitution that addresses privileges and immunities. Section 1 of the Fourteenth Amendment provides: "No state shall make or enforce any law which shall abridge the privileges or immunities of citizens of the United States." Unlike the Privileges and Immunities Clause in Article IV, the Fourteenth Amendment speaks of the "privileges *or* immunities" of "citizens of the United States." We will consider this provision in Chapter 7.

In reading the following case, consider whether a state is discriminating against out-of-state residents, whether the discrimination is likely to jeopardize interstate harmony, and whether any state interest might justify the discrimination.

BALDWIN V. FISH AND GAME COMMISSION OF MONTANA

436 U.S. 371 (1978)

MR. JUSTICE BLACKMUN delivered the opinion of the Court.

Appellant Lester Baldwin is a Montana resident. He also is an outfitter holding a state license as a hunting guide. The majority of his customers are nonresidents who come to Montana to hunt elk and other big game. Appellants Carlson, Huseby, Lee and Moris are residents of Minnesota. They have hunted big game, particularly elk, in Montana in past years and wish to continue to do so.

In 1975, the five appellants, disturbed by the difference in the kinds of Montana elk-hunting licenses available to nonresidents, as contrasted with those available to residents of the State, and by the difference in the fees the nonresident and the resident must pay for their respective licenses, instituted the present federal suit for declaratory and injunctive relief and for reimbursement, in part, of fees already paid. * * *

The relevant facts are not in any real controversy and many of them are agreed. * * * For the 1975 hunting season, a Montana resident could purchase a license solely for elk for $4. The nonresident, however, in order to hunt elk, was required to purchase a combination license at a cost of $151; this entitled him to take one elk and two deer. For the 1976 season, the Montana resident could purchase a license solely for elk for $9. The nonresident, in order to hunt elk, was required to purchase a combination license at a cost of $225; this entitled him to take one elk, one deer, one black bear, and game birds, and to fish with hook and line. A resident was not required to buy any combination of licenses, but if he did, the cost to him of all the privileges granted by the nonresident combination license was $30. The nonresident thus paid 7 1/2 times as much as the resident, and if the nonresident wished to hunt only elk, he paid 25 times as much as the resident.

Appellants strongly urge here that the Montana licensing scheme for the hunting of elk violates the Privileges and Immunities Clause of Art. IV, § 2, of our Constitution. That Clause is not one the contours of which have been precisely shaped by the process and wear of constant litigation and judicial interpretation over the years since 1789. * * *

Perhaps because of the imposition of the Fourteenth Amendment upon our constitutional consciousness and the extraordinary emphasis that the Amendment received, it is not surprising that the contours of Art. IV, § 2, cl. 1, are not well developed, and that the relationship, if any, between the Privileges and Immunities Clause and the "privileges or immunities" language of the Fourteenth Amendment is less than clear. We are, nevertheless, not without some pronouncements by this Court as to the Clause's significance and reach. There are at least three general comments that deserve mention:

The first is that of Mr. Justice Field, writing for a unanimous Court in *Paul v. Virginia*, 75 U.S. (8 Wall.) 168, 180 (1869). He emphasized nationalism, the proscription of discrimination, and the assurance of equality of all citizens within any State:

> "It was undoubtedly the object of the clause in question to place the citizens of each State upon the same footing with citizens of other States, so far as the advantages resulting from citizenship in those States are concerned. It relieves them from the disabilities of alienage in other States; it inhibits discriminating legislation against them by other States; it gives them the right of free ingress into other States, and egress from

> them; it insures to them in other States the same freedom possessed by the citizens of those States in the acquisition and enjoyment of property and in the pursuit of happiness; and it secures to them in other States the equal protection of their laws. It has been justly said that no provision in the Constitution has tended so strongly to constitute the citizens of the United States one people as this."

The second came 70 years later when Mr. Justice Roberts, writing for himself and Mr. Justice Black in *Hague v. CIO*, 307 U.S. 496, 511 (1939), summed up the history of the Clause and pointed out what he felt to be the difference in analysis in the earlier cases from the analysis in later ones:

> "[P]rior to the adoption of the Fourteenth Amendment, there had been no constitutional definition of citizenship of the United States, or of the rights, privileges, and immunities secured thereby or springing therefrom. At one time it was thought that this section recognized a group of rights which, according to the jurisprudence of the day, were classed as 'natural rights'; and that the purpose of the section was to create rights of citizens of the United States by guaranteeing the citizens of every State the recognition of this group of rights by every other State. * * * While this description of the civil rights of the citizens of the States has been quoted with approval, it has come to be the settled view that Article IV, § 2, does not import that a citizen of one State carries with him into another fundamental privileges and immunities which come to him necessarily by the mere fact of his citizenship in the State first mentioned, but, on the contrary, that in any State every citizen of any other State is to have the same privileges and immunities which the citizens of that State enjoy. The section, in effect, prevents a State from discriminating against citizens of other States in favor of its own."

The third and most recent general pronouncement is that authored by Mr. Justice Marshall for a nearly unanimous Court in *Austin v. New Hampshire*, 420 U.S. 656, 660–661 (1975), stressing the Clause's "norm of comity" and the Framers' concerns:

> "The Clause thus establishes a norm of comity without specifying the particular subjects as to which citizens of one State coming within the jurisdiction of another are guaranteed equality of treatment. The origins of the Clause do reveal, however, the concerns of central import to the Framers. During the preconstitutional period, the practice of some States denying to outlanders the treatment that its citizens demanded for themselves was widespread. The fourth of the Articles of Confederation

was intended to arrest this centrifugal tendency with some particularity. . . . The discriminations at which this Clause was aimed were by no means eradicated during the short life of the Confederation, and the provision was carried over into the comity article of the Constitution in briefer form but with no change of substance or intent, unless it was to strengthen the force of the Clause in fashioning a single nation."

When the Privileges and Immunities Clause has been applied to specific cases, it has been interpreted to prevent a State from imposing unreasonable burdens on citizens of other States in their pursuit of common callings within the State, *Ward v. Maryland*, 12 Wall. 418 (1871); in the ownership and disposition of privately held property within the State, *Blake v. McClung*, 172 U.S. 239 (1898); and in access to the courts of the State, *Canadian Northern R. Co. v. Eggen*, 252 U.S. 553 (1920).

Take Note

The Court gives examples of the kinds of discrimination that do, and that do not, jeopardize interstate harmony. Is it possible to discern a broader principle from these examples?

It has not been suggested, however, that state citizenship or residency may never be used by a State to distinguish among persons. Suffrage, for example, always has been understood to be tied to an individual's identification with a particular State. No one would suggest that the Privileges and Immunities Clause requires a State to open its polls to a person who declines to assert that the State is the only one where he claims a right to vote. The same is true as to qualification for an elective office of the State. Nor must a State always apply all its laws or all its services equally to anyone, resident or nonresident, who may request it so to do. Some distinctions between residents and nonresidents merely reflect the fact that this is a Nation composed of individual States, and are permitted; other distinctions are prohibited because they hinder the formation, the purpose, or the development of a single Union of those States. Only with respect to those "privileges" and "immunities" bearing upon the vitality of the Nation as a single entity must the State treat all citizens, resident and nonresident, equally. Here we must decide into which category falls a distinction with respect to access to recreational big-game hunting.

Does the distinction made by Montana between residents and nonresidents in establishing access to elk hunting threaten a basic right in a way that offends the Privileges and Immunities Clause? Merely to ask the question seems to provide the answer. We repeat much of what already has been said above: Elk hunting by nonresidents in Montana is a recreation and a sport. In itself—wholly apart from license fees—it is costly and obviously available only to the wealthy nonresident or to the one so taken with the sport that he sacrifices other values in order to indulge in it and to enjoy what it offers. It is not a means to the nonresident's livelihood. The mastery of the animal and the trophy are the ends that are sought; appellants are not totally excluded from these. The elk supply, which has been entrusted to the care of the State by the people of Montana, is finite and must be carefully tended in order to be preserved.

Appellants' interest in sharing this limited resource on more equal terms with Montana residents simply does not fall within the purview of the Privileges and Immunities Clause. Equality in access to Montana elk is not basic to the maintenance or well-being of the Union. Appellants do not—and cannot—contend that they are deprived of a means of a livelihood by the system or of access to any part of the State to which they may seek to travel. We do not decide the full range of activities that are sufficiently basic to the livelihood of the Nation that the States may not interfere with a nonresident's participation therein without similarly interfering with a resident's participation. Whatever rights or activities may be "fundamental" under the Privileges and Immunities Clause, we are persuaded, and hold, that elk hunting by nonresidents in Montana is not one of them.

POINTS FOR DISCUSSION

a. Elements of the Rule

How did the Montana law discriminate against out-of-state residents? Was the discrimination likely to jeopardize interstate harmony? Did Montana have to show that the discrimination was necessary to further an important state interest? Should it have been required to make such a showing?

b. The Dormant Commerce Clause Doctrine and Equal Protection

How would you analyze the Montana law under the Dormant Commerce Clause Doctrine or under the Equal Protection Clause? Why didn't the Court analyze it under those provisions?

SUPREME COURT OF NEW HAMPSHIRE V. PIPER

470 U.S. 274 (1985)

JUSTICE POWELL delivered the opinion of the Court.

The Rules of the Supreme Court of New Hampshire limit bar admission to state residents. We here consider whether this restriction violates the Privileges and Immunities Clause of the United States Constitution, Art. IV, § 2.

Kathryn Piper lives in Lower Waterford, Vermont, about 400 yards from the New Hampshire border. In 1979, she applied to take the February 1980 New Hampshire bar examination. Piper submitted with her application a statement of intent to become a New Hampshire resident. Following an investigation, the Board of Bar Examiners found that Piper was of good moral character and met the other requirements for admission. She was allowed to take, and passed, the examination. Piper was informed by the Board that she would have to establish a home address in New Hampshire prior to being sworn in.

On May 7, 1980, Piper requested from the Clerk of the New Hampshire Supreme Court a dispensation from the residency requirement. Although she had a "possible job" with a lawyer in Littleton, New Hampshire, Piper stated that becoming a resident of New Hampshire would be inconvenient. Her house in Vermont was secured by a mortgage with a favorable interest rate, and she and her husband recently had become parents. * * * [After the Clerk informed Piper that her request had been denied, she] formally petitioned the New Hampshire Supreme Court for permission to become a member of the bar. * * * The Supreme Court denied Piper's formal request on December 31, 1980. [She filed suit in United States District Court asserting that Rule 42 of the New Hampshire Supreme Court, which excludes nonresidents from the bar, violates the Privileges and Immunities Clause of Art. IV, § 2, of the United States Constitution. The District Court concluded that the residency requirement violated the Privileges and Immunities Clause, and the Court of Appeals affirmed.]

[The Privileges and Immunities] Clause was intended to "fuse into one Nation a collection of independent, sovereign States." *Toomer v. Witsell*, 334 U.S. 385, 395 (1948). Recognizing this purpose, we have held that it is "[o]nly with respect to those 'privileges' and 'immunities' bearing on the vitality of the Nation as a single entity" that a State must accord residents and nonresidents equal treatment. *Baldwin v. Montana Fish & Game Comm'n*, 436 U.S. 371, 383 (1978).

Derived, like the Commerce Clause, from the fourth of the Articles of Confederation, the Privileges and Immunities Clause was intended to create a national economic union. It is therefore not surprising that this Court repeatedly has found that "one of the privileges which the Clause guarantees to citizens of State A is that of doing business in State B on terms of substantial equality with the citizens of that State." *Toomer*, 334 U.S., at 396. In *Ward v. Maryland*, 12 Wall. 418 (1871), the Court invalidated a statute under which nonresidents were required to pay $300 per year for a license to trade in goods not manufactured in Maryland, while resident traders paid a fee varying from $12 to $150. Similarly, in *Toomer*, the Court held that nonresident fishermen could not be required to pay a license fee of $2,500 for each shrimp boat owned when residents were charged only $25 per boat. Finally, in *Hicklin v. Orbeck*, 437 U.S. 518 (1978), we [invalidated] a statute containing a resident hiring preference for all employment related to the development of the State's oil and gas resources.

There is nothing in *Ward, Toomer,* or *Hicklin* suggesting that the practice of law should not be viewed as a "privilege" under Art. IV, § 2. Like the occupations considered in our earlier cases, the practice of law is important to the national economy. As the Court noted in *Goldfarb v. Virginia State Bar*, 421 U.S. 773, 788 (1975), the "activities of lawyers play an important part in commercial intercourse."

The lawyer's role in the national economy is not the only reason that the opportunity to practice law should be considered a "fundamental right." We believe that the legal profession has a noncommercial role and duty that reinforce the view that the practice of law falls within the ambit of the Privileges and Immunities Clause. Out-of-state lawyers may—and often do—represent persons who raise unpopular federal claims. In some cases, representation by nonresident counsel may be the only means available for the vindication of federal rights. The lawyer who champions unpopular causes surely is as important to the "maintenance or well-being of the Union," *Baldwin,* 436 U.S., at 388, as was the shrimp fisherman in *Toomer,* or the pipeline worker in *Hicklin.*

The conclusion that Rule 42 deprives nonresidents of a protected privilege does not end our inquiry. The Clause does not preclude discrimination against nonresidents where (i) there is a substantial reason for the difference in treatment; and (ii) the discrimination practiced against nonresidents bears a substantial relationship to the State's objective. *Toomer,* 334 U.S., at 396. In deciding whether the discrimination bears a close or substantial relationship to the State's objective, the Court has considered the availability of less restrictive means.

The Supreme Court of New Hampshire offers several justifications for its refusal to admit nonresidents to the bar. It asserts that nonresident members would be less likely (i) to become, and remain, familiar with local rules and procedures; (ii) to behave ethically; (iii) to be available for court proceedings; and (iv) to do *pro bono* and other volunteer work in the State. We find that none of these reasons meets the test of "substantiality," and that the means chosen do not bear the necessary relationship to the State's objectives.

There is no evidence to support appellant's claim that nonresidents might be less likely to keep abreast of local rules and procedures. Nor may we assume that a nonresident lawyer—any more than a resident—would disserve his clients by failing to familiarize himself with the rules. As a practical matter, we think that unless a lawyer has, or anticipates, a considerable practice in the New Hampshire courts, he would be unlikely to take the bar examination and pay the annual dues of $125.

[There is also] no reason to believe that a nonresident lawyer will conduct his practice in a dishonest manner. The nonresident lawyer's professional duty and interest in his reputation should provide the same incentive to maintain high ethical standards as they do for resident lawyers. * * * Furthermore, [the] Supreme Court of New Hampshire has the authority to discipline all members of the bar, regardless of where they reside. See N.H.Sup.Ct. Rule 37.

There is more merit to the appellant's assertion that a nonresident member of the bar at times would be unavailable for court proceedings. In the course of litigation, pretrial hearings on various matters often are held on short notice. At times a court will need to confer immediately with counsel. Even the most conscientious lawyer residing in a distant State may find himself unable to appear in court for an unscheduled hearing or proceeding. Nevertheless, we do not believe that this type of problem justifies the exclusion of nonresidents from the state bar. One may assume that a high percentage of nonresident lawyers willing to take the state bar examination and pay the annual dues will reside in places reasonably convenient to New Hampshire. Furthermore, in those cases where the nonresident counsel will be unavailable on short notice, the State can protect its interests through less restrictive means. The trial court, by rule or as an exercise of discretion, may require any lawyer who resides at a great distance to retain a local attorney who will be available for unscheduled meetings and hearings.

The final reason advanced by appellant is that nonresident members of the state bar would be disinclined to do their share of *pro bono* and volunteer work. Perhaps this is true to a limited extent, particularly where the member resides in a distant location. We think it is reasonable to believe, however, that most lawyers who become members of a state bar will endeavor to perform their share of these services. This sort of participation, of course, would serve the professional interest of a lawyer who practices in the State. Furthermore, a nonresident bar member, like the resident member, could be required to represent indigents and perhaps to participate in formal legal-aid work.

In summary, appellant neither advances a "substantial reason" for its discrimination against nonresident applicants to the bar, nor demonstrates that the discrimination practiced bears a close relationship to its proffered objectives. We conclude that New Hampshire's bar residency requirement violates the

Privileges and Immunities Clause of Art. IV, § 2, of the United States Constitution. * * * Accordingly, we affirm the judgment of the Court of Appeals.

[JUSTICE WHITE's opinion concurring in the result has been omitted.]

JUSTICE REHNQUIST, dissenting.

[The Court] clearly disregards the fact that the practice of law is—almost by definition—fundamentally different from those other occupations that are practiced across state lines without significant deviation from State to State. The fact that each State is free, in a large number of areas, to establish independently of the other States its own laws for the governance of its citizens, is a fundamental precept of our Constitution that, I submit, is of equal stature with the need for the States to form a cohesive union.

The reason that the practice of law should be treated differently is that law is one occupation that does not readily translate across state lines. Certain aspects of legal practice are distinctly and intentionally *non-national;* in this regard one might view this country's legal system as the antithesis of the norms embodied in the Art. IV Privileges and Immunities Clause. Put simply, the State has a substantial interest in creating its own set of laws responsive to its own local interests, and it is reasonable for a State to decide that those people who have been trained to analyze law and policy are better equipped to write those state laws and adjudicate cases arising under them. The State therefore may decide that it has an interest in maximizing the number of resident lawyers, so as to increase the quality of the pool from which its lawmakers can be drawn. A residency law such as the one at issue is the obvious way to accomplish these goals.

In addition, I find the Court's "less restrictive means" analysis both ill-advised and potentially unmanageable. [Such] an analysis, when carried too far, will ultimately lead to striking down almost any statute on the ground that the Court could think of another "less restrictive" way to write it. This approach to judicial review, far more than the usual application of a standard of review, tends to place courts in the position of second-guessing legislators on legislative matters. Surely this is not a consequence to be desired. * * * [I]n any event courts should not play the game that the Court has played here—independently scrutinizing each asserted state interest to see if it could devise a better way than the State to accomplish that goal.

POINTS FOR DISCUSSION

a. Defining Privileges and Immunities

In a footnote omitted here, the Court stated that a state "may restrict to its residents * * * the right to hold state elective office." If a state may prohibit out-of-state residents from serving in office, why can't it prohibit out-of-state residents from practicing law in the state? Is it because holding office is not a "privilege" of citizenship, or because the state has a stronger interest in limiting elective office to residents? Are there any other jobs that the states can make available only to residents?

b. Justifying Discrimination Against Out-of-State Residents

Under the Court's decision, a state can justify discrimination against out-of-state residents if there is a substantial reason for the difference in treatment and the discrimination bears a substantial relationship to the State's objective. How deferential to the state's justifications should the Court be in conducting this inquiry? We will consider the question of deference in Volume 2 when we consider the various tiers of scrutiny.

D. STATE POWER TO REGULATE THE HOUSE AND SENATE

Chapter 3, which addressed federal powers, began with the landmark case of *McCulloch v. Maryland.* That case presented two issues. Recall that the first issue was whether Congress has the power to create a national bank. The Supreme Court, relying in part on the Necessary and Proper Clause, concluded that Congress has this power. The second issue was whether the states could impose a tax on the notes issued by the national bank. The Court held that the state could not. Indeed, since *McCulloch*, the Court has announced that, as a general rule, instrumentalities of the federal government are immune from state taxes and regulations. California cannot tax the U.S. Postal Service, New York cannot tell the U.S. Navy how to operate its ships, and so forth. This principle serves as a general limitation on the power of the states, derived from the structure of the Constitution and the relationship between the states and the federal government.

But the scope of this limitation on state authority is somewhat uncertain. A major test of federal immunity from state regulation occurred in the early 1990s. A grass-roots movement arose throughout the country to impose term limits on members of Congress. The movement stemmed from a belief that members of Congress had become interested primarily in seeking reelection and therefore had become ineffective in running the country. Limiting the terms that a member of Congress could serve was thought to provide a solution to this problem.

Legislatures in 23 states passed measures to restrict the ability of senior members of the House of Representatives and the Senate to seek reelection. If these restrictions were constitutional, at least 72 members of Congress would have been barred from standing for reelection in 1996. Many more would have faced term limits in the future. So when the Supreme Court agreed to consider the issue in the following case, quite a few politicians anxiously awaited its decision. See Deborah Kalb & Doug Obey, *Members Applaud, Decry Decision on Term Limits*, The Hill (May 24, 1995).

The Constitution includes provisions that speak directly to the question of the qualifications for Members of Congress. These provisions were predictably quite important in the challenge to the state term-limit provisions.

> **U.S. Constitution, Article I, Section 3**
>
> **Clause 2.** "No Person shall be a Representative who shall not have attained to the Age of twenty five Years, and been seven Years a Citizen of the United States, and who shall not, when elected, be an Inhabitant of that State in which he shall be chosen."
>
> **Clause 3.** "No Person shall be a Senator who shall not have attained to the Age of thirty Years, and been nine Years a Citizen of the United States, and who shall not, when elected, be an Inhabitant of that State for which he shall be chosen."

U.S. TERM LIMITS, INC. V. THORNTON

514 U.S. 779 (1995)

JUSTICE STEVENS delivered the opinion of the Court.

At the general election on November 3, 1992, the voters of Arkansas adopted Amendment 73, [which had been proposed as a "Term Limitation Amendment,"] to their State Constitution. * * * Section 3 [of the Amendment], the provision at issue in these cases, applies to the Arkansas Congressional Delegation. It provides:

> "(a) Any person having been elected to three or more terms as a member of the United States House of Representatives from Arkansas shall not be certified as a candidate and shall not be eligible to have his/her name placed on the ballot for election to the United States House of Representatives from Arkansas.
>
> "(b) Any person having been elected to two or more terms as a member of the United States Senate from Arkansas shall not be certified as a

> candidate and shall not be eligible to have his/her name placed on the ballot for election to the United States Senate from Arkansas."

Amendment 73 states that it is self-executing and shall apply to all persons seeking election after January 1, 1993.

On November 13, 1992, respondent Bobbie Hill, on behalf of herself, similarly situated Arkansas "citizens, residents, taxpayers and registered voters," and the League of Women Voters of Arkansas, filed a complaint in the Circuit Court for Pulaski County, Arkansas, seeking a declaratory judgment that § 3 of Amendment 73 is "unconstitutional and void." * * *

Twenty-six years ago, in *Powell v. McCormack,* 395 U.S. 486 (1969), we reviewed the history and text of the Qualifications Clauses in a case involving an attempted exclusion of a duly elected Member of Congress. The principal issue was whether the power granted to each House in Art. I, § 5, cl. 1, to judge the "Qualifications of its own Members" includes the power to impose qualifications other than those set forth in the text of the Constitution. In an opinion by Chief Justice Warren for eight Members of the Court, we held that it does not. * * *

Make the Connection

We considered the Court's decision in *Powell* in Chapter 2, when we discussed the political question doctrine.

[In *Powell,*] we viewed the Convention debates as manifesting the Framers' intent that the qualifications in the Constitution be fixed and exclusive. We found particularly revealing the debate concerning a proposal made by the Committee of Detail that would have given Congress the power to add property qualifications. James Madison argued that such a power would vest "an improper & dangerous power in the Legislature," by which the Legislature "can by degrees subvert the Constitution." 395 U.S. at 533–534, quoting 2 Records of the Federal Convention of 1787, pp. 249–250 (M. Farrand ed. 1911). Madison continued: "A Republic may be converted into an aristocracy or oligarchy as well by limiting the number capable of being elected, as the number authorised to elect." 395 U.S. at 534, quoting 2 Farrand 250.

The Framers further revealed their concerns about congressional abuse of power when Gouverneur Morris suggested modifying the proposal of the Committee of Detail to grant Congress unfettered power to add qualifications. We noted that Hugh Williamson "expressed concern that if a majority of the legislature should happen to be 'composed of any particular description of men, of lawyers for example, . . . the future elections might be secured to their own body.' " *Id.* at 535, quoting 2 Farrand 250. We noted, too, that Madison emphasized the British Parliament's attempts to regulate qualifications, and that he observed: "[T]he abuse they had made of it was a lesson worthy of our attention." 395 U.S. at 535, quoting 2 Farrand 250. We found significant that the Convention rejected both Morris' modification and the Committee's proposal.

We also recognized in *Powell* that the post Convention ratification debates confirmed that the Framers understood the qualifications in the Constitution to be fixed and unalterable by Congress. For example, we noted that in response to the antifederalist charge that the new Constitution favored the wealthy and well born, Alexander Hamilton wrote:

> "The truth is that there is no method of securing to the rich the preference apprehended but by prescribing qualifications of property either for those who may elect or be elected. But this forms no part of the power to be conferred upon the national government. . . . *The qualifications of the persons who may choose or be chosen, as has been remarked upon other occasions, are defined and fixed in the Constitution, and are unalterable by the legislature.*" 395 U.S., at 539, quoting The Federalist No. 60, p. 371 (C. Rossiter ed. 1961) (emphasis added) (hereinafter The Federalist).

The exercise by Congress of its power to judge the qualifications of its Members further confirmed this understanding. We concluded that, during the first 100 years of its existence, "Congress strictly limited its power to judge the qualifications of its members to those enumerated in the Constitution." 395 U.S. at 542.

As this elaborate summary reveals, our historical analysis in *Powell* was both detailed and persuasive. We thus conclude now, as we did in *Powell,* that history shows that, with respect to Congress, the Framers intended the Constitution to establish fixed qualifications.

Our reaffirmation of *Powell* does not necessarily resolve the specific questions presented in these cases. For petitioners argue that whatever the constitutionality of additional qualifications for membership imposed by Congress, the historical and textual materials discussed in *Powell* do not support the conclusion that the Constitution prohibits additional qualifications imposed by States. In the absence of such a constitutional prohibition, petitioners argue, the Tenth Amendment and the principle of reserved powers require that States be allowed to add such qualifications.

Take Note

The Court concludes that the Framers intended the Constitution to establish fixed qualifications for members of Congress. Why isn't this conclusion alone sufficient to resolve this case?

Contrary to petitioners' assertions, the power to add qualifications is not part of the original powers of sovereignty that the Tenth Amendment reserved to the States. Petitioners' Tenth Amendment argument misconceives the nature of the right at issue because that Amendment could only "reserve" that which existed before. As Justice Story recognized, "the states can exercise no powers whatsoever, which exclusively spring out of the existence of the national government, which the constitution does not delegate to them. . . . No state can say, that it has reserved, what it never possessed." 1 Story § 627.

Justice Story's position thus echoes that of Chief Justice Marshall in *McCulloch v. Maryland*, 4 Wheat. 316 (1819). In *McCulloch*, the Court rejected the argument that the Constitution's silence on the subject of state power to tax corporations chartered by Congress implies that the States have "reserved" power to tax such federal instrumentalities. As Chief Justice Marshall pointed out, an "original right to tax" such federal entities "never existed, and the question whether it has been surrendered, cannot arise." *Id.*, at 430.

With respect to setting qualifications for service in Congress, no such right existed before the Constitution was ratified. [Under the Articles of Confederation,] "the States retained most of their sovereignty, like independent nations bound together only by treaties." *Wesberry v. Sanders*, 376 U.S. 1, 9 (1964). * * * In adopting [the Constitution], the Framers envisioned a uniform national system, rejecting the notion that the Nation was a collection of States, and instead creating a direct link between the National Government and the people of the United States. In that National Government, representatives owe primary allegiance not to the people of a State, but to the people of the Nation.

In short, as the Framers recognized, electing representatives to the National Legislature was a new right, arising from the Constitution itself. The Tenth Amendment thus provides no basis for concluding that the States possess reserved power to add qualifications to those that are fixed in the Constitution. Instead, any state power to set the qualifications for membership in Congress must derive not from the reserved powers of state sovereignty, but rather from the delegated powers of national sovereignty. In the absence of any constitutional delegation to the States of power to add qualifications to those enumerated in the Constitution, such a power does not exist.

The available affirmative evidence indicates the Framers' intent that States have no role in the setting of qualifications. In The Federalist No. 52, dealing with the House of Representatives, Madison addressed the "qualifications of the electors and the elected." Madison first noted the difficulty in achieving uniformity in the qualifications for electors, which resulted in the Framers' decision to require only that the qualifications for federal electors be the same as those for state electors. Madison argued that such a decision "must be satisfactory to every State, because it is comfortable to the standard already established, or which may be established, by the State itself." Madison then explicitly contrasted the state control over the qualifications of electors with the lack of state control over the qualifications of the elected:

> "The qualifications of the elected, being less carefully and properly defined by the State constitutions, and being at the same time more susceptible of uniformity, have been very properly considered and regulated by the convention. A representative of the United States must be of the age of twenty-five years; must have been seven years a citizen of the United States; must, at the time of his election be an inhabitant of the State he is to represent; and, during the time of his service must be in no office under the United States. Under these reasonable limitations, the door of this part of the federal government is open to merit of every description, whether native or adoptive, whether young or old, and without regard to poverty or wealth, or to any particular profession of religious faith."

We also find compelling the complete absence in the ratification debates of any assertion that States had the power to add qualifications. In those debates, the question whether to require term limits, or "rotation," was a major source of controversy. The draft of the Constitution that was submitted for ratification contained no provision for rotation. In arguments that echo in the preamble to Arkansas' Amendment 73, opponents of ratification condemned the absence of a rotation requirement, noting that "there is no doubt that senators will hold their office perpetually; and in this situation, they must of necessity lose their dependence, and their attachments to the people."

Regardless of which side has the better of the debate over rotation, it is most striking that nowhere in the extensive ratification debates have we found any statement by either a proponent or an opponent of rotation that the draft constitution would permit States to require rotation for the representatives of their own citizens. If the participants in the debate had believed that the States retained the authority to impose term limits, it is inconceivable that the Federalists would not have made this obvious response to the arguments of the pro-rotation forces. The absence in an otherwise freewheeling debate of any suggestion that States had the power to impose additional qualifications unquestionably reflects the Framers' common understanding that States lacked that power.

Our conclusion that States lack the power to impose qualifications vindicates the same "fundamental principle of our representative democracy" that we recognized in *Powell,* namely, that "the people should choose whom they please to govern them." *Id.*

Petitioners argue that, even if States may not add qualifications, Amendment 73 is constitutional because it is not such a qualification, and because Amendment 73 is a permissible exercise of state power to regulate the "Times, Places and Manner of holding Elections." We reject these contentions. In our view, Amendment 73 is an indirect attempt to accomplish what the Constitution prohibits Arkansas from accomplishing directly. * * *

JUSTICE THOMAS, with whom THE CHIEF JUSTICE, JUSTICE O'CONNOR, and JUSTICE SCALIA join, dissenting.

The Court holds [that] neither the elected legislature of [a] State nor the people themselves (acting by ballot initiative) may prescribe any qualifications for [federal] representatives. The majority therefore defends the right of the people of Arkansas to "choose whom they please to govern them" by invalidating a provision that won nearly 60% of the votes cast in a direct election and that carried every congressional district in the State.

When they adopted the Federal Constitution, of course, the people of each State surrendered some of their authority to the United States (and hence to entities accountable to the people of other States as well as to themselves). They affirmatively deprived their States of certain powers, see, *e.g.,* Art. I, § 10, and they affirmatively conferred certain powers upon the Federal Government, see, *e.g.,* Art. I, § 8. Because the people of the several States are the only true source of power, however, the Federal Government enjoys no authority beyond what the Constitution confers: The Federal Government's powers are limited and enumerated. In the words of Justice Black: "The United States is entirely a creature of the Constitution. Its power and authority have no other source." *Reid v. Covert,* 354 U.S. 1, 5–6 (1957) (plurality opinion).

In each State, the remainder of the people's powers—"[t]he powers not delegated to the United States by the Constitution, nor prohibited by it to the States," Amdt. 10—are either delegated to the state government or retained by the people. The Federal Constitution does not specify which of these two possibilities obtains; it is up to the various state constitutions to declare which powers the people of each State have delegated to their state government. As far as the Federal Constitution is concerned, then, the States can exercise all powers that the Constitution does not withhold from them. The Federal Government and the States thus face different default rules: Where the Constitution is silent about the exercise of a particular power—that is, where the Constitution does not speak either expressly or by necessary implication—the Federal Government lacks that power and the States enjoy it.

The majority's essential logic is that the state governments could not "reserve" any powers that they did not control at the time the Constitution was drafted. But it was not the state governments that were doing the reserving. The Constitution derives its authority instead from the consent of *the people* of the States. Given the fundamental principle that all governmental powers stem from the people of the States, it would simply be incoherent to assert that the people of the States could not reserve any powers that they had not previously controlled.

The majority also seeks support for its view of the Tenth Amendment in *McCulloch v. Maryland*, 4 Wheat. 316 (1819). But this effort is misplaced. * * * [The Court] held that the Constitution affirmatively prohibited Maryland's tax on the bank created by [a federal] statute. The Court relied principally on concepts that it deemed inherent in the Supremacy Clause of Article VI, [concluding] that the very nature of state taxation on the bank's operations was "incompatible with, and repugnant to," the federal statute creating the bank. * * * For the majority, however, *McCulloch* apparently turned on the fact that before the Constitution was adopted, the States had possessed no power to tax the instrumentalities of the governmental institutions that the Constitution created. This understanding of *McCulloch* makes most of Chief Justice Marshall's opinion irrelevant; according to the majority, there was no need to inquire into whether federal law deprived Maryland of the power in question, because the power could not fall into the category of "reserved" powers anyway.

I take it to be established, then, that the people of Arkansas do enjoy "reserved" powers over the selection of their representatives in Congress. Purporting to exercise those reserved powers, they have agreed among themselves that the candidates covered by § 3 of Amendment 73—those whom they have already elected to three or more terms in the House of Representatives or to two or more terms in the Senate—should not be eligible to appear on the ballot for reelection, but should nonetheless be returned to Congress if enough voters are sufficiently enthusiastic about their candidacy to write in their names. Whatever one might think of the wisdom of this arrangement, we may not override the decision of the people of Arkansas unless something in the Federal Constitution deprives them of the power to enact such measures.

At least on their face, * * * the Qualifications Clauses do nothing to prohibit the people of a State from establishing additional eligibility requirements for their own representatives. Joseph Story thought that such a prohibition was nonetheless implicit in the constitutional list of qualifications, because "[f]rom the very nature of such a provision, the affirmation of these qualifications would seem to imply a negative of all others." 1 Commentaries on the Constitution of the United States § 624 (1833). This argument rests on the maxim *expressio unius est exclusio alterius.* When the Framers decided which qualifications to include in the Constitution, they also decided not to include any other qualifications in the Constitution. In Story's view, it would conflict with this latter decision for the people of the individual States to decide, as a matter of state law, that they would like their own representatives in Congress to meet additional eligibility requirements.

Definition

Expressio unius est exclusio alterius means "to say one thing is to exclude the other." The *expressio unius* maxim says that an express inclusion of some things in a law implies the exclusion of others. What would this maxim mean with respect to the requirements included in Article I for members of the House and Senate?

To spell out the logic underlying this argument is to expose its weakness. Even if one were willing to ignore the distinction between requirements enshrined in the Constitution and other requirements that the Framers were content to leave within the reach of ordinary law, Story's application of the *expressio unius* maxim takes no account of federalism. At most, the specification of certain nationwide disqualifications in the Constitution implies the negation of other *nationwide* disqualifications; it does not imply that individual States or their people are barred from adopting their own disqualifications on a state-by-state basis. Thus, the one delegate to the Philadelphia Convention who voiced anything approaching Story's argument said only that a recital of qualifications in the Constitution would imply that *Congress* lacked any qualification-setting power. See 2 Farrand 123 (remarks of John Dickinson).

The Qualifications Clauses do prevent the individual States from abolishing all eligibility requirements for Congress. This restriction on state power reflects the fact that when the people of one State send immature, disloyal, or unknowledgeable representatives to Congress, they jeopardize not only their own interests but also the interests of the people of other States. Because Congress wields power over all the States, the people of each State need some guarantee that the legislators elected by the people of other States will meet minimum standards of competence. The Qualifications Clauses provide that guarantee:

They list the requirements that the Framers considered essential to protect the competence of the National Legislature.

If the people of a State decide that they would like their representatives to possess additional qualifications, however, they have done nothing to frustrate the policy behind the Qualifications Clauses. Anyone who possesses all of the constitutional qualifications, plus some qualifications required by state law, still has all of the federal qualifications. Accordingly, the fact that the Constitution specifies certain qualifications that the Framers deemed necessary to protect the competence of the National Legislature does not imply that it strips the people of the individual States of the power to protect their own interests by adding other requirements for their own representatives.

> **Take Note**
>
> The dissent concludes that the Qualifications Clause imposes a floor, not a ceiling. The majority, in contrast, concluded that the same text imposes not only a floor but also a ceiling. Which view do you find more persuasive?

The people of other States could legitimately complain if the people of Arkansas decide, in a particular election, to send a 6-year-old to Congress. But the Constitution gives the people of other States no basis to complain if the people of Arkansas elect a freshman representative in preference to a long-term incumbent. That being the case, it is hard to see why the rights of the people of other States have been violated when the people of Arkansas decide to enact a more general disqualification of long-term incumbents. Such a disqualification certainly is subject to scrutiny under other constitutional provisions, such as the First and Fourteenth Amendments. But as long as the candidate whom they send to Congress meets the constitutional age, citizenship, and inhabitancy requirements, the people of Arkansas have not violated the Qualifications Clauses.

In seeking ratification of the Constitution, James Madison did assert that "[u]nder these reasonable limitations [set out in the House Qualifications Clause], the door of this part of the federal government is open to merit of every description. . . ." The Federalist No. 52. The majority stresses this assertion, and others to the same effect, in support of its "egalitarian concept." But there is no reason to interpret these statements as anything more than claims that the Constitution itself imposes relatively few disqualifications for congressional office. One should not lightly assume that Madison and his colleagues, who were attempting to win support at the state level for the new Constitution, were proclaiming the inability of the people of the States or their state legislatures to prescribe any eligibility requirements for their own Representatives or Senators. Instead, they were merely responding to the charge that the Constitution was undemocratic and would lead to aristocracies in office. The statement that the qualifications imposed in the Constitution are not unduly restrictive hardly implies that the Constitution withdrew the power of the people of each State to prescribe additional eligibility requirements for their own Representatives if they so desired.

[S]tate practice immediately after the ratification of the Constitution refutes the majority's suggestion that the Qualifications Clauses were commonly understood as being exclusive. Five States supplemented the constitutional disqualifications in their very first election laws, and the surviving records suggest that the legislatures of these States considered and rejected the interpretation of the Constitution that the majority adopts today. [T]he first Virginia election law erected a property qualification for Virginia's contingent in the Federal House of Representatives. See Virginia Election Law (Nov. 20, 1788), in 2 Documentary History of the First Federal Elections, 1788–1790, pp. 293, 294 (G. DenBoer ed. 1984) (hereinafter First Federal Elections) (restricting possible candidates to "freeholder[s]"). What is more, while the Constitution merely requires representatives to be inhabitants of their State, the legislatures of five of the seven States that divided themselves into districts for House elections added that representatives also had to be inhabitants of the district that elected them. Three of these States adopted durational residency requirements too, insisting that representatives have resided within their districts for at least a year (or, in one case, three years) before being elected.[31]

It is radical enough for the majority to hold that the Constitution implicitly precludes the people of the States from prescribing any eligibility requirements for the congressional candidates who seek their votes. This holding, after all, does not stop with negating the term limits that many States have seen fit to impose on their Senators and Representatives. Today's decision also means that no State may disqualify congressional candidates whom a court has found to be mentally incompetent, see, e.g., Fla. Stat. §§ 97.041(2), 99.021(1)(a) (1991), who are currently in prison, see, e.g., Ill. Comp. Stat. Ann., ch. 10, §§ 5/3–5, 5/7–10, 5/10–5 (1993 and West Supp.1995), or who have past vote-fraud convictions, see, e.g.,

31 See Georgia Election Law (Jan. 23, 1789) (restricting representatives from each district to "resident[s] of three years standing in the district"), in 2 First Federal Elections 456, 457; Maryland Election Law (Dec. 22, 1788) (simple district residency requirement), in 2 First Federal Elections 136, 138; Massachusetts Election Resolutions (Nov. 20, 1788) (same), in 1 First Federal Elections 508, 509 (M. Jensen & R. Becker eds. 1976); North Carolina Election Law (Dec. 16, 1789) (requiring the person elected from each district to have been "a Resident or Inhabitant of that Division for which he is elected, during the Space or Term of one Year before, and at the Time of Election"), in 4 First Federal Elections 347; Virginia Election Law (Nov. 20, 1788) (requiring each candidate to have been "a bona fide resident for twelve months within such District"), in 2 First Federal Elections 293, 294. Upon being admitted to the Union in 1796, Tennessee also required its Members in the Federal House of Representatives to have been Tennessee residents for three years and district residents for one year before their election. Act of Apr. 20, 1796, ch. 10, in Laws of the State of Tennessee 81 (1803).

Ga. Code Ann. §§ 21–2–2(25), 21–2–8 (1993 and Supp.1994). Likewise, after today's decision, the people of each State must leave open the possibility that they will trust someone with their vote in Congress even though they do not trust him with a vote in the election for Congress. See, e.g., R.I. Gen. Laws § 17–14–1.2 (1988) (restricting candidacy to people "qualified to vote").

POINTS FOR DISCUSSION

a. Method of Constitutional Interpretation

Do the majority and dissent disagree about whether the issue in this case should be determined by discerning the original meaning of the Constitution or do they just disagree about what the original meaning of the Constitution is?

b. Qualifications Other than Term Limits

The dissent lists various statutes that impose qualifications on members of Congress other than term limits. Are all of these statutes unconstitutional? What might be the practical consequences of invalidating all of these statutes?

c. U.S. Term Limits and *McCulloch*

Recall that the decision in *McCulloch* addressed both (1) whether the states had "reserved" powers to regulate the national government and (2) whether under the Constitution sovereignty remained solely in the constituent political communities in the states or rather also lay in a national political community. Was the Court's approach in U.S. *Term Limits* consistent with the Court's approach in *McCulloch*? What about the approach of the dissent in U.S. *Term Limits*?

Executive Summary of This Chapter

This chapter covers several important constitutional limitations on state power. These limitations concern the role of the states in the federal system. The limitations address the relationship of state law to federal law, the power of the states to regulate what the federal government also may regulate, the relations between states and citizens of other states, and state power to restrict the membership of Congress.

Under the Supremacy Clause, federal law can preempt (i.e., supplant) state law expressly or impliedly. Congress impliedly preempts state law in two ways:

(1) **Field Preemption**: "If Congress evidences an intent to occupy a given field, any state law falling within that field is preempted."

(2) **Conflict Preemption**: "If Congress has not entirely displaced state regulation over the matter in question, state law is still preempted to the

extent it actually conflicts with federal law. . . ." *Silkwood v. Kerr-McKee* (1984).

The **Dormant Commerce Clause Doctrine** says that a state law affecting interstate commerce is invalid in the following situations:

(1) The state law concerns a subject for which **national uniformity** is necessary. *Cooley v. Board of Wardens* (1851); *Wabash, St. Louis & Pacific Ry. Co. v. Illinois* (1886).

(2) The state law **discriminates against interstate commerce** either on its face or in its effects, unless the discrimination is necessary to further a legitimate state interest. *Dean Milk v. City of Madison* (1951), *Hughes v. Oklahoma* (1979).

(3) The state law imposes a **burden on interstate commerce** that is excessive in relation to legitimate local interests. *South Carolina Department of Transportation v. Barnwell Brothers* (1938), *Southern Pacific v. Arizona* (1945), *Kassel v. Consolidated Freightways Corp.* (1981).

In applying these limitations under the Dormant Commerce Clause Doctrine, the Court has followed the following principles:

(1) **Legitimate state interests** include protecting health and safety and conserving natural resources, but they do not include protecting local businesses from competition, *Dean Milk v. City of Madison* (1951), or isolating the state from a problem common to many states (like disposing of trash or avoiding traffic on state highways), *Kassel v. Consolidated Freightways Corp.* (1981); *City of Philadelphia v. New Jersey* (1978).

(2) The term "**interstate commerce**" has the same meaning for determining limitations on states under the Dormant Commerce Clause Doctrine as it does for determining the power of Congress under the Commerce Clause. *City of Philadelphia v. New Jersey* (1978); *Camps Newfound/Owatonna, Inc. v. Town of Harrison, Maine* (1996).

(3) Under the **Market-Participant Exception** to the Dormant Commerce Clause Doctrine, a state may discriminate against interstate commerce when buying or selling goods or services in the market (as opposed to regulating the market). *South-Central Timber Development, Inc. v. Wunnicke* (1982).

(4) A state does not discriminate against interstate commerce by enacting **laws that favor local government** as opposed to local citizens

or businesses. *United Haulers Ass'n, Inc. v. Oneida-Herkimer Solid Waste Management Authority* (2007).

(5) In legislation enacted under its power to regulate interstate commerce, **Congress may consent to state laws** that would otherwise violate the Dormant Commerce Clause Doctrine. *Prudential Life Insurance Co. v. Benjamin* (1946). But even if discriminatory state laws do not violate the Dormant Commerce Clause Doctrine, they may violate the **Equal Protection Clause**. *Metropolitan Life Ins. Co. v. Ward* (1985).

The Privileges and Immunities Clause prohibits discrimination against out-of-state residents or citizens (but not corporations or aliens) if the discrimination might jeopardize interstate harmony, unless the discrimination is necessary to promote a substantial state interest. *Baldwin v. Fish & Game Commission* (1978); *Supreme Court of New Hampshire v. Piper* (1985).

States generally cannot regulate the House and Senate by restricting their membership. Article I sets forth the only qualifications for members of Congress, and the states may not attempt to impose additional qualifications by limiting the ability of candidates to have their names appear on general ballots. *U.S. Term Limits, Inc. v. Thornton* (1995).

PART IV

Separation of Powers

Our consideration of federalism was, in a very important sense, a consideration of the separation of powers—specifically, a consideration of the separation of powers between the federal government and the states, and among the states themselves. In addition, our consideration in Chapter 2 of the judicial power, which focused on the courts' relationship to the states and (more important for present purposes) to the other branches of the federal government, was a subset of the more general topic of the separation of powers.

We turn now directly to a consideration of the separation of powers among the branches of the federal government. In Chapter 5, we take up the scope of federal executive power. In Chapter 6, we will address the scope of the federal legislative power. Although we cover these topics in separate chapters, they are closely related. Indeed, when we consider the scope of the President's power, it is often in relation to a (potential) competing claim of power by Congress. And when we discuss the legislative power, the President's role in that process—and Congress's authority to place limits on that role—will often be front and center. As we consider these questions, pay close attention to the broad themes that are common to them.

On May 30, 1787, at the Constitutional Convention in Philadelphia, Gouverneur Morris proposed that "a national government ought to be established consisting of a supreme Legislature, Executive, and Judiciary." 1 Records of the Federal Convention of 1787 38–39 (Max Farrand ed. 1937). The

> **FYI**
>
> Gouverneur Morris was a delegate from Pennsylvania. At the Constitutional Convention, he spoke more than any other delegate, even more than James Madison, who was the next most loquacious. Morris was principally responsible for drafting the grand preamble of the Constitution and for putting much of the Constitution in its final, elegant form. Note that "Gouverneur" was his first name; it is not a title. (Gouverneur Morris was named after his mother, Sarah Gouverneur.)

Convention adopted this proposal to separate the federal government into three branches. The Constitution embodies the separation of powers in the first sections of Article I, Article II, and Article III.

U.S. Constitution

Article I, § 1. "All legislative Powers herein granted shall be vested in a Congress of the United States, which shall consist of a Senate and House of Representatives."

Article II, § 1. "The executive Power shall be vested in a President of the United States of America."

Article III, § 1. "The judicial Power of the United States shall be vested in one supreme Court, and in such inferior Courts as the Congress may from time to time ordain and establish."

The Framers of the Constitution believed that separating the basic powers of government and distributing them among different branches would protect the people. If the powers were not separated, then there might be no check on abuses by the government. As James Madison wrote in The Federalist No. 47: "The accumulation of all powers legislative, executive and judiciary in the same hands, whether of one, a few or many, and whether hereditary, self appointed, or elective, may justly be pronounced the very definition of tyranny."

This view continues to have influence. In modern times, no one disputes the basic idea that our system has and should have separated powers. But if the theory of the separation of powers is easy to state, its application in practice has often proved elusive. How should we read the grants of authority to the President and to Congress, which often are phrased in vague and general language? Does the actual structure of government created by the Constitution obviate the need for judicial intervention in inter-branch disputes? These are questions on which we will focus in the next two chapters.

But the Constitution also mixes the powers of the branches in several important respects. Congress has the legislative power, but the President has the power of the veto. The President has the power of appointment, but the Senate has the power of "advice and consent." This mixing in many cases blurs the inquiry over the proper allocation of government power.

As we will see, sometimes a branch of government attempts to aggrandize its own power by exercising powers reserved to another branch. At other times, a branch will attempt to encroach on the power of another branch, by limiting that branch's power without attempting to exercise it itself. Still other times, one branch will attempt to yield its powers to another branch. The Supreme Court has decided several very important cases determining what the Constitution permits and what it does not. Pay close attention to the contexts in which these conflicts arise, and the particular way in which the separation of powers is alleged to have been violated.

CHAPTER 5

Federal Executive Power

INTRODUCTION

As noted above, Article II of the Constitution begins by declaring: "The executive Power shall be vested in a President of the United States of America." Executive power in general is the power to carry out and enforce federal laws, to represent the United States in its foreign relations, and to run the government. Sections 2 and 3 of Article II provide some details about the President and the President's executive power: The President is the Commander in Chief of the Armed Forces. The President may grant pardons. With the advice and consent of the Senate, the President may make treaties with foreign nations. Also with the advice and consent of the Senate, the President may appoint judges, ambassadors, and all other officers of the United States. In addition, the President may establish diplomatic relations with foreign nations by receiving their ambassadors. And the President must "take Care that the Laws be faithfully executed."

This chapter does not proceed with a clause-by-clause examination of the President's powers and duties. Instead, it focuses on difficult issues that have arisen when the President has pressed presidential authority to its limits. In reading the cases that follow, consider not only the rules announced by the Supreme Court, but also why the President may have felt a need to assert the disputed powers. Consider as well what the cases reveal about whether the Court should aggressively police the boundaries of presidential authority, and what checks might exist absent judicial intervention.

A. DOMESTIC AFFAIRS

When acting with respect to domestic affairs (i.e., non-international subjects), the President clearly can exercise any powers given to him by the Constitution or by (otherwise constitutional) federal legislation. For an example of a constitutional power, consider Article II, § 2, cl. 2, which says that the President may grant pardons. A pardon is an official act that eliminates consequences that the recipient of the pardon otherwise would suffer for having committed a crime. Even when a pardon is politically controversial—such as the pardon President Gerald Ford gave to former President Richard Nixon—no one doubts that the President has the power to grant the pardon. For an example of a statutory power, consider the Antiquities Act, 54 U.S.C. § 320301, which authorizes the President to protect historic landmarks on federally owned land by designating them as national monuments. Pursuant to this Act, the President clearly has the power to establish national monuments. *See, e.g.*, *United States v. California*, 436 U.S. 32 (1978). (We will consider Congress's power to delegate decision-making authority of this sort when we discuss the Federal Legislative Power in Chapter 6.)

A more difficult question is whether the President may take actions with respect to domestic affairs that both go beyond any statutory authorization and find no obvious sanction in expressly enumerated constitutional provisions. An argument against finding implied executive powers is that Article II contains no equivalent of the Necessary and Proper clause found in Article I. But an argument for finding implied executive powers is that the wording of the first section of Article I and the wording of the first section of Article II are subtly different. Unlike Article I, which purports to vest only the legislative powers "herein granted" in Congress, Article II simply vests the "executive Power" in the President. As noted above, some specific powers are listed in Article II. But is there reason to read Article II to permit the President to rely on unenumerated, inherent authority that he enjoys simply by virtue of the importance of the office?

The following case says that the answer is no. "The President's power, if any," according to the Court, "must stem either from an act of Congress or from the Constitution itself." As you read the case, consider why the President believed that he needed an additional power, the exercise of which gave rise to the challenge in the case.

YOUNGSTOWN SHEET & TUBE CO. V. SAWYER

343 U.S. 579 (1952)

MR. JUSTICE BLACK delivered the opinion of the Court.

We are asked to decide whether the President was acting within his constitutional power when he issued an order directing the Secretary of Commerce to take possession of and operate most of the Nation's steel mills. The mill owners argue that the President's order amounts to lawmaking, a legislative function which the Constitution has expressly confided to the Congress and not to the President. The Government's position is that the order was made on findings of the President that his action was necessary to avert a national catastrophe which would inevitably result from a stoppage of steel production, and that in meeting this grave emergency the President was acting within the aggregate of his constitutional powers as the Nation's Chief Executive and the Commander in Chief of the Armed Forces of the United States. The issue emerges here from the following series of events:

In the latter part of 1951 [during the Korean War], a dispute arose between the steel companies and their employees over terms and conditions that should be included in new collective bargaining agreements. Long-continued conferences failed to resolve the dispute. On December 18, 1951, the employees' representative, United Steelworkers of America, C.I.O., gave notice of an intention to strike when the existing bargaining agreements expired on December 31. The Federal Mediation and Conciliation Service then intervened in an effort to get labor and management to agree. This failing, the President on December 22, 1951, referred the dispute to the Federal Wage Stabilization Board to investigate and make recommendations for fair and equitable terms of settlement. This Board's report resulted in no settlement. On April 4, 1952, the Union gave notice of a nation-wide strike called to begin at 12:01 a.m. April 9. The indispensability of steel as a component of substantially all weapons and other war materials led the President to believe that the proposed work stoppage would immediately jeopardize our national defense and that governmental seizure of the steel mills was necessary in order to assure the continued availability of steel. Reciting these considerations for his action, the President, a few hours before the strike was to begin, issued Executive Order 10340, [which] directed the Secretary of Commerce to take possession of most of the steel mills and keep them running. The Secretary immediately issued his own possessory orders, calling upon the presidents of the various seized companies to serve as operating managers for the United States. They were directed to carry on their activities in accordance with regulations and directions of the Secretary. The next morning the President sent a message to Congress reporting his action. Twelve days later he sent a second message. Congress has taken no action.

Obeying the Secretary's orders under protest, the companies brought proceedings against him in the District Court. Their complaints charged that the seizure was not authorized by an act of Congress or by any constitutional provisions. The District Court was asked to declare the orders of the President and the Secretary invalid and to issue preliminary and permanent injunctions restraining their enforcement. * * * [The] District Court on April 30 issued a preliminary injunction restraining the Secretary from "continuing the seizure and possession of the plant * * * and from acting under the purported authority of Executive Order No. 10340." On the same day the Court of Appeals stayed the District Court's injunction. Deeming it best that the issues raised be promptly decided by this Court, we granted certiorari on May 3 and set the cause for argument on May 12.

The President's power, if any, to issue the order must stem either from an act of Congress or from the Constitution itself. There is no statute that expressly authorizes the President to take possession of property as he did here. Nor is there any act of Congress to which our attention has been directed from which such a power can fairly be implied. Indeed, we do not understand the Government to rely on statutory authorization for this seizure. There are two statutes [the Selective Service Act and the Defense Production Act of 1950] which do authorize the President to take both personal and real property under certain conditions.

Food for Thought

Why are the two statutes cited in these paragraphs relevant to the Court's analysis? Does the Court hold that the President violated these two statutes? Or is the Court suggesting something else?

However, the Government admits that these conditions were not met and that the President's order was not rooted in either of the statutes. The Government refers to the seizure provisions of [the Defense Production Act] as "much too cumbersome, involved, and time-consuming for the crisis which was at hand."

Moreover, the use of the seizure technique to solve labor disputes in order to prevent work stoppages was not only unauthorized by any congressional enactment; prior to this controversy, Congress had refused to adopt that method of settling labor disputes. When the Taft-Hartley Act was under consideration in 1947, Congress rejected an amendment which would have authorized such governmental seizures in cases of emergency. Apparently it was thought that the technique of seizure, like that of compulsory arbitration, would interfere with the process of collective bargaining. Consequently, the plan Congress adopted in that Act did not provide for seizure under any circumstances. Instead, the plan sought to bring about settlements by use of the customary devices of mediation, conciliation, investigation by boards of inquiry, and public reports.

It is clear that if the President had authority to issue the order he did, it must be found in some provisions of the Constitution. And it is not claimed that express constitutional language grants this power to the President. The contention is that presidential power should be implied from the aggregate of his powers under the Constitution. Particular reliance is placed on provisions in Article II which say that "the executive Power shall be vested in a President * * *"; that "he shall take Care that the Laws be faithfully executed"; and that he "shall be Commander in Chief of the Army and Navy of the United States."

The order cannot properly be sustained as an exercise of the President's military power as Commander in Chief of the Armed Forces. The Government attempts to do so by citing a number of cases upholding broad powers in military commanders engaged in day-to-day fighting in a theater of war. Such cases need not concern us here. Even though "theater of war" be an expanding concept, we cannot with faithfulness to our constitutional system hold that the Commander in Chief of the Armed Forces has the ultimate power as such to take possession of private property in order to keep labor disputes from stopping production. This is a job for the Nation's lawmakers, not for its military authorities.

Make the Connection

In *McCulloch v. Maryland*, which we considered in Chapter 3, the Court held that Congress enjoys implied powers. Is the Court saying here that the same isn't true for the President?

Nor can the seizure order be sustained because of the several constitutional provisions that grant executive power to the President. In the framework of our Constitution, the President's power to see that the laws are faithfully executed refutes the idea that he is to be a lawmaker. The Constitution limits his functions in the lawmaking process to the recommending of laws he thinks wise and the vetoing of laws he thinks bad. And the Constitution is neither silent nor equivocal about who shall make laws which the President is to execute. The first section of the first article says that "All legislative Powers herein granted shall be vested in a Congress of the United States * * *." After granting many powers to the Congress, Article I goes on to provide that Congress may "make all Laws which shall be necessary and proper for carrying into Execution the foregoing Powers and all other Powers vested by this Constitution in the Government of the United States, or in any Department or Officer thereof."

Make the Connection

The Court states that Congress had power to authorize the seizure of the steel plants. What would have been the source of Congress's authority to do so? Would such an action have been consistent with the Fifth Amendment?

The President's order does not direct that a congressional policy be executed in a manner prescribed by Congress—it directs that a presidential policy be executed in a manner prescribed by the President. The preamble of the order itself, like that of many statutes, sets out reasons why the President believes certain policies should be adopted, proclaims these policies as rules of conduct to be followed, and again, like a statute, authorizes a government official to promulgate additional rules and regulations consistent with the policy proclaimed and needed to carry that policy into execution. The power of Congress to adopt such public policies as those proclaimed by the order is beyond question. It can authorize the taking of private property for public use. It can make laws regulating the relationships between employers and employees, prescribing rules designed to settle labor disputes, and fixing wages and working conditions in certain fields of our economy. The Constitution did not subject this law-making power of Congress to presidential or military supervision or control.

It is said that other Presidents without congressional authority have taken possession of private business enterprises in order to settle labor disputes. But even if this be true, Congress has not thereby lost its exclusive constitutional authority to make laws necessary and proper to carry out the powers vested by the Constitution "in the Government of the United States, or in any Department or Officer thereof."

The Founders of this Nation entrusted the law making power to the Congress alone in both good and bad times. It would do no good to recall the historical events, the fears of power and the hopes for freedom that lay behind their choice. Such a review would but confirm our holding that this seizure order cannot stand.

MR. JUSTICE FRANKFURTER, concurring.

[For the Founders of this Nation,] the doctrine of separation of powers was not mere theory; it was a felt necessity. Not so long ago it was fashionable to find our system of checks and balances obstructive to effective government. It was easy to ridicule that system as outmoded—too easy. The experience through which the world has passed in our own day has made vivid the realization that the Framers of our Constitution were not inexperienced doctrinaires. These long-headed statesmen had no illusion that our people enjoyed biological or psychological or sociological immunities from the hazards of concentrated power.

The question before the Court comes in this setting. Congress has frequently—at least 16 times since 1916—specifically provided for executive seizure of production, transportation, communications, or storage facilities. In every case it has qualified this grant of power with limitations and safeguards. * * * It cannot be contended that the President would have had power to issue this order had Congress explicitly negated such authority in formal legislation. Congress has expressed its will to withhold this power from the President as though it had said so in so many words. * * * It is one thing to draw an intention of Congress from general language and to say that Congress would have explicitly written what is inferred, where Congress has not addressed itself to a specific situation. It is quite impossible, however, when Congress did specifically address itself to a problem, as Congress did to that of seizure, to find secreted in the interstices of legislation the very grant of power which Congress consciously withheld. To find authority so explicitly withheld is not merely to disregard in a particular instance the clear will of Congress. It is to disrespect the whole legislative process and the constitutional division of authority between President and Congress.

The Constitution is a framework for government. Therefore the way the framework has consistently operated fairly establishes that it has operated according to its true nature. Deeply embedded traditional ways of conducting government cannot supplant the Constitution or legislation, but they give meaning to the words of a text or supply them. It is an inadmissibly narrow conception of American constitutional law to confine it to the words of the Constitution and to disregard the gloss which life has written upon them. In short, a systematic, unbroken, executive practice, long pursued to the knowledge of the Congress and never before questioned, engaged in by Presidents who have also sworn to uphold the Constitution, making as it were such exercise of power part of the structure of our government, may be treated as a gloss on "executive Power" vested in the President by § 1 of Art. II. * * *

Down to the World War II period, [the] record is barren of instances comparable to the one before us. Of twelve seizures by President Roosevelt prior to the enactment of the War Labor Disputes Act in June, 1943, three were sanctioned by existing law, and six others were effected after Congress, on December 8, 1941, had declared the existence of a state of war. In this case, reliance on the powers that flow from declared war has been commendably disclaimed by the Solicitor General. Thus the list of executive assertions of the power of seizure in circumstances comparable to the present reduces to three in the six-month period from June to December of 1941. We need not split hairs in comparing those actions to the one before us, though much might be said by way of differentiation. Without passing on their validity, as we are not called upon to do, it suffices to say that these three isolated instances do not add up, either in number, scope, duration or contemporaneous legal justification, to the kind of executive construction of the Constitution [that would justify the action at issue]. Nor do they come to us sanctioned by long-continued acquiescence of Congress giving decisive weight to a construction by the Executive of its powers.

MR. JUSTICE JACKSON, concurring in the judgment and opinion of the court.

A judge, like an executive adviser, may be surprised at the poverty of really useful and unambiguous authority applicable to concrete problems of executive power as they actually present themselves. Just what our forefathers did envision, or would have envisioned had they foreseen modern conditions, must be divined from materials almost as enigmatic as the dreams Joseph was called upon to interpret for Pharaoh. A century and a half of partisan debate and scholarly speculation yields no net result but only supplies more or less apt quotations from respected sources on each side of any question. They largely cancel each other. And court decisions are indecisive because of the judicial practice of dealing with the largest questions in the most narrow way.

The actual art of governing under our Constitution does not and cannot conform to judicial definitions of the power of any of its branches based on isolated clauses or even single Articles torn from context. While the Constitution diffuses power the better to secure liberty, it also contemplates that practice will integrate the dispersed powers into a workable government. It enjoins upon its branches separateness but interdependence, autonomy but reciprocity. Presidential powers are not fixed but fluctuate, depending upon their disjunction or conjunction with those of Congress. We may well begin by a somewhat over-simplified grouping of practical situations in which a President may doubt, or others may challenge, his powers, and by distinguishing roughly the legal consequences of this factor of relativity.

> **Take Note**
>
> Although only a concurrence, Justice Jackson's description of the three categories of executive action quickly captured judicial imaginations. Scores of subsequent opinions, including several in this chapter, have cited it. Can you think of examples for each category?
>
> Does Justice Jackson's identification of these three situations actually help resolve questions of presidential power? Consider three situations. Situation #1: Congress passes a resolution directing the President to pardon a convict, and the President then pardons the convict. Situation #2: Congress passes no resolution concerning the convict, and the President pardons the convict. Situation #3: Congress passes a resolution telling the President not to pardon the convict but the President pardons the convict anyway. In which situation did the President act with the greatest and least constitutional authority? Or is the President's authority, when conferred by Article II, the same regardless of the position taken by Congress?

1. When the President acts pursuant to an express or implied authorization of Congress, his authority is at its maximum, for it includes all that he possesses in his own right plus all that Congress can delegate. In these circumstances, and in these only, may he be said (for what it may be worth), to personify the federal sovereignty. If his act is held unconstitutional under these

circumstances, it usually means that the Federal Government as an undivided whole lacks power. A seizure executed by the President pursuant to an Act of Congress would be supported by the strongest of presumptions and the widest latitude of judicial interpretation, and the burden of persuasion would rest heavily upon any who might attack it.

2. When the President acts in absence of either a congressional grant or denial of authority, he can only rely upon his own independent powers, but there is a zone of twilight in which he and Congress may have concurrent authority, or in which its distribution is uncertain. Therefore, congressional inertia, indifference or quiescence may sometimes, at least as a practical matter, enable, if not invite, measures on independent presidential responsibility. In this area, any actual test of power is likely to depend on the imperatives of events and contemporary imponderables rather than on abstract theories of law.

3. When the President takes measures incompatible with the expressed or implied will of Congress, his power is at its lowest ebb, for then he can rely only upon his own constitutional powers minus any constitutional powers of Congress over the matter. Courts can sustain exclusive Presidential control in such a case only by disabling the Congress from acting upon the subject. Presidential claim to a power at once so conclusive and preclusive must be scrutinized with caution, for what is at stake is the equilibrium established by our constitutional system.

Into which of these classifications does this executive seizure of the steel industry fit? It is eliminated from the first by admission, for it is conceded that no congressional authorization exists for this seizure. That takes away also the support of the many precedents and declarations which were made in relation, and must be confined, to this category.

Can it then be defended under flexible tests available to the second category? It seems clearly eliminated from that class because Congress has not left seizure of private property an open field but has covered it by three statutory policies inconsistent with this seizure. * * *

> **Take Note**
>
> Why didn't the President's action fall into Justice Jackson's second category, which involves congressional silence on the action in question? In Justice Jackson's view, has Congress been silent on the issue? How can one tell the difference among implied congressional authorization (category 1), implied congressional prohibition (category 3), and congressional silence (category 2)?

This leaves the current seizure to be justified only by the severe tests under the third grouping, where it can be supported only by any remainder of executive power after subtraction of such powers as Congress may have over the subject. In short, we can sustain the President only by holding that seizure of such strike-bound industries is within his domain and beyond control by Congress.

The Solicitor General seeks the power of seizure in three clauses of the Executive Article, the first reading, "The executive Power shall be vested in a President of the United States of America." Lest I be thought to exaggerate, I quote the interpretation which his brief puts upon it: "In our view, this clause constitutes a grant of all the executive powers of which the Government is capable." If that be true, it is difficult to see why the forefathers bothered to add several specific items, including some trifling ones.

The example of such unlimited executive power that must have most impressed the forefathers was the prerogative exercised by George III, and the description of its evils in the Declaration of Independence leads me to doubt that they were creating their new Executive in his image. Continental European examples were no more appealing. And if we seek instruction from our own times, we can match it only from the executive powers in those governments we disparagingly describe as totalitarian. I cannot accept the view that this clause is a grant in bulk of all conceivable executive power but regard it as an allocation to the presidential office of the generic powers thereafter stated.

The clause on which the Government next relies is that "The President shall be Commander in Chief of the Army and Navy of the United States * * *." These cryptic words have given rise to some of the most persistent controversies in our constitutional history. Of course, they imply something more than an empty title. But just what authority goes with the name has plagued Presidential advisers who would not waive or narrow it by nonassertion yet cannot say where it begins or ends. It undoubtedly puts the Nation's armed forces under Presidential command. Hence, this loose appellation is sometimes advanced as support for any Presidential action, internal or external, involving use of force, the idea being that it vests power to do anything, anywhere, that can be done with an army or navy.

That seems to be the logic of an argument tendered at our bar—that the President having, on his own responsibility, sent American troops abroad derives from that act "affirmative power" to seize the means of producing a supply of steel for them. To quote, "Perhaps the most forceful illustrations of the scope of Presidential power in this connection is the fact that American troops in Korea, whose safety and effectiveness are so directly involved here, were sent to the field by an exercise of the President's constitutional powers." Thus, it is said he has invested himself with "war powers."

> **FYI**
>
> Congress did not declare war in the Korean conflict. The United States contributed troops after the United Nations condemned North Korea's invasion of South Korea. President Truman characterized the United States' participation in the conflict as a "police action."

I cannot foresee all that it might entail if the Court should indorse this argument. Nothing in our Constitution is plainer than that declaration of a war is entrusted only to Congress. Of course, a state of war may in fact exist without a formal declaration. But no doctrine that the Court could promulgate would seem to me more sinister and alarming than that a President whose conduct of foreign affairs is so largely uncontrolled, and often even is unknown, can vastly enlarge his mastery over the internal affairs of the country by his own commitment of the Nation's armed forces to some foreign venture. I do not, however, find it necessary or appropriate to consider the legal status of the Korean enterprise to discountenance argument based on it. * * *

There are indications that the Constitution did not contemplate that the title Commander-in-Chief of the Army and Navy will constitute him also Commander-in-Chief of the country, its industries and its inhabitants. He has no monopoly of "war powers," whatever they are. While Congress cannot deprive the President of the command of the army and navy, only Congress can provide him an army or navy to command. It is also empowered to make rules for the "Government and Regulation of land and naval forces," by which it may to some unknown extent impinge upon even command functions. That military powers of the Commander-in-Chief were not to supersede representative government of internal affairs seems obvious from the Constitution and from elementary American history.

We should not use this occasion to circumscribe, much less to contract, the lawful role of the President as Commander-in-Chief. I should indulge the widest latitude of interpretation to sustain his exclusive function to command the instruments of national force, at least when turned against the outside world for the security of our society. But, when it is turned inward, not because of rebellion but because of a lawful economic struggle between industry and labor, it should have no such indulgence. His command power is not such an absolute as might be implied from that office in a militaristic system but is subject to limitations consistent with a constitutional Republic whose law and policy-making branch is a representative Congress. The purpose of lodging dual titles in one man was to insure that the civilian would control the military, not to enable the military to subordinate the presidential office. * * * What the power of command may include I do not try to envision, but I think it is not a military prerogative, without support of law, to seize persons or property because they are important or even essential for the military and naval establishment.

The third clause in which the Solicitor General finds seizure powers is that "he shall take Care that the Laws be faithfully executed * * *." That authority must be matched against words of the Fifth Amendment that "No person shall be * * * deprived of life, liberty, or property, without due process of law * * *." One gives a governmental authority that reaches so far as there is law, the other gives a private right that authority shall go no farther. These signify about all there is of the principle that ours is a government of laws, not of men, and that we submit ourselves to rulers only if under rules.

The Solicitor General lastly grounds support of the seizure upon nebulous, inherent powers never expressly granted but said to have accrued to the office from the customs and claims of preceding administrations. The plea is for a resulting power to deal with a crisis or an emergency according to the necessities of the case, the unarticulated assumption being that necessity knows no law.

The appeal, however, that we declare the existence of inherent powers *ex necessitate* to meet an emergency asks us to do what many think would be wise, although it is something the forefathers omitted. They knew what emergencies were, knew the pressures they engender for authoritative action, knew, too, how they afford a ready pretext for usurpation. We may also suspect that they suspected that emergency powers would tend to kindle emergencies. Aside from suspension of the privilege of the writ of habeas corpus in time of rebellion or invasion, when the public safety may require it, they made no express provision for exercise of extraordinary authority because of a crisis. I do not think we rightfully may so amend their work, and, if we could, I am not convinced it would be wise to do so, although many modern nations have forthrightly recognized that war and economic crises may upset the normal balance between liberty and authority. * * *

With all its defects, delays and inconveniences, men have discovered no technique for long preserving free government except that the Executive be under the law, and that the law be made by parliamentary deliberations. Such institutions may be destined to pass away. But it is the duty of the Court to be last, not first, to give them up.

[JUSTICE DOUGLAS's concurring opinion and JUSTICE BURTON'S and JUSTICE CLARK'S opinions concurring in the judgment are omitted.]

MR. CHIEF JUSTICE VINSON, with whom MR. JUSTICE REED and MR. JUSTICE MINTON join, dissenting.

In passing upon the question of Presidential powers in this case, we must first consider the context in which those powers were exercised. Those who suggest that this is a case involving extraordinary powers should be mindful that these are extraordinary times. A world not yet recovered from the devastation of World War II has been forced to face the threat of another and more terrifying global conflict.

The President has the duty to execute the [legislative programs that Congress created to support the Korean War effort]. Their successful execution depends upon continued production of steel and stabilized prices for steel. [T]he President acted to avert a complete shutdown of steel production. * * * One is not here called upon even to consider the possibility of executive seizure of a farm, a corner grocery store or even a single industrial plant. Such considerations arise only when one ignores the central fact of this case—that the Nation's entire basic steel production would have shut down completely if there had been no Government seizure. * * * Accordingly, if the President has any power under the Constitution to meet a critical situation in the absence of express statutory authorization, there is no basis whatever for criticizing the exercise of such power in this case.

The whole of the "executive Power" is vested in the President. * * * This comprehensive grant of the executive power to a single person was bestowed soon after the country had thrown the yoke of monarchy. Only by instilling initiative and vigor in all of the three departments of Government, declared Madison, could tyranny in any form be avoided. * * * It is thus apparent that the Presidency was deliberately fashioned as an office of power and independence. [The Framers did not] create an automaton impotent to exercise the powers of Government at a time when the survival of the Republic itself may be at stake.

A review of executive action demonstrates that our Presidents have on many occasions exhibited the leadership contemplated by the Framers when they made the President Commander in Chief, and imposed upon him the trust to "take Care that the Laws be faithfully executed." With or without explicit statutory authorization, Presidents have at such times dealt with national emergencies by acting promptly and resolutely to enforce legislative programs, at least to save those programs until Congress could act. Congress and the courts have responded to such executive initiative with consistent approval. * * *

The fact that temporary executive seizures of industrial plants to meet an emergency have not been directly tested in this Court furnishes not the slightest suggestion that such actions have been illegal. Rather, the fact that Congress and the courts have consistently recognized and given their support to such executive action indicates that such a power of seizure has been accepted throughout our history. * * *

Much of the argument in this case has been directed at straw men. We do not now have before us the case of a President acting solely on the basis of his own notions of the public welfare. Nor is there any question of unlimited executive power in this case. The President himself closed the door to any such claim when he sent his Message to Congress stating his purpose to abide by any action of Congress, whether approving or disapproving his seizure action. Here, the President immediately made sure that Congress was fully informed of the temporary action he had taken only to preserve the legislative programs from destruction until Congress could act. * * *

Seizure of plaintiffs' property is not a pleasant undertaking. Similarly unpleasant to a free country are the draft which disrupts the home and military procurement which causes economic dislocation and compels adoption of price controls, wage stabilization and allocation of materials. The President informed Congress that even a temporary Government operation of plaintiffs' properties was "thoroughly distasteful" to him, but was necessary to prevent immediate paralysis of the mobilization program. Presidents have been in the past, and any man worthy of the Office should be in the future, free to take at least interim action necessary to execute legislative programs essential to survival of the Nation. A sturdy judiciary should not be swayed by the unpleasantness or unpopularity of necessary executive action, but must independently determine for itself whether the President was acting, as required by the Constitution, to "take Care that the Laws be faithfully executed."

POINTS FOR DISCUSSION

a. What Did the President Do Wrong?

Did the Court conclude that the President had acted in violation of a specific constitutional or statutory provision, or instead just that the President did not have authority to act? If the President lacked authority for his order, what effect if any could it have?

b. The Government's Argument

In defending the President's seizure of the steel mills in the district court, Assistant Attorney General Holmes Baldridge told the court: "It is our position that the President is accountable only to the country, and that the President's decisions are conclusive." District Judge David A. Pine asked in response: "Then the Constitution limits the Judiciary, but does not limit the Executive?" The Assistant Attorney General responded: "That is the way we read the constitution." See William H. Rehnquist, *The Supreme Court* 160 (2002) (recounting the proceedings in the District Court). What language in Article II might support the government's position? In what sense is the President accountable "to the country"? What consequences might flow from the government's position if the courts had accepted it? Can you think of a better argument for the government?

c. President Lincoln

During the Civil War, President Abraham Lincoln took a number of controversial executive actions, such as suspending the writ of habeas corpus (i.e., the power of courts to order the government to release persons who have been detained without a valid legal basis). When confronted with objections that he was violating the Constitution, Lincoln asked in response whether it is "possible to lose the nation and yet preserve the Constitution?" What was President Lincoln implying? What precedential value should Lincoln's actions have?

d. Inherent Powers

The Court concluded that the President does not enjoy inherent power to act, but instead is limited to those powers granted in the Constitution and by statute. If an attack by a hostile power rendered Congress unable to act, would the President have power to take all necessary responsive actions? If so, doesn't that mean that the President has powers beyond those clearly enumerated in the Constitution, and that sometimes the President can act even without express constitutional or statutory authorization? And if not, is our constitutional structure sensible?

e. Emergency Powers

Several provisions of the Constitution refer to exigent circumstances that might arise because of war or other national emergencies. See, e.g., Art. I, § 9, cl. 2 ("The Privilege of the Writ of Habeas Corpus shall not be suspended, unless when in Cases of Rebellion or Invasion the public Safety may require it."); Art. I, § 8, cl. 15 ("The Congress shall have the Power * * * To provide for calling forth the Militia to execute the Laws of the Union, suppress Insurrections and repel Invasions."); Amend. III ("No Soldier shall, in time of peace be quartered in any house, without the consent of the Owner, nor in time of war, but in a manner to be prescribed by law."); Amend. V ("No person shall be held to answer for a capital, or otherwise infamous crime, unless on a presentment or indictment of a Grand Jury, except in cases arising in the land or naval forces, or in the Militia, when in actual service in time of War or public danger."). Yet there is no provision in the Constitution expressly conferring upon either the President or Congress broad powers to act in the face of an emergency.

Should the Court find such a power to be implied? If so, was *Youngstown* the case in which to do it?

B. FOREIGN AFFAIRS

In *Youngstown Sheet & Tube Co. v. Sawyer*, the Supreme Court said that when acting with respect to domestic affairs the President has only the powers expressly or by implication conferred by the Constitution or by statute. Might the President have additional powers—powers not explicitly conferred by the Constitution or statute—when acting with respect to foreign affairs?

DAMES & MOORE V. REGAN

453 U.S. 654 (1981)

JUSTICE REHNQUIST delivered the opinion of the Court.

On November 4, 1979, the American Embassy in Tehran was seized and our diplomatic personnel were captured and held hostage. In response to that crisis, President Carter, acting pursuant to the International Emergency Economic Powers Act, 91 Stat. 1626 (hereinafter IEEPA), declared a national emergency on November 14, 1979, and blocked the removal or transfer of "all property and interests in property of the Government of Iran, its instrumentalities and controlled entities and the Central Bank of Iran which are or become subject to the jurisdiction of the United States. . . ."

On January 20, 1981, the Americans held hostage were released by Iran pursuant to an Agreement entered into the day before and embodied in two Declarations of the Democratic and Popular Republic of Algeria. The Agreement stated that "[i]t is the purpose of [the United States and Iran] . . . to terminate all litigation as between the Government of each party and the nationals of the other, and to bring about the settlement and termination of all such claims through binding arbitration." In furtherance of this goal, the Agreement called for the establishment of an Iran-United States Claims Tribunal which would arbitrate any claims not settled within six months. Awards of the Claims Tribunal are to be "final and binding" and "enforceable . . . in the courts of any nation in accordance with its laws." * * *

[To implement the Agreement, the President issued executive orders and the Treasury Department issued regulations. These executive orders and regulations sought to move pending cases from domestic courts to the Claims Tribunal. Among other things, they required courts to suspend pending litigation against Iran. These executive orders affected petitioner Dames & Moore which had sued the Government of Iran, the Atomic Energy Organization of Iran, and a number of Iranian banks in federal court, claiming that it was owed more than $3 million for breach of contract.]

On April 28, 1981, petitioner filed this action in the District Court for declaratory and injunctive relief against the United States and the Secretary of the Treasury, seeking to prevent enforcement of the Executive Orders and Treasury Department regulations implementing the Agreement with Iran. In its complaint, petitioner alleged that the actions of the President and the Secretary of the Treasury implementing the Agreement with Iran were beyond their statutory and constitutional powers and, in any event, were unconstitutional to the extent they adversely affect petitioner's final judgment against the Government of Iran and the Atomic Energy Organization, its execution of that judgment in the State of Washington, its prejudgment attachments, and its ability to continue to litigate against the Iranian banks. * * *

The parties and the lower courts, confronted with the instant questions, have all agreed that much relevant analysis is contained in *Youngstown Sheet & Tube v. Sawyer*, 343 U.S. 579 (1952). * * * Although we have in the past found and do today find Justice Jackson's classification of executive actions into three general categories analytically useful, * * * Jackson himself recognized that his three categories represented "a somewhat over-simplified grouping," 343 U.S. at 635, and it is doubtless the case that executive action in any particular instance falls, not neatly in one of three pigeonholes, but rather at some point along a spectrum running from explicit congressional authorization to explicit congressional prohibition. This is particularly true as respects cases such as the one before us, involving responses to international crises the nature of which Congress can hardly have been expected to anticipate in any detail.

Take Note

The Court here treats Justice Jackson's opinion in *Youngstown* as containing the proper framework for analyzing claims of presidential power, even though that opinion was merely a concurrence. Indeed, Jackson's opinion has been the most enduring of the several opinions in *Youngstown*. It might also interest you to learn that Chief Justice Rehnquist clerked for Justice Jackson after graduating from law school.

[The Court concluded that the IEEPA provided specific congressional authorization to the President to nullify the attachments and order the transfer of Iranian assets, but that neither the IEEPA nor the Hostage Act, 22 U.S.C. § 1732, authorized the suspension of the claims of American citizens against Iran.]

Although we have declined to conclude that the IEEPA or the Hostage Act directly authorizes the President's suspension of claims for the reasons noted, we cannot ignore the general tenor of Congress' legislation in this area in trying to determine whether the President is acting alone or at least with the acceptance of Congress. As we have noted, Congress cannot anticipate and legislate with regard to every possible action the President may find it necessary to take or every possible situation in which he might act. Such failure of Congress specifically to delegate authority does not, "especially . . . in the areas of foreign policy and national security," imply "congressional disapproval" of action taken by the Executive. *Haig v. Agee*, 453 U.S. 280, 291 (1981). On the contrary, the enactment of legislation closely related to the question of the President's authority in a particular case which evinces legislative intent to accord the President broad discretion may be considered to "invite" "measures on independent presidential responsibility," *Youngstown*, 343 U.S., at 637 (Jackson, J., concurring). At least this is so where there is no contrary indication of legislative intent and when, as here, there is a history of congressional acquiescence in conduct of the sort engaged in by the President. It is to that history which we now turn.

> **Take Note**
>
> How does the Court's statement here of the test for Presidential authority differ from Justice Jackson's statement in *Youngstown*?

Not infrequently in affairs between nations, outstanding claims by nationals of one country against the government of another country are "sources of friction" between the two sovereigns. *United States v. Pink*, 315 U.S. 203, 225 (1942). To resolve these difficulties, nations have often entered into agreements settling the claims of their respective nationals. As one treatise writer puts it, international agreements settling claims by nationals of one state against the government of another "are established international practice reflecting traditional international theory." L. Henkin, Foreign Affairs and the Constitution 262 (1972). Consistent with that principle, the United States has repeatedly exercised its sovereign authority to settle the claims of its nationals against foreign countries. Though those settlements have sometimes been made by treaty, there has also been a longstanding practice of settling such claims by executive agreement without the advice and consent of the Senate. Under such agreements, the President has agreed to renounce or extinguish claims of United States nationals against foreign governments in return for lump-sum payments or the establishment of arbitration procedures. To be sure, many of these settlements were encouraged by the United States claimants themselves, since a claimant's only hope of obtaining any payment at all might lie in having his Government negotiate a diplomatic settlement on his behalf. But it is also undisputed that the

"United States has sometimes disposed of the claims of its citizens without their consent, or even without consultation with them, usually without exclusive regard for their interests, as distinguished from those of the nation as a whole." Henkin, *supra*, at 262–263. It is clear that the practice of settling claims continues today. Since 1952, the President has entered into at least 10 binding settlements with foreign nations, including an $80 million settlement with the People's Republic of China.

Crucial to our decision today is the conclusion that Congress has implicitly approved the practice of claim settlement by executive agreement. This is best demonstrated by Congress' enactment of the International Claims Settlement Act of 1949, 64 Stat. 13, as amended, 22 U.S.C. § 1621 *et seq.* (1976 ed. and Supp. IV). The Act had two purposes: (1) to allocate to United States nationals funds received in the course of an executive claims settlement with Yugoslavia, and (2) to provide a procedure whereby funds resulting from future settlements could be distributed. To achieve these ends Congress created the International Claims Commission, now the Foreign Claims Settlement Commission, and gave it jurisdiction to make final and binding decisions with respect to claims by United States nationals against settlement funds. By creating a procedure to implement future settlement agreements, Congress placed its stamp of approval on such agreements. Indeed, the legislative history of the Act observed that the United States was seeking settlements with countries other than Yugoslavia and that the bill contemplated settlements of a similar nature in the future.

Over the years Congress has frequently amended the International Claims Settlement Act to provide for particular problems arising out of settlement agreements, thus demonstrating Congress' continuing acceptance of the President's claim settlement authority. With respect to the Executive Agreement with the People's Republic of China, for example, Congress established an allocation formula for distribution of the funds received pursuant to the Agreement. As with legislation involving other executive agreements, Congress did not question the fact of the settlement or the power of the President to have concluded it. In 1976, Congress authorized the Foreign Claims Settlement Commission to adjudicate the merits of claims by United States nationals against East Germany, prior to any settlement with East Germany, so that the Executive would "be in a better position to negotiate an adequate settlement . . . of these claims." S. Rep. No. 94–1188, p. 2 (1976). Similarly, Congress recently amended the International Claims Settlement Act to facilitate the settlement of claims against Vietnam. * * *

In addition to congressional acquiescence in the President's power to settle claims, prior cases of this Court have also recognized that the President does have some measure of power to enter into executive agreements without obtaining the advice and consent of the Senate. In *United States v. Pink*, 315 U.S. 203 (1942), for example, the Court upheld the validity of the Litvinov Assignment, which was part of an Executive Agreement whereby the Soviet Union assigned to the United States amounts owed to it by American nationals so that outstanding claims of other American nationals could be paid. The Court explained that the resolution of such claims was integrally connected with normalizing United States' relations with a foreign state:

> "Power to remove such obstacles to full recognition as settlement of claims of our nationals . . . certainly is a modest implied power of the President. . . . No such obstacle can be placed in the way of rehabilitation of relations between this country and another nation, unless the historic conception of the powers and responsibilities . . . is to be drastically revised." *Id.*, at 229–230.

In light of all of the foregoing—the inferences to be drawn from the character of the legislation Congress has enacted in the area, such as the IEEPA and the Hostage Act, and from the history of acquiescence in executive claims settlement—we conclude that the President was authorized to suspend pending claims pursuant to Executive Order No. 12294. As Justice Frankfurter pointed out in *Youngstown*, 343 U.S., at 610–611, "a systematic, unbroken, executive practice, long pursued to the knowledge of the Congress and never before questioned . . . may be treated as a gloss on 'Executive Power' vested in the President by § 1 of Art. II." Past practice does not, by itself, create power, but "long-continued practice, known to and acquiesced in by Congress, would raise a presumption that the [action] had been [taken] in pursuance of its consent. . . ." *United States v. Midwest Oil Co.*, 236 U.S. 459, 474 (1915). Such practice is present here and such a presumption is also appropriate. In light of the fact that Congress may be considered to have consented to the President's action in suspending claims, we cannot say that action exceeded the President's powers.

Food for Thought

The Court places emphasis on the historic practice of Presidents in settling claims and of Congress in acquiescing in this practice. Why should what the President and Congress have done in the past be relevant to the question whether the President has a particular power? Can Congress and the President create precedents comparable to those established in judicial decisions?

Just as importantly, Congress has not disapproved of the action taken here. Though Congress has held hearings on the Iranian Agreement itself, Congress has not enacted legislation, or even passed a resolution, indicating its displeasure with the Agreement. Quite the contrary, the relevant Senate Committee has stated that the establishment of the Tribunal is "of vital importance to the United States." S. Rep. No. 97–71, p. 5 (1981). We are thus clearly not confronted with a situation in which Congress has in some way resisted the exercise of Presidential authority.

Finally, we re-emphasize the narrowness of our decision. We do not decide that the President possesses plenary power to settle claims, even as against foreign governmental entities. * * * But where, as here, the settlement of claims has been determined to be a necessary incident to the resolution of a major foreign policy dispute between our country and another, and where, as here, we can conclude that Congress acquiesced in the President's action, we are not prepared to say that the President lacks the power to settle such claims.

POINTS FOR DISCUSSION

a. Domestic Affairs v. Foreign Affairs

Recall that the Court held in the *Youngstown* case that the President does not enjoy inherent authority to act; instead, the President has power to act only if the Constitution or a congressional statute confers such authority. Although the case involved President Truman's actions during the Korean War, the Court viewed his act nationalizing the steel industry as one pertaining to matters of domestic affairs. After the decision in *Dames & Moore*, does the same approach apply when the President acts in the arena of foreign affairs? If not, in what way is the approach different? Does the Court adequately explain why the two contexts are different? And how can the Court identify when a President's actions concern domestic affairs and when they concern foreign affairs?

b. Nature of the President's Action

Does the Court hold that the President's executive order is federal law that is supreme over state law? If not, how can the President's order supersede private claims and liens under state law? Is this result consistent with the Supremacy Clause?

c. Executive Agreements

Article II, § 2 of the Constitution provides that the President "shall have Power, by and with the Advice and Consent of the Senate, to make Treaties, provided two thirds of the Senators present concur." An executive agreement, in contrast, is an agreement negotiated with a foreign nation by the President without subsequent ratification by the Senate. Are executive agreements constitutional? Some commentators have argued that they are not. See Bradford Clark, *Domesticating Sole Executive Agreements*, 93 Va. L. Rev. 1573, 1611–1612 (2007). Does the Constitution's treatment of the *states'* authority to enter agreements with foreign nations shed any light on the issue? Article I, § 10, cl. 1 provides that "[n]o State shall enter into any Treaty, Alliance, or Confederation," but clause 3 states that "[n]o State shall, without the Consent of Congress, * * * enter into any Agreement or Compact with another State, or with a foreign Power." Does this suggest that there is a difference under the Constitution between "treaties" and "agreements"? If so, what is it?

The Court's opinion in *Dames & Moore* suggested that the President has greater leeway to act in matters of foreign affairs, but the Court still largely adhered to the *Youngstown* case's account of the scope of the President's powers. Does the Court's embrace of *Youngstown* suggest that the President does not enjoy any extra-constitutional powers when dealing with matters of international affairs? Consider the two cases that follow.

The issue in the following case requires some background to understand. In ordinary circumstances, Congress establishes federal criminal offenses by enacting statutes that specify conduct that is unlawful. The President then (through other officers) enforces the legislation by prosecuting offenders. For example, one provision of the Federal Criminal Code, 18 U.S.C. § 1002, makes it a federal crime to possess forged or counterfeit documents for the purpose of defrauding the government. The President, through the Justice Department, enforces the statute by bringing charges against and prosecuting suspected criminals. But suppose that Congress wanted to alter this usual model to give the President more authority and discretion. For example, suppose that Congress amended § 1002 to say that it shall be unlawful to possess forged or counterfeit documents for the purpose of defrauding the government "if and when the President by proclamation declares that this conduct shall be a crime." Would this statute be constitutional? At the time of the *Curtiss-Wright* decision, there was a serious argument that the answer was no because the hypothetical statute would impermissibly delegate legislative power (i.e., the power to decide what is a crime and what is not) to the President. In *Curtiss-Wright* the Court considered whether Congress could give the President greater discretion in the context of foreign affairs.

Make the Connection

We will discuss Congress's power to delegate decision-making authority to the President and to other officers in the course of our discussion of the federal legislative power, in Chapter 6.

UNITED STATES V. CURTISS-WRIGHT EXPORT CORPORATION

299 U.S. 304 (1936)

MR. JUSTICE SUTHERLAND delivered the opinion of the Court.

On January 27, 1936, an indictment was returned in the court below, the first count of which charges that appellees, beginning with the 29th day of May, 1934, conspired to sell in the United States certain arms of war, namely, fifteen machine guns, to Bolivia, a country then engaged in armed conflict in the Chaco, in violation of the Joint Resolution of Congress approved May 28, 1934, and the provisions of a proclamation issued on the same day by the President of the United States pursuant to authority conferred by section 1 of the resolution. In pursuance of the conspiracy, the commission of certain overt acts was alleged, details of which need not be stated. The Joint Resolution (chapter 365, 48 Stat. 811) follows:

> **FYI**
>
> In the 1930s, Bolivia and Paraguay fought a war in the Chaco, a plain that covers parts of Argentina, Bolivia, and Paraguay. American arms manufacturers were selling weapons to both sides in the conflict, complicating diplomatic relations.

> Resolved by the Senate and House of Representatives of the United States of America in Congress assembled, That if the President finds that the prohibition of the sale of arms and munitions of war in the United States to those countries now engaged in armed conflict in the Chaco may contribute to the reestablishment of peace between those countries, and if after consultation with the governments of other American Republics and with their cooperation, as well as that of such other governments as he may deem necessary, he makes proclamation to that effect, it shall be unlawful to sell, except under such limitations and exceptions as the President prescribes, any arms or munitions of war in any place in the United States to the countries now engaged in that armed conflict, or to any person, company, or association acting in the interest of either country, until otherwise ordered by the President or by Congress.
>
> Sec. 2. Whoever sells any arms or munitions of war in violation of section 1 shall, on conviction, be punished by a fine not exceeding $10,000 or by imprisonment not exceeding two years, or both.

> **FYI**
>
> A joint resolution is a resolution passed by both houses of Congress and presented to the President for his signature or veto. It has the force of law. (In contrast, a concurrent resolution is passed by both Houses of Congress but does not have the force of law because it is not presented to the President.)

The President's proclamation (48 Stat. 1744, No. 2087), after reciting the terms of the Joint Resolution, declares:

> Now, Therefore, I, Franklin D. Roosevelt, President of the United States of America, acting under and by virtue of the authority conferred in me by the said joint resolution of Congress, do hereby declare and proclaim that I have found that the prohibition of the sale of arms and munitions of war in the United States to those countries now engaged in armed conflict in the Chaco may contribute to the reestablishment of peace between those countries, and that I have consulted with the governments of other American Republics and have been assured of the cooperation of such governments as I have deemed necessary as contemplated by the said joint resolution; and I do hereby admonish all citizens of the United States and every person to abstain from every violation of the provisions of the joint resolution above set forth, hereby made applicable to Bolivia and Paraguay, and I do hereby warn them that all violations of such provisions will be rigorously prosecuted.

Appellees severally demurred to [the indictment] on the [ground] that the Joint Resolution effects an invalid delegation of legislative power to the executive * * *.

Definition

The verb "demur" means to "object to the legal sufficiency of a claim [or criminal charge] alleged in a pleading without admitting or denying the truth of the facts stated." *Black's Law Dictionary* (10th ed. 2014).

Whether, if the Joint Resolution had related solely to internal affairs, it would be open to the challenge that it constituted an unlawful delegation of legislative power to the Executive, we find it unnecessary to determine. The whole aim of the resolution is to affect a situation entirely external to the United States, and falling within the category of foreign affairs. The determination which we are called to make, therefore, is whether the Joint Resolution, as applied to that situation, is vulnerable to attack under the rule that forbids a delegation of the lawmaking power. In other words, assuming (but not deciding) that the challenged delegation, if it were confined to internal affairs, would be invalid, may it nevertheless be sustained on the ground that its exclusive aim is to afford a remedy for a hurtful condition within foreign territory?

> **Take Note**
>
> The Court acknowledges that it might have concluded that the joint resolution might have been an unconstitutional delegation of power if it concerned internal affairs. But the Court makes clear that a different standard applies in matters of foreign affairs.

It will contribute to the elucidation of the question if we first consider the differences between the powers of the federal government in respect of foreign or external affairs and those in respect of domestic or internal affairs. That there are differences between them, and that these differences are fundamental, may not be doubted.

The two classes of powers are different, both in respect of their origin and their nature. The broad statement that the federal government can exercise no powers except those specifically enumerated in the Constitution, and such implied powers as are necessary and proper to carry into effect the enumerated powers, is categorically true only in respect of our internal affairs. In that field, the primary purpose of the Constitution was to carve from the general mass of legislative powers then possessed by the states such portions as it was thought desirable to vest in the federal government, leaving those not included in the enumeration still in the states. That this doctrine applies only to powers which the states had is self-evident. And since the states severally never possessed international powers, such powers could not have been carved from the mass of state powers but obviously were transmitted to the United States from some other source. During the Colonial period, those powers were possessed exclusively by and were entirely under the control of the Crown. By the Declaration of Independence, "the Representatives of the United States of America" declared the United (not the several) Colonies to be free and independent states, and as such to have "full Power to levy War, conclude Peace, contract Alliances, establish Commerce and to do all other Acts and Things which Independent States may of right do."

As a result of the separation from Great Britain by the colonies, acting as a unit, the powers of external sovereignty passed from the Crown not to the colonies severally, but to the colonies in their collective and corporate capacity as the United States of America. Even before the Declaration, the colonies were a unit in foreign affairs, acting through a common agency—namely, the Continental Congress, composed of delegates from the thirteen colonies. That agency exercised the powers of war and peace, raised an army, created a navy, and finally adopted the Declaration of Independence. Rulers come and go; governments end and forms of government change; but sovereignty survives. A political society cannot endure without a supreme will somewhere. Sovereignty is never held in suspense. When, therefore, the external sovereignty of Great Britain in respect of the colonies ceased, it immediately passed to the Union. That fact was given practical application almost at once. The treaty of peace, made on September 3, 1783, was concluded between his Brittanic Majesty and the "United States of America." 8 Stat., European Treaties, 80.

The Union existed before the Constitution, which was ordained and established among other things to form "a more perfect Union." Prior to that event, it is clear that the Union, declared by the Articles of Confederation to be "perpetual," was the sole possessor of external sovereignty, and in the Union it remained without change save in so far as the Constitution in express terms qualified its exercise. The Framers' Convention was called and exerted its powers upon the irrefutable postulate that though the states were several their people in respect of foreign affairs were one.

> **Take Note**
>
> In this passage, the Court concludes that the federal government has extra-constitutional powers, which are powers that do not "depend upon the affirmative grants of the Constitution." Where did these powers come from? What (and who) defines them?

It results that the investment of the federal government with the powers of external sovereignty did not depend upon the affirmative grants of the Constitution. The powers to declare and wage war, to conclude peace, to make treaties, to maintain diplomatic relations with other sovereignties, if they had never been mentioned in the Constitution, would have vested in the federal government as necessary concomitants of nationality. Neither the Constitution nor the laws passed in pursuance of it have any force in foreign territory unless in respect of our own citizens; and operations of the nation in such territory must be governed by treaties, international understandings and compacts, and the principles of international law. As a member of the family of nations, the right and power of the United States in that field are equal to the right and power of the other members of the international family. Otherwise, the United States is not completely sovereign. The power to acquire territory by discovery and occupation, the power to expel undesirable aliens, the power to make such international agreements as do not constitute treaties in the constitutional sense, none of which is expressly affirmed by the Constitution, nevertheless exist as inherently inseparable from the conception of nationality. This the court recognized, and in each of the cases cited found the warrant for its conclusions not in the provisions of the Constitution, but in the law of nations.

> **Definition**
>
> The terms "international law" and "law of nations" refer to the principles "governing the relationships between countries." *Black's Law Dictionary* (10th ed. 2014). Treaties have established some of the principles, while tradition and practice have established others.

Not only, as we have shown, is the federal power over external affairs in origin and essential character different from that over internal affairs, but participation in the exercise of the power is significantly limited. In this vast external realm, with its important, complicated, delicate and manifold problems, the President alone has the power to speak or listen as a representative of the nation. He makes treaties with the advice and consent of the Senate; but he alone negotiates. Into the field of negotiation the Senate cannot intrude; and Congress itself is powerless to invade it. As Marshall said in his great argument of March 7, 1800, in the House of Representatives, "The President is the sole organ of the nation in its external relations, and its sole representative with foreign nations." Annals, 6th Cong., col. 613. * * * It is important to bear in mind that we are here dealing not alone with an authority vested in the President by an exertion of legislative power, but with such an authority plus the very delicate, plenary and exclusive power of the President as the sole organ of the federal government in the field of international relations—a power which does not require as a basis for its exercise an act of Congress, but which, of course, like every other governmental power, must be exercised in subordination to the applicable provisions of the Constitution. It is quite apparent that if, in the maintenance of our international relations, embarrassment—perhaps serious embarrassment—is to be avoided and success for our aims achieved, congressional legislation which is to be made effective through negotiation and inquiry within the international field must often accord to the President a degree of discretion and freedom from statutory restriction which would not be admissible were domestic affairs alone involved.

Take Note

The Court explains here why Congress might need to give the President more discretion "within the international field" than with respect to "domestic affairs." What is the Court's reasoning? What kind of "serious embarrassment" might result if the President could not have discretion?

Moreover, he, not Congress, has the better opportunity of knowing the conditions which prevail in foreign countries, and especially is this true in time of war. He has his confidential sources of information. He has his agents in the form of diplomatic, consular and other officials. Secrecy in respect of information gathered by them may be highly necessary, and the premature disclosure of it productive of harmful results. Indeed, so clearly is this true that the first President refused to accede to a request to lay before the House of Representatives the instructions, correspondence and documents relating to the negotiation of the Jay Treaty—a refusal the wisdom of which was recognized by the House itself and has never since been doubted. In his reply to the request, President Washington said:

> "The nature of foreign negotiations requires caution, and their success must often depend on secrecy; and even when brought to a conclusion a full disclosure of all the measures, demands, or eventual concessions which may have been proposed or contemplated would be extremely impolitic; for this might have a pernicious influence on future negotiations, or produce immediate inconveniences, perhaps danger and mischief, in relation to other powers. The necessity of such caution and secrecy was one cogent reason for vesting the power of making treaties in the President, with the advice and consent of the Senate, the principle on which that body was formed confining it to a small number of members. To admit, then, a right in the House of Representatives to demand and to have as a matter of course all the papers respecting a negotiation with a foreign power would be to establish a dangerous precedent." 1 Messages and Papers of the Presidents, p. 194.

In the light of the foregoing observations, it is evident that this court should not be in haste to apply a general rule which will have the effect of condemning legislation like that under review as constituting an unlawful delegation of legislative power. The principles which justify such legislation find overwhelming support in the unbroken legislative practice which has prevailed almost from the inception of the national government to the present day.

Practically every volume of the United States Statutes contains one or more acts or joint resolutions of Congress authorizing action by the President in respect of subjects affecting foreign relations, which either leave the exercise of the power to his unrestricted judgment, or provide a standard far more general than that which has always been considered requisite with regard to domestic affairs.

Food for Thought

According to the Court's reasoning, are statutes delegating authority to the President a necessary predicate for the President's exercise of authority in the arena of foreign affairs?

The uniform, long-continued and undisputed legislative practice just disclosed rests upon an admissible view of the Constitution which, even if the practice found far less support in principle than we think it does, we should not feel at liberty at this late day to disturb.

[W]e conclude there is sufficient warrant for the broad discretion vested in the President to determine whether the enforcement of the statute will have a beneficial effect upon the re-establishment of peace in the affected countries; whether he shall make proclamation to bring the resolution into operation; whether and when the resolution shall cease to operate and to make proclamation accordingly; and to prescribe limitations and exceptions to which the enforcement of the resolution shall be subject.

POINTS FOR DISCUSSION

a. "*Curtiss-Wright*, So I'm Right."

Presidents often justify controversial actions that they have taken in the field of foreign affairs by citing the *Curtiss-Wright* decision. (A longstanding inside joke among Justice Department lawyers is that the President's argument in the Supreme Court often boils down to "*Curtiss-Wright*, so I'm right.") Yet if the President has extra-constitutional powers over foreign affairs, how far do these powers extend? What limitations does the Court suggest might exist? And is the approach of the Court in *Youngstown* reconcilable with the approach of the Court in *Curtiss-Wright*?

b. Sovereignty and History

Not everyone agrees with the Court's understanding of the Revolutionary period. One prominent scholar has described the historical account of sovereignty as "shockingly inaccurate," contending that the various state governments actually exercised many foreign affairs powers following independence. See Charles A. Lofgren, United States v. Curtiss-Wright Export Corporation*: An Historical Reassessment*, 83 Yale L.J. 1, 30–32 (1973). Others believe that the Court's account (at least with respect to this question) was largely correct. See, e.g., Jack N. Rakove, *The Origins of Judicial Review: A Plea for New Contexts*, 49 Stan. L. Rev. 1031, 1043 (1997). How important is a correct assessment of history to the Court's conclusion?

c. Congressional Power over Foreign Affairs

What is Congress's role in foreign affairs? Under Article I, Congress has authority to regulate commerce with foreign nations; to lay and collect duties (which presumably permits Congress to impose retaliatory sanctions on other nations' goods); to raise, support, and regulate the armed forces; and to declare war. This suggests at least some role for Congress in foreign affairs. Did the Court's analysis in *Curtiss-Wright* properly take account of that role?

The Constitution specifies the manner in which the United States can enter into treaties with foreign countries. Article II, section 2, clause 2 says that the President "shall have Power, by and with the Advice and Consent of the Senate, to make Treaties, provided two thirds of the Senators present concur." Oddly, though, the Constitution does not specify a procedure for the United States to withdraw from treaties.

The Supreme Court ruled in *Whitney v. Robertson*, 124 U.S. 190 (1888), that Congress and the President, acting together, can abrogate a treaty by passing a statute that overrides the treaty. In that case, the United States made a treaty with the Republic of San Domingo (now the Dominican Republic) saying that the United States would not impose a higher duty on articles imported from San Domingo than from other countries. Congress subsequently passed a statute that contradicted this treaty by exempting Hawaii (then an independent nation), but not San Domingo, from duties on centrifugal and molasses sugars. The Court rejected an argument by importers from San Domingo that, under the treaty, they should not have to pay a duty. The Court reasoned:

> By the constitution, a treaty is placed on the same footing, and made of like obligation, with an act of legislation. Both are declared by that instrument to be the supreme law of the land, and no superior efficacy is given to either over the other. When the two relate to the same subject, the courts will always endeavor to construe them so as to give effect to both, if that can be done without violating the language of either; but, if the two are inconsistent, the one last in date will control the other: provided, always, the stipulation of the treaty on the subject is self-executing.

Id. at 194.

The following case concerns the question whether it is possible for the President unilaterally, i.e., without the concurrence of Congress (or the Senate alone), to cause the United States to withdraw from a treaty. A little history is necessary for understanding what happened in the case. After World War II, two rival Chinese forces fought for control of China, and they formed two rival governments. The communist forces, led by Mao Zedong, established the People's Republic of China (PRC) with its capital in Peking (now known as Beijing). The nationalist forces, led by Chiang Kai-shek, established the Republic of China (ROC), with its capital on the island of Taiwan. Each government claimed to rule all of China. But in reality the PRC controlled the mainland, while the ROC controlled only Taiwan. In 1949, the United States entered into diplomatic relations and a mutual defense treaty with the ROC. But in 1978, President Carter announced that the United States would recognize the PRC as the sole government of China, effective January 1, 1979, and would simultaneously withdraw recognition from the ROC and terminate the mutual defense treaty. When Senator Barry Goldwater and others sued to enjoin this action, arguing that President Carter's action would violate the treaty, the Court of Appeals for the D.C. Circuit held that the President had not exceeded his authority. The case then went to the Supreme Court. Resolution of the issue divided the Court so much that a majority of justices could not agree on the proper analysis. But when all was said and done, the President did succeed in withdrawing the United States from the mutual defense treaty because neither the Supreme Court nor anyone else effectively intervened.

GOLDWATER V. CARTER

444 U.S. 996 (1979)

ORDER

The petition for a writ of certiorari is granted. The judgment of the Court of Appeals is vacated and the case is remanded to the District Court with directions to dismiss the complaint.

MR. JUSTICE MARSHALL concurs in the result.

MR. JUSTICE POWELL, concurring.

Although I agree with the result reached by the Court, I would dismiss the complaint as not ripe for judicial review. This Court has recognized that an issue should not be decided if it is not ripe for judicial review. *Buckley v. Valeo*, 424 U.S. 1, 113–114 (1976) (*per curiam*). Prudential considerations persuade me that a dispute between Congress and the President is not ready for judicial review unless and until each branch has taken action asserting its constitutional authority. Differences between the President and the Congress are commonplace under our system. The differences should, and almost invariably do, turn on political rather than legal considerations. The Judicial Branch should not decide issues affecting the allocation of power between the President and Congress until the political branches reach a constitutional impasse. Otherwise, we would encourage small groups or even individual Members of Congress to seek judicial resolution of issues before the normal political process has the opportunity to resolve the conflict.

> **Take Note**
>
> A majority of the Supreme Court agreed that the judgment of the Court of Appeals should be vacated and the case should be dismissed. But no group of five Justices could agree on the rationale for this result. So the Court simply issued this two-sentence order. Various Justices then wrote opinions explaining their views.

In this case, a few Members of Congress claim that the President's action in terminating the treaty with Taiwan has deprived them of their constitutional role with respect to a change in the supreme law of the land. Congress has taken no official action. In the present posture of this case, we do not know whether there ever will be an actual confrontation between the Legislative and Executive Branches. Although the Senate has considered a resolution declaring that Senate approval is necessary for the termination of any mutual defense treaty, see 125 Cong.Rec. S7015, S7038–S7039 (June 6, 1979), no final vote has been taken on the resolution. See *id.*, at S16683–S16692 (Nov. 15, 1979). Moreover, it is unclear whether the resolution would have retroactive effect. See *id.*, at S7054–S7064 (June 6, 1979); *id.*, at S7862 (June 18, 1979). It cannot be said that either the Senate or the House has rejected the President's claim. If the Congress chooses not to confront the President, it is not our task to do so. I therefore concur in the dismissal of this case.

MR. JUSTICE REHNQUIST, with whom THE CHIEF JUSTICE, MR. JUSTICE STEWART, and MR. JUSTICE STEVENS join, concurring in the judgment.

Take Note

Justice Rehnquist's opinion was supported by four justices. It is the "plurality opinion" because it received more votes than any other opinion. But it is still only a concurrence in the judgment, rather than a majority opinion.

I am of the view that the basic question presented by the petitioners in this case is "political" and therefore nonjusticiable because it involves the authority of the President in the conduct of our country's foreign relations and the extent to which the Senate or the Congress is authorized to negate the action of the President. * * * Here, while the Constitution is express as to the manner in which the Senate shall participate in the ratification of a treaty, it is silent as to that body's participation in the abrogation of a treaty. In this respect the case is directly analogous to *Coleman v. Miller*, 307 U.S. 433 (1939) [in which a plurality decided that the question whether a state ratified or rejected a constitutional amendment is a non-justiciable political question].

In light of the absence of any constitutional provision governing the termination of a treaty, and the fact that different termination procedures may be appropriate for different treaties, the instant case in my view also "must surely be controlled by political standards [rather than standards easily characterized as judicially manageable]." [*Dyer v. Blair*, 390 F. Supp. 1291, 1302 (N.D.Ill.1975) (three-judge court).] I think that the justifications for concluding that the question here is political in nature are even more compelling * * * because it involves foreign relations—specifically a treaty commitment to use military force in the defense of a foreign government if attacked.

Make the Connection

We discussed the political question doctrine in Chapter 2, in our consideration of the judicial power.

The present case differs in several important respects from *Youngstown Sheet & Tube Co. v. Sawyer*, 343 U.S. 579 (1952), cited by petitioners as authority both for reaching the merits of this dispute and for reversing the Court of Appeals. In *Youngstown*, private litigants brought a suit contesting the President's authority under his war powers to seize the Nation's steel industry, an action of profound and demonstrable domestic impact. Here, by contrast, we are asked to settle a dispute between coequal branches of our Government, each of which has resources available to protect and assert its interests, resources not available to private litigants outside the judicial forum. Moreover, as in *Curtiss-Wright,* the effect of this action, as far as we can tell, is "entirely external to the United States, and [falls] within the category of foreign affairs." Finally, as already noted, the situation presented here is closely akin to that presented in *Coleman,* where the Constitution spoke only to the procedure for ratification of an amendment, not to its rejection.

MR. JUSTICE BLACKMUN, with whom MR. JUSTICE WHITE joins, dissenting in part.

In my view, the time factor and its importance are illusory; if the President does not have the power to terminate the treaty (a substantial issue that we should address only after briefing and oral argument), the notice of intention to terminate surely has no legal effect. It is also indefensible, without further study, to pass on the issue of justiciability or on the issues of standing or ripeness. While I therefore join in the grant of the petition for certiorari, I would set the case for oral argument and give it the plenary consideration it so obviously deserves.

MR. JUSTICE BRENNAN, dissenting.

In stating that this case presents a nonjusticiable "political question," Mr. Justice Rehnquist, in my view, profoundly misapprehends the political-question principle as it applies to matters of foreign relations. Properly understood, the political-question doctrine restrains courts from reviewing an exercise of foreign policy judgment by the coordinate political branch to which authority to make that judgment has been "constitutional[ly] commit[ted]." *Baker v. Carr*, 369 U.S. 186, 211–213, 217 (1962). But the doctrine does not pertain when a court is faced with the *antecedent* question whether a particular branch has been constitutionally designated as the repository of political decisionmaking power. *Cf. Powell v. McCormack,* 395 U.S. 486, 519–521 (1969). The issue of decisionmaking authority must be resolved as a matter of constitutional law, not political discretion; accordingly, it falls within the competence of the courts.

The constitutional question raised here is prudently answered in narrow terms. Abrogation of the defense treaty with Taiwan was a necessary incident to Executive recognition of the Peking Government, because the defense treaty was predicated upon the now-abandoned view that the Taiwan Government was the only legitimate political authority in China. Our cases firmly establish that the Constitution commits to the President alone the power to recognize, and withdraw recognition from, foreign regimes. That mandate being clear, our judicial inquiry into the treaty rupture can go no further.

POINTS FOR DISCUSSION

a. Counting the Votes

How many Justices thought that the President had the authority to terminate the treaty? How many Justices thought that he did not? How many Justices thought that the Supreme Court could not decide the issue because it was not ripe? How many Justices thought that the Supreme Court could not decide the issue because it was a non-justiciable political question?

b. Advising the President

Suppose that the President wants to withdraw from a treaty with another country. Because the President is concerned that Congress will not support this move by passing legislation abrogating the treaty, the President is contemplating acting alone. The President asks you, "Can I pull the United States out of the treaty all by myself?" What legal and practical advice would you give the President?

c. Role for Congress

Justice Powell concluded that the case was not yet ripe for review. Did he think that it might have become ripe for review in the future? What steps could Congress have taken in opposing the President's actions other than having individual members of Congress bring a lawsuit?

Problem

Although the United States formally recognized Israel in 1948, as of 2015 no United States President had recognized Israeli sovereignty over Jerusalem. Instead, the Executive Branch maintained that "the status of Jerusalem . . . should be decided not unilaterally but in consultation with all concerned." United Nations Gen. Assembly Official Records, 5th Emergency Sess., 1554th Plenary Meetings, United Nations Doc. No. 1 A/PV.1554, p. 10 (July 14, 1967). The President's position on Jerusalem was reflected in State Department policy regarding passports and consular reports of birth abroad. Understanding that passports will be construed as reflections of American policy, the State Department's Foreign Affairs Manual instructs its employees, in general, to record the place of birth on a passport as the "country [having] present sovereignty over the actual area of birth." Dept. of State, 7 Foreign Affairs Manual (FAM) § 1383.4 (1987). The FAM, however, did not allow citizens to list a sovereign that conflicts with Executive Branch policy. See generally *id.*, § 1383. Because the United States does not recognize any country as having sovereignty over Jerusalem, the FAM instructed employees to record the place of birth for citizens born there as "Jerusalem."

In 2002, Congress passed the Foreign Relations Authorization Act, Fiscal Year 2003, 116 Stat. 1350. Section 214 of the Act, titled "United States Policy with Respect to Jerusalem as the Capital of Israel," sought to override the FAM by allowing citizens born in Jerusalem to list their place of birth as "Israel." § 214(d). Later that year, Menachem Binyamin Zivotofsky was born to United States citizens living in Jerusalem. In December 2002, Zivotofsky's mother visited the American Embassy in Tel Aviv to request both a passport and a consular report of birth abroad for her son. She asked that his place of birth be listed as "Jerusalem, Israel." The Embassy clerks explained that, pursuant to State Department policy, the passport would list only "Jerusalem." Zivotofsky's parents objected and, as his guardians, brought suit on his behalf in the United States District Court for the District of Columbia, seeking to enforce § 214(d). The Executive Branch defended by asserting that the President has the exclusive power of "recognition," which is a "formal acknowledgement" that a particular "entity possesses the qualifications for statehood" or "that a particular regime is the effective government of a state." Restatement (Third) of Foreign Relations Law of the United States § 203, Comment a, p. 84 (1986). The Executive Branch relied on Article II, § 3 of the U.S. Constitution, which provides that the President "shall receive Ambassadors and other public Ministers."

How should the Court rule? Does the Constitution expressly or implicitly address the power to recognize the boundaries of foreign nations? If not, is this power of recognition, in the words of *Curtiss-Wright,* one of the "necessary concomitants of nationality" that all sovereign nations possess? If so, is it a power that the President must enjoy exclusively, or should it be shared with Congress?

When the Supreme Court confronted this issue, it held that "judicial precedent and historical practice teach that it is for the President alone to make the specific decision of what foreign power he will recognize as legitimate, both for the Nation as a whole and for the purpose of making his own position clear within the context of recognition in discussions and negotiations with foreign nations." Accordingly, the Court concluded that Section 214(d) was invalid. See *Zivotofsky v. Kerry*, 576 U.S. 1 (2015). Should the Court have concluded that the case presented a non-justiciable political question?

In 2017, two years after the Court's decision, President Trump announced that the United States recognizes Jerusalem as Israel's capital.

C. THE PRESIDENT'S POWERS IN TIMES OF WAR

The Court in *Goldwater* declined to resolve an interbranch controversy over the respective powers of the President and Congress in a matter of foreign affairs. That controversy existed at least in part because the Constitution divides responsibility over matters of foreign affairs—and on the subject of treaties in particular—between the President and Congress.

Controversies have also long existed over the scope of the President's powers in times of war, in large part because the Constitution similarly divides responsibility between the President and Congress over matters related to war. The President is the Commander in Chief of the Armed Forces. But the Constitution also vests Congress with substantial authority over matters of war, including the power to "declare War" and to "make Rules concerning Captures on Land and Water," Art. I, § 8, cl. 11, to "raise and support Armies" and "provide and maintain a Navy," Art. I, § 8, cl. 12 & 13, and to "make Rules for the * * * Regulation of the land and naval Forces," Art. I, § 8, cl. 14. Not surprisingly given this arrangement, questions have often arisen about the respective roles of the President and Congress in matters of war. And, as in the *Goldwater* case, some of those questions have never been resolved.

Consider the case of the War Powers Resolution of 1973. After the United States had been involved in the Vietnam War for many years without a formal congressional declaration of war, Congress adopted a joint resolution to govern and limit the President's authority to involve the armed forces in hostilities. The stated purpose of the resolution was to "fulfill the intent of the framers of the Constitution of the United States and insure that the collective judgment of both the Congress and the President will apply to the introduction of United States Armed Forces into hostilities, or into situations where imminent involvement in hostilities is clearly indicated by the circumstances, and to the continued use of such forces in hostilities or in such situations." Although President Nixon vetoed the resolution, stating that it "would attempt to take away, by a mere legislative act, authorities which the President has properly exercised under the Constitution for almost 200 years," Congress overrode the veto with a super-majority vote in both houses.

The Resolution provides in relevant part:

> § 2(c). The constitutional powers of the President as Commander-in-Chief to introduce United States Armed Forces into hostilities, or into situations where imminent involvement in hostilities is clearly indicated

by the circumstances, are exercised only pursuant to (1) a declaration of war, (2) specific statutory authorization, or (3) a national emergency created by attack upon the United States, its territories or possessions, or its armed forces.

[§ 3 requires the President "in every possible instance" to "consult" with Congress before introducing the armed forces into hostilities and then regularly for the duration of the hostilities.]

§ 4(a). In the absence of a declaration of war, in any case in which United States Armed Forces are introduced [into hostilities,] the President shall submit within 48 hours to the Speaker of the House of Representatives and to the President pro tempore of the Senate a report, in writing, setting forth—(A) the circumstances necessitating the introduction of United States Armed Forces; (B) the constitutional and legislative authority under which such introduction took place; and (C) the estimated scope and duration of the hostilities or involvement.

[§ 4(b) requires the President to provide "such other information as the Congress may request."]

§ 5(b). Within sixty calendar days after a report is submitted or is required to be submitted pursuant to section 4(a)(1), whichever is earlier, the President shall terminate any use of United States Armed Forces with respect to which such report was submitted (or required to be submitted), unless the Congress (1) has declared war or has enacted a specific authorization for such use of United States Armed Forces, (2) has extended by law such sixty-day period, or (3) is physically unable to meet as a result of an armed attack upon the United States. Such sixty-day period shall be extended for not more than an additional thirty days if the President determines and certifies to the Congress in writing that unavoidable military necessity respecting the safety of United States Armed Forces requires the continued use of such armed forces in the course of bringing about a prompt removal of such forces.

§ 5(c). Notwithstanding subsection (b), at any time that United States Armed Forces are engaged in hostilities outside the territory of the United States, its possessions and territories without a declaration of war or specific statutory authorization, such forces shall be removed by the President if the Congress so directs by concurrent resolution.

Is the War Powers Resolution constitutional? Is it merely an implementation of Congress's authority to declare war—and effectively Congress's attempt to define what counts as war? Or is it an impermissible interference with the President's role as Commander-in-Chief? Does Congress possess any other authority, short of declaring war, effectively to control the President's commitment of the armed forces to hostilities?

Presidents of both parties have taken the position that the War Powers Resolution is unconstitutional. They have also read it narrowly. For example, Presidents of both parties have taken the view that the Resolution "recognizes and presupposes the existence of unilateral Presidential authority" to "introduce troops into hostilities or potential hostilities without prior authorization by the Congress." Opinion of the Office of Legal Counsel on the Deployment of United States Armed Forces Into Haiti (Sept. 27, 1994). (Do you agree with this interpretation?) Since 1973, Presidents have sometimes complied with the Resolution's reporting requirements; other times they have not.

The Court has never addressed the constitutionality of the War Powers Resolution. Is the absence of judicial resolution of this question problematic? Or does it leave the question of authority over matters of war in the proper forum?

When the Nation goes to war, the President not only must make decisions about how to use military force, but also must make decisions about how to deal with persons captured in the course of armed conflicts. We focus here on a question that has taken on particular urgency in recent years, in the wake of the terrorist attacks of September 11, 2001: the President's power to detain and create rules for trying persons accused of acting as enemy combatants.

The following very heavily edited case arose out of America's use of military force following the terrorist attack of September 11, 2001. We include it, rather than earlier decisions, because of its obvious contemporary significance and because it contains the latest words on the President's war powers. But a small amount of background about two significant earlier cases might be useful. In *Ex parte Milligan*, 71 U.S. 2 (1866), the Court granted a writ of habeas corpus to Milligan, a citizen of Indiana who had not served in the armed forces during the Civil War. Milligan had been detained in 1864 by the United States military and accused of plotting against military authorities. He was tried, before the war ended, by a military commission and sentenced to death. Although a civilian grand jury convened after the end of the Civil War failed to indict Milligan, the government announced its intention to proceed with Milligan's execution. Milligan challenged that decision in federal court. Justice Davis, who had been Lincoln's friend and campaign manager, wrote the opinion shortly after the former President's assassination. The Court held that Milligan could not be tried by a military commission. The Court explained: "Civil liberty and this kind of martial law cannot endure together * * * [and] can never exist where the courts are open, and in the proper and unobstructed exercise of their jurisdiction."

Ex parte Quirin, 317 U.S. 1 (1942), concerned eight Nazi saboteurs who used a German submarine to sneak into the United States during World War II with orders to commit a series of attacks in the United States. After the saboteurs were captured, President Roosevelt ordered the men tried by a military commission. The government charged the saboteurs with violating the laws of war by, among other things, crossing military lines out of uniform. The men, at least one of whom was an American citizen, unsuccessfully challenged the legality of the tribunal. The Court distinguished *Ex parte Milligan* on the ground that the petitioners had been charged with violating the laws of war rather than domestic law. *Ex parte Quirin* is a famous but controversial case. It appears that two of the saboteurs never intended to carry out the plan, and that after landing they informed the FBI about the plot. They nevertheless were tried before the military commission and (at least initially) sentenced to death. In addition, the historical record reveals that President Roosevelt's Attorney General personally lobbied the Justices of the Supreme Court to uphold the military tribunal commissioned to try the eight men. The Court issued its opinion in the case only after six of the men (those who had not informed law enforcement authorities of the plot) had already been executed. See Jonathan Turley, *Art and the Constitution: The Supreme Court and the Rise of the Impressionist School of Constitutional Interpretation*, 2004 Cato Sup. Ct. Rev. 69.

Finally, in 1948, Congress enacted the Non-Detention Act, 18 U.S.C. § 4001(a), which provides: "No citizen shall be imprisoned or otherwise detained by the United States except pursuant to an Act of Congress." It was against this background that the Court decided the most recent cases on the scope of the President's authority to detain enemy combatants. In reading the case that follows, you will see that although the Court concluded that Congress gave the President authority to use military force, substantial questions still arose about the scope of that authority. Pay particularly close attention to two points: (1) the division of opinions among the Justices on basic issues regarding the President's war powers; and (2) the Justices' treatment of precedents from the World War II era.

HAMDI V. RUMSFELD

542 U.S. 507 (2004)

JUSTICE O'CONNOR announced the judgment of the Court and delivered an opinion, in which THE CHIEF JUSTICE, JUSTICE KENNEDY, and JUSTICE BREYER join.

> **Take Note**
>
> Justice O'Connor's opinion was supported by four justices. It is the "plurality opinion" because it received more votes than any other.

At this difficult time in our Nation's history, we are called upon to consider the legality of the Government's detention of a United States citizen on United States soil as an "enemy combatant" and to address the process that is constitutionally owed to one who seeks to challenge his classification as such. The United States Court of Appeals for the Fourth Circuit held that petitioner's detention was legally authorized and that he was entitled to no further opportunity to challenge his enemy-combatant label. We now vacate and remand. We hold that although Congress authorized the detention of combatants in the narrow circumstances alleged here, due process demands that a citizen held in the United States as an enemy combatant be given a meaningful opportunity to contest the factual basis for that detention before a neutral decisionmaker.

On September 11, 2001, the al Qaeda terrorist network used hijacked commercial airliners to attack prominent targets in the United States. Approximately 3,000 people were killed in those attacks. One week later, in response to these "acts of treacherous violence," Congress passed a resolution authorizing the President to "use all necessary and appropriate force against those nations, organizations, or persons he determines planned, authorized, committed, or aided the terrorist attacks" or "harbored such organizations or persons, in order to prevent any future acts of international terrorism against the United States by such nations, organizations or persons." Authorization for Use of Military Force ("the AUMF"), 115 Stat. 224. Soon thereafter, the President ordered United States Armed Forces to Afghanistan, with a mission to subdue al Qaeda and quell the Taliban regime that was known to support it.

This case arises out of the detention of a man whom the Government alleges took up arms with the Taliban during this conflict. His name is Yaser Esam Hamdi. Born an American citizen in Louisiana in 1980, Hamdi moved with his family to Saudi Arabia as a child. By 2001, the parties agree, he resided in Afghanistan. At some point that year, he was seized by members of the Northern Alliance, a coalition of military groups opposed to the Taliban government, and eventually was turned over to the United States military.

The Government asserts that it initially detained and interrogated Hamdi in Afghanistan before transferring him to the United States Naval Base in Guantanamo Bay in January 2002. In April 2002, upon learning that Hamdi is an American citizen, authorities transferred him to a naval brig in Norfolk, Virginia, where he remained until a recent transfer to a brig in Charleston, South Carolina. The Government contends that Hamdi is an "enemy combatant," and that this status justifies holding him in the United States indefinitely—without formal charges or proceedings—unless and until it makes the determination that access to counsel or further process is warranted.

The threshold question before us is whether the Executive has the authority to detain citizens who qualify as "enemy combatants." There is some debate as to the proper scope of this term, and the Government has never provided any court with the full criteria that it uses in classifying individuals as such. It has made clear, however, that, for purposes of this case, the "enemy combatant" that it is seeking to detain is an individual who, it alleges, was "part of or supporting forces hostile to the United States or coalition partners" in Afghanistan and who "engaged in an armed conflict against the United States" there. Brief for Respondents 3. We therefore answer only the narrow question before us: whether the detention of citizens falling within that definition is authorized.

> **FYI**
>
> Hamdi's father challenged Hamdi's detention by filing a petition for a writ of habeas corpus. A writ of habeas corpus requires the government to release a prisoner unless the government can show legal cause for the detention. The power of courts to grant writs of habeas corpus is an important safeguard against tyranny because it prevents the government from arbitrarily detaining persons (including opponents of the government or supporters of unpopular causes). The Constitution's "Suspension Clause" in Article I, § 9, cl. 2, protects the writ by saying: "The Privilege of the Writ of Habeas Corpus shall not be suspended, unless when in Cases of Rebellion or Invasion the public Safety may require it." No one contended in this case that Congress or the President had suspended the writ of habeas corpus.

The Government maintains that no explicit congressional authorization is required, because the Executive possesses plenary authority to detain pursuant to Article II of the Constitution. We do not reach the question whether Article II provides such authority, however, because we agree with the Government's alternative position, that Congress has in fact authorized Hamdi's detention, through the AUMF.

The AUMF authorizes the President to use "all necessary and appropriate force" against "nations, organizations, or persons" associated with the September 11, 2001, terrorist attacks. 115 Stat. 224. There can be no doubt that individuals who fought against the United States in Afghanistan as part of the Taliban, an organization known to have supported the al Qaeda terrorist network responsible for those attacks, are individuals Congress sought to target in passing the AUMF. We conclude that detention of individuals falling into the limited category we are considering, for the duration of the particular conflict in which they were captured, is so fundamental and accepted an incident to war as to be an exercise of the "necessary and appropriate force" Congress has authorized the President to use.

The capture and detention of lawful combatants and the capture, detention, and trial of unlawful combatants, by "universal agreement and practice," are "important incident[s] of war." Ex parte Quirin, 317 U.S. 1 (1942). The purpose of detention is to prevent captured individuals from returning to the field of battle and taking up arms once again.

There is no bar to this Nation's holding one of its own citizens as an enemy combatant. In *Quirin,* one of the detainees, Haupt, alleged that he was a naturalized United States citizen. 317 U.S., at 20. We held that "[c]itizens who associate themselves with the military arm of the enemy government, and with its aid, guidance and direction enter this country bent on hostile acts, are enemy belligerents within the meaning of . . . the law of war." *Id.,* at 37–38. While Haupt was tried for violations of the law of war, nothing in *Quirin* suggests that his citizenship would have precluded his mere detention for the duration of the relevant hostilities. See *id.,* at 30–31. Nor can we see any reason for drawing such a line here. A citizen, no less than an alien, can be "part of or supporting forces hostile to the United States or coalition partners" and "engaged in an armed conflict against the United States," Brief for Respondents 3; such a citizen, if released, would pose the same threat of returning to the front during the ongoing conflict.

In light of these principles, it is of no moment that the AUMF does not use specific language of detention. Because detention to prevent a combatant's return to the battlefield is a fundamental incident of waging war, in permitting the use of "necessary and appropriate force," Congress has clearly and unmistakably authorized detention in the narrow circumstances considered here.

> **Take Note**
>
> Do you agree that Congress has "clearly and unmistakably" authorized detention in the particular circumstances at issue in this case? Would it matter if Congress had done so merely by implication?

Hamdi objects, nevertheless, that Congress has not authorized the *indefinite* detention to which he is now subject. The Government responds that "the detention of enemy combatants during World War II was just as 'indefinite' while that war was being fought." We take Hamdi's objection to be not to the lack of certainty regarding the date on which the conflict will end, but to the substantial prospect of perpetual detention. We recognize that the national security underpinnings of the "war on terror," although crucially important, are broad and malleable. As the Government concedes, "given its unconventional nature, the current conflict is unlikely to end with a formal cease-fire agreement." The prospect Hamdi raises is therefore not far-fetched. If the Government does not consider this unconventional war won for two generations, and if it maintains during that time that Hamdi might, if released, rejoin forces fighting against the United States, then the position it has taken throughout the litigation of this case suggests that Hamdi's detention could last for the rest of his life. It is a clearly established principle of the law of war that detention may last no longer than active hostilities. See Article 118 of the Geneva Convention (III) Relative to the Treatment of Prisoners of War, Aug. 12, 1949, [1955] 6 U.S.T. 3316, 3406, T.I.A.S. No. 3364 ("Prisoners of war shall be released and repatriated without delay after the cessation of active hostilities").

Hamdi contends that the AUMF does not authorize indefinite or perpetual detention. Certainly, we agree that indefinite detention for the purpose of interrogation is not authorized. Further, we understand Congress' grant of authority for the use of "necessary and appropriate force" to include the authority to detain for the duration of the relevant conflict, and our understanding is based on longstanding law-of-war principles. If the practical circumstances of a given conflict are entirely unlike those of the conflicts that informed the development of the law of war, that understanding may unravel. But that is not the situation we face as of this date. Active combat operations against Taliban fighters apparently are ongoing in Afghanistan. The United States may detain, for the duration of these hostilities, individuals legitimately determined to be Taliban combatants who "engaged in an armed conflict against the United States." If the record establishes that United States troops are still involved in active combat in Afghanistan, those detentions are part of the exercise of "necessary and appropriate force," and therefore are authorized by the AUMF.

[Although the plurality concluded that the AUMF authorized the President to detain enemy combatants, it concluded that the Due Process Clause requires that "a citizen-detainee seeking to challenge his classification as an enemy combatant * * * receive notice of the factual basis for his classification, and a fair opportunity to rebut the Government's factual assertions before a neutral decisionmaker."]

In so holding, we necessarily reject the Government's assertion that separation of powers principles mandate a heavily circumscribed role for the courts in such circumstances. Indeed, the position that the courts must forgo any examination of the individual case and focus exclusively on the legality of the broader detention scheme cannot be mandated by any reasonable view of separation of powers, as this approach serves only to condense power into a single branch of government. We have long since made clear that a state of war is not a blank check for the President when it comes to the rights of the Nation's citizens. *Youngstown Sheet & Tube v. Sawyer*, 343 U.S. 579, 587 (1952). Whatever power the United States Constitution envisions for the Executive in its exchanges with other nations or with enemy organizations in times of conflict, it most assuredly envisions a role for all three branches when individual liberties are at stake. * * * Thus, while we do not question that our due process assessment must pay keen attention to the particular burdens faced by the Executive in the context of military action, it would turn our system of checks and balances on its head to suggest that a citizen could not make his way to court with a challenge to the factual basis for his detention by his Government, simply because the Executive opposes making available such a challenge.

[The Court remanded the case to allow for a determination whether Hamdi actually was an enemy combatant.]

JUSTICE SOUTER, with whom JUSTICE GINSBURG joins, concurring in part, dissenting in part, and concurring in the judgment.

The threshold issue is how broadly or narrowly to read the Non-Detention Act, the tone of which is severe: "No citizen shall be imprisoned or otherwise detained by the United States except pursuant to an Act of Congress." 18 U.S.C. § 4001(a). Should the severity of the Act be relieved when the Government's stated factual justification for incommunicado detention is a war on terrorism, so that the Government may be said to act "pursuant" to congressional terms that fall short of explicit authority to imprison individuals? With one possible though important qualification, the answer has to be no.

The fact that Congress intended to guard against a repetition of the World War II internments when it * * * gave us § 4001(a) provides a powerful reason to think that § 4001(a) was meant to require clear congressional authorization before any citizen can be placed in a cell. It is not merely that the legislative history shows that § 4001(a) was thought necessary in anticipation of times just

> **Make the Connection**
>
> We consider the government's internment of Japanese-American citizens during World War II, and the Court's decision in *Korematsu v. United States*, in Volume 2.

like the present, in which the safety of the country is threatened. To appreciate what is most significant, one must only recall that the internments of the 1940s were accomplished by Executive action.

[E]ven if history had spared us the cautionary example of the internments in World War II, * * * there would be a compelling reason to read § 4001(a) to demand manifest authority to detain before detention is authorized. The defining character of American constitutional government is its constant tension between security and liberty, serving both by partial helpings of each. In a government of separated powers, deciding finally on what is a reasonable degree of guaranteed liberty whether in peace or war (or some condition in between) is not well entrusted to the Executive Branch of Government, whose particular responsibility is to maintain security. For reasons of inescapable human nature, the branch of the Government asked to counter a serious threat is not the branch on which to rest the Nation's entire reliance in striking the balance between the will to win and the cost in liberty on the way to victory; the responsibility for security will naturally amplify the claim that security legitimately raises. A reasonable balance is more likely to be reached on the judgment of a different branch * * *. Hence the need for an assessment by Congress before citizens are subject to lockup, and likewise the need for a clearly expressed congressional resolution of the competing claims.

Under this principle of reading § 4001(a) robustly to require a clear statement of authorization to detain, none of the Government's arguments suffices to justify Hamdi's detention. * * * Since the Force Resolution was adopted one week after the attacks of September 11, 2001, it naturally speaks with some generality, but its focus is clear, and that is on the use of military power. It is fairly read to authorize the use of armies and weapons, whether against other armies or individual terrorists. But * * * it never so much as uses the word detention, and there is no reason to think Congress might have perceived any need to augment Executive power to deal with dangerous citizens within the United States, given the well-stocked statutory arsenal of defined criminal offenses covering the gamut of actions that a citizen sympathetic to terrorists might commit. See, *e.g.*, 18 U.S.C. § 2339A (material support for various terrorist acts); § 2339B (material support to a foreign terrorist organization); § 2332a (use of a weapon of mass destruction, including conspiracy and attempt); § 2332b(a)(1) (acts of terrorism "transcending national boundaries," including threats, conspiracy, and attempt); 18 U.S.C. § 2339C (financing of certain terrorist acts); see also 18 U.S.C. § 3142(e) (pretrial detention).

Since the Government has given no reason either to deflect the application of § 4001(a) or to hold it to be satisfied, I need to go no further; the Government hints of a constitutional challenge to the statute, but it presents none here. I will, however, stray across the line between statutory and constitutional territory just far enough to note the weakness of the Government's mixed claim of inherent, extrastatutory authority under a combination of Article II of the Constitution and the usages of war. It is in fact in this connection that the Government developed its argument that the exercise of war powers justifies the detention, and what I have just said about its inadequacy applies here as well. Beyond that, it is instructive to recall Justice Jackson's observation that the President is not Commander in Chief of the country, only of the military. *Youngstown Sheet & Tube Co. v. Sawyer*, 343 U.S. 579, 643–644 (1952) (concurring opinion); see also *id.*, at 637–638 (Presidential authority is "at its lowest ebb" where the President acts contrary to congressional will).

There may be room for one qualification to Justice Jackson's statement, however: in a moment of genuine emergency, when the Government must act with no time for deliberation, the Executive may be able to detain a citizen if there is reason to fear he is an imminent threat to the safety of the Nation and its people. This case, however, does not present that question, because an emergency power of necessity must at least be limited by the emergency; Hamdi has been locked up for over two years. Cf. Ex parte Milligan, 4 Wall. 2, 127 (1866) (martial law justified only by "actual and present" necessity as in a genuine invasion that closes civilian courts). * * * Whether insisting on the careful scrutiny of emergency claims or on a vigorous reading of § 4001(a), we are heirs to a tradition given voice 800 years ago by Magna Carta, which, on the barons' insistence, confined executive power by "the law of the land."

Because I find Hamdi's detention forbidden by § 4001(a) and unauthorized by the Force Resolution, I would not reach any questions of what process he may be due in litigating disputed issues in a proceeding under the habeas statute or prior to the habeas enquiry itself. * * * Since this disposition does not command a majority of the Court, however, the need to give practical effect to the conclusions of eight Members of the Court rejecting the Government's position calls for me to join with the plurality in ordering remand on terms closest to those I would impose.

Take Note

Why did Justice Souter decide that the President does not have authority to detain Hamdi? If Hamdi had been killed by American forces in armed combat on a battlefield in Afghanistan, would that action have been authorized? If so, why can't the government take the lesser step of detaining him in the United States indefinitely?

JUSTICE SCALIA, with whom JUSTICE STEVENS joins, dissenting.

Where the Government accuses a citizen of waging war against it, our constitutional tradition has been to prosecute him in federal court for treason or some other crime. Where the exigencies of war prevent that, the Constitution's Suspension Clause, Art. I, § 9, cl. 2, allows Congress to relax the usual protections temporarily. Absent suspension, however, the Executive's assertion of military exigency has not been thought sufficient to permit detention without charge. No one contends that the congressional Authorization for Use of Military Force, on which the Government relies to justify its actions here, is an implementation of the Suspension Clause. Accordingly, I would reverse the decision below.

The very core of liberty secured by our Anglo-Saxon system of separated powers has been freedom from indefinite imprisonment at the will of the Executive. * * * The gist of the Due Process Clause, as understood at the founding and since, was to force the Government to follow those common-law procedures traditionally deemed necessary before depriving a person of life, liberty, or property. * * * These due process rights have historically been vindicated by the writ of habeas corpus. In England before the founding, the writ developed into a tool for challenging executive confinement. * * * The writ of habeas corpus was preserved in the Constitution—the only common-law writ to be explicitly mentioned. See Art. I, § 9, cl. 2.

The allegations here, of course, are no ordinary accusations of criminal activity. [Hamdi] has been imprisoned because the Government believes he participated in the waging of war against the United States. The relevant question, then, is whether there is a different, special procedure for imprisonment of a citizen accused of wrongdoing by aiding the enemy in wartime. [The plurality] asserts that captured enemy combatants (other than those suspected of war crimes) have traditionally been detained until the cessation of hostilities and then released. That is probably an accurate description of wartime practice with respect to enemy aliens. The tradition with respect to American citizens, however, has been quite different. Citizens aiding the enemy have been treated as traitors subject to the criminal process.

There are times when military exigency renders resort to the traditional criminal process impracticable. English law accommodated such exigencies by allowing legislative suspension of the writ of habeas corpus for brief periods. * * * Our Federal Constitution contains a provision explicitly permitting suspension, but limiting the situations in which it may be invoked: "The privilege of the Writ of Habeas Corpus shall not be suspended, unless when in Cases of Rebellion or Invasion the public Safety may require it." Art. I, § 9, cl. 2. Although this provision does not state that suspension must be effected by, or authorized by, a legislative act, it has been so understood, consistent with English practice and the Clause's placement in Article I. See Ex parte Merryman, 17 F. Cas. 144, 151–152 (Cir. Ct. D Md. 1861) (Taney, C. J., rejecting Lincoln's unauthorized suspension); 3 J. Story, Commentaries on the Constitution of the United States § 1336, at 208–209 (1833).

The Suspension Clause was by design a safety valve, the Constitution's only "express provision for exercise of extraordinary authority because of a crisis," *Youngstown Sheet & Tube Co. v. Sawyer*, 343 U.S. 579, 650 (1952) (Jackson, J., concurring). Very early in the Nation's history, President Jefferson unsuccessfully sought a suspension of habeas corpus to deal with Aaron Burr's conspiracy to overthrow the Government. See 16 Annals of Congress 402–425 (1807). During the Civil War, Congress passed its first Act authorizing Executive suspension of the writ of habeas corpus, see Act of Mar. 3, 1863, 12 Stat. 755, to the relief of those many who thought President Lincoln's unauthorized proclamations of suspension (*e.g.*, Proclamation No. 1, 13 Stat. 730 (1862)) unconstitutional. Later Presidential proclamations of suspension relied upon the congressional authorization, *e.g.*, Proclamation No. 7, 13 Stat. 734 (1863). During Reconstruction, Congress passed the Ku Klux Klan Act, which included a provision authorizing suspension of the writ, invoked by President Grant in quelling a rebellion in nine South Carolina counties.

[T]he reasoning and conclusion of *Milligan* logically cover the present case. The Government justifies imprisonment of Hamdi on principles of the law of war and admits that, absent the war, it would have no such authority. But if the law of war cannot be applied to citizens where courts are open, then Hamdi's imprisonment without criminal trial is no less unlawful than Milligan's trial by military tribunal.

The proposition that the Executive lacks indefinite wartime detention authority over citizens is consistent with the Founders' general mistrust of military power permanently at the Executive's disposal. In the Founders' view, the "blessings of liberty" were threatened by "those military establishments which must gradually poison its very fountain." The Federalist No. 45, p. 238 (J. Madison). * * * Except for the actual command of military forces, all authorization for their maintenance and all explicit authorization for their use is placed in the control of Congress under Article I, rather than the President under Article II. As Hamilton explained, the President's military authority would be "much inferior" to that of the British King. [The Federalist No. 69, p. 357.] A view of the Constitution that gives the Executive authority to use military force rather than the force of law against citizens on American soil flies in the face of the mistrust that engendered these provisions.

The Government argues that our more recent jurisprudence ratifies its indefinite imprisonment of a citizen within the territorial jurisdiction of federal courts. * * * In [Ex parte Quirin, 317 U.S. 1 (1942),] it was uncontested that the petitioners were members of enemy forces. * * * But where those jurisdictional facts are not conceded—where the petitioner insists that he is not a belligerent—*Quirin* left the pre-existing law in place: Absent suspension of the writ, a citizen held where the courts are open is entitled either to criminal trial or to a judicial decree requiring his release.

It follows from what I have said that Hamdi is entitled to a habeas decree requiring his release unless (1) criminal proceedings are promptly brought, or (2) Congress has suspended the writ of habeas corpus. A suspension of the writ could, of course, lay down conditions for continued detention, similar to those that today's opinion prescribes under the Due Process Clause. But there is a world of difference between the people's representatives' determining the need for that suspension (and prescribing the conditions for it), and this Court's doing so.

The plurality finds justification for Hamdi's imprisonment in the Authorization for Use of Military Force. * * * This is not remotely a congressional suspension of the writ, and no one claims that it is. Contrary to the plurality's view, I do not think this statute even authorizes detention of a citizen with the clarity necessary * * * to overcome [18 U.S.C. § 4001(a).] But even if it did, I would not permit it to overcome Hamdi's entitlement to habeas corpus relief. The Suspension Clause of the Constitution, which carefully circumscribes the conditions under which the writ can be withheld, would be a sham if it could be evaded by congressional prescription of requirements other than the common-law requirement of committal for criminal prosecution that render the writ, though available, unavailing. If the Suspension Clause does not guarantee the citizen that he will either be tried or released, unless the conditions for suspending the writ exist and the grave action of suspending the writ has been taken; if it merely guarantees the citizen that he will not be detained unless Congress by ordinary legislation says he can be detained; it guarantees him very little indeed.

Several limitations give my views in this matter a relatively narrow compass. They apply only to citizens, accused of being enemy combatants, who are detained within the territorial jurisdiction of a federal court. * * * Where the citizen is captured outside and held outside the United States, the constitutional requirements may be different. Moreover, even within the United States, the accused citizen-enemy combatant may lawfully be detained once prosecution is in progress or in contemplation.

I frankly do not know whether these tools are sufficient to meet the Government's security needs, including the need to obtain intelligence through interrogation. It is far beyond my competence, or the Court's competence, to determine that. But it is not beyond Congress's. If the situation demands it, the Executive can ask Congress to authorize suspension of the writ—which can be made subject to whatever conditions Congress deems appropriate, including even the procedural novelties invented by the plurality today. To be sure, suspension is limited by the Constitution to cases of rebellion or invasion. But whether the attacks of September 11, 2001, constitute an "invasion," and whether those attacks still justify suspension several years later, are questions for Congress rather than this Court. If civil rights are to be curtailed during wartime, it must be done openly and democratically, as the Constitution requires, rather than by silent erosion through an opinion of this Court.

> **Take Note**
>
> Justice Scalia suggests that the question whether the circumstances justifying suspension exist is a non-justiciable political question. If Congress can simply declare an emergency and suspend the writ indefinitely, without judicial oversight, is there sufficient protection for the liberty interests that Justice Scalia said are protected by the writ in the first place? See Amanda L. Tyler, *Is Suspension a Political Question?* 59 Stan. L. Rev. 333 (2006).

The Founders well understood the difficult tradeoff between safety and freedom. [They] warned us about the risk, and equipped us with a Constitution designed to deal with it. Many think it not only inevitable but entirely proper that liberty give way to security in times of national crisis * * *. Whatever the general merits of the view that war silences law or modulates its voice, that view has no place in the interpretation and application of a Constitution designed precisely to confront war and, in a manner that accords with democratic principles, to accommodate it. Because the Court has proceeded to meet the current emergency in a manner the Constitution does not envision, I respectfully dissent.

JUSTICE THOMAS, dissenting.

The Executive Branch, acting pursuant to the powers vested in the President by the Constitution and with explicit congressional approval, has determined that Hamdi is an enemy combatant and should be detained. This detention falls squarely within the Federal Government's war powers, and we lack the expertise and capacity to second-guess that decision.

[B]ecause the Founders understood that they could not foresee the myriad potential threats to national security that might later arise, they chose to create a Federal Government that necessarily possesses sufficient power to handle any threat to the security of the Nation. * * * The Founders intended that the President have primary responsibility—along with the necessary power—to protect the national security and to conduct the Nation's foreign relations. They did so principally because the structural advantages of a unitary Executive are essential in these domains.

These structural advantages are most important in the national-security and foreign-affairs contexts. * * * To this end, the Constitution vests in the President "[t]he executive Power," Art. II, § 1, provides that he "shall be Commander in Chief of the" Armed Forces, § 2, and places in him the power to recognize foreign governments, § 3. This Court has long recognized these features and has accordingly held that the President has constitutional authority to protect the national security and that this authority carries with it broad discretion. * * * Congress, to be sure, has a substantial and essential role in both foreign affairs and national security. But it is crucial to recognize that judicial interference in these domains destroys the purpose of vesting primary responsibility in a unitary Executive.

For these institutional reasons and because "Congress cannot anticipate and legislate with regard to every possible action the President may find it necessary to take or every possible situation in which he might act," it should come as no surprise that "[s]uch failure of Congress does not, especially in the areas of foreign policy and national security, imply congressional disapproval of action taken by the Executive." *Dames & Moore v. Regan*, 453 U.S. 654, 678 (1981). Rather, in these domains, the fact that Congress has provided the President with broad authorities does not imply—and the Judicial Branch should not infer—that Congress intended to deprive him of particular powers not specifically enumerated. See *Dames & Moore*, 453 U.S. at 678.

I acknowledge that the question whether Hamdi's executive detention is lawful is a question properly resolved by the Judicial Branch, though the question comes to the Court with the strongest presumptions in favor of the Government. The plurality agrees that Hamdi's detention is lawful if he is an enemy combatant. But the question whether Hamdi is actually an enemy combatant is "of a kind for which the Judiciary has neither aptitude, facilities nor responsibility and which has long been held to belong in the domain of political power not subject to judicial intrusion or inquiry." *Chicago & Southern Air Lines, Inc. v. Waterman S.S. Corp.*, 333 U.S. 103, 111 (1948). That is, although it is appropriate for the Court to determine the judicial question whether the President has the asserted authority, we lack the information and expertise to question whether Hamdi is actually an enemy combatant, a question the resolution of which is committed to other branches.

Although the President very well may have inherent authority to detain those arrayed against our troops, I agree with the plurality that we need not decide that question because Congress [in the AUMF] has authorized the President to do so. * * * But I do not think that the plurality has adequately explained the breadth of the President's authority to detain enemy combatants, an authority that includes making virtually conclusive factual findings. In my view, the structural considerations discussed above, as recognized in our precedent, demonstrate that we lack the capacity and responsibility to second-guess this determination. In a case strikingly similar to this one, the Court addressed a Governor's authority to detain for an extended period a person the executive believed to be responsible, in part, for a local insurrection. Justice Holmes wrote for a unanimous Court:

> "When it comes to a decision by the head of the State upon a matter involving its life, the ordinary rights of individuals must yield to what *he deems* the necessities of the moment. Public danger warrants the substitution of executive process for judicial process. This was admitted with regard to killing men in the actual clash of arms, and we think it obvious, although it was disputed, that the same is true of temporary detention to prevent apprehended harm." *Moyer v. Peabody*, 212 U.S. 78 (1909).

The Court answered Moyer's claim that he had been denied due process by emphasizing that

> "it is familiar that what is due process of law depends on circumstances. It varies with the subject-matter and the necessities of the situation. Thus summary proceedings suffice for taxes, and executive decisions for exclusion from the country. . . . Such arrests are not necessarily for punishment, but are by way of precaution to prevent the exercise of hostile power." *Id.,* at 84–85 (citations omitted).

In this context, due process requires nothing more than a good-faith executive determination. To be clear: The Court has held that an executive, acting pursuant to statutory and constitutional authority may, consistent with the Due Process Clause, unilaterally decide to detain an individual if the executive deems this necessary for the public safety *even if he is mistaken.*

POINTS FOR DISCUSSION

a. Comparing the Opinions

How is Justice Scalia's opinion different from Justice Souter's opinion? How would each of them rule on a case involving the detention of a *non*-citizen? How is Justice O'Connor's opinion different from Justice Thomas's opinion? What are the various Justices' views about the President's statutory authority to detain a citizen? The President's constitutional authority?

b. Deference to the Executive

Justice Thomas agreed with the plurality opinion by Justice O'Connor that the Authorization to Use Military Force allowed the President to order the detention of enemy combatants. But he disagreed with the plurality's conclusion that the President's determination of who was an enemy combatant was subject to judicial interference. (Although Justice Thomas's position on this issue received only one vote at the Supreme Court, it was the view of the court of appeals. See *Hamdi v. Rumsfeld*, 316 F.3d 450 (4th Cir. 2003).) If the President or his military subordinate orders an airstrike against suspected enemy combatants, may a court assert jurisdiction to determine whether the intended targets actually are enemy combatants? If not, why is this case different?

c. Aftermath of the Decision

Following this decision, the Department of Defense created Combatant Status Review Tribunals (i.e., hearing bodies composed of military officers) to determine whether individual detainees in fact were combatants. Much litigation has followed over the adequacy of the procedures followed by these tribunals. The United States returned Yaser Hamdi to Saudi Arabia on October 11, 2004, pursuant to an agreement in which Hamdi renounced his American citizenship and promised not to leave Saudi Arabia for five years. Saudi Arabia took no action against him. See Joel Brinkley, *From Afghanistan to Saudi Arabia, via Guantanamo*, N.Y. Times, Oct. 16, 2004, at A4.

d. Detaining Citizens Captured in the United States

Hamdi concerned the President's power to detain a citizen captured on a battlefield abroad and alleged to be an enemy combatant. What are the limits on the President's power to detain a citizen captured *in the United States*? The Court was presented with this question in *Rumsfeld v. Padilla*, 542 U.S. 426 (2004), but a five-Justice majority declined to decide the issue, concluding that the respondent had filed his petition for a writ of habeas corpus in the wrong district court and against the wrong defendant. Justice Stevens, joined by Justices Souter, Ginsburg, and Breyer, dissented, concluding that Congress had not, in the AUMF, authorized the detention of an American citizen arrested in the United States. (Justice Breyer had reached the opposite conclusion in *Hamdi* with respect to citizens captured abroad.) Justice Stevens asserted:

> "At stake in this case is nothing less than the essence of a free society. Even more important than the method of selecting the people's rulers and their successors is the character of the constraints imposed on the Executive by the rule of law. Unconstrained executive detention for the purpose of investigating and preventing subversive activity is the hallmark of the Star Chamber. Access to counsel for the purpose of protecting the citizen from official mistakes and mistreatment is the hallmark of due process. Executive detention of subversive citizens, like detention of enemy soldiers to keep them off the battlefield, may sometimes be justified to prevent persons from launching or becoming missiles of destruction. It may not, however, be justified by the naked interest in using unlawful procedures to extract information. Incommunicado detention for months on end is such a procedure. Whether the information so procured is more or less reliable than that acquired by more extreme forms of torture is of no consequence. For if this Nation is to remain true to the ideals symbolized by its flag, it must not wield the tools of tyrants even to resist an assault by the forces of tyranny."

Justice Scalia's opinion in *Hamdi* makes clear that he would have agreed, in a properly filed case, that the President lacks authority (absent a suspension of the writ of habeas corpus) to detain without charges or access to a lawyer a citizen captured in the United States. Accordingly, five members of the Court (at least in 2004) appear to have believed that the President lacked such authority.

Do the Executive's reasons for detaining a citizen matter in resolving the question whether the Constitution permits detention without access to lawyers or judicial process? Should they?

In *Hamdi*, the Supreme Court considered whether the President had authority to order the military to detain, without trial or access to lawyers, American citizens alleged to be enemy combatants. Does the President have power to order the use of military tribunals to try *non*-citizen enemy combatants for war crimes? In 2001, President Bush issued an order to govern the "Detention, Treatment, and Trial of Certain Non-Citizens in the War Against Terrorism." 66 Fed. Reg. 57833. The order authorized trials by "military commissions" for non-citizens for whom the President determines "there is reason to believe" that he or she (1) "is or was" a member of al Qaeda or (2) has engaged or participated in terrorist activities aimed at or harmful to the United States. A Yemeni national charged with conspiring with Osama bin Laden and others to engage in acts of terrorism and deemed eligible for trial by military commission sought writs of habeas corpus and mandamus to challenge the Executive Branch's proposed means of prosecuting him on the charges.

In *Hamdan v. Rumsfeld*, 548 U.S. 557 (2006), the Court held that the President's order was inconsistent with a statutory requirement imposed by the Uniform Code of Military Justice (UCMJ) and also violated the laws of war as embodied in the Third Geneva Convention of 1949 on the Treatment of Prisoners of War. Citing *Youngstown Sheet & Tube Co. v. Sawyer*, 343 U.S. 579, 637 (1952), the Court declared, "Whether or not the President has independent power, absent congressional authorization, to convene military commissions, he may not disregard limitations that Congress has, in proper exercise of its own war powers, placed on his powers." The Court also concluded that neither the Authorization for Use of Military Force nor the Detainee Treatment Act (DTA), Pub. L. 109–163, 119 Stat 3136, 3474 (Jan. 6, 2006), which Congress had enacted after Hamdan's commission had been convened, provided "specific, overriding authorization" for the military commission that had been convened to try Hamdan.

Justice Thomas, joined in part by two other Justices, dissented. In his view, in the domains of foreign policy and national security, "the fact that Congress has provided the President with broad authorities does not imply—and the Judicial Branch should not infer—that Congress intended to deprive him of particular powers not specifically enumerated." Instead, he asserted that the President's decision was "entitled to a heavy measure of deference." He would have concluded that the AUMF authorized the President's order. In addition, he would have concluded that the proposed procedures for the military commissions were consistent with the UCMJ and the laws of war.

Congress responded to the Court's decision in *Hamdan* by enacting the Military Commissions Act of 2006, Pub. L. No. 109–366, 120 Stat 2600 (Oct. 17, 2006). Among other things, this Act authorized the President to use military commissions to try suspected terrorists and allowed the commissions' procedures to differ from those of courts-martial. Congress specifically amended the UCMJ to overrule the Court's interpretation, rejecting Justice Stevens's view and adopting Justice Thomas's. See 10 U.S.C. § 836(1). In *Boumediene v. Bush*, 553 U.S. 723 (2008), however, the Court held that persons detained at Guantanamo Bay enjoy the privilege of habeas corpus because Guantanamo Bay is under the de facto control of the United States military, and that the procedures that Congress provided in the Detainee Treatment Act of 2005 and the Military Commissions

Act of 2006 for those detainees were not an "adequate and effective substitute for habeas corpus." Because Congress had not formally suspended the writ of habeas corpus, the Court concluded that these procedures operated as "an unconstitutional suspension of the writ." The Court did not reach the question whether the President had authority to detain the petitioners, leaving that question "to be resolved in the first instance by the District Court."

Did the Court's decisions in *Hamdan* and *Boumediene* meaningfully constrain the President's authority to detain and try persons whom he considers threats to the United States? Did they constrain Congress's power to authorize the President to do so? If so, are those constraints justified?

D. EXECUTIVE PRIVILEGE

A privilege is an exception to a general duty. For example, a witness who is properly called before a grand jury may have a general duty to testify. But the witness may assert certain privileges that limit this duty. For example, the Fifth Amendment privilege against self-incrimination may give the witness the right not to make statements exposing the witness to criminal liability. The attorney-client privilege similarly may allow the witness to refuse to disclose the content of prior communications with the witness's lawyer.

Presidents since Washington have claimed that the Constitution creates an "executive privilege" that allows them to keep secret their communications with close advisors. Presidents often assert this privilege when Congress is investigating executive actions and demands that the White House provide information. But the privilege also can arise in judicial proceedings, as the following case shows. In reading the decision, consider the arguments for concluding that an executive privilege exists and the nature of the restrictions that the Supreme Court places on the privilege that it recognizes.

Prior to the 1972 Presidential election, supporters of President Nixon were caught trying to break into the Democratic Party headquarters in the Watergate complex in Washington, D.C. There is no evidence that President Nixon knew about the crime in advance. But President Nixon and his advisors plotted to cover up the incident because they correctly predicted that the attempted burglary would have negative political consequences. At the request of a special prosecutor appointed by the Attorney General, a grand jury subsequently investigated whether President Nixon and others had conspired to obstruct justice. The grand jury wanted access to tape recordings that President Nixon had made of his conversations with advisors in the White House concerning the cover-up. President Nixon's refusal to disclose them led to the decision that follows.

President Richard Nixon (1913–1994)
Library of Congress

UNITED STATES V. NIXON

418 U.S. 683 (1974)

MR. CHIEF JUSTICE BURGER delivered the opinion of the Court.

On March 1, 1974, a grand jury of the United States District Court for the District of Columbia returned an indictment charging seven named individuals with various offenses, including conspiracy to defraud the United States and to obstruct justice. Although he was not designated as such in the indictment, the grand jury named the President, among others, as an unindicted coconspirator. On April 18, 1974, upon motion of the Special Prosecutor, a *subpoena duces tecum* was issued pursuant to Rule 17(c) to the President by the United States District Court and made returnable on May 2, 1974. This subpoena required the production, in advance of the September 9 trial date, of certain tapes, memoranda, papers, transcripts or other writings relating to

> **Definition**
>
> A *subpoena duces tecum* is an order directing a witness to appear and bring documents or other items. *Black's Law Dictionary* (9th ed. 2009).

> **FYI**
>
> The Supreme Court granted certiorari before the Court of Appeals decided the case. This is very rare, but the Court did so "because of the public importance of the issues presented and the need for their prompt resolution."

certain precisely identified meetings between the President and others. The Special Prosecutor was able to fix the time, place, and persons present at these discussions because the White House daily logs and appointment records had been delivered to him. On April 30, the President publicly released edited transcripts of 43 conversations; portions of 20 conversations subject to subpoena in the present case were included. On May 1, 1974, the President's counsel filed a "special appearance" and a motion to quash the subpoena under Rule 17(c). This motion was accompanied by a formal claim of privilege.

JUSTICIABILITY

In the District Court, the President's counsel argued that the court lacked jurisdiction to issue the subpoena because the matter was an intra-branch dispute between a subordinate and superior officer of the Executive Branch and hence not subject to judicial resolution. That argument has been renewed in this Court with emphasis on the contention that the dispute does not present a "case" or "controversy" which can be adjudicated in the federal courts. The President's counsel [views] the present dispute as essentially a "jurisdictional" dispute within the Executive Branch which he analogizes to a dispute between two congressional committees. Since the Executive Branch has exclusive authority and absolute discretion to decide whether to prosecute a case, it is contended that a President's decision is final in determining what evidence is to be used in a given criminal case. * * * The Special Prosecutor's demand for the items therefore presents, in the view of the President's counsel, a political

> **FYI**
>
> Early in the controversy over the Watergate break-in, Attorney General Elliot Richardson appointed Archibald Cox, a law professor, as a special prosecutor to investigate the affair. After Cox subpoenaed recordings that the President had secretly made of conversations in the Oval Office, President Nixon ordered Richardson to fire Cox. Richardson and his deputy, William Ruckelshaus, resigned rather than fire Cox. (These resignations became known as the "Saturday Night Massacre.") Solicitor General Robert Bork then fired Cox. After criticism of Cox's firing, the Nixon administration appointed a new special prosecutor, Leon Jaworski, who sought the evidence at issue here. For Robert Bork's perspective, see Robert H. Bork, *Saving Justice: Watergate, The Saturday Night Massacre, and other Adventures of a Solicitor General* (2013). Bork reveals that Richardson and Ruckelshaus supported Nixon's request that they fire Cox but could not do it themselves because of promises they had made to the Senate. Richardson even urged Bork to fire Cox.

question under *Baker v. Carr*, 369 U.S. 186 (1962), since it involves a "textually demonstrable" grant of power under Art. II.

Our starting point is the nature of the proceeding for which the evidence is sought—here a pending criminal prosecution. It is a judicial proceeding in a federal court alleging violation of federal laws and is brought in the name of the United States as sovereign. Under the authority of Art. II, § 2, Congress has vested in the Attorney General the power to conduct the criminal litigation of the United States Government. It has also vested in him the power to appoint subordinate officers to assist him in the discharge of his duties. Acting pursuant to those statutes, the Attorney General has delegated the authority to represent the United States in these particular matters to a Special Prosecutor with unique authority and tenure.[8] The regulation gives the Special Prosecutor explicit power to contest the invocation of executive privilege in the process of seeking evidence deemed relevant to the performance of these specially delegated duties.

[I]t is theoretically possible for the Attorney General to amend or revoke the regulation defining the Special Prosecutor's authority. But he has not done so. So long as this regulation remains in force the Executive Branch is bound by it, and indeed the United States as the sovereign composed of the three branches is bound to respect and to enforce it. Moreover, the delegation of authority to the Special Prosecutor in this case is not an ordinary delegation by the Attorney General to a subordinate officer: with the authorization of the President, the Acting Attorney General provided in the regulation that the Special Prosecutor

---

[8] The regulation issued by the Attorney General pursuant to his statutory authority vests in the Special Prosecutor plenary authority to control the course of investigations and litigation related to "all offenses arising out of the 1972 Presidential Election for which the Special Prosecutor deems it necessary and appropriate to assume responsibility, allegations involving the President, members of the White House staff, or Presidential appointees, and any other matters which he consents to have assigned to him by the Attorney General." 38 Fed.Reg. 30739, as amended by 38 Fed.Reg. 32805. In particular, the Special Prosecutor was given full authority, inter alia, "to contest the assertion of 'Executive Privilege' . . . and handl(e) all aspects of any cases within his jurisdiction." Id., at 30739. The regulations then go on to provide:

> "In exercising this authority, the Special Prosecutor will have the greatest degree of independence that is consistent with the Attorney General's statutory accountability for all matters falling within the jurisdiction of the Department of Justice. The Attorney General will not countermand or interfere with the Special Prosecutor's decisions or actions. The Special Prosecutor will determine whether and to what extent he will inform or consult with the Attorney General about the conduct of his duties and responsibilities. In accordance with assurances given by the President to the Attorney General that the President will not exercise his Constitutional powers to effect the discharge of the Special Prosecutor or to limit the independence that he is hereby given, the Special Prosecutor will not be removed from his duties except for extraordinary improprieties on his part and without the President's first consulting the Majority and the Minority Leaders and Chairmen and ranking Minority Members of the Judiciary Committees of the Senate and House of Representatives and ascertaining that their consensus is in accord with his proposed action."

was not to be removed without the "consensus" of eight designated leaders of Congress.

The demands of and the resistance to the subpoena present an obvious controversy in the ordinary sense, but that alone is not sufficient to meet constitutional standards. In the constitutional sense, controversy means more than disagreement and conflict; rather it means the kind of controversy courts traditionally resolve. Here at issue is the production or nonproduction of specified evidence deemed by the Special Prosecutor to be relevant and admissible in a pending criminal case. It is sought by one official of the Executive Branch within the scope of his express authority; it is resisted by the Chief Executive on the ground of his duty to preserve the confidentiality of the communications of the President. Whatever the correct answer on the merits, these issues are "of a type which are traditionally justiciable." The independent Special Prosecutor with his asserted need for the subpoenaed material in the underlying criminal prosecution is opposed by the President with his steadfast assertion of privilege against disclosure of the material. This setting assures there is "that concrete adverseness which sharpens the presentation of issues upon which the court so largely depends for illumination of difficult constitutional questions." *Baker v. Carr*, 369 U.S., at 204. Moreover, since the matter is one arising in the regular course of a federal criminal prosecution, it is within the traditional scope of Art. III power.

THE CLAIM OF PRIVILEGE

The first contention is a broad claim that the separation of powers doctrine precludes judicial review of a President's claim of privilege. The second contention is that if he does not prevail on the claim of absolute privilege, the court should hold as a matter of constitutional law that the privilege prevails over the subpoena. In the performance of assigned constitutional duties each branch of the Government must initially interpret the Constitution, and the interpretation of its powers by any branch is due great respect from the others. * * * Many decisions of this Court, however, have unequivocally reaffirmed the holding of *Marbury v. Madison* that "[i]t is emphatically the province and duty of the judicial department to say what the law is." * * * * Since this Court has consistently exercised the power to construe and delineate claims arising under express powers, it must follow that the Court has authority to interpret claims with respect to powers alleged to derive from enumerated powers.

In support of his claim of absolute privilege, the President's counsel urges two grounds, one of which is common to all governments and one of which is peculiar to our system of separation of powers. The first ground is the valid need for protection of communications between high Government officials and those who advise and assist them in the performance of their manifold duties; the importance of this confidentiality is too plain to require further discussion. Human experience teaches that those who expect public dissemination of their remarks may well temper candor with a concern for appearances and for their own interests to the detriment of the decisionmaking process. Whatever the nature of the privilege of confidentiality of Presidential communications in the exercise of Art. II powers, the privilege can be said to derive from the supremacy of each branch within its own assigned area of constitutional duties. Certain powers and privileges flow from the nature of enumerated powers; the protection of the confidentiality of Presidential communications has similar constitutional underpinnings.

Take Note

Does the claimed executive privilege find support in the text of the Constitution? If not, where did President Nixon argue that it comes from?

The second ground asserted by the President's counsel in support of the claim of absolute privilege rests on the doctrine of separation of powers. Here it is argued that the independence of the Executive Branch within its own sphere insulates a President from a judicial subpoena in an ongoing criminal prosecution, and thereby protects confidential Presidential communications.

However, neither the doctrine of separation of powers, nor the need for confidentiality of high-level communications, without more, can sustain an absolute, unqualified Presidential privilege of immunity from judicial process under all circumstances. The President's need for complete candor and objectivity from advisers calls for great deference from the courts. However, when the privilege depends solely on the broad, undifferentiated claim of public interest in the confidentiality of such conversations, a confrontation with other values arises. Absent a claim of need to protect military, diplomatic, or sensitive national security secrets, we find it difficult to accept the argument that even the very important interest in confidentiality of Presidential communications is significantly diminished by production of such material for *in camera* inspection with all the protection that a district court will be obliged to provide.

Definition

In camera means "in the judge's private chambers." *Black's Law Dictionary* (9th ed. 2009).

The impediment that an absolute, unqualified privilege would place in the way of the primary constitutional duty of the Judicial Branch to do justice in criminal prosecutions would plainly conflict with the function of the courts under Art. III. In designing the structure of our Government and dividing and allocating the sovereign power among three co-equal branches, the Framers of the Constitution sought to provide a comprehensive system, but the separate powers were not intended to operate with absolute independence. To read the Art. II powers of the President as providing an absolute privilege as against a subpoena essential to enforcement of criminal statutes on no more than a generalized claim of the public interest in confidentiality of nonmilitary and nondiplomatic discussions would upset the constitutional balance of "a workable government" and gravely impair the role of the courts under Art. III.

Since we conclude that the legitimate needs of the judicial process may outweigh Presidential privilege, it is necessary to resolve those competing interests in a manner that preserves the essential functions of each branch. The right and indeed the duty to resolve that question does not free the Judiciary from according high respect to the representations made on behalf of the President.

The expectation of a President to the confidentiality of his conversations and correspondence, like the claim of confidentiality of judicial deliberations, for example, has all the values to which we accord deference for the privacy of all citizens and, added to those values, is the necessity for protection of the public interest in candid, objective, and even blunt or harsh opinions in Presidential decisionmaking. A President and those who assist him must be free to explore alternatives in the process of shaping policies and making decisions and to do so in a way many would be unwilling to express except privately. These are the considerations justifying a presumptive privilege for Presidential communications. The privilege is fundamental to the operation of Government and inextricably rooted in the separation of powers under the Constitution. * * *

But this presumptive privilege must be considered in light of our historic commitment to the rule of law. This is nowhere more profoundly manifest than in our view that "the twofold aim (of criminal justice) is that guilt shall not escape or innocence suffer." *Berger v. United States*, 295 U.S. 78, 88 (1935). We have elected to employ an adversary system of criminal justice in which the parties contest all issues before a court of law. The need to develop all relevant facts in the adversary system is both fundamental and comprehensive. The ends of criminal justice would be defeated if judgments were to be founded on a partial or speculative presentation of the facts. The very integrity of the judicial system and public confidence in the system depend on full disclosure of all the facts, within the framework of the rules of evidence. To ensure that justice is done, it is imperative to the function of courts that compulsory process be available for the production of evidence needed either by the prosecution or by the defense.

In this case we must weigh the importance of the general privilege of confidentiality of Presidential communications in performance of the President's responsibilities against the inroads of such a privilege on the fair administration of criminal justice. The interest in preserving confidentiality is weighty indeed and entitled to great respect. However, we cannot conclude that advisers will be moved to temper the candor of their remarks by the infrequent occasions of disclosure because of the possibility that such conversations will be called for in the context of a criminal prosecution.

On the other hand, the allowance of the privilege to withhold evidence that is demonstrably relevant in a criminal trial would cut deeply into the guarantee of due process of law and gravely impair the basic function of the courts. A President's acknowledged need for confidentiality in the communications of his office is general in nature, whereas the constitutional need for production of relevant evidence in a criminal proceeding is specific and central to the fair adjudication of a particular criminal case in the administration of justice. Without access to specific facts a criminal prosecution may be totally frustrated. The President's broad interest in confidentiality of communications will not be vitiated by disclosure of a limited number of conversations preliminarily shown to have some bearing on the pending criminal cases.

We conclude that when the ground for asserting privilege as to subpoenaed materials sought for use in a criminal trial is based only on the generalized interest in confidentiality, it cannot prevail over the fundamental demands of due process of law in the fair administration of criminal justice. The generalized assertion of privilege must yield to the demonstrated, specific need for evidence in a pending criminal trial.

[The Court concluded by describing how a judge, when confronted with a claim of privilege, should inspect the evidence *in camera* before making a ruling.]

Affirmed.

POINTS FOR DISCUSSION

a. Legal Question or Policy Question?

Is the question whether the President should have an executive privilege a legal question or a policy question? What legal sources does the Court cite in support of the privilege? What legal sources does the Court cite for limiting it? What policy considerations does the Court take into account?

b. Disputes with Congress

Suppose that Congress demands that the President turn over sensitive documents, and the President refuses to turn them over on grounds of executive privilege. How can Congress and the President settle the dispute over production of the documents? Is the Court's role in such a controversy different from the Court's role in *Nixon*?

E. EXECUTIVE IMMUNITY

The following two cases consider important and related questions. The first is whether Presidents face civil liability for actions that they take in their official capacity. This question is significant. If Presidents face no liability, then they might not take care to avoid violating the rights of individuals. On the other hand, if Presidents may incur civil liability for their official actions, then they may hesitate to carry out their duties for fear of being sued. The second question is whether courts may entertain a civil lawsuit against a President during the President's term of office for unofficial actions taken before the President's term in office. Allowing these lawsuits may burden the President because litigation can be time-consuming and distracting. But barring them may deny justice to plaintiffs who have valid claims.

NIXON V. FITZGERALD

457 U.S. 731 (1982)

JUSTICE POWELL delivered the opinion of the Court.

In January 1970 the respondent A. Ernest Fitzgerald lost his job as a management analyst with the Department of the Air Force. Fitzgerald's dismissal occurred in the context of a departmental reorganization and reduction in force, in which his job was eliminated. In announcing the reorganization, the Air Force characterized the action as taken to promote economy and efficiency in the Armed Forces.

Respondent's discharge attracted unusual attention in Congress and in the press. Fitzgerald had attained national prominence approximately one year earlier, during the waning months of the Presidency of Lyndon B. Johnson. On November 13, 1968, Fitzgerald appeared before the Subcommittee on Economy in Government of the Joint Economic Committee of the United States Congress. To the evident embarrassment of his superiors in the Department of Defense,

Fitzgerald testified that cost-overruns on the C-5A transport plane could approximate $2 billion. He also revealed that unexpected technical difficulties had arisen during the development of the aircraft.

[Claiming that he had suffered retaliation for his congressional testimony, Fitzgerald sued former President Richard Nixon and others for damages. President Nixon claimed that he had absolute immunity from liability for any action that he may have taken against Fitzgerald while he was President.]

This Court consistently has recognized that government officials are entitled to some form of immunity from suits for civil damages. In *Spalding v. Vilas*, 161 U.S. 483 (1896), the Court considered the immunity available to the Postmaster General in a suit for damages based upon his official acts. Drawing upon principles of immunity developed in English cases at common law, the Court concluded that "[t]he interests of the people" required a grant of absolute immunity to public officers. *Id.*, at 498. In the absence of immunity, the Court reasoned, executive officials would hesitate to exercise their discretion in a way "injuriously affect[ing] the claims of particular individuals," *id.*, at 499, even when the public interest required bold and unhesitating action. Considerations of "public policy and convenience" therefore compelled a judicial recognition of immunity from suits arising from official acts.

> **Definition**
>
> Qualified immunity shields certain government officials from lawsuits claiming that their actions were unlawful, as long as the actions, even though ultimately judged to have been unlawful, were not inconsistent with "clearly established law." See, e.g., *Harlow v. Fitzgerald*, 457 U.S. 800 (1982). Absolute immunity, in contrast, shields certain government officials from lawsuits regardless of the legality of the challenged conduct.

In *Scheuer v. Rhodes*, 416 U.S. 232 (1974), the Court considered the immunity available to state executive officials in a 42 U.S.C § 1983 suit alleging the violation of constitutional rights. * * * As construed by subsequent cases, *Scheuer* established a two-tiered division of immunity defenses in § 1983 suits. To most [state] executive officers *Scheuer* accorded qualified immunity. For them the scope of the defense varied in proportion to the nature of their official functions and the range of decisions that conceivably might be taken in "good faith." This "functional" approach also defined a second tier, however, at which the especially sensitive duties of certain officials—notably judges and prosecutors—required the continued recognition of absolute immunity. See, *e.g.*, *Imbler v. Pachtman*, 424 U.S. 409 (1976) (state prosecutors possess absolute immunity with respect to the initiation and pursuit of prosecutions); *Stump v. Sparkman*, 435 U.S. 349 (1978) (state judge possesses absolute immunity for all judicial acts).

This approach was reviewed in detail in *Butz v. Economou*, 438 U.S. 478 (1978), when we considered for the first time the kind of immunity possessed by *federal* executive officials who are sued for constitutional violations. In *Butz* the Court rejected an argument, based on decisions involving federal officials charged with common-law torts, that all high federal officials have a right to absolute immunity from constitutional damages actions. Concluding that a blanket recognition of absolute immunity would be anomalous in light of the qualified immunity standard applied to state executive officials, *id.* at 504, we held that federal officials generally have the same qualified immunity possessed by state officials in cases under § 1983. In so doing we reaffirmed our holdings that some officials, notably judges and prosecutors, "because of the special nature of their responsibilities," *id.*, at 511, "require a full exemption from liability." *Id.* at 508. In *Butz* [we] left open the question whether other federal officials could show that "public policy requires an exemption of that scope." *Id.* at 506.

Here a former President asserts his immunity from civil damages claims of two kinds. He stands named as a defendant in a direct action under the Constitution and in two statutory actions under federal laws of general applicability. In neither case has Congress taken express legislative action to subject the President to civil liability for his official acts.

Applying the principles of our cases to claims of this kind, we hold that petitioner, as a former President of the United States, is entitled to absolute immunity from damages liability predicated on his official acts. We consider this immunity a functionally mandated incident of the President's unique office, rooted in the constitutional tradition of the separation of powers and supported by our history. Justice Story's analysis remains persuasive:

> "There are . . . incidental powers, belonging to the executive department, which are necessarily implied from the nature of the functions, which are confided to it. Among these, must necessarily be included the power to perform them. . . . The president cannot, therefore, be liable to arrest, imprisonment, or detention, while he is in the discharge of the duties of his office; and for this purpose his person must be deemed, in civil cases at least, to possess an official inviolability." 3 J. Story, Commentaries on the Constitution of the United States § 1563, pp. 418–419 (1st ed. 1833).

The President occupies a unique position in the constitutional scheme. Article II, § 1, of the Constitution provides that "[t]he executive Power shall be vested in a President of the United States." This grant of authority establishes the President as the chief constitutional officer of the Executive Branch, entrusted with supervisory and policy responsibilities of utmost discretion and sensitivity. These include the enforcement of federal law—it is the President who is charged constitutionally to "take Care that the Laws be faithfully executed"; the conduct of foreign affairs—a realm in which the Court has recognized that "[i]t would be intolerable that courts, without the relevant information, should review and perhaps nullify actions of the Executive taken on information properly held secret"; and management of the Executive Branch—a task for which "imperative reasons requir[e] an unrestricted power [in the President] to remove the most important of his subordinates in their most important duties."

In arguing that the President is entitled only to qualified immunity, the respondent relies on cases in which we have recognized immunity of this scope for governors and cabinet officers. *E.g., Butz v. Economou*, 438 U.S. 478 (1978); *Scheuer v. Rhodes*, 416 U.S. 232 (1974). We find these cases to be inapposite. The President's unique status under the Constitution distinguishes him from other executive officials.[31]

Because of the singular importance of the President's duties, diversion of his energies by concern with private lawsuits would raise unique risks to the effective functioning of government. As is the case with prosecutors and judges—for whom absolute immunity now is established—a President must concern himself with matters likely to "arouse the most intense feelings." *Pierson v. Ray*, 386 U.S. 547, 554 (1967). Yet, as our decisions have recognized, it is in precisely such cases that there exists the greatest public interest in providing an official "the maximum ability to deal fearlessly and impartially with" the duties of his office. *Ferri v. Ackerman*, 444 U.S. 193, 203 (1979). This concern is compelling where the officeholder must make the most sensitive and far-reaching decisions entrusted to any official under our constitutional system.[32] Nor can the sheer prominence of

---

[31] Noting that the Speech and Debate Clause provides a textual basis for congressional immunity, respondent argues that the Framers must be assumed to have rejected any similar grant of executive immunity. This argument is unpersuasive. First, a specific textual basis has not been considered a prerequisite to the recognition of immunity. No provision expressly confers judicial immunity. Yet the immunity of judges is well settled. Second, this Court already has established that absolute immunity may be extended to certain officials of the Executive Branch. Third, there is historical evidence from which it may be inferred that the Framers assumed the President's immunity from damages liability. At the Constitutional Convention several delegates expressed concern that subjecting the President even to impeachment would impair his capacity to perform his duties of office. See 2 M. Farrand, Records of the Federal Convention of 1787, p. 64 (1911) (remarks of Gouverneur Morris); id., at 66 (remarks of Charles Pinckney). The delegates of course did agree to an Impeachment Clause. But nothing in their debates suggests an expectation that the President would be subjected to the distraction of suits by disappointed private citizens. * * *

[32] Among the most persuasive reasons supporting official immunity is the prospect that damages liability may render an official unduly cautious in the discharge of his official duties. As Judge Learned Hand wrote in *Gregoire v. Biddle*, 177 F.2d 579, 581 (CA2 1949), *cert. denied*, 339 U.S. 949 (1950), "[t]he justification for [denying recovery] is that it is impossible to know whether the claim is well founded until the case has been tried, and

the President's office be ignored. In view of the visibility of his office and the effect of his actions on countless people, the President would be an easily identifiable target for suits for civil damages. Cognizance of this personal vulnerability frequently could distract a President from his public duties, to the detriment of not only the President and his office but also the Nation that the Presidency was designed to serve.

In defining the scope of an official's absolute privilege, this Court has recognized that the sphere of protected action must be related closely to the immunity's justifying purposes. *** In view of the special nature of the President's constitutional office and functions, we think it appropriate to recognize absolute Presidential immunity from damages liability for acts within the "outer perimeter" of his official responsibility.

Here respondent argues that petitioner Nixon would have acted outside the outer perimeter of his duties by ordering the discharge of an employee who was lawfully entitled to retain his job in the absence of " 'such cause as will promote the efficiency of the service.' " Brief for Respondent 39, citing 5 U.S.C. § 7512(a). Because Congress has granted this legislative protection, respondent argues, no federal official could, within the outer perimeter of his duties of office, cause Fitzgerald to be dismissed without satisfying this standard in prescribed statutory proceedings.

This construction would subject the President to trial on virtually every allegation that an action was unlawful, or was taken for a forbidden purpose. Adoption of this construction thus would deprive absolute immunity of its intended effect. It clearly is within the President's constitutional and statutory authority to prescribe the manner in which the Secretary will conduct the business of the Air Force. See 10 U.S.C. § 8012(b). Because this mandate of office must include the authority to prescribe reorganizations and reductions in force, we conclude that petitioner's alleged wrongful acts lay well within the outer perimeter of his authority.

A rule of absolute immunity for the President will not leave the Nation without sufficient protection against misconduct on the part of the Chief Executive. There remains the constitutional remedy of impeachment. In addition, there are formal and informal checks on Presidential action that do not apply with equal force to other executive officials. The President is subjected to constant scrutiny by the press. Vigilant oversight by Congress also may serve to deter Presidential abuses of office, as well as to make credible the threat of

---

to submit all officials, the innocent as well as the guilty, to the burden of a trial and to the inevitable danger of its outcome, would dampen the ardor of all but the most resolute. . . ."

impeachment. Other incentives to avoid misconduct may include a desire to earn reelection, the need to maintain prestige as an element of Presidential influence, and a President's traditional concern for his historical stature.

The existence of alternative remedies and deterrents establishes that absolute immunity will not place the President "above the law." For the President, as for judges and prosecutors, absolute immunity merely precludes a particular private remedy for alleged misconduct in order to advance compelling public ends.

JUSTICE WHITE, with whom JUSTICE BRENNAN, JUSTICE MARSHALL, and JUSTICE BLACKMUN join, dissenting.

[According to the Court, the] President, acting within the outer boundaries of what Presidents normally do, may, without liability, deliberately cause serious injury to any number of citizens even though he knows his conduct violates a statute or tramples on the constitutional rights of those who are injured. Even if the President in this case ordered Fitzgerald fired by means of a trumped-up reduction in force, knowing that such a discharge was contrary to the civil service laws, he would be absolutely immune from suit. By the same token, if a President, without following the statutory procedures which he knows apply to himself as well as to other federal officials, orders his subordinates to wiretap or break into a home for the purpose of installing a listening device, and the officers comply with his request, the President would be absolutely immune from suit. He would be immune regardless of the damage he inflicts, regardless of how violative of the statute and of the Constitution he knew his conduct to be, and regardless of his purpose.

The possibility of liability may, in some circumstances, distract officials from the performance of their duties and influence the performance of those duties in ways adverse to the public interest. * * * The Court's response, until today, to this problem has been to apply the argument to individual functions, not offices, and to evaluate the effect of liability on governmental decisionmaking within that function, in light of the substantive ends that are to be encouraged or discouraged. In this case, therefore, the Court should examine the functions implicated by the causes of action at issue here and the effect of potential liability on the performance of those functions.

The wholesale claim that the President is entitled to absolute immunity in all of his actions stands on no firmer ground than did the claim that all Presidential communications are entitled to an absolute privilege, which was rejected in favor of a functional analysis, by a unanimous Court in *United States v. Nixon*, 418 U.S. 683 (1974). Therefore, whatever may be true of the necessity of such a broad immunity in certain areas of executive responsibility, the only question that must be answered here is whether the dismissal of employees falls within a constitutionally assigned executive function, the performance of which would be substantially impaired by the possibility of a private action for damages. I believe it does not.

Absolute immunity is appropriate when the threat of liability may bias the decisionmaker in ways that are adverse to the public interest. But as the various regulations and statutes protecting civil servants from arbitrary executive action illustrate, this is an area in which the public interest is demonstrably on the side of encouraging less "vigor" and more "caution" on the part of decisionmakers. That is, the very steps that Congress has taken to assure that executive employees will be able freely to testify in Congress and to assure that they will not be subject to arbitrary adverse actions indicate that those policy arguments that have elsewhere justified absolute immunity are not applicable here. Absolute immunity would be nothing more than a judicial declaration of policy that directly contradicts the policy of protecting civil servants reflected in the statutes and regulations.

POINTS FOR DISCUSSION

a. Another Legal Question or Policy Question?

We previously have considered whether the executive privilege is rooted in law or policy. What about the question whether the President should have absolute immunity? Is that a legal question or a question of policy? Do the majority and dissenting opinions disagree on this question? Is it possible to find a justification in the Constitution's structure even if not in any express provision?

b. Political Checks

Is there an adequate political check on presidential over-reaching such that judicial intervention is unnecessary? If not, is the conclusion in *Fitzgerald* nevertheless defensible?

c. Status of Presidential Immunity

The Court notes that Congress had not purported to authorize suits against the President. Could Congress enact a statute over-riding the President's immunity in some class of cases? In all cases?

d. The President's Subordinates

Suppose the President orders a subordinate to torture a suspected terrorist, in violation of the law. Would the President be liable for damages? Would the subordinate?

CLINTON V. JONES

520 U.S. 681 (1997)

JUSTICE STEVENS delivered the opinion of the Court.

Petitioner, William Jefferson Clinton, was elected to the Presidency in 1992, and re-elected in 1996. His term of office expires on January 20, 2001. In 1991 he was the Governor of the State of Arkansas. Respondent, Paula Corbin Jones, is a resident of California. In 1991 she lived in Arkansas, and was an employee of the Arkansas Industrial Development Commission.

On May 6, 1994, she commenced this action in the United States District Court for the Eastern District of Arkansas by filing a complaint naming petitioner and Danny Ferguson, a former Arkansas State Police officer, as defendants. The complaint alleges two federal claims, and two state-law claims over which the federal court has jurisdiction because of the diverse citizenship of the parties. As the case comes to us, we are required to assume the truth of the detailed—but as yet untested—factual allegations in the complaint.

Those allegations principally describe events that are said to have occurred on the afternoon of May 8, 1991, during an official conference held at the Excelsior Hotel in Little Rock, Arkansas. The Governor delivered a speech at the conference; respondent—working as a state employee—staffed the registration desk. She alleges that Ferguson persuaded her to leave her desk and to visit the Governor in a business suite at the hotel, where he made "abhorrent" sexual advances that she vehemently rejected. She further claims that her superiors at work subsequently dealt with her in a hostile and rude manner, and changed her duties to punish her for rejecting those advances. Finally, she alleges that after petitioner was elected President, Ferguson defamed her by making a statement to a reporter that implied she had accepted petitioner's alleged overtures, and that various persons authorized to speak for the President publicly branded her a liar by denying that the incident had occurred. * * * [I]t is perfectly clear that the alleged misconduct of petitioner was unrelated to any of his official duties as President of the United States and, indeed, occurred before he was elected to that office.

Take Note

"Defamation" is a tort that consists of causing "[m]alicious or groundless harm to the reputation or good name of another by the making of a false statement to a third person." *Black's Law Dictionary* (10th ed. 2014).

In response to the complaint, petitioner promptly advised the District Court that he intended to file a motion to dismiss on grounds of Presidential immunity, and requested the court to defer all other pleadings and motions until after the immunity issue was resolved. [T]he court granted the request. Petitioner thereupon filed a motion "to dismiss . . . without prejudice and to toll any statutes of limitation [that may be applicable] until he is no longer President, at which time the plaintiff may refile the instant suit." * * * The District Judge denied the motion to dismiss on immunity grounds and ruled that discovery in the case could go forward, but ordered any trial stayed until the end of petitioner's Presidency. Although she recognized that a "thin majority" in *Nixon v. Fitzgerald*, 457 U.S. 731 (1982), had held that "the President has absolute immunity from civil damage actions arising out of the execution of official duties of office," she was not convinced that "a President has absolute immunity from civil causes of action arising prior to assuming the office." She was, however, persuaded by some of the reasoning in our opinion in *Fitzgerald* that deferring the trial if one were required would be appropriate. Relying in part on the fact that respondent had failed to bring her complaint until two days before the 3-year period of limitations expired, she concluded that the public interest in avoiding litigation that might hamper the President in conducting the duties of his office outweighed any demonstrated need for an immediate trial.

Both parties appealed. A divided panel of the Court of Appeals affirmed the denial of the motion to dismiss, but because it regarded the order postponing the trial until the President leaves office as the "functional equivalent" of a grant of temporary immunity, it reversed that order. * * *

Petitioner's principal submission—that "in all but the most exceptional cases," the Constitution affords the President temporary immunity from civil damages litigation arising out of events that occurred before he took office—cannot be sustained on the basis of precedent.

Only three sitting Presidents have been defendants in civil litigation involving their actions prior to taking office. Complaints against Theodore Roosevelt and Harry Truman had been dismissed before they took office; the dismissals were affirmed after their respective inaugurations. Two companion cases arising out of an automobile accident were filed against John F. Kennedy in 1960 during the Presidential campaign. After taking office, he unsuccessfully argued that his status as Commander in Chief gave him a right to a stay under the Soldiers' and Sailors' Civil Relief Act of 1940. The motion for a stay was denied by the District Court, and the matter was settled out of court. Thus, none of those cases sheds any light on the constitutional issue before us.

The principal rationale for affording certain public servants immunity from suits for money damages arising out of their official acts is inapplicable to unofficial conduct. In cases involving prosecutors, legislators, and judges we have repeatedly explained that the immunity serves the public interest in enabling such officials to perform their designated functions effectively without fear that a particular decision may give rise to personal liability. * * * That rationale provided the principal basis for our holding that a former President of the United States was "entitled to absolute immunity from damages liability predicated on his official acts," *Fitzgerald,* 457 U.S. at 749. Our central concern was to avoid rendering the President "unduly cautious in the discharge of his official duties." 457 U.S., at 752, n. 32.

This reasoning provides no support for an immunity for *unofficial* conduct. As we explained in *Fitzgerald,* "the sphere of protected action must be related closely to the immunity's justifying purposes." *Id.,* at 755. Because of the President's broad responsibilities, we recognized in that case an immunity from damages claims arising out of official acts extending to the "outer perimeter of his authority." *Id.,* at 757. But we have never suggested that the President, or any other official, has an immunity that extends beyond the scope of any action taken in an official capacity.

Moreover, when defining the scope of an immunity for acts clearly taken *within* an official capacity, we have applied a functional approach. "Frequently our decisions have held that an official's absolute immunity should extend only to acts in performance of particular functions of his office." *Id.,* at 755. Hence, for example, a judge's absolute immunity does not extend to actions performed in a purely administrative capacity. See *Forrester v. White,* 484 U.S. 219, 229–230 (1988). As our opinions have made clear, immunities are grounded in "the nature of the function performed, not the identity of the actor who performed it." *Id.,* at 229. Petitioner's effort to construct an immunity from suit for unofficial acts grounded purely in the identity of his office is unsupported by precedent.

We are also unpersuaded by the evidence from the historical record to which petitioner has called our attention. He points to a comment by Thomas Jefferson protesting the subpoena *duces tecum* Chief Justice Marshall directed to him in the Burr trial, a statement in the diaries kept by Senator William Maclay of the first Senate debates, in which then-Vice President John Adams and Senator Oliver Ellsworth are recorded as having said that "the President personally [is] not . . . subject to any process whatever," lest it be "put . . . in the power of a common Justice to exercise any Authority over him and Stop the Whole Machine of Government," and to a quotation from Justice Story's Commentaries on the Constitution. None of these sources sheds much light on the question at hand.

Respondent, in turn, has called our attention to conflicting historical evidence. Speaking in favor of the Constitution's adoption at the Pennsylvania

Convention, James Wilson—who had participated in the Philadelphia Convention at which the document was drafted—explained that, although the President "is placed [on] high," "not a single privilege is annexed to his character; far from being above the laws, he is amenable to them in his private character as a citizen, and in his public character by impeachment." 2 J. Elliot, Debates on the Federal Constitution 480 (2d ed. 1863). This description is consistent with both the doctrine of Presidential immunity as set forth in *Fitzgerald* and rejection of the immunity claim in this case. With respect to acts taken in his "public character"—that is, official acts—the President may be disciplined principally by impeachment, not by private lawsuits for damages. But he is otherwise subject to the laws for his purely private acts.

> **Take Note**
>
> Was the President seeking absolute immunity from suit? Or simply immunity while in office? If the latter, wasn't the President's claim substantially less sweeping than the claim upheld in *Fitzgerald*?

Petitioner's strongest argument supporting his immunity claim is based on the text and structure of the Constitution. He does not contend that the occupant of the Office of the President is "above the law," in the sense that his conduct is entirely immune from judicial scrutiny. The President argues merely for a postponement of the judicial proceedings that will determine whether he violated any law. His argument is grounded in the character of the office that was created by Article II of the Constitution, and relies on separation-of-powers principles that have structured our constitutional arrangement since the founding.

As a starting premise, petitioner contends that he occupies a unique office with powers and responsibilities so vast and important that the public interest demands that he devote his undivided time and attention to his public duties. He submits that—given the nature of the office—the doctrine of separation of powers places limits on the authority of the Federal Judiciary to interfere with the Executive Branch that would be transgressed by allowing this action to proceed.

We have no dispute with the initial premise of the argument. * * * It does not follow, however, that separation-of-powers principles would be violated by allowing this action to proceed. The doctrine of separation of powers is concerned with the allocation of official power among the three coequal branches of our Government. * * *

Of course the lines between the powers of the three branches are not always neatly defined. But in this case there is no suggestion that the Federal Judiciary is being asked to perform any function that might in some way be described as "executive." Respondent is merely asking the courts to exercise their core Article

III jurisdiction to decide cases and controversies. Whatever the outcome of this case, there is no possibility that the decision will curtail the scope of the official powers of the Executive Branch. The litigation of questions that relate entirely to the unofficial conduct of the individual who happens to be the President poses no perceptible risk of misallocation of either judicial power or executive power.

Rather than arguing that the decision of the case will produce either an aggrandizement of judicial power or a narrowing of executive power, petitioner contends that—as a byproduct of an otherwise traditional exercise of judicial power—burdens will be placed on the President that will hamper the performance of his official duties. We have recognized that "[e]ven when a branch does not arrogate power to itself . . . the separation-of-powers doctrine requires that a branch not impair another in the performance of its constitutional duties." *Loving v. United States*, 517 U.S. 748, 757 (1996). As a factual matter, petitioner contends that this particular case—as well as the potential additional litigation that an affirmance of the Court of Appeals' judgment might spawn—may impose an unacceptable burden on the President's time and energy, and thereby impair the effective performance of his office.

Petitioner's predictive judgment finds little support in either history or the relatively narrow compass of the issues raised in this particular case. As we have already noted, in the more than 200-year history of the Republic, only three sitting Presidents have been subjected to suits for their private actions. If the past is any indicator, it seems unlikely that a deluge of such litigation will ever engulf the Presidency. As for the case at hand, if properly managed by the District Court, it appears to us highly unlikely to occupy any substantial amount of petitioner's time.

Food for Thought

Are courts well suited to making predictions of this sort? Was the Court's prediction here a good one?

The District Court has broad discretion to stay proceedings as an incident to its power to control its own docket. See, *e.g., Landis v. North American Co.*, 299 U.S. 248, 254 (1936). As we have explained, "[e]specially in cases of extraordinary public moment, [a plaintiff] may be required to submit to delay not immoderate in extent and not oppressive in its consequences if the public welfare or convenience will thereby be promoted." *Id.*, at 256. Although we have rejected the argument that the potential burdens on the President violate separation-of-powers principles, those burdens are appropriate matters for the District Court to evaluate in its management of the case. The high respect that is owed to the office of the Chief Executive, though not justifying a rule of categorical immunity, is a matter that should inform the conduct of the entire proceeding, including the timing and scope of discovery.

Nevertheless, we are persuaded that it was an abuse of discretion for the District Court to defer the trial until after the President leaves office. Such a lengthy and categorical stay takes no account whatever of the respondent's interest in bringing the case to trial. The complaint was filed within the statutory limitations period—albeit near the end of that period—and delaying trial would increase the danger of prejudice resulting from the loss of evidence, including the inability of witnesses to recall specific facts, or the possible death of a party.

The decision to postpone the trial was, furthermore, premature. The proponent of a stay bears the burden of establishing its need. In this case, at the stage at which the District Court made its ruling, there was no way to assess whether a stay of trial after the completion of discovery would be warranted. Other than the fact that a trial may consume some of the President's time and attention, there is nothing in the record to enable a judge to assess the potential harm that may ensue from scheduling the trial promptly after discovery is concluded. We think the District Court may have given undue weight to the concern that a trial might generate unrelated civil actions that could conceivably hamper the President in conducting the duties of his office. If and when that should occur, the court's discretion would permit it to manage those actions in such fashion (including deferral of trial) that interference with the President's duties would not occur. But no such impingement upon the President's conduct of his office was shown here.

Take Note

The Court here refers to "discovery." Before a civil case proceeds to trial, each party has a right to discover relevant information known by the other party. A party may submit requests for written answers to questions ("interrogatories"), may schedule an interview conducted under oath (a "deposition"), or may request that that other party admit certain facts or produce certain documents or other potential evidence. The use of these methods is called "discovery."

If Congress deems it appropriate to afford the President stronger protection, it may respond with appropriate legislation. As petitioner notes in his brief, Congress has enacted more than one statute providing for the deferral of civil litigation to accommodate important public interests. See, *e.g.,* 11 U.S.C. § 362 (litigation against debtor stayed upon filing of bankruptcy petition); Soldiers' and Sailors' Civil Relief Act of 1940, 50 U.S.C. App. §§ 501–525 (provisions governing, *inter alia,* tolling or stay of civil claims by or against military personnel during course of active duty). * * *

JUSTICE BREYER, concurring in the judgment.

I agree with the majority that the Constitution does not automatically grant the President an immunity from civil lawsuits based upon his private conduct. Nor does the "doctrine of separation of powers require federal courts to stay" virtually "all private actions against the President until he leaves office." * * * To obtain a postponement the President must "bear the burden of establishing its need."

Food for Thought

In 1997, both Houses of Congress were controlled by the Republican party. President Clinton was a Democrat. Is the possibility of legislation conferring immunity, in such circumstances or more generally, a realistic form of protection for the President?

In my view, however, once the President sets forth and explains a conflict between judicial proceeding and public duties, the matter changes. At that point, the Constitution permits a judge to schedule a trial in an ordinary civil damages action (where postponement normally is possible without overwhelming damage to a plaintiff) only within the constraints of a constitutional principle—a principle that forbids a federal judge in such a case to interfere with the President's discharge of his public duties. I have no doubt that the Constitution contains such a principle applicable to civil suits, based upon Article II's vesting of the entire "executive Power" in a single individual, implemented through the Constitution's structural separation of powers, and revealed both by history and case precedent. I recognize that this case does not require us now to apply the principle specifically, thereby delineating its contours; nor need we now decide whether lower courts are to apply it directly or categorically through the use of presumptions or rules of administration. Yet I fear that to disregard it now may appear to deny it.

The Constitution states that the "executive Power shall be vested in a President." Art. II, § 1. This constitutional delegation means that a sitting President is unusually busy, that his activities have an unusually important impact upon the lives of others, and that his conduct embodies an authority bestowed by the entire American electorate. He (along with his constitutionally subordinate Vice President) is the only official for whom the entire Nation votes, and is the only elected officer to represent the entire Nation both domestically and abroad. * * * [T]his constitutional structure means that the President is not like Congress, for Congress can function as if it were whole, even when up to half of its members are absent, see U.S. Const., Art. I, § 5, cl. 1. It means that the President is not like the Judiciary, for judges often can designate other judges, e.g., from other judicial circuits, to sit even should an entire court be detained by personal litigation. It means that, unlike Congress, which is regularly out of session, U.S. Const., Art. I, §§ 4, 5, 7, the President never adjourns.

Nixon v. Fitzgerald strongly supports the principle that judges hearing a private civil damages action against a sitting President may not issue orders that could significantly distract a President from his official duties. * * * The majority [overlooks] the fact that *Fitzgerald* set forth a single immunity (an absolute immunity) applicable both to sitting and former Presidents. Its reasoning focused upon both. Its key paragraph, explaining why the President enjoys an absolute immunity rather than a qualified immunity, contains seven sentences, four of which focus primarily upon time and energy *distraction* and three of which focus primarily upon official decision *distortion.*

This case is a private action for civil damages in which, as the District Court here found, it is possible to preserve evidence and in which later payment of interest can compensate for delay. The District Court in this case determined that the Constitution required the postponement of trial during the sitting President's term. It may well be that the trial of this case cannot take place without significantly interfering with the President's ability to carry out his official duties. Yet, I agree with the majority that there is no automatic temporary immunity and that the President should have to provide the District Court with a reasoned explanation of why the immunity is needed; and I also agree that, in the absence of that explanation, the court's postponement of the trial date was premature. For those reasons, I concur in the result.

POINTS FOR DISCUSSION

a. Subsequent History

When Paula Jones's sexual harassment lawsuit went forward, Jones's attorneys deposed President Clinton. During the deposition, President Clinton misleadingly answered questions about his sexual activities with another subordinate, Monica Lewinsky, an intern at the White House. This testimony led President Clinton to be suspended from the bar, fined by the district court, and impeached by the House of Representatives (although not convicted of an offense by the Senate). Needless to say, the entire event caused a major disruption in the work of the President. Should the Court have anticipated this possible consequence of allowing a civil lawsuit to proceed? Judge Richard Posner has written: "In retrospect * * * allowing Paula Jones's suit against the President to go forward before he left office [appears to be one of the Supreme Court's] naive, unintended, unpragmatic, and gratuitous body blows to the Presidency." Richard A. Posner, *An Affair of State: The Investigation, Impeachment, and Trial of President Clinton* 13 (1999).

b. Congressional Action

Could Congress grant the President protection from lawsuits while he is in office? If so, how would you draft a statute for this purpose? Would protection from all civil lawsuits while in office be a good idea?

TRUMP V. VANCE

140 S.Ct. 2412 (2020)

CHIEF JUSTICE ROBERTS delivered the opinion of the Court.

In our judicial system, "the public has a right to every man's evidence." Since the earliest days of the Republic, "every man" has included the President of the United States. Beginning with Jefferson and carrying on through Clinton, Presidents have uniformly testified or produced documents in criminal proceedings when called upon by federal courts. This case involves—so far as we and the parties can tell—the first *state* criminal subpoena directed to a President. The President contends that the subpoena is unenforceable. We granted certiorari to decide whether Article II and the Supremacy Clause categorically preclude, or require a heightened standard for, the issuance of a state criminal subpoena to a sitting President.

In the summer of 2018, the New York County District Attorney's Office opened an investigation into what it opaquely describes as "business transactions involving multiple individuals whose conduct may have violated state law." A year later, the office—acting on behalf of a grand jury—served a subpoena *duces tecum* (essentially a request to produce evidence) on Mazars USA, LLP, the personal accounting firm of President Donald J. Trump. The subpoena directed Mazars to produce financial records relating to the President and business organizations affiliated with him, including "[t]ax returns and related schedules," from "2011 to the present."

The President, acting in his personal capacity, sued the district attorney and Mazars in Federal District Court to enjoin enforcement of the subpoena. * * * Mazars, concluding that the dispute was between the President and the district attorney, took no position on the legal issues raised by the President. The District Court * * * ruled that the President was not entitled to injunctive relief. [T]he Court of Appeals agreed with the District Court's denial of a preliminary injunction. * * *

[In 1807, the federal government prosecuted Aaron Burr, the former Vice President, for treason. Burr had hatched a plan with General James Wilkinson, the Governor of the Louisiana Territory, to establish a new territory in Mexico, then controlled by Spain.] Both men anticipated that war between the United States and Spain was imminent, and when it broke out they intended to invade Spanish territory at the head of a private army. But while Burr was rallying allies to his cause, tensions with Spain eased and rumors began to swirl that Burr was conspiring to detach States by the Allegheny Mountains from the Union. Wary of being exposed as the principal co-conspirator, Wilkinson * * * sent a series of letters to President Jefferson accusing Burr of plotting to attack New Orleans and revolutionize the Louisiana Territory.

Jefferson, who despised his former running mate Burr for trying to steal the 1800 presidential election from him, was predisposed to credit Wilkinson's version of events. [Jefferson directed prosecutors to try Burr for treason. Chief Justice John Marshall presided as Circuit Justice for Virginia. Before trial, Burr moved for a subpoena *duces tecum*, directing Jefferson to produce a letter from Wilkinson and accompanying documents, which Jefferson had referenced in a message to Congress.] The prosecution opposed the request, arguing that a President could not be subjected to such a subpoena and that the letter might contain state secrets. Following four days of argument, Marshall [ruled that the President] does not "stand exempt from the general provisions of the constitution" or, in particular, the Sixth Amendment's guarantee that those accused have compulsory process for obtaining witnesses for their defense. *United States* v. *Burr*, 25 F. Cas. 30, 33–34 (No. 14,692d) (CC Va. 1807). At common law the "single reservation" to the duty to testify in response to a subpoena was "the case of the king," whose "dignity" was seen as "incompatible" with appearing "under the process of the court." *Id.*, at 34. But, as Marshall explained, a king is born to power and can "do no wrong." *Ibid.* The President, by contrast, is "of the people" and subject to the law. *Ibid.* According to Marshall, the sole argument for exempting the President from testimonial obligations was that his "duties as chief magistrate demand his whole time for national objects." *Ibid.* But, in Marshall's assessment, those demands were "not unremitting." *Ibid.* And should the President's duties preclude his attendance at a particular time and place, a court could work that out upon return of the subpoena. *Ibid.*

Marshall also rejected the prosecution's argument that the President was immune from a subpoena *duces tecum* because executive papers might contain state secrets. "A subpoena duces tecum," he said, "may issue to any person to whom an ordinary subpoena may issue." *Ibid.* * * * As for "the propriety of introducing any papers," that would "depend on the character of the paper, not on the character of the person who holds it." *Id.*, at 34. Marshall acknowledged that the papers sought by Burr could contain information "the disclosure of which would endanger the public safety," but stated that, again, such concerns would have "due consideration" upon the return of the subpoena. *Id.*, at 37.

While the arguments unfolded, Jefferson, who had received word of the motion, wrote to the prosecutor indicating that he would—subject to the prerogative to decide which executive communications should be withheld—"furnish on all occasions, whatever the purposes of justice may require." Letter from T. Jefferson to G. Hay (June 12, 1807), in 10 Works of Thomas Jefferson 398, n. (P. Ford ed. 1905). His "personal attendance," however, was out of the question, for it "would leave the nation without" the "sole branch which the constitution requires to be always in function." Letter from T. Jefferson to G. Hay (June 17, 1807), in *id.*, at 400–401, n.

Before Burr received the subpoenaed documents, Marshall rejected the prosecution's core legal theory for treason and Burr was accordingly acquitted. * * * Committed to salvaging a conviction, [Jefferson] directed the prosecutors to proceed with a misdemeanor (yes, misdemeanor) charge for inciting war against Spain. Burr then renewed his request for Wilkinson's October 21 letter, which he later received a copy of, and subpoenaed a second letter, dated November 12, 1806, which the prosecutor claimed was privileged. Acknowledging that the President may withhold information to protect public safety, Marshall instructed that Jefferson should "state the particular reasons" for withholding the letter. *United States* v. *Burr*, 25 F. Cas. 187, 192 (No. 14,694) (CC Va. 1807). [The need to decide whether to compel disclosure of the letter] was averted when [it] became clear that the prosecution lacked the evidence to convict [on the misdemeanor charge].

In the two centuries since the Burr trial, successive Presidents have accepted Marshall's ruling that the Chief Executive is subject to subpoena. [Presidents from James Monroe to Bill Clinton] have uniformly agreed to testify when called in criminal proceedings, provided they could do so at a time and place of their choosing. * * *

The bookend to Marshall's ruling came in 1974 when the question he never had to decide—whether to compel the disclosure of official communications over the objection of the President—came to a head. The [Court in *United States* v. *Nixon*, 418 U. S. 683, 705 (1974),] readily acknowledged the importance of preserving the confidentiality of communications "between high Government officials and those who advise and assist them." But, like Marshall two centuries prior, the Court recognized the countervailing interests at stake. * * * The Court [concluded] that the President's "generalized assertion of privilege must yield to the demonstrated, specific need for evidence in a pending criminal trial." *Id.*, at 713. Two weeks later, President Nixon dutifully released the tapes.

[This history] involved *federal* criminal proceedings. Here we are confronted for the first time with a subpoena issued to the President by a local grand jury operating under the supervision of a *state* court.[5] In the President's view, that distinction makes all the difference. He argues that the Supremacy Clause gives a sitting President absolute immunity from state criminal subpoenas because compliance with those subpoenas would categorically impair a President's performance of his Article II functions. The Solicitor General, arguing on behalf of the United States, [urges] us to resolve this case by holding that a state grand jury subpoena for a sitting President's personal records must, at the very least, "satisfy a heightened standard of need," which the Solicitor General contends was not met here.

We begin with the question of absolute immunity. No one doubts that Article II guarantees the independence of the Executive Branch. As the head of that branch, the President "occupies a unique position in the constitutional scheme." *Nixon* v. *Fitzgerald*, 457 U. S. 731, 749 (1982). His duties, which range from faithfully executing the laws to commanding the Armed Forces, are of unrivaled gravity and breadth. Quite appropriately, those duties come with protections that safeguard the President's ability to perform his vital functions. See, *e.g.*, *ibid.* (concluding that the President enjoys "absolute immunity from damages liability predicated on his official acts"); *Nixon*, 418 U. S., at 708 (recognizing that presidential communications are presumptively privileged).

In addition, the Constitution guarantees "the entire independence of the General Government from any control by the respective States." *Farmers and Mechanics Sav. Bank of Minneapolis* v. *Minnesota*, 232 U. S. 516, 521 (1914). As we have often repeated, "States have no power . . . to retard, impede, burden, or in any manner control the operations of the constitutional laws enacted by Congress." *McCulloch* v. *Maryland*, 4 Wheat. 316, 436 (1819). It follows that States also lack the power to impede the President's execution of those laws.

Marshall's ruling in *Burr*, entrenched by 200 years of practice and our decision in *Nixon*, confirms that *federal* criminal subpoenas do not "rise to the level of constitutionally forbidden impairment of the Executive's ability to perform its constitutionally mandated functions." *Clinton v. Jones*, 520 U. S. 681, 702–703 (1997). But the President * * * argues that *state* criminal subpoenas pose a unique

---

[5] While the subpoena was directed to the President's accounting firm, the parties agree that the papers at issue belong to the President and that Mazars is merely the custodian. Thus, for purposes of immunity, it is functionally a subpoena issued to the President.

threat of impairment and thus demand greater protection. To be clear, the President does not contend here that *this* subpoena, in particular, is impermissibly burdensome. Instead he makes a *categorical* argument about the burdens generally associated with state criminal subpoenas, focusing on three: diversion, stigma, and harassment. * * *

The President's primary contention, which the Solicitor General supports, is that complying with state criminal subpoenas would necessarily divert the Chief Executive from his duties. He grounds that concern in *Nixon* v. *Fitzgerald*, which recognized a President's "absolute immunity from damages liability predicated on his official acts." 457 U. S., at 749. In explaining the basis for that immunity, this Court observed that the prospect of such liability could "distract a President from his public duties, to the detriment of not only the President and his office but also the Nation that the Presidency was designed to serve." *Id.*, at 753. The President contends that the diversion occasioned by a state criminal subpoena imposes an equally intolerable burden on a President's ability to perform his Article II functions.

But *Fitzgerald* did not hold that distraction was sufficient to confer absolute immunity. We instead drew a careful analogy to the common law absolute immunity of judges and prosecutors, concluding that a President, like those officials, must "deal fearlessly and impartially with the duties of his office"—not be made "unduly cautious in the discharge of [those] duties" by the prospect of civil liability for official acts. *Id.*, at 751–752, and n. 32. Indeed, we expressly rejected immunity based on distraction alone 15 years later in *Clinton* v. *Jones*. [In holding that a sitting President does not enjoy absolute immunity from civil liability for private conduct, we explained that] the "dominant concern" in *Fitzgerald* was not mere distraction but the distortion of the Executive's "decisionmaking process" with respect to official acts that would stem from "worry as to the possibility of damages." 520 U. S., at 694, n. 19. * * *

The same is true of criminal subpoenas. Just as a "properly managed" civil suit is generally "unlikely to occupy any substantial amount of" a President's time or attention, *id.,* at 702, two centuries of experience confirm that a properly tailored criminal subpoena will not normally hamper the performance of the President's constitutional duties. If anything, we expect that in the mine run of cases, where a President is subpoenaed during a proceeding targeting someone else, as Jefferson was, the burden on a President will ordinarily be lighter than the burden of defending against a civil suit.

The President, however, believes the district attorney is investigating him and his businesses. In such a situation, he contends, the "toll that criminal process . . .

exacts from the President is even heavier" than the distraction at issue in *Fitzgerald* and *Clinton*, because "criminal litigation" poses unique burdens on the President's time and will generate a "considerable if not overwhelming degree of mental preoccupation." But the President is not seeking immunity from the diversion occasioned by the prospect of future criminal *liability*. Instead he concedes—consistent with the position of the Department of Justice—that state grand juries are free to investigate a sitting President with an eye toward charging him after the completion of his term. The President's objection therefore must be limited to the *additional* distraction caused by the subpoena itself. But that argument runs up against the 200 years of precedent establishing that Presidents, and their official communications, are subject to judicial process, even when the President is under investigation, see *Nixon*, 418 U. S., at 706.

The President next claims that the stigma of being subpoenaed will undermine his leadership at home and abroad. Notably, the Solicitor General does not endorse this argument, perhaps because we have twice denied absolute immunity claims by Presidents in cases involving allegations of serious misconduct. See *Clinton*, 520 U. S., at 685; *Nixon*, 418 U. S., at 687. But even if a tarnished reputation were a cognizable impairment, there is nothing inherently stigmatizing about a President performing "the citizen's normal duty of . . . furnishing information relevant" to a criminal investigation. *Branzburg* v. *Hayes*, 408 U. S. 665, 691 (1972). Nor can we accept that the risk of association with persons or activities under criminal investigation can absolve a President of such an important public duty. Prior Presidents have weathered these associations in federal cases, and there is no reason to think any attendant notoriety is necessarily greater in state court proceedings. * * * Additionally, while the current suit has cast the Mazars subpoena into the spotlight, longstanding rules of grand jury secrecy aim to prevent the very stigma the President anticipates. * * *

Finally, the President and the Solicitor General warn that subjecting Presidents to state criminal subpoenas will make them "easily identifiable target[s]" for harassment. *Fitzgerald*, 457 U. S., at 753. But we rejected a nearly identical argument in *Clinton* * * *. The President and the Solicitor General nevertheless argue that state criminal subpoenas pose a heightened risk [because,] while federal prosecutors are accountable to and removable by the President, the 2,300 district attorneys in this country are responsive to local constituencies, local interests, and local prejudices, and might "use criminal process to register their dissatisfaction with" the President. * * *

We recognize, as does the district attorney, that harassing subpoenas could, under certain circumstances, threaten the independence or effectiveness of the

Executive. [But] here again the law already seeks to protect against the predicted abuse. First, grand juries are prohibited from engaging in "arbitrary fishing expeditions" and initiating investigations "out of malice or an intent to harass." *United States* v. *R. Enterprises, Inc.*, 498 U. S. 292, 299 (1991). [In] the event of such harassment, a President would be entitled to the protection of federal courts. * * * Second, [the] Supremacy Clause prohibits state judges and prosecutors from interfering with a President's official duties. See, *e.g.*, *Tennessee* v. *Davis*, 100 U. S. 257, 263 (1880) ("No State government can . . . obstruct [the] authorized officers" of the Federal Government.). Any effort to manipulate a President's policy decisions or to "retaliat[e]" against a President for official acts through issuance of a subpoena, would thus be an unconstitutional attempt to "influence" a superior sovereign "exempt" from such obstacles, see *McCulloch*, 4 Wheat., at 427. * * *

Given these safeguards and the Court's precedents, we cannot conclude that absolute immunity is necessary or appropriate under Article II or the Supremacy Clause. * * * On that point the Court is unanimous.

We next consider whether a state grand jury subpoena seeking a President's private papers must satisfy a heightened need standard. The Solicitor General would require a threshold showing that the evidence sought is "critical" for "specific charging decisions" and that the subpoena is a "last resort," meaning the evidence is "not available from any other source" and is needed "now, rather than at the end of the President's term." JUSTICE ALITO [largely] agrees * * *.

We disagree, for three reasons. First, such a heightened standard would extend protection designed for official documents to the President's private papers. As the Solicitor General and JUSTICE ALITO acknowledge, their proposed test is derived from executive privilege cases that trace back to *Burr*. * * * But this argument does not account for the relevant passage from *Burr*: "If there be a paper in the possession of the executive, which is *not of an official nature*, he must stand, as respects that paper, in nearly the same situation with any other individual." *Id.*, at 191 (emphasis added). * * *

Second, neither the Solicitor General nor JUSTICE ALITO has established that heightened protection against state subpoenas is necessary for the Executive to fulfill his Article II functions. Beyond the risk of harassment, which we addressed above, the only justification they offer for the heightened standard is protecting Presidents from "unwarranted burdens." In effect, they argue that even if federal subpoenas to a President are warranted whenever evidence is material, state subpoenas are warranted "only when [the] evidence is essential." But that double standard has no basis in law. For if the state subpoena is not issued to manipulate, the documents themselves are not protected, and the Executive is not impaired, then nothing in Article II or the Supremacy Clause supports holding state subpoenas to a higher standard than their federal counterparts.

Finally, in the absence of a need to protect the Executive, the public interest in fair and effective law enforcement cuts in favor of comprehensive access to evidence. Requiring a state grand jury to meet a heightened standard of need would hobble the grand jury's ability to acquire "all information that might possibly bear on its investigation." *R. Enterprises, Inc.*, 498 U. S., at 297. And, even assuming the evidence withheld under that standard were preserved until the conclusion of a President's term, in the interim the State would be deprived of investigative leads that the evidence might yield, allowing memories to fade and documents to disappear. This could frustrate the identification, investigation, and indictment of third parties (for whom applicable statutes of limitations might lapse). More troubling, it could prejudice the innocent by depriving the grand jury of *exculpatory* evidence.

Rejecting a heightened need standard does not leave Presidents with "no real protection." To start, a President may avail himself of the same protections available to every other citizen. These include the right to challenge the subpoena on any grounds permitted by state law, which usually include bad faith and undue burden or breadth. And, as in federal court, "[t]he high respect that is owed to the office of the Chief Executive . . . should inform the conduct of the entire proceeding, including the timing and scope of discovery." *Clinton*, 520 U. S., at 707. * * * In addition, the Executive can—as the district attorney concedes—argue that compliance with a particular subpoena would impede his constitutional duties. Incidental to the functions confided in Article II is "the power to perform them, without obstruction or impediment." 3 J. Story, Commentaries on the Constitution of the United States § 1563, pp. 418–419 (1833). As a result, "once the President sets forth and explains a conflict between judicial proceeding and public duties," or shows that an order or subpoena would "significantly interfere with his efforts to carry out" those duties, "the matter changes." *Clinton*, 520 U. S., at 710, 714 (opinion of BREYER, J.). At that point, a court should use its inherent authority to quash or modify the subpoena, if necessary to ensure that such "interference with the President's duties would not occur." *Id.*, at 708 (opinion of the Court).

Two hundred years ago, a great jurist of our Court established that no citizen, not even the President, is categorically above the common duty to produce evidence when called upon in a criminal proceeding. We reaffirm that principle today and hold that the President is neither absolutely immune from state criminal subpoenas seeking his private papers nor entitled to a heightened standard of need. * * *

The arguments presented here and in the Court of Appeals were limited to absolute immunity and heightened need. The Court of Appeals, however, has directed that the case be returned to the District Court, where the President may raise further arguments as appropriate. 941 F. 3d, at 646, n. 19. We affirm the judgment of the Court of Appeals and remand the case for further proceedings consistent with this opinion.

JUSTICE KAVANAUGH, with whom JUSTICE GORSUCH joins, concurring in the judgment.

In our system of government, as this Court has often stated, no one is above the law. That principle applies, of course, to a President. At the same time, in light of Article II of the Constitution, this Court has repeatedly declared—and the Court indicates again today—that a court may not proceed against a President as it would against an ordinary litigant. The question here, then, is how to balance the State's interests and the Article II interests. The longstanding precedent that has applied to federal criminal subpoenas for official, privileged Executive Branch information is *United States* v. *Nixon*, 418 U. S. 683 (1974). That landmark case requires that a prosecutor establish a "demonstrated, specific need" for the President's information. *Id.*, at 713.

The *Nixon* "demonstrated, specific need" standard is a tried-and-true test that accommodates both the interests of the criminal process and the Article II interests of the Presidency. The *Nixon* standard ensures that a prosecutor's interest in subpoenaed information is sufficiently important to justify an intrusion on the Article II interests of the Presidency. The *Nixon* standard also reduces the risk of subjecting a President to unwarranted burdens, because it provides that a prosecutor may obtain a President's information only in certain defined circumstances.

Because this case again entails a clash between the interests of the criminal process and the Article II interests of the Presidency, I would apply the longstanding *Nixon* "demonstrated, specific need" standard to this case. * * * I agree that the case should be remanded to the District Court for further proceedings, where the President may raise constitutional and legal objections to the state grand jury subpoena as appropriate.

JUSTICE THOMAS, dissenting.

* * * I agree with the majority that the President does not have absolute immunity from the issuance of a grand jury subpoena. Unlike the majority,

however, I do not reach this conclusion based on a primarily functionalist analysis. Instead, I reach it based on the text of the Constitution, which, as understood by the ratifying public and incorporated into an early circuit opinion by Chief Justice Marshall, does not support the President's claim of absolute immunity.

The text of the Constitution explicitly addresses the privileges of some federal officials, but it does not afford the President absolute immunity. Members of Congress are "privileged from Arrest during their Attendance at the Session of their respective Houses, and in going to and returning from the same," except for "Treason, Felony and Breach of the Peace." Art. I, § 6, cl. 1. The Constitution further specifies that, "for any Speech or Debate in either House, they shall not be questioned in any other Place." *Ibid.* By contrast, the text of the Constitution contains no explicit grant of absolute immunity from legal process for the President. As a Federalist essayist noted during ratification, the President's "person is not so much protected as that of a member of the House of Representatives" because he is subject to the issuance of judicial process "like any other man in the ordinary course of law." An American Citizen I (Sept. 26, 1787), in 2 Documentary History of the Ratification of the Constitution 141 (M. Jansen ed. 1976) (emphasis deleted). * * * Based on the evidence of original meaning and Chief Justice Marshall's early interpretation in *Burr*, the better reading of the text of the Constitution is that the President has no absolute immunity from the issuance of a grand jury subpoena.

Take Note

Under Justice Thomas's approach, was *Nixon v. Fitzgerald* correctly decided?

In *Burr*, after explaining that the President was not absolutely immune from issuance of a subpoena, Chief Justice Marshall proceeded to explain that the President might be excused from the enforcement of one. * * * Chief Justice Marshall set out the pertinent standard: To avoid enforcement of the subpoena, the President must "sho[w]" that "his duties as chief magistrate demand his whole time for national objects." 25 F. Cas. at 34. Although *Burr* involved a federal subpoena, the same principle applies to a state subpoena. * * * Accordingly, a federal court may provide injunctive and declaratory relief to stay enforcement of a state subpoena when the President meets the *Burr* standard.

The *Burr* standard places the burden on the President but also requires courts to take pains to respect the demands on the President's time. * * * The President has vast responsibilities both abroad and at home. * * * A subpoena imposes both demands on the President's limited time and a mental burden, even when the President is not directly engaged in complying. This understanding of the

Presidency should guide courts in deciding whether to enforce a subpoena for the President's documents.

Courts must also recognize their own limitations. When the President asserts that matters of foreign affairs or national defense preclude his compliance with a subpoena, the Judiciary will rarely have a basis for rejecting that assertion. * * * Here, too, Chief Justice Marshall was correct. A court should "fee[l] many, perhaps, peculiar motives for manifesting as guarded a respect for the chief magistrate of the Union as is compatible with its official duties." *Burr*, 25 F. Cas., at 37. Courts should have the same "circumspection" as Chief Justice Marshall before "tak[ing] any step which would in any manner relate to that high personage." *Id.*, at 35.[3]

I agree with the majority that the President has no absolute immunity from the issuance of this subpoena. The President also sought relief from enforcement of the subpoena, however, and he asked this Court to allow further proceedings on that question if we rejected his claim of absolute immunity. The Court inexplicably fails to address this request, although its decision leaves the President free to renew his request for an injunction against enforcement immediately on remand. I would vacate and remand to allow the District Court to determine whether enforcement of this subpoena should be enjoined because the President's "duties as chief magistrate demand his whole time for national objects." Accordingly, I respectfully dissent.

JUSTICE ALITO, dissenting.

This case is almost certain to be portrayed as a case about the current President and the current political situation, but the case has a much deeper significance. While the decision will of course have a direct effect on President Trump, what the Court holds today will also affect all future Presidents—which is to say, it will affect the Presidency, and that is a matter of great and lasting importance to the Nation.

The event that precipitated this case is unprecedented. Respondent Vance, an elected state prosecutor, launched a criminal investigation of a sitting President and obtained a grand jury subpoena for his records. The specific question before us—whether the subpoena may be enforced—cannot be answered adequately

3 * * * I agree with the majority's decision not to adopt [the "heightened need"] standard, but for different reasons. The constitutional question in this case is whether the President is able to perform the duties of his office, whereas a heightened need standard addresses a logically independent issue. Under a heightened-need standard, a grand jury with only the usual need for particular information would be refused it when the President is perfectly able to comply, while a grand jury with a heightened need would be entitled to it even if compliance would place undue obligations on the President. This result makes little sense and lacks any basis in the original understanding of the Constitution. I would leave questions of the grand jury's need to state law.

without considering the broader question that frames it: whether the Constitution imposes restrictions on a State's deployment of its criminal law enforcement powers against a sitting President. If the Constitution sets no such limits, then a local prosecutor may prosecute a sitting President. And if that is allowed, it follows *a fortiori* that the subpoena at issue can be enforced. On the other hand, if the Constitution does not permit a State to prosecute a sitting President, the next logical question is whether the Constitution restrains any other prosecutorial or investigative weapons.

In evaluating these questions, two important structural features must be taken into account. The first is the nature and role of the Presidency. * * * The Constitution entrusts the President with responsibilities that are essential to the country's safety and well-being. The President is Commander in Chief of the Armed Forces. Art. II, § 2, cl. 1. He is responsible for the defense of the country from the moment he enters office until the moment he leaves. The President also has the lead role in foreign relations. * * * As the head of the Executive Branch, the President is ultimately responsible for everything done by all the departments and agencies of the Federal Government and a federal civilian work force that includes millions of employees. These weighty responsibilities impose enormous burdens on the time and energy of any occupant of the Presidency. * * *

The second structural feature is the relationship between the Federal Government and the States. [The] Constitution * * * provided for the Federal Government to be independent of and, within its allotted sphere, supreme over the States. Art. VI, cl. 2. Accordingly, a State may not block or interfere with the lawful work of the National Government. This was an enduring lesson of Chief Justice Marshall's landmark opinion for the Court in *McCulloch* v. *Maryland*, 4 Wheat. 316 (1819). * * * Building on [the decision], two centuries of case law prohibit the States from taxing, regulating, or otherwise interfering with the lawful work of federal agencies, instrumentalities, and officers. * * *

[In] a similar way, a State's sovereign power to enforce its criminal laws must accommodate the indispensable role that the Constitution assigns to the Presidency. This must be the rule with respect to a state prosecution of a sitting President. * * * It has been aptly said that the President is the "sole indispensable man in government," and subjecting a sitting President to criminal prosecution would severely hamper his ability to carry out the vital responsibilities that the Constitution puts in his hands.

The constitutional provisions on impeachment provide further support for the rule that a President may not be prosecuted while in office. The Framers foresaw the need to provide for the possibility that a President might be implicated in the commission of a serious offense, and they did not want the country to be forced to endure such a President for the remainder of his term in office. But when a President has been elected by the people pursuant to the procedures set out in the Constitution, it is no small thing to overturn that choice. The Framers therefore crafted a special set of procedures to deal with that contingency. They put the charging decision in the hands of a body that represents all the people (the House of Representatives), not a single prosecutor or the members of a local grand jury. And they entrusted the weighty decision whether to remove a President to a supermajority of Senators, who were expected to exercise reasoned judgment and not the political passions of the day or the sentiments of a particular region.

The Constitution [also] specifies the consequences of a judgment adverse to the President. After providing that the judgment cannot impose any punishment beyond removal from the Presidency and disqualification from holding any other federal office, the Constitution states that "the Party convicted shall nevertheless be liable and subject to Indictment, Trial, Judgment, and Punishment, according to Law." Art. I, § 3, cl. 7. The plain implication is that criminal prosecution, like removal from the Presidency and disqualification from other offices, is a consequence that can come about only after the Senate's judgment, not during or prior to the Senate trial.

In the proceedings below, neither respondent, nor the District Court, nor the Second Circuit was willing to concede the fundamental point that a sitting President may not be prosecuted by a local district attorney. [Such a scenario would be striking.] If a sitting President were charged in New York County, would he be arrested and fingerprinted? * * * Could he be sent to Rikers Island or be required to post bail? Could the judge impose restrictions on his travel? * * * If the President were charged with a complicated offense requiring a long trial, would he have to put his Presidential responsibilities aside for weeks on end while sitting in a Manhattan courtroom? * * * This entire imagined scene is farcical. * * *

While the prosecution of a sitting President provides the most dramatic example of a clash between the indispensable work of the Presidency and a State's exercise of its criminal law enforcement powers, other examples are easy to imagine. Suppose state officers obtained and sought to execute a search warrant for a sitting President's private quarters in the White House. Suppose a state court authorized surveillance of a telephone that a sitting President was known to use. Or suppose that a sitting President was subpoenaed to testify before a state grand jury and, as is generally the rule, no Presidential aides, even those carrying the so-called "nuclear football," were permitted to enter the grand jury room. What these examples illustrate is a principle that this Court has recognized: legal proceedings involving a sitting President must take the responsibilities and demands of the office into account. See *Clinton* v. *Jones*, 520 U. S. 681, 707 (1997).

It is not enough to recite sayings like "no man is above the law" and "the public has a right to every man's evidence." These sayings are true—and important—but they beg the question. The law applies equally to all persons, including a person who happens for a period of time to occupy the Presidency. But there is no question that the nature of the office demands in some instances that the application of laws be adjusted at least until the person's term in office ends.

[T]he specific investigative weapon at issue in the case before us * * * is less intrusive in an immediate sense than those mentioned above. Since the records are held by, and the subpoena was issued to, a third party, compliance would not require much work on the President's part. * * * But [if] we say that a subpoena to a third party is insufficient to undermine a President's performance of his duties, what about a subpoena served on the President himself? Surely in that case, the President could turn over the work of gathering the requested documents to attorneys or others recruited to perform the task. And if one subpoena is permitted, what about two? Or three? Or ten? Drawing a line based on such factors would involve the same sort of "perplexing inquiry, so unfit for the judicial department" that Marshall rejected in *McCulloch*, 4 Wheat., at 430.

The Court faced a similar issue when it considered whether a President can be sued for an allegedly unlawful act committed in the performance of official duties. See *Nixon* v. *Fitzgerald*, 457 U. S. 731 (1982). We did not ask whether the particular suit before us would have interfered with the carrying out of Presidential duties. (It could not have had that effect because President Nixon had already left office.) Instead, we adopted a rule for all such suits, and we should take a similar approach here. The rule should take into account both the effect of subpoenas on the functioning of the Presidency and the risk that they will be used for harassment.

* * * When the issuance of such a subpoena is part of an investigation that regards the President as a "target" or "subject," the subpoena can easily impair a President's "energetic performance of [his] constitutional duties." *Cheney* v. *United States Dist. Court for D. C.*, 542 U. S. 367, 382 (2004). Few individuals will simply brush off an indication that they may be within a prosecutor's crosshairs. Few will put the matter out of their minds and go about their work unaffected. For many, the prospect of prosecution will be the first and last thing on their minds every day. [There is also potential for the] use of subpoenas to harass * * *. There are

more than 2,300 local prosecutors and district attorneys in the country. Many local prosecutors are elected, and many prosecutors have ambitions for higher elected office. * * * If a sitting President is intensely unpopular in a particular district—and that is a common condition—targeting the President may be an alluring and effective electoral strategy. But it is a strategy that would undermine our constitutional structure.

In light of the above, a subpoena like the one now before us should not be enforced unless it meets a test that takes into account the need to prevent interference with a President's discharge of the responsibilities of the office. I agree with the Court that not all such subpoenas should be barred. There may be situations in which there is an urgent and critical need for the subpoenaed information. The situation in the Burr trial, where the documents at issue were sought by a criminal defendant to defend against a charge of treason, is a good example. But in a case like the one at hand, a subpoena should not be allowed unless a heightened standard is met.

[W]e should not treat this subpoena like an ordinary grand jury subpoena and should not relegate a President to the meager defenses that are available when an ordinary grand jury subpoena is challenged. * * * The Presidency deserves greater protection. Thus, in a case like this one, a prosecutor should be required (1) to provide at least a general description of the possible offenses that are under investigation, (2) to outline how the subpoenaed records relate to those offenses, and (3) to explain why it is important that the records be produced and why it is necessary for production to occur while the President is still in office. In the present case, the district attorney made a brief proffer, but important questions were left hanging. It would not be unduly burdensome to insist on answers before enforcing the subpoena. * * * I therefore respectfully dissent.

POINTS FOR DISCUSSION

a. Absolute Immunity

All nine Justices rejected the President's claim that he is absolutely immune from all forms of criminal process. Is it obvious to you that the Court reached the correct conclusion on this issue? What are the strongest arguments for the President's position?

b. Enforcing a Subpoena Against a Sitting President

The Justices disagreed over the appropriate standard for enforcing a subpoena against the President in a criminal proceeding. Under the Court's approach, no heightened standard applies when a subpoena is directed at the President. Do you agree that the enforcement of subpoenas against sitting Presidents is not likely unduly to impair the President's ability to fulfill the duties of his office? According to the Court, under what circumstances might a court appropriately decline to enforce such a subpoena? Conversely, under the various standards expressed in Justices Kavanaugh's, Thomas's, and Alito's opinions, are you confident that the needs of the criminal justice system will be adequately accommodated?

c. Can a Sitting President Be Indicted?

Suppose that, on remand, the court enforces the subpoena and the President complies. If the documents reveal criminal wrongdoing, could the New York District Attorney indict the President for violation of the state's criminal laws? The Court did not address whether a sitting President is immune from criminal prosecution (state or federal), but Justice Alito asserted in his dissent that a President enjoys such immunity, at a minimum from state prosecutions. Is there an argument that a sitting President should not enjoy such immunity? Does it matter what the nature of the crime is?

TRUMP V. MAZARS USA, LLP

140 S.Ct. 2019 (2020)

CHIEF JUSTICE ROBERTS delivered the opinion of the Court.

Over the course of five days in April 2019, three committees of the U.S. House of Representatives issued four subpoenas seeking information about the finances of President Donald J. Trump, his children, and affiliated businesses. We have held that the House has authority under the Constitution to issue subpoenas to assist it in carrying out its legislative responsibilities. The House asserts that the financial information sought here—encompassing a decade's worth of transactions by the President and his family—will help guide legislative reform in areas ranging from money laundering and terrorism to foreign involvement in U.S. elections. The President contends that the House lacked a valid legislative aim and instead sought these records to harass him, expose personal matters, and conduct law enforcement activities beyond its authority. The question presented is whether the subpoenas exceed the authority of the House under the Constitution.

We have never addressed a congressional subpoena for the President's information. Two hundred years ago, it was established that Presidents may be subpoenaed during a federal criminal proceeding, *United States* v. *Burr*, 25 F. Cas. 30 (No. 14,692d) (CC Va. 1807) (Marshall, Cir. J.), and earlier today we extended that ruling to state criminal proceedings, *Trump* v. *Vance*. Nearly fifty years ago, we held that a federal prosecutor could obtain information from a President despite assertions of executive privilege, *United States* v. *Nixon*, 418 U.S. 683 (1974), and more recently we ruled that a private litigant could subject a President to a damages suit and appropriate discovery obligations in federal court, *Clinton* v. *Jones*, 520 U.S. 681 (1997).

This case is different. Here the President's information is sought not by prosecutors or private parties in connection with a particular judicial proceeding, but by committees of Congress that have set forth broad legislative objectives. Congress and the President—the two political branches established by the Constitution—have an ongoing relationship that the Framers intended to feature both rivalry and reciprocity. See The Federalist No. 51, p. 349 (J. Cooke ed. 1961) (J. Madison); *Youngstown Sheet & Tube Co.* v. *Sawyer*, 343 U.S. 579, 635 (1952) (Jackson, J., concurring). That distinctive aspect necessarily informs our analysis of the question before us.

I

[The House Committee on Financial Services issued broad subpoenas to two banks, Deutsche Bank and Capitol One, seeking financial records concerning the President, his children, their immediate family members, and several businesses. The Committee sought these documents as part of its efforts "to close loopholes that allow corruption, terrorism, and money laundering to infiltrate our country's financial system." The Permanent Select Committee on Intelligence issued an identical subpoena to Deutsche Bank. The subpoena was part of an investigation into foreign efforts to undermine the U.S. political process. The House Committee on Oversight and Reform issued a subpoena to Mazars USA, LLP, an accounting firm. The subpoena sought financial document and records of communications between Mazars and the President and his businesses. The purpose of the subpoena was to determine whether the President had accurately represented his financial affairs.]

Petitioners—the President in his personal capacity, along with his children and affiliated businesses—filed two suits challenging the subpoenas. They contested the subpoena issued by the Oversight Committee in the District Court for the District of Columbia and the subpoenas issued by the Financial Services and Intelligence Committees in the Southern District of New York. In both cases, petitioners contended that the subpoenas lacked a legitimate legislative purpose and violated the separation of powers. The President did not, however, resist the subpoenas by arguing that any of the requested records were protected by executive privilege. For relief, petitioners asked for declaratory judgments and injunctions preventing Mazars and the banks from complying with the subpoenas. Although named as defendants, Mazars and the banks took no positions on the legal issues in these cases, and the House committees intervened to defend the subpoenas. [The lower courts denied relief.]

II

A

The question presented is whether the subpoenas exceed the authority of the House under the Constitution. Historically, disputes over congressional demands for presidential documents have not ended up in court. Instead, they have been hashed out in the "hurly-burly, the give-and-take of the political process between the legislative and the executive." Hearings on S. 2170 et al. before the Subcommittee on Intergovernmental Relations of the Senate Committee on Government Operations, 94th Cong., 1st Sess., 87 (1975) (A. Scalia, Assistant Attorney General, Office of Legal Counsel).

That practice began with George Washington and the early Congress. In 1792, a House committee requested Executive Branch documents pertaining to General St. Clair's campaign against the Indians in the Northwest Territory, which had concluded in an utter rout of federal forces when they were caught by surprise near the present-day border between Ohio and Indiana. See T. Taylor, Grand Inquest: The Story of Congressional Investigations 19–23 (1955). Since this was the first such request from Congress, President Washington called a Cabinet meeting, wishing to take care that his response "be rightly conducted" because it could "become a precedent." 1 Writings of Thomas Jefferson 189 (P. Ford ed. 1892).

The meeting, attended by the likes of Alexander Hamilton, Thomas Jefferson, Edmund Randolph, and Henry Knox, ended with the Cabinet of "one mind": The House had authority to "institute inquiries" and "call for papers" but the President could "exercise a discretion" over disclosures, "communicat[ing] such papers as the public good would permit" and "refus[ing]" the rest. *Id.*, at 189–190. President Washington then dispatched Jefferson to speak to individual congressmen and "bring them by persuasion into the right channel." *Id.*, at 190. The discussions were apparently fruitful, as the House later narrowed its request and the documents were supplied without recourse to the courts. See 3 Annals of Cong. 536 (1792); Taylor, *supra*, at 24.

Jefferson, once he became President, followed Washington's precedent. In early 1807, after Jefferson had disclosed that "sundry persons" were conspiring to invade Spanish territory in North America with a private army, 16 Annals of Cong. 686–687, the House requested that the President produce any information in his possession touching on the conspiracy (except for information that would harm the public interest), *id.*, at 336, 345, 359. Jefferson chose not to divulge the entire "voluminous" correspondence on the subject, explaining that much of it was "private" or mere "rumors" and "neither safety nor justice" permitted him to "expos[e] names" apart from identifying the conspiracy's "principal actor": Aaron Burr. *Id.*, at 39–40. Instead of the entire correspondence, Jefferson sent Congress particular documents and a special message summarizing the conspiracy. *Id.*, at 39–43; see generally *Vance*, *ante*, at 3–4. Neither Congress nor the President asked the Judiciary to intervene.

Ever since, congressional demands for the President's information have been resolved by the political branches without involving this Court. * * *

This dispute therefore represents a significant departure from historical practice. Although the parties agree that this particular controversy is justiciable, we recognize that it is the first of its kind to reach this Court; that disputes of this sort can raise important issues concerning relations between the branches; that related disputes involving congressional efforts to seek official Executive Branch information recur on a regular basis, including in the context of deeply partisan controversy; and that Congress and the Executive have nonetheless managed for over two centuries to resolve such disputes among themselves without the benefit of guidance from us. Such longstanding practice "is a consideration of great weight" in cases concerning "the allocation of power between [the] two elected branches of Government," and it imposes on us a duty of care to ensure that we not needlessly disturb "the compromises and working arrangements that [those] branches . . . themselves have reached." *NLRB* v. *Noel Canning*, 573 U.S. 513, 524–526 (2014) (quoting *The Pocket Veto Case*, 279 U.S. 655, 689 (1929)). With that in mind, we turn to the question presented.

B

Congress has no enumerated constitutional power to conduct investigations or issue subpoenas, but we have held that each House has power "to secure needed information" in order to legislate. *McGrain* v. *Daugherty*, 273 U.S. 135, 161 (1927). This "power of inquiry—with process to enforce it—is an essential and appropriate auxiliary to the legislative function." *Id.*, at 174. Without information, Congress would be shooting in the dark, unable to legislate "wisely or effectively." *Id.*, at 175. The congressional power to obtain information is "broad" and "indispensable." *Watkins* v. *United States*, 354 U.S. 178, 187, 215 (1957). It encompasses inquiries into the administration of existing laws, studies of proposed laws, and "surveys of defects in our social, economic or political system for the purpose of enabling the Congress to remedy them." *Id.*, at 187.

Because this power is "justified solely as an adjunct to the legislative process," it is subject to several limitations. *Id.*, at 197. Most importantly, a congressional subpoena is valid only if it is "related to, and in furtherance of, a legitimate task of the Congress." *Id.*, at 187. The subpoena must serve a "valid legislative purpose," *Quinn* v. *United States*, 349 U.S. 155, 161 (1955); it must "concern[ ] a subject on which legislation 'could be had,' " *Eastland* v. *United States Servicemen's Fund*, 421 U.S. 491, 506 (1975) (quoting *McGrain*, 273 U.S., at 177).

Furthermore, Congress may not issue a subpoena for the purpose of "law enforcement," because "those powers are assigned under our Constitution to the Executive and the Judiciary." *Quinn*, 349 U.S., at 161. Thus Congress may not use subpoenas to "try" someone "before [a] committee for any crime or wrongdoing." *McGrain*, 273 U. S., at 179. Congress has no " 'general' power to inquire into private affairs and compel disclosures," *id.*, at 173–174, and "there is no congressional power to expose for the sake of exposure," *Watkins*, 354 U.S., at 200. "Investigations conducted solely for the personal aggrandizement of the investigators or to 'punish' those investigated are indefensible." *Id.*, at 187.

Finally, recipients of legislative subpoenas retain their constitutional rights throughout the course of an investigation. See *id.*, at 188, 198. And recipients have long been understood to retain common law and constitutional privileges with respect to certain materials, such as attorney-client communications and governmental communications protected by executive privilege. See, *e.g.*, Congressional Research Service, *supra,* at 16–18 (attorney-client privilege); *Senate Select Committee*, 498 F.2d, at 727, 730–731 (executive privilege).

C

The President contends, as does the Solicitor General appearing on behalf of the United States, that the usual rules for congressional subpoenas do not govern here because the President's papers are at issue. They argue for a more demanding standard based in large part on cases involving the Nixon tapes—recordings of conversations between President Nixon and close advisers discussing the break-in at the Democratic National Committee's headquarters at the Watergate complex. The tapes were subpoenaed by a Senate committee and the Special Prosecutor investigating the break-in, prompting President Nixon to invoke executive privilege and leading to two cases addressing the showing necessary to require the President to comply with the subpoenas. See *Nixon*, 418 U.S. 683; *Senate Select Committee*, 498 F.2d 725.

Those cases, the President and the Solicitor General now contend, establish the standard that should govern the House subpoenas here. Quoting *Nixon*, the President asserts that the House must establish a "demonstrated, specific need" for the financial information, just as the Watergate special prosecutor was required to do in order to obtain the tapes. 418 U.S., at 713. And drawing on *Senate Select Committee*—the D.C. Circuit case refusing to enforce the Senate subpoena for the tapes—the President and the Solicitor General argue that the House must show that the financial information is "demonstrably critical" to its legislative purpose. 498 F.2d, at 731.

Make the Connection

The President did not argue that the executive privilege that the Supreme Court recognized in *United States v. Nixon* protects the subpoenaed documents. Instead, he argued only that a House committee must show a "demonstrated, specific need" for the subpoenaed documents. Why aren't the documents at issue in this case covered by executive privilege? What arguments support the requirement of "demonstrated, specific need" in *Nixon*? Do those arguments apply here?

We disagree that these demanding standards apply here. Unlike the cases before us, *Nixon* and *Senate Select Committee* involved Oval Office communications over which the President asserted executive privilege. That privilege safeguards the public interest in candid, confidential deliberations within the Executive Branch; it is "fundamental to the operation of Government." *Nixon*, 418 U.S., at 708. As a result, information subject to executive privilege deserves "the greatest protection consistent with the fair administration of justice." *Id.*, at 715. We decline to transplant that protection root and branch to cases involving nonprivileged, private information, which by definition does not implicate sensitive Executive Branch deliberations.

The standards proposed by the President and the Solicitor General—if applied outside the context of privileged information—would risk seriously impeding Congress in carrying out its responsibilities. The President and the Solicitor General would apply the same exacting standards to *all* subpoenas for the President's information, without recognizing distinctions between privileged and nonprivileged information, between official and personal information, or between various legislative objectives. Such a categorical approach would represent a significant departure from the longstanding way of doing business between the branches, giving short shrift to Congress's important interests in conducting inquiries to obtain the information it needs to legislate effectively. Confounding the legislature in that effort would be contrary to the principle that:

> It is the proper duty of a representative body to look diligently into every affair of government and to talk much about what it sees. It is meant to be the eyes and the voice, and to embody the wisdom and will of its constituents. Unless Congress have and use every means of acquainting itself with the acts and the disposition of the administrative agents of the government, the country must be helpless to learn how it is being served.

United States v. *Rumely*, 345 U.S. 41, 43 (1953) (internal quotation marks omitted).

Legislative inquiries might involve the President in appropriate cases; as noted, Congress's responsibilities extend to "every affair of government." *Ibid.* Because the President's approach does not take adequate account of these significant congressional interests, we do not adopt it.

D

The House meanwhile would have us ignore that these suits involve the President. Invoking our precedents concerning investigations that did not target the President's papers, the House urges us to uphold its subpoenas because they "relate[] to a valid legislative purpose" or "concern[] a subject on which legislation could be had." Brief for Respondent 46 (quoting *Barenblatt* v. *United States*, 360 U.S. 109, 127 (1959), and *Eastland*, 421 U.S., at 506)). That approach is appropriate, the House argues, because the cases before us are not "momentous separation-of-powers disputes."

The House's approach fails to take adequate account of the significant separation of powers issues raised by congressional subpoenas for the President's information. Congress and the President have an ongoing institutional relationship as the "opposite and rival" political branches established by the Constitution. The Federalist No. 51, at 349. As a result, congressional subpoenas directed at the President differ markedly from congressional subpoenas we have previously reviewed, *e.g.*, *Barenblatt*, 360 U.S., at 127; *Eastland*, 421 U.S., at 506, and they bear little resemblance to criminal subpoenas issued to the President in the course of a specific investigation, see *Nixon*, 418 U. S. 683. Unlike those subpoenas, congressional subpoenas for the President's information unavoidably pit the political branches against one another. Cf. *In re Sealed Case*, 121 F.3d 729, 753 (D.C. Cir. 1997) ("The President's ability to withhold information from Congress implicates different constitutional considerations than the President's ability to withhold evidence in judicial proceedings.").

Far from accounting for separation of powers concerns, the House's approach aggravates them by leaving essentially no limits on the congressional power to subpoena the President's personal records. Any personal paper possessed by a President could potentially "relate to" a conceivable subject of legislation, for Congress has broad legislative powers that touch a vast number of subjects. The President's financial records could relate to economic reform, medical records to health reform, school transcripts to education reform, and so on. Indeed, at argument, the House was unable to identify *any* type of information that lacks some relation to potential legislation.

Without limits on its subpoena powers, Congress could "exert an imperious controul" over the Executive Branch and aggrandize itself at the President's expense, just as the Framers feared. The Federalist No. 71, at 484 (A. Hamilton); see *id.*, No. 48, at 332–333 (J. Madison); *Bowsher* v. *Synar*, 478 U.S. 714, 721–722, 727 (1986). And a limitless subpoena power would transform the "established practice" of the political branches. *Noel Canning*, 573 U.S., at 524. Instead of negotiating over information requests, Congress could simply walk away from the bargaining table and compel compliance in court.

The interbranch conflict here does not vanish simply because the subpoenas seek personal papers or because the President sued in his personal capacity. The President is the only person who alone composes a branch of government. As a result, there is not always a clear line between his personal and official affairs. "The interest of the man" is often "connected with the constitutional rights of the place." The Federalist No. 51, at 349. Given the close connection between the Office of the President and its occupant, congressional demands for the President's papers can implicate the relationship between the branches regardless whether those papers are personal or official. Either way, a demand may aim to harass the President or render him "complaisan[t] to the humors of the Legislature." *Id.*, No. 71, at 483. In fact, a subpoena for personal papers may pose a heightened risk of such impermissible purposes, precisely because of the documents' personal nature and their less evident connection to a legislative task. No one can say that the controversy here is less significant to the relationship between the branches simply because it involves personal papers. Quite the opposite. That appears to be what makes the matter of such great consequence to the President and Congress.

E

Congressional subpoenas for the President's personal information implicate weighty concerns regarding the separation of powers. Neither side, however, identifies an approach that accounts for these concerns. For more than two centuries, the political branches have resolved information disputes using the wide variety of means that the Constitution puts at their disposal. The nature of such interactions would be transformed by judicial enforcement of either of the approaches suggested by the parties, eroding a "[d]eeply embedded traditional way[ ] of conducting government." *Youngstown Sheet & Tube Co.*, 343 U.S., at 610 (Frankfurter, J., concurring).

A balanced approach is necessary, one that takes a "considerable impression" from "the practice of the government," *McCulloch* v. *Maryland*, 4 Wheat. 316, 401 (1819), and "resist[s]" the "pressure inherent within each of the separate Branches to exceed the outer limits of its power," *INS* v. *Chadha*, 462 U.S. 919, 951 (1983). We therefore conclude that, in assessing whether a subpoena directed at the President's personal information is "related to, and in furtherance of, a legitimate task of the Congress," *Watkins*, 354 U.S., at 187, courts must perform a careful analysis that takes adequate account of the separation of powers principles at stake, including both the significant legislative interests of Congress and the "unique position" of the President, *Clinton*, 520 U.S., at 698. Several special considerations inform this analysis.

Take Note

The Court describes here the "special considerations" upon which the validity of the subpoenas depends. Why does the Court remand the case so that the lower courts can take these special considerations into account instead of making its own decision?

First, courts should carefully assess whether the asserted legislative purpose warrants the significant step of involving the President and his papers. " '[O]ccasion[s] for constitutional confrontation between the two branches' should be avoided whenever possible." *Cheney* v. *United States Dist. Court for D. C.*, 542 U.S. 367, 389–390 (2004) (quoting *Nixon*, 418 U.S., at 692). Congress may not rely on the President's information if other sources could reasonably provide Congress the information it needs in light of its particular legislative objective. The President's unique constitutional position means that Congress may not look to him as a "case study" for general legislation.

Unlike in criminal proceedings, where "[t]he very integrity of the judicial system" would be undermined without "full disclosure of all the facts," *Nixon*, 418 U.S., at 709, efforts to craft legislation involve predictive policy judgments that are "not hamper[ed] . . . in quite the same way" when every scrap of potentially relevant evidence is not available, *Cheney*, 542 U.S., at 384; see *Senate Select Committee*, 498 F.2d, at 732. While we certainly recognize Congress's important interests in obtaining information through appropriate inquiries, those interests are not sufficiently powerful to justify access to the President's personal papers when other sources could provide Congress the information it needs.

Second, to narrow the scope of possible conflict between the branches, courts should insist on a subpoena no broader than reasonably necessary to support Congress's legislative objective. The specificity of the subpoena's request "serves as an important safeguard against unnecessary intrusion into the operation of the Office of the President." *Cheney*, 542 U.S., at 387.

Third, courts should be attentive to the nature of the evidence offered by Congress to establish that a subpoena advances a valid legislative purpose. The more detailed and substantial the evidence of Congress's legislative purpose, the better. See *Watkins*, 354 U.S., at 201, 205 (preferring such evidence over "vague" and "loosely worded" evidence of Congress's purpose). That is particularly true when Congress contemplates legislation that raises sensitive constitutional issues, such as legislation concerning the Presidency. In such cases, it is "impossible" to conclude that a subpoena is designed to advance a valid legislative purpose unless Congress adequately identifies its aims and explains why the President's information will advance its consideration of the possible legislation. *Id.*, at 205–206, 214–215.

Fourth, courts should be careful to assess the burdens imposed on the President by a subpoena. We have held that burdens on the President's time and attention stemming from judicial process and litigation, without more, generally do not cross constitutional lines. See *Vance*; *Clinton*, 520 U.S., at 704–705. But burdens imposed by a congressional subpoena should be carefully scrutinized, for they stem from a rival political branch that has an ongoing relationship with the President and incentives to use subpoenas for institutional advantage.

Other considerations may be pertinent as well; one case every two centuries does not afford enough experience for an exhaustive list.

When Congress seeks information "needed for intelligent legislative action," it "unquestionably" remains "the duty of *all* citizens to cooperate." *Watkins*, 354 U.S., at 187 (emphasis added). Congressional subpoenas for information from the President, however, implicate special concerns regarding the separation of powers. The courts below did not take adequate account of those concerns. The judgments of the Courts of Appeals for the D. C. Circuit and the Second Circuit are vacated, and the cases are remanded for further proceedings consistent with this opinion.

JUSTICE THOMAS, dissenting.

[Following a lengthy analysis of the text of the constitution and historical practice, Justice Thomas concluded that it is "readily apparent that the Committees have no constitutional authority to subpoena private, nonofficial documents."] If the Committees wish to investigate alleged wrongdoing by the

President and obtain documents from him, the Constitution provides Congress with a special mechanism for doing so: impeachment.

* * * The founding generation understood impeachment as a check on Presidential abuses. In response to charges that impeachment "confounds legislative and judiciary authorities in the same body," Alexander Hamilton called it "an essential check in the hands of [Congress] upon the encroachments of the executive." The Federalist No. 66, at 401–402. And, in the Virginia ratifying convention, James Madison identified impeachment as a check on Presidential abuse of the treaty power. 10 Documentary History 1397.

The power to impeach includes a power to investigate and demand documents. Impeachments in the States often involved an investigation. In 1781, the Virginia Legislature began what Edmund Randolph called an "impeachment" of then-Governor Thomas Jefferson. P. Hoffer & N. Hull, Impeachment in America, 1635–1805, p. 85 (1984). This "most publicized and far-reaching impeachment inquiry for incompetence" included an "inquir[y] into the conduct of the executive of this state for the last two months." *Ibid.* The legislatures of New Jersey, *id.*, at 92, and Pennsylvania, *id.*, at 93–95, similarly investigated officials through impeachment proceedings.

Reinforcing this understanding, the founding generation repeatedly referred to impeachment as an "inquest." See 4 Debates on the Constitution 44 (J. Elliot ed. 1854) (speech of A. Maclaine) (referring to the House as "the grand inquest of the Union at large"); The Federalist No. 65, at 397 (Hamilton) (referring to the House as "a method of NATIONAL INQUEST"); 2 Records of the Federal Convention 154 (M. Farrand ed. 1911) (record from the Committee of Detail stating that "[t]he House of Representatives shall be the grand Inquest of this Nation; and all Impeachments shall be made by them"); see also Mass. Const., ch. 1, § 3, Art. VI (1780) (referring to the Massachusetts House of Representatives as "the Grand Inquest of this Commonwealth"). At the time, an "inquest" referred to an "[i]nquiry, especially that made by a Jury" or "the Jury itself." N. Bailey, Universal Etymological Dictionary (22d ed. 1770).

The Founders were also aware of the contemporaneous impeachment of Warren Hastings in England, in which the House of Commons heard witnesses before voting to impeach. P. Marshall, The Impeachment of Warren Hastings 40–41, 58 (1965). In the first impeachment under the new Constitution, Congressmen cited the Hastings impeachment as precedent for several points, including the power to take testimony before impeaching. 7 Annals of Cong. 456 (1797) (Rep. Rutledge); *id.*, at 459 (Rep. Sitgreaves); *id.*, at 460 (Rep. Gallatin).

Other evidence from the 1790s confirms that the power to investigate includes the power to demand documents. When the House of Representatives sought documents related to the Jay Treaty from President George Washington, he refused to provide them on the ground that the House had no legislative powers relating to the ratification of treaties. 5 Annals of Cong. 760–762 (1796). But he carefully noted that "[i]t does not occur that the inspection of the papers asked for can be relative to any purpose under the cognizance of the House of Representatives, except that of an impeachment; which the resolution has not expressed." *Id.,* at 760. In other words, he understood that the House can demand documents as part of its power to impeach.

This Court has also long recognized the power of the House to demand documents. Even as it questioned the power to issue legislative subpoenas, the Court in *Kilbourn* acknowledged the ability to "compel the attendance of witnesses, and their answer to proper questions" when "the question of . . . impeachment is before either body acting in its appropriate sphere on that subject." 103 U. S., at 190.

I express no view today on the boundaries of the power to demand documents in connection with impeachment proceedings. But the power of impeachment provides the House with authority to investigate and hold accountable Presidents who commit high crimes or misdemeanors. That is the proper path by which the Committees should pursue their demands.

JUSTICE ALITO, dissenting.

JUSTICE THOMAS makes a valuable argument about the constitutionality of congressional subpoenas for a President's personal documents. In these cases, however, I would assume for the sake of argument that such subpoenas are not categorically barred. Nevertheless, legislative subpoenas for a President's personal documents are inherently suspicious. Such documents are seldom of any special value in considering potential legislation, and subpoenas for such documents can easily be used for improper non-legislative purposes. Accordingly, courts must be very sensitive to separation of powers issues when they are asked to approve the enforcement of such subpoenas.

In many cases, disputes about subpoenas for Presidential documents are fought without judicial involvement. If Congress attempts to obtain such documents by subpoenaing a President directly, those two heavyweight institutions can use their considerable weapons to settle the matter. But when Congress issues such a subpoena to a third party, Congress must surely appreciate that the Judiciary may be pulled into the dispute, and Congress should not expect that the courts will allow the subpoena to be enforced without seriously examining its legitimacy.

Whenever such a subpoena comes before a court, Congress should be required to make more than a perfunctory showing that it is seeking the documents for a legitimate legislative purpose and not for the purpose of exposing supposed Presidential wrongdoing. See *ante*, at 12. The House can inquire about possible Presidential wrongdoing pursuant to its impeachment power, see *ante* (THOMAS, J., dissenting), but the Committees do not defend these subpoenas as ancillary to that power.

Instead, they claim that the subpoenas were issued to gather information that is relevant to legislative issues, but there is disturbing evidence of an improper law enforcement purpose. See 940 F.3d 710, 767–771 (D.C. Cir. 2019) (Rao, J., dissenting). In addition, the sheer volume of documents sought calls out for explanation.

The Court recognizes that the decisions below did not give adequate consideration to separation of powers concerns. Therefore, after setting out a non-exhaustive list of considerations for the lower courts to take into account, the Court vacates the judgments of the Courts of Appeals and sends the cases back for reconsideration. I agree that the lower courts erred and that these cases must be remanded, but I do not think that the considerations outlined by the Court can be properly satisfied unless the House is required to show more than it has put forward to date.

Specifically, the House should provide a description of the type of legislation being considered, and while great specificity is not necessary, the description should be sufficient to permit a court to assess whether the particular records sought are of any special importance. The House should also spell out its constitutional authority to enact the type of legislation that it is contemplating, and it should justify the scope of the subpoenas in relation to the articulated legislative needs. In addition, it should explain why the subpoenaed information, as opposed to information available from other sources, is needed. Unless the House is required to make a showing along these lines, I would hold that enforcement of the subpoenas cannot be ordered. Because I find the terms of the Court's remand inadequate, I must respectfully dissent.

Food for Thought

In what way is Justice Alito's standard for the validity of a subpoena to the President more demanding than the Court's opinion?

POINTS FOR DISCUSSION

a. Special Considerations?

The Court announces four "special considerations" that should "inform" a court's assessment of a subpoena directed at the President but says that other considerations may also be pertinent. What authority does the Court cite for each of the four identified special considerations? How might those instructions play out in this case? What other considerations might be relevant?

b. Victory or Defeat?

The Court did not decide whether the subpoenas were enforceable but instead remanded the case so that the lower courts could address several "special considerations" before making their decisions. Despite this limited result, some observers saw this case as very helpful to President Trump, predicting that litigation would likely drag out until after the election in November 2020. For example, an author in an influential Capitol Hill newspaper immediately predicted that the decision "will frustrate the House's effort to get President Donald Trump's [personal and business information] before the November election." Todd Ruger, *Supreme Court Caps Congressional Power to Subpoena Presidential Records*, Roll Call, Jul. 9, 2020. Few if any commentators appeared to be concerned that a delay in enforcing the subpoenas would hinder the House's stated efforts to develop legislation. Does the focus on the presidential election rather than the stated purposes for which the subpoenaed documents were sought call into question the validity of the subpoenas? Or does it underscore valid reasons why Congress might want the information in the first place?

Executive Summary of This Chapter

The Constitution establishes the **separation of powers** in the first sections of Articles I, II, and III by assigning legislative authority to Congress, executive authority to the President, and judicial authority to the Supreme Court (and inferior federal courts). Violations of the separation of powers may occur when one branch of government tries to exercise power that belongs to another branch, or when one branch tries to surrender its power to other branches.

With respect to **domestic affairs**, the Supreme Court has held that the President may exercise only those powers granted expressly or implicitly by a statute or by the Constitution. *Youngstown Sheet & Tube v. Sawyer* (1952). Accordingly, the President did not have the power to seize private property outside the theater of war except pursuant to a statute.

The President may enter into **international agreements** settling claims by United States citizens against a foreign government even in the absence of express statutory or constitutional authority and even if the agreements abrogate state-law rights. *Dames & Moore v. Regan* (1981).

With respect to **international affairs**, the theory of the "**extra-constitutional origin of the foreign affairs power"** says that the United States may exercise not only the powers that the Constitution expressly grants, but also other foreign affairs powers enjoyed by all sovereigns. *United States v. Curtiss-Wright Export* (1936).

As a practical matter, the President can exercise some foreign affairs powers not expressly granted in the Constitution, because the federal courts will decline to review the President's actions under the political question doctrine or other doctrines. For example, the Supreme Court declined in *Goldwater v. Carter* (1979) to decide whether the President had **the power to rescind treaty obligations**, effectively allowing the President to rescind the treaty.

The President also has the exclusive power of "recognition"—that is, the power to "make the specific decision of what foreign power he will recognize as legitimate, both for the Nation as a whole and for the purpose of making his own position clear within the context of recognition in discussions and negotiations with foreign nations." *Zivotofsky v. Kerry* (2015). Accordingly, Congress cannot require the President to "contradict his own statement regarding a determination of formal recognition." *Id.*

If federal legislation grants the President authority to use military force, but does not specify the details, the President has only the powers granted by the Constitution, by other statutes, and by the laws of war. Exercising these powers, the President may detain enemy combatants, if they are accorded certain requirements imposed by the Due Process Clause. *Hamdi v. Rumsfeld* (2004). But the President may not try them by military commissions if the procedures of those military commissions would violate other federal statutes or the laws of war. *Hamdan v. Rumsfeld* (2006).

The Executive Privilege doctrine, which is constitutionally implied by the need for the effective discharge of executive power, says that the President has a qualified privilege to keep confidential any communications with executive advisors. Although the privilege is not absolute, it generally will protect any communications with executive advisors regarding "military, diplomatic, or sensitive national security secrets." Conversely, "the demonstrated, specific need for evidence in a pending criminal trial" can overcome the assertion of executive privilege. *United States v. Nixon* (1974).

The President has absolute immunity from civil liability for official acts taken while President. *Nixon v. Fitzgerald* (1982). But the President does not have immunity from, and does not have a right to delay lawsuits for, private acts, even while still serving as President. *Clinton v. Jones* (1997).

The President is not absolutely immune from grand jury subpoenas nor are such subpoenas subject to a heightened standard of review. The President may challenge the subpoenas on grounds permitted to all citizens by state law. In addition, the President can challenge subpoenas on the ground that compliance would impede the President's constitutional duties. *Trump v. Vance* (2020).

If the House or Senate seeks information about the President and issues subpoenas to third-parties (such as banks or accountants) to obtain the information, the President may challenge the subpoenas on the ground that they exceed the authority of the House or Senate. The validity of the subpoenas depends on several "special considerations," including: (1) whether the asserted legislative purpose warrants the significant step of involving the President and his papers; (2) whether the subpoenas are no broader than reasonably necessary to support Congress's legislative objective; (3) what kind of evidence Congress has offered to establish that the subpoenas advance a valid legislative purpose; and (4) how great are the burdens imposed on the President by the subpoenas. *Trump v. Mazars USA, LLP* (2020).

POINT-COUNTERPOINT

Did the Court strike the right balance between the President's power and Congress's power in the "war on terror"?

POINT: PETER J. SMITH

In *Hamdi v. Rumsfeld*, 542 U.S. 507 (2004), and the other modern cases on the President's power in the "war on terror," the Court properly imposed limits on the President's authority to act in the face of congressional prohibition. The power that the President asserted in those cases was truly breathtaking, and fundamentally inconsistent with our constitutional design.

In our constitutional scheme, the President, like any other person, is subject to the rule of law. And generally speaking, it is Congress that creates the law, not the President. To be sure, it oversimplifies matters to suggest, as did Justice Black in *Youngstown Sheet & Tube Co. v. Sawyer*, 343 U.S. 579 (1952), that one can answer the question of the scope of the President's power by noting that the President is not a "lawmaker." After all, the Court has long recognized that Congress may delegate broad policy-making authority to the President. But when Congress affirmatively prohibits the President from acting, or when the President seeks without congressional authorization to take actions that touch on individual rights in matters that the Constitution commits in large part to congressional control, claims of presidential authority must be viewed with a skeptical eye.

The cases arising from the war on terror involved assertions of presidential power in just such circumstances. Article I specifically empowers Congress, and not the President, to "declare War," to "make Rules for * * * the Regulation of the land and naval Forces," and to "make Rules concerning Captures on Land and Water," powers that, together, appear to embrace rules about how to detain and interrogate persons accused of taking up arms against the United States. And Congress has exercised those powers to impose limits on the detention, treatment, and trial of such persons. To be sure, the Constitution also makes the President the Commander in Chief of the armed forces. But that clause was designed largely to make clear that the military would be subject to civilian control—and thus to the rule of law. See The Federalist No. 69.

It is in light of this background that one must evaluate claims of presidential authority in the war on terror. Of course, the Constitution should not be read so inflexibly as to prevent the President from acting in an emergency, without congressional authorization, to protect the nation. For example, few doubt that the President would have authority, even before Congress has had the opportunity to act, to repel an imminent invasion. But the authority that the President claimed in the recent war on terror cases went far beyond this modest and unobjectionable power.

In *Hamdi*, the President essentially asserted the power to round up American citizens, declare them enemies of the state, and then, on the basis of nothing more than his personal, unsubstantiated declaration, detain them indefinitely—with no right to a lawyer or a hearing, and no opportunity for the courts or the Congress ever to intervene. The Court properly declined to find such a power in the broadly worded Authorization to Use Military Force. Indeed, such a power—even if exercised in good faith and with the best intentions—is fundamentally inconsistent with the rule of law and long-held constitutional values.

Resolving the proper relationship between Congress and the President is, of course, only one part of the task that confronts the courts in cases arising from the war on terror. Wholly aside from separation-of-powers concerns, constitutional protections for individual rights might preclude the President from taking these actions even *with* express congressional authorization, and *Hamdi* may well be vulnerable to criticism for failing fully to recognize those protections. But if nothing else, the Court made clear that the President is subject to the rule of law. This is an essential step in the process of determining the proper balance of power between the President and Congress, even in matters of war and national security.

COUNTERPOINT: GREGORY E. MAGGS

The Supreme Court's first four war on terror cases together raise a serious separation of powers problem, but the problem does not concern the separation between the President and Congress. In each case, the President in fact acted with statutory authority from Congress. Instead, the problem concerns the actions of the Supreme Court. Although the Court began with restraint, it increasingly usurped the role of the political branches.

In *Hamdi v. Rumsfeld*, 542 U.S. 507 (2004), the President claimed that Congress by legislation had authorized him to use military force and that under this authority he could detain enemy combatants, including U.S. citizens. Five members of the Court correctly agreed, provided that the President properly determined that the persons detained actually were enemy combatants. This case is largely unremarkable from a separation of powers point of view.

In *Rasul v. Bush*, 542 U.S. 466 (2004), the President claimed that the habeas corpus statute enacted by Congress did not give the Court jurisdiction over a detainee held at Guantanamo Bay, Cuba. A majority of the Court, however, overruled prior precedent and misread the habeas corpus statute so that the Court could assert jurisdiction. The Court thus insinuated itself into policy matters that belonged to Congress and the President. In a bipartisan move, Congress promptly rebuked the Court for this usurpation by enacting the Detainee Treatment Act of 2005, which re-stripped the Court of habeas corpus jurisdiction.

In *Hamdan v. Rumsfeld*, 548 U.S. 557 (2006), the Supreme Court also abused its power by again misinterpreting congressional legislation. The Court wrongly held that the Detainee Treatment Act of 2005 did not apply to pending cases, contrary to its usual construction of jurisdictional statutes. It also incorrectly held that the Uniform Code of Military Justice (UCMJ) prohibited the President from trying war criminals by military commission when the military commission procedures differed from those used by courts-martial. This decision was wrong because, although UCMJ imposed a uniformity requirement, the requirement meant only that Army military commissions had to be the same as Navy and Air Force military commissions. It did not mean that military commissions had to be uniform with courts-martial. In the Military Commissions Act of 2006, a bipartisan Congress again rebuked the Court by overruling both statutory interpretations in *Hamdan* and again granting authority to the President.

Finally, in *Boumediene v. Bush*, 553 U.S. 723 (2008), the Court apparently realized that it could no longer play games with the President and Congress by misconstruing legislation. Instead, it held that the Military Commissions Act of 2006 was unconstitutional. Again disregarding precedent, the Court ruled that enemy combatants detained outside the United States may have a constitutional right to habeas corpus. This incorrect decision represents the most serious separation of powers problem to date. Because the Court couched its usurpation in constitutional terms, Congress and the President have no means to respond. As a result, the Supreme Court is now in charge of an important part of military policy.

CHAPTER 6

The Separation of Powers: The Legislative Process

INTRODUCTION

In Chapter 5, we considered the Federal Executive Power. The discussion necessarily touched not only on the President's constitutional powers, but also the powers of Congress; after all, challenges to the President's assertion of power often are based on an assertion that the President has encroached on the powers of Congress, or at least acted in conflict with Congress's assertion of its own powers.

In this chapter, we consider the federal legislative power more directly. But in so doing, we of course cannot treat Congress's power in isolation. Indeed, most of the cases that we consider in this chapter involve either a conflict between Congress's power and the President's power or a claim that Congress has impermissibly given away its power to another branch. The issues that we raised in Chapter 5, therefore, remain highly relevant here. In the sections that follow, we consider Congress's authority to delegate power to other governmental actors, including the President and officials at administrative agencies; congressional attempts to exclude the President from the legislative process; the implications of the requirements of "bicameralism and presentment"; Congress's power to control Executive officials; and the limits imposed on Congress's power by the constitutional prohibition on Bills of Attainder.

A. DELEGATION OF LEGISLATIVE POWER

In the traditional account of the law-making process, Congress passes specific laws, which the executive branch then carries out or enforces. The federal criminal law is the classic example of this process. Congress has passed statutes making it a criminal offense to rob a federally insured bank, to counterfeit money, to launder money, or to assassinate government officials. These statutes specify all of the elements of these offenses because Congress has made all of the legislative choices about what they should be. The role of the executive branch is simply to enforce them by obtaining indictments against suspected offenders and then prosecuting them.

On this account, Congress makes the important policy decisions in enacting the law—to take one of the examples above, Congress has decided that robbing a federally insured bank is an offense worthy of punishment, and has identified the specific elements of the offense, see 18 U.S.C. § 2113—and prosecutors in the executive branch merely enforce those decisions, by seeking indictments and prosecuting persons accused of violating the law.

Not every federal statute, however, contemplates this allocation of authority between Congress and the executive branch. Particularly since the emergence of the modern administrative state, Congress has passed general laws that give administrative agencies or other executive officers discretion to make and then enforce rules, regulations, and decisions for achieving the goals and objectives of the general laws. Indeed, this approach to law making is perhaps now more common. As the federal government has become enormous, the kinds of problems that it seeks to solve have become more complex. Congress, for example, wants to regulate the environment, the energy industry, the manufacture of food and drugs, and so forth. But Congress recognizes that its members do not have the knowledge or the time to figure out all of the details, or to respond to rapidly changing facts on the ground. As a result, Congress does not try to specify all of the regulatory details in the statutes that it passes. Instead, Congress passes laws that give administrative agencies discretion to formulate the necessary regulations for achieving various goals.

For example, Congress might pass statutes giving the Environmental Protection Agency (EPA) discretion to issue regulations to protect the air or water. Or Congress might pass laws giving the Food and Drug Administration (FDA) discretion to regulate drug safety. Any regulations promulgated by the EPA or FDA under these statutes have the force of law, and the executive branch will enforce them.

Perspective and Analysis

Consider the following account of how Congress relies on administrative agencies:

> Congress typically assigns to an agency responsibility for constructing a regulatory or benefit program that is consistent with a long, complicated statute. When that statute emerges from the sausage factory that is the legislative process, it invariably includes scores of gaps, ambiguities, and internally inconsistent provisions. * * * An agency's task in this typical situation is to construct a coherent regulatory program within the boundaries created by the statutes that limit the agency's discretion.

Richard Pierce, *Reconciling Chevron and Stare Decisis*, 85 Geo. L.J. 2225, 2235 (1997).

Such statutes, which delegate a substantial amount of policy-making authority to actors outside Congress, raise some constitutional questions. After all, Article I, § 1 gives the "legislative power" of the federal government to Congress; if only Congress is permitted to exercise that authority, then at some point a delegation of policy-making authority will be tantamount to a delegation of the legislative power itself. But the issue is substantially more complicated than it might seem at first blush.

First, the constitutional text does not expressly forbid Congress from delegating the legislative power to other government actors. Indeed, the comparable language in Article II—which vests the "executive Power" in the President—has never been thought to prevent the President from delegating to other officers the authority to enforce federal law. (As a result, the President may permit, for example, the Attorney General to make decisions about whom to indict, even though such a decision is a quintessentially executive function.) Some scholars have argued that the grant of the legislative power in Article I should be read the same way, to permit Congress to delegate its authority to other government actors. See Thomas W. Merrill, *Rethinking Article I, Section 1: From Nondelegation to Exclusive Delegation*, 104 Colum. L. Rev. 2097 (2004).

The Court, however, has always treated the grant of legislative power in Article I differently, concluding that Congress may not delegate its legislative power. The Court has ruled that "Congress may not delegate the power to make laws and so may delegate no more than the authority to make policies and rules that implement its statutes." *Loving v. United States*, 517 U.S. 748, 771 (1996). The

Court has sometimes noted that this view derives from the writings of John Locke, a British political philosopher whose work was highly influential with the Framers. See, *e.g.*, *Industrial Union Dept., AFL-CIO v. American Petroleum Inst.*, 448 U.S. 607, 672–73 (1980) (Rehnquist, J., concurring in the judgment) ("Locke wrote that '[t]he power of the legislative [branch], being derived from the people by a positive voluntary grant and institution, can be no other than what that positive grant conveyed, which being only to make laws, and not to make legislators, the legislative [branch] can have no power to transfer their authority of making laws and place it in other hands.' " (quoting J. Locke, *Second Treatise of Civil Government*, in the *Tradition of Freedom*, ¶ 141, p. 244 (M. Mayer ed. 1957)).

Second, even once one concludes that the Constitution prohibits delegation of the legislative power, difficult questions of definition arise. Article I, after all, does not define the term "legislative power." Must Congress make every policy choice, leaving to the executive branch only the ministerial task of enforcement? This, as it turns out, would be virtually impossible. Even specific statutes, such as the criminal laws mentioned above, inevitably delegate some policy-making authority to the individuals who will enforce them. To take just one example, should the money-laundering statute be applied to a person who conceals money under the floorboards of his car as a way of obscuring its illegal origins? See *United States v. Cuellar*, 478 F.3d 282 (5th Cir. 2007). As Justice Scalia has explained, "Once it is conceded, as it must be, that no statute can be entirely precise, and that some judgments, even some judgments involving policy considerations, must be left to the officers executing the law and to the judges applying it, the debate over unconstitutional delegation becomes a debate not over a point of principle but over a question of degree." *Mistretta v. United States*, 488 U.S. 361, 415 (1989) (Scalia, J., dissenting).

The Supreme Court has addressed this issue in numerous cases. The Court has concluded that Congress impermissibly delegates legislative power only when it fails to provide an "intelligible principle" to guide the agency's or the executive official's exercise of discretion. *Id.* This is known as the "**non-delegation doctrine**."

In actual practice, the Supreme Court has rejected almost all challenges claiming that Congress has impermissibly delegated legislative authority. For example, in *National Broadcasting Co. v. United States*, 319 U.S. 190, 216–217 (1943), the Supreme Court upheld a statute so broad that it granted the Federal Communications Commission authority to regulate radio broadcasting according to "public interest, convenience, or necessity." Indeed, the Supreme Court has found delegations unconstitutional in only a few cases. In *A.L.A. Schechter Poultry*

Corp. v. United States, 295 U.S. 495 (1935), and *Panama Refining Co. v. Ryan*, 293 U.S. 388 (1935), the Supreme Court held that Congress had gone too far in the National Industrial Recovery Act when it authorized the President to prescribe "codes of fair competition" in business without giving the President further guidance. The Court decided these cases at a time when it was regularly invalidating New Deal legislation as beyond Congress's power to regulate under the Commerce Clause.

Make the Connection

We saw a hint of these cases in Chapter 3 when we considered the Court's decision in *Carter v. Carter Coal.*

The following case involves the non-delegation doctrine. In reading the case, consider why Congress might have wanted to give broad discretion to the EPA and why the Supreme Court chose not to interfere.

WHITMAN V. AMERICAN TRUCKING ASSOCIATIONS

531 U.S. 457 (2001)

JUSTICE SCALIA delivered the opinion of the Court.

Section 109(a) of the [Clean Air Act (CAA)] requires the Administrator of the EPA to promulgate [national ambient air quality standards (NAAQS)] for each air pollutant for which "air quality criteria" have been issued under § 108. Once a NAAQS has been promulgated, the Administrator must review the standard (and the criteria on which it is based) "at five-year intervals" and make "such revisions . . . as may be appropriate." CAA § 109(d)(1). These cases arose when, on July 18, 1997, the Administrator revised the NAAQS for particulate matter and ozone. American Trucking Associations, Inc., and its co-respondents—which include, in addition to other private companies, the States of Michigan, Ohio, and West Virginia—challenged the new standards in the Court of Appeals for the District of Columbia Circuit * * *.

Take Note

Three states challenged the regulations at issue in this case. Does the case raise a federalism issue? If not, why did these states file a challenge?

The District of Columbia Circuit accepted some of the challenges and rejected others. It agreed * * * that § 109(b)(1) delegated legislative power to the Administrator in contravention of the United States Constitution, Art. I, § 1, because it found that the EPA had interpreted the statute to provide no "intelligible principle" to guide the agency's exercise of authority. * * *

[S]ince the first step in assessing whether a statute delegates legislative power is to determine what authority the statute confers, we address that issue of interpretation first and reach respondents' constitutional arguments [afterward]. Section 109(b)(1) instructs the EPA to set primary ambient air quality standards "the attainment and maintenance of which . . . are requisite to protect the public health" with "an adequate margin of safety." Were it not for the hundreds of pages of briefing respondents have submitted on the issue, one would have thought it fairly clear that this text does not permit the EPA to consider costs in setting the standards. The language, as one scholar has noted, "is absolute." D. Currie, Air Pollution: Federal Law and Analysis 4–15 (1981). The EPA, "based on" the information about health effects contained in the technical "criteria" documents compiled under § 108(a)(2), is to identify the maximum airborne concentration of a pollutant that the public health can tolerate, decrease the concentration to provide an "adequate" margin of safety, and set the standard at that level. Nowhere are the costs of achieving such a standard made part of that initial calculation.

The Court of Appeals held that [section 109(b)(1)] as interpreted by the Administrator did not provide an "intelligible principle" to guide the EPA's exercise of authority in setting NAAQS. "[The] EPA," it said, "lack[ed] any determinate criteria for drawing lines. It has failed to state intelligibly how much is too much." The court hence found that the EPA's interpretation (but not the statute itself) violated the nondelegation doctrine. We disagree.

In a delegation challenge, the constitutional question is whether the statute has delegated legislative power to the agency. Article I, § 1, of the Constitution vests "[a]ll legislative Powers herein granted . . . in a Congress of the United States." This text permits no delegation of those powers, *Loving v. United States,* 517 U.S. 748, 771 (1996), and so we repeatedly have said that when Congress confers decisionmaking authority upon agencies *Congress* must "lay down by legislative act an intelligible principle to which the person or body authorized to [act] is directed to conform." *J.W. Hampton, Jr., & Co. v. United States,* 276 U.S. 394, 409 (1928).

We agree with the Solicitor General that the text of § 109(b)(1) of the CAA at a minimum requires that "[f]or a discrete set of pollutants and based on published air quality criteria that reflect the latest scientific knowledge, [the] EPA must establish uniform national standards at a level that is requisite to protect public health from the adverse effects of the pollutant in the ambient air." Tr. of Oral Arg., p. 5. Requisite, in turn, "mean[s] sufficient, but not more than necessary." *Id.,* at 7. These limits on the EPA's discretion are strikingly similar to the ones we approved in *Touby v. United States,* 500 U.S. 160 (1991), which permitted the Attorney General to designate a drug as a controlled substance for purposes of criminal drug enforcement if doing so was "necessary to avoid an imminent hazard to the public safety." They also resemble the Occupational Safety and Health Act of 1970 provision requiring the agency to "set the standard which most adequately assures, to the extent feasible, on the basis of the best available evidence, that no employee will suffer any impairment of health"—which the Court upheld in *Industrial Union Dept., AFL-CIO v. American Petroleum Institute,* 448 U.S. 607, 646 (1980), and which even then-Justice REHNQUIST, who alone in that case thought the statute violated the nondelegation doctrine, see *id.* (opinion concurring in judgment), would have upheld if, like the statute here, it did not permit economic costs to be considered. See *American Textile Mfrs. Institute, Inc. v. Donovan,* 452 U.S. 490, 545 (1981) (REHNQUIST, J., dissenting).

> **Take Note**
>
> In this paragraph, the Court describes an "identifiable principle" that serves to channel the EPA's discretion. What is the principle? Can you think of regulations that might violate this principle?

The scope of discretion § 109(b)(1) allows is in fact well within the outer limits of our nondelegation precedents. In the history of the Court we have found the requisite "intelligible principle" lacking in only two statutes, one of which provided literally no guidance for the exercise of discretion, and the other of which conferred authority to regulate the entire economy on the basis of no more precise a standard than stimulating the economy by assuring "fair competition." See *Panama Refining Co. v. Ryan,* 293 U.S. 388 (1935); *A.L.A. Schechter Poultry Corp. v. United States,* 295 U.S. 495 (1935). We have, on the other hand, upheld the validity of § 11(b)(2) of the Public Utility Holding Company Act of 1935, 49 Stat. 821, which gave the Securities and Exchange Commission authority to modify the structure of holding company systems so as to ensure that they are not "unduly or unnecessarily complicate[d]" and do not "unfairly or inequitably distribute voting power among security holders." *American Power & Light Co. v. SEC,* 329 U.S. 90, 104 (1946). We have approved the wartime conferral of agency power to fix the prices of commodities at a level that "will be generally fair and equitable and will effectuate the [in some respects conflicting] purposes of th[e] Act." *Yakus v. United States,* 321 U.S. 414, 420 (1944). And we have found an "intelligible principle" in various statutes authorizing regulation in the "public interest." See, *e.g., National Broadcasting Co. v. United States,* 319 U.S. 190, 225–226 (1943) (Federal Communications Commission's power to regulate airwaves); *New York Central Securities Corp. v. United States,* 287 U.S. 12, 24–25 (1932) (Interstate Commerce Commission's power to approve railroad consolidations). In short, we have "almost never felt qualified to second-guess Congress regarding the permissible degree of policy judgment that can be left to those executing or applying the law."

Mistretta v. United States, 488 U.S. 361, 416 (1989) (SCALIA, J., dissenting); see id., at 373 (majority opinion).

It is true enough that the degree of agency discretion that is acceptable varies according to the scope of the power congressionally conferred. While Congress need not provide any direction to the EPA regarding the manner in which it is to define "country elevators," which are to be exempt from new-stationary-source regulations governing grain elevators, it must provide substantial guidance on setting air standards that affect the entire national economy. But even in sweeping regulatory schemes we have never demanded, as the Court of Appeals did here, that statutes provide a "determinate criterion" for saying "how much [of the regulated harm] is too much." In *Touby* for example, we did not require the statute to decree how "imminent" was too imminent, or how "necessary" was necessary enough, or even—most relevant here—how "hazardous" was too hazardous. 500 U.S., at 165–167. Similarly, the statute at issue in *Lichter v. United States,* 334 U.S. 742, 783 (1948), authorized agencies to recoup "excess profits" paid under wartime Government contracts, yet we did not insist that Congress specify how much profit was too much. It is therefore not conclusive for delegation purposes that, as respondents argue, ozone and particulate matter are "nonthreshold" pollutants that inflict a continuum of adverse health effects at any airborne concentration greater than zero, and hence require the EPA to make judgments of degree. "[A] certain degree of discretion, and thus of lawmaking, inheres in most executive or judicial action." *Mistretta v. United States, supra,* at 417 (SCALIA, J., dissenting) (emphasis deleted). Section 109(b)(1) of the CAA, which to repeat we interpret as requiring the EPA to set air quality standards at the level that is "requisite"—that is, not lower or higher than is necessary—to protect the public health with an adequate margin of safety, fits comfortably within the scope of discretion permitted by our precedent.

> **Food for Thought**
>
> Is it possible to imagine a statute that leaves no discretion at all for the actor administering the statute? Suppose that the statute required the EPA to set a standard for particulate matter at the level that, "regardless of cost, ensured that no person would suffer any material health impairment." Would that statute leave policy-making discretion to the person administering it?

JUSTICE THOMAS, concurring.

The parties to these cases who briefed the constitutional issue wrangled over constitutional doctrine with barely a nod to the text of the Constitution. Although this Court since 1928 has treated the "intelligible principle" requirement as the only constitutional limit on congressional grants of power to administrative agencies, see *J.W. Hampton, Jr., & Co. v. United States,* 276 U.S. 394, 409 (1928), the

Constitution does not speak of "intelligible principles." Rather, it speaks in much simpler terms: "*All* legislative Powers herein granted shall be vested in a Congress." U.S. Const., Art. 1, § 1 (emphasis added). I am not convinced that the intelligible principle doctrine serves to prevent all cessions of legislative power. I believe that there are cases in which the principle is intelligible and yet the significance of the delegated decision is simply too great for the decision to be called anything other than "legislative."

> **Food for Thought**
>
> Justice Thomas laments that the parties did not explain how the text of the Constitution addresses the question in this case. What, if anything, does the text of the Constitution require? Does that text answer the question in this case?

As it is, none of the parties to these cases has examined the text of the Constitution or asked us to reconsider our precedents on cessions of legislative power. On a future day, however, I would be willing to address the question whether our delegation jurisprudence has strayed too far from our Founders' understanding of separation of powers.

JUSTICE STEVENS, with whom JUSTICE SOUTER joins, concurring in part and concurring in the judgment.

The Court has two choices. We could choose to articulate our ultimate disposition of this issue by frankly acknowledging that the power delegated to the EPA is "legislative" but nevertheless conclude that the delegation is constitutional because adequately limited by the terms of the authorizing statute. Alternatively, we could pretend, as the Court does, that the authority delegated to the EPA is somehow not "legislative power." * * * I am persuaded that it would be both wiser and more faithful to what we have actually done in delegation cases to admit that agency rulemaking authority is "legislative power."

The proper characterization of governmental power should generally depend on the nature of the power, not on the identity of the person exercising it. If the NAAQS that the EPA promulgated had been prescribed by Congress, everyone would agree that those rules would be the product of an exercise of "legislative power." The same characterization is appropriate when an agency exercises rulemaking authority pursuant to a permissible delegation from Congress.

My view is not only more faithful to normal English usage, but is also fully consistent with the text of the Constitution. In Article I, the Framers vested "All legislative Powers" in the Congress, Art. I, § 1, just as in Article II they vested the "executive Power" in the President, Art. II, § 1. Those provisions do not purport to limit the authority of either recipient of power to delegate authority to others. * * *

It seems clear that an executive agency's exercise of rulemaking authority pursuant to a valid delegation from Congress is "legislative." As long as the delegation provides a sufficiently intelligible principle, there is nothing inherently unconstitutional about it.

[JUSTICE BREYER's opinion concurring in part and concurring in the judgment is omitted.]

POINTS FOR DISCUSSION

a. The Need for Broad Discretion

Why might Congress have thought that it needed to give the EPA broad discretion to set "ambient air quality standards"? Could Congress have set those standards itself?

b. Justification for the Intelligible Principle Requirement

Why must legislation that gives an administrative agency authority to pass rules and regulations contain an "intelligible principle" to guide the agency's discretion? Is the administrative agency in effect legislating if it does not act under the constraint of some intelligible principle? Is it accurate to say that the administrative agency is not legislating if Congress does give the agency an intelligible principle to follow? If so, is it still true if the "intelligible principle" is phrased in very general terms?

c. Constitutional Text

Justice Thomas urged the Court to focus more on the constitutional text, presumably Article I, § 1. Yet other constitutional provisions appear to contemplate the existence of something like an administrative state. The Necessary and Proper Clause, for example, speaks of powers vested "in the Government of the United States, or in any Department or Officer thereof," Art. I, § 8, cl. 18, even though the Constitution doesn't specifically vest power in anyone other than Congress, the President, and the federal courts. The Opinion Clause, Art. II, § 2, cl. 1, similarly contemplates "executive Departments" with "principal Officer[s]" who will have legal "Duties." The Appointments Clause, Art. II, § 2, cl. 2, likewise contemplates "Officers" and "Departments." Do these provisions cast any light on the permissibility of delegation of decision-making authority?

d. History

Some scholars have criticized the modern non-delegation doctrine as being inconsistent with the original meaning. See, e.g., Gary Lawson, *Delegation and Original*

Meaning, 88 Va. L. Rev. 327 (2002). But others have argued that early practice—under which Congress gave administrators broad statutory authority to regulate—suggests that modern cases are perhaps much closer to the original understanding of Congress's power to delegate authority than critics have suggested. See Jerry L. Mashaw, *Recovering American Administrative Law: Federalist Foundations, 1787–1801*, 115 Yale L.J. 1256 (2006).

e. Judicial Deference

As the *American Trucking* case makes clear, the Court affords Congress a good deal of leeway in reviewing cases challenging delegations of authority. Why has the Court been so deferential? Is the Court better suited than Congress to decide which policy choices Congress alone ought to make?

B. EXCLUDING THE PRESIDENT FROM THE LEGISLATIVE PROCESS

The consequence of the Court's approach to delegation is that officials in the executive branch often have considerable power to make policy decisions. As we have seen, often Congress passes general rules, and administrative agencies then fill in many of the details. Congress recognizes that it cannot possibly make all of the policies necessary for running the government. But that does not mean that Congress wants to cede total control over all important policy making. Over the past several decades, Congress has looked for ways to oversee or check some of the policy-making by administrative agencies.

Congress's most common method of oversight involves calling executive branch officials to testify before congressional committees. For example, suppose that the Food and Drug Administration (FDA) refuses to approve as safe and effective a drug that many people think deserves approval. Someone might complain to the House or Senate committee charged with oversight of the FDA. The committee then might call FDA officials to participate in a hearing on the subject on Capitol Hill. The committee might ask the FDA officials about the decision. If the committee disagrees with the FDA's position, members of the committee might berate the officials publicly and ask for a change of policy. Members of Congress might even threaten the agency with the loss of funds for essential operations.

In many instances, oversight hearings persuade officials from administrative agencies to back down and change their policies. These officials may wish to appease Congress, even though the officials are part of the executive branch. They know that Congress ultimately has the power to pass legislation overruling their decisions or to retaliate against the agency by limiting its future funding.

But sometimes, fundamental policy disputes occur, and mere oversight by Congress does not suffice to cause executive branch officials to change an agency's position. Congress, in these instances, sometimes carries through with its threats to pass legislation overruling the agency. But Congress faces several practical difficulties in attempting to control administrative agencies by enacting new statutes. Passing legislation is a long and difficult process. Even if Congress successfully acts, it may not be able to undo a particular unpopular decision because of limits on Congress's power to legislate retroactively. And even if Congress can enact a bill, the President has a veto, and may use it to support the agency's position over that of Congress.

The shortcomings in these methods of exercising control over administrative agencies led Congress in the 20th century to devise a controversial alternative tactic. The invention was the inclusion of "**legislative veto**" provisions in statutes conferring discretion on administrative agencies. Legislative veto provisions typically said that Congress—or the House or the Senate acting alone—could rescind certain actions taken by agencies simply by passing a resolution. Legislative veto provisions thus made agency actions conditional. The agency could act, but the action would become invalid if one or both Houses of Congress disapproved.

In the following landmark case, the Supreme Court determined that legislative veto provisions are unconstitutional. In reading the case, consider why Congress desired the legislative veto and why the Supreme Court concluded that Congress could not give itself this tool.

IMMIGRATION AND NATURALIZATION SERVICE V. CHADHA

462 U.S. 919 (1983)

CHIEF JUSTICE BURGER delivered the opinion of the Court.

Chadha is an East Indian who was born in Kenya and holds a British passport. He was lawfully admitted to the United States in 1966 on a nonimmigrant student visa. His visa expired on June 30, 1972. On October 11, 1973, the District Director of the Immigration and Naturalization Service ordered Chadha to show cause why he should not be deported for having "remained in the United States for a longer time than permitted." Pursuant to § 242(b) of the Immigration and Nationality Act, a deportation hearing was held before an immigration judge on January 11, 1974. Chadha conceded that he was deportable for overstaying his visa and the hearing was adjourned to enable him to file an application for suspension of deportation under § 244(a)(1) of the Act. Section 244(a)(1) provides [for suspension of deportation for persons of "good moral character" in certain cases of "extreme hardship."]

> **FYI**
>
> No one knows why the House exercised its legislative veto with respect to Chadha. One controversial theory, often discussed but never proved, was that members of Congress or their staff used the veto power to seek bribes. Chadha's attorney, Alan Morrison (who later became a colleague of this book's authors), believed the "committee was just showing who was the boss, that they had the power and they wanted to be sure that the Immigration Service understood it." *See* Oral History of Alan Morrison: Interviews conducted by Daniel Marcus (2008).

The immigration judge found that Chadha met the requirements of § 244(a)(1): he had resided continuously in the United States for over seven years, was of good moral character, and would suffer "extreme hardship" if deported. Pursuant to § 244(c)(1) of the Act, the immigration judge suspended Chadha's deportation * * *. [This suspension became the Attorney General's recommendation.] Once the Attorney General's recommendation for suspension of Chadha's deportation was conveyed to Congress, Congress had the power under § 244(c)(2) of the Act to veto[2] the Attorney General's determination that Chadha should not be deported. Section 244(c)(2) provides:

> **FYI**
>
> At the time of the decision in this case, the Immigration and Naturalization Service was a component of the Department of Justice. Chadha's deportation hearing was held before an "administrative law judge," an agency official with a good deal of independence from political decision-makers. But under the statute, the Attorney General was the final decision-maker for the agency. Does this structure itself raise concerns about the separation of powers?

"(2) In the case of an alien specified in paragraph (1) of subsection (a) of this subsection—if during the session of the Congress at which a case is reported, or prior to the close of the session of the Congress next following the session at which a case is reported, either the Senate or the House of Representatives passes a resolution stating in substance that it does not favor the suspension of such deportation, the Attorney General shall thereupon deport such alien or authorize the alien's voluntary departure at his own expense under the order of deportation in the manner provided by law. If, within the time above specified, neither the Senate nor

2 In constitutional terms, "veto" is used to describe the President's power under Art. I, § 7 of the Constitution. It appears, however, that Congressional devices of the type authorized by § 244(c)(2) have come to be commonly referred to as a "veto." We refer to the Congressional "resolution" authorized by § 244(c)(2) as a "one-House veto" of the Attorney General's decision to allow a particular deportable alien to remain in the United States.

the House of Representatives shall pass such a resolution, the Attorney General shall cancel deportation proceedings."

On December 12, 1975, Representative Eilberg, Chairman of the Judiciary Subcommittee on Immigration, Citizenship, and International Law, introduced a resolution opposing "the granting of permanent residence in the United States to [six] aliens," including Chadha. The resolution was referred to the House Committee on the Judiciary. On December 16, 1975, the resolution was discharged from further consideration by the House Committee on the Judiciary and submitted to the House of Representatives for a vote. The resolution had not been printed and was not made available to other Members of the House prior to or at the time it was voted on. So far as the record before us shows, the House consideration of the resolution was based on Representative Eilberg's statement from the floor that

FYI

Before Congress enacted § 244, suspension of deportation was done by "private bills," which are bills passed by both Houses of Congress and presented to the President and that relate only to one or a small number of persons or entities. Why do you suppose Congress changed that system?

> "[i]t was the feeling of the committee, after reviewing 340 cases, that the aliens contained in the resolution [Chadha and five others] did not meet these statutory requirements, particularly as it relates to hardship; and it is the opinion of the committee that their deportation should not be suspended." *Ibid.*

The resolution was passed without debate or recorded vote. Since the House action was pursuant to § 244(c)(2), the resolution was not treated as an Article I legislative act; it was not submitted to the Senate or presented to the President for his action.

After the House veto of the Attorney General's decision to allow Chadha to remain in the United States, the immigration judge reopened the deportation proceedings to implement the House order deporting Chadha. Chadha moved to terminate the proceedings on the ground that § 244(c)(2) is unconstitutional.

Take Note

Chadha raised his separation of powers argument as a defense to a deportation proceeding. Is the Court's role in addressing such a challenge different from the Court's role when the dispute is directly between Congress and an Executive official—or the President himself?

The Presentment Clauses

The records of the Constitutional Convention reveal that the requirement that all legislation be presented to the President before becoming law was uniformly accepted by the Framers. Presentment to the President and the Presidential veto were considered so imperative that the draftsmen took special pains to assure that these requirements could not be circumvented. During the final debate on Art. I, § 7, cl. 2, James Madison expressed concern that it might easily be evaded by the simple expedient of calling a proposed law a "resolution" or "vote" rather than a "bill." 2 M. Farrand, The Records of the Federal Convention of 1787 301–302. As a consequence, Art. I, § 7, cl. 3, was added. *Id.*, at 304–305.

Jagdish Chadha and his attorney Alan B. Morrison on the steps of the U.S. Supreme Court
Alan B. Morrison

The decision to provide the President with a limited and qualified power to nullify proposed legislation by veto was based on the profound conviction of the Framers that the powers conferred on Congress were the powers to be most carefully circumscribed. It is beyond doubt that lawmaking was a power to be shared by both Houses and the President. In The Federalist No. 73, Hamilton focused on the President's role in making laws:

> "If even no propensity had ever discovered itself in the legislative body to invade the rights of the Executive, the rules of just reasoning and theoretic propriety would of themselves teach us that the one ought not to be left to the mercy of the other, but ought to possess a constitutional and effectual power of self-defense."

The President's role in the lawmaking process also reflects the Framers' careful efforts to check whatever propensity a particular Congress might have to enact oppressive, improvident, or ill-considered measures. [See The Federalist No. 73.] * * * The Court also has observed that the Presentment Clauses serve the important purpose of assuring that a "national" perspective is grafted on the legislative process * * *. *Myers v. United States*, 272 U.S. 52, 123 (1926).

Bicameralism

The bicameral requirement of Art. I, §§ 1, 7 was of scarcely less concern to the Framers than was the Presidential veto and indeed the two concepts are interdependent. By providing that no law could take effect without the concurrence of the prescribed majority of the Members of both Houses, the Framers reemphasized their belief, already remarked upon in connection with the Presentment Clauses, that legislation should not be enacted unless it has been carefully and fully considered by the Nation's elected officials. In the Constitutional Convention debates on the need for a bicameral legislature, James Wilson, later to become a Justice of this Court, commented:

> "Despotism comes on mankind in different shapes. Sometimes in an Executive, sometimes in a military, one. Is there danger of a Legislative despotism? Theory & practice both proclaim it. If the Legislative authority be not restrained, there can be neither liberty nor stability; and it can only be restrained by dividing it within itself, into distinct and independent branches. In a single house there is no check, but the inadequate one, of the virtue & good sense of those who compose it." 1 M. Farrand, Records of the Federal Convention of 1787, p. 254 (1911).

Hamilton argued that [were] the Nation to adopt a Constitution providing for only one legislative organ, "we shall finally accumulate, in a single body, all the most important prerogatives of sovereignty, and thus * * * create in reality that very tyranny which the adversaries of the new Constitution either are, or affect to be, solicitous to avert." The Federalist No. 22. These observations are consistent with what many of the Framers expressed, none more cogently than Hamilton* in pointing up the need to divide and disperse power in order to protect liberty: "In republican government, the legislative authority necessarily predominates. The remedy for this inconveniency is to divide the legislature into different branches; and to render them, by different modes of election and different principles of action, as little connected with each other as the nature of their common functions and their common dependence on the society will admit." The Federalist No. 51.

We see therefore that the Framers were acutely conscious that the bicameral requirement and the Presentment Clauses would serve essential constitutional functions. The President's participation in the legislative process was to protect the Executive Branch from Congress and to protect the whole people from improvident laws. The division of the Congress into two distinctive bodies assures

---

* The Court mistakenly attributed The Federalist No. 51 to Hamilton. The consensus of scholars is that James Madison wrote The Federalist No. 51, one of the most-cited Federalist Papers of all time. See Ira C. Lupu, *The Most-Cited Federalist Papers*, 15 Const. Comment. 403 (1997).—*Eds.*

that the legislative power would be exercised only after opportunity for full study and debate in separate settings. The President's unilateral veto power, in turn, was limited by the power of two thirds of both Houses of Congress to overrule a veto thereby precluding final arbitrary action of one person. It emerges clearly that the prescription for legislative action in Art. I, §§ 1, 7 represents the Framers' decision that the legislative power of the Federal government be exercised in accord with a single, finely wrought and exhaustively considered, procedure.

Not every action taken by either House is subject to the bicameralism and presentment requirements of Art. I. Whether actions taken by either House are, in law and fact, an exercise of legislative power depends not on their form but upon "whether they contain matter which is properly to be regarded as legislative in its character and effect." S. Rep. No. 1335, 54th Cong., 2d Sess., 8 (1897).

Examination of the action taken here by one House pursuant to § 244(c)(2) reveals that it was essentially legislative in purpose and effect. In purporting to exercise power defined in Art. I, § 8, cl. 4 to "establish an uniform Rule of Naturalization," the House took action that had the purpose and effect of altering the legal rights, duties and relations of persons, including the Attorney General, Executive Branch officials and Chadha, all outside the legislative branch. Section 244(c)(2) purports to authorize one House of Congress to require the Attorney General to deport an individual alien whose deportation otherwise would be cancelled under § 244. The one-House veto operated in this case to overrule the Attorney General and mandate Chadha's deportation; absent the House action, Chadha would remain in the United States. Congress has *acted* and its action has altered Chadha's status.

Take Note

The Court says that the requirements of bicameralism and presentment apply only to "legislative" action. In reading the rest of the opinion, observe how the Court decides whether what the House did here is a form of legislative action. What actions by Congress do not count as "legislative" action? What is the test for what counts?

The legislative character of the one-House veto in this case is confirmed by the character of the Congressional action it supplants. Neither the House of Representatives nor the Senate contends that, absent the veto provision in § 244(c)(2), either of them, or both of them acting together, could effectively require the Attorney General to deport an alien once the Attorney General, in the exercise of legislatively delegated authority,[16] had determined the alien should

16 Congress protests that affirming the Court of Appeals in this case will sanction "lawmaking by the Attorney General." To be sure, some administrative agency action—rule making, for example—may resemble "lawmaking." [But when] the Attorney General performs his duties pursuant to § 244, he does not exercise "legislative" power. The bicameral process is not necessary as a check on the Executive's administration of the

remain in the United States. Without the challenged provision in § 244(c)(2), this could have been achieved, if at all, only by legislation requiring deportation. Similarly, a veto by one House of Congress under § 244(c)(2) cannot be justified as an attempt at amending the standards set out in § 244(a)(1), or as a repeal of § 244 as applied to Chadha. Amendment and repeal of statutes, no less than enactment, must conform with Art. I.

Finally, we see that when the Framers intended to authorize either House of Congress to act alone and outside of its prescribed bicameral legislative role, they narrowly and precisely defined the procedure for such action. There are but four provisions in the Constitution, explicit and unambiguous, by which one House may act alone with the unreviewable force of law, not subject to the President's veto: (a) The House of Representatives alone was given the power to initiate impeachments. Art. I, § 2, cl. 6; (b) The Senate alone was given the power to conduct trials following impeachment on charges initiated by the House and to convict following trial. Art. I, § 3, cl. 5; (c) The Senate alone was given final unreviewable power to approve or to disapprove presidential appointments. Art. II, § 2, cl. 2; (d) The Senate alone was given unreviewable power to ratify treaties negotiated by the President. Art. II, § 2, cl. 2. * * * Clearly, when the Draftsmen sought to confer special powers on one House, independent of the other House, or of the President, they did so in explicit, unambiguous terms.

Since it is clear that the action by the House under § 244(c)(2) was not within any of the express constitutional exceptions authorizing one House to act alone, and equally clear that it was an exercise of legislative power, that action was subject to the standards prescribed in Article I.

The veto authorized by § 244(c)(2) doubtless has been in many respects a convenient shortcut; the "sharing" with the Executive by Congress of its authority over aliens in this manner is, on its face, an appealing compromise. In purely practical terms, it is obviously easier for action to be taken by one House without submission to the President; but it is crystal clear from the records of the Convention, contemporaneous writings and debates, that the Framers ranked

---

laws because his administrative activity cannot reach beyond the limits of the statute that created it—a statute duly enacted pursuant to Art. I, §§ 1, 7. The constitutionality of the Attorney General's execution of the authority delegated to him by § 244 involves only a question of delegation doctrine. * * * Executive action under legislatively delegated authority that might resemble "legislative" action in some respects is not subject to the approval of both Houses of Congress and the President for the reason that the Constitution does not so require. That kind of Executive action is always subject to check by the terms of the legislation that authorized it; and if that authority is exceeded it is open to judicial review as well as the power of Congress to modify or revoke the authority entirely. A one-House veto is clearly legislative in both character and effect and is not so checked; the need for the check provided by Art. I, §§ 1, 7 is therefore clear. Congress' authority to delegate portions of its power to administrative agencies provides no support for the argument that Congress can constitutionally control administration of the laws by way of a Congressional veto.

other values higher than efficiency. The records of the Convention and debates in the States preceding ratification underscore the common desire to define and limit the exercise of the newly created federal powers affecting the states and the people. There is unmistakable expression of a determination that legislation by the national Congress be a step-by-step, deliberate and deliberative process. We hold that the Congressional veto provision in § 244(c)(2) is severable from the Act and that it is unconstitutional.

> **Definition**
>
> A "severable statute" is a statute "that remains operative in its remaining provisions even if a portion of the law is declared unconstitutional." *Black's Law Dictionary* (2014 ed.)

JUSTICE POWELL, concurring in the judgment.

The Court's decision, based on the Presentment Clauses, apparently will invalidate every use of the legislative veto. * * * One reasonably may disagree with Congress' assessment of the veto's utility, but the respect due its judgment as a coordinate branch of Government cautions that our holding should be no more extensive than necessary to decide this case. In my view, the case may be decided on a narrower ground. When Congress finds that a particular person does not satisfy the statutory criteria for permanent residence in this country it has assumed a judicial function in violation of the principle of separation of powers.

> **Make the Connection**
>
> This concern led the Framers explicitly to prohibit Congress from enacting "Bills of Attainder," legislative acts that impose punishment. We will consider that prohibition later in this chapter.

[The Framers were concerned] that trial by a legislature lacks the safeguards necessary to prevent the abuse of power. * * * On its face, the House's action appears clearly adjudicatory. The House did not enact a general rule; rather it made its own determination that six specific persons did not comply with certain statutory criteria. It thus undertook the type of decision that traditionally has been left to other branches.

The impropriety of the House's assumption of this function is confirmed by the fact that its action raises the very danger the Framers sought to avoid—the exercise of unchecked power. In deciding whether Chadha deserves to be deported, Congress is not subject to any internal constraints that prevent it from arbitrarily depriving him of the right to remain in this country. Unlike the judiciary or an administrative agency, Congress is not bound by established substantive rules. Nor is it subject to the procedural safeguards, such as the right to counsel and a hearing before an impartial tribunal, that are present when a court or an agency adjudicates individual rights. The only effective constraint on Congress' power is political, but Congress is most accountable politically when it prescribes rules of general applicability. When it decides rights of specific persons, those rights are subject to "the tyranny of a shifting majority."

JUSTICE WHITE, dissenting.

Today the Court not only invalidates § 244(c)(2) of the Immigration and Nationality Act, but also sounds the death knell for nearly 200 other statutory provisions in which Congress has reserved a "legislative veto." For this reason, the Court's decision is of surpassing importance. And it is for this reason that the Court would have been well-advised to decide the case, if possible, on the narrower grounds of separation of powers, leaving for full consideration the constitutionality of other congressional review statutes operating on such varied matters as war powers and agency rulemaking, some of which concern the independent regulatory agencies.

The prominence of the legislative veto mechanism in our contemporary political system and its importance to Congress can hardly be overstated. It has become a central means by which Congress secures the accountability of executive and independent agencies. Without the legislative veto, Congress is faced with a Hobson's choice: either to refrain from delegating the necessary authority, leaving itself with a hopeless task of writing laws with the requisite specificity to cover endless special circumstances across the entire policy landscape, or in the alternative, to abdicate its law-making function to the executive branch and independent agencies. To choose the former leaves major national problems unresolved; to opt for the latter risks unaccountable policymaking by those not elected to fill that role. Accordingly, over the past five decades, the legislative veto has been placed in nearly 200 statutes. The device is known in every field of governmental concern: reorganization, budgets, foreign affairs, war powers, and regulation of trade, safety, energy, the environment and the economy.

> **Take Note**
>
> Why does Justice White think that Congress needs the legislative veto? Does he make a constitutional argument or a policy argument for upholding the legislative veto?

The history of the legislative veto also makes clear that it has not been a sword with which Congress has struck out to aggrandize itself at the expense of the other branches—the concerns of Madison and Hamilton. Rather, the veto has been a means of defense, a reservation of ultimate authority necessary if Congress is to fulfill its designated role under Article I as the nation's lawmaker. While the President has often objected to particular legislative vetoes, generally those left in the hands of congressional committees, the Executive has more often agreed to legislative review as the price for a broad delegation of authority. To be sure, the

President may have preferred unrestricted power, but that could be precisely why Congress thought it essential to retain a check on the exercise of delegated authority.

If the legislative veto were as plainly unconstitutional as the Court strives to suggest, its broad ruling today would be more comprehensible. But, the constitutionality of the legislative veto is anything but clearcut. * * * The reality of the situation is that the constitutional question posed today is one of immense difficulty over which the executive and legislative branches—as well as scholars and judges—have understandably disagreed. That disagreement stems from the silence of the Constitution on the precise question: The Constitution does not directly authorize or prohibit the legislative veto. Thus, our task should be to determine whether the legislative veto is consistent with the purposes of Art. I and the principles of Separation of Powers which are reflected in that Article and throughout the Constitution. We should not find the lack of a specific constitutional authorization for the legislative veto surprising, and I would not infer disapproval of the mechanism from its absence. * * * [O]ur Federal Government was intentionally chartered with the flexibility to respond to contemporary needs without losing sight of fundamental democratic principles.

The power to exercise a legislative veto is not the power to write new law without bicameral approval or presidential consideration. The veto must be authorized by statute and may only negative what an Executive department or independent agency has proposed. On its face, the legislative veto no more allows one House of Congress to make law than does the presidential veto confer such power upon the President.

If Congress may delegate lawmaking power to independent and executive agencies, it is most difficult to understand Article I as forbidding Congress from also reserving a check on legislative power for itself. Absent the veto, the agencies receiving delegations of legislative or quasi-legislative power may issue regulations having the force of law without bicameral approval and without the President's signature. It is thus not apparent why the reservation of a veto over the exercise of that legislative power must be subject to a more exacting test. In both cases, it is enough that the initial statutory authorizations comply with the Article I requirements. * * * Under the Court's analysis, the Executive Branch and the independent agencies may make rules with the effect of law while Congress, in whom the Framers confided the legislative power, may not exercise a veto which precludes such rules from having operative force.

The central concern of the presentation and bicameralism requirements of Article I is that when a departure from the legal status quo is undertaken, it is done with the approval of the President and both Houses of Congress—or, in the event of a presidential veto, a two-thirds majority in both Houses. This interest is fully satisfied by the operation of § 244(c)(2). The President's approval is found in the Attorney General's action in recommending to Congress that the deportation order for a given alien be suspended. The House and the Senate indicate their approval of the Executive's action by not passing a resolution of disapproval within the statutory period. Thus, a change in the legal status quo—the deportability of the alien—is consummated only with the approval of each of the three relevant actors. The disagreement of any one of the three maintains the alien's pre-existing status: the Executive may choose not to recommend suspension; the House and Senate may each veto the recommendation. The effect on the rights and obligations of the affected individuals and upon the legislative system is precisely the same as if a private bill were introduced but failed to receive the necessary approval.

[T]he history of the separation of powers doctrine is [a] history of accommodation and practicality. Apprehensions of an overly powerful branch have not led to undue prophylactic measures that handicap the effective working of the national government as a whole. The Constitution does not contemplate total separation of the three branches of Government.

The legislative veto provision does not "prevent the Executive Branch from accomplishing its constitutionally assigned functions." * * * § 244 grants the executive only a qualified suspension authority and it is only that authority which the President is constitutionally authorized to execute. Moreover, the Court believes that the legislative veto we consider today is best characterized as an exercise of legislative or quasi-legislative authority. Under this characterization, the practice does not, even on the surface, constitute an infringement of executive or judicial prerogative. * * * Nor does § 244 infringe on the judicial power, as Justice POWELL would hold. * * * Congressional action does not substitute for judicial review of the Attorney General's decisions.

[The Court's holding] reflects a profoundly different conception of the Constitution than that held by the Courts which sanctioned the modern administrative state. Today's decision strikes down in one fell swoop provisions in more laws enacted by Congress than the Court has cumulatively invalidated in its history. * * * I must dissent.

POINTS FOR DISCUSSION

a. The Reach of *Chadha*

Justice White observes that nearly 200 federal statutes contained legislative veto provisions. In light of the Court's decision, all of these federal statutes were (at least in part) unconstitutional. For this reason, *INS v. Chadha* could be said to have invalidated more federal statutes than any other case in the history of the United States. Was the number of statutes containing legislative veto provisions a reason for pause, or was it instead a reason for the Court to act as it did?

b. Aggrandizement v. Delegation

In the first part of this chapter, we saw that the Court is not overly concerned about the possibility that Congress might delegate some of its power to administrative agencies. But here we see the Court is concerned when Congress reserves to itself a new method to check the exercise of those delegated powers. Why might the Court have seen this reservation as a more troubling separation of powers problem than delegation?

c. Formalism v. Functionalism

Chief Justice Burger and Justice White both were concerned about preserving the separation of powers, but they clearly viewed the substantive content of that concept—and the Court's role in enforcing it—differently. Chief Justice Burger insisted that the Constitution creates a set form for the law-making process, and that any deviation from that form must therefore be unconstitutional. He reasoned, in other words, that the contours of the separation of powers are determined by constitutional form. Justice White, in contrast, reasoned that the Court's task was to determine whether the legislative veto presented an actual, functional threat to the notion of the separation of powers. If the legislative veto did not substantially or meaningfully shift the balance of power to one branch, he suggested, then the Court should not intervene.

What are the virtues of these two approaches—formalism and functionalism—to separation of powers issues? As you read the rest of the cases in this chapter, be sensitive to the types of arguments on which the Court relies, and consider whether the Court is better suited for applying one or the other approach.

C. IMPLICATIONS OF BICAMERALISM AND PRESENTMENT

Congress often passes bills that include thousands of pages of new tax, spending, and regulatory provisions. The President traditionally has had a binary choice in dealing with these bills: the President either can sign such bills or veto them. If the President signs a bill, the President approves the bill in total, and all of the bill's provisions become law. If the President vetoes the bill, the President disapproves it, and none of the provisions becomes law. The President does not have the option to approve some of the bill but not the rest.

In many states, the system is different; state constitutions may allow governors to sign bills but selectively disapprove of some of their provisions. This power is typically called a "**line-item veto**." The bill becomes law, except for the items in the bill that the governor has disapproved. The following case concerns the question whether Congress may give the President similar authority.

CLINTON V. NEW YORK

524 U.S. 417 (1998)

JUSTICE STEVENS delivered the opinion of the Court.

The Line Item Veto Act gives the President the power to "cancel in whole" three types of provisions that have been signed into law: "(1) any dollar amount of discretionary budget authority; (2) any item of new direct spending; or (3) any limited tax benefit." 2 U.S.C. § 691(a) [110 Stat. 1200].

The Act requires the President to adhere to precise procedures whenever he exercises his cancellation authority. In identifying items for cancellation he must consider the legislative history, the purposes, and other relevant information about the items. See § 691(b). He must determine, with respect to each cancellation, that it will "(i) reduce the Federal budget deficit; (ii) not impair any essential Government functions; and (iii) not harm the national interest." § 691(a)(3)(A). Moreover, he must transmit a special message to Congress notifying it of each cancellation within five calendar days (excluding Sundays) after the enactment of the canceled provision. See § 691(a)(3)(B).

Food for Thought

Putting aside the particular separation of powers issue that the Court addresses in this case, does the Act contain an intelligible principle to guide the President's exercise of authority under the Act? Do the requirements in § 691 limit the President's policy-making discretion in any meaningful way?

A cancellation takes effect upon receipt by Congress of the special message from the President. See § 691b(a). If, however, a "disapproval bill" pertaining to a special message is enacted into law, the cancellations set forth in that message become "null and void." *Ibid.* The Act sets forth a detailed expedited procedure for the consideration of a "disapproval bill," see § 691d, but no such bill was passed for either of the cancellations involved in these cases. A majority vote of both Houses is sufficient to enact a disapproval bill. The Act does not grant the

President the authority to cancel a disapproval bill, see § 691(c), but he does, of course, retain his constitutional authority to veto such a bill.

[Following these procedures, the President exercised his authority to cancel one provision in the Balanced Budget Act of 1997, 111 Stat. 251, 515, and two provisions in the Taxpayer Relief Act of 1997, 111 Stat. 788, 895–896, 990–993. The cancelled provision in the Balanced Budget Act would have, in effect, increased federal subsidies for medical care in the state of New York. The cancelled provisions in the Tax Payer Relief Act would have, in effect, reduced the taxes imposed on the sale of certain food refineries to farmers' cooperatives.]

The effect of a cancellation is plainly stated in § 691e, which defines the principal terms used in the Act. With respect to both an item of new direct spending and a limited tax benefit, the cancellation prevents the item "from having legal force or effect." §§ 691e(4)(B)–(C). Thus, under the plain text of the statute, the two actions of the President that are challenged in these cases prevented one section of the Balanced Budget Act of 1997 and one section of the Taxpayer Relief Act of 1997 "from having legal force or effect." The remaining provisions of those statutes * * * continue to have the same force and effect as they had when signed into law.

> **Food for Thought**
>
> Why do you suppose Congress enacted the Line Item Veto Act? If it is to prevent wasteful spending, why can't Congress simply stop including wasteful provisions in its bills?

In both legal and practical effect, the President has amended two Acts of Congress by repealing a portion of each. "[R]epeal of statutes, no less than enactment, must conform with Art. I." *INS v. Chadha,* 462 U.S. 919, 954 (1983). There is no provision in the Constitution that authorizes the President to enact, to amend, or to repeal statutes. Both Article I and Article II assign responsibilities to the President that directly relate to the lawmaking process, but neither addresses the issue presented by these cases. * * * [A]fter a bill has passed both Houses of Congress, but "before it become[s] a Law," it must be presented to the President. If he approves it, "he shall sign it, but if not he shall return it, with his Objections to that House in which it shall have originated, who shall enter the Objections at large on their Journal, and proceed to reconsider it." Art. I, § 7, cl. 2. His "return" of a bill, which is usually described as a "veto," is subject to being overridden by a two-thirds vote in each House.

There are important differences between the President's "return" of a bill pursuant to Article I, § 7, and the exercise of the President's cancellation authority pursuant to the Line Item Veto Act. The constitutional return takes place *before* the bill becomes law; the statutory cancellation occurs *after* the bill becomes law.

The constitutional return is of the entire bill; the statutory cancellation is of only a part. Although the Constitution expressly authorizes the President to play a role in the process of enacting statutes, it is silent on the subject of unilateral Presidential action that either repeals or amends parts of duly enacted statutes.

There are powerful reasons for construing constitutional silence on this profoundly important issue as equivalent to an express prohibition. The procedures governing the enactment of statutes set forth in the text of Article I were the product of the great debates and compromises that produced the Constitution itself. Familiar historical materials provide abundant support for the conclusion that the power to enact statutes may only "be exercised in accord with a single, finely wrought and exhaustively considered, procedure." *Chadha*, 462 U.S., at 951. Our first President understood the text of the Presentment Clause as requiring that he either "approve all the parts of a Bill, or reject it in toto." [Writings of George Washington 96 (J. Fitzpatrick ed., 1940).] What has emerged in these cases from the President's exercise of his statutory cancellation powers, however, are truncated versions of two bills that passed both Houses of Congress. They are not the product of the "finely wrought" procedure that the Framers designed.

> **Take Note**
>
> The Court explains here why the Constitution does not permit the President to approve or disapprove parts of bills. What kinds of reasoning does the Court use? Is it functionalist or formalist?

The Government advances two related arguments to support its position that despite the unambiguous provisions of the Act, cancellations do not amend or repeal properly enacted statutes in violation of the Presentment Clause. First, relying primarily on *Field v. Clark,* 143 U.S. 649 (1892), the Government contends that the cancellations were merely exercises of discretionary authority granted to the President by the Balanced Budget Act and the Taxpayer Relief Act read in light of the previously enacted Line Item Veto Act. Second, the Government submits that the substance of the authority to cancel tax and spending items "is, in practical effect, no more and no less than the power to 'decline to spend' specified sums of money, or to 'decline to implement' specified tax measures." Neither argument is persuasive.

In *Field v. Clark,* the Court upheld the constitutionality of the Tariff Act of 1890. Act of Oct. 1, 1890, 26 Stat. 567. That statute contained a "free list" of almost 300 specific articles that were exempted from import duties "unless otherwise specially provided for in this act." *Id.,* at 602. Section 3 was a special provision that directed the President to suspend that exemption for sugar, molasses, coffee, tea, and hides "whenever, and so often" as he should be satisfied that any country producing and exporting those products imposed duties on the agricultural products of the United States that he deemed to be "reciprocally unequal and unreasonable." *Id.,* at 612. The section then specified the duties to be imposed on those products during any such suspension. The Court provided this explanation for its conclusion that § 3 had not delegated legislative power to the President:

> "[W]hen [the President] ascertained the fact [made relevant by the statute,] it became his duty to issue a proclamation declaring the suspension, as to that country, which Congress had determined should occur. He had no discretion in the premises except in respect to the duration of the suspension so ordered. But that related only to the enforcement of the policy established by Congress. As the suspension was absolutely required when the President ascertained the existence of a particular fact, it cannot be said that in ascertaining that fact and in issuing his proclamation, in obedience to the legislative will, he exercised the function of making laws. . . . It was a part of the law itself as it left the hands of Congress that the provisions, full and complete in themselves, permitting the free introduction of sugars, molasses, coffee, tea and hides, from particular countries, should be suspended, in a given contingency, and that in case of such suspensions certain duties should be imposed." *Id.,* at 693.

This passage identifies three critical differences between the power to suspend the exemption from import duties and the power to cancel portions of a duly enacted statute. First, the exercise of the suspension power was contingent upon a condition that did not exist when the Tariff Act was passed: the imposition of "reciprocally unequal and unreasonable" import duties by other countries. In contrast, the exercise of the cancellation power within five days after the enactment of the Balanced Budget and Tax Reform Acts necessarily was based on the same conditions that Congress evaluated when it passed those statutes. Second, under the Tariff Act, when the President determined that the contingency had arisen, he had a duty to suspend; in contrast, while it is true that the President was required by the Act to make three determinations before he canceled a provision, those determinations did not qualify his discretion to cancel or not to cancel. Finally, whenever the President suspended an exemption under the Tariff Act, he was executing the policy that Congress had embodied in the statute. In contrast, whenever the President cancels an item of new direct spending or a limited tax benefit he is rejecting the policy judgment made by Congress and relying on his own policy judgment. Thus, the conclusion in *Field v. Clark* that the suspensions mandated by the Tariff Act were not exercises of legislative power does not undermine our opinion that cancellations pursuant to the Line Item Veto Act are the functional equivalent of partial repeals of Acts of Congress that fail to satisfy Article I, § 7. * * * The Line Item Veto Act authorizes the President himself to effect the repeal of laws, for his own policy reasons, without observing the procedures set out in Article I, § 7. The fact that Congress intended such a result is of no moment. Although Congress presumably anticipated that the President might cancel some of the items in the Balanced Budget Act and in the Taxpayer Relief Act, Congress cannot alter the procedures set out in Article I, § 7, without amending the Constitution.

Neither are we persuaded by the Government's contention that the President's authority to cancel new direct spending and tax benefit items is no greater than his traditional authority to decline to spend appropriated funds. The Government has reviewed in some detail the series of statutes in which Congress has given the Executive broad discretion over the expenditure of appropriated funds. For example, the First Congress appropriated "sum[s] not exceeding" specified amounts to be spent on various Government operations. See, *e.g.*, Act of Sept. 29, 1789, ch. 23, § 1, 1 Stat. 95; Act of Mar. 26, 1790, ch. 4, 1 Stat. 104; Act of Feb. 11, 1791, ch. 6, 1 Stat. 190. In those statutes, as in later years, the President was given wide discretion with respect to both the amounts to be spent and how the money would be allocated among different functions. It is argued that the Line Item Veto Act merely confers comparable discretionary authority over the expenditure of appropriated funds. The critical difference between this statute and all of its predecessors, however, is that unlike any of them, this Act gives the President the unilateral power to change the text of duly enacted statutes. None of the Act's predecessors could even arguably have been construed to authorize such a change.

JUSTICE KENNEDY, concurring.

A Nation cannot plunder its own treasury without putting its Constitution and its survival in peril. The statute before us, then, is of first importance, for it seems undeniable the Act will tend to restrain persistent excessive spending. Nevertheless, for the reasons given by Justice STEVENS in the opinion for the Court, the statute must be found invalid. Failure of political will does not justify unconstitutional remedies.

JUSTICE SCALIA, with whom JUSTICE O'CONNOR joins, and with whom JUSTICE BREYER joins as to Part III, concurring in part and dissenting in part.

[Art. I, § 7] no more categorically prohibits the Executive reduction of congressional dispositions in the course of implementing statutes that authorize such reduction, than it categorically prohibits the Executive augmentation of congressional dispositions in the course of implementing statutes that authorize such augmentation—generally known as substantive rulemaking. There are, to be sure, limits upon the former just as there are limits upon the latter * * *. Those limits are established, however, not by some categorical prohibition of Art. I, § 7, [but] by what has come to be known as the doctrine of unconstitutional delegation of legislative authority: When authorized Executive reduction or augmentation is allowed to go too far, it usurps the nondelegable function of Congress and violates the separation of powers. It is this doctrine, and not the Presentment Clause, that was discussed in the *Field* opinion, and it is this doctrine, and not the Presentment Clause, that is the issue presented by the statute before us here. Insofar as the degree of political, "lawmaking" power conferred upon the Executive is concerned, there is not a dime's worth of difference between Congress's authorizing the President to cancel a spending item, and Congress's authorizing money to be spent on a particular item at the President's discretion. And the latter has been done since the founding of the Nation.

The short of the matter is this: Had the Line Item Veto Act authorized the President to "decline to spend" any item of spending contained in the Balanced Budget Act of 1997, there is not the slightest doubt that authorization would have been constitutional. What the Line Item Veto Act does instead—authorizing the President to "cancel" an item of spending—is technically different. But the technical difference does *not* relate to the technicalities of the Presentment Clause, which have been fully complied with; and the doctrine of unconstitutional delegation, which *is* at issue here, is preeminently *not* a doctrine of technicalities. The title of the Line Item Veto Act, which was perhaps designed to simplify for public comprehension, or perhaps merely to comply with the terms of a campaign pledge, has succeeded in faking out the Supreme Court. The President's action it authorizes in fact is not a line-item veto and thus does not offend Art. I, § 7; and insofar as the substance of that action is concerned, it is no different from what Congress has permitted the President to do since the formation of the Union.

Food for Thought

Why does Justice Scalia think that this case does not involve a genuine line-item veto?

JUSTICE BREYER, with whom JUSTICE O'CONNOR and JUSTICE SCALIA join as to Part III, dissenting.

When our Nation was founded, Congress could easily have provided the President with [the kind of power at issue here]. In that time period, our population was less than 4 million, federal employees numbered fewer than 5,000, [and] annual federal budget outlays totaled approximately $4 million. At that time, a Congress, wishing to give a President the power to select among appropriations, could simply have embodied each appropriation in a separate bill, each bill subject to a separate Presidential veto. Today, however, our population is about 250 million, the Federal Government employs more than 4 million people, the annual federal budget is $1.5 trillion, and a typical budget appropriations bill may have a dozen titles, hundreds of sections, and spread across more than 500 pages of the Statutes at Large. Congress cannot divide such a bill into thousands, or tens of thousands, of separate appropriations bills, each one of which the President would have to sign, or to veto, separately. Thus, the question is whether the Constitution permits Congress to choose a particular novel means to achieve this same, constitutionally legitimate, end.

[We should] interpret nonliteral separation-of-powers principles in light of the need for "workable government." *Youngstown Sheet & Tube Co. v. Sawyer*, 343 U.S. 579, 635 (1952), (Jackson, J., concurring). If we apply those principles in light of that objective, as this Court has applied them in the past, the Act is constitutional.

The Court believes that the Act violates the literal text of the Constitution.* A simple syllogism captures its basic reasoning: Major Premise: The Constitution sets forth an exclusive method for enacting, repealing, or amending laws. Minor Premise: The Act authorizes the President to "repea[l] or amen[d]" laws in a different way, namely by announcing a cancellation of a portion of a previously enacted law. Conclusion: The Act is inconsistent with the Constitution. I find this syllogism unconvincing, however, because its Minor Premise is faulty. When the President "canceled" the two appropriation measures now before us, he did not *repeal* any law nor did he *amend* any law. He simply *followed* the law, leaving the statutes, as they are literally written, intact.

To understand why one cannot say, *literally speaking*, that the President has repealed or amended any law, imagine [that] the canceled New York health care tax provision at issue here [had instead specifically said that] "*the President may prevent the just-mentioned provision from having legal force or effect if he determines x, y, and*

* Justices O'Connor and Scalia joined this paragraph and the two that follow it.—*Eds.*

z." (Assume x, y and z to be the same determinations required by the Line Item Veto Act). Whatever a person might say, or think, about the constitutionality of this imaginary law, [the] English language would prevent one from saying [that] a President who [prevents the tax from having legal force or effect] has either *repealed* or *amended* this particular hypothetical statute. Rather, the President has *followed* that law to the letter. He has exercised the power it explicitly delegates to him. He has executed the law, not repealed it.

It could make no significant difference to this linguistic point were the italicized proviso to appear, not as part of what I have called Section One, but, instead, at the bottom of the statute page, say, referenced by an asterisk, with a statement that it applies to every spending provision in the Act next to which a similar asterisk appears. And that being so, it could make no difference if that proviso appeared, instead, in a different, earlier enacted law, along with legal language that makes it applicable to every future spending provision picked out according to a specified formula. * * * But, of course, this last mentioned possibility is this very case.

Because I disagree with the Court's holding of literal violation, I must consider whether the Act nonetheless violates separation-of-powers principles. * * * Viewed conceptually, the power the Act conveys [is] "executive." As explained above, an exercise of that power "executes" the Act. * * * The fact that one could also characterize this kind of power as "legislative," say, if Congress itself (by amending the appropriations bill) prevented a provision from taking effect, is beside the point. This Court has frequently found that the exercise of a particular power [can] fall within the constitutional purview of more than one branch of Government.

[O]ne cannot say that the Act "encroaches" upon Congress' power, when Congress retained the power to insert, by simple majority, into any future appropriations bill, into any section of any such bill, or into any phrase of any section, a provision that says the Act will not apply. See 2 U.S.C. § 691f(c)(1) (1994 ed., Supp. II). Congress also retained the power to "disapprov[e]," and thereby reinstate, any of the President's cancellations. See 2 U.S.C. § 691b(a). And it is Congress that drafts and enacts the appropriations statutes that are subject to the Act in the first place—and thereby defines the outer limits of the President's cancellation authority. * * * Nor can one say the Act's grant of power "aggrandizes" the Presidential office. The grant is limited [to] the power to spend, or not to spend, particular appropriated items, and the power to permit, or not to permit, specific limited exemptions from generally applicable tax law from taking effect. These powers [resemble] those the President has exercised in the past on other occasions.

The "nondelegation" doctrine [raises] a more serious constitutional obstacle here. [The standards in the Act] are broad. But this Court has upheld standards that are equally broad, or broader. [In addition, the] President, unlike most agency decisionmakers, is an elected official. He is responsible to the voters, who, in principle, will judge the manner in which he exercises his delegated authority. Whether the President's expenditure decisions, for example, are arbitrary is a matter that in the past has been left primarily to those voters to consider.

[I] recognize that the Act before us is novel. In a sense, it skirts a constitutional edge. But that edge has to do with means, not ends. The means chosen do not amount literally to the enactment, repeal, or amendment of a law. * * * Those means do not violate any basic separation-of-powers principle. They do not improperly shift the constitutionally foreseen balance of power from Congress to the President. Nor, since they comply with separation-of-powers principles, do they threaten the liberties of individual citizens. They represent an experiment that may, or may not, help representative government work better. The Constitution, in my view, authorizes Congress and the President to try novel methods in this way. Consequently, with respect, I dissent.

POINTS FOR DISCUSSION

a. Aggrandizement?

Does this case involve an attempt by Congress to aggrandize its own powers? If not, why should the Court care whether Congress has given the President additional powers? If Congress becomes concerned about the President's abuse of authority conferred by the statute, can't Congress simply repeal the Act?

b. Political Logrolling

The term "logrolling" in politics refers to a common way of accommodating differences of opinion when passing legislation. Politicians may support opponents' proposals, to induce these opponents to support their own objectives. For example, suppose that in setting the federal budget, Republicans want to increase defense spending, while Democrats desire to raise education spending. Rather than blocking each other's proposals, the two parties might agree to pass a single spending bill that increases both defense spending and education spending. How would giving the President a line-item veto affect logrolling compromises of this kind? What benefits and drawbacks might result? Compare J. Gregory Sidak, *The Line-Item Veto Amendment*, 80 Cornell L. Rev. 1498, 1498 (1995) ("The absence of a presidential line-item veto may have contributed to the seemingly irreversible growth of the federal government."), with Adrian Vermeule, *The Constitutional Law of Congressional Procedure*, 71 U. Chi. L. Rev. 361, 413 n. 169 (2004) ("Logrolling may permit, of course, either socially beneficial trades or the infliction of socially harmful externalities * * *. Much depends on the details of the situation.").

c. Constitutional Alternatives?

After the decision in *Clinton*, is it possible to craft a constitutional statute that gives the President the authority to trim wasteful spending from the budget?

D. CONGRESSIONAL CONTROL OVER EXECUTIVE OFFICIALS

As we have seen, Article II vests the executive power of the United States in the President. But of course the President cannot administer the entire federal government alone. Instead, the President must act through subordinates, like the Secretary of State, the Attorney General, the Secretary of Defense, and so forth. The Constitution specifically requires the President to "take Care that the Laws be faithfully executed," Art. II, § 3, and it provides that the President "may require the Opinion, in writing, of the principal Officer in each of the executive Departments, upon any Subject relating to the Duties of their respective Offices," Art. II, § 2.

But a question not fully addressed by the text of the Constitution is how or to what extent the President may control the actions of subordinates. The conventional way that a President, like any other supervisor, exercises control over subordinates is through the power to hire and to fire. The Constitution's assignment of responsibility for hiring and firing, therefore, is of the utmost importance in determining the extent of the President's authority to control the actions of subordinates.

The Constitution makes clear, in the Appointments Clause, Art. II, § 2, cl. 2, that the President has authority (subject to the "the Advice and Consent of the Senate") to appoint "Officers" of the United States, and that Congress may (but need not) vest in the President the power to appoint "inferior Officers," as well.

U.S. Constitution, Article II, Section 2, Clause 2

[The President] shall nominate, and by and with the Advice and Consent of the Senate, shall appoint Ambassadors, other public Ministers and Consuls, Judges of the supreme Court, and all other Officers of the United States, whose Appointments are not herein otherwise provided for, and which shall be established by Law: but the Congress may by Law vest the Appointment of such inferior Officers, as they think proper, in the President alone, in the Courts of Law, or in the Heads of Departments.

The Court has held that Congress may not assign *to itself* the power to appoint executive officers. See *Buckley v. Valeo*, 424 U.S. 1, 139 (1976) (holding that Congress could not constitutionally authorize Members of Congress to appoint members of the Federal Election Commission). But a Congress that seeks to limit the President's authority to control his subordinates might be able to achieve its goal by vesting the power to appoint in someone other than the President. As the language of the Appointments Clause makes clear, whether Congress can do so turns on whether the official whose appointment is at issue is an "Officer" or instead an "inferior Officer." We will defer until later in this chapter—specifically in the discussion of the Court's decision in *Morrison v. Olson*—how the Court distinguishes between these two classes of officials. But do those categories of officials together include every person who works for the federal government? Consider the case that follows.

LUCIA V. SECURITIES AND EXCHANGE COMMISSION

138 S.Ct. 2044 (2018)

JUSTICE KAGAN delivered the opinion of the Court.

The Appointments Clause of the Constitution lays out the permissible methods of appointing "Officers of the United States," a class of government officials distinct from mere employees. Art. II, § 2, cl. 2. This case requires us to decide whether administrative law judges (ALJs) of the Securities and Exchange Commission (SEC or Commission) qualify as such "Officers."

The SEC has statutory authority to enforce the nation's securities laws. One way it can do so is by instituting an administrative proceeding against an alleged wrongdoer. By law, the Commission may itself preside over such a proceeding. See 17 CFR § 201.110 (2017). But the Commission also may, and typically does, delegate that task to an ALJ. The SEC currently has five ALJs. Other staff members, rather than the Commission proper, selected them all.

An ALJ assigned to hear an SEC enforcement action has extensive powers—the "authority to do all things necessary and appropriate to discharge his or her duties" and ensure a "fair and orderly" adversarial proceeding. §§ 201.111, 200.14(a). Those powers "include, but are not limited to," supervising discovery; issuing, revoking, or modifying subpoenas; deciding motions; ruling on the admissibility of evidence; administering oaths; hearing and examining witnesses; generally "[r]egulating the course of" the proceeding and the "conduct of the parties and their counsel"; and imposing sanctions for "[c]ontemptuous conduct" or violations of procedural requirements. §§ 201.111, 201.180; see §§ 200.14(a), 201.230. As that list suggests, an SEC ALJ exercises authority "comparable to" that of a federal district judge conducting a bench trial. *Butz* v. *Economou*, 438 U.S. 478, 513 (1978).

After a hearing ends, the ALJ issues an "initial decision." § 201.360(a)(1). That decision must set out "findings and conclusions" about all "material issues of fact [and] law"; it also must include the "appropriate order, sanction, relief, or denial thereof." § 201.360(b). The Commission can then review the ALJ's decision, either upon request or *sua sponte*. See § 201.360(d)(1). But if it opts against review, the Commission "issue[s] an order that the [ALJ's] decision has become final." § 201.360(d)(2). At that point, the initial decision is "deemed the action of the Commission." § 78d–1(c).

> **Food for Thought**
>
> ALJs preside over adjudicatory proceedings at administrative agencies. Their decisions are usually subject to review by the head(s) of the agency, whose decisions are in turn usually subject to review in Article III courts. Is this process consistent with your understanding of Article III and the Due Process Clause?

This case began when the SEC instituted an administrative proceeding against petitioner Raymond Lucia and his investment company. Lucia marketed a retirement savings strategy called "Buckets of Money." In the SEC's view, Lucia used misleading slideshow presentations to deceive prospective clients. The SEC charged Lucia under the Investment Advisers Act, § 80b–1 *et seq.*, and assigned ALJ Cameron Elliot to adjudicate the case. After nine days of testimony and argument, Judge Elliot issued an initial decision concluding that Lucia had violated the Act and imposing sanctions, including civil penalties of $300,000 and a lifetime bar from the investment industry. [After a remand from the Commission for more factfinding, Judge Elliot] made additional findings of deception and issued a revised initial decision, with the same sanctions.

On appeal to the SEC, Lucia argued that the administrative proceeding was invalid because Judge Elliot had not been constitutionally appointed [because] the

Commission had left the task of appointing ALJs, including Judge Elliot, to SEC staff members. As a result, Lucia contended, Judge Elliot lacked constitutional authority to do his job.

> **FYI**
>
> In the court of appeals, the federal government defended the Commission's position that SEC ALJs are not officers. After the presidential election, the government switched sides, arguing that the ALJs are officers and that their appointment was unconstitutional. The Court appointed an *amicus curiae* to defend the judgment below.

The Commission rejected Lucia's argument. [A panel of the Court of Appeals for the D. C. Circuit concluded that SEC ALJs are employees rather than officers, and so are not subject to the Appointments Clause. The Court of Appeals heard argument *en banc* but divided evenly, resulting in a *per curiam* order denying Lucia's claim. See 868 F. 3d 1021 (2017).]

The sole question here is whether the Commission's ALJs are "Officers of the United States" or simply employees of the Federal Government. The Appointments Clause prescribes the exclusive means of appointing "Officers." Only the President, a court of law, or a head of department can do so. See Art. II, § 2, cl. 2.[3] And as all parties agree, none of those actors appointed Judge Elliot before he heard Lucia's case; instead, SEC staff members gave him an ALJ slot. So if the Commission's ALJs are constitutional officers, Lucia raises a valid Appointments Clause claim. The only way to defeat his position is to show that those ALJs are not officers at all, but instead non-officer employees—part of the broad swath of "lesser functionaries" in the Government's workforce. *Buckley* v. *Valeo*, 424 U. S. 1, 126, n. 162 (1976) (*per curiam*). For if that is true, the Appointments Clause cares not a whit about who named them. See *United States* v. *Germaine*, 99 U. S. 508, 510 (1879).

Two decisions set out this Court's basic framework for distinguishing between officers and employees. *Germaine* held that "civil surgeons" (doctors hired to perform various physical exams) were mere employees because their duties were "occasional or temporary" rather than "continuing and permanent." *Id.,* at 511–512. Stressing "ideas of tenure [and] duration," the Court there made clear that an individual must occupy a "continuing" position established by law to qualify as an officer. *Id.,* at 511. *Buckley* then set out another requirement, central to this case. It determined that members of a federal commission were officers

---

[3] That statement elides a distinction, not at issue here, between "principal" and "inferior" officers. See *Edmond* v. *United States*, 520 U. S. 651, 659–660 (1997). * * * Both the Government and Lucia view the SEC's ALJs as inferior officers and acknowledge that the Commission, as a head of department, can constitutionally appoint them.

only after finding that they "exercis[ed] significant authority pursuant to the laws of the United States." 424 U. S., at 126. The inquiry thus focused on the extent of power an individual wields in carrying out his assigned functions.

The standard is no doubt framed in general terms, tempting advocates to add whatever glosses best suit their arguments. And maybe one day we will see a need to refine or enhance the test *Buckley* set out so concisely. But that day is not this one, because in *Freytag* v. *Commissioner*, 501 U. S. 868 (1991), we applied the unadorned "significant authority" test to adjudicative officials who are near-carbon copies of the Commission's ALJs. As we now explain, our analysis there * * * necessarily decides this case.

The officials at issue in *Freytag* were the "special trial judges" (STJs) of the United States Tax Court. * * * This Court held that the Tax Court's STJs are officers, not mere employees. Citing *Germaine*, the Court first found that STJs hold a continuing office established by law. See 501 U. S., at 881. They serve on an ongoing, rather than a "temporary [or] episodic[,] basis"; and their "duties, salary, and means of appointment" are all specified in the Tax Code. *Ibid.* The Court then considered, as *Buckley* demands, the "significance" of the "authority" STJs wield. 501 U. S., at 881. * * * Describing the responsibilities involved in presiding over adversarial hearings, the Court said: STJs "take testimony, conduct trials, rule on the admissibility of evidence, and have the power to enforce compliance with discovery orders." *Id.*, at 881–882. And the Court observed that "[i]n the course of carrying out these important functions, the [STJs] exercise significant discretion." *Id.*, at 882. That fact meant they were officers, even when their decisions were not final.

Freytag says everything necessary to decide this case. To begin, the Commission's ALJs, like the Tax Court's STJs, hold a continuing office established by law. Far from serving temporarily or episodically, SEC ALJs "receive[ ] a career appointment." 5 CFR § 930.204(a) (2018). And that appointment is to a position created by statute, down to its "duties, salary, and means of appointment." *Freytag*, 501 U. S., at 881; see 5 U. S. C. §§ 556–557, 5372, 3105.

Still more, the Commission's ALJs exercise the same "significant discretion" when carrying out the same "important functions" as STJs do. *Freytag*, 501 U. S., at 882. Both sets of officials have all the authority needed to ensure fair and orderly adversarial hearings—indeed, nearly all the tools of federal trial judges. See *Butz*, 438 U. S., at 513. * * * And at the close of those proceedings, ALJs issue decisions much like that in *Freytag*—except with potentially more independent effect. * * * In a major case like *Freytag*, a regular Tax Court judge must always review an STJ's opinion. And that opinion counts for nothing unless the regular judge adopts it as his own. See 501 U. S., at 873. By contrast, the SEC can decide against reviewing an ALJ decision at all. And when the SEC declines review (and issues an order saying so), the ALJ's decision itself "becomes final" and is "deemed the action of the Commission." § 201.360(d)(2); 15 U. S. C. § 78d–1(c). That last-word capacity makes this an *a fortiori* case: If the Tax Court's STJs are officers, as *Freytag* held, then the Commission's ALJs must be too.

The only issue left is remedial. * * * Judge Elliot heard and decided Lucia's case without the kind of appointment the [Appointments] Clause requires. * * * This Court has also held that the "appropriate" remedy for an adjudication tainted with an appointments violation is a new "hearing before a properly appointed" official. *Ryder* v. *United States*, 515 U. S. 177, 183, 188 (1995). And we add today one thing more. That official cannot be Judge Elliot, even if he has by now received (or receives sometime in the future) a constitutional appointment. Judge Elliot has already both heard Lucia's case and issued an initial decision on the merits. He cannot be expected to consider the matter as though he had not adjudicated it before.[5] To cure the constitutional error, another ALJ (or the Commission itself) must hold the new hearing to which Lucia is entitled.[6]

We accordingly reverse the judgment of the Court of Appeals and remand the case for further proceedings consistent with this opinion.

JUSTICE THOMAS, with whom JUSTICE GORSUCH joins, concurring.

I agree with the Court that this case is indistinguishable from *Freytag* v. *Commissioner*, 501 U. S. 868 (1991). * * * Moving forward, however, this Court will not be able to decide every Appointments Clause case by comparing it to *Freytag*. And, as the Court acknowledges, our precedents in this area do not provide much guidance. While precedents like *Freytag* discuss what is *sufficient* to make someone an officer of the United States, our precedents have never clearly defined what is

---

[5] JUSTICE BREYER disagrees with our decision to wrest further proceedings from Judge Elliot, arguing that "[f]or him to preside once again would not violate the structural purposes [of] the Appointments Clause." But our Appointments Clause remedies are designed not only to advance those purposes directly, but also to create "[ ]incentive[s] to raise Appointments Clause challenges." *Ryder* v. *United States*, 515 U. S. 177, 183 (1995). We best accomplish that goal by providing a successful litigant with a hearing before a new judge. That is especially so because (as JUSTICE BREYER points out) the old judge would have no reason to think he did anything wrong on the merits—and so could be expected to reach all the same judgments. * * *

[6] While this case was on judicial review, the SEC issued an order "ratif[ying]" the prior appointments of its ALJs. Order (Nov. 30, 2017), online at https://www.sec.gov/litigation/opinions/2017/33-10440.pdf (as last visited June 18, 2018). Lucia argues that the order is invalid. We see no reason to address that issue. The Commission has not suggested that it intends to assign Lucia's case on remand to an ALJ whose claim to authority rests on the ratification order. The SEC may decide to conduct Lucia's rehearing itself. Or it may assign the hearing to an ALJ who has received a constitutional appointment independent of the ratification.

necessary. I would resolve that question based on the original public meaning of "Officers of the United States." * * *

The Founders likely understood the term "Officers of the United States" to encompass all federal civil officials who perform an ongoing, statutory duty—no matter how important or significant the duty. Mascott, *Who Are "Officers of the United States"?* 70 Stan. L. Rev. 443, 454 (2018). "Officers of the United States" was probably not a term of art that the Constitution used to signify some special type of official. Based on how the Founders used it and similar terms, the phrase "of the United States" was merely a synonym for "federal," and the word "Office[r]" carried its ordinary meaning. See *id.*, at 471–479. The ordinary meaning of "officer" was anyone who performed a continuous public duty. See *id.*, at 484–507; *e.g.*, *United States* v. *Maurice*, 26 F. Cas. 1211, 1214 (No. 15,747) (CC Va. 1823) (defining officer as someone in "a public charge or employment" who performed a "continuing" duty); 8 Annals of Cong. 2304–2305 (1799) (statement of Rep. Harper) (explaining that the word officer "is derived from the Latin word *officium*" and "includes all persons holding posts which require the performance of some public duty"). For federal officers, that duty is "established by Law"—that is, by statute. Art. II, § 2, cl. 2. The Founders considered individuals to be officers even if they performed only ministerial statutory duties—including recordkeepers, clerks, and tidewaiters (individuals who watched goods land at a customhouse). See Mascott 484–507. Early congressional practice reflected this understanding. With exceptions not relevant here, Congress required all federal officials with ongoing statutory duties to be appointed in compliance with the Appointments Clause. See *id.*, at 507–545.

Applying the original meaning here, the administrative law judges of the Securities and Exchange Commission easily qualify as "Officers of the United States." These judges exercise many of the agency's statutory duties, including issuing initial decisions in adversarial proceedings. See 15 U. S. C. § 78d–1(a); 17 CFR §§ 200.14, 200.30–9 (2017). As explained, the importance or significance of these statutory duties is irrelevant. All that matters is that the judges are continuously responsible for performing them. * * * Because the Court reaches the same conclusion by correctly applying *Freytag*, I join its opinion.

JUSTICE BREYER, with whom JUSTICE GINSBURG and JUSTICE SOTOMAYOR join as to Part III, concurring in the judgment in part and dissenting in part.

[I] [The Administrative Procedure Act] governs the appointment of administrative law judges. It provides [that] "[e]ach agency shall appoint as many administrative law judges as are necessary for" hearings governed by the Administrative Procedure Act. 5 U. S. C. § 3105. In the case of the Securities and

Exchange Commission, the relevant "agency" is the Commission itself. But the Commission did not appoint the Administrative Law Judge who presided over Lucia's hearing. Rather, the Commission's staff appointed that Administrative Law Judge, without the approval of the Commissioners themselves.

I do not believe that the Administrative Procedure Act permits the Commission to delegate its power to appoint its administrative law judges to its staff. We have held that, for purposes of the Constitution's Appointments Clause, the Commission itself is a "Hea[d]" of a "Departmen[t]." *Free Enterprise Fund, supra*, at 512–513. Thus, reading the statute as referring to the Commission itself, and not to its staff, avoids a difficult constitutional question, namely, the very question that the Court answers today: whether the Commission's administrative law judges are constitutional "inferior Officers" whose appointment Congress may vest only in the President, the "Courts of Law," or the "Heads of Departments." * * * The upshot, in my view, is that for statutory, not constitutional, reasons, the Commission did not lawfully appoint the Administrative Law Judge here at issue. And this Court should decide no more than that.

[II] [I]n my view, [the] Appointments Clause is properly understood to grant Congress a degree of leeway as to whether particular Government workers are officers or instead mere employees not subject to the Appointments Clause. * * * The use of the words "by Law" [in the Appointments Clause] to describe the establishment and means of appointment of "Officers of the United States," together with the fact that Article I of the Constitution vests the legislative power in Congress, suggests that (other than the officers the Constitution specifically lists) Congress, not the Judicial Branch alone, must play a major role in determining who is an "Office[r] of the United States." And Congress' intent in this specific respect is often highly relevant. Congress' leeway is not, of course, absolute—it may not, for example, say that positions the Constitution itself describes as "Officers" are not "Officers." But given the constitutional language, the Court, when deciding whether other positions are "Officers of the United States" under the Appointments Clause, should give substantial weight to Congress' decision.

I would not answer the question whether the Securities and Exchange Commission's administrative law judges are constitutional "Officers" without first deciding * * * what effect that holding would have on the statutory "for cause" removal protections that Congress provided for administrative law judges. If [saying] administrative law judges are "inferior Officers" will cause them to lose their "for cause" removal protections, then I would likely hold that the administrative law judges are not "Officers," for to say otherwise would be to contradict Congress' enactment of those protections in the Administrative Procedure Act. * * *

[III] Separately, I also disagree with the majority's conclusion that the proper remedy in this case requires a hearing before a *different* administrative law judge. The Securities and Exchange Commission has now itself appointed the Administrative Law Judge in question, and I see no reason why he could not rehear the case. After all, when a judge is reversed on appeal and a new trial ordered, typically the judge who rehears the case is the same judge who heard it the first time. The reversal here is based on a technical constitutional question, and the reversal implies no criticism at all of the original judge or his ability to conduct the new proceedings. For him to preside once again would not violate the structural purposes that we have said the Appointments Clause serves, nor would it, in any obvious way, violate the Due Process Clause.

JUSTICE SOTOMAYOR, with whom JUSTICE GINSBURG joins, dissenting.

The Court today and scholars acknowledge that this Court's Appointments Clause jurisprudence offers little guidance on who qualifies as an "Officer of the United States." * * * This confusion can undermine the reliability and finality of proceedings and result in wasted resources.

As the majority notes, this Court's decisions currently set forth at least two prerequisites to officer status: (1) an individual must hold a "continuing" office established by law, *United States* v. *Germaine*, 99 U. S. 508, 511–512 (1879), and (2) an individual must wield "significant authority," *Buckley* v. *Valeo*, 424 U. S. 1, 126 (1976) (*per curiam*). The first requirement is relatively easy to grasp; the second, less so. To be sure, to exercise "significant authority," the person must wield considerable powers in comparison to the average person who works for the Federal Government. As this Court has noted, the vast majority of those who work for the Federal Government are not "Officers of the United States." See *Free Enterprise Fund* v. *Public Company Accounting Oversight Bd.*, 561 U. S. 477, 506, n. 9 (2010) (indicating that well over 90% of those who render services to the Federal Government and are paid by it are not constitutional officers). But this Court's decisions have yet to articulate the types of powers that will be deemed significant enough to constitute "significant authority."

To provide guidance to Congress and the Executive Branch, I would hold that one requisite component of "significant authority" is the ability to make final, binding decisions on behalf of the Government. Accordingly, a person who merely advises and provides recommendations to an officer would not herself qualify as an officer. * * *

Turning to the question presented here, it is true that the administrative law judges (ALJs) of the Securities and Exchange Commission wield "extensive powers." * * * Nevertheless, I would hold that Commission ALJs are not officers because they lack final decisionmaking authority. * * * Commission ALJs can issue only "initial" decisions. 5 U. S. C. § 557(b). The Commission can review any initial decision upon petition or on its own initiative. 15 U. S. C. § 78d–1(b). The Commission's review of an ALJ's initial decision is *de novo.* 5 U. S. C. § 557(c). It can "make any findings or conclusions that in its judgment are proper and on the basis of the record." 17 CFR § 201.411(a) (2017). * * * Even where the Commission does not review an ALJ's initial decision, as in cases in which no party petitions for review and the Commission does not act *sua sponte*, the initial decision still only becomes final when the Commission enters a finality order. 17 CFR § 201.360(d)(2). And by operation of law, every action taken by an ALJ "shall, for all purposes, . . . be deemed the action of the *Commission.*" 15 U. S. C. § 78d–1(c) (emphasis added). In other words, Commission ALJs do not exercise significant authority because they do not, and cannot, enter final, binding decisions against the Government or third parties. * * * I would conclude that Commission ALJs are not officers for purposes of the Appointments Clause * * *.

POINTS FOR DISCUSSION

a. Officers, Inferior Officers, and Employees

As we will see soon, the Court has struggled to distinguish between officers, who must be appointed by the President subject to Senate advice and consent, and inferior officers, who can, if Congress so provides, be appointed by Heads of Departments or the Courts of Law. Does the Constitution also contemplate "employees" who work for the federal government but who can be hired by other means? What is the Court's test for distinguishing between inferior officers and employees? Under the Court's test, is an Assistant United States Attorney—one of the thousands of federal prosecutors who staff regional offices around the country—an inferior officer or an employee? What about under Justice Thomas's test? If the head of an agency can simply "ratify" the appointment of such a person, and thereby appoint her consistent with the Appointments Clause, does it matter if we call her an inferior officer or instead an employee?

b. Inferior Officers, Employees, and Multiple Layers of Protection from Removal

In *Free Enterprise Fund v. Public Company Accounting Oversight Board*, 561 U.S. 477 (2010), which we will consider later in this chapter, the Court held that Congress cannot create two layers of "for-cause" protection from removal—that is, Congress cannot restrict the President's power to remove a principal officer who in turn is restricted in his ability to remove an inferior officer who determines the policy and enforces the laws of the United States. Because the President can terminate Commissioners of the SEC only for cause, the Solicitor General of the United States argued in Lucia that Congress could not also impose strict good-cause limits on the Commissioners' power to remove ALJs. Would there be any problem with such a conclusion?

ALJs adjudicate claims between the government and private citizens. Although they do not enjoy the protections for independence that Article III confers on federal judges, they have long enjoyed statutory protection from interference by the political appointees at the agency, to ensure a fair and unbiased hearing. If Commissioners at the SEC could terminate them at will, then they would lose much of that independence. But is it problematic to create a class of government officials who exercise power beyond the meaningful control of the President?

Would it make more sense to conclude that agencies lack constitutional power to adjudicate matters involving private parties? Or would that approach substantially undermine the functioning of the administrative state?

We will return to the Appointments Clause later in this chapter, and in particular to the distinction between officers and inferior officers and Congress's power to give someone other than the President the power to appoint. But assume for present pruposes that the President gets to appoint an officer. Even officers whom the President has appointed might sometimes seek to make decisions with which the President disagrees. Suppose, for example, that the President disagrees with the Secretary of the Treasury on a matter of policy or the President views the Secretary of Treasury's performance as unsatisfactory. What can the President do? Traditionally, the President has exercised control in these kinds of situations either by firing, or threatening to fire, subordinates who do not conform to the President's requirements. Indeed, the President might be able to control the decision-making even of officers whom he has *not* appointed if he has the power to remove them from office.

The next two cases consider the question whether Congress by statute can limit the President's ability to discharge subordinates and thus restrict the ability of the President to control the executive branch. The two decisions, however, are not easy to reconcile. As a noted commentator has written, *Myers v. United States* "stands for the broad proposition that any congressional limits on the [the President's] removal power are unconstitutional," Erwin Chemerinsky, *Constitutional Law: Principles and Policies* 350 (3d ed. 2006), at least with respect to "Officers" of the United States. But *Humphrey's Executor v. United States* holds that, at least with respect to the heads of some administrative agencies, Congress "may limit removal to situations where there is just cause for firing." *Id.* at 351. In reading the cases, consider how the Court reconciles the difference.

MYERS V. UNITED STATES

272 U.S. 52 (1926)

MR. CHIEF JUSTICE TAFT delivered the opinion of the Court.

> **FYI**
>
> William Howard Taft was the President of the United States from 1909–1913. In his tremendous legal and political career, he also served as Chief Justice of the United States, a federal circuit judge, the solicitor general of the United States, the civil governor of the Philippines, and a professor at Yale Law School.

This case presents the question whether under the Constitution the President has the exclusive power of removing executive officers of the United States whom he has appointed by and with the advice and consent of the Senate.

Myers, appellant's intestate, was on July 21, 1917, appointed by the President, by and with the advice and consent of the Senate, to be a postmaster of the first class at Portland, Or., for a term of four years. On January 20, 1920, Myers' resignation was demanded. He refused the demand. On February 2, 1920, he was removed from office by order of the Postmaster General, acting by direction of the President. * * * On April 21, 1921, he brought this suit in the Court of Claims for his salary from the date of his removal, which * * * amounted to $8,838.71. In August, 1920, the President made a recess appointment of one Jones, who took office September 19, 1920.

> **Definitions**
>
> "Intestate" means having died without a will. In many states, after a person dies, the "administrator" (or administratrix, if female) of a person's estate pays any debts the person owes, collects any payments owed to the person, and then distributes the person's assets to the person's heirs. A "recess appointment" is a temporary appointment of a person to a federal office made by the President while the Senate is in recess and cannot vote on the appointment.

By the sixth section of the Act of Congress of July 12, 1876, 19 Stat. 80, under which Myers was appointed with the advice and consent of the Senate as a first-class postmaster, it is provided that:

> "Postmasters of the first, second, and third classes shall be appointed and may be removed by the President by and with the advice and consent of the Senate, and shall hold their offices for four years unless sooner removed or suspended according to law."

The Senate did not consent to the President's removal of Myers during his term. If this statute in its requirement that his term should be four years unless sooner removed by the President by and with the consent of the Senate is valid, the appellant, Myers' administratrix, is entitled to recover his unpaid salary for his full term and the judgment of the Court of Claims must be reversed. The government maintains that the requirement is invalid, for the reason that under article 2 of the Constitution the President's power of removal of executive officers appointed by him with the advice and consent of the Senate is full and complete without consent of the Senate. If this view is sound, the removal of Myers by the President without the Senate's consent was legal, and the judgment of the Court of Claims against the appellant was correct, and must be affirmed * * *. We are therefore confronted by the constitutional question and cannot avoid it.

In the House of Representatives of the First Congress, on Tuesday, May 18, 1789, Mr. Madison moved in the committee of the whole that there should be established three executive departments, one of Foreign Affairs, another of the Treasury, and a third of War, at the head of each of which there should be a Secretary, to be appointed by the President by and with the advice and consent of the Senate, and to be removable by the President. The committee agreed to the establishment of a Department of Foreign Affairs, but a discussion ensued as to making the Secretary removable by the President. 1 Annals of Congress, 370, 371. "The question was now taken and carried, by a considerable majority, in favor of declaring the power of removal to be in the President." 1 Annals of Congress, 383.

> **FYI**
>
> During the debate on Madison's proposal, a discussion of removal of officers arose. A small number of Representatives believed that impeachment was the only way to remove an officer, and the rest of the Members were divided roughly evenly among the following three views: (1) removal is the President's prerogative alone; (2) removal, like appointment, is vested jointly in the President and the Senate; and (3) because the Constitution is silent, Congress can settle the question of removal pursuant to its power under the Necessary and Proper Clause. See Edward S. Corwin, *Tenure of Office and the Removal Power Under the Constitution*, 27 Colum. L. Rev. 353 (1927). Proponents of the first view and the third view ultimately joined to confer the power on the President. Is it a fair inference from this record that the original understanding was that the removal power resided solely in the President?

It is convenient in the course of our discussion of this case to review the reasons advanced by Mr. Madison and his associates for their conclusion, supplementing them, so far as may be, by additional considerations which lead this court to concur therein.

The debates in the Constitutional Convention indicated an intention to create a strong executive, and after a controversial discussion the executive power of the government was vested in one person and many of his important functions were specified so as to avoid the humiliating weakness of the Congress during the Revolution and under the Articles of Confederation.

Mr. Madison and his associates in the discussion in the House dwelt at length upon the necessity there was for construing article 2 to give the President the sole power of removal in his responsibility for the conduct of the executive branch, and enforced this by emphasizing his duty expressly declared in the third section of the article to "take care that the laws be faithfully executed." Madison, 1 Annals of Congress, 496, 497.

The vesting of the executive power in the President was essentially a grant of the power to execute the laws. But the President alone and unaided could not execute the laws. He must execute them by the assistance of subordinates. This view has since been repeatedly affirmed by this court. As he is charged specifically to take care that they be faithfully executed, the reasonable implication, even in the absence of express words, was that as part of his executive power he should select those who were to act for him under his direction in the execution of the laws. The further implication must be, in the absence of any express limitation respecting removals, that as his selection of administrative officers is essential to the execution of the laws by him, so must be his power of removing those for whom he cannot continue to be responsible. Fisher Ames, 1 Annals of Congress, 474.

Take Note

The Court explains in this paragraph why the President must have the power to remove subordinates and explains in the next paragraph why Congress should not play a role in the removal decisions. What is the Court's reasoning? Does the Court offer legal or policy arguments?

The power to prevent the removal of an officer who has served under the President is different from the authority to consent to or reject his appointment. When a nomination is made, it may be presumed that the Senate is, or may become, as well advised as to the fitness of the nominee as the President, but in the nature of things the defects in ability or intelligence or loyalty in the administration of the laws of one who has served as an officer under the President are facts as to which the President, or his trusted subordinates, must be better informed than the Senate, and the power to remove him may therefore be regarded as confined for very sound and practical reasons, to the governmental authority which has administrative control. The power of removal is incident to the power of appointment, not to the power of advising and consenting to appointment, and when the grant of the executive power is enforced by the express mandate to take care that the laws be faithfully executed, it emphasizes the necessity for including within the executive power as conferred the exclusive power of removal.

We come now to consider an argument, advanced and strongly pressed on behalf of the complainant, that this case concerns only the removal of a postmaster, that a postmaster is an inferior officer, and that such an office was not included within the legislative decision of 1789, which related only to superior officers to be appointed by the President by and with the advice and consent of the Senate.* * *

Section 2 of article 2, after providing that the President shall nominate and with the consent of the Senate appoint ambassadors, other public ministers, consuls, judges of the Supreme Court and all other officers of the United States whose appointments are not herein otherwise provided for, and which shall be established by law, contains the proviso:

> "But the Congress may by law vest the appointment of such inferior officers, as they think proper, in the President alone, in the courts of law or in the heads of departments."

The power to remove inferior executive officers, like that to remove superior executive officers, is an incident of the power to appoint them, and is in its nature an executive power. The authority of Congress given by the excepting clause to vest the appointment of such inferior officers in the heads of departments carries with it authority incidentally to invest the heads of departments with power to remove. It has been the practice of Congress to do so and this court has recognized that power. * * * But the court never has held, nor reasonably could hold, although it is argued to the contrary on behalf of the appellant, that the excepting clause enables Congress to draw to itself, or to either branch of it, the power to remove or the right to participate in the exercise of that power. To do this would be to go beyond the words and implications of that clause, and to infringe the constitutional principle of the separation of governmental powers.

Food for Thought

If Congress can vest the authority to appoint an "inferior" officer in someone other than the President, then why can't it limit the President's authority to fire such an officer, as well? Is the defect here not that Congress limited the *President's* right to remove, but instead that Congress reserved the power to *itself*?

For the reasons given, we must therefore hold that the provision of the law of 1876 by which the unrestricted power of removal of first-class postmasters is denied to the President is in violation of the Constitution and invalid.

POINTS FOR DISCUSSION

a. Original Understanding

To what extent does the Court rely on the original understanding of the Constitution to support its conclusion? Is the evidence of the original understanding cited by the Court persuasive? What inference should we draw from the fact that the Constitution specifies the President's and the Senate's role in appointments, but is silent with respect to the President's power of removal? What weight should we put on the fact that Congress has the power to impeach and remove Officers of the United States? See Article II, § 4; Article I, § 2, cl. 5; Article I, § 3, cl. 6.

b. President Andrew Johnson's Firing of the Secretary of War

Vice President Andrew Johnson became President when Abraham Lincoln was assassinated in 1865. President Johnson soon disagreed with Secretary of War Edwin Stanton about the treatment of the defeated Southern states. Congress, which generally sided with Stanton, passed the Tenure of Office Act of 1867, 14 Stat 430 (over Johnson's veto) to prevent Johnson from firing Stanton and other officials. When Johnson removed Stanton in violation of this Act, the House of Representatives impeached him. But the Senate did not remove Johnson from office, acquitting him by a single vote. Does this historical incident support or undermine the Court's conclusion in *Myers*? To read more about this history, see Steven G. Calabresi & Christopher S. Yoo, *The Unitary Executive During the Second Half-Century*, 26 Harv. J. L & Pub. Pol'y 667, 737–759 (2003).

HUMPHREY'S EXECUTOR V. UNITED STATES

295 U.S. 602 (1935)

MR. JUSTICE SUTHERLAND delivered the opinion of the Court.

Plaintiff brought suit in the Court of Claims against the United States to recover a sum of money alleged to be due the deceased for salary as a Federal Trade Commissioner from October 8, 1933, when the President undertook to remove him from office, to the time of his death on February 14, 1934. The court below has certified to this court two questions in respect of the power of the President to make the removal. The material facts which give rise to the questions are as follows:

> **FYI**
>
> At the time this case was decided, the judges on the Court of Claims had the power to ask the Supreme Court to review legal issues by "certifying" them to the Supreme Court. *See* William Howard Taft, *The Jurisdiction of the Supreme Court Under the Act of February 13, 1925*, 35 Yale L.J. 1, 4 (1925).

William E. Humphrey, the decedent, on December 10, 1931, was nominated by President Hoover to succeed himself as a member of the Federal Trade Commission, and was confirmed by the United States Senate. He was duly commissioned for a term of seven years, expiring September 25, 1938; and, after taking the required oath of office, entered upon his duties. On July 25, 1933, President Roosevelt addressed a letter to the commissioner asking for his resignation, on the ground "that the aims and purposes of the Administration with respect to the work of the Commission can be carried out most effectively with personnel of my own selection," but disclaiming any reflection upon the commissioner personally or upon his services. The commissioner replied, asking time to consult his friends. After some further correspondence upon the subject, the President on August 31, 1933, wrote the commissioner expressing the hope that the resignation would be forthcoming, and saying: "You will, I know, realize that I do not feel that your mind and my mind go along together on either the policies or the administering of the Federal Trade Commission, and, frankly, I think it is best for the people of this country that I should have a full confidence."

The commissioner declined to resign; and on October 7, 1933, the President wrote him: "Effective as of this date you are hereby removed from the office of Commissioner of the Federal Trade Commission."

Humphrey never acquiesced in this action, but continued thereafter to insist that he was still a member of the commission, entitled to perform its duties and receive the compensation provided by law at the rate of $10,000 per annum. Upon these and other facts set forth in the certificate, which we deem it unnecessary to recite, the following questions are certified:

> 1. Do the provisions of section 1 of the Federal Trade Commission Act, stating that "any commissioner may be removed by the President for inefficiency, neglect of duty, or malfeasance in office," restrict or limit the power of the President to remove a commissioner except upon one or more of the causes named?
>
> If the foregoing question is answered in the affirmative, then—
>
> 2. If the power of the President to remove a commissioner is restricted or limited as shown by the foregoing interrogatory and the answer made thereto, is such a restriction or limitation valid under the Constitution of the United States?

[The Court answered the first question in the affirmative.]

Second. To support its contention that the removal provision of section 1, as we have just construed it, is an unconstitutional interference with the executive power of the President, the government's chief reliance is *Myers v. United States*, 272 U.S. 52 (1926). * * *

The office of a postmaster is so essentially unlike the office now involved that the decision in the *Myers* Case cannot be accepted as controlling our decision here. A postmaster is an executive officer restricted to the performance of executive functions. He is charged with no duty at all related to either the legislative or judicial power. The actual decision in the *Myers* Case finds support in the theory that such an officer is merely one of the units in the executive department and, hence, inherently subject to the exclusive and illimitable power of removal by the Chief Executive, whose subordinate and aid he is. Putting aside dicta, which may be followed if sufficiently persuasive but which are not controlling, the necessary reach of the decision goes far enough to include all purely executive officers. It goes no farther; much less does it include an officer who occupies no place in the executive department and who exercises no part of the executive power vested by the Constitution in the President.

> **Take Note**
>
> How does the Court distinguish *Myers v. United States*? Do you find the distinction convincing? Is there any other way to distinguish *Myers*?

The Federal Trade Commission is an administrative body created by Congress to carry into effect legislative policies embodied in the statute in accordance with the legislative standard therein prescribed, and to perform other specified duties as a legislative or as a judicial aid. Such a body cannot in any proper sense be characterized as an arm or an eye of the executive. Its duties are performed without executive leave and, in the contemplation of the statute, must be free from executive control. In administering the provisions of the statute in respect of "unfair methods of competition," that is to say, in filling in and administering the details embodied by that general standard, the commission acts in part quasi legislatively and in part quasi judicially. In making investigations and reports thereon for the information of Congress under section 6, in aid of the legislative power, it acts as a legislative agency. Under section 7, which authorizes the commission to act as a master in chancery under rules prescribed by the court, it acts as an agency of the judiciary. To the extent that it exercises any executive function, as distinguished from executive power in the constitutional sense, it does so in the discharge and effectuation of its quasi legislative or quasi judicial powers, or as an agency of the legislative or judicial departments of the government.

We think it plain under the Constitution that illimitable power of removal is not possessed by the President in respect of officers of the character of those just named. The authority of Congress, in creating quasi legislative or quasi judicial agencies, to require them to act in discharge of their duties independently of executive control cannot well be doubted; and that authority includes, as an appropriate incident, power to fix the period during which they shall continue, and to forbid their removal except for cause in the meantime. For it is quite evident that one who holds his office only during the pleasure of another cannot be depended upon to maintain an attitude of independence against the latter's will.

The fundamental necessity of maintaining each of the three general departments of government entirely free from the control or coercive influence, direct or indirect, of either of the others, has often been stressed and is hardly open to serious question. So much is implied in the very fact of the separation of the powers of these departments by the Constitution; and in the rule which recognizes their essential coequality. The sound application of a principle that makes one master in his own house precludes him from imposing his control in the house of another who is master there. * * *

The power of removal here claimed for the President falls within this principle, since its coercive influence threatens the independence of a commission, which is not only wholly disconnected from the executive department, but which, as already fully appears, was created by Congress as a means of carrying into operation legislative and judicial powers, and as an agency of the legislative and judicial departments.

> **Take Note**
>
> The Court concludes here that Congress may restrict the President's power to remove officers at agencies exercising quasi-judicial or quasi-legislative power. How can Congress, consistent with the separation of powers, create an agency that exercises "quasi-judicial" or "quasi-legislative" power?

The result of what we now have said is this: Whether the power of the President to remove an officer shall prevail over the authority of Congress to condition the power by fixing a definite term and precluding a removal except for cause will depend upon the character of the office; the *Myers* decision, affirming the power of the President alone to make the removal, is confined to purely executive officers; and as to officers of the kind here under consideration, we hold that no removal can be made during the prescribed term for which the officer is appointed, except for one or more of the causes named in the applicable statute.

POINTS FOR DISCUSSION

a. The "Unitary Executive"

Proponents of the theory of the "unitary executive" generally oppose efforts to vest executive power in persons whom the President cannot control. Does *Humphrey's Executor* suggest that our government now has two executive branches, one that is under the complete control of the President and another that operates largely independent of the President? Is a non-unitary executive branch consistent with the text of Article II, section 1? Or do other provisions in the Constitution contemplate officers beyond the complete control of the President?

b. Independent Administrative Agencies

Federal administrative agencies that are led by an official whom the President can fire only for good cause are now called "Independent Administrative Agencies." These agencies include the Central Intelligence Agency, the Federal Communications Commission, the Board of Governors of the Federal Reserve System, and the Federal Trade Commission. What do these agencies have in common? Do they all perform quasi-legislative or quasi-judicial functions? Should the President really have limited control over the important functions carried out by these governmental bodies? Conversely, why might independence be desirable for some or all of those agencies?

As we will see shortly, the tension between *Myers* and *Humphrey's Executor* created an unstable place for the law to rest. But even assuming that, in deciding whether Congress can limit the President's power to remove an officer, the Court's focus on the "character of the office" is sensible, we must have some way to determine when in fact an officer exercises "executive," rather than "quasi-judicial" or "quasi-legislative," power. This can be a surprisingly difficult inquiry, particularly in certain contexts.

The legislative branch of government includes more than the 100 senators in the Senate and the 435 representatives in the House. These politicians all have staffs that help them in their work. In addition, Congress employs important officials, such as the Sergeant at Arms, the Librarian of the Library of Congress, and the Architect of the Capitol, who all help carry out the functions of the legislative branch. No one doubts that Congress may employ these officials and restrict the President's ability to interfere with them. A separate question, however, is whether Congress can assign executive powers to them. The following case says that the answer is no. But determining whether an officer is in fact in the legislative branch of government and whether the official actually exercises executive power are not always easy tasks. Consider how the Court answers these questions in this case.

BOWSHER V. SYNAR

478 U.S. 714 (1986)

CHIEF JUSTICE BURGER delivered the opinion of the Court.

On December 12, 1985, the President signed into law the Balanced Budget and Emergency Deficit Control Act of 1985, Pub.L. 99–177, 99 Stat. 1038, popularly known as the "Gramm-Rudman-Hollings Act." The purpose of the Act is to eliminate the federal budget deficit. To that end, the Act sets a "maximum deficit amount" for federal spending for each of fiscal years 1986 through 1991. The size of that maximum deficit amount progressively reduces to zero in fiscal year 1991. If in any fiscal year the federal budget deficit exceeds the maximum deficit amount by more than a specified sum, the Act requires across-the-board cuts in federal spending to reach the targeted deficit level, with half of the cuts made to defense programs and the other half made to nondefense programs. The Act exempts certain priority programs from these cuts.

> **FYI**
>
> OMB is an entity within the Executive Office of the President. The Director of OMB is removable at will by the President. The CBO is in the Legislative Branch. The Comptroller General is the head of the Government Accountability Office (formerly called the General Accounting Office), which is charged with investigating how the federal government spends taxpayer dollars.

These "automatic" reductions are accomplished through a rather complicated procedure, spelled out in § 251, the so-called "reporting provisions" of the Act. Each year, the Directors of the Office of Management and Budget (OMB) and the

Congressional Budget Office (CBO) independently estimate the amount of the federal budget deficit for the upcoming fiscal year. If that deficit exceeds the maximum targeted deficit amount for that fiscal year by more than a specified amount, the Directors of OMB and CBO independently calculate, on a program-by-program basis, the budget reductions necessary to ensure that the deficit does not exceed the maximum deficit amount. The Act then requires the Directors to report jointly their deficit estimates and budget reduction calculations to the Comptroller General.

The Comptroller General, after reviewing the Directors' reports, then reports his conclusions to the President. The President in turn must issue a "sequestration" order mandating the spending reductions specified by the Comptroller General. There follows a period during which Congress may by legislation reduce spending to obviate, in whole or in part, the need for the sequestration order. If such reductions are not enacted, the sequestration order becomes effective and the spending reductions included in that order are made.

Within hours of the President's signing of the Act, Congressman Synar, who had voted against the Act, filed a complaint seeking declaratory relief that the Act was unconstitutional. Eleven other Members later joined Congressman Synar's suit. A virtually identical lawsuit was also filed by the National Treasury Employees Union. The Union alleged that its members had been injured as a result of the Act's automatic spending reduction provisions, which have suspended certain cost-of-living benefit increases to the Union's members.

We noted recently that "[t]he Constitution sought to divide the delegated powers of the new Federal Government into three defined categories, Legislative, Executive, and Judicial." *INS v. Chadha,* 462 U.S. 919, 951 (1983). The declared purpose of separating and dividing the powers of government, of course, was to "diffus[e] power the better to secure liberty." *Youngstown Sheet & Tube Co. v. Sawyer,* 343 U.S. 579, 635 (1952) (Jackson, J., concurring). Justice Jackson's words echo the famous warning of Montesquieu, quoted by James Madison in The Federalist No. 47, that "there can be no liberty where the legislative and executive powers are united in the same person, or body of magistrates."

Even a cursory examination of the Constitution reveals the influence of Montesquieu's thesis that checks and balances were the foundation of a structure of government that would protect liberty. The Framers provided a vigorous Legislative Branch and a separate and wholly independent Executive Branch, with each branch responsible ultimately to the people. The Framers also provided for a Judicial Branch equally independent with "[t]he judicial Power . . . extend[ing] to all Cases, in Law and Equity, arising under this Constitution, and the Laws of the United States." Art. III, § 2.

Other, more subtle, examples of separated powers are evident as well. Unlike parliamentary systems such as that of Great Britain, no person who is an officer of the United States may serve as a Member of the Congress. Art. I, § 6. Moreover, unlike parliamentary systems, the President, under Article II, is responsible not to the Congress but to the people, subject only to impeachment proceedings which are exercised by the two Houses as representatives of the people. Art. II, § 4. And even in the impeachment of a President the presiding officer of the ultimate tribunal is not a member of the Legislative Branch, but the Chief Justice of the United States. Art. I, § 3.

The Constitution does not contemplate an active role for Congress in the supervision of officers charged with the execution of the laws it enacts. The President appoints "Officers of the United States" with the "Advice and Consent of the Senate. . . ." Art. II, § 2. Once the appointment has been made and confirmed, however, the Constitution explicitly provides for removal of Officers of the United States by Congress only upon impeachment by the House of Representatives and conviction by the Senate. An impeachment by the House and trial by the Senate can rest only on "Treason, Bribery or other high Crimes and Misdemeanors." Article II, § 4. A direct congressional role in the removal of officers charged with the execution of the laws beyond this limited one is inconsistent with separation of powers.

This Court first directly addressed this issue in *Myers v. United States,* 272 U.S. 52 (1925). At issue in *Myers* was a statute providing that certain postmasters could be removed only "by and with the advice and consent of the Senate." * * * Chief Justice Taft, writing for the Court, declared the statute unconstitutional on the ground that for Congress to "draw to itself, or to either branch of it, the power to remove or the right to participate in the exercise of that power . . . would be . . . to infringe the constitutional principle of the separation of governmental powers." *Id.,* at 161.

A decade later, in *Humphrey's Executor v. United States,* 295 U.S. 602 (1935), relied upon heavily by appellants, a Federal Trade Commissioner who had been removed by the President sought backpay. *Humphrey's Executor* involved an issue not presented either in the *Myers* case or in this case—*i.e.,* the power of Congress to limit the President's powers of removal of a Federal Trade Commissioner.[4] The

[4] Appellants therefore are wide of the mark in arguing that an affirmance in this case requires casting doubt on the status of "independent" agencies because no issues involving such agencies are presented here. The statutes establishing independent agencies typically specify either that the agency members are removable

relevant statute permitted removal "by the President," but only "for inefficiency, neglect of duty, or malfeasance in office." * * * The Court distinguished *Myers,* reaffirming its holding that congressional participation in the removal of executive officers is unconstitutional. * * *

In light of these precedents, we conclude that Congress cannot reserve for itself the power of removal of an officer charged with the execution of the laws except by impeachment. To permit the execution of the laws to be vested in an officer answerable only to Congress would, in practical terms, reserve in Congress control over the execution of the laws. * * * The structure of the Constitution does not permit Congress to execute the laws; it follows that Congress cannot grant to an officer under its control what it does not possess. * * * With these principles in mind, we turn to consideration of whether the Comptroller General is controlled by Congress.

The critical factor lies in the provisions of the statute defining the Comptroller General's office relating to removability. Although the Comptroller General is nominated by the President from a list of three individuals recommended by the Speaker of the House of Representatives and the President *pro tempore* of the Senate, see 31 U.S.C. § 703(a)(2), and confirmed by the Senate, he is removable only at the initiative of Congress. He may be removed not only by impeachment but also by joint resolution of Congress "at any time" resting on any one of the following bases: "(i) permanent disability"; "(ii) inefficiency"; "(iii) neglect of duty"; "(iv) malfeasance"; or "(v) a felony or conduct involving moral turpitude." 31 U.S.C. § 703(e)(1)(B).[7]

This provision was included, as one Congressman explained in urging passage of the Act, because Congress "felt that [the Comptroller General] should be brought under the sole control of Congress, so that Congress at any moment when it found he was inefficient and was not carrying on the duties of his office as he should and as the Congress expected, could remove him without the long, tedious process of a trial by impeachment." 61 Cong. Rec. 1081 (1921).

---

by the President for specified causes, see, *e.g.,* 15 U.S.C. § 41 (members of the Federal Trade Commission may be removed by the President "for inefficiency, neglect of duty, or malfeasance in office"), or else do not specify a removal procedure, see, *e.g.,* 2 U.S.C. § 437c (Federal Election Commission). This case involves nothing like these statutes, but rather a statute that provides for direct congressional involvement over the decision to remove the Comptroller General. Appellants have referred us to no independent agency whose members are removable by the Congress for certain causes short of impeachable offenses, as is the Comptroller General * * *.

[7] Although the President could veto such a joint resolution, the veto could be overridden by a two-thirds vote of both Houses of Congress. Thus, the Comptroller General could be removed in the face of Presidential opposition. Like the District Court, 626 F.Supp., at 1393, n. 21, we therefore read the removal provision as authorizing removal by Congress alone.

The removal provision was an important part of the legislative scheme, as a number of Congressmen recognized. Representative Hawley commented: "[H]e is our officer, in a measure, getting information for us. . . . If he does not do his work properly, we, as practically his employers, ought to be able to discharge him from his office." 58 Cong. Rec. 7136 (1919). Representative Sisson observed that the removal provisions would give "[t]he Congress of the United States . . . absolute control of the man's destiny in office." 61 Cong. Rec. 987 (1921). The ultimate design was to "give the legislative branch of the Government control of the audit, not through the power of appointment, but through the power of removal." 58 Cong. Rec. 7211 (1919) (Rep. Temple).

Over the years, the Comptrollers General have also viewed themselves as part of the Legislative Branch. In one of the early Annual Reports of Comptroller General, the official seal of his office was described as reflecting

> "the independence of judgment to be exercised by the General Accounting Office, subject to the control of the legislative branch. . . . The combination represents an agency of the Congress independent of other authority auditing and checking the expenditures of the Government as required by law and subjecting any questions arising in that connection to quasi-judicial determination." GAO Ann. Rep. 5–6 (1924).

Against this background, we see no escape from the conclusion that, because Congress has retained removal authority over the Comptroller General, he may not be entrusted with executive powers. The remaining question is whether the Comptroller General has been assigned such powers in the Balanced Budget and Emergency Deficit Control Act of 1985.

Take Note

The Court recognizes that the Comptroller General traditionally has been viewed as an official within the legislative branch. Does this fact determine the outcome of the case, or are other facts more significant?

The primary responsibility of the Comptroller General under the instant Act is the preparation of a "report." This report must contain detailed estimates of projected federal revenues and expenditures. The report must also specify the reductions, if any, necessary to reduce the deficit to the target for the appropriate fiscal year. The reductions must be set forth on a program-by-program basis.

In preparing the report, the Comptroller General is to have "due regard" for the estimates and reductions set forth in a joint report submitted to him by the Director of CBO and the Director of OMB, the President's fiscal and budgetary adviser. However, the Act plainly contemplates that the Comptroller General will exercise his independent judgment and evaluation with respect to those estimates. The Act also provides that the Comptroller General's report "shall explain fully any differences between the contents of such report and the report of the Directors." § 251(b)(2).

> **Food for Thought**
>
> Do you agree that "interpreting a law enacted by Congress" is the "very essence" of the executive function? Who else might be called upon to perform that function? And is "interpretation" really what the Comptroller General is required to do under the scheme at issue here?

Appellants suggest that the duties assigned to the Comptroller General in the Act are essentially ministerial and mechanical so that their performance does not constitute "execution of the law" in a meaningful sense. On the contrary, we view these functions as plainly entailing execution of the law in constitutional terms. Interpreting a law enacted by Congress to implement the legislative mandate is the very essence of "execution" of the law. Under § 251, the Comptroller General must exercise judgment concerning facts that affect the application of the Act. He must also interpret the provisions of the Act to determine precisely what budgetary calculations are required. Decisions of that kind are typically made by officers charged with executing a statute.

The executive nature of the Comptroller General's functions under the Act is revealed in § 252(a)(3) which gives the Comptroller General the ultimate authority to determine the budget cuts to be made. Indeed, the Comptroller General commands the President himself to carry out, without the slightest variation (with exceptions not relevant to the constitutional issues presented), the directive of the Comptroller General as to the budget reductions:

> **Food for Thought**
>
> If the President must "carry out" the Comptroller General's directive, then isn't the Comptroller General's power more "legislative" in nature? Who ordinarily is responsible for deciding how much money the government will appropriate for its programs?

> "The [Presidential] order *must provide* for reductions in the manner specified in section 251(a)(3), *must incorporate* the provisions of the [Comptroller General's] report submitted under section 251(b), and *must be consistent with such report in all respects*. The President *may not modify or recalculate any of the estimates, determinations, specifications, bases, amounts, or percentages* set forth in the report submitted under section 251(b) in determining the reductions to be specified in the order with respect to programs, projects, and activities, or with respect to budget activities, within an account. . . ." § 252(a)(3) (emphasis added).

Congress of course initially determined the content of the Balanced Budget and Emergency Deficit Control Act; and undoubtedly the content of the Act determines the nature of the executive duty. However, as *Chadha* makes clear, once Congress makes its choice in enacting legislation, its participation ends. Congress can thereafter control the execution of its enactment only indirectly—by passing new legislation. *Chadha,* 462 U.S., at 958. By placing the responsibility for execution of the Balanced Budget and Emergency Deficit Control Act in the hands of an officer who is subject to removal only by itself, Congress in effect has retained control over the execution of the Act and has intruded into the executive function. The Constitution does not permit such intrusion. We conclude that the District Court correctly held that the powers vested in the Comptroller General under § 251 violate the command of the Constitution that the Congress play no direct role in the execution of the laws.

JUSTICE STEVENS, with whom JUSTICE MARSHALL joins, concurring in the judgment.

I agree with the Court that the "Gramm-Rudman-Hollings" Act contains a constitutional infirmity so severe that the flawed provision may not stand. I disagree with the Court, however, on the reasons why the Constitution prohibits the Comptroller General from exercising the powers assigned to him by § 251(b) and § 251(c)(2) of the Act. It is not the dormant, carefully circumscribed congressional removal power that represents the primary constitutional evil. Nor do I agree with the conclusion of both the majority and the dissent that the analysis depends on a labeling of the functions assigned to the Comptroller General as "executive powers." Rather, I am convinced that the Comptroller General must be characterized as an agent of Congress because of his longstanding statutory responsibilities; that the powers assigned to him under the Gramm-Rudman-Hollings Act require him to make policy that will bind the Nation; and that, when Congress, or a component or an agent of Congress, seeks to make policy that will bind the Nation, it must follow the procedures mandated by Article I of the Constitution—through passage by both Houses and presentment to the President. In short, Congress may not exercise its fundamental power to formulate national policy by delegating that power to one of its two Houses, to a legislative committee, or to an individual agent of the Congress such as the Speaker of the House of Representatives, the Sergeant at Arms of the Senate, or the Director

Take Note

According to Justice Stevens, what is the nature of the power exercised by the Comptroller General? If he disagrees with the Court on this question, then why does he agree that the Act is unconstitutional?

of the Congressional Budget Office. *INS v. Chadha*, 462 U.S. 919 (1983). That principle, I believe, is applicable to the Comptroller General.

JUSTICE WHITE, dissenting.

The Court, acting in the name of separation of powers, takes upon itself to strike down the Gramm-Rudman-Hollings Act, one of the most novel and far-reaching legislative responses to a national crisis since the New Deal. * * * I will not purport to speak to the wisdom of the policies incorporated in the legislation the Court invalidates * * *. I will, however, address the wisdom of the Court's willingness to interpose its distressingly formalistic view of separation of powers as a bar to the attainment of governmental objectives through the means chosen by the Congress and the President in the legislative process established by the Constitution. * * * [T]he Court's decision rests on a feature of the legislative scheme that is of minimal practical significance and that presents no substantial threat to the basic scheme of separation of powers.

It is evident (and nothing in the Court's opinion is to the contrary) that the powers exercised by the Comptroller General under the Gramm-Rudman-Hollings Act are not such that vesting them in an officer not subject to removal at will by the President would in itself improperly interfere with Presidential powers. Determining the level of spending by the Federal Government is not by nature a function central either to the exercise of the President's enumerated powers or to his general duty to ensure execution of the laws; rather, appropriating funds is a peculiarly legislative function, and one expressly committed to Congress by Art. I, § 9, which provides that "No Money shall be drawn from the Treasury, but in Consequence of Appropriations made by Law." In enacting Gramm-Rudman-Hollings, Congress has chosen to exercise this legislative power to establish the level of federal spending by providing a detailed set of criteria for reducing expenditures below the level of appropriations in the event that certain conditions are met. Delegating the execution of this legislation—that is, the power to apply the Act's criteria and make the required calculations—to an officer independent of the President's will does not deprive the President of any power that he would otherwise have or that is essential to the performance of the duties of his office. Rather, the result of such a delegation, from the standpoint of the President, is no different from the result of more traditional forms of appropriation: under either system, the level of funds available to the Executive Branch to carry out its duties is not within the President's discretionary control.

I have no quarrel with the proposition that the powers exercised by the Comptroller under the Act may be characterized as "executive" in that they involve the interpretation and carrying out of the Act's mandate. I can also accept the general proposition that although Congress has considerable authority in designating the officers who are to execute legislation, the constitutional scheme of separated powers does prevent Congress from reserving an executive role for itself or for its "agents." I cannot accept, however, that the exercise of authority by an officer removable for cause by a joint resolution of Congress is analogous to the impermissible execution of the law by Congress itself, nor would I hold that the congressional role in the removal process renders the Comptroller an "agent" of the Congress, incapable of receiving "executive" power.

The question to be answered is whether the threat of removal of the Comptroller General for cause through joint resolution as authorized by the Budget and Accounting Act renders the Comptroller sufficiently subservient to Congress that investing him with "executive" power can be realistically equated with the unlawful retention of such power by Congress itself; more generally, the question is whether there is a genuine threat of "encroachment or aggrandizement of one branch at the expense of the other," *Buckley v. Valeo*, 424 U.S. 1, 122 (1976). Common sense indicates that the existence of the removal provision poses no such threat to the principle of separation of powers.

The statute does not permit anyone to remove the Comptroller at will; removal is permitted only for specified cause, with the existence of cause to be determined by Congress following a hearing. * * * These [limitations] on the removal power militate strongly against the characterization of the Comptroller as a mere agent of Congress by virtue of the removal authority.

More importantly, the substantial role played by the President in the process of removal through joint resolution reduces to utter insignificance the possibility that the threat of removal will induce subservience to the Congress. * * * [A] joint resolution must be presented to the President and is ineffective if it is vetoed by him, unless the veto is overridden by the constitutionally prescribed two-thirds majority of both Houses of Congress. The requirement of Presidential approval obviates the possibility that the Comptroller will perceive himself as so completely at the mercy of Congress that he will function as its tool. If the Comptroller's conduct in office is not so unsatisfactory to the President as to convince the latter that removal is required under the statutory standard, Congress will have no independent power to coerce the Comptroller unless it can muster a two-thirds majority in both Houses—a feat of bipartisanship more difficult than that required to impeach and convict. The incremental *in terrorem* effect of the possibility of congressional removal in the face of a Presidential veto is therefore exceedingly unlikely to have any discernible impact on the extent of congressional influence over the Comptroller.

The practical result of the removal provision is not to render the Comptroller unduly dependent upon or subservient to Congress, but to render him one of the most independent officers in the entire federal establishment. Those who have studied the office agree that the procedural and substantive limits on the power of Congress and the President to remove the Comptroller make dislodging him against his will practically impossible. * * * Realistic consideration of the nature of the Comptroller General's relation to Congress thus reveals that the threat to separation of powers conjured up by the majority is wholly chimerical.

The wisdom of vesting "executive" powers in an officer removable by joint resolution may indeed be debatable—as may be the wisdom of the entire scheme of permitting an unelected official to revise the budget enacted by Congress—but such matters are for the most part to be worked out between the Congress and the President through the legislative process, which affords each branch ample opportunity to defend its interests. Under such circumstances, the role of this Court should be limited to determining whether the Act so alters the balance of authority among the branches of government as to pose a genuine threat to the basic division between the lawmaking power and the power to execute the law. Because I see no such threat, I cannot join the Court in striking down the Act.

JUSTICE BLACKMUN, dissenting.

The only relief sought in this case is nullification of the automatic budget-reduction provisions of the Deficit Control Act, and that relief should not be awarded even if the Court is correct that those provisions are constitutionally incompatible with Congress' authority to remove the Comptroller General by joint resolution. Any incompatibility, I feel, should be cured by refusing to allow congressional removal—if it ever is attempted—and not by striking down the central provisions of the Deficit Control Act. However wise or foolish it may be, that statute unquestionably ranks among the most important federal enactments of the past several decades. I cannot see the sense of invalidating legislation of this magnitude in order to preserve a cumbersome, 65-year-old removal power that has never been exercised and appears to have been all but forgotten until this litigation.

In the absence of express statutory direction, I think it is plain that, as both Houses urge, invalidating the Comptroller General's functions under the Deficit Control Act would frustrate congressional objectives far more seriously than would refusing to allow Congress to exercise its removal authority under the 1921 law. The majority suggests that the removal authority plays an important role in furthering Congress' desire to keep the Comptroller General under its control. But as Justice WHITE demonstrates, the removal provision serves feebly for such purposes, especially in comparison to other, more effective means of supervision at Congress' disposal. Unless Congress institutes impeachment proceedings—a course all agree the Constitution would permit—the 1921 law authorizes Congress to remove the Comptroller General only for specified cause, only after a hearing, and only by passing the procedural equivalent of a new public law. Congress has never attempted to use this cumbersome procedure, and the Comptroller General has shown few signs of subservience. If Congress in 1921 wished to make the Comptroller General its lackey, it did a remarkably poor job.

I do not claim that the 1921 removal provision is a piece of statutory deadwood utterly without contemporary significance. But it comes close. Rarely if ever invoked even for symbolic purposes, the removal provision certainly pales in importance beside the legislative scheme the Court strikes down today—an extraordinarily far-reaching response to a deficit problem of unprecedented proportions. Because I believe that the constitutional defect found by the Court cannot justify the remedy it has imposed, I respectfully dissent.

POINTS FOR DISCUSSION

a. An Alternative Remedy?

The Court announced that Congress cannot give the Comptroller General the executive powers that he would have under the Balanced Budget Act and at the same time reserve the power to remove him. Justice Blackmun reasoned in dissent that striking down the part of the Balanced Budget Act that gives the Comptroller General executive power is not the best solution to this problem. What would be another solution?

b. What Is Executive Power?

The Court concluded that the Comptroller General exercised executive power under the Act. Did Justice White disagree? Is the line between executive and legislative authority obvious, particularly in this context? What was Justice Stevens's reasoning in agreeing with the Court's resolution of the case?

c. Who Controls the Comptroller General?

The Court reasoned that because Congress could override a presidential veto of a resolution approving the Comptroller General's removal, the removal provision in effect authorized "removal by Congress alone." Such an override vote would require a two-thirds majority in each House of Congress. See Article I, § 7, cl. 2. Yet Congress has authority to remove an executive official by impeachment and conviction, see Article II, § 4, and it can do so by a mere majority vote in the House and then a two-thirds vote in the Senate. See Article I, § 2, cl. 5; Article I, § 3, cl. 6. More important, the President has no authority to veto such a decision. In light of this scheme, is the Court's assertion about Congress's control over the Comptroller General convincing? Is it relevant that the Constitution authorizes impeachment only for high crimes and misdemeanors?

d. The *Myers* Principle

The members of the Court disagreed about the nature of the Comptroller General's authority and the extent of Congress's control over him. But notice that once one concludes (1) that he exercises executive power and (2) that he is subject to congressional control, the narrower principle of the *Myers* case—that Congress cannot *reserve to itself* the power to remove an executive official—controlled the outcome of the case.

Bowsher stands at least for the proposition that Congress cannot reserve to itself the power to remove an officer exercising executive authority. But can Congress limit the *President*'s authority to remove such officers if it does not preserve a role for itself in the removal decision? Viewed together, *Myers* and *Humphrey's Executor* gave a somewhat unsatisfying answer to the question.

The case that follows addresses the question squarely. It concerns a very important conflict of ideas. In general, no one doubts that prosecuting criminal suspects is an executive branch function. But leaving prosecutorial decisions solely to the executive branch might be problematic if the criminal suspects are themselves government officials within the executive branch. After the Watergate scandal, Congress addressed this issue with the Ethics in Government Act of 1978, which allowed a panel of federal judges to appoint an independent counsel to investigate and, if necessary, to prosecute executive branch officials.

MORRISON V. OLSON

487 U.S. 654 (1988)

CHIEF JUSTICE REHNQUIST delivered the opinion of the Court.

This case presents us with a challenge to the independent counsel provisions of the Ethics in Government Act of 1978. We hold today that these provisions of the Act do not violate the Appointments Clause of the Constitution, Art. II, § 2, cl. 2, or the limitations of Article III, nor do they impermissibly interfere with the President's authority under Article II in violation of the constitutional principle of separation of powers.

Title VI of the Ethics in Government Act allows for the appointment of an "independent counsel" to investigate and, if appropriate, prosecute certain high-ranking Government officials for violations of federal criminal laws. The Act requires the Attorney General, upon receipt of information that he determines is "sufficient to constitute grounds to investigate whether any person [covered by the Act] may have violated any Federal criminal law," to conduct a preliminary investigation of the matter. When the Attorney General has completed this investigation, or 90 days has elapsed, he is required to report to a special court (the Special Division) created by the Act "for the purpose of appointing independent counsels."[3] If the Attorney General determines that "there are no reasonable grounds to believe that further investigation is warranted," then he must notify the Special Division of this result. In such a case, "the division of the court shall have no power to appoint an independent counsel." If, however, the Attorney General has determined that there are "reasonable grounds to believe that further investigation or prosecution is warranted," then he "shall apply to the division of the court for the appointment of an independent counsel." The Attorney General's application to the court "shall contain sufficient information to assist the [court] in selecting an independent counsel and in defining that independent counsel's prosecutorial jurisdiction." Upon receiving this application, the Special Division "shall appoint an appropriate independent counsel and shall define that independent counsel's prosecutorial jurisdiction."

With respect to all matters within the independent counsel's jurisdiction, the Act grants the counsel "full power and independent authority to exercise all investigative and prosecutorial functions and powers of the Department of Justice, the Attorney General, and any other officer or employee of the Department of Justice." * * * [The] procedure for removing an independent counsel [is governed by section 596(a)(1), which] provides:

> "An independent counsel appointed under this chapter may be removed from office, other than by impeachment and conviction, only by the personal action of the Attorney General and only for good cause, physical disability, mental incapacity, or any other condition that substantially impairs the performance of such independent counsel's duties."

---

3 The Special Division is a division of the United States Court of Appeals for the District of Columbia Circuit. The court consists of three circuit court judges or justices appointed by the Chief Justice of the United States. One of the judges must be a judge of the United States Court of Appeals for the District of Columbia Circuit, and no two of the judges may be named to the Special Division from a particular court. The judges are appointed for 2-year terms, with any vacancy being filled only for the remainder of the 2-year period.

[In 1983, the White House refused to turn over certain documents regarding environmental policies to Congress on grounds of executive privilege. Congress called appellee, Theodore Olson, who was then the Assistant Attorney General for the Office of Legal Counsel (OLC), to testify about the Justice Department's role in this matter. Questions subsequently arose about whether Olson had testified truthfully. The Special Division eventually appointed Alexia Morrison (appellant) as an independent counsel to investigate the charges. In May and June 1987, appellant caused a grand jury to issue and serve subpoenas *ad testificandum* and *duces tecum* on Olson and two other government officials (appellees). All three appellees moved to quash the subpoenas on the ground that the Ethics in Government Act was unconstitutional.]

FYI

After this case was decided, the Independent Counsel ultimately decided that no charges against Olson were warranted. Olson later represented President George W. Bush in litigation over the 2000 presidential election, and he subsequently became the Solicitor General of the United States.

[Appellees first claim that the Act violates the Appointments Clause, Article II, § 2, cl. 2.] The parties do not dispute that "[t]he Constitution for purposes of appointment . . . divides all its officers into two classes." *United States v. Germaine,* 99 U.S. (9 Otto) 508, 509 (1879). As we stated in *Buckley v. Valeo,* 424 U.S. 1, 132 (1976): "[P]rincipal officers are selected by the President with the advice and consent of the Senate. Inferior officers Congress may allow to be appointed by the President alone, by the heads of departments, or by the Judiciary." The initial question is, accordingly, whether appellant is an "inferior" or a "principal" officer. If she is the latter, as the Court of Appeals concluded, then the Act is in violation of the Appointments Clause.

Take Note

The Court in this part of the opinion reaches two conclusions. First, the independent counsel is an "inferior officer" of the United States. Second, Congress can vest in the courts of law the power to appoint inferior officers who exercise (at least some types of) executive authority. What leads the Court to these conclusions? Could Congress vest in the courts the power to appoint all inferior officers of the United States?

The line between "inferior" and "principal" officers is one that is far from clear, and the Framers provided little guidance into where it should be drawn. We need not attempt here to decide exactly where the line falls between the two types of officers, because in our view appellant clearly falls on the "inferior officer" side of that line. Several factors lead to this conclusion.

First, appellant is subject to removal by a higher Executive Branch official. Although appellant may not be "subordinate" to the Attorney General (and the

President) insofar as she possesses a degree of independent discretion to exercise the powers delegated to her under the Act, the fact that she can be removed by the Attorney General indicates that she is to some degree "inferior" in rank and authority. Second, appellant is empowered by the Act to perform only certain, limited duties. An independent counsel's role is restricted primarily to investigation and, if appropriate, prosecution for certain federal crimes. Admittedly, the Act delegates to appellant "full power and independent authority to exercise all investigative and prosecutorial functions and powers of the Department of Justice," but this grant of authority does not include any authority to formulate policy for the Government or the Executive Branch, nor does it give appellant any administrative duties outside of those necessary to operate her office. The Act specifically provides that in policy matters appellant is to comply to the extent possible with the policies of the Department.

Third, appellant's office is limited in jurisdiction. Not only is the Act itself restricted in applicability to certain federal officials suspected of certain serious federal crimes, but an independent counsel can only act within the scope of the jurisdiction that has been granted by the Special Division pursuant to a request by the Attorney General. Finally, appellant's office is limited in tenure. There is concededly no time limit on the appointment of a particular counsel. Nonetheless, the office of independent counsel is "temporary" in the sense that an independent counsel is appointed essentially to accomplish a single task, and when that task is over the office is terminated, either by the counsel herself or by action of the Special Division. Unlike other prosecutors, appellant has no ongoing responsibilities that extend beyond the accomplishment of the mission that she was appointed for and authorized by the Special Division to undertake. In our view, these factors relating to the "ideas of tenure, duration . . . and duties" of the independent counsel, *Germaine, supra,* 9 Otto, at 511, are sufficient to establish that appellant is an "inferior" officer in the constitutional sense.

This does not, however, end our inquiry under the Appointments Clause. Appellees argue that even if appellant is an "inferior" officer, the Clause does not empower Congress to place the power to appoint such an officer outside the Executive Branch. They contend that the Clause does not contemplate congressional authorization of "interbranch appointments," in which an officer of one branch is appointed by

Food for Thought

Could Congress vest the head of the FTC with the power to appoint the clerk of a United States District Court? The Chief Justice with the power to appoint the Deputy Secretary of Defense? If not, why is this case different? Does it make sense to read the absence of a specific limitation on interbranch appointments implicitly to permit them?

officers of another branch. * * * On its face, [the Appointments Clause] admits of no limitation on interbranch appointments. Indeed, the inclusion of "as they think proper" seems clearly to give Congress significant discretion to determine whether it is "proper" to vest the appointment of, for example, executive officials in the "courts of Law." * * *

We also note that the history of the Clause provides no support for appellees' position. Throughout most of the process of drafting the Constitution, the Convention concentrated on the problem of who should have the authority to appoint judges. * * * [T]here was little or no debate on the question whether the Clause empowers Congress to provide for interbranch appointments, and there is nothing to suggest that the Framers intended to prevent Congress from having that power.

We do not mean to say that Congress' power to provide for interbranch appointments of "inferior officers" is unlimited. [Congress'] decision to vest the appointment power in the courts would be improper if there was some "incongruity" between the functions normally performed by the courts and the performance of their duty to appoint. In this case, however, we do not think it impermissible for Congress to vest the power to appoint independent counsel in a specially created federal court. We thus disagree with the Court of Appeals' conclusion that there is an inherent incongruity about a court having the power to appoint prosecutorial officers. We have recognized that courts may appoint private attorneys to act as prosecutor for judicial contempt judgments.

Appellees next contend that the powers vested in the Special Division by the Act conflict with Article III of the Constitution. * * * As a general rule, we have broadly stated that "executive or administrative duties of a nonjudicial nature may not be imposed on judges holding office under Art. III of the Constitution." *Buckley,* 424 U.S., at 123. The purpose of this limitation is to help ensure the independence of the Judicial Branch and to prevent the Judiciary from encroaching into areas reserved for the other branches.

Take Note

The Court concludes here that Congress can give federal judges powers as "incident[s]" to the power of appointing inferior officers. Does the Court identify a clear test for what these powers include?

In our view, Congress' power under the Clause to vest the "Appointment" of inferior officers in the courts may, in certain circumstances, allow Congress to give the courts some discretion in defining the nature and scope of the appointed official's authority. Particularly when, as here, Congress creates a temporary "office" the nature and duties of which will by necessity vary with the factual circumstances giving rise to the need for an appointment in the first place, it may vest the power to define the scope of the office in the court as an incident to the appointment of the officer pursuant to the Appointments Clause. * * *

[W]e do not think that Article III absolutely prevents Congress from vesting [other] miscellaneous powers in the Special Division pursuant to the Act. * * * [T]he miscellaneous powers [to grant extensions and refer matters to the counsel] do not impermissibly trespass upon the authority of the Executive Branch. * * * [These functions] are not inherently "Executive"; indeed, they are directly analogous to functions that federal judges perform in other contexts, such as deciding whether to allow disclosure of matters occurring before a grand jury, deciding to extend a grand jury investigation, or awarding attorney's fees. [Although] the Special Division's power to terminate the office of the independent counsel pursuant to § 596(b)(2) * * * is not a power that could be considered typically "judicial," * * * we do not, as did the Court of Appeals, view this provision as a significant judicial encroachment upon executive power or upon the prosecutorial discretion of the independent counsel. * * * The termination provisions of the Act do not give the Special Division anything approaching the power to *remove* the counsel while an investigation or court proceeding is still underway—this power is vested solely in the Attorney General. As we see it, "termination" may occur only when the duties of the counsel are truly "completed" or "so substantially completed" that there remains no need for any continuing action by the independent counsel. It is basically a device for removing from the public payroll an independent counsel who has served his or her purpose, but is unwilling to acknowledge the fact. So construed, the Special Division's power to terminate does not pose a sufficient threat of judicial intrusion into matters that are more properly within the Executive's authority to require that the Act be invalidated as inconsistent with Article III.

We now turn to consider whether the Act is invalid under the constitutional principle of separation of powers. Two related issues must be addressed: The first is whether the provision of the Act restricting the Attorney General's power to remove the independent counsel to only those instances in which he can show "good cause," taken by itself, impermissibly interferes with the President's exercise of his constitutionally appointed functions. The second is whether, taken as a whole, the Act violates the separation of powers by reducing the President's ability to control the prosecutorial powers wielded by the independent counsel.

Unlike both *Bowsher v. Synar,* 478 U.S. 714 (1986), and *Myers v. United States,* 272 U.S. 52 (1926), this case does not involve an attempt by Congress itself to gain a role in the removal of executive officials other than its established powers of impeachment and conviction.

The Act instead puts the removal power squarely in the hands of the Executive Branch; an independent counsel may be removed from office, "only by the personal action of the Attorney General, and only for good cause." There is no requirement of congressional approval of the Attorney General's removal decision, though the decision is subject to judicial review. In our view, the removal provisions of the Act make this case more analogous to *Humphrey's Executor v. United States,* 295 U.S. 602 (1935), than to *Myers* or *Bowsher.*

Appellees [argue] that our decision in *Humphrey's Executor* rests on a distinction between "purely executive" officials and officials who exercise "quasi-legislative" and "quasi-judicial" powers. In their view, when a "purely executive" official is involved, the governing precedent is *Myers*, not *Humphrey's Executor.* And, under *Myers*, the President must have absolute discretion to discharge "purely" executive officials at will.

We undoubtedly did rely on the terms "quasi-legislative" and "quasi-judicial" to distinguish the officials involved in *Humphrey's Executor* [from] those in *Myers*, but our present considered view is that the determination of whether the Constitution allows Congress to impose a "good cause"-type restriction on the President's power to remove an official cannot be made to turn on whether or not that official is classified as "purely executive." The analysis contained in our removal cases is designed not to define rigid categories of those officials who may or may not be removed at will by the President, but to ensure that Congress does not interfere with the President's exercise of the "executive power" and his constitutionally appointed duty to "take care that the laws be faithfully executed" under Article II. *Myers* was undoubtedly correct in its holding, and in its broader suggestion that there are some "purely executive" officials who must be removable by the President at will if he is to be able to accomplish his constitutional role. * * * At the other end of the spectrum[,] the characterization of the [agency] in *Humphrey's Executor* [as] "quasi-legislative" or "quasi-judicial" in large part reflected our judgment that it was not essential to the President's proper execution of his Article II powers that these agencies be headed up by individuals who were removable at will. We do not mean to suggest that an analysis of the functions served by the officials at issue is irrelevant. But the real question is whether the removal restrictions are of such a nature that they impede the President's ability to perform his constitutional duty, and the functions of the officials in question must be analyzed in that light.

Considering for the moment the "good cause" removal provision in isolation from the other parts of the Act at issue in this case, we cannot say that the imposition of a "good cause" standard for removal by itself unduly trammels on executive authority. There is no real dispute that the functions performed by the independent counsel are "executive" in the sense that they are law enforcement functions that typically have been undertaken by officials within the Executive Branch. As we noted above, however, the independent counsel is an inferior officer under the Appointments Clause, with limited jurisdiction and tenure and lacking policymaking or significant administrative authority. Although the counsel exercises no small amount of discretion and judgment in deciding how to carry out his or her duties under the Act, we simply do not see how the President's need to control the exercise of that discretion is so central to the functioning of the Executive Branch as to require as a matter of constitutional law that the counsel be terminable at will by the President.

The final question to be addressed is whether the Act, taken as a whole, violates the principle of separation of powers by unduly interfering with the role of the Executive Branch. * * * We observe first that this case does not involve an attempt by Congress to increase its own powers at the expense of the Executive Branch. Unlike some of our previous cases, most recently *Bowsher v. Synar,* this case simply does not pose a "dange[r] of congressional usurpation of Executive Branch functions." 478 U.S., at 727; see also *INS v. Chadha,* 462 U.S. 919, 958 (1983). Indeed, with the exception of the power of impeachment—which applies to all officers of the United States—Congress retained for itself no powers of control or supervision over an independent counsel. The Act does empower certain Members of Congress to request the Attorney General to apply for the appointment of an independent counsel, but the Attorney General has no duty to comply with the request, although he must respond within a certain time limit. Other than that, Congress' role under the Act is limited to receiving reports or other information and oversight of the independent counsel's activities, functions that we have recognized generally as being incidental to the legislative function of Congress. See *McGrain v. Daugherty,* 273 U.S. 135, 174 (1927).

> **Food for Thought**
>
> The Court says here that the Act does not "unduly" interfere with executive authority. Does the Court indicate what kind of measures would constitute an undue interference? If not, are there manageable standards that a court can apply?

Similarly, we do not think that the Act works any *judicial* usurpation of properly executive functions. As should be apparent from our discussion of the Appointments Clause above, the power to appoint inferior officers such as independent counsel is not in itself an "executive" function in the constitutional sense, at least when Congress has exercised its power to vest the appointment of an inferior office in the "courts of Law." We note nonetheless that under the Act the Special Division has no power to appoint an independent counsel *sua sponte;* it may only do so upon the specific request of the Attorney General, and the courts are specifically prevented from reviewing the Attorney General's decision not to seek appointment. In addition, once the court has appointed a counsel and defined his or her jurisdiction, it has no power to supervise or control the activities of the counsel. As we pointed out in our discussion of the Special Division in relation to Article III, the various powers delegated by the statute to the Division are not supervisory or administrative, nor are they functions that the Constitution requires be performed by officials within the Executive Branch. The Act does give a federal court the power to review the Attorney General's decision to remove an independent counsel, but in our view this is a function that is well within the traditional power of the Judiciary.

JUSTICE KENNEDY took no part in the consideration or decision of this case.

JUSTICE SCALIA, dissenting.

Article II, § 1, cl. 1, of the Constitution provides: "The executive Power shall be vested in a President of the United States." That is what this suit is about. Power. The allocation of power among Congress, the President, and the courts in such fashion as to preserve the equilibrium the Constitution sought to establish—so that "a gradual concentration of the several powers in the same department," The Federalist No. 51 (J. Madison), can effectively be resisted. Frequently an issue of this sort will come before the Court clad, so to speak, in sheep's clothing: the potential of the asserted principle to effect important change in the equilibrium of power is not immediately evident, and must be discerned by a careful and perceptive analysis. But this wolf comes as a wolf.

[B]y the application of this statute in the present case, Congress has effectively compelled a criminal investigation of a high-level appointee of the President in connection with his actions arising out of a bitter power dispute between the President and the Legislative Branch. Mr. Olson may or may not be guilty of a crime; we do not know. But we do know that the investigation of him has been commenced, not necessarily because the President or his authorized subordinates believe it is in the interest of the United States, in the sense that it warrants the diversion of resources from other efforts, and is worth the cost in money and in possible damage to other governmental interests; and not even, leaving aside those normally considered factors, because the President or his authorized subordinates necessarily believe that an investigation is likely to unearth a violation worth prosecuting; but only because the Attorney General cannot affirm, as Congress demands, that there are no reasonable grounds to believe that further investigation is warranted. The decisions regarding the scope of that further investigation, its duration, and, finally, whether or not prosecution should ensue, are likewise beyond the control of the President and his subordinates. If to describe this case is not to decide it, the concept of a government of separate and coordinate powers no longer has meaning.

To repeat, Article II, § 1, cl. 1, of the Constitution provides: "The executive Power shall be vested in a President of the United States." This does not mean *some of* the executive power, but *all of* the executive power. It seems to me, therefore, that the decision of the Court of Appeals invalidating the present statute must be upheld on fundamental separation-of-powers principles if the following two questions are answered affirmatively: (1) Is the conduct of a criminal prosecution (and of an investigation to decide whether to prosecute) the exercise of purely executive power? (2) Does the statute deprive the President of the United States of exclusive control over the exercise of that power? Surprising to say, the Court appears to concede an affirmative answer to both questions, but seeks to avoid the inevitable conclusion that since the statute vests some purely executive power in a person who is not the President of the United States it is void.

Governmental investigation and prosecution of crimes is a quintessentially executive function. As for the second question, whether the statute before us deprives the President of exclusive control over that quintessentially executive activity: * * * That is indeed the whole object of the statute. * * * [I]t is ultimately irrelevant *how much* the statute reduces Presidential control. * * * It is not for us to determine, and we have never presumed to determine, how much of the purely executive powers of government must be within the full control of the President. The Constitution prescribes that they *all* are.

> **Take Note**
>
> Justice Scalia here advances the theory of the "Unitary Executive." What are constitutional arguments for and against this theory? As a matter of policy, what are the possible benefits and drawbacks to having a unitary executive?

The utter incompatibility of the Court's approach with our constitutional traditions can be made more clear, perhaps, by applying it to the powers of the other two branches. Is it conceivable that if Congress passed a statute depriving itself of less than full and entire control over some insignificant area of legislation, we would inquire whether the matter was "so central to the functioning of the Legislative Branch" as really to require complete control, or whether the statute gives Congress "sufficient control over the surrogate legislator to ensure that Congress is able to perform its constitutionally assigned duties"? Of course we would have none of that. * * * Or to bring the point closer to home, consider a statute giving to non-Article III judges just a tiny bit of purely judicial power in a relatively insignificant field, with substantial control, though not total control, in the courts * * *. We would say that our "constitutionally assigned duties" include complete control over all exercises of the judicial power.

Is it unthinkable that the President should have such exclusive power, even when alleged crimes by him or his close associates are at issue? No more so than that Congress should have the exclusive power of legislation, even when what is at issue is its own exemption from the burdens of certain laws. See Civil Rights Act of 1964, Title VII (prohibiting "employers," not defined to include the United States, from discriminating on the basis of race, color, religion, sex, or national origin). No more so than that this Court should have the exclusive power to pronounce the final decision on justiciable cases and controversies, even those pertaining to the constitutionality of a statute reducing the salaries of the Justices. See *United States v. Will,* 449 U.S. 200, 211–217 (1980). A system of separate and coordinate powers necessarily involves an acceptance of exclusive power that can theoretically be abused. * * * While the separation of powers may prevent us from righting every wrong, it does so in order to ensure that we do not lose liberty. The checks against any branch's abuse of its exclusive powers are twofold: First, retaliation by one of the other branch's use of *its* exclusive powers: Congress, for example, can impeach the executive who willfully fails to enforce the laws * * *. Second, and ultimately, there is the political check that the people will replace those in the political branches * * * who are guilty of abuse. Political pressures produced special prosecutors—for Teapot Dome and for Watergate, for example—long before this statute created the independent counsel.

> **FYI**
>
> The Teapot Dome Scandal in the early 1920s concerned allegations that Secretary of the Interior Albert Bacon Fall took bribes from oil companies seeking leases of federal land. The Watergate Scandal in the early 1970s involved allegations that President Richard Nixon's supporters broke into the Democratic Party headquarters and that President Nixon and his subordinates later obstructed the FBI's investigation of the matter.

The Court has, nonetheless, replaced the clear constitutional prescription that the executive power belongs to the President with a "balancing test." What are the standards to determine how the balance is to be struck, that is, how much removal of Presidential power is too much? * * * Once we depart from the text of the Constitution, just where short of that do we stop? The most amazing feature of the Court's opinion is that it does not even purport to give an answer. It simply announces, with no analysis, that the ability to control the decision whether to investigate and prosecute the President's closest advisers, and indeed the President himself, is not "so central to the functioning of the Executive Branch" as to be constitutionally required to be within the President's control. * * * Evidently, the governing standard is to be what might be called the unfettered wisdom of a majority of this Court, revealed to an obedient people on a case-by-case basis. This is not only not the government of laws that the Constitution established; it is not a government of laws at all.

[T]he independent counsel is not an inferior officer because she is not subordinate to any officer in the Executive Branch (indeed, not even to the President). * * * To be sure, it is not a *sufficient* condition for "inferior" officer status that one be subordinate to a principal officer. Even an officer who is subordinate to a department head can be a principal officer. * * * But it is surely a *necessary* condition for inferior officer status that the officer be subordinate to another officer. * * * Because appellant is not subordinate to another officer, she is not an "inferior" officer and her appointment other than by the President with the advice and consent of the Senate is unconstitutional.

[T]he restrictions upon the removal of the independent counsel also violate our established precedent dealing with that specific subject. * * * Since our 1935 decision in *Humphrey's Executor*—which was considered by many at the time the product of an activist, anti-New Deal Court bent on reducing the power of President Franklin Roosevelt—it has been established that the line of permissible restriction upon removal of principal officers lies at the point at which the powers exercised by those officers are no longer purely executive. * * * It has often been observed, correctly in my view, that the line between "purely executive" functions and "quasi-legislative" or "quasi-judicial" functions is not a clear one or even a rational one. But at least it permitted the identification of certain officers, and certain agencies, whose functions were entirely within the control of the President. * * * Today, however, *Humphrey's Executor* is swept into the dustbin of repudiated constitutional principles. * * * "[O]ur present considered view" is simply that any executive officer's removal can be restricted, so long as the President remains "able to accomplish his constitutional role." There are now no lines. If the removal of a prosecutor, the virtual embodiment of the power to "take care that the laws be faithfully executed," can be restricted, what officer's removal cannot? This is an open invitation for Congress to experiment. What about a special Assistant Secretary of State, with responsibility for one very narrow area of foreign policy, who would

Food for Thought

Do you agree that Congress is likely to use the power that the Court permits here to damage the Presidency? What other limits might there be on Congress's power to do so?

not only have to be confirmed by the Senate but could also be removed only pursuant to certain carefully designed restrictions? Could this possibly render the President "[un]able to accomplish his constitutional role"? Or a special Assistant Secretary of Defense for Procurement? The possibilities are endless, and the Court does not understand what the separation of powers, what "[a]mbition . . . counteract[ing] ambition," The Federalist No. 51 (J. Madison), is all about, if it does not expect Congress to try them.

Under our system of government, the primary check against prosecutorial abuse is a political one. The prosecutors who exercise this awesome discretion are selected and can be removed by a President, whom the people have trusted enough to elect. Moreover, when crimes are not investigated and prosecuted fairly, nonselectively, with a reasonable sense of proportion, the President pays the cost in political damage to his administration. * * *

That is the system of justice the rest of us are entitled to, but what of that select class consisting of present or former high-level Executive Branch officials? * * * An independent counsel is selected, and the scope of his or her authority prescribed, by a panel of judges. What if they are politically partisan, as judges have been known to be, and select a prosecutor antagonistic to the administration, or even to the particular individual who has been selected for this special treatment? * * * The independent counsel thus selected proceeds to assemble a staff. [I]n the nature of things this has to be done by finding lawyers who are willing to lay aside their current careers for an indeterminate amount of time, to take on a job that has no prospect of permanence and little prospect for promotion. One thing is certain, however: it involves investigating and perhaps prosecuting a particular individual. * * * What would be the reaction if, in an area not covered by this statute, the Justice Department posted a public notice inviting applicants to assist in an investigation and possible prosecution of a certain prominent person? [T]o be sure, the investigation must relate to the area of criminal offense specified by the life-tenured judges. But [should] the independent counsel or his or her staff come up with something beyond that scope, nothing prevents him or her from asking the judges to expand his or her authority.

Food for Thought

Justice Scalia here effectively predicted the controversy that would arise over Independent Counsel Kenneth Starr's investigation of President Clinton. Does subsequent history vindicate Justice Scalia's view? If so, as a matter of policy? Of constitutional law?

The mini-Executive that is the independent counsel, [operating] in an area where so little is law and so much is discretion, is intentionally cut off from the unifying influence of the Justice Department, and from the perspective that multiple responsibilities provide. What would normally be regarded as a technical violation (there are no rules defining such things), may in his or her small world assume the proportions of an indictable offense. What would normally be regarded as an investigation that has reached the level of pursuing such picayune matters that it should be concluded, may to him or her be an investigation that ought to go on for another year. How frightening it must be to have your own independent counsel and staff appointed, with nothing else to do but to investigate you until investigation is no longer worthwhile—with whether it is worthwhile not depending upon what such judgments usually hinge on, competing responsibilities. And to have that counsel and staff decide, with no basis for comparison, whether what you have done is bad enough, willful enough, and provable enough, to warrant an indictment. How admirable the constitutional system that provides the means to avoid such a distortion. And how unfortunate the judicial decision that has permitted it.

POINTS FOR DISCUSSION

a. The Appointments Clause

According to the Court's test, is the Deputy Secretary of Defense for War Planning a principal or inferior officer? If the latter, what does that suggest about the Court's test?

b. Functionalism v. Formalism

The Court took a functionalist approach to the separation of powers issues presented, asking whether the arrangement that Congress created is inconsistent with the values that the separation of powers is designed to protect and with a properly functioning governmental system. Justice Scalia, in contrast, took a formalist approach to the issues, asking whether the independent counsel exercises "executive" power and then concluding that the Constitution imposes rigid limits on Congress's power to limit the President's control over officials who exercise such power. But Justice Scalia also offered, in the final few paragraphs of his opinion, a functional response to the Court's argument. Who gave a more convincing assessment of the likely effect of the independent counsel regime on the operation of the separation of powers between Congress and the Executive Branch?

c. Need for an Independent Counsel

The Ethics in Government Act was a response to the Watergate scandal, and the independent counsel provisions were a specific response to President Nixon's termination of the first special prosecutor that his Attorney General had appointed to investigate the scandal. In enacting the statute, Congress presumably concluded that the President faced a conflict of interest in deciding whether to permit investigation of wrong-doing by high-ranking Executive Branch officials, including the President.

How does Justice Scalia address the concern that an independent counsel is needed to prosecute government officials within the executive branch? Is his reasoning convincing? It apparently was persuasive, eventually, to Congress. The Ethics in Government Act expired in 1992. Congress renewed it in 1994, but then let it expire again in 1999, after independent counsels had pursued investigations of a number of executive branch officials, including President William Jefferson Clinton. Scholar Erwin Chemerinsky writes:

> "The ultimate question is whether the benefits in terms of independent investigations outweigh the costs with regard to the loss of accountability when there is a special prosecutor. After Watergate [when there was no independent counsel to investigate Nixon administration officials], the answer seemed clearly yes. Now after the Whitewater special prosecutor [who investigated President Clinton and other members of the Clinton administration] * * * the answer to many seems clearly no. Not surprisingly, President Clinton is among those who have experienced this shift in views. The independent counsel law expired in 1992, and it was not renewed until 1994, when President Clinton took office and supported it. It is reported that subsequently President Clinton told [former Senator Majority Leader] Bob Dole, an opponent of renewing the Ethics in Government Act, "You were right and I was wrong on the independent counsel."

Erwin Chemerinsky, *Learning the Wrong Lessons from History: Why There Must be an Independent Counsel Law*, 5 WTR Widener L. Symp. J. 1, 9 (2000).

d. No Error or Harmless Error?

Did the Court conclude that no separation of powers violation had occurred or just that any separation of powers violation was so minor that it was harmless? Exactly what standard does the Court establish for application to future cases?

FREE ENTERPRISE FUND V. PUBLIC COMPANY ACCOUNTING OVERSIGHT BOARD

561 U.S. 477 (2010)

CHIEF JUSTICE ROBERTS delivered the opinion of the Court.

[The Sarbanes-Oxley Act of 2002, 116 Stat. 745, created a new five-member "Public Company Accounting Oversight Board" to supervise the accounting industry. The Board has five members, appointed to 5-year terms by the Securities and Exchange Commission (SEC). The Board has power to enforce the Act, the rules of the Board, and provisions of the securities laws relating to the preparation and issuance of audit reports and the obligations and liabilities of accountants. 15 U.S.C. § 7215(b)(1). The Board also may impose sanctions for violations, including revocation of a firm's registration and money penalties up to $15 million. *Id.* § 7215(c)(4).

The SEC has supervisory authority over the Board's functions, but can remove Board members only "for good cause shown," including willful violation of the Act, willful abuse of authority, or failing to enforce compliance with applicable rule and standards. *Id.* § 7217(d)(3). The Commissioners who make up the SEC have similar protection for their positions. On this point, the Court said: "The parties agree that the Commissioners cannot themselves be removed by the President except under the *Humphrey's Executor* standard of 'inefficiency, neglect of duty, or malfeasance in office,' 295 U.S. 602, 620 (1935) (internal quotation marks omitted), and we decide the case with that understanding."]

Our Constitution divided the "powers of the new Federal Government into three defined categories, Legislative, Executive, and Judicial." *INS v. Chadha*, 462 U.S. 919, 951 (1983). Article II vests "[t]he executive Power . . . in a President of the United States of America," who must "take Care that the Laws be faithfully executed." Art. II, § 1, cl. 1; *id.*, § 3. In light of "[t]he impossibility that one man should be able to perform all the great business of the State," the Constitution provides for executive officers to "assist the supreme Magistrate in discharging the duties of his trust." 30 *Writings of George Washington* 334 (J. Fitzpatrick ed.1939).

Since 1789, the Constitution has been understood to empower the President to keep these officers accountable—by removing them from office, if necessary. See generally *Myers v. United States*, 272 U.S. 52 (1926). This Court has determined, however, that this authority is not without limit. In *Humphrey's Executor v. United States*, 295 U.S. 602 (1935), we held that Congress can, under certain circumstances, create independent agencies run by principal officers appointed by the President, whom the President may not remove at will but only for good cause. Likewise, in *United States v. Perkins*, 116 U.S. 483 (1886), and *Morrison v. Olson*, 487 U.S. 654 (1988), the Court sustained similar restrictions on the power of principal executive officers—themselves responsible to the

FYI

In *Perkins*, the Court upheld the claim of a cadet engineer in the Navy that he had improperly been discharged. Although a federal statute prohibited dismissals of naval officers in times of peace, except after conviction and sentencing by a court-martial, the Secretary of the Navy asserted that he had power to discharge Perkins at will. In rejecting that assertion, the Court stated: "We have no doubt that when congress, by law, vests the appointment of inferior officers in the heads of departments, it may limit and restrict the power of removal as it deems best for the public interest."

President—to remove their own inferiors. The parties do not ask us to reexamine any of these precedents, and we do not do so.

We are asked, however, to consider a new situation not yet encountered by the Court. The question is whether these separate layers of protection may be combined. May the President be restricted in his ability to remove a principal officer, who is in turn restricted in his ability to remove an inferior officer, even though that inferior officer determines the policy and enforces the laws of the United States?

We hold that such multilevel protection from removal is contrary to Article II's vesting of the executive power in the President. The President cannot "take Care that the Laws be faithfully executed" if he cannot oversee the faithfulness of the officers who execute them. Here the President cannot remove an officer who enjoys more than one level of good-cause protection, even if the President determines that the officer is neglecting his duties or discharging them improperly. That judgment is instead committed to another officer, who may or may not agree with the President's determination, and whom the President cannot remove simply because that officer disagrees with him. This contravenes the President's "constitutional obligation to ensure the faithful execution of the laws." *Morrison*, 487 U.S. at 693.

The removal of executive officers was discussed extensively in Congress when the first executive departments were created. The view that "prevailed, as most consonant to the text of the Constitution" and "to the requisite responsibility and harmony in the Executive Department," was that the executive power included a power to oversee executive officers through removal; because that traditional executive power was not "expressly taken away, it remained with the President." Letter from James Madison to Thomas Jefferson (June 30, 1789), 16 Documentary History of the First Federal Congress 893 (2004). "This Decision of 1789 provides contemporaneous and weighty evidence of the Constitution's meaning since many of the Members of the First Congress had taken part in framing that instrument." *Bowsher v. Synar*, 478 U.S. 714, 723–724 (1986). And it soon became the "settled and well understood construction of the Constitution." *Ex parte Hennen*, 38 U.S. 230 (1839).

As explained, we have previously upheld limited restrictions on the President's removal power [in *Perkins*, *Humphrey's Executor*, and *Morrison*]. In those cases, however, only one level of protected tenure separated the President from an officer exercising executive power. It was the President—or a subordinate he could remove at will—who decided whether the officer's conduct merited removal under the good-cause standard.

The Act before us does something quite different. It not only protects Board members from removal except for good cause, but withdraws from the President any decision on whether that good cause exists. That decision is vested instead in other tenured officers—the Commissioners—none of whom is subject to the President's direct control. The result is a Board that is not accountable to the President, and a President who is not responsible for the Board.

The added layer of tenure protection makes a difference. Without a layer of insulation between the Commission and the Board, the Commission could remove a Board member at any time, and therefore would be fully responsible for what the Board does. The President could then hold the Commission to account for its supervision of the Board, to the same extent that he may hold the Commission to account for everything else it does.

A second level of tenure protection changes the nature of the President's review. Now the Commission cannot remove a Board member at will. The President therefore cannot hold the Commission fully accountable for the Board's conduct, to the same extent that he may hold the Commission accountable for everything else that it does. The Commissioners are not responsible for the Board's actions. They are only responsible for their own determination of whether the Act's rigorous good-cause standard is met. And even if the President disagrees with their determination, he is powerless to intervene—unless that determination is so unreasonable as to constitute "inefficiency, neglect of duty, or malfeasance in office." *Humphrey's Executor*, 295 U.S., at 620.

This novel structure does not merely add to the Board's independence, but transforms it. Neither the President, nor anyone directly responsible to him, nor even an officer whose conduct he may review only for good cause, has full control over the Board. The President is stripped of the power our precedents have preserved, and his ability to execute the laws—by holding his subordinates accountable for their conduct—is impaired.

That arrangement is contrary to Article II's vesting of the executive power in the President. Without the ability to oversee the Board, or to attribute the Board's failings to those whom he *can* oversee, the President is no longer the judge of the Board's conduct. He is not the one who decides whether Board members are abusing their offices or neglecting their duties. He can neither ensure that the laws are faithfully executed, nor be held responsible for a Board member's breach of faith. This violates the

> **Food for Thought**
>
> Why would Congress enact a provision that insulates the Board members from supervision in this manner? Do the possible benefits of insulating the Board members from political oversight come at any possible costs?

basic principle that the President "cannot delegate ultimate responsibility or the active obligation to supervise that goes with it," because Article II "makes a single President responsible for the actions of the Executive Branch." *Clinton v. Jones*, 520 U.S. 681, 712–713 (1997) (BREYER, J., concurring in judgment).

Indeed, if allowed to stand, this dispersion of responsibility could be multiplied. If Congress can shelter the bureaucracy behind two layers of good-cause tenure, why not a third? At oral argument, the Government was unwilling to concede that even *five* layers between the President and the Board would be too many. The officers of such an agency—safely encased within a Matryoshka doll of tenure protections—would be immune from Presidential oversight, even as they exercised power in the people's name.

Perhaps an individual President might find advantages in tying his own hands. But the separation of powers does not depend on the views of individual Presidents, nor on whether "the encroached-upon branch approves the encroachment," *New York v. United States*, 505 U.S. 144, 182 (1992). The President can always choose to restrain himself in his dealings with subordinates. He cannot, however, choose to bind his successors by diminishing their powers, nor can he escape responsibility for his choices by pretending that they are not his own.

The diffusion of power carries with it a diffusion of accountability. The people do not vote for the "Officers of the United States." Art. II, § 2, cl. 2. They instead look to the President to guide the "assistants or deputies . . . subject to his superintendence." The Federalist No. 72, p. 487 (J. Cooke ed. 1961) (A. Hamilton). Without a clear and effective chain of command, the public cannot "determine on whom the blame or the punishment of a pernicious measure, or series of pernicious measures ought really to fall." *Id.*, No. 70, at 476 (same). That is why the Framers sought to ensure that "those who are employed in the execution of the law will be in their proper situation, and the chain of dependence be preserved; the lowest officers, the middle grade, and the highest, will depend, as they ought, on the President, and the President on the community." 1 Annals of Cong., at 499 (J. Madison).

Food for Thought

Isn't the Court's argument in this paragraph also an argument against any limits on the President's authority to remove any officer? If so, why doesn't the Court revisit *Humphrey's Executor* and *Morrison*?

By granting the Board executive power without the Executive's oversight, this Act subverts the President's ability to ensure that the laws are faithfully executed—as well as the public's ability to pass judgment on his efforts. The Act's restrictions are incompatible with the Constitution's separation of powers.

Petitioners' complaint argued that the Board's "freedom from Presidential oversight and control" rendered it "and all power and authority exercised by it" in violation of the Constitution. We reject such a broad holding. Instead, we agree with the Government that the unconstitutional tenure provisions are severable from the remainder of the statute. * * * The Sarbanes-Oxley Act remains "fully operative as a law" with these tenure restrictions excised.

> **Take Note**
>
> Is the standard that the Court announces here for distinguishing between principal and inferior officers the same standard that the Court applied in *Morrison*? Does it give sufficient guidance for making the distinction? Does it suggest that all officers except Heads of Departments are inferior officers?

Petitioners [also] argue that Board members are principal officers requiring Presidential appointment with the Senate's advice and consent. We held in *Edmond v. United States*, 520 U.S. 651 (1997), that "[w]hether one is an 'inferior' officer depends on whether he has a superior," and that " 'inferior officers' are officers whose work is directed and supervised at some level" by other officers appointed by the President with the Senate's consent. In particular, we noted that "[t]he power to remove officers" at will and without cause "is a powerful tool for control" of an inferior. *Id.*, at 664. As explained above, the statutory restrictions on the Commission's power to remove Board members are unconstitutional and void. Given that the Commission is properly viewed, under the Constitution, as possessing the power to remove Board members at will, and given the Commission's other oversight authority, we have no hesitation in concluding that under *Edmond* the Board members are inferior officers whose appointment Congress may permissibly vest in a "Hea[d] of Departmen[t]."

JUSTICE BREYER, with whom JUSTICE STEVENS, JUSTICE GINSBURG, and JUSTICE SOTOMAYOR join, dissenting.

In answering the question presented, we cannot look to more specific constitutional text, such as the text of the Appointments Clause or the Presentment Clause, upon which the Court has relied in other separation-of-powers cases. That is because, with the exception of the general "vesting" and "take care" language, the Constitution is completely "silent with respect to the power of removal from office." *Ex parte Hennen*, 13 Pet. 230, 258 (1839); see also *Morrison v. Olson*, 487 U.S. 654, 723 (1988) (SCALIA, J., dissenting) ("There is, of course, no provision in the Constitution stating who may remove executive officers.").

Nor does history offer significant help. The President's power to remove Executive Branch officers "was not discussed in the Constitutional Convention."

Myers v. United States, 272 U.S. 52, 109–110 (1926). The First Congress enacted federal statutes that limited the President's ability to *oversee* Executive Branch officials, including the Comptroller of the United States, federal district attorneys (precursors to today's United States Attorneys), and, to a lesser extent, the Secretary of the Treasury. But those statutes did not directly limit the President's authority to *remove* any of those officials—"a subject" that was "much disputed" during "the early history of this government," "and upon which a great diversity of opinion was entertained." *Hennen*. Scholars, like Members of this Court, have continued to disagree, not only about the inferences that should be drawn from the inconclusive historical record, but also about the nature of the original disagreement.

Nor does this Court's precedent fully answer the question presented. At least it does not clearly invalidate the provision in dispute. In *Myers*, the Court invalidated—for the first and only time—a congressional statute on the ground that it unduly limited the President's authority to remove an Executive Branch official. But soon thereafter the Court expressly disapproved most of *Myers*' broad reasoning. See *Humphrey's Executor*, 295 U.S., at 626–627. Moreover, the Court has since said that "the essence of the decision in *Myers* was the judgment that the Constitution prevents Congress from '*draw[ing] to itself* . . . the power to remove or the right to participate in the exercise of that power.' " *Morrison* (emphasis added). And that feature of the statute—a feature that would *aggrandize* the power of Congress—is not present here. Congress has not granted itself any role in removing the members of the Accounting Board.

When previously deciding this kind of nontextual question, the Court has emphasized the importance of examining how a particular provision, taken in context, is likely to function. * * * [T]oday vast numbers of statutes governing vast numbers of subjects, concerned with vast numbers of different problems, provide for, or foresee, their execution or administration through the work of administrators organized within many different kinds of administrative structures, exercising different kinds of administrative authority, to achieve their legislatively mandated objectives. And, given the nature of the Government's work, it is not surprising that administrative units come in many different shapes and sizes. The functional approach required by our precedents recognizes this administrative complexity and, more importantly, recognizes the various ways presidential power operates within this context—and the various ways in which a removal provision might affect that power.

[We should] conclude that the "for cause" restriction before us will not restrict presidential power significantly. For one thing, the restriction directly limits, not the President's power, but the power of an already independent agency. The Court seems to have forgotten that fact when it identifies its central constitutional problem: According to the Court, the President "is powerless to intervene" if he has determined that the Board members' "conduct merit[s] removal" because "[t]hat decision is vested instead in other tenured officers—the Commissioners—none of whom is subject to the President's direct control." But so long as the President is *legitimately* foreclosed from removing the *Commissioners* except for cause (as the majority assumes), nullifying the Commission's power to remove Board members only for cause will not resolve the problem the Court has identified: The President will *still* be "powerless to intervene" by removing the Board members if the Commission reasonably decides not to do so.

In other words, the Court fails to show why *two* layers of "for cause" protection—Layer One insulating the Commissioners from the President, and Layer Two insulating the Board from the Commissioners—impose any more serious limitation upon the *President's* powers than *one* layer. Consider the four scenarios that might arise:

1. The President and the Commission both want to keep a Board member in office. Neither layer is relevant.

2. The President and the Commission both want to dismiss a Board member. Layer Two stops them both from doing so without cause. The President's ability to remove the Commission (Layer One) is irrelevant, for he and the Commission are in agreement.

3. The President wants to dismiss a Board member, but the Commission wants to keep the member. Layer One allows the Commission to make that determination notwithstanding the President's contrary view. Layer Two is irrelevant because the Commission does not seek to remove the Board member.

4. The President wants to keep a Board member, but the Commission wants to dismiss the Board member. Here, Layer Two *helps the President*, for it hinders the Commission's ability to dismiss a Board member whom the President wants to keep in place.

Thus, the majority's decision to eliminate only *Layer Two* accomplishes virtually nothing. And that is because a removal restriction's effect upon presidential power depends not on the presence of a "double-layer" of for-cause removal, as the majority pretends, but rather on the real-world nature of the President's relationship with the Commission. If the President confronts a Commission that seeks to *resist* his policy preferences—a distinct possibility when, as here, a Commission's membership must reflect both political parties, 15 U.S.C. § 78d(a)—the restriction on the *Commission's* ability to remove a Board member is either irrelevant (as in scenario 3) or may actually help the President (as in scenario 4). And if the President faces a Commission that seeks to implement his policy preferences, Layer One is irrelevant, for the President and Commission see eye to eye.

POINTS FOR DISCUSSION

a. Differing Views of *Humphrey's Executor* and *Morrison v. Olson*?

Both the majority and dissent recognized that *Humphrey's Executor* and *Morrison* allow Congress to impose some restrictions on the President's ability to remove executive branch officials. Is it a fair inference that the majority was skeptical about the basis for *Humphrey's Executor* and *Morrison* and did not want to carry their principles further, whereas the dissent agreed with those decisions and saw no harm in extending them?

b. Functional Considerations

The dissent recommended that, when the Court is confronted with questions about the constitutionality of a statute that the text of the Constitution does not answer, the Court should consider how the statute "taken in context, is likely to function." Do you have confidence in the Court's ability to make such an assessment, and to create workable rules of constitutional law based on such an assessment? Conversely, is the Court's approach problematic because it did not dwell on such considerations?

SEILA LAW LLC V. CONSUMER FINANCIAL PROTECTION BUREAU

140 S.Ct. 2183 (2020)

CHIEF JUSTICE ROBERTS delivered the opinion of the Court with respect to Parts I, II, and III.

I

[In the wake of the 2008 financial crisis, Congress established the Consumer Financial Protection Bureau (CFPB).] Congress tasked the CFPB with "implement[ing]" and "enforc[ing]" a large body of financial consumer protection laws to "ensur[e] that all consumers have access to markets for consumer financial products and services and that markets for consumer financial products and services are fair, transparent, and competitive." 12 U.S.C. § 5511(a). Congress transferred the administration of 18 existing federal statutes to the CFPB, including the Fair Credit Reporting Act, the Fair Debt Collection Practices Act, and the Truth in Lending Act. See §§ 5512(a), 5481(12), (14). In addition, Congress enacted a new prohibition on "any unfair, deceptive, or abusive act or practice" by certain participants in the consumer-finance sector. § 5536(a)(1)(B). Congress authorized the CFPB to implement that broad standard (and the 18 pre-existing statutes placed under the agency's purview) through binding regulations. §§ 5531(a)–(b), 5581(a)(1)(A), (b).

Congress also vested the CFPB with potent enforcement powers. The agency has the authority to conduct investigations, issue subpoenas and civil investigative demands, initiate administrative adjudications, and prosecute civil actions in federal court. §§ 5562, 5564(a), (f). To remedy violations of federal consumer financial law, the CFPB may seek restitution, disgorgement, and injunctive relief, as well as civil penalties of up to $1,000,000 (inflation adjusted) for each day that a violation occurs. §§ 5565(a), (c)(2); 12 CFR § 1083.1(a), Table (2019). Since its inception, the CFPB has obtained over $11 billion in relief for over 25 million consumers, including a $1 billion penalty against a single bank in 2018.

The CFPB's rulemaking and enforcement powers are coupled with extensive adjudicatory authority. The agency may conduct administrative proceedings to "ensure or enforce compliance with" the statutes and regulations it administers. 12 U. S. C. § 5563(a). When the CFPB acts as an adjudicator, it has "jurisdiction to grant any appropriate legal or equitable relief." § 5565(a)(1). * * *

* * * Rather than create a traditional independent agency headed by a multimember board or commission, Congress elected to place the CFPB under the leadership of a single Director. 12 U.S.C. § 5491(b)(1). The CFPB Director is appointed by the President with the advice and consent of the Senate. § 5491(b)(2). The Director serves for a term of five years, during which the President may remove the Director from office only for "inefficiency, neglect of duty, or malfeasance in office." §§ 5491(c)(1), (3).

Seila Law LLC is a California-based law firm that provides debt-related legal services to clients. In 2017, the CFPB issued a civil investigative demand to Seila Law to determine whether the firm had "engag[ed] in unlawful acts or practices in the advertising, marketing, or sale of debt relief services." The demand (essentially a subpoena) directed Seila Law to produce information and documents related to its business practices. Seila Law asked the CFPB to set aside the demand, objecting that the agency's leadership by a single Director removable only for cause violated the separation of powers. The CFPB declined to address that claim and directed Seila Law to comply with the demand. [When the CFB sued Seila

Take Note

In arguing this case at U.S. Court of Appeals for the Ninth Circuit, government lawyers employed by the CFPB successfully contended that the CFPB's structure was constitutional. But when Seila Law sought certiorari at the Supreme Court, the Solicitor General chose to side with Seila Law and filed a response supporting the grant of certiorari and arguing that the CFPB's structure was unconstitutional. As is customary in such situations, the Supreme Court invited a prominent advocate to file an amicus brief (without compensation) defending the judgment of the Court of Appeals. Paul Clement, a former Solicitor General, had previously argued 95 cases before the Supreme Court.

Law to enforce the demand, the District Court and Court of Appeals rejected Seila's constitutional challenges.]

II

[The Court held in Part II that Seila Law had standing to challenge the structure of the CFPB.]

III

We hold that the CFPB's leadership by a single individual removable only for inefficiency, neglect, or malfeasance violates the separation of powers.

Article II provides that "[t]he executive Power shall be vested in a President," who must "take Care that the Laws be faithfully executed." Art. II, § 1, cl. 1; *id.*, § 3. The entire "executive Power" belongs to the President alone. But because it would be "impossib[le]" for "one man" to "perform all the great business of the State," the Constitution assumes that lesser executive officers will "assist the supreme Magistrate in discharging the duties of his trust." 30 Writings of George Washington 334 (J. Fitzpatrick ed. 1939).

These lesser officers must remain accountable to the President, whose authority they wield. As Madison explained, "[I]f any power whatsoever is in its nature Executive, it is the power of appointing, overseeing, and controlling those who execute the laws." 1 Annals of Cong. 463 (1789). That power, in turn, generally includes the ability to remove executive officials, for it is "only the authority that can remove" such officials that they "must fear and, in the performance of [their] functions, obey." *Bowsher v. Synar*, 478 U.S. 714, 726 (1986).

The President's removal power has long been confirmed by history and precedent. It "was discussed extensively in Congress when the first executive departments were created" in 1789. *Free Enterprise Fund*, 561 U.S., at 492. "The view that 'prevailed, as most consonant to the text of the Constitution' and 'to the requisite responsibility and harmony in the Executive Department,' was that the executive power included a power to oversee executive officers through removal." *Ibid.* (quoting Letter from James Madison to Thomas Jefferson (June 30, 1789), 16 Documentary History of the First Federal Congress 893 (2004)). The First

Congress's recognition of the President's removal power in 1789 "provides contemporaneous and weighty evidence of the Constitution's meaning," *Bowsher*, 478 U.S., at 723, and has long been the "settled and well understood construction of the Constitution," *Ex parte Hennen*, 13 Pet. 230, 259 (1839).

The Court recognized the President's prerogative to remove executive officials in *Myers v. United States*. Chief Justice Taft, writing for the Court, conducted an exhaustive examination of the First Congress's determination in 1789, the views of the Framers and their contemporaries, historical practice, and our precedents up until that point. He concluded that Article II "grants to the President" the "general administrative control of those executing the laws, including the power of appointment *and removal* of executive officers." Just as the President's "selection of administrative officers is essential to the execution of the laws by him, so must be his power of removing those for whom he cannot continue to be responsible." *Id.*, at 117. "[T]o hold otherwise," the Court reasoned, "would make it impossible for the President . . . to take care that the laws be faithfully executed." *Id.*, at 164.

We recently reiterated the President's general removal power in *Free Enterprise Fund.* "Since 1789," we recapped, "the Constitution has been understood to empower the President to keep these officers accountable—by removing them from office, if necessary." 561 U.S., at 483. Although we had previously sustained congressional limits on that power in certain circumstances, we declined to extend those limits to "a new situation not yet encountered by the Court"—an official insulated by *two* layers of for-cause removal protection. *Id.,* at 483.

Free Enterprise Fund left in place two exceptions to the President's unrestricted removal power. First, in *Humphrey's Executor*, decided less than a decade after *Myers*, the Court upheld a statute that protected the Commissioners of the FTC from removal except for "inefficiency, neglect of duty, or malfeasance in office." 295 U.S. at 620. In reaching that conclusion, the Court stressed that Congress's ability to impose such removal restrictions "will depend upon the character of the office." 295 U.S. at 631.

Because the Court limited its holding "to officers of the kind here under consideration," *id.,* at 632, the contours of the *Humphrey's Executor* exception depend upon the characteristics of the agency before the Court. Rightly or wrongly, the Court viewed the FTC (as it existed in 1935) as exercising "no part of the executive power." *Id.,* at 628. Instead, it was "an administrative body" that performed "specified duties as a legislative or as a judicial aid." *Ibid.* It acted "as a legislative agency" in "making investigations and reports" to Congress and "as an agency of the judiciary" in making recommendations to courts as a master in chancery. *Ibid.* "To the extent that [the FTC] exercise[d] any executive *function*[,] as distinguished from executive *power* in the constitutional sense," it did so only in the discharge of its "quasi-legislative or quasi-judicial powers." *Ibid.* (emphasis added).

The Court identified several organizational features that helped explain its characterization of the FTC as non-executive. Composed of five members—no more than three from the same political party—the Board was designed to be "non-partisan" and to "act with entire impartiality." *Id.*, at 624, 619–620. The FTC's duties were "neither political nor executive," but instead called for "the trained judgment of a body of experts" "informed by experience." *Id.*, at 624. And the Commissioners' staggered, seven-year terms enabled the agency to accumulate technical expertise and avoid a "complete change" in leadership "at any one time." *Ibid.*

In short, *Humphrey's Executor* permitted Congress to give for-cause removal protections to a multimember body of experts, balanced along partisan lines, that performed legislative and judicial functions and was said not to exercise any executive power. Consistent with that understanding, the Court later applied "[t]he philosophy of *Humphrey's Executor*" to uphold for-cause removal protections for the members of the War Claims Commission—a three-member "adjudicatory body" tasked with resolving claims for compensation arising from World War II. *Wiener v. United States*, 357 U.S. 349, 356 (1958).

While recognizing an exception for multimember bodies with "quasi-judicial" or "quasi-legislative" functions, *Humphrey's Executor* reaffirmed the core holding of *Myers* that the President has "unrestrictable power . . . to remove purely executive officers." 295 U.S. at 632. The Court acknowledged that between purely executive officers on the one hand, and officers that closely resembled the FTC Commissioners on the other, there existed "a field of doubt" that the Court left "for future consideration." *Ibid.*

We have recognized a second exception for *inferior* officers in two cases, *United States* v. *Perkins*, 116 U.S. 483 (1886), and *Morrison* v. *Olson*, 487 U.S. 654 (1988). In *Perkins*, we upheld tenure protections for a naval cadet-engineer. And, in *Morrison*, we upheld a provision granting good-cause tenure protection to an independent counsel appointed to investigate and prosecute particular alleged crimes by high-ranking Government officials. Backing away from the reliance in *Humphrey's Executor* on the concepts of "quasi-legislative" and "quasi-judicial" power, we viewed the ultimate question as whether a removal restriction is of "such a nature that [it] impede[s] the President's ability to perform his constitutional duty." 487 U.S. at 691. Although the independent counsel was a single person and performed "law enforcement functions that typically have been undertaken by officials within the Executive Branch," we concluded that the removal protections did not unduly interfere with the functioning of the Executive Branch because "the independent counsel [was] an inferior officer under the Appointments Clause, with limited jurisdiction and tenure and lacking policymaking or significant administrative authority." *Ibid.*

These two exceptions—one for multimember expert agencies that do not wield substantial executive power, and one for inferior officers with limited duties and no policymaking or administrative authority—"represent what up to now have been the outermost constitutional limits of permissible congressional restrictions on the President's removal power." *PHH Corp. v. CFPB*, 881 F.3d 75, 196 (2018) (Kavanaugh, J., dissenting).

> **Food for Thought**
>
> Does the Court's description of the Court's holding and reasoning in *Morrison* reflect your understanding of the case? Or did the Court in *Morrison* have a more flexible understanding of congressional power to restrict the President's power to remove officials?

Neither *Humphrey's Executor* nor *Morrison* resolves whether the CFPB Director's insulation from removal is constitutional. Start with *Humphrey's Executor*. Unlike the New Deal-era FTC upheld there, the CFPB is led by a single Director who cannot be described as a "body of experts" and cannot be considered "non-partisan" in the same sense as a group of officials drawn from both sides of the aisle. 295 U.S. at 624. Moreover, while the staggered terms of the FTC Commissioners prevented complete turnovers in agency leadership and guaranteed that there would always be some Commissioners who had accrued significant expertise, the CFPB's single-Director structure and five-year term guarantee abrupt shifts in agency leadership and with it the loss of accumulated expertise.

In addition, the CFPB Director is hardly a mere legislative or judicial aid. Instead of making reports and recommendations to Congress, as the 1935 FTC did, the Director possesses the authority to promulgate binding rules fleshing out 19 federal statutes, including a broad prohibition on unfair and deceptive practices in a major segment of the U.S. economy. And instead of submitting recommended dispositions to an Article III court, the Director may unilaterally issue final decisions awarding legal and equitable relief in administrative adjudications. Finally, the Director's enforcement authority includes the power to seek daunting monetary penalties against private parties on behalf of the United States in federal court—a quintessentially executive power not considered in *Humphrey's Executor*.

The logic of *Morrison* also does not apply. Everyone agrees the CFPB Director is not an inferior officer, and her duties are far from limited. Unlike the independent counsel, who lacked policymaking or administrative authority, the Director has the sole responsibility to administer 19 separate consumer-protection statutes that cover everything from credit cards and car payments to mortgages and student loans. It is true that the independent counsel in *Morrison* was empowered to initiate criminal investigations and prosecutions, and in that respect wielded core executive power. But that power, while significant, was trained inward to high-ranking Governmental actors identified by others, and was confined to a specified matter in which the Department of Justice had a potential conflict of interest. By contrast, the CFPB Director has the authority to bring the coercive power of the state to bear on millions of private citizens and businesses, imposing even billion-dollar penalties through administrative adjudications and civil actions.

In light of these differences, the constitutionality of the CFPB Director's insulation from removal cannot be settled by *Humphrey's Executor* or *Morrison* alone.

The question instead is whether to extend those precedents to the "new situation" before us, namely an independent agency led by a single Director and vested with significant executive power. *Free Enterprise Fund*, 561 U.S., at 483. We decline to do so. Such an agency has no basis in history and no place in our constitutional structure.

After years of litigating the agency's constitutionality, the Courts of Appeals, parties, and *amici* have identified "only a handful of isolated" incidents in which Congress has provided good-cause tenure to principal officers who wield power alone rather than as members of a board or commission. *Ibid.* "[T]hese few scattered examples"—four to be exact—shed little light. *NLRB v. Noel Canning*, 573 U.S. 513, 538 (2014).

First, the CFPB's defenders point to the Comptroller of the Currency, who enjoyed removal protection for *one year* during the Civil War. That example has rightly been dismissed as an aberration. It was "adopted without discussion" during the heat of the Civil War and abandoned before it could be "tested by executive or judicial inquiry." *Myers*, 272 U.S., at 165.

Second, the supporters of the CFPB point to the Office of the Special Counsel (OSC), which has been headed by a single officer since 1978. But this first enduring single-leader office, created nearly 200 years after the Constitution was ratified, drew a contemporaneous constitutional objection from the Office of Legal Counsel under President Carter and a subsequent veto on constitutional grounds by President Reagan. In any event, the OSC exercises only limited jurisdiction to enforce certain rules governing Federal Government employers and employees. It does not bind private parties at all or wield regulatory authority comparable to the CFPB.

Third, the CFPB's defenders note that the Social Security Administration (SSA) has been run by a single Administrator since 1994. That example, too, is comparatively recent and controversial. President Clinton questioned the constitutionality of the SSA's new single-Director structure upon signing it into law. In addition, unlike the CFPB, the SSA lacks the authority to bring enforcement actions against private parties. Its role is largely limited to adjudicating claims for Social Security benefits.

The only remaining example is the Federal Housing Finance Agency (FHFA), created in 2008 to assume responsibility for Fannie Mae and Freddie Mac. It regulates primarily Government-sponsored enterprises, not purely private actors. And its single-Director structure is a source of ongoing controversy. Indeed, it was recently held unconstitutional by the Fifth Circuit, sitting en banc. See *Collins v. Mnuchin*, 938 F.3d 553, 587–588 (2019).

The Framers deemed an energetic executive essential to "the protection of the community against foreign attacks," "the steady administration of the laws," "the protection of property," and "the security of liberty." [The Federalist No. 70, at 475 (A. Hamilton)] No. 70, at 471. Accordingly, they chose not to bog the Executive down with the "habitual feebleness and dilatoriness" that comes with a "diversity of views and opinions." *Id.*, at 476. Instead, they gave the Executive the "[d]ecision, activity, secrecy, and dispatch" that "characterise the proceedings of one man." *Id.*, at 472.

To justify and check *that* authority—unique in our constitutional structure—the Framers made the President the most democratic and politically accountable official in Government. Only the President (along with the Vice President) is elected by the entire Nation. And the President's political accountability is enhanced by the solitary nature of the Executive Branch, which provides "a single object for the jealousy and watchfulness of the people." *Id.,* at 479. The President "cannot delegate ultimate responsibility or the active obligation to supervise that goes with it," because Article II "makes a single President responsible for the actions of the Executive Branch." *Free Enterprise Fund,* 561 U.S., at 496–497 (quoting *Clinton v. Jones*, 520 U.S. 681, 712–713 (1997) (BREYER, J., concurring in judgment)).

> **Food for Thought**
>
> Under the Court's reasoning, should restrictions on the President's power to remove Commissioners of a multi-member body such as the Federal Trade Commission be unconstitutional, as well?

The CFPB's single-Director structure contravenes this carefully calibrated system by vesting significant governmental power in the hands of a single individual accountable to no one. The Director is neither elected by the people nor meaningfully controlled (through the threat of removal) by someone who is. The Director does not even depend on Congress for annual appropriations. See The Federalist No. 58, at 394 (J. Madison) (describing the "power over the purse" as the "most compleat and effectual weapon" in representing the interests of the people). Yet the Director may *unilaterally*, without meaningful supervision, issue final regulations, oversee adjudications, set enforcement priorities, initiate prosecutions, and determine what penalties to impose on private parties. With no colleagues to persuade, and no boss or electorate looking over her shoulder, the Director may dictate and enforce policy for a vital segment of the economy affecting millions of Americans.

Because the CFPB is headed by a single Director with a five-year term, some Presidents may not have any opportunity to shape its leadership and thereby influence its activities. A President elected in 2020 would likely not appoint a CFPB Director until 2023, and a President elected in 2028 may *never* appoint one. That means an unlucky President might get elected on a consumer-protection platform and enter office only to find herself saddled with a holdover Director from a competing political party who is dead set *against* that agenda. To make matters worse, the agency's single-Director structure means the President will not have the opportunity to appoint any other leaders—such as a chair or fellow members of a Commission or Board—who can serve as a check on the Director's authority and help bring the agency in line with the President's preferred policies.

IV

* * * The provisions of the Dodd-Frank Act bearing on the CFPB's structure and duties remain fully operative without the offending tenure restriction. Those provisions are capable of functioning independently, and there is nothing in the text or history of the Dodd-Frank Act that demonstrates Congress would have preferred *no* CFPB to a CFPB supervised by the President. Quite the opposite. Unlike the Sarbanes-Oxley Act at issue in *Free Enterprise Fund*, the Dodd-Frank Act contains an express severability clause. There is no need to wonder what Congress would have wanted if "any provision of this Act" is "held to be unconstitutional" because it has told us: "the remainder of this Act" should "not be affected." 12 U.S.C. § 5302.

Because we find the Director's removal protection severable from the other provisions of Dodd-Frank that establish the CFPB, we remand for the Court of Appeals to consider whether the civil investigative demand was validly ratified.

JUSTICE THOMAS, with whom JUSTICE GORSUCH joins, concurring in part and dissenting in part.

Continued reliance on *Humphrey's Executor* to justify the existence of independent agencies creates a serious, ongoing threat to our Government's design. Leaving these unconstitutional agencies in place does not enhance this Court's legitimacy; it subverts political accountability and threatens individual liberty. We have a "responsibility to 'examin[e] without fear, and revis[e] without reluctance,' any 'hasty and crude decisions' rather than leaving 'the character of [the] law impaired, and the beauty and harmony of the [American constitutional] system destroyed by the perpetuity of error.' " *Gamble* v. *United States*, 587 U. S. ___ (2019) (THOMAS, J., concurring) (quoting 1 J. Kent, Commentaries on American Law 444 (1826)). We simply cannot compromise when it comes to our Government's structure. Today, the Court does enough to resolve this case, but in the future, we should reconsider *Humphrey's Executor in toto*. And I hope that we will have the will to do so.

While I think that the Court correctly resolves the merits of the constitutional question, I do not agree with its decision to sever the removal restriction in 12 U.S.C. § 5491(c)(3). To resolve this case, I would simply deny the Consumer Financial Protection Bureau (CFPB) petition to enforce the civil investigative demand.

Because the power of judicial review does not allow courts to revise statutes, the Court's severability doctrine must be rooted in statutory interpretation. But, even viewing severability as an interpretive question, I remain skeptical of our doctrine. As I have previously explained, "the severability doctrine often requires courts to weigh in on statutory provisions that no party has standing to challenge, bringing courts dangerously close to issuing advisory opinions." *Murphy*, 138 S.Ct., at 1487 (concurring opinion). And the application of the doctrine "does not follow basic principles of statutory interpretation." *Id.*, at 1486. Instead of determining the meaning of a statute's text, severability involves "nebulous inquir[ies] into hypothetical congressional intent." *Booker*, *supra*, at 320, n. 7 (THOMAS, J., dissenting in part).

JUSTICE KAGAN, with whom JUSTICE GINSBURG, JUSTICE BREYER, and JUSTICE SOTOMAYOR join, concurring in the judgment with respect to severability and dissenting in part.

The text of the Constitution, the history of the country, the precedents of this Court, and the need for sound and adaptable governance—all stand against the majority's opinion. They point not to the majority's "general rule" of "unrestricted removal power" with two grudgingly applied "exceptions." Rather, they bestow discretion on the legislature to structure administrative institutions as the times demand, so long as the President retains the ability to carry out his constitutional duties. And most relevant here, they give Congress wide leeway to limit the President's removal power in the interest of enhancing independence from politics in regulatory bodies like the CFPB.

What does the Constitution say about the separation of powers—and particularly about the President's removal authority? (Spoiler alert: about the latter, nothing at all.) * * * It is of course true that the Framers lodged three different kinds of power in three different entities. And that they did so for a crucial purpose—because, as James Madison wrote, "there can be no liberty where the legislative and executive powers are united in the same person[ ] or body" or where "the power of judging [is] not separated from the legislative and executive powers." The Federalist No. 47, p. 325 (J. Cooke ed. 1961) (quoting Baron de Montesquieu).

The problem lies * * * in failing to recognize that the separation of powers is, by design, neither rigid nor complete. Blackstone, whose work influenced the Framers on this subject as on others, observed that "every branch" of government "supports and is supported, regulates and is regulated, by the rest." 1 W. Blackstone, Commentaries on the Laws of England 151 (1765). So as James Madison stated, the creation of distinct branches "did not mean that these departments ought to have no partial agency in, or no controul over the acts of each other." The Federalist No. 47, at 325 (emphasis deleted). To the contrary, Madison explained, the drafters of the Constitution—like those of then-existing state constitutions—opted against keeping the branches of government "absolutely separate and distinct." *Id.*, at 327. Or as Justice Story reiterated a half-century later: "[W]hen we speak of a separation of the three great departments of government," it is "not meant to affirm, that they must be kept wholly and entirely separate." 2 J. Story, Commentaries on the Constitution of the United States § 524, p. 8 (1833). Instead, the branches have—as they must for the whole arrangement to work—"common link[s] of connexion [and] dependence." *Ibid.*

One way the Constitution reflects that vision is by giving Congress broad authority to establish and organize the Executive Branch. Article II presumes the existence of "Officer[s]" in "executive Departments." § 2, cl. 1. But it does not, as you might think from reading the majority opinion, give the President authority to decide what kinds of officers—in what departments, with what responsibilities—the Executive Branch requires. Instead, Article I's Necessary and Proper Clause puts those decisions in the legislature's hands. Congress has the power "[t]o make all Laws which shall be necessary and proper for carrying into Execution" not just its own enumerated powers but also "all other Powers vested by this Constitution in the Government of the United States, or in any Department or Officer thereof." § 8, cl. 18. Similarly, the Appointments Clause reflects Congress's central role in structuring the Executive Branch. Yes, the President can appoint principal officers, but only as the legislature "shall . . . establish[ ] by Law" (and of course subject to the Senate's advice and consent). Art. II, § 2, cl. 2. And Congress has plenary power to decide not only what inferior officers will exist but also who (the President or a head of department) will appoint them. So as Madison told the first Congress, the legislature gets to "create[ ] the office, define[ ] the powers, [and] limit[ ] its duration." 1 Annals of Cong. 582 (1789). The President, as to the construction of his own branch of government, can only try to work his will through the legislative process.

The majority relies for its contrary vision on Article II's Vesting Clause, but the provision can't carry all that weight. Or as Chief Justice Rehnquist wrote of a similar claim in *Morrison v. Olson*, 487 U.S. 654, (1988), "extrapolat[ing]" an unrestricted removal power from such "general constitutional language"—which says only that "[t]he executive Power shall be vested in a President"—is "more than the text will bear." *Id.,* at 690, n. 29. Dean John Manning has well explained why, even were it not obvious from the Clause's "open-ended language." Separation of Powers as Ordinary Interpretation, 124 Harv. L. Rev. 1939, 1971 (2011). The Necessary and Proper Clause, he writes, makes it impossible to "establish a constitutional violation simply by showing that Congress has constrained the way '[t]he executive Power' is implemented"; that is exactly what the Clause gives Congress the power to do. *Id.,* at 1967. Only "a *specific* historical understanding" can bar Congress from enacting a given constraint. *Id.,* at 2024. And nothing of that sort broadly prevents Congress from limiting the President's removal power. * * *

Nor can the Take Care Clause come to the majority's rescue. * * * [T]he text of the Take Care Clause requires only enough authority to make sure "the laws [are] faithfully executed"—meaning with fidelity to the law itself, not to every presidential policy preference. As this Court has held, a President can ensure " 'faithful execution' of the laws"—thereby satisfying his "take care" obligation—with a removal provision like the one here. *Morrison*, 487 U.S., at 692. A for-cause standard gives him "ample authority to assure that [an official] is competently performing [his] statutory responsibilities in a manner that comports with the [relevant legislation's] provisions." *Ibid.*

Finally, recall the Constitution's telltale silence: Nowhere does the text say anything about the President's power to remove subordinate officials at will. * * * That's because removal is a *tool*—one means among many, even if sometimes an important one, for a President to control executive officials. To find that authority hidden in the Constitution as a "general rule" is to discover what is nowhere there.

History no better serves the majority's cause. * * * Begin with evidence from the Constitution's ratification. And note that this moment is indeed the beginning: Delegates to the Constitutional Convention never discussed whether or to what extent the President would have power to remove executive officials. As a result, the Framers advocating ratification had no single view of the matter. In Federalist No. 77, Hamilton presumed that under the new Constitution "[t]he consent of [the Senate] would be necessary to displace as well as to appoint" officers of the United States. *Id.,* at 515. He thought that scheme would promote "steady administration": "Where a man in any station had given satisfactory evidence of his fitness for it, a new president would be restrained" from substituting "a person more agreeable to him." *Ibid.* By contrast, Madison thought the Constitution allowed Congress to decide how any executive official could be removed. He explained in Federalist No. 39: "The tenure of the ministerial offices generally will be a subject of legal regulation, conformably to the reason of the case, and the example of the State Constitutions." *Id.,* at 253. Neither view, of course, at all supports the majority's story.

What is more, the Court's precedents before today have accepted the role of independent agencies in our governmental system. * * * *Humphrey's* found constitutional a statute identical to the one here, providing that the President could remove FTC Commissioners for "inefficiency, neglect of duty, or malfeasance in office." 295 U.S., at 619. The *Humphrey's* Court, as the majority notes, relied in substantial part on what kind of work the Commissioners performed. (By contrast, nothing in the decision turned—as the majority suggests, on any of the agency's organizational features.) According to *Humphrey's*, the Commissioners' primary work was to "carry into effect legislative policies"—"filling in and administering the details embodied by [a statute's] general standard." 295 U.S., at 627–628. In addition, the Court noted, the Commissioners recommended dispositions in court cases, much as a special master does. Given those "quasi-legislative" and "quasi-judicial"—as opposed to "purely executive"—functions, Congress could limit the President's removal authority. *Id.,* at 628. Or said another way, Congress could give the FTC some "independen[ce from] executive control." *Id.,* at 629.

* * * *Morrison* both extended *Humphrey's* domain and clarified the standard for addressing removal issues. The *Morrison* Court, over a one-Justice dissent, upheld for-cause protections afforded to an independent counsel with power to investigate and prosecute crimes committed by high-ranking officials. The Court well understood that those law enforcement functions differed from the rulemaking and adjudicatory duties highlighted in *Humphrey's* * * *. But that difference did not resolve the issue. An official's functions, *Morrison* held, were relevant to but not dispositive of a removal limit's constitutionality. The key question in all the cases, *Morrison* saw, was whether such a restriction would "impede the President's ability to perform his constitutional duty." 487 U.S., at 691. Only if it did so would it fall outside Congress's power. And the protection for the independent counsel, the Court found, did not. Even though the counsel's functions were "purely executive," the President's "need to control the exercise of [her] discretion" was not "so central to the functioning of the Executive Branch as to require" unrestricted removal authority. *Id.,* at 690–691. True enough, the Court acknowledged, that the for-cause standard prevented the President from firing the counsel for discretionary decisions or judgment calls. But it preserved "ample authority" in the President "to assure that the counsel is competently performing" her "responsibilities in a manner that comports with" all legal requirements. *Id.,* at 692. That meant the President could meet his own constitutional obligation "to ensure 'the faithful execution' of the laws." *Ibid.*

The majority's description of *Morrison* is not true to the decision. (Mostly, it seems, the majority just wishes the case would go away.) First, *Morrison* is no "exception" to a broader rule from *Myers*. *Morrison* echoed all of *Humphrey's* criticism of the by-then infamous *Myers* "dicta." 487 U.S., at 687. It again rejected the notion of an "all-inclusive" removal power. *Ibid.* It yet further confined *Myers*' reach, making clear that Congress could restrict the President's removal of officials carrying out even the most traditional executive functions. And the decision, with care, set out the governing rule—again, that removal restrictions are permissible so long as they do not impede the President's performance of his own constitutionally assigned duties. Second, as all that suggests, *Morrison* is not limited to inferior officers. In the eight pages addressing the removal issue, the Court constantly spoke of "officers" and "officials" in general. 487 U.S., at 685–

693. By contrast, the Court there used the word "inferior" in just one sentence (which of course the majority quotes), when applying its general standard to the case's facts. *Id.,* at 691. Indeed, Justice Scalia's dissent emphasized that the counsel's inferior-office status played no role in the Court's decision. See *id.,* at 724 ("The Court could have resolved the removal power issue in this case by simply relying" on that status, but did not). As Justice Scalia noted, the Court in *United States v. Perkins*, 116 U.S. 483, 484–485 (1886), had a century earlier allowed Congress to restrict the President's removal power over inferior officers. See *Morrison*, 487 U.S., at 723–724. Were that *Morrison*'s basis, a simple citation would have sufficed.

The question here, which by now you're well equipped to answer, is whether including that for-cause standard in the statute creating the CFPB violates the Constitution. Applying our longstanding precedent, the answer is clear: It does not. This Court, as the majority acknowledges, has sustained the constitutionality of the FTC and similar independent agencies. The for-cause protections for the heads of those agencies, the Court has found, do not impede the President's ability to perform his own constitutional duties, and so do not breach the separation of powers. There is nothing different here. The CFPB wields the same kind of power as the FTC and similar agencies. And all of their heads receive the same kind of removal protection. No less than those other entities—by now part of the fabric of government—the CFPB is thus a permissible exercise of Congress's power under the Necessary and Proper Clause to structure administration.

And Congress's choice to put a single director, rather than a multimember commission, at the CFPB's head violates no principle of separation of powers. The purported constitutional problem here is that an official has "slip[ped] from the Executive's control" and "supervision"—that he has become unaccountable to the President. So to make sense on the majority's own terms, the distinction between singular and plural agency heads must rest on a theory about why the former more easily "slip" from the President's grasp. But the majority has nothing to offer. In fact, the opposite is more likely to be true: To the extent that such matters are measurable, individuals are easier than groups to supervise.

To begin with, trying to generalize about these matters is something of a fool's errand. Presidential control * * * can operate through many means—removal to be sure, but also appointments, oversight devices (*e.g.,* centralized review of rulemaking or litigating positions), budgetary processes, personal outreach, and more. The effectiveness of each of those control mechanisms, when present, can then depend on a multitude of agency-specific practices, norms, rules, and organizational features. In that complex stew, the difference between a singular and plural agency head will often make not a whit of difference. * * *

But if the demand is for generalization, then the majority's distinction cuts the opposite way: More powerful control mechanisms are needed (if anything) for commissions. Holding everything else equal, those are the agencies more likely to "slip from the Executive's control." Just consider your everyday experience: It's easier to get one person to do what you want than a gaggle. So too, you know exactly whom to blame when an individual—but not when a group—does a job badly. The same is true in bureaucracies. A multimember structure reduces accountability to the President because it's harder for him to oversee, to influence—or to remove, if necessary—a group of five or more commissioners than a single director. Indeed, that is *why* Congress so often resorts to hydra-headed agencies. * * *

[In addition,] the premise of the majority's argument—that the CFPB head is a mini-dictator, not subject to meaningful presidential control—is wrong. As this Court has seen in the past, independent agencies are not fully independent. A for-cause removal provision, as noted earlier, leaves "ample" control over agency heads in the hands of the President. *Morrison*, 487 U.S., at 692. He can discharge them for failing to perform their duties competently or in accordance with law, and so ensure that the laws are "faithfully executed." And he can use the many other tools attached to the Office of the Presidency—including in the CFPB's case, rulemaking review—to exert influence over discretionary policy calls. * * *

Recall again how this dispute got started. In the midst of the Great Recession, Congress and the President came together to create an agency [to] protect consumers from the reckless financial practices that had caused the then-ongoing economic collapse. Not only Congress but also the President thought that the new agency, to fulfill its mandate, needed a measure of independence. So the two political branches, acting together, gave the CFPB Director the same job protection that innumerable other agency heads possess. * * * And now consider how the dispute ends—with five unelected judges rejecting the result of that democratic process. * * * The majority does so even though the Constitution grants to Congress, acting with the President's approval, the authority to create and shape administrative bodies. And even though those branches, as compared to courts, have far greater understanding of political control mechanisms and agency design. * * * Because this Court ignores that sensible—indeed, that obvious—division of tasks, I respectfully dissent.

POINTS FOR DISCUSSION

a. *Humphrey's Executor*

The Court distinguishes *Humphrey's Executor* v. *United States*, 295 U.S. 602 (1935), on the ground that it concerned expert agencies led by a *group* of principal officers removable by the President only for good cause, while this case involved a single officer removable for good cause. The dissent finds this distinction unpersuasive because individuals are easier to supervise than groups. Which view is correct? If this case is indistinguishable from *Humphrey's Executor*, are Justice Thomas and Justice Gorsuch correct in asserting that the validity of *Humphrey's Executor* should be questioned? What would be the consequence of overturning *Humphrey's Executor*?

b. *Morrison v. Olson*

The Court distinguishes *Morrison v. Olson* on the ground that it concerned removal restrictions on an *inferior* officer. How does the dissent respond? Does the Court's position call *Morrison v. Olson* into question?

E. BILLS OF ATTAINDER

Article I, section 9, clause 3 provides that Congress cannot pass a "bill of attainder." (Article I, section 10, clause 1 imposes the same prohibition on the states.) As understood in modern times, a bill of attainder is a legislative act that imposes a forbidden type of punishment. The Supreme Court has said: "In deciding whether a statute inflicts forbidden punishment, we have recognized three necessary inquiries: (1) whether the challenged statute falls within the historical meaning of legislative punishment; (2) whether the statute, 'viewed in terms of the type and severity of burdens imposed, reasonably can be said to further nonpunitive legislative purposes'; and (3) whether the legislative record 'evinces a congressional intent to punish.' " *Selective Service System v. Minnesota Public Interest Research Group*, 468 U.S. 841, 852 (1984) (quoting *Nixon v. Administrator of General Services*, 433 U.S. 425, 473, 475–476, 478 (1977)). Impermissible legislative punishments historically have included the death penalty, imprisonment, banishment, confiscation of property, and bars to participating in specific employments and professions. For example, suppose that Congress, following the attacks of September 11, 2001, had passed a law saying: "Osama bin

> **Food for Thought**
>
> Litigants often challenge federal and state laws as being unconstitutional bills of attainder. Between 2000 and 2010, over 1100 reported cases addressed the Bill of Attainder clauses in Article I, sections 9 and 10. The courts, however, very rarely have determined that legislation actually violates these clauses. Does this mean that the clauses are not important?

Laden, when captured, shall be immediately put to death for his role in the attacks." This hypothetical law would be a bill of attainder, and it would be unconstitutional.

Bills of attainder, in a sense, violate the separation of powers. In passing a bill of attainder, Congress would be seeking to serve not only a legislative function, but also an executive and judicial function. In the example, Congress would be deciding that Bin Laden should face the prospect of punishment (instead of leaving this decision to the executive branch) and would be deciding what punishment he deserves (instead of leaving this decision to the judiciary). Bills of attainder, of course, also deprive the person being punished of important individual rights, such as due process of law. (Recall that Justice Powell thought that the exercise of legislative power in *Chadha* was tantamount to a bill of attainder.)

Perhaps no bill of attainder could raise more serious separation of power questions than one aimed against the President of the United States. Congress not only would be asserting executive power, but would be using it against the Chief Executive. The following case considers whether this extreme use of a bill of attainder occurred when Congress acted to take custody of President Richard Nixon's papers and tape recordings. In reading the case, consider how the Court decides whether Congress acted to punish President Nixon.

NIXON V. ADMINISTRATOR OF GENERAL SERVICES

433 U.S. 425 (1977)

MR. JUSTICE BRENNAN delivered the opinion of the Court.

Title I of Pub. L. 93–526, 88 Stat. 1695, the Presidential Recordings and Materials Preservation Act (hereafter Act), directs the Administrator of General Services, official of the Executive Branch, to take custody of the Presidential papers and tape recordings of appellant, former President Richard M. Nixon, and promulgate regulations that (1) provide for the orderly processing and screening by Executive Branch archivists of such materials for the purpose of returning to appellant those that are personal and private in nature, and (2) determine the terms and conditions upon which public access may eventually be had to those materials that are retained. The question for decision is whether Title I is unconstitutional on its face as a violation of * * * the Bill of Attainder Clause.

The materials at issue consist of some 42 million pages of documents and some 880 tape recordings of conversations. Upon his resignation, appellant directed Government archivists to pack and ship the materials to him in California. This shipment was delayed when the Watergate Special Prosecutor advised President Ford of his continuing need for the materials. At the same time, President Ford requested that the Attorney General give his opinion respecting ownership of the materials. The Attorney General advised that the historical practice of former Presidents and the absence of any governing statute to the contrary supported ownership in the appellant. * * *

Make the Connection

In Chapter 5, we considered how President Nixon sought to invoke executive privilege to shield disclosure of tape recordings. This case is related. Congress passed the law at issue here because it was concerned that President Nixon might destroy some of his papers and tape recordings, including materials that might be relevant to the Watergate investigation.

[The Court first rejected former President Nixon's claim that the Act violated the separation of powers and his claim of executive privilege.]

[Appellant's] argument is that Congress acted on the premise that he had engaged in "misconduct," was an "unreliable custodian" of his own documents, and generally was deserving of a "legislative judgment of blameworthiness." Thus, he argues, the Act is pervaded with the key features of a bill of attainder: a law that legislatively determines guilt and inflicts punishment upon an identifiable individual without provision of the protections of a judicial trial.

Appellant's argument relies almost entirely upon *United States v. Brown*, 381 U.S. 437 (1965), the Court's most recent decision addressing the scope of the Bill of Attainder Clause. It is instructive, therefore, to sketch the broad outline of that case. *Brown* invalidated § 504 of the Labor-Management Reporting and Disclosure Act of 1959, that made it a crime for a Communist Party member to serve as an officer of a labor union. After detailing the infamous history of bills of attainder, the Court found that the Bill of Attainder Clause was an important ingredient of the doctrine of "separation of powers," one of the organizing principles of our system of government. 381 U.S., at 442–443. Just as Art. III confines the Judiciary to the task of adjudicating concrete "cases or controversies," so too the Bill of Attainder Clause was found to "reflect . . . the Framers' belief that the Legislative Branch is not so well suited as politically independent judges and juries to the task of ruling upon the blameworthiness of, and levying appropriate punishment upon, specific persons." *Id.* at 445. *Brown* thus held that § 504 worked a bill of attainder by focusing upon easily identifiable members of a class—members of the Communist Party—and imposing on them the sanction of mandatory forfeiture of a job or office, long deemed to be punishment with the contemplation of the Bill of Attainder Clause.

In essence, he argues that *Brown* establishes that the Constitution is offended whenever a law imposes undesired consequences on an individual or on a class that is not defined at a proper level of generality. The Act in question therefore is faulted for singling out appellant, as opposed to all other Presidents or members of the Government, for disfavored treatment.

Appellant's characterization of the meaning of a bill of attainder obviously proves far too much. By arguing that an individual or defined group is attainted whenever he or it is compelled to bear burdens which the individual or group dislikes, appellant removes the anchor that ties the bill of attainder guarantee to realistic conceptions of classification and punishment. His view would cripple the very process of legislating, for any individual or group that is made the subject of adverse legislation can complain that the lawmakers could and should have defined the relevant affected class at a greater level of generality. Furthermore, every person or group made subject to legislation which he or it finds burdensome may subjectively feel, and can complain, that he or it is being subjected to unwarranted punishment. However expansive the prohibition against bills of attainder, it surely was not intended to serve as a variant of the equal protection doctrine, invalidating every Act of Congress or the States that legislatively burdens some persons or groups but not all other plausible individuals. In short, while the Bill of Attainder Clause serves as an important "bulwark against tyranny," *United States v. Brown*, 381 U.S., at 443, it does not do so by limiting Congress to the choice of legislating for the universe, or legislating only benefits, or not legislating at all.

Thus, in the present case, the Act's specificity—the fact that it refers to appellant by name—does not automatically offend the Bill of Attainder Clause. Indeed, viewed in context, the focus of the enactment can be fairly and rationally understood. It is true that Title I deals exclusively with appellant's papers. But Title II casts a wider net by establishing a special commission to study and recommend appropriate legislation regarding the preservation of the records of future Presidents and all other federal officials. In this light, Congress' action to preserve only appellant's records is easily explained by the fact that at the time of the Act's passage, only his materials demanded immediate attention. The Presidential papers of all former Presidents from Hoover to Johnson were already housed in functioning Presidential libraries. Congress had reason for concern solely with the preservation of appellant's materials, for he alone had entered into a depository agreement, the Nixon-Sampson agreement, which by its terms called for the destruction of certain of the materials. Indeed, as the federal appellees argue, "appellant's depository agreement . . . created an imminent danger that the tape recordings would be destroyed if appellant, who had contracted phlebitis, were to die." In short, appellant constituted a legitimate class of one, and this provides a basis for Congress' decision to proceed with dispatch with respect to his materials while accepting the status of his predecessors' papers and ordering the further consideration of generalized standards to govern his successors.

Moreover, even if the specificity element were deemed to be satisfied here, the Bill of Attainder Clause would not automatically be implicated. Forbidden legislative punishment is not involved merely because the Act imposes burdensome consequences. Rather, we must inquire further whether Congress, by lodging appellant's materials in the custody of the General Services Administration pending their screening by Government archivists and the promulgation of further regulations, "inflict(ed) punishment" within the constitutional proscription against bills of attainder. *United States v. Lovett*, 328 U.S. 303, 315 (1946).

In England a bill of attainder originally connoted a parliamentary Act sentencing a named individual or identifiable members of a group to death. Article I, § 9, however, also proscribes enactments originally characterized as bills of pains and penalties, that is, legislative Acts inflicting punishment other than execution. Generally addressed to persons considered disloyal to the Crown or State, "pains and penalties" historically consisted of a wide array of punishments: commonly included were imprisonment, banishment, and the punitive confiscation of property by the sovereign. Our country's own experience with bills of attainder resulted in the addition of another sanction to the list of impermissible legislative punishments: a legislative enactment barring designated individuals or groups from participation in specified employments or vocations, a mode of punishment commonly employed against those legislatively branded as disloyal. See, e.g., *Cummings v. Missouri*, 71 U.S. (4 Wall.) 277, 323 (1867) (barring clergymen from ministry in the absence of subscribing to a loyalty oath); *United States v. Lovett* (barring named individuals from Government employment); *United States v. Brown* (barring Communist Party members from offices in labor unions).

Needless to say, appellant cannot claim to have suffered any of these forbidden deprivations at the hands of the Congress. While it is true that Congress ordered the General Services Administration to retain control over records that appellant claims as his property, § 105 of the Act makes provision for an award by the District Court of "just compensation." This undercuts even a colorable contention that the Government has punitively confiscated appellant's property, for the "owner (thereby) is to be put in the same position monetarily as he would have occupied if his property has not been taken." *United States v. Reynolds*, 397 U.S. 14, 16 (1970). Thus, no feature of the challenged Act falls within the historical meaning of legislative punishment.

But our inquiry is not ended by the determination that the Act imposes no punishment traditionally judged to be prohibited by the Bill of Attainder Clause. Our treatment of the scope of the Clause has never precluded the possibility that new burdens and deprivations might be legislatively fashioned that are inconsistent with the bill of attainder guarantee. The Court, therefore, often has looked beyond mere historical experience and has applied a functional test of the existence of punishment, analyzing whether the law under challenge, viewed in terms of the type and severity of burdens imposed, reasonably can be said to further nonpunitive legislative purposes. Where such legitimate legislative purposes do not appear, it is reasonable to conclude that punishment of individuals disadvantaged by the enactment was the purpose of the decisionmakers.

Application of the functional approach to this case leads to rejection of appellant's argument that the Act rests upon a congressional determination of his blameworthiness and a desire to punish him. For, as noted previously, legitimate justifications for passage of the Act are readily apparent. First, in the face of the Nixon-Sampson agreement which expressly contemplated the destruction of some of appellant's materials, Congress stressed the need to preserve "[i]nformation included in the materials of former President Nixon [that] is needed to complete the prosecutions of Watergate-related crimes." H.R. Rep. No. 93–1507, p. 2 (1974). Second, again referring to the Nixon-Sampson agreement, Congress expressed its desire to safeguard the "public interest in gaining appropriate access to materials of the Nixon Presidency which are of general historical significance. The information in these materials will be of great value to the political health and vitality of the United States." *Ibid.* Indeed, these same objectives are stated in the text of the Act itself, § 104(a), where Congress instructs the General Services Administration to promulgate regulations that further these ends and at the same time protect the constitutional and legal rights of any individual adversely affected by the Administrator's retention of appellant's materials.

A third recognized test of punishment is strictly a motivational one: inquiring whether the legislative record evinces a congressional intent to punish. See, e.g., *United States v. Lovett*, 328 U.S., at 308–314. The District Court unequivocally found: "There is no evidence presented to us, nor is there any to be found in the legislative record, to indicate that Congress' design was to impose a penalty upon

Mr. Nixon . . . as punishment for alleged past wrongdoings. . . . The legislative history leads to only one conclusion, namely, that the Act before us is regulatory and not punitive in character." We find no cogent reason for disagreeing with this conclusion.

POINTS FOR DISCUSSION

a. Intent to Punish?

Why would Congress pass this law and single out President Nixon if it did not intend to punish him? Is the Court's definition of punishment unduly narrow?

b. Compensation

In 1998, President Nixon's estate and the United States finally reached a settlement in which the United States paid the estate $18 million for the confiscated papers and tape recordings, some of which may have been President Nixon's personal property. See Christopher Marquis, *Government Agrees to Pay Nixon Estate*, N.Y. Times, Jun. 13, 2000, at A18.

Executive Summary of This Chapter

The non-delegation doctrine says that Congress may not delegate its legislative authority to the executive branch. But Congress may give the executive branch discretion to promulgate rules and regulations so long as Congress guides the discretion with some "intelligible principle." *Whitman v. American Trucking* (2007).

Congress may exercise legislative power only by acting pursuant to the Bicameralism and Presentment requirements in Article I, § 7. *INS v. Chadha* (1983); *Clinton v. City of New York* (1998). Legislative power consists of actions that have "the purpose and effect of altering the legal rights, duties, and relations of persons outside of the legislative branch." *INS v. Chadha* (1983).

In general, the President has the authority to remove the heads of executive agencies for any reason because the power to remove officials is incident to the power to appoint their replacements. *Myers v. United States* (1926). But this general power is qualified in some circumstances by Congress's power by statute to limit the President's power to remove to cases of good cause. Congress may impose such a restriction on the President's power to remove (1) members of multimember expert agencies that do not wield substantial executive power, *Humphrey's Executor v. United States* (1935), and (2) inferior officers with limited duties and no policymaking or administrative authority, *Morrison v. Olson* (1988). *Seila Law LLC v. Consumer Financial Protection Bureau* (2020).

The Court has also stated that a for-cause limitation on the President's removal power is invalid if the "standard for removal by itself unduly trammels on executive authority," *Morrison v. Olson* (1988), but it is not clear if this remains the test. At a minimum, Congress may not restrict the President's ability to remove a principal officer if that officer, in turn, is restricted in his ability to remove an inferior officer who is responsible for determining the policy and enforcing the laws of the United States. *Free Enterprise Fund v. Public Company Accounting Oversight Board* (2010). As a corollary to the foregoing rules, in general legislation cannot give executive powers to officials whom Congress can remove other than by impeachment and conviction. *Bowsher v. Synar* (1986).

Administrative law judges who have power to adjudicate matters involving private parties generally count as "inferior officers" whose appointment must conform to the requirements of the Appointments Clause, rather than as "employees" who can be appointed by figures other than the President, the Heads of Departments, or the courts of law. *Lucia v. SEC* (2018). The line between principal and inferior officers is not clear, but the difference turns on whether the person is subordinate to another officer and the scope, jurisdiction, and duration of the person's duties and tenure. *Morrison v. Olson* (1988).

The Appointments Clause permits Congress to vest in the courts the power of appointing inferior executive officers, such as prosecutors, and to give the courts some discretion in defining the nature and scope of the appointed officer's jurisdiction. *Morrison v. Olson* (1988). In addition, Article III permits federal judges to exercise ministerial functions not traditionally limited to the executive branch. *Morrison v. Olson* (1988).

In determining whether a law is a **bill of attainder**, the courts will consider precedent and a variety of factors, including (1) whether the challenged statute falls within the historical meaning of legislative punishment; (2) whether the statute furthers nonpunitive legislative purposes; and (3) whether the legislative record evinces an intent to punish. But a law is not a bill of attainder merely because it imposes burdens on only one person. *Nixon v. Admin. of General Services* (1977).

PART V

Constitutional Limitations on Non-Governmental Conduct

Throughout this book, we have seen many examples of how state and federal governmental units and governmental officials have taken actions that have violated the Constitution. Congress, for instance, has infringed the Constitution by enacting laws that contravene the freedom of speech. See, e.g., *Buckley v. Valeo,* 424 U.S. 1 (1976). The President has sometimes violated the Constitution by taking actions for which he lacks authority. See *Youngstown Sheet & Tube Co. v. Sawyer*, 343 U.S 579 (1952). And the states have enacted laws that violate the Equal Protection Clause, see, e.g., *Loving v. Virginia*, 388 U.S. 1 (1967), and other provisions.

But do acts by private individuals or corporations ever violate the Constitution? The general answer to this question, subject to important exceptions, is no. The **state action doctrine** says that while the Constitution imposes limits on the action of the state and federal governments and governmental officials—action that is called "state action" for simplicity—the Constitution generally does not limit the actions of private parties.

The state action doctrine has a textual explanation. Most provisions in the Constitution by their terms address the government rather than private individuals. For example, suppose that parents require their minor children to attend a particular church. Are the parents violating the First Amendment's protection of the free exercise of religion? Simply reading the First Amendment reveals the answer. The First Amendment says that "*Congress* shall make *no law* respecting an establishment of religion, or prohibiting the free exercise thereof * * *." The Amendment does not purport to address non-governmental action that has some effect on religious practice. The parents' action therefore does not violate the constitutional protection of the free exercise of religion.

There are, however, some very important exceptions to this doctrine. First, the Thirteenth Amendment, which prohibits slavery and involuntary servitude, does not confine its prohibition to governmental action. Instead, it provides that neither "shall *exist* within the United States, or any place subject to their jurisdiction" (emphasis added). Indeed, slavery, although supported and enabled in many ways by state and federal legal institutions, was principally a problem of private action, and it is unsurprising that the constitutional prohibition on the institution does not limit itself to governmental conduct. And in the *Civil Rights Cases*, 109 U.S. 3 (1883), discussed below, the Supreme Court interpreted the Thirteenth Amendment to apply to both state and private conduct.

FYI

The Eighteenth Amendment also applied to private action, prohibiting the "manufacture, sale, or transportation of intoxicating liquors" in the United States. It was repealed, however, by the Twenty-First Amendment.

Second, as we will see in this part, even when provisions of the Constitution that by their terms limit only governmental action are at issue, the state action doctrine is subject to exceptions or special cases. In particular, the **traditional public function exception** says that if private individuals are performing actions that have traditionally been performed exclusively by the government, their actions may be deemed to be state action. The **judicial enforcement exception** provides that, at least in some instances, a court's decision to uphold a private action may violate the Constitution. Finally, under the **joint participation exception**, sometimes when a private party and a state actor jointly participate in an activity, they are both engaged in state action.

POINTS FOR DISCUSSION

a. Structural and Institutional Considerations

As a matter of policy, why would the drafters of the Constitution have chosen to address—with the one significant exception discussed above—only state action and not the action of private citizens? The Supreme Court has explained that the state action requirement "preserves an area of individual freedom by limiting the reach of federal law and federal judicial power." *Lugar v. Edmonson Oil Co.*, 457 U.S. 922, 936 (1982). Can you think of an illustration of this idea? Can you think of any alternative explanation for why the drafters focused only on the conduct of the state and federal governments?

b. New Proposals

The ill-fated experiment with "Prohibition"—the constitutional ban on the manufacture, sale, or transportation of "intoxicating liquors"—for many years served as a cautionary tale for those who hoped to amend the Constitution to apply to private conduct. Nevertheless, in the last few decades there have been several proposals to amend the Constitution to prohibit certain forms of private action, though all have failed in Congress.

For example, a proposed amendment to prohibit "physical desecration of the flag" passed the House of Representatives in 2005 by the requisite two-thirds vote but fell one vote short in the Senate the following year. And a proposed amendment to define marriage as "the union of a man and a woman" failed to obtain the two-thirds majority in both houses of Congress. Why do you think that these amendments failed? Is it solely because of the strong feelings about the particular conduct regulated? Or did they fail in part because of a strong belief that the Constitution generally is not an appropriate vehicle for the regulation of private conduct?

Make the Connection

The proposed "flag burning" amendment was a response to the Supreme Court's decision in *Texas v. Johnson,* which we consider in Volume 2.

CHAPTER 7

The State Action Doctrine

A. THE GENERAL REQUIREMENT OF STATE ACTION

The decision in the *Civil Rights Cases*, 109 U.S. 3 (1883), which we consider below, concerned a collection of lawsuits arising under the Civil Rights Act of 1875. This sweeping legislation, enacted 89 years before the Civil Rights Act of 1964, would have banned most private racial discrimination in the United States. But the Supreme Court held that the legislation was unconstitutional, concluding that Congress lacked the power to address racial discrimination by private parties under either § 5 of the Fourteenth Amendment or § 2 of the Thirteenth Amendment.

> **Make the Connection**
>
> We consider Congress's power to enforce the Reconstruction Amendments in Volume 2.

The civil rights legislation and the decision are very important in the history of racial inequality in the United States. Most law students are familiar with how the Supreme Court led the drive to end discrimination in the mid-twentieth century in landmark decisions such as *Shelley v. Kraemer*, 334 U.S. 1 (1948), and *Brown v. Board of Education*, 347 U.S. 483 (1954). Some readers may be surprised to learn that Congress had sought to outlaw private racial discrimination in a sweeping law enacted decades earlier, but that the Supreme Court had invalidated the legislation.

The decision in the *Civil Rights Cases* is also significant because of the clarity with which it addressed the state action doctrine. A significant part of the Court's analysis under the Fourteenth Amendment concerned the fact that the challenged statute addressed private discrimination as opposed to discrimination by the government. Read the case carefully to discern the Court's logic.

THE CIVIL RIGHTS CASES

109 U.S. 3 (1883)

BRADLEY, J.

These cases are all founded on the first and second sections of the act of congress known as the "Civil Rights Act," passed March 1, 1875, entitled "An act to protect all citizens in their civil and legal rights." Two of the cases, those against Stanley and Nichols, are indictments for denying to persons of color the accommodations and privileges of an inn or hotel; two of them, those against Ryan and Singleton, are [for] denying to individuals the privileges and accommodations of a theater * * *. The case of Robinson and wife against the Memphis & Charleston Railroad Company [is] to recover the penalty of $500 given by the second section of the act; and the *gravamen* was the refusal by the conductor of the railroad company to allow the wife to ride in the ladies' car, for the reason, as stated in one of the counts, that she was a person of African descent. * * *

The Grand Opera House was the largest theater in New York City. Its proprietor, Singleton, was indicted for violating the Civil Rights Act by denying a person the full enjoyment of the Opera House because of his race.
James Dabney McCabe, *Lights and Shadows of New York Life* 474 (1872)

It is obvious that the primary and important question in all the cases is the constitutionality of the law; for if the law is unconstitutional none of the prosecutions can stand. * * * The sections of the law referred to provide as follows:

> Section 1. That all persons within the jurisdiction of the United States shall be entitled to the full and equal enjoyment of the accommodations, advantages, facilities, and privileges of inns, public conveyances on land or water, theaters, and other places of public amusement; subject only to the conditions and limitations established

by law, and applicable alike to citizens of every race and color, regardless of any previous condition of servitude.

Sec. 2. That any person who shall violate the foregoing section by denying to any citizen, except for reasons by law applicable to citizens of every race and color, and regardless of any previous condition of servitude, the full enjoyment of any of the accommodations, advantages, facilities, or privileges in said section enumerated, or by aiding or inciting such denial, shall, for every such offense, forfeit and pay the sum of $500 to the person aggrieved thereby, to be recovered in an action of debt, with full costs; and shall, also, for every such offense, be deemed guilty of a misdemeanor, and upon conviction thereof shall be fined not less than $500 nor more than $1,000, or shall be imprisoned not less than 30 days nor more than one year * * *.

Make the Connection

In Chapter 3, we saw in *Heart of Atlanta Motel v. United States* that the Court concluded that Congress had the power to enact the Civil Rights Act of 1964 under the Commerce Clause. How is the Civil Rights Act of 1875 different from that law?

Has congress constitutional power to make such a law? * * *

The first section of the fourteenth amendment—which is the one relied on—after declaring who shall be citizens of the United States, and of the several states, is prohibitory in its character, and prohibitory upon the states. * * * It is state action of a particular character that is prohibited. Individual invasion of individual rights is not the subject-matter of the amendment. It has a deeper and broader scope. It nullifies and makes void all state legislation, and state action of every kind, which impairs the privileges and immunities of citizens of the United States, or which injures them in life, liberty, or property without due process of law, or which denies to any of them the equal protection of the laws. It not only does this, but, in order that the national will, thus declared, may not be a mere *brutum fulmen*, the last section of the amendment invests congress with power to enforce it by appropriate legislation. To enforce what? To enforce the prohibition. To adopt appropriate legislation for correcting the effects of such prohibited state law and state acts, and thus to render them effectually null, void, and innocuous. This is the legislative power conferred upon congress, and this is the whole of it. It does not invest congress with power to legislate upon subjects which are within the domain of state

Definition

Brutum fulmen is Latin for "inert thunder"; figuratively, the phrase means "an empty noise" or "empty threat" or something that is ineffectual. See *Black's Law Dictionary* (9th ed. 2009).

legislation; but to provide modes of relief against state legislation, or state action, of the kind referred to. It does not authorize congress to create a code of municipal law for the regulation of private rights; but to provide modes of redress against the operation of state laws, and the action of state officers, executive or judicial, when these are subversive of the fundamental rights specified in the amendment. Positive rights and privileges are undoubtedly secured by the fourteenth amendment; but they are secured by way of prohibition against state laws and state proceedings affecting those rights and privileges, and by power given to congress to legislate for the purpose of carrying such prohibition into effect; and such legislation must necessarily be predicated upon such supposed state laws or state proceedings, and be directed to the correction of their operation and effect. * * *

Take Note

In these paragraphs, the Court concludes that the Fourteenth Amendment addresses only state action. Why does this conclusion matter in this case, which involves claims arising not under the Fourteenth Amendment but instead under a federal statute?

And so in the present case, until some state law has been passed, or some state action through its officers or agents has been taken, adverse to the rights of citizens sought to be protected by the fourteenth amendment, no legislation of the United States under said amendment, nor any proceeding under such legislation, can be called into activity, for the prohibitions of the amendment are against state laws and acts done under state authority. * * *

In this connection it is proper to state that civil rights, such as are guarantied by the constitution against state aggression, cannot be impaired by the wrongful acts of individuals, unsupported by state authority in the shape of laws, customs, or judicial or executive proceedings. The wrongful act of an individual, unsupported by any such authority, is simply a private wrong, or a crime of that individual; an invasion of the rights of the injured party, it is true, whether they affect his person, his property, or his reputation; but if not sanctioned in some way by the state, or not done under state authority, his rights remain in full force, and may presumably be vindicated by resort to the laws of the state for redress. An individual cannot deprive a man of his right to vote, to hold property, to buy and to sell, to sue in the courts, or to be a witness or a juror; he may, by force or fraud, interfere with the enjoyment of the right in a particular case; he may commit an assault against the person, or commit murder, or use ruffian violence at the polls, or slander the good name of a fellow-citizen; but unless protected in these wrongful acts by some shield of state law or state authority, he cannot destroy or injure the right; he will only render himself amenable to satisfaction or punishment; and amenable therefor to the laws of the state where the wrongful acts are committed. Hence, in all those cases where the constitution seeks to protect the rights of the citizen against discriminative and unjust laws of the state by prohibiting such laws, it is not individual offenses, but abrogation and denial of rights, which it denounces, and for which it clothes the congress with power to provide a remedy. This abrogation and denial of rights, for which the states alone were or could be responsible, was the great seminal and fundamental wrong which was intended to be remedied. And the remedy to be provided must necessarily be predicated upon that wrong. It must assume that in the cases provided for, the evil or wrong actually committed rests upon some state law or state authority for its excuse and perpetration.

Of course, these remarks do not apply to those cases in which congress is clothed with direct and plenary powers of legislation over the whole subject, accompanied with an express or implied denial of such power to the states, as in the regulation of commerce with foreign nations, among the several states, and with the Indian tribes, the coining of money, the establishment of post-offices and post-roads, the declaring of war, etc. In these cases congress has power to pass laws for regulating the subjects specified, in every detail, and the conduct and transactions of individuals respect thereof. But where a subject is not submitted to the general legislative power of congress, but is only submitted thereto for the purpose of rendering effective some prohibition against particular state legislation or state action in reference to that subject, the power given is limited by its object, and any legislation by congress in the matter must necessarily be corrective in its character, adapted to counteract and redress the operation of such prohibited state laws or proceedings of state officers.

[T]he power of congress to adopt direct and primary, as distinguished from corrective, legislation on the subject in hand, is sought, in the second place, from the thirteenth amendment, which abolishes slavery. * * * This amendment, as well as the fourteenth, is undoubtedly self-executing without any ancillary legislation, so far as its terms are applicable to any existing state of circumstances. By its own unaided force it abolished slavery, and established universal freedom. Still, legislation may be necessary and proper to meet all the various cases and circumstances to be affected by it, and to prescribe proper modes of redress for its violation in letter or spirit. And such legislation may be primary and direct in

> **Take Note**
>
> The Court here begins to discuss the Thirteenth Amendment, which it recognizes addresses private as well as state action. Why then does the Thirteenth Amendment not give Congress the power to pass the law at issue in this case?

its character; for the amendment is not a mere prohibition of state laws establishing or upholding slavery, but an absolute declaration that slavery or involuntary servitude shall not exist in any part of the United States.

Make the Connection

We discuss Congress's power to enforce the Thirteenth Amendment, and in particular the Court's decision in *Jones v. Alfred H. Mayer Co.*, 392 U.S. 409, 440 (1968), in Volume 2. The Court in *Jones* relied on this language in the *Civil Rights Cases*, and then concluded that "Congress has the power under the Thirteenth Amendment rationally to determine what are the badges and the incidents of slavery, and the authority to translate that determination into effective legislation."

It is true that slavery cannot exist without law any more than property in lands and goods can exist without law, and therefore the thirteenth amendment may be regarded as nullifying all state laws which establish or uphold slavery. But it has a reflex character also, establishing and decreeing universal civil and political freedom throughout the United States; and it is assumed that the power vested in congress to enforce the article by appropriate legislation, clothes congress with power to pass all laws necessary and proper for abolishing all badges and incidents of slavery in the United States; and upon this assumption it is claimed that this is sufficient authority for declaring by law that all persons shall have equal accommodations and privileges in all inns, public conveyances, and places of public amusement; the argument being that the denial of such equal accommodations and privileges is in itself a subjection to a species of servitude within the meaning of the amendment. Conceding the major proposition to be true, that congress has a right to enact all necessary and proper laws for the obliteration and prevention of slavery, with all its badges and incidents, is the minor proposition also true, that the denial to any person of admission to the accommodations and privileges of an inn, a public conveyance, or a theater, does subject that person to any form of servitude, or tend to fasten upon him any badge of slavery? If it does not, then power to pass the law is not found in the thirteenth amendment.

The long existence of African slavery in this country gave us very distinct notions of what it was, and what were its necessary incidents. Compulsory service of the slave for the benefit of the master, restraint of his movements except by the master's will, disability to hold property, to make contracts, to have a standing in court, to be a witness against a white person, and such like burdens and incapacities were the inseparable incidents of the institution. Severer punishments for crimes were imposed on the slave than on free persons guilty of the same offenses. * * * The only question under the present head, therefore, is, whether the refusal to any persons of the accommodations of an inn, or a public conveyance, or a place of public amusement, by an individual, and without any sanction or support from any state law or regulation, does inflict upon such persons any manner of servitude, or form of slavery, as those terms are understood in this country? * * *

After giving to these questions all the consideration which their importance demands, we are forced to the conclusion that such an act of refusal has nothing to do with slavery or involuntary servitude, and that if it is violative of any right of the party, his redress is to be sought under the laws of the state; or, if those laws are adverse to his rights and do not protect him, his remedy will be found in the corrective legislation which congress has adopted, or may adopt, for counteracting the effect of state laws, or state action, prohibited by the fourteenth amendment. It would be running the slavery argument into the ground to make it apply to every act of discrimination which a person may see fit to make as to the guests he will entertain, or as to the people he will take into his coach or cab or car, or admit to his concert or theater, or deal with in the matters of intercourse or business. Innkeepers and public carriers, by the laws of all the states, so far as we are aware, are bound, to the extent of their facilities, to furnish proper accommodation to all unobjectionable persons who in good faith apply for them. If the laws themselves make any unjust discrimination, amenable to the prohibitions of the fourteenth amendment, congress has full power to afford a remedy under that amendment and in accordance with it.

HARLAN, J., dissenting.

The thirteenth amendment, my brethren concede, did something more than to prohibit slavery as an *institution*, resting upon distinctions of race, and upheld by positive law. They admit that it established and decreed universal *civil freedom* throughout the United States. But did the freedom thus established involve nothing more than exemption from actual slavery? Was nothing more intended than to forbid one man from owning another as property? Was it the purpose of the nation simply to destroy the institution, and then remit the race, theretofore held in bondage, to the several states for such protection, in their civil rights, necessarily growing out of freedom, as those states, in their discretion, choose to provide? Were the states, against whose solemn protest the institution was destroyed, to be left perfectly free, so far as national interference was concerned, to make or allow discriminations against that race, as such, in the enjoyment of those fundamental rights that inhere in a state of freedom? * * *

Congress has not, in these matters, entered the domain of state control and supervision. It does not assume to prescribe the general conditions and limitations under which inns, public conveyances, and places of public amusement shall be conducted or managed. It simply declares in effect that since the nation has established universal freedom in this country for all time, there shall be no discrimination, based merely upon race or color, in respect of the legal rights in the accommodations and advantages of public conveyances, inns, and places of public amusement.

I am of the opinion that such discrimination practiced by corporations and individuals in the exercise of their public or quasi-public functions is a badge of servitude, the imposition of which congress may prevent under its power [by] appropriate legislation, to enforce the thirteenth amendment; and consequently, without reference to its enlarged power under the fourteenth amendment, the act of March 1, 1875, is not, in my judgment, repugnant to the constitution.

It remains now to consider these cases with reference to the power congress has possessed since the adoption of the fourteenth amendment. The assumption that this amendment consists wholly of prohibitions upon state laws and state proceedings in hostility to its provisions, is unauthorized by its language. The first clause of the first section—"all persons born or naturalized in the United States, and subject to the jurisdiction thereof, are citizens of the United States, and of the state wherein they reside"—is of a distinctly affirmative character. In its application to the colored race, previously liberated, it created and granted, as well citizenship of the United States, as citizenship of the state in which they respectively resided. It introduced all of that race, whose ancestors had been imported and sold as slaves, at once, into the political community known as the "People of the United States." They became, instantly, citizens of the United States, and of their respective states. Further, they were brought, by this supreme act of the nation, within the direct operation of that provision of the constitution which declares that "the citizens of each state shall be entitled to all privileges and immunities of citizens in the several states."

But what was secured to colored citizens of the United States—as between them and their respective states—by the grant to them of state citizenship? With what rights, privileges, or immunities did this grant from the nation invest them? There is one, if there be no others—exemption from race discrimination in respect of any civil right belonging to citizens of the white race in the same state. That, surely, is their constitutional privilege when within the jurisdiction of other states. And such must be their constitutional right, in their own state, unless the recent amendments be "splendid baubles," thrown out to delude those who deserved fair and generous treatment at the hands of the nation. Citizenship in this country necessarily imports equality of civil rights among citizens of every race in the same state. It is fundamental in American citizenship that, in respect of such rights, there shall be no discrimination by the state, or its officers, or by individuals, or corporations exercising public functions or authority, against any citizen because of his race or previous condition of servitude. * * *

POINTS FOR DISCUSSION

a. The Fourteenth Amendment

The "syllogism" is a form of reasoning that consists of a major premise, a minor premise, and a conclusion. A classic example of a syllogism is as follows: All men are mortal; Socrates is a man; therefore, Socrates is mortal. In the *Civil Rights Cases*, the syllogism for the Fourteenth Amendment issue appears to be this: Section 5 of the Fourteenth Amendment gives Congress only the power to address violations of § 1 of the Fourteenth Amendment; private discrimination does not violate § 1 of the Fourteenth Amendment; therefore, § 5 does not give Congress the power to address private discrimination.

How does the Court explain its minor premise (i.e. that private discrimination does not violate § 1)? Why does the dissent disagree with the majority on this point? Note that the Supreme Court used the same reasoning in *United States v. Morrison*, 529 U.S. 598 (2000), which we consider (in relevant part) in Volume 2. In *Morrison*, the Court concluded that Congress could not use its power under § 5 of the Fourteenth Amendment to prohibit gender-motivated violence by private actors because § 1 of the Amendment does not apply to purely private conduct. If the Court's minor premise in the *Civil Rights Cases* was wrong, does that mean that the Court was wrong in *Morrison*, as well?

b. The Thirteenth Amendment

According to the Court, what justifies the conclusion that only state action can violate the Fourteenth Amendment even though (in its view) certain types of private action can violate the Thirteenth Amendment? What is the disagreement between the majority and dissent with respect to the Thirteenth Amendment?

c. The State Action Doctrine and Federalism

If the Constitution does not limit the actions of private individuals, then any restrictions on their actions must come from legislation or the common law. If Congress lacks the power to regulate certain forms of private conduct, then any limitations on that conduct must come from state law (if at all). Does it make sense to leave to the states the sole authority to determine the legality of private discrimination? Even if it makes sense today, did it make sense in 1883, when the Court decided the *Civil Rights Cases*? What does the Court's reasoning suggest more generally about the ability of the United States to address social problems? What has history shown?

d. Missed Opportunity to End Racial Discrimination?

How different would the United States have been if the Supreme Court had upheld the Civil Rights Act of 1875? Immediately after the Supreme Court decided the *Civil Rights Cases*, did Congress miss an opportunity to use the Commerce Clause as an alternative source of power for enacting the law? In a portion of the opinion omitted here, the Court suggested that Congress might have power to end discrimination in the territories and the District of Columbia, which are subject to plenary regulation by Congress. Should Congress at least have responded to the Court's decision by enacting such a statute?

B. THE PUBLIC FUNCTION EXCEPTION

As explained above, the state action doctrine rests on the conclusion that the Constitution generally addresses the conduct of the government but not private parties. This principle raises several important questions: What happens when private parties assume the functions traditionally undertaken by the state? Can the government evade the Constitution's requirements by outsourcing governmental functions to private parties? For example, suppose that a town's police department hires a private detective to look for clues. Can the private detective search any building without a warrant and then successfully argue that the search did not violate the Fourth Amendment because a private detective is not a state actor?

The Supreme Court has addressed these questions by creating what has become known as the **public function exception** to the state action doctrine. Under the public function exception, private parties may be deemed to be state actors when they engage in activities "traditionally exclusively reserved to the State." *Jackson v. Metropolitan Edison Co.*, 419 U.S. 345, 352 (1974). In reading the cases that follow, attempt to discern which public functions are "traditionally exclusively" reserved to the state.

MARSH V. STATE OF ALABAMA

326 U.S. 501 (1946)

MR. JUSTICE BLACK delivered the opinion of the Court.

In this case we are asked to decide whether a State, consistently with the First and Fourteenth Amendments, can impose criminal punishment on a person who undertakes to distribute religious literature on the premises of a company-owned town contrary to the wishes of the town's management. The town, a suburb of Mobile, Alabama, known as Chickasaw, is owned by the Gulf Shipbuilding Corporation. Except for that it has all the characteristics of any other American town. The property consists of residential buildings, streets, a system of sewers, a sewage disposal plant and a "business block" on which business places are situated. A deputy of the Mobile County Sheriff, paid by the company, serves as the town's policeman. Merchants and service establishments have rented the stores and business places on the business block and the United States uses one of the places as a post office from which six carriers deliver mail to the people of Chickasaw and the adjacent area. The town and the surrounding neighborhood, which cannot be distinguished from the Gulf property by anyone not familiar with the property lines, are thickly settled, and according to all indications the residents use the business block as their regular shopping center. To do so, they now, as they have for many years, make use of a company-owned paved street and sidewalk located alongside the store fronts in order to enter and leave the stores and the post office. Intersecting company-owned roads at each end of the business block lead into a four-lane public highway which runs parallel to the business block at a distance of thirty feet. There is nothing to stop highway traffic from coming onto the business block and upon arrival a traveler may make free use of the facilities available there. In short the town and its shopping district are accessible to and freely used by the public in general and there is nothing to distinguish them from any other town and shopping center except the fact that the title to the property belongs to a private corporation.

Appellant, a Jehovah's Witness, came onto the sidewalk we have just described, stood near the post-office and undertook to distribute religious literature. In the stores the corporation had posted a notice which read as follows: "This Is Private Property, and Without Written Permission, No Street, or House Vendor, Agent or Solicitation of Any Kind Will Be Permitted." Appellant was warned that she could not distribute the literature without a permit and told that no permit would be issued to her. She protested that the company rule could not be constitutionally applied so as to prohibit her from distributing religious writings. When she was asked to leave the sidewalk and Chickasaw she declined. The deputy sheriff arrested her and she was charged in the state court with violating Title 14, Section 426 of the 1940 Alabama Code which makes it a crime to enter or remain on the premises of another after having been warned not to do so. Appellant contended that to construe the state statute as applicable to her activities would abridge her right to freedom of press and religion contrary to the First and Fourteenth Amendments to the Constitution. This contention was rejected and she was convicted. * * *

Had the title to Chickasaw belonged not to a private but to a municipal corporation and had appellant been arrested for violating a municipal ordinance rather than a ruling by those appointed by the corporation to manage a company-town it would have been clear that appellant's conviction must be reversed. Under our decision in *Lovell v. Griffin*, 303 U.S. 444 (1938), and others which have followed that case, neither a state nor a municipality can completely bar the distribution of literature containing religious or political ideas on its streets, sidewalks and public places or make the right to distribute dependent on a flat license tax or permit to be issued by an official who could deny it at will. * * * From these decisions it is clear that had the people of Chickasaw owned all the homes, and all the stores, and all the streets, and all the sidewalks, all those owners together could not have set up a municipal government with sufficient power to pass an ordinance completely barring the distribution of religious literature. Our question then narrows down to this: Can those people who live in or come to Chickasaw be denied freedom of press and religion simply because a single company has legal title to all the town? For it is the state's contention that the mere fact that all the property interests in the town are held by a single company is enough to give that company power, enforceable by a state statute, to abridge these freedoms.

> **Make the Connection**
>
> Why does the First Amendment prohibit an ordinary municipality from barring the distribution of literature on a public sidewalk? We address questions of this sort in Volume 2.

We do not agree that the corporation's property interests settle the question. The State urges in effect that the corporation's right to control the inhabitants of Chickasaw is coextensive with the right of a homeowner to regulate the conduct of his guests. We can not accept that contention. Ownership does not always mean absolute dominion. The more an owner, for his advantage, opens up his property for use by the public in general, the more do his rights become circumscribed by the statutory and constitutional rights of those who use it. Thus, the owners of privately held bridges, ferries, turnpikes and railroads may not operate them as freely as a farmer does his farm. Since these facilities are built and operated primarily to benefit the public and since their operation is essentially a public function, it is subject to state regulation. And, though the issue is not directly analogous to the one before us we do want to point out by way of illustration that such regulation may not result in an operation of these facilities, even by privately owned companies, which unconstitutionally interferes with and discriminates against interstate commerce. * * *

We do not think it makes any significant constitutional difference as to the relationship between the rights of the owner and those of the public that here the State, instead of permitting the corporation to operate a highway, permitted it to use its property as a town, operate a "business block" in the town and a street and sidewalk on that business block. Whether a corporation or a municipality owns or possesses the town the public in either case has an identical interest in the functioning of the community in such manner that the channels of communication remain free. As we have heretofore stated, the town of Chickasaw does not function differently from any other town. The "business block" serves as the community shopping center and is freely accessible and open to the people in the area and those passing through. The managers appointed by the corporation cannot curtail the liberty of press and religion of these people consistently with the purposes of the Constitutional guarantees, and a state statute, as the one here involved, which enforces such action by criminally punishing those who attempt to distribute religious literature clearly violates the First and Fourteenth Amendments to the Constitution.

Many people in the United States live in company-owned towns. These people, just as residents of municipalities, are free citizens of their State and country. Just as all other citizens they must make decisions which affect the welfare of community and nation. To act as good citizens they must be informed. In order to enable them to be properly informed their information must be uncensored. There is no more reason for depriving these people of the liberties guaranteed by the First and Fourteenth Amendments than there is for curtailing these freedoms with respect to any other citizen. * * * Reversed and remanded.

MR. JUSTICE REED, [joined by the CHIEF JUSTICE and MR. JUSTICE BURTON,] dissenting.

Our Constitution guarantees to every man the right to express his views in an orderly fashion. An essential element of "orderly" is that the man shall also have a right to use the place he chooses for his exposition. The rights of the owner, which the Constitution protects as well as the right of free speech, are not outweighed by the interests of the trespasser, even though he trespasses in behalf of religion or free speech. We cannot say that Jehovah's Witnesses can claim the privilege of a license, which has never been granted, to hold their meetings in other private places, merely because the owner has admitted the public to them for other limited purposes. Even though we have reached the point where this Court is required to force private owners to open their property for the practice there of religious activities or propaganda distasteful to the owner, because of the public interest in freedom of speech and religion, there is no need for the application of such a doctrine here. Appellant, as we have said, was free to engage in such practices on the public highways, without becoming a trespasser on the company's property.

POINTS FOR DISCUSSION

a. Competing First Amendment Rights?

The Court discusses some of the consequences that might flow if the Court were to conclude that this case did not involve state action. In particular, the opinion asserts that millions of Americans who live in company towns would not have the full protection that the Constitution provides in traditional, state-run municipalities. But what are the consequences of the Court's decision that there *is* state action? Must the Gulf Ship Building Company provide all of the rights that a state would? For example, must it hold elections for a local government?

What are the implications of the holding in *Marsh* for ordinary rights of free association? Suppose that all of the property in the town were owned not by a corporation but instead by one private individual. Does the Court's holding mean that this private individual would not be able to choose which messages, religious or otherwise, are distributed on his property? Do ordinary property owners face a similar limitation? If not, doesn't the Court's holding in *Marsh* abridge the free speech or associational rights of the property owner?

b. Public Function Exception or State Involvement?

Is the Court's conclusion in *Marsh* based on the fact that the company that owns the town is effectively acting in a "public" capacity? The Court reasoned that if individual owners of property joined together to establish a municipality, they could not evade the limits that the Constitution imposes on state action, and that the company here similarly was effectively acting in a public capacity. But the Court also stated that "a state statute, as the one here involved, which enforces [the exclusion of the appellant] by criminally punishing those who attempt to distribute religious literature clearly violates the First and Fourteenth Amendments to the Constitution." Does that mean that the state action requirement was satisfied by the judicial enforcement of the state ordinance that makes it a crime to enter or remain on the premises of another after having been warned not to do so? We will consider this theory of state action below, when we discuss *Shelley v. Kraemer*.

c. Company Towns

Company towns flourished in the United States at the start of the twentieth century. Businesses built them near factories and mines to house employees who otherwise could not afford housing or could not travel long distances to work because they lacked transportation. Company towns became less common with the advent of cars, and only a few traditional company towns still exist. Indeed, in modern times, a complete reversal has occurred; to promote employment and economic growth, some communities now provide sites for factories. See Marilyn Geewax, "*Company Towns" are Back, but not Like the Old Days*, Atlanta Const., Jan. 7, 1996, at G3.

The Court held in *Marsh v. Alabama* that a company town serves a traditional public function. This conclusion certainly seems plausible because towns ordinarily are run by governments, not by businesses. But what about something smaller than a company town, such as a large shopping mall that serves only some, but not all, of the functions of a town? This question vexed the Supreme Court for many years, but was finally resolved in the case that follows.

HUDGENS V. NATIONAL LABOR RELATIONS BOARD

424 U.S. 507 (1976)

MR. JUSTICE STEWART delivered the opinion of the Court.

A group of labor union members who engaged in peaceful primary picketing within the confines of a privately owned shopping center were threatened by an agent of the owner with arrest for criminal trespass if they did not depart. * * * The petitioner, Scott Hudgens, is the owner of the North DeKalb Shopping Center, located in suburban Atlanta, Ga. The center consists of a single large building with an enclosed mall. Surrounding the building is a parking area which can accommodate 2,640 automobiles. The shopping center houses 60 retail stores leased to various businesses. One of the lessees is the Butler Shoe Co. Most of the stores, including Butler's, can be entered only from the interior mall.

In January 1971, warehouse employees of the Butler Shoe Co. went on strike to protest the company's failure to agree to demands made by their union in contract negotiations. The strikers decided to picket not only Butler's warehouse but its nine retail stores in the Atlanta area as well, including the store in the North DeKalb Shopping Center. On January 22, 1971, four of the striking warehouse employees entered the center's enclosed mall carrying placards which read: "Butler Shoe Warehouse on Strike, AFL-CIO, Local 315." The general manager of the shopping center informed the employees that they could not picket within the mall or on the parking lot and threatened them with arrest if they did not leave. The employees departed but returned a short time later and began picketing in an area of the mall immediately adjacent to the entrances of the Butler store. After the picketing had continued for approximately 30 minutes, the shopping center manager again informed the pickets that if they did not leave they would be arrested for trespassing. The pickets departed.

It is, of course, a commonplace that the constitutional guarantee of free speech is a guarantee only against abridgment by government, federal or state. Thus, while statutory or common law may in some situations extend protection or provide redress against a private corporation or person who seeks to abridge the free expression of others, no such protection or redress is provided by the Constitution itself.

This elementary proposition is little more than a truism. But even truisms are not always unexceptionably true, and an exception to this one was recognized almost 30 years ago in *Marsh v. Alabama*, 326 U.S. 501 (1946). * * * It was the *Marsh* case that in 1968 provided the foundation for the Court's decision in *Amalgamated Food Employees Union v. Logan Valley Plaza*, 391 U.S. 308 (1968). That case involved peaceful picketing within a large shopping center near Altoona, Pa. One of the tenants of the shopping center was a retail store that employed a wholly nonunion staff. Members of a local union picketed the store, carrying signs proclaiming that it was nonunion and that its employees were not receiving union wages or other union benefits. The picketing took place on the shopping center's property in the immediate vicinity of the store. A Pennsylvania court issued an injunction that required all picketing to be confined to public areas outside the shopping center, and the Supreme Court of Pennsylvania affirmed the issuance of this injunction. This Court held that the doctrine of the *Marsh* case required reversal of that judgment.

The Court's opinion pointed out that the First and Fourteenth Amendments would clearly have protected the picketing if it had taken place on a public sidewalk: "[S]treets, sidewalks, parks, and other similar public places are so historically associated with the exercise of First Amendment rights that access to them for the purpose of exercising such rights cannot constitutionally be denied broadly and absolutely." The Court's opinion then reviewed the *Marsh* case in detail, emphasized the similarities between the business block in Chickasaw, Ala., and the Logan Valley shopping center and unambiguously concluded: "The shopping center here is clearly the functional equivalent of the business district of Chickasaw involved in *Marsh*." Upon the basis of that conclusion, the Court held that the First and Fourteenth Amendments required reversal of the judgment of the Pennsylvania Supreme Court.

Four years later the Court had occasion to reconsider the *Logan Valley* doctrine in *Lloyd Corp. v. Tanner*, 407 U.S. 551 (1972). That case involved a shopping center covering some 50 acres in downtown Portland, Ore. On a

November day in 1968 five young people entered the mall of the shopping center and distributed handbills protesting the then ongoing American military operations in Vietnam. Security guards told them to leave, and they did so, "to avoid arrest." They subsequently brought suit in a Federal District Court, seeking declaratory and injunctive relief. The trial court ruled in their favor, holding that the distribution of handbills on the shopping center's property was protected by the First and Fourteenth Amendments. The Court of Appeals for the Ninth Circuit affirmed the judgment, expressly relying on this Court's *Marsh* and *Logan Valley* decisions. This Court reversed the judgment of the Court of Appeals.

The Court in its *Lloyd* opinion did not say that it was overruling the *Logan Valley* decision. Indeed a substantial portion of the Court's opinion in *Lloyd* was devoted to pointing out the differences between the two cases, noting particularly that, in contrast to the hand-billing in *Lloyd*, the picketing in *Logan Valley* had been specifically directed to a store in the shopping center and the pickets had had no other reasonable opportunity to reach their intended audience. But the fact is that the reasoning of the Court's opinion in *Lloyd* cannot be squared with the reasoning of the Court's opinion in *Logan Valley*.

It matters not that some Members of the Court may continue to believe that the *Logan Valley* case was rightly decided. Our institutional duty is to follow until changed the law as it now is, not as some Members of the Court might wish it to be. And in the performance of that duty we make clear now, if it was not clear before, that the rationale of *Logan Valley* did not survive the Court's decision in the *Lloyd* case.

If a large self-contained shopping center is the functional equivalent of a municipality, as *Logan Valley* held, then the First and Fourteenth Amendments would not permit control of speech within such a center to depend upon the speech's content. For while a municipality may constitutionally impose reasonable time, place, and manner regulations on the use of its streets and sidewalks for First Amendment purposes, and may even forbid altogether such use of some of its facilities, what a municipality may not do under the First and Fourteenth Amendments is to discriminate in the regulation of expression on the basis of the content of that expression. * * * It conversely follows, therefore, that if the respondents in the *Lloyd* case did not have a First Amendment right to enter that shopping center to distribute handbills concerning Vietnam, then the pickets in the present case did not have a First Amendment right to enter this shopping center for the purpose of advertising their strike against the Butler Shoe Co.

We conclude, in short, that under the present state of the law the constitutional guarantee of free expression has no part to play in a case such as this. * * * Vacated and remanded.

MR. JUSTICE MARSHALL, with whom MR. JUSTICE BRENNAN joins, dissenting.

The Court adopts the view that *Marsh* has no bearing on this case because the privately owned property in *Marsh* involved all the characteristics of a typical town. But there is nothing in *Marsh* to suggest that its general approach was limited to the particular facts of that case. The underlying concern in *Marsh* was that traditional public channels of communication remain free, regardless of the incidence of ownership. Given that concern, the crucial fact in *Marsh* was that the company owned the traditional forums essential for effective communication; it was immaterial that the company also owned a sewer system and that its property in other respects resembled a town.

In *Logan Valley* we recognized what the Court today refuses to recognize[:] that the owner of the modern shopping center complex, by dedicating his property to public use as a business district, to some extent displaces the "State" from control of historical First Amendment forums, and may acquire a virtual monopoly of places suitable for effective communication. The roadways, parking lots, and walkways of the modern shopping center may be as essential for effective speech as the streets and sidewalks in the municipal or company-owned town. I simply cannot reconcile the Court's denial of any role for the First Amendment in the shopping center with *Marsh*'s recognition of a full rule for the First Amendment on the streets and sidewalks of the company-owned town.

POINTS FOR DISCUSSION

a. Distinguishing a Company Town from a Shopping Center

The Court in *Marsh* made clear that the owner of a company town serves a traditional public function, whereas the Court in *Hudgens* concluded that the owner of a large shopping mall does not. Accordingly, the former is a state actor limited by the First Amendment, while the latter is not. What factors differentiate the two? What factors should be most important? Does the Court's willingness in *Hudgens* to overrule *Logan Valley* suggest that *Marsh* is vulnerable to the same fate?

b. Universities and Company Towns

Private university campuses are sometimes similar to company towns. They have residence halls where students sleep, cafeterias where they eat, stores where they can shop, buildings where they study and work, sidewalks, stadiums, open gathering places, and so forth. If a private university limits speech on campus, does it violate the First Amendment under the public function exception to the state action doctrine? In other words, is a private university more like a company town or a shopping mall? What arguments might you make for each side? Can the issue be avoided by concluding that higher education is not traditionally an *exclusively* public function? See *Greenya v. George Washington University*, 512 F.2d 556, 561 n.10 (1975).

C. THE JUDICIAL ENFORCEMENT EXCEPTION

The **judicial enforcement exception** to the state action doctrine provides that some private action can effectively become public action when a court acts to uphold the private action. The exception begins with the unobjectionable premise that judicial decisions are a form of state action; after all, judges and courts are part of the government. The theory of the exception is that although private conduct alone does not violate the Constitution, a court's enforcement of that private conduct may constitute state action. Thus, in the famous case of *Shelley v. Kraemer*, 334 U.S. 1 (1948), the Supreme Court concluded that although private homeowners do not violate the Constitution by engaging in race discrimination against prospective neighbors, a state court violates the Equal Protection Clause by enforcing such private discrimination. In reading the case, think carefully about how far this logic should extend.

SHELLEY V. KRAEMER

334 U.S. 1 (1948)

MR. CHIEF JUSTICE VINSON delivered the opinion of the Court.

On February 16, 1911, thirty out of a total of thirty-nine owners of property fronting both sides of Labadie Avenue between Taylor Avenue and Cora Avenue in the city of St. Louis signed an agreement, which was subsequently recorded, providing in part:

> [T]he said property is hereby restricted to the use and occupancy for the term of Fifty (50) years from this date, so that it shall be a condition all the time and [in] subsequent conveyances and shall attach to the land, as a condition precedent to the sale of the same, that hereafter no part of said property or any portion thereof shall be, for said term of Fifty-years, occupied by any person not of the Caucasian race * * *.

On August 11, 1945, pursuant to a contract of sale, petitioners Shelley, who are Negroes, for valuable consideration received from one Fitzgerald a warranty deed to [a house subject to this restrictive covenant]. * * * On October 9, 1945, respondents, as owners of other property subject to the terms of the restrictive covenant, brought suit in Circuit Court of the city of St. Louis praying that petitioners Shelley be restrained from taking possession of the property and that judgment be entered divesting title out of petitioners Shelley and revesting title in the immediate grantor or in such other person as the court should direct. * * * The Supreme Court of Missouri sitting en banc * * * held the agreement effective and concluded that enforcement of its provisions violated no rights guaranteed to petitioners by the Federal Constitution. At the time the court rendered its decision, petitioners were occupying the property in question. [A companion case involved the enforcement of a similar restrictive covenant.]

Take Note

To transfer land to a buyer, the seller must sign a written document called a "deed," which describes the property being sold. A "warranty deed" contains guarantees assuring the buyer that the others will not challenge the transfer in various ways. The "valuable consideration" is the price that the Shelleys paid for the property.

It is * * * clear that restrictions on the right of occupancy of the sort sought to be created by the private agreements in these cases could not be squared with the requirements of the Fourteenth Amendment if imposed by state statute or local ordinance. We do not understand respondents to urge the contrary. In the case of *Buchanan v. Warley*, 245 U.S. 60 (1917), a unanimous Court declared unconstitutional the provisions of a city ordinance which denied to colored persons the right to occupy houses in blocks in which the greater number of houses were occupied by white persons, and imposed similar restrictions on white persons with respect to blocks in which the greater number of houses were occupied by colored persons. During the course of the opinion in that case, this Court stated: "The Fourteenth Amendment and these statutes enacted in furtherance of its purpose operate to qualify and entitle a colored man to acquire property without state legislation discriminating against him solely because of color."

FYI

Buchanan v. Warley was litigated by the NAACP and was one of the organization's earliest judicial victories in campaigning for equal rights. Although the decision did not end all discrimination in residential housing, it was still "a symbolic watershed, showing that civil rights progress could be made through the courts." Susan D. Carle, *Race, Class, and Legal Ethics in the Early NAACP (1910–1920)*, 20 Law & Hist. Rev. 97, 128 (2002).

But the present cases, unlike those just discussed, do not involve action by state legislatures or city councils. Here the particular patterns of discrimination and the areas in which the restrictions are to operate, are determined, in the first instance, by the terms of agreements among private individuals. Participation of the State consists in the enforcement of the restrictions so defined. The crucial issue with which we are here confronted is whether this distinction removes these cases from the operation of the prohibitory provisions of the Fourteenth Amendment.

Since the decision of this Court in the *Civil Rights Cases*, 109 U.S. 3 (1883), the principle has become firmly embedded in our constitutional law that the action inhibited by the first section of the Fourteenth Amendment is only such action as may fairly be said to be that of the States. That Amendment erects no shield against merely private conduct, however discriminatory or wrongful.

We conclude, therefore, that the restrictive agreements standing alone cannot be regarded as a violation of any rights guaranteed to petitioners by the Fourteenth Amendment. So long as the purposes of those agreements are effectuated by voluntary adherence to their terms, it would appear clear that there has been no action by the State and the provisions of the Amendment have not been violated.

But here there was more. These are cases in which the purposes of the agreements were secured only by judicial enforcement by state courts of the restrictive terms of the agreements. The respondents urge that judicial enforcement of private agreements does not amount to state action; or, in any event, the participation of the State is so attenuated in character as not to amount to state action within the meaning of the Fourteenth Amendment. Finally, it is suggested, even if the States in these cases may be deemed to have acted in the constitutional sense, their action did not deprive petitioners of rights guaranteed by the Fourteenth Amendment. We move to a consideration of these matters.

That the action of state courts and of judicial officers in their official capacities is to be regarded as action of the State within the meaning of the Fourteenth Amendment, is a proposition which has long been established by decisions of this Court. That principle was given expression in the earliest cases involving the construction of the terms of the Fourteenth Amendment. * * *

One of the earliest applications of the prohibitions contained in the Fourteenth Amendment to action of state judicial officials occurred in cases in which Negroes had been excluded from jury service in criminal prosecutions by reason of their race or color. These cases demonstrate, also, the early recognition by this Court that state action in violation of the Amendment's provisions is equally repugnant to the constitutional commands whether directed by state statute or taken by a judicial official in the absence of statute. Thus, in *Strauder v. West Virginia*, 100 U.S. 303 (1880), this Court declared invalid a state statute restricting jury service to white persons as amounting to a denial of the equal protection of the laws to the colored defendant in that case. * * *

> **Make the Connection**
>
> We consider the Court's decision in *Strauder*, and discrimination on the basis of race, in Volume 2.

We have no doubt that there has been state action in these cases in the full and complete sense of the phrase. The undisputed facts disclose that petitioners were willing purchasers of properties upon which they desired to establish homes. The owners of the properties were willing sellers; and contracts of sale were accordingly consummated. It is clear that but for the active intervention of the state courts, supported by the full panoply of state power, petitioners would have been free to occupy the properties in question without restraint.

These are not cases, as has been suggested, in which the States have merely abstained from action, leaving private individuals free to impose such discriminations as they see fit. Rather, these are cases in which the States have made available to such individuals the full coercive power of government to deny to petitioners, on the grounds of race or color, the enjoyment of property rights in premises which petitioners are willing and financially able to acquire and which the grantors are willing to sell. The difference between judicial enforcement and nonenforcement of the restrictive covenants is the difference to petitioners between being denied rights of property available to other members of the community and being accorded full enjoyment of those rights on an equal footing.

> **Take Note**
>
> The Court explains here why this case involves state action even if private racial discrimination is not state action. Suppose that the case involved instead a claim for an injunction to enforce a contractual provision that prohibited the parties from publicly discussing the terms of a prior settlement. Would a court's grant of such an injunction to enforce a private agreement constitute state action in violation of the First Amendment? If not, why is this case different?

Respondents urge, however, that since the state courts stand ready to enforce restrictive covenants excluding white persons from the ownership or occupancy of property covered by such agreements, enforcement of covenants excluding colored persons may not be deemed a denial of equal protection of the laws to the colored persons who are thereby affected. This contention does not bear scrutiny. * * * The rights created by the first section of the Fourteenth Amendment are, by its terms, guaranteed to the individual. The rights established are personal rights. It is, therefore, no answer to these petitioners to say that the courts may also be induced to deny white persons rights of ownership and occupancy on grounds of race or color. Equal protection of the laws is not achieved through indiscriminate imposition of inequalities. Nor do we find merit in the suggestion that property owners who are parties to these agreements are denied equal protection of the laws if denied access to the courts to enforce the terms of restrictive covenants and to assert property rights which the state courts have held to be created by such agreements. The Constitution confers upon no individual the right to demand action by the State which results in the denial of equal protection of the laws to other individuals. And it would appear beyond question that the power of the State to create and enforce property interests must be exercised within the boundaries defined by the Fourteenth Amendment. Cf. *Marsh v. Alabama*, 326 U.S. 501 (1946).

[Reversed.]

POINTS FOR DISCUSSION

a. How Far Does *Shelley's* Reasoning Extend?

The Court concluded in *Shelley* that judicial enforcement of the racially restrictive covenants would involve state action because judges and courts are state actors. Many scholars have questioned this reasoning. Dean Erwin Chemerinsky, for example, writes:

> If any decision by a state court represents state action, then ultimately all private actions must comply with the Constitution. Anyone who believes that his or her rights have been violated can sue in state court. If the court dismisses the case because the state law does not forbid the violation, there is state action sustaining the infringement of the right * * *. It is difficult to imagine anything that cannot be transformed into state action under this reasoning. * * * The Court [never] has taken *Shelley* this far, but nor has it articulated any clear limiting principles.

Erwin Chemerinsky, *Constitutional Law: Principles and Policies* 528 (3d ed. 2006). See also Kimberly A. Yuracko, *Education Off the Grid: Constitutional Constraints on Homeschooling*, 96 Cal. L. Rev. 123, 151–178 (2008) (discussing three different views about how far *Shelley* should be interpreted to extend).

Consider this example: In *Hudgens v. National Labor Relations Board*, 424 U.S. 507 (1976), the Supreme Court held that a private shopping mall's decision to exclude picketers was not state action. The Court therefore upheld the action. Wasn't the Supreme Court's action in enforcing the shopping mall's decision to exclude the picketers itself a form of state action? Did the Court's action convert the shopping mall's otherwise private action into state action? If not, how does this example differ from the circumstances at issue in *Shelley*? Can you articulate a limiting principle for the rule announced in *Shelley*?

b. Current Federal Law and Discrimination in Housing

When the Court decided *Shelley*, racially restrictive covenants did not violate federal (or, for that matter, state) statutory law. It also was not clear at the time whether Congress had power (even assuming that it had the will) under the Commerce Clause to prohibit the use or enforcement of such restrictive covenants. Given the analytical problems that the decision raises, is it fair to conclude that the Court's resolution of the question in *Shelley* reflected more the Court's concern that there was no effective way to stop this invidious practice than it did the Court's view about the state action doctrine?

Congress eventually did act. Title VIII of the Civil Rights Act of 1968 now prohibits discrimination on the basis of race (or other status-based distinctions) in the sale, rental, or financing of housing. 42 U.S.C. § 3601 *et seq.* In light of the Court's reasoning in *Shelley*, did Congress have authority to enact this statute pursuant to its authority to enforce the Fourteenth Amendment? (We consider that power in Volume 2.) If not, does the Commerce Clause as currently interpreted confer the requisite authority? (Recall our consideration in Chapter 3 of Congress's power under the Commerce Clause.)

D. THE JOINT PARTICIPATION (OR ENTANGLEMENT) EXCEPTION

The Supreme Court also has recognized the **joint participation exception** (sometimes called the **entanglement exception**) to the state action doctrine. Under this doctrine, some private parties will be deemed to be state actors in certain circumstances when they are acting with the state or state officers. The Supreme Court has held that a private party may be held liable for a deprivation of a constitutional right if two elements are present:

> First, the deprivation must be caused by the exercise of some right or privilege created by the State or by a rule of conduct imposed by the state or by a person for whom the State is responsible. * * * Second, the party charged with the deprivation must be a person who may fairly be said to be a state actor. This may be because he is a state official, because he has acted together with or has obtained significant aid from state officials, or because his conduct is otherwise chargeable to the State.

Lugar v. Edmondson Oil Co., 457 U.S. 922, 937 (1982).

The second of these two elements—that the private party "may fairly be said to be a state actor"—is, as its terms suggest, an indefinite standard. The only way to determine whether this element is satisfied is to consider all the facts and to compare them to the Court's precedents. Consider the cases that follow.

BURTON V. WILMINGTON PARKING AUTHORITY

365 U.S. 715 (1961)

MR. JUSTICE CLARK delivered the opinion of the Court.

In this action for declaratory and injunctive relief it is admitted that the Eagle Coffee Shoppe, Inc., a restaurant located within an off-street automobile parking building in Wilmington, Delaware, has refused to serve appellant food or drink solely because he is a Negro. The parking building is owned and operated by the Wilmington Parking Authority, an agency of the State of Delaware, and the restaurant is the Authority's lessee. Appellant claims that such refusal abridges his rights under the Equal Protection Clause of the Fourteenth Amendment to the United States Constitution. The Supreme Court of Delaware has held that Eagle was acting in "a purely private capacity" under its lease; that its action was not that of the Authority and was not, therefore, state action within the contemplation of the prohibitions contained in that Amendment. It also held that under 24 Del. Code § 1501,[1] Eagle was a restaurant * * * and that as such it "is not required (under Delaware law) to serve any and all persons entering its place of business." * * *

FYI

William "Dutch" Burton was a city councilman in Wilmington. His lawyer was Louis Redding. Redding had been the only black person in the Harvard Law School class of 1928, and he was the first black attorney in the state of Delaware. Previously, Redding had worked with Thurgood Marshall in litigating *Brown v. Board of Education*, 347 U.S. 483 (1954), the famous school desegregation case. Redding said that he took Burton's case in part because the Eagle Coffee Shoppe had also denied service to him (Redding). For more about the case, see Annette Woolard-Provine, *Integrating Delaware: The Reddings of Wilmington* (2003).

The Authority was created by the City of Wilmington pursuant to 22 Del. Code §§ 501–515. It is "a public body corporate and politic, exercising public powers of the State as an agency thereof." Its statutory purpose is to provide adequate parking facilities for the convenience of the public and thereby relieve the "parking crisis, which threatens the welfare of the community * * *."

---

1 The statute provides that: "No keeper of an inn, tavern, hotel, or restaurant, or other place of public entertainment or refreshment of travelers, guests, or customers shall be obliged, by law, to furnish entertainment or refreshment to persons whose reception or entertainment by him would be offensive to the major part of his customers, and would injure his business. As used in this section, 'customer' includes all who have occasion for entertainment or refreshment."

The first project undertaken by the Authority was the erection of a parking facility on Ninth Street in downtown Wilmington. * * * Before it began actual construction of the facility, the Authority was advised by its retained experts that the anticipated revenue from the parking of cars and proceeds from sale of its bonds would not be sufficient to finance the construction costs of the facility. Moreover, the bonds were not expected to be marketable if payable solely out of parking revenues. To secure additional capital needed for its "debt-service" requirements, and thereby to make bond financing practicable, the Authority decided it was necessary to enter long-term leases with responsible tenants for commercial use of some of the space available in the projected "garage building." The public was invited to bid for these leases.

In April 1957 such a private lease, for 20 years and renewable for another 10 years, was made with Eagle Coffee Shoppe, Inc., for use as a "restaurant, dining room, banquet hall, cocktail lounge and bar and for no other use and purpose." The multi-level space of the building which was let to Eagle, although "within the exterior walls of the structure, has no marked public entrance leading from the parking portion of the facility into the restaurant proper [whose main entrance] is located on Ninth Street." In its lease the Authority covenanted to complete construction expeditiously, including completion of "the decorative finishing of the leased premises and utilities therefor, without cost to Lessee," including necessary utility connections, toilets, hung acoustical tile and plaster ceilings; vinyl asbestos, ceramic tile and concrete floors; connecting stairs and wrought iron railings; and wood-floored show windows. Eagle spent some $220,000 to make the space suitable for its operation and, to the extent such improvements were so attached to realty as to become part thereof, Eagle to the same extent enjoys the Authority's tax exemption.

Other portions of the structure were leased to other tenants, including a bookstore, a retail jeweler, and a food store. Upon completion of the building, the Authority located at appropriate places thereon official signs indicating the public character of the building, [and] they flew from mastheads on the roof both the state and national flags.

In August 1958 appellant parked his car in the building and walked around to enter the restaurant by its front door on Ninth Street. Having entered and sought service, he was refused it. Thereafter he filed this declaratory judgment action in the Court of Chancery. * * *

[T]he Delaware Supreme Court seems to have placed controlling emphasis on its conclusion, as to the accuracy of which there is doubt, that only some 15% of the total cost of the facility was "advanced" from public funds; that the cost of the entire facility was allocated three-fifths to the space for commercial leasing and two-fifths to parking space; that anticipated revenue from parking was only some 30.5% of the total income, the balance of which was expected to be earned by the leasing; that the Authority had no original intent to place a restaurant in the building, it being only a happenstance resulting from the bidding; that Eagle expended considerable moneys on furnishings; that the restaurant's main and marked public entrance is on Ninth Street without any public entrance direct from the parking area; and that "the only connection Eagle has with the public facility [is] the furnishing of the sum of $28,700 annually in the form of rent which is used by the Authority to defray a portion of the operating expense of an otherwise unprofitable enterprise." While these factual considerations are indeed validly accountable aspects of the enterprise upon which the State has embarked, we cannot say that they lead inescapably to the conclusion that state action is not present. Their persuasiveness is diminished when evaluated in the context of other factors which must be acknowledged.

The land and building were publicly owned. As an entity, the building was dedicated to "public uses" in performance of the Authority's "essential governmental functions." The costs of land acquisition, construction, and maintenance are defrayed entirely from donations by the City of Wilmington, from loans and revenue bonds and from the proceeds of rentals and parking services out of which the loans and bonds were payable. Assuming that the distinction would be significant, the commercially leased areas were not surplus state property, but constituted a physically and financially integral and, indeed, indispensable part of the State's plan to operate its project as a self-sustaining unit. Upkeep and maintenance of the building, including necessary repairs, were responsibilities of the Authority and were payable out of public funds. It cannot be doubted that the peculiar relationship of the restaurant to the parking facility in which it is located confers on each an incidental variety of mutual benefits. Guests of the restaurant are afforded a convenient place to park their automobiles, even if they cannot enter the restaurant directly from the parking area. Similarly, its convenience for diners may well provide additional demand for the Authority's parking facilities. Should any improvements effected in the leasehold by Eagle become part of the realty, there is no possibility of increased taxes being passed on to it since the fee is held by a tax-exempt government agency. Neither can it be ignored, especially in view of Eagle's affirmative allegation that for it to serve Negroes would injure its business, that profits earned by discrimination not only contribute to, but also are indispensable elements in, the financial success of a governmental agency.

Addition of all these activities, obligations and responsibilities of the Authority, the benefits mutually conferred, together with the obvious fact that the restaurant is operated as an integral part of a public building devoted to a public parking service, indicates that degree of state participation and involvement in discriminatory action which it was the design of the Fourteenth Amendment to condemn. It is irony amounting to grave injustice that in one part of a single building, erected and maintained with public funds by an agency of the State to serve a public purpose, all persons have equal rights, while in another portion, also serving the public, a Negro is a second-class citizen, offensive because of his race, without rights and unentitled to service, but at the same time fully enjoys equal access to nearby restaurants in wholly privately owned buildings. As the Chancellor pointed out, in its lease with Eagle the Authority could have affirmatively required Eagle to discharge the responsibilities under the Fourteenth Amendment imposed upon the private enterprise as a consequence of state participation. But no State may effectively abdicate its responsibilities by either ignoring them or by merely failing to discharge them whatever the motive may be. It is of no consolation to an individual denied the equal protection of the laws that it was done in good faith. * * * By its inaction, the Authority, and through it the State, has not only made itself a party to the refusal of service, but has elected to place its power, property and prestige behind the admitted discrimination. The State has so far insinuated itself into a position of interdependence with Eagle that it must be recognized as a joint participant in the challenged activity, which, on that account, cannot be considered to have been so "purely private" as to fall without the scope of the Fourteenth Amendment.

> **Take Note**
>
> The Court acknowledges here that no simple test exists for when the joint participation exception applies to convert otherwise private action into state action. Instead, the answer depends on all the facts and circumstances. Can you identify the facts that were dispositive here?

Because readily applicable formulae may not be fashioned, the conclusions drawn from the facts and circumstances of this record are by no means declared as universal truths on the basis of which every state leasing agreement is to be tested. Owing to the very "largeness" of government, a multitude of relationships might appear to some to fall within the Amendment's embrace, but that, it must be remembered, can be determined only in the framework of the peculiar facts or circumstances present. Therefore respondents' prophecy of nigh universal application of a constitutional precept so peculiarly dependent for its invocation upon appropriate facts fails to take into account "Differences in circumstances (which) beget appropriate differences in law," *Whitney v. State Tax Comm.*, 309 U.S. 530, 542 (1940). Specifically defining the limits of our inquiry, what we hold today is that when a State leases public property in the manner and for the purpose shown to have been the case here, the proscriptions of the Fourteenth Amendment must be complied with by the lessee as certainly as though they were binding covenants written into the agreement itself. [Reversed.]

MR. JUSTICE STEWART, concurring.

I agree that the judgment must be reversed, but I reach that conclusion by a route much more direct than the one traveled by the Court. In upholding Eagle's right to deny service to the appellant solely because of his race, the Supreme Court of Delaware relied upon a statute of that State which permits the proprietor of a restaurant to refuse to serve "persons whose reception or entertainment by him would be offensive to the major part of his customers." There is no suggestion in the record that the appellant as an individual was such a person. The highest court of Delaware has thus construed this legislative enactment as authorizing discriminatory classification based exclusively on color. Such a law seems to me clearly violative of the Fourteenth Amendment. I think, therefore, that the appeal was properly taken, and that the statute, as authoritatively construed by the Supreme Court of Delaware, is constitutionally invalid.

MR. JUSTICE HARLAN, whom MR. JUSTICE WHITTAKER joins, dissenting.

The Court's opinion, by a process of first undiscriminatingly throwing together various factual bits and pieces and then undermining the resulting structure by an equally vague disclaimer, seems to me to leave completely at sea just what it is in this record that satisfies the requirement of "state action."

POINTS FOR DISCUSSION

a. The Standard for Application of the Joint Participation Exception

What exactly is the standard for application of the joint participation exception? Is it simply that otherwise private action is state action when the private actor can "fairly be said to be a state actor"? See *Lugar v. Edmondson Oil Co.*, 457 U.S. 922 (1982). What are the advantages and disadvantages of such an open-ended standard?

b. What Facts Are Significant?

Suppose that the Eagle Coffee Shop were not a tenant in the government-owned garage, but instead were simply a neighbor next door to the parking garage. Would the case have come out the same way? If not, exactly which facts were significant for the Court's conclusion in *Burton*?

c. Alternative Grounds for Finding State Action

Justice Stewart did not rest his concurrence on the joint participation exception. Instead, he concluded that the statute that authorized the Eagle Coffee Shop to exclude Burton itself was unconstitutional, because it permitted "discriminatory classification based exclusively on color." Given the state action doctrine, is this a valid basis for granting relief to Mr. Burton? What if the statute had conferred a right on private store owners to refuse to serve persons "for any reason, or no reason"? Would such a statute also, in Justice Stewart's view, violate the Fourteenth Amendment?

EDMONSON V. LEESVILLE CONCRETE CO., INC.

500 U.S. 614 (1991)

JUSTICE KENNEDY delivered the opinion of the Court.

Thaddeus Donald Edmonson, a construction worker, was injured in a jobsite accident at Fort Polk, Louisiana * * *. Edmonson sued Leesville Concrete Company for negligence in [federal district court], claiming that a Leesville employee permitted one of the company's trucks to roll backward and pin him against some construction equipment. Edmonson invoked his Seventh Amendment right to a trial by jury.

> **Definition**
>
> In a jury trial, jurors are selected from a group, traditionally called the "venire," of potential jurors. Attorneys for both sides are permitted to question the potential jurors through a process called "*voir dire*." Following *voir dire*, each party can challenge any juror for cause (e.g., bias) and can challenge a limited number of jurors without giving any cause. Challenges made without giving cause are called "peremptory challenges." See *Black's Law Dictionary* (9th ed. 2009).

During *voir dire,* Leesville used two of its three peremptory challenges authorized by statute to remove black persons from the prospective jury. Citing our decision in *Batson v. Kentucky,* 476 U.S. 79 (1986), Edmonson, who is himself black, requested that the District Court require Leesville to articulate a race-neutral explanation for striking the two jurors. The District Court denied the request on the ground that *Batson* does not apply in civil proceedings. * * *

> **Make the Connection**
>
> In *Batson v. Kentucky,* the Supreme Court held that a prosecutor—who is clearly a state actor—may not use peremptory challenges in a racially discriminatory manner. We briefly consider this decision in Volume 2, in conjunction with our discussion of *Strauder v. West Virginia.*

The Constitution structures the National Government, confines its actions, and, in regard to certain individual liberties and other specified matters, confines the actions of the States. With a few exceptions, such as the provisions of the Thirteenth Amendment, constitutional guarantees of individual liberty and equal protection do not apply to the actions of private entities. This fundamental limitation on the scope of constitutional guarantees "preserves an area of individual freedom by limiting the reach of federal law" and "avoids imposing on the State, its agencies or officials, responsibility for conduct for which they cannot fairly be blamed." *Lugar v. Edmondson Oil Co.,* 457 U.S. 922, 936–937 (1982). One great object of the Constitution is to permit citizens to structure their private relations as they choose subject only to the constraints of statutory or decisional law.

To implement these principles, courts must consider from time to time where the governmental sphere ends and the private sphere begins. Although the conduct of private parties lies beyond the Constitution's scope in most instances, governmental authority may dominate an activity to such an extent that its participants must be deemed to act with the authority of the government and, as a result, be subject to constitutional constraints. This is the jurisprudence of state action, which explores the "essential dichotomy" between the private sphere and the public sphere, with all its attendant constitutional obligations.

We begin our discussion within the framework for state-action analysis set forth in *Lugar.* There we considered the state-action question in the context of a due process challenge to a State's procedure allowing private parties to obtain prejudgment attachments. We asked first whether the claimed constitutional deprivation resulted from the exercise of a right or privilege having its source in state authority, and second, whether the private party charged with the deprivation could be described in all fairness as a state actor.

There can be no question that the first part of the *Lugar* inquiry is satisfied here. By their very nature, peremptory challenges have no significance outside a court of law. Their sole purpose is to permit litigants to assist the government in the selection of an impartial trier of fact. While we have recognized the value of peremptory challenges in this regard, particularly in the criminal context, there is no constitutional obligation to allow them. Peremptory challenges are permitted only when the government, by statute or decisional law, deems it appropriate to allow parties to exclude a given number of persons who otherwise would satisfy the requirements for service on the petit jury.

Given that the statutory authorization for the challenges exercised in this case is clear, the remainder of our state-action analysis centers around the second part of the *Lugar* test, whether a private litigant in all fairness must be deemed a government actor in the use of peremptory challenges. Although we have recognized that this aspect of the analysis is often a factbound inquiry, [our] precedents establish that, in determining whether a particular action or course of conduct is governmental in character, it is relevant to examine the following: the extent to which the actor relies on governmental assistance and benefits, see *Burton v. Wilmington Parking Authority,* 365 U.S. 715 (1961); whether the actor is performing a traditional governmental function, see *Marsh v. Alabama,* 326 U.S. 501 (1946); and whether the injury caused is aggravated in a unique way by the incidents of governmental authority, see *Shelley v. Kraemer,* 334 U.S. 1 (1948). Based on our application of these three principles to the circumstances here, we hold that the exercise of peremptory challenges by the defendant in the District Court was pursuant to a course of state action.

* * * It cannot be disputed that, without the overt, significant participation of the government, the peremptory challenge system, as well as the jury trial system of which it is a part, simply could not exist. As discussed above, peremptory challenges have no utility outside the jury system, a system which the government alone administers. * * * The trial judge exercises substantial control over *voir dire* in the federal system. The judge determines the range of information that may be discovered about a prospective juror, and so affects the exercise of both challenges for cause and peremptory challenges. In some cases, judges may even conduct the entire *voir dire* by themselves, a common practice in the District Court where the instant case was tried. The judge oversees the exclusion of jurors for cause, in this way determining which jurors remain eligible for the exercise of peremptory strikes. In cases involving multiple parties, the trial judge decides how peremptory challenges shall be allocated among them. When a lawyer exercises a peremptory challenge, the judge advises the juror he or she has been excused.

As we have outlined here, a private party could not exercise its peremptory challenges absent the overt, significant assistance of the court. The government summons jurors, constrains their freedom of movement, and subjects them to public scrutiny and examination. * * * By enforcing a discriminatory peremptory challenge, the court "has not only made itself a party to the [biased act], but has elected to place its power, property and prestige behind the [alleged] discrimination." *Burton v. Wilmington Parking Authority,* 365 U.S., at 725. * * * [Reversed and remanded.]

JUSTICE O'CONNOR, with whom THE CHIEF JUSTICE and JUSTICE SCALIA join, dissenting.

The Court concludes that the action of a private attorney exercising a peremptory challenge is attributable to the government and therefore may compose a constitutional violation. This conclusion is based on little more than that the challenge occurs in the course of a trial. Not everything that happens in a courtroom is state action. A trial, particularly a civil trial is by design largely a stage on which private parties may act; it is a forum through which they can resolve their disputes in a peaceful and ordered manner. The government erects the platform; it does not thereby become responsible for all that occurs upon it. As much as we would like to eliminate completely from the courtroom the specter of racial discrimination, the Constitution does not sweep that broadly. Because I believe that a peremptory strike by a private litigant is fundamentally a matter of private choice and not state action, I dissent.

JUSTICE SCALIA, dissenting.

The concrete benefits of the Court's newly discovered constitutional rule are problematic. It will not necessarily be a net help rather than hindrance to minority litigants in obtaining racially diverse juries. In criminal cases, *Batson v. Kentucky,* 476 U.S. 79 (1986), already prevents the *prosecution* from using race-based strikes. The effect of today's decision (which logically must apply to criminal prosecutions) will be to prevent the *defendant* from doing so—so that the minority defendant can no longer seek to prevent an all-white jury, or to seat as many jurors of his own race as possible. To be sure, it is ordinarily more difficult to *prove* race-based strikes of white jurors, but defense counsel can generally be relied upon to do what we say the Constitution requires. So in criminal cases, today's decision represents a net loss to the minority litigant. In civil cases that is probably not true—but it does not represent an unqualified gain either. *Both* sides have peremptory challenges, and they are sometimes used to *assure* rather than to *prevent* a racially diverse jury.

POINTS FOR DISCUSSION

a. The Court's Approach

The Court identified three "principles" to help to guide the decision whether a particular course of action was "governmental in character." Which, if any, of these three principles did the Court rely upon in concluding that a private litigant's racially discriminatory exercise of peremptory challenges constitutes state action?

b. Justice O'Connor's Dissent

Did Justice O'Connor disagree with the open-ended standard applied by the Court or just the Court's application of that standard? If the latter, which facts were dispositive in her view?

c. Justice Scalia's Dissent

Justice Scalia's prediction came to pass. In a subsequent case, *Georgia v. McCollum,* 505 U.S. 42, 52 (1992), the Supreme Court extended *Edmonson* and held that a criminal defendant could not use peremptory challenges in a racially discriminatory manner. Can a criminal defendant, on trial by the state, "be fairly said to be a state actor"?

In the previous two cases, in which the Court concluded that private parties and the government were jointly participating in an activity, it was the private party that engaged in the action that allegedly violated someone's constitutional rights. The following case is a "mirror image" joint participation case. Again a private party and the government are ostensibly jointly participating in an activity, but in this case it is the government that takes the action that allegedly violates someone's constitutional rights. In such a case, can the private party be held responsible for the government's action?

NATIONAL COLLEGIATE ATHLETIC ASSOCIATION V. TARKANIAN

488 U.S. 179 (1988)

JUSTICE STEVENS delivered the opinion of the Court.

When he became head basketball coach at the University of Nevada, Las Vegas (UNLV), in 1973, Jerry Tarkanian inherited a team with a mediocre 14–14 record. Four years later the team won 29 out of 32 games and placed third in the championship tournament sponsored by the National Collegiate Athletic Association (NCAA), to which UNLV belongs.

Yet in September 1977 UNLV informed Tarkanian that it was going to suspend him. No dissatisfaction with Tarkanian, once described as "the 'winningest' active basketball coach," motivated his suspension. Rather, the impetus was a report by the NCAA detailing 38 violations of NCAA rules by UNLV personnel, including 10 involving Tarkanian. The NCAA had placed the university's basketball team on probation for two years and ordered UNLV to show cause why the NCAA should not impose further penalties unless UNLV severed all ties during the probation between its intercollegiate athletic program and Tarkanian.

Facing demotion and a drastic cut in pay, Tarkanian brought suit in Nevada state court, alleging that he had been deprived of his Fourteenth Amendment due process rights in violation of 42 U.S.C. § 1983. Ultimately Tarkanian obtained injunctive relief and an award of attorney's fees against both UNLV and the NCAA. NCAA's liability may be upheld only if its participation in the events that led to Tarkanian's suspension constituted "state action" prohibited by the Fourteenth Amendment and was performed "under color of" state law within the meaning of § 1983. We granted certiorari to review the Nevada Supreme Court's holding that the NCAA engaged in state action when it conducted its investigation and recommended that Tarkanian be disciplined. We now reverse.

UNLV is a branch of the University of Nevada, a state-funded institution. The university is organized and operated pursuant to provisions of Nevada's State Constitution, statutes, and regulations. In performing their official functions, the executives of UNLV unquestionably act under color of state law.

The NCAA is an unincorporated association of approximately 960 members, including virtually all public and private universities and 4-year colleges conducting major athletic programs in the United States. Basic policies of the NCAA are determined by the members at annual conventions. Between conventions, the Association is governed by its Council, which appoints various committees to implement specific programs.

One of the NCAA's fundamental policies "is to maintain intercollegiate athletics as an integral part of the educational program and the athlete as an integral part of the student body, and by so doing, retain a clear line of demarcation between college athletics and professional sports." It has therefore adopted rules, which it calls "legislation," governing the conduct of the intercollegiate athletic programs of its members. This NCAA legislation applies to a variety of issues, such as academic standards for eligibility, admissions, financial aid, and the recruiting of student athletes. By joining the NCAA, each member agrees to abide by and to enforce such rules.

The NCAA's bylaws provide that its enforcement program shall be administered by a Committee on Infractions. The Committee supervises an investigative staff, makes factual determinations concerning alleged rule violations, and is expressly authorized to "impose appropriate penalties on a member found to be in violation, or recommend to the Council suspension or termination of membership." In particular, the Committee may order a member institution to show cause why that member should not suffer further penalties unless it imposes a prescribed discipline on an employee; it is not authorized, however, to sanction a member institution's employees directly. The bylaws also provide that representatives of member institutions "are expected to cooperate fully" with the administration of the enforcement program. * * *

[From 1972 to 1976, the Committee on Infractions investigated allegations that Tarkanian and others at UNLV had violated NCAA requirements governing the recruitment of student athletes.] It requested UNLV to investigate and provide detailed information concerning each alleged incident. * * * With the assistance of the Attorney General of Nevada and private counsel, UNLV conducted a thorough investigation of the charges. On October 27, 1976, it filed a comprehensive response containing voluminous exhibits and sworn affidavits. The response denied all of the allegations and specifically concluded that Tarkanian was completely innocent of wrongdoing. Thereafter, the Committee conducted four days of hearings at which counsel for UNLV and Tarkanian presented their views of the facts and challenged the credibility of the NCAA investigators and their informants. Ultimately the Committee decided that many of the charges could not be supported, but it did find 38 violations of NCAA rules, including 10 committed by Tarkanian. Most serious was the finding that Tarkanian had violated the University's obligation to provide full cooperation with the NCAA investigation. * * *

The Committee proposed a series of sanctions against UNLV, including a 2-year period of probation during which its basketball team could not participate in postseason games or appear on television. The Committee also requested UNLV to show cause why additional penalties should not be imposed against UNLV if it failed to discipline Tarkanian by removing him completely from the University's intercollegiate athletic program during the probation period. UNLV appealed most of the Committee's findings and proposed sanctions to the NCAA Council. After hearing arguments from attorneys representing UNLV and Tarkanian, the Council on August 25, 1977, unanimously approved the Committee's investigation and hearing process and adopted all its recommendations.

Promptly after receiving the NCAA report, the president of UNLV directed the University's vice president to schedule a hearing to determine whether the Committee's recommended sanctions should be applied. Tarkanian and UNLV were represented at that hearing; the NCAA was not. Although the vice president expressed doubt concerning the sufficiency of the evidence supporting the Committee's findings, he concluded that "given the terms of our adherence to the NCAA we cannot substitute—biased as we must be—our own judgment on the credibility of witnesses for that of the infractions committee and the Council." With respect to the proposed sanctions, he advised the president that he had three options:

> "1. Reject the sanction requiring us to disassociate Coach Tarkanian from the athletic program and take the risk of still heavier sanctions, *e.g.*, possible extra years of probation.
>
> 2. Recognize the University's delegation to the NCAA of the power to act as ultimate arbiter of these matters, thus reassigning Mr. Tarkanian

from his present position—though tenured and without adequate notice—even while believing that the NCAA was wrong.

3. Pull out of the NCAA completely on the grounds that you will not execute what you hold to be their unjust judgments."

Pursuant to the vice president's recommendation, the president accepted the second option and notified Tarkanian that he was to "be completely severed of any and all relations, formal or informal, with the University's Intercollegiate athletic program during the period of the University's NCAA probation."

The day before his suspension was to become effective, Tarkanian filed an action in Nevada state court for declaratory and injunctive relief * * *. [After lengthy proceedings, the state courts concluded that the suspension violated the Due Process Clause of the Fourteenth Amendment. The courts enjoined UNLV from suspending Tarkanian and enjoined the NCAA from conducting "any further proceedings against the University," from enforcing its show-cause order, and from taking any other action against the University. The Nevada trial court also awarded Tarkanian attorney's fees of almost $196,000, of which the NCAA had to pay 90%. The NCAA challenged its liability on grounds that it was not a state actor.]

> **Food for Thought**
>
> The state court held that both UNLV and the NCAA had violated Tarkanian's rights. But only the NCAA sought review in the Supreme Court. Why didn't UNLV seek review of the judgment, as well?

In the typical case raising a state-action issue, a private party has taken the decisive step that caused the harm to the plaintiff, and the question is whether the State was sufficiently involved to treat that decisive conduct as state action. * * * Thus, in the usual case we ask whether the State provided a mantle of authority that enhanced the power of the harm-causing individual actor.

> **Make the Connection**
>
> We consider the doctrine of "procedural due process," and its application to state efforts to terminate employees, in Volume 2.

This case uniquely mirrors the traditional state-action case. Here the final act challenged by Tarkanian—his suspension—was committed by UNLV. A state university without question is a state actor. When it decides to impose a serious disciplinary sanction upon one of its tenured employees, it must comply with the terms of the Due Process Clause of the Fourteenth Amendment * * *. Thus when UNLV notified Tarkanian that he was being separated from all relations with the university's basketball program, it acted under color of state law within the meaning of 42 U.S.C. § 1983.

The mirror image presented in this case requires us to step through an analytical looking glass to resolve the case. Clearly UNLV's conduct was influenced by the rules and recommendations of the NCAA, the private party. But it was UNLV, the state entity, that actually suspended Tarkanian. Thus the question is not whether UNLV participated to a critical extent in the NCAA's activities, but whether UNLV's actions in compliance with the NCAA rules and recommendations turned the NCAA's conduct into state action.

We examine first the relationship between UNLV and the NCAA regarding the NCAA's rulemaking. UNLV is among the NCAA's members and participated in promulgating the Association's rules; it must be assumed, therefore, that Nevada had some impact on the NCAA's policy determinations. Yet the NCAA's several hundred other public and private member institutions each similarly affected those policies. Those institutions, the vast majority of which were located in States other than Nevada, did not act under color of Nevada law. It necessarily follows that the source of the legislation adopted by the NCAA is not Nevada but the collective membership, speaking through an organization that is independent of any particular State.

Tarkanian further asserts that the NCAA's investigation, enforcement proceedings, and consequent recommendations constituted state action because they resulted from a delegation of power by UNLV. UNLV, as an NCAA member, subscribed to the statement in the Association's bylaws that NCAA "enforcement procedures are an essential part of the intercollegiate athletic program of each member institution." It is, of course, true that a State may delegate authority to a private party and thereby make that party a state actor. Thus, we recently held that a private physician who had contracted with a state prison to attend to the inmates' medical needs was a state actor. *West v. Atkins*, 487 U.S. 42 (1988). But UNLV delegated no power to the NCAA to take specific action against any university employee. The commitment by UNLV to adhere to NCAA enforcement procedures was enforceable only by sanctions that the NCAA might impose on UNLV itself.

Indeed, the notion that UNLV's promise to cooperate in the NCAA enforcement proceedings was tantamount to a partnership agreement or the transfer of certain university powers to the NCAA is belied by the history of this case. It is quite obvious that UNLV used its best efforts to retain its winning coach—a goal diametrically opposed to the NCAA's interest in ascertaining the truth of its investigators' reports. During the several years that the NCAA investigated the alleged violations, the NCAA and UNLV acted much more like adversaries than like partners engaged in a dispassionate search for the truth. The

NCAA cannot be regarded as an agent of UNLV for purposes of that proceeding. It is more correctly characterized as an agent of its remaining members which, as competitors of UNLV, had an interest in the effective and evenhanded enforcement of the NCAA's recruitment standards. Just as a state-compensated public defender acts in a private capacity when he or she represents a private client in a conflict against the State, *Polk County v. Dodson,* 454 U.S. 312, 320 (1981), the NCAA is properly viewed as a private actor at odds with the State when it represents the interests of its entire membership in an investigation of one public university.

Finally, Tarkanian argues that the power of the NCAA is so great that [UNLV] had no practical alternative to compliance with its demands. We are not at all sure this is true, but even if we assume that a private monopolist can impose its will on a state agency by a threatened refusal to deal with it, it does not follow that such a private party is therefore acting under color of state law.

In final analysis the question is whether "the conduct allegedly causing the deprivation of a federal right [can] be fairly attributable to the State." *Lugar v. Edmondson Oil Co.*, 457 U.S. 922, 937 (1982). It would be ironic indeed to conclude that the NCAA's imposition of sanctions against UNLV—sanctions that UNLV and its counsel, including the Attorney General of Nevada, steadfastly opposed during protracted adversary proceedings—is fairly attributable to the State of Nevada. It would be more appropriate to conclude that UNLV has conducted its athletic program under color of the policies adopted by the NCAA, rather than that those policies were developed and enforced under color of Nevada law. [Reversed and remanded.]

JUSTICE WHITE, with whom JUSTICE BRENNAN, JUSTICE MARSHALL, and JUSTICE O'CONNOR join, dissenting.

* * * Had UNLV refused to suspend Tarkanian, and the NCAA responded by imposing sanctions against UNLV, it would be hard indeed to find any state action that harmed Tarkanian. But that is not this case. Here, UNLV did suspend Tarkanian, and it did so because it embraced the NCAA rules governing conduct of its athletic program and adopted the results of the hearings conducted by the NCAA concerning Tarkanian, as it had agreed that it would. Under these facts, I would find that the NCAA acted jointly with UNLV and therefore is a state actor.

POINTS FOR DISCUSSION

a. Opposing Goals

The Court concluded in *Tarkanian* that the NCAA was not a state actor, even though it jointly engaged in some activity with UNLV, because the NCAA and UNLV were diametrically opposed to each other in their goals. Suppose that the university's leadership had in fact been appalled by Coach Tarkanian's alleged misconduct and wanted to oust him from his position to remove a stain on the university's name, even if the consequence would be a less powerful basketball program. (Remember, anything is possible in a hypothetical question.) Would the case have come out differently?

b. Another Mirror Image Case

In *Dennis v. Sparks*, 449 U.S. 24 (1980), the Duval County Ranch Company bribed a Texas state judge to issue an injunction preventing Orville Dennis from producing oil on his property. When Dennis learned of the bribery, he sued the company, its owners, and the judge under 42 U.S.C. § 1983, claiming that through the bribery they had conspired to deprive him of his right to due process under the Fourteenth Amendment. The private parties argued that they could not have deprived Dennis of his right to due process because they were not state actors. But the Supreme Court concluded:

> [T]o act "under color of" state law for § 1983 purposes does not require that the defendant be an officer of the State. It is enough that he is a willful participant in joint action with the State or its agents. [H]ere the allegations were that an official act of the defendant judge was the product of a corrupt conspiracy involving bribery of the judge. Under these allegations, the private parties conspiring with the judge were acting under color of state law; and it is of no consequence in this respect that the judge himself is immune from damages liability.

Id. at 28. In what way was *Dennis* a "mirror image" joint participation case? Why was the result different from the result in *Tarkanian*?

Problem

The following statement of facts comes from *Manhattan Community Access Corporation v. Halleck*, 139 S.Ct. 1921 (2019):

> Time Warner * * * operates a cable system in Manhattan. Under state law, Time Warner must set aside some channels on its cable system for public access. New York City * * * has designated a private

nonprofit corporation named Manhattan Neighborhood Network (MNN) * * * to operate Time Warner's public access channels in Manhattan. * * *

DeeDee Halleck and Jesus Papoleto Melendez produced public access programming in Manhattan. They made a film about MNN's alleged neglect of the East Harlem community. Halleck submitted the film to MNN for airing on MNN's public access cannels, and MNN later televised the film. Afterwards, MNN fielded multiple complaints about the film's content. In response, MNN temporarily suspended Halleck from using the public access channels.

Halleck and Papoleto subsequently claimed that MNN violated their freedom of speech under the First Amendment by suspending them. Although MNN is not a governmental entity, Halleck and Papoleto argued that it was a state actor limited by the First Amendment for three reasons:

(1) MNN exercises a function traditionally and exclusively performed by the government, namely, providing a public forum.

(2) MNN is highly regulated by state law.

(3) The government has so much regulatory control over the public access channels that it "effectively owns" them, and MNN manages this "property" for the government.

Should the Court conclude that MNN is a state actor?

Executive Summary of This Chapter

The **state action doctrine** recognizes that the Constitution restrains the actions of federal, state, and local governments and government officials, but generally does not limit the actions of private individuals and corporations. *The Civil Rights Cases,* 109 U.S. 3 (1883).

The **public function exception** to the state action doctrine requires courts to apply constitutional limitations to private entities when they engage in functions traditionally exclusively reserved to the government. Under this doctrine, the Court has held that a company town must afford speakers the protection of the First Amendment, *Marsh v. State of Alabama,* 326 U.S. 501 (1946), but that a shopping center need not, *Hudgens v. NLRB*, 424 U.S. 507 (1976).

The **judicial enforcement exception** to the state action doctrine says that a court's enforcement of a private agreement may constitute state action.

Accordingly, judicial enforcement of a restrictive covenant that requires a party to discriminate on the basis of race violates the Fourteenth Amendment. *Shelley v. Kraemer*, 334 U.S. 1 (1948). But the Supreme Court has not extended this rationale to its logical limits, perhaps because any private action could be upheld by a court and thus transformed into state action.

The **joint participation** exception (sometimes called the **entanglement exception**) to the state action doctrine provides that a private party may be held liable for a deprivation of a right if two elements are present: (1) the deprivation is caused by the exercise of some right or privilege created by the State or by a rule of conduct imposed by the state or by a person for whom the State is responsible; and (2) the party charged with the deprivation may fairly be said to be a state actor. *Lugar v. Edmondson Oil Co.*, 457 U.S. 922, 937 (1982). Whether someone can "fairly be said to be a state actor" depends on all the facts and circumstances. Applying this test, the Court has concluded that a private litigant who exercised a peremptory challenge in a racially discriminatory fashion engaged in state action. See *id.* Similarly, a private restaurant that had a lease in a government-owned building was deemed to be a state actor when it discriminated against a customer. *Burton v. Wilmington Parking Authority*, 365 U.S. 715 (1961). But a private intercollegiate sports organization was deemed not to be a state actor, even though it jointly acted with a state university, because the two institutions had opposing goals. *National Collegiate Athletic Association v. Tarkanian*, 488 U.S. 179 (1988).

APPENDIX

The Constitution of the United States of America

We the People of the United States, in Order to form a more perfect Union, establish Justice, insure domestic Tranquility, provide for the common defence, promote the general Welfare, and secure the Blessings of Liberty to ourselves and our Posterity, do ordain and establish this Constitution for the United States of America.

ARTICLE I

SECTION 1. All legislative Powers herein granted shall be vested in a Congress of the United States, which shall consist of a Senate and House of Representatives.

SECTION 2. [1] The House of Representatives shall be composed of Members chosen every second Year by the People of the several States, and the Electors in each State shall have the Qualifications requisite for Electors of the most numerous Branch of the State Legislature.

[2] No Person shall be a Representative who shall not have attained to the Age of twenty five Years, and been seven Years a Citizen of the United States, and who shall not, when elected, be an Inhabitant of that State in which he shall be chosen.

[3] [Representatives and direct Taxes shall be apportioned among the several States which may be included within this Union, according to their respective Numbers, which shall be determined by adding to the whole Number of free Persons, including those bound to Service for a Term of Years, and excluding Indians not taxed, three fifths of all other Persons.] The actual Enumeration shall be made within three Years after the first Meeting of the Congress of the United States, and within every subsequent Term of ten Years, in such

Take Note

The bracketed text has been modified by Section 2 of the Fourteenth Amendment.

Manner as they shall by Law direct. The Number of Representatives shall not exceed one for every thirty Thousand, but each State shall have at Least one Representative; and until such enumeration shall be made, the State of New Hampshire shall be entitled to chuse three, Massachusetts eight, Rhode-Island and Providence Plantations one, Connecticut five, New-York six, New Jersey four, Pennsylvania eight, Delaware one, Maryland six, Virginia ten, North Carolina five, South Carolina five, and Georgia three.

[4] When vacancies happen in the Representation from any State, the Executive Authority thereof shall issue Writs of Election to fill such Vacancies.

[5] The House of Representatives shall chuse their Speaker and other Officers; and shall have the sole Power of Impeachment.

SECTION 3. [1] The Senate of the United States shall be composed of two Senators from each State, [chosen by the Legislature thereof for six Years]; and each Senator shall have one Vote.

Take Note

The bracketed text in the first two clauses of Section 3 has been modified by the Seventeenth Amendment.

[2] Immediately after they shall be assembled in Consequence of the first Election, they shall be divided as equally as may be into three Classes. The Seats of the Senators of the first Class shall be vacated at the Expiration of the second Year, of the second Class at the Expiration of the fourth Year, and of the third Class at the Expiration of the sixth Year, so that one third may be chosen every second Year; [and if Vacancies happen by Resignation, or otherwise, during the Recess of the Legislature of any State, the Executive thereof may make temporary Appointments until the next Meeting of the Legislature, which shall then fill such Vacancies.]

[3] No Person shall be a Senator who shall not have attained to the Age of thirty Years, and been nine Years a Citizen of the United States, and who shall not, when elected, be an Inhabitant of that State for which he shall be chosen.

[4] The Vice President of the United States shall be President of the Senate, but shall have no Vote, unless they be equally divided.

[5] The Senate shall chuse their other Officers, and also a President pro tempore, in the Absence of the Vice President, or when he shall exercise the Office of President of the United States.

[6] The Senate shall have the sole Power to try all Impeachments. When sitting for that Purpose, they shall be on Oath or Affirmation. When the President

of the United States is tried, the Chief Justice shall preside: And no Person shall be convicted without the Concurrence of two thirds of the Members present.

[7] Judgment in Cases of Impeachment shall not extend further than to removal from Office, and disqualification to hold and enjoy any Office of honor, Trust or Profit under the United States: but the Party convicted shall nevertheless be liable and subject to Indictment, Trial, Judgment and Punishment, according to Law.

SECTION 4. [1] The Times, Places and Manner of holding Elections for Senators and Representatives, shall be prescribed in each State by the Legislature thereof; but the Congress may at any time by Law make or alter such Regulations, except as to the Places of chusing Senators.

[2] The Congress shall assemble at least once in every Year, and such Meeting shall be [on the first Monday in December], unless they shall by Law appoint a different Day.

Take Note

The bracketed text has been modified by Section 2 of the Twentieth Amendment.

SECTION 5. [1] Each House shall be the Judge of the Elections, Returns and Qualifications of its own Members, and a Majority of each shall constitute a Quorum to do Business; but a smaller Number may adjourn from day to day, and may be authorized to compel the Attendance of absent Members, in such Manner, and under such Penalties as each House may provide.

[2] Each House may determine the Rules of its Proceedings, punish its Members for disorderly Behaviour, and, with the Concurrence of two thirds, expel a Member.

[3] Each House shall keep a Journal of its Proceedings, and from time to time publish the same, excepting such Parts as may in their Judgment require Secrecy; and the Yeas and Nays of the Members of either House on any question shall, at the Desire of one fifth of those Present, be entered on the Journal.

[4] Neither House, during the Session of Congress, shall, without the Consent of the other, adjourn for more than three days, nor to any other Place than that in which the two Houses shall be sitting.

SECTION 6. [1] The Senators and Representatives shall receive a Compensation for their Services, to be ascertained by Law, and paid out of the Treasury of the United States. They shall in all Cases, except Treason, Felony and Breach of the Peace, be privileged from Arrest during their Attendance at the Session of their respective Houses, and in going to and returning from the same;

and for any Speech or Debate in either House, they shall not be questioned in any other Place.

[2] No Senator or Representative shall, during the Time for which he was elected, be appointed to any civil Office under the Authority of the United States, which shall have been created, or the Emoluments whereof shall have been encreased during such time; and no Person holding any Office under the United States, shall be a Member of either House during his Continuance in Office.

SECTION 7. [1] All Bills for raising Revenue shall originate in the House of Representatives; but the Senate may propose or concur with Amendments as on other Bills.

[2] Every Bill which shall have passed the House of Representatives and the Senate, shall, before it become a Law, be presented to the President of the United States: If he approve he shall sign it, but if not he shall return it, with his Objections to that House in which it shall have originated, who shall enter the Objections at large on their Journal, and proceed to reconsider it. If after such Reconsideration two thirds of that House shall agree to pass the Bill, it shall be sent, together with the Objections, to the other House, by which it shall likewise be reconsidered, and if approved by two thirds of that House, it shall become a Law. But in all such Cases the Votes of both Houses shall be determined by yeas and Nays, and the Names of the Persons voting for and against the Bill shall be entered on the Journal of each House respectively. If any Bill shall not be returned by the President within ten Days (Sundays excepted) after it shall have been presented to him, the Same shall be a Law, in like Manner as if he had signed it, unless the Congress by their Adjournment prevent its Return, in which Case it shall not be a Law.

[3] Every Order, Resolution, or Vote to which the Concurrence of the Senate and House of Representatives may be necessary (except on a question of Adjournment) shall be presented to the President of the United States; and before the Same shall take Effect, shall be approved by him, or being disapproved by him, shall be repassed by two thirds of the Senate and House of Representatives, according to the Rules and Limitations prescribed in the Case of a Bill.

SECTION 8. [1] The Congress shall have Power To lay and collect Taxes, Duties, Imposts and Excises, to pay the Debts and provide for the common Defence and general Welfare of the United States; but all Duties, Imposts and Excises shall be uniform throughout the United States;

[2] To borrow Money on the credit of the United States;

[3] To regulate Commerce with foreign Nations, and among the several States, and with the Indian Tribes;

[4] To establish an uniform Rule of Naturalization, and uniform Laws on the subject of Bankruptcies throughout the United States;

[5] To coin Money, regulate the Value thereof, and of foreign Coin, and fix the Standard of Weights and Measures;

[6] To provide for the Punishment of counterfeiting the Securities and current Coin of the United States;

[7] To establish Post Offices and post Roads;

[8] To promote the Progress of Science and useful Arts, by securing for limited Times to Authors and Inventors the exclusive Right to their respective Writings and Discoveries;

[9] To constitute Tribunals inferior to the supreme Court;

[10] To define and punish Piracies and Felonies committed on the high Seas, and Offences against the Law of Nations;

[11] To declare War, grant Letters of Marque and Reprisal, and make Rules concerning Captures on Land and Water;

[12] To raise and support Armies, but no Appropriation of Money to that Use shall be for a longer Term than two Years;

[13] To provide and maintain a Navy;

[14] To make Rules for the Government and Regulation of the land and naval Forces;

[15] To provide for calling forth the Militia to execute the Laws of the Union, suppress Insurrections and repel Invasions;

[16] To provide for organizing, arming, and disciplining, the Militia, and for governing such Part of them as may be employed in the Service of the United States, reserving to the States respectively, the Appointment of the Officers, and the Authority of training the Militia according to the discipline prescribed by Congress;

[17] To exercise exclusive Legislation in all Cases whatsoever, over such District (not exceeding ten Miles square) as may, by Cession of particular States, and the Acceptance of Congress, become the Seat of the Government of the United States, and to exercise like Authority over all Places purchased by the

Consent of the Legislature of the State in which the Same shall be, for the Erection of Forts, Magazines, Arsenals, dock-Yards, and other needful Buildings;—And

[18] To make all Laws which shall be necessary and proper for carrying into Execution the foregoing Powers, and all other Powers vested by this Constitution in the Government of the United States, or in any Department or Officer thereof.

SECTION 9. [1] The Migration or Importation of such Persons as any of the States now existing shall think proper to admit, shall not be prohibited by the Congress prior to the Year one thousand eight hundred and eight, but a Tax or duty may be imposed on such Importation, not exceeding ten dollars for each Person.

[2] The Privilege of the Writ of Habeas Corpus shall not be suspended, unless when in Cases of Rebellion or Invasion the public Safety may require it.

[3] No Bill of Attainder or ex post facto Law shall be passed.

Take Note

The bracketed text has been modified by the Sixteenth Amendment.

[4] No Capitation, or other direct, Tax shall be laid, [unless in Proportion to the Census or enumeration herein before directed to be taken.]

[5] No Tax or Duty shall be laid on Articles exported from any State.

[6] No Preference shall be given by any Regulation of Commerce or Revenue to the Ports of one State over those of another; nor shall Vessels bound to, or from, one State, be obliged to enter, clear, or pay Duties in another.

[7] No Money shall be drawn from the Treasury, but in Consequence of Appropriations made by Law; and a regular Statement and Account of the Receipts and Expenditures of all public Money shall be published from time to time.

[8] No Title of Nobility shall be granted by the United States: And no Person holding any Office of Profit or Trust under them, shall, without the Consent of the Congress, accept of any present, Emolument, Office, or Title, of any kind whatever, from any King, Prince, or foreign State.

SECTION 10. [1] No State shall enter into any Treaty, Alliance, or Confederation; grant Letters of Marque and Reprisal; coin Money; emit Bills of Credit; make any Thing but gold and silver Coin a Tender in Payment of Debts; pass any Bill of Attainder, ex post facto Law, or Law impairing the Obligation of Contracts, or grant any Title of Nobility.

[2] No State shall, without the Consent of the Congress, lay any Imposts or Duties on Imports or Exports, except what may be absolutely necessary for executing [its] inspection Laws: and the net Produce of all Duties and Imposts, laid by any State on Imports or Exports, shall be for the Use of the Treasury of the United States; and all such Laws shall be subject to the Revision and Controul of the Congress.

[3] No State shall, without the Consent of Congress, lay any Duty of Tonnage, keep Troops, or Ships of War in time of Peace, enter into any Agreement or Compact with another State, or with a foreign Power, or engage in War, unless actually invaded, or in such imminent Danger as will not admit of delay.

ARTICLE II

SECTION 1. [1] The executive Power shall be vested in a President of the United States of America. He shall hold his Office during the Term of four Years, and, together with the Vice President, chosen for the same Term, be elected, as follows:

[2] Each State shall appoint, in such Manner as the Legislature thereof may direct, a Number of Electors, equal to the whole Number of Senators and Representatives to which the State may be entitled in the Congress: but no Senator or Representative, or Person holding an Office of Trust or Profit under the United States, shall be appointed an Elector.

> **Take Note**
>
> The bracketed text has been superseded by the Twelfth Amendment, part of which in turn was modified by Section 3 of the Twentieth Amendment.

[3] [The Electors shall meet in their respective States, and vote by Ballot for two Persons, of whom one at least shall not be an Inhabitant of the same State with themselves. And they shall make a List of all the Persons voted for, and of the Number of Votes for each; which List they shall sign and certify, and transmit sealed to the Seat of the Government of the United States, directed to the President of the Senate. The President of the Senate shall, in the Presence of the Senate and House of Representatives, open all the Certificates, and the Votes shall then be counted. The Person having the greatest Number of Votes shall be the President, if such Number be a Majority of the whole Number of Electors appointed; and if there be more than one who have such Majority, and have an equal Number of Votes, then the House of Representatives shall immediately chuse by Ballot one of them for President; and if no Person have a Majority, then from the five highest on the List the said House shall in like Manner chuse the

President. But in chusing the President, the Votes shall be taken by States, the Representation from each State having one Vote; A quorum for this purpose shall consist of a Member or Members from two thirds of the States, and a Majority of all the States shall be necessary to a Choice. In every Case, after the Choice of the President, the Person having the greatest Number of Votes of the Electors shall be the Vice President. But if there should remain two or more who have equal Votes, the Senate shall chuse from them by Ballot the Vice President.]

[4] The Congress may determine the Time of chusing the Electors, and the Day on which they shall give their Votes; which Day shall be the same throughout the United States.

[5] No Person except a natural born Citizen, or a Citizen of the United States, at the time of the Adoption of this Constitution, shall be eligible to the Office of President; neither shall any Person be eligible to that Office who shall not have attained to the Age of thirty five Years, and been fourteen Years a Resident within the United States.

Take Note

The bracketed text has been modified by the Twenty-Fifth Amendment.

[6] [In Case of the Removal of the President from Office, or of his Death, Resignation, or Inability to discharge the Powers and Duties of the said Office, the Same shall devolve on the Vice President, and the Congress may by Law provide for the Case of Removal, Death, Resignation or Inability, both of the President and Vice President, declaring what Officer shall then act as President, and such Officer shall act accordingly, until the Disability be removed, or a President shall be elected.]

[7] The President shall, at stated Times, receive for his Services, a Compensation, which shall neither be increased nor diminished during the Period for which he shall have been elected, and he shall not receive within that Period any other Emolument from the United States, or any of them.

[8] Before he enter on the Execution of his Office, he shall take the following Oath or Affirmation:—"I do solemnly swear (or affirm) that I will faithfully execute the Office of President of the United States, and will to the best of my Ability, preserve, protect and defend the Constitution of the United States."

SECTION 2. [1] The President shall be Commander in Chief of the Army and Navy of the United States, and of the Militia of the several States, when called into the actual Service of the United States; he may require the Opinion, in writing, of the principal Officer in each of the executive Departments, upon any Subject relating to the Duties of their respective Offices, and he shall have Power to grant

Reprieves and Pardons for Offences against the United States, except in Cases of Impeachment.

[2] He shall have Power, by and with the Advice and Consent of the Senate, to make Treaties, provided two thirds of the Senators present concur; and he shall nominate, and by and with the Advice and Consent of the Senate, shall appoint Ambassadors, other public Ministers and Consuls, Judges of the supreme Court, and all other Officers of the United States, whose Appointments are not herein otherwise provided for, and which shall be established by Law: but the Congress may by Law vest the Appointment of such inferior Officers, as they think proper, in the President alone, in the Courts of Law, or in the Heads of Departments.

[3] The President shall have Power to fill up all Vacancies that may happen during the Recess of the Senate, by granting Commissions which shall expire at the End of their next Session.

SECTION 3. He shall from time to time give to the Congress Information of the State of the Union, and recommend to their Consideration such Measures as he shall judge necessary and expedient; he may, on extraordinary Occasions, convene both Houses, or either of them, and in Case of Disagreement between them, with Respect to the Time of Adjournment, he may adjourn them to such Time as he shall think proper; he shall receive Ambassadors and other public Ministers; he shall take Care that the Laws be faithfully executed, and shall Commission all the Officers of the United States.

SECTION 4. The President, Vice President and all civil Officers of the United States, shall be removed from Office on Impeachment for, and Conviction of, Treason, Bribery, or other high Crimes and Misdemeanors.

ARTICLE III

SECTION 1. The judicial Power of the United States shall be vested in one supreme Court, and in such inferior Courts as the Congress may from time to time ordain and establish. The Judges, both of the supreme and inferior Courts, shall hold their Offices during good Behaviour, and shall, at stated Times, receive for their Services a Compensation, which shall not be diminished during their Continuance in Office.

SECTION 2. [1] The judicial Power shall extend to all Cases, in Law and Equity, arising under this Constitution, the Laws of the United States, and Treaties made, or which shall be made, under their Authority;—to all Cases affecting Ambassadors, other public Ministers and Consuls;—to all Cases of admiralty and maritime Jurisdiction;—to Controversies to which the United States shall be a Party;—to Controversies between two or more States;[—between a State and

> **Take Note**
>
> The bracketed text has been modified by the Eleventh Amendment.

Citizens of another State;]—between Citizens of different States;—between Citizens of the same State claiming Lands under Grants of different States, [and between a State, or the Citizens thereof, and foreign States, Citizens or Subjects.]

[2] In all Cases affecting Ambassadors, other public Ministers and Consuls, and those in which a State shall be Party, the supreme Court shall have original Jurisdiction. In all the other Cases before mentioned, the supreme Court shall have appellate Jurisdiction, both as to Law and Fact, with such Exceptions, and under such Regulations as the Congress shall make.

[3] The Trial of all Crimes, except in Cases of Impeachment, shall be by Jury; and such Trial shall be held in the State where the said Crimes shall have been committed; but when not committed within any State, the Trial shall be at such Place or Places as the Congress may by Law have directed.

SECTION 3. [1] Treason against the United States, shall consist only in levying War against them, or in adhering to their Enemies, giving them Aid and Comfort. No Person shall be convicted of Treason unless on the Testimony of two Witnesses to the same overt Act, or on Confession in open Court.

[2] The Congress shall have Power to declare the Punishment of Treason, but no Attainder of Treason shall work Corruption of Blood, or Forfeiture except during the Life of the Person attainted.

ARTICLE IV

SECTION 1. Full Faith and Credit shall be given in each State to the public Acts, Records, and judicial Proceedings of every other State. And the Congress may by general Laws prescribe the Manner in which such Acts, Records and Proceedings shall be proved, and the Effect thereof.

SECTION 2. [1] The Citizens of each State shall be entitled to all Privileges and Immunities of Citizens in the several States.

[2] A Person charged in any State with Treason, Felony, or other Crime, who shall flee from Justice, and be found in another State, shall on Demand of the executive Authority of the State from which he fled, be delivered up, to be removed to the State having Jurisdiction of the Crime.

[3] [No Person held to Service or Labour in one State, under the Laws thereof, escaping into another, shall, in Consequence of any Law or Regulation

therein, be discharged from such Service or Labour, but shall be delivered up on Claim of the Party to whom such Service or Labour may be due.]

Take Note

The bracketed text has been superseded by the Thirteenth Amendment.

SECTION 3. [1] New States may be admitted by the Congress into this Union; but no new State shall be formed or erected within the Jurisdiction of any other State; nor any State be formed by the Junction of two or more States, or Parts of States, without the Consent of the Legislatures of the States concerned as well as of the Congress.

[2] The Congress shall have Power to dispose of and make all needful Rules and Regulations respecting the Territory or other Property belonging to the United States; and nothing in this Constitution shall be so construed as to Prejudice any Claims of the United States, or of any particular State.

SECTION 4. The United States shall guarantee to every State in this Union a Republican Form of Government, and shall protect each of them against Invasion; and on Application of the Legislature, or of the Executive (when the Legislature cannot be convened), against domestic Violence.

ARTICLE V

The Congress, whenever two thirds of both Houses shall deem it necessary, shall propose Amendments to this Constitution, or, on the Application of the Legislatures of two thirds of the several States, shall call a Convention for proposing Amendments, which, in either Case, shall be valid to all Intents and Purposes, as Part of this Constitution, when ratified by the Legislatures of three fourths of the several States, or by Conventions in three fourths thereof, as the one or the other Mode of Ratification may be proposed by the Congress; Provided that no Amendment which may be made prior to the Year One thousand eight hundred and eight shall in any Manner affect the first and fourth Clauses in the Ninth Section of the first Article; and that no State, without its Consent, shall be deprived of its equal Suffrage in the Senate.

ARTICLE VI

[1] All Debts contracted and Engagements entered into, before the Adoption of this Constitution, shall be as valid against the United States under this Constitution, as under the Confederation.

[2] This Constitution, and the Laws of the United States which shall be made in Pursuance thereof; and all Treaties made, or which shall be made, under the Authority of the United States, shall be the supreme Law of the Land; and the

Judges in every State shall be bound thereby, any Thing in the Constitution or Laws of any State to the Contrary notwithstanding.

[3] The Senators and Representatives before mentioned, and the Members of the several State Legislatures, and all executive and judicial Officers, both of the United States and of the several States, shall be bound by Oath or Affirmation, to support this Constitution; but no religious Test shall ever be required as a Qualification to any Office or public Trust under the United States.

ARTICLE VII

The Ratification of the Conventions of nine States, shall be sufficient for the Establishment of this Constitution between the States so ratifying the Same.

ARTICLES IN ADDITION TO, AND AMENDMENT OF THE CONSTITUTION OF THE UNITED STATES OF AMERICA, PROPOSED BY CONGRESS, AND RATIFIED BY THE LEGISLATURES OF THE SEVERAL STATES, PURSUANT TO THE FIFTH ARTICLE OF THE ORIGINAL CONSTITUTION:

AMENDMENT I [1791]

Congress shall make no law respecting an establishment of religion, or prohibiting the free exercise thereof; or abridging the freedom of speech, or of the press; or the right of the people peaceably to assemble, and to petition the Government for a redress of grievances.

AMENDMENT II [1791]

A well regulated Militia, being necessary to the security of a free State, the right of the people to keep and bear Arms, shall not be infringed.

> **Food for Thought**
>
> The Amendments are listed at the end of the text of the original document. Would it matter, for purposes of interpreting the Constitution, if instead the text of the Amendments was integrated with the language of the original document, in the relevant provisions? For example, would it matter if the text of the Eleventh Amendment were incorporated into Section 2 of Article 3, rather than simply included here at the end?

AMENDMENT III [1791]

No Soldier shall, in time of peace be quartered in any house, without the consent of the Owner, nor in time of war, but in a manner to be prescribed by law.

AMENDMENT IV [1791]

The right of the people to be secure in their persons, houses, papers, and effects, against unreasonable searches and seizures, shall not be violated, and no Warrants shall issue, but upon probable cause, supported by Oath or affirmation, and particularly describing the place to be searched, and the persons or things to be seized.

AMENDMENT V [1791]

No person shall be held to answer for a capital, or otherwise infamous crime, unless on a presentment or indictment of a Grand Jury, except in cases arising in the land or naval forces, or in the Militia, when in actual service in time of War or public danger; nor shall any person be subject for the same offence to be twice put in jeopardy of life or limb; nor shall be compelled in any criminal case to be a witness against himself, nor be deprived of life, liberty, or property, without due process of law; nor shall private property be taken for public use, without just compensation.

AMENDMENT VI [1791]

In all criminal prosecutions, the accused shall enjoy the right to a speedy and public trial, by an impartial jury of the State and district wherein the crime shall have been committed, which district shall have been previously ascertained by law, and to be informed of the nature and cause of the accusation; to be confronted with the witnesses against him; to have compulsory process for obtaining witnesses in his favor, and to have the Assistance of Counsel for his defence.

AMENDMENT VII [1791]

In Suits at common law, where the value in controversy shall exceed twenty dollars, the right of trial by jury shall be preserved, and no fact tried by a jury, shall be otherwise re-examined in any Court of the United States, than according to the rules of the common law.

AMENDMENT VIII [1791]

Excessive bail shall not be required, nor excessive fines imposed, nor cruel and unusual punishments inflicted.

AMENDMENT IX [1791]

The enumeration in the Constitution, of certain rights, shall not be construed to deny or disparage others retained by the people.

AMENDMENT X [1791]

The powers not delegated to the United States by the Constitution, nor prohibited by it to the States, are reserved to the States respectively, or to the people.

AMENDMENT XI [1798]

The Judicial power of the United States shall not be construed to extend to any suit in law or equity, commenced or prosecuted against one of the United States by Citizens of another State, or by Citizens or Subjects of any Foreign State.

AMENDMENT XII [1804]

The Electors shall meet in their respective states and vote by ballot for President and Vice-President, one of whom, at least, shall not be an inhabitant of the same state with themselves; they shall name in their ballots the person voted for as President, and in distinct ballots the person voted for as Vice-President, and they shall make distinct lists of all persons voted for as President, and of all persons voted for as Vice-President, and of the number of votes for each, which lists they shall sign and certify, and transmit sealed to the seat of the government of the United States, directed to the President of the Senate;—the President of the Senate shall, in the presence of the Senate and House of Representatives, open all the certificates and the votes shall then be counted;—The person having the greatest number of votes for President, shall be the President, if such number be a majority of the whole number of Electors appointed; and if no person have such majority, then from the persons having the highest numbers not exceeding three on the list of those voted for as President, the House of Representatives shall choose immediately, by ballot, the President. But in choosing the President, the votes shall be taken by states, the representation from each state having one vote; a quorum for this purpose shall consist of a member or members from two-thirds of the states, and a majority of all the states shall be necessary to a choice. [And if the House of Representatives shall not choose a President whenever the right of choice shall devolve upon them, before the fourth day of March next following, then the Vice-President shall act as President, as in case of the death or other constitutional disability of the President.] The person having the greatest number of votes as Vice-President, shall be the Vice-President, if such number be a majority of the whole number of Electors appointed, and if no person have a majority, then from the two highest numbers on the list, the Senate shall choose the Vice-President; a quorum for the purpose shall consist of two-thirds of the whole number of Senators, and a majority of the whole number shall be necessary to a choice. But no person constitutionally ineligible to the office of President shall be eligible to that of Vice-President of the United States.

Take Note

The bracketed text has been superseded by the Twentieth Amendment.

AMENDMENT XIII [1865]

SECTION 1. Neither slavery nor involuntary servitude, except as a punishment for crime whereof the party shall have been duly convicted, shall exist within the United States, or any place subject to their jurisdiction.

SECTION 2. Congress shall have power to enforce this article by appropriate legislation.

AMENDMENT XIV [1868]

SECTION 1. All persons born or naturalized in the United States, and subject to the jurisdiction thereof, are citizens of the United States and of the State wherein they reside. No State shall make or enforce any law which shall abridge the privileges or immunities of citizens of the United States; nor shall any State deprive any person of life, liberty, or property, without due process of law; nor deny to any person within its jurisdiction the equal protection of the laws.

SECTION 2. Representatives shall be apportioned among the several States according to their respective numbers, counting the whole number of persons in each State, excluding Indians not taxed. [But when the right to vote at any election for the choice of electors for President and Vice-President of the United States, Representatives in Congress, the Executive and Judicial officers of a State, or the members of the Legislature thereof, is denied to any of the male inhabitants of such State, being twenty-one years of age, and citizens of the United States, or in any way abridged, except for participation in rebellion, or other crime, the basis of representation therein shall be reduced in the proportion which the number of such male citizens shall bear to the whole number of male citizens twenty-one years of age in such State.]

Take Note

The bracketed text has been modified by the Twenty-Sixth Amendment.

SECTION 3. No person shall be a Senator or Representative in Congress, or elector of President and Vice-President, or hold any office, civil or military, under the United States, or under any State, who, having previously taken an oath, as a member of Congress, or as an officer of the United States, or as a member of any State legislature, or as an executive or judicial officer of any State, to support the Constitution of the United States, shall have engaged in insurrection or rebellion against the same, or given aid or comfort to the enemies thereof. But Congress may by a vote of two-thirds of each House, remove such disability.

SECTION 4. The validity of the public debt of the United States, authorized by law, including debts incurred for payment of pensions and bounties for services in suppressing insurrection or rebellion, shall not be questioned. But neither the

United States nor any State shall assume or pay any debt or obligation incurred in aid of insurrection or rebellion against the United States, or any claim for the loss or emancipation of any slave; but all such debts, obligations and claims shall be held illegal and void.

SECTION 5. The Congress shall have the power to enforce, by appropriate legislation, the provisions of this article.

AMENDMENT XV [1870]

SECTION 1. The right of citizens of the United States to vote shall not be denied or abridged by the United States or by any State on account of race, color, or previous condition of servitude.

SECTION 2. The Congress shall have the power to enforce this article by appropriate legislation.

AMENDMENT XVI [1913]

The Congress shall have power to lay and collect taxes on incomes, from whatever source derived, without apportionment among the several States, and without regard to any census or enumeration.

AMENDMENT XVII [1913]

[1] The Senate of the United States shall be composed of two Senators from each State, elected by the people thereof, for six years; and each Senator shall have one vote. The electors in each State shall have the qualifications requisite for electors of the most numerous branch of the State legislatures.

[2] When vacancies happen in the representation of any State in the Senate, the executive authority of such State shall issue writs of election to fill such vacancies: Provided, That the legislature of any State may empower the executive thereof to make temporary appointments until the people fill the vacancies by election as the legislature may direct.

[3] This amendment shall not be so construed as to affect the election or term of any Senator chosen before it becomes valid as part of the Constitution.

AMENDMENT XVIII [1919]

> **Take Note**
>
> The Eighteenth Amendment was repealed by the Twenty-First Amendment.

SECTION 1. After one year from the ratification of this article the manufacture, sale, or transportation of intoxicating liquors within, the importation thereof into, or the exportation thereof from the United States and all territory subject to the jurisdiction thereof for beverage purposes is hereby prohibited.

SECTION 2. The Congress and the several States shall have concurrent power to enforce this article by appropriate legislation.

SECTION 3. This article shall be inoperative unless it shall have been ratified as an amendment to the Constitution by the legislatures of the several States, as provided in the Constitution, within seven years from the date of the submission hereof to the States by the Congress.

AMENDMENT XIX [1920]

[1] The right of citizens of the United States to vote shall not be denied or abridged by the United States or by any State on account of sex.

[2] Congress shall have power to enforce this article by appropriate legislation.

AMENDMENT XX [1933]

SECTION 1. The terms of the President and the Vice President shall end at noon on the 20th day of January, and the terms of Senators and Representatives at noon on the 3d day of January, of the years in which such terms would have ended if this article had not been ratified; and the terms of their successors shall then begin.

SECTION 2. The Congress shall assemble at least once in every year, and such meeting shall begin at noon on the 3d day of January, unless they shall by law appoint a different day.

SECTION 3. If, at the time fixed for the beginning of the term of the President, the President elect shall have died, the Vice President elect shall become President. If a President shall not have been chosen before the time fixed for the beginning of his term, or if the President elect shall have failed to qualify, then the Vice President elect shall act as President until a President shall have qualified; and the Congress may by law provide for the case wherein neither a President elect nor a Vice President shall have qualified, declaring who shall then act as President, or the manner in which one who is to act shall be selected, and such person shall act accordingly until a President or Vice President shall have qualified.

SECTION 4. The Congress may by law provide for the case of the death of any of the persons from whom the House of Representatives may choose a President whenever the right of choice shall have devolved upon them, and for the case of the death of any of the persons from whom the Senate may choose a Vice President whenever the right of choice shall have devolved upon them.

SECTION 5. Sections 1 and 2 shall take effect on the 15th day of October following the ratification of this article.

SECTION 6. This article shall be inoperative unless it shall have been ratified as an amendment to the Constitution by the legislatures of three-fourths of the several States within seven years from the date of its submission.

AMENDMENT XXI [1933]

SECTION 1. The eighteenth article of amendment to the Constitution of the United States is hereby repealed.

SECTION 2. The transportation or importation into any State, Territory, or Possession of the United States for delivery or use therein of intoxicating liquors, in violation of the laws thereof, is hereby prohibited.

SECTION 3. This article shall be inoperative unless it shall have been ratified as an amendment to the Constitution by conventions in the several States, as provided in the Constitution, within seven years from the date of the submission hereof to the States by the Congress.

AMENDMENT XXII [1951]

SECTION 1. No person shall be elected to the office of the President more than twice, and no person who has held the office of President, or acted as President, for more than two years of a term to which some other person was elected President shall be elected to the office of President more than once. But this Article shall not apply to any person holding the office of President when this Article was proposed by Congress, and shall not prevent any person who may be holding the office of President, or acting as President, during the term within which this Article becomes operative from holding the office of President or acting as President during the remainder of such term.

SECTION 2. This article shall be inoperative unless it shall have been ratified as an amendment to the Constitution by the legislatures of three-fourths of the several States within seven years from the date of its submission to the States by the Congress.

AMENDMENT XXIII [1961]

SECTION 1. The District constituting the seat of Government of the United States shall appoint in such manner as Congress may direct:

A number of electors of President and Vice President equal to the whole number of Senators and Representatives in Congress to which the District would be entitled if it were a State, but in no event more than the least populous State;

they shall be in addition to those appointed by the States, but they shall be considered, for the purposes of the election of President and Vice President, to be electors appointed by a State; and they shall meet in the District and perform such duties as provided by the twelfth article of amendment.

SECTION 2. The Congress shall have power to enforce this article by appropriate legislation.

AMENDMENT XXIV [1964]

SECTION 1. The right of citizens of the United States to vote in any primary or other election for President or Vice President, for electors for President or Vice President, or for Senator or Representative in Congress, shall not be denied or abridged by the United States or any State by reason of failure to pay poll tax or other tax.

SECTION 2. The Congress shall have power to enforce this article by appropriate legislation.

AMENDMENT XXV [1967]

SECTION 1. In case of the removal of the President from office or of his death or resignation, the Vice President shall become President.

SECTION 2. Whenever there is a vacancy in the office of the Vice President, the President shall nominate a Vice President who shall take office upon confirmation by a majority vote of both Houses of Congress.

SECTION 3. Whenever the President transmits to the President pro tempore of the Senate and the Speaker of the House of Representatives his written declaration that he is unable to discharge the powers and duties of his office, and until he transmits to them a written declaration to the contrary, such powers and duties shall be discharged by the Vice President as Acting President.

SECTION 4. [1] Whenever the Vice President and a majority of either the principal officers of the executive departments or of such other body as Congress may by law provide, transmit to the President pro tempore of the Senate and the Speaker of the House of Representatives their written declaration that the President is unable to discharge the powers and duties of his office, the Vice President shall immediately assume the powers and duties of the office as Acting President.

[2] Thereafter, when the President transmits to the President pro tempore of the Senate and the Speaker of the House of Representatives his written declaration that no inability exists, he shall resume the powers and duties of his office unless the Vice President and a majority of either the principal officers of

the executive department or of such other body as Congress may by law provide, transmit within four days to the President pro tempore of the Senate and the Speaker of the House of Representatives their written declaration that the President is unable to discharge the powers and duties of his office. Thereupon Congress shall decide the issue, assembling within forty-eight hours for that purpose if not in session. If the Congress, within twenty-one days after receipt of the latter written declaration, or, if Congress is not in session, within twenty-one days after Congress is required to assemble, determines by two-thirds vote of both Houses that the President is unable to discharge the powers and duties of his office, the Vice President shall continue to discharge the same as Acting President; otherwise, the President shall resume the powers and duties of his office.

AMENDMENT XXVI [1971]

SECTION 1. The right of citizens of the United States, who are eighteen years of age or older, to vote shall not be denied or abridged by the United States or by any State on account of age.

SECTION 2. The Congress shall have power to enforce this article by appropriate legislation.

FYI

The Twenty-Seventh Amendment was proposed on September 25, 1789, along with the Amendments that became the Bill of Rights. The amendment was ratified quickly by six states, but not by the rest of the states. The amendment had no "sunset provision," however, and over time it was ratified by other states until, in 1992, Michigan became the 38th state to ratify it, satisfying the three-fourths requirement.

AMENDMENT XXVII [1992]

No law, varying the compensation for the services of the Senators and Representatives, shall take effect, until an election of representatives shall have intervened.

Index